LAST VOICES
VOICES
of the IRISH
REVOLUTION

LAST
VOICES
of the IRISH
REVOLUTION

TOM HURLEY

Gill Books

Gill Books
Hume Avenue
Park West
Dublin 12
www.gillbooks.ie

Gill Books is an imprint of M.H. Gill and Co.

© Tom Hurley 2023

9780717199785

Designed by Typo•glyphix, Burton-on-Trent, DE14 3HE
Edited by Gráinne Treanor
Proofread by Geraldine Begley
Printed and bound in Great Britain by CPI Group (UK) Ltd, Croydon, CR0 4YY
This book is typeset in Elena Basic Light 10pt on 12pt leading.

The paper used in this book comes from the wood pulp of sustainably managed forests.

For permission to reproduce photos, the author and publisher gratefully acknowledge
the following:

© Denis Minihane/*The Echo/Irish Examiner*: xiv.a; © *The Corkman*: xv.g; Courtesy of
Edwina Vaughan: xiv.b; Courtesy of Michael Clancy: xiv.c; Courtesy of Elizabeth
Burke: xiv.d; Courtesy of Allison Murphy: xiv.e; Courtesy of Noel Cleary: xiv.f;
Courtesy of Anthony Fitzgerald: xiv.g; Courtesy of Carina Markett: xiv.h; Courtesy of
The Longford Eye: xv.a; Courtesy of Patsy Holmes: xv.b; Courtesy of Eileen Keating: xv.c;
Courtesy of Gerard Kelly: xv.d; Courtesy of Muiris McGinley: xv.e; Courtesy of
Fergal Griffin: xv.f; Courtesy of Eddie and Marion O'Donovan: xv.h; Courtesy of
Alan Parkinson: xv.i; Courtesy of Dawn DeSantis: xv.j; Courtesy of Lucy and
Gerry Smyth: xv.k; Courtesy of Michael McMahon: xv.l.

A CIP catalogue record for this book is available from the British Library.

5 4 3 2 1

Dedicated to the memory of the 20 contributors to this book who are now enjoying their eternal rewards:

George Carpenter
Michael Casey
Seán Clancy
George Cooper
Norman Douglas
Jack Duff
Patrick Fitzgerald
William Geary
Patrick Greene
Patsy Holmes
Dan Keating
John Kelly
Anthony McGinley
Mai McMahon (née Grogan)
Kathleen Noonan (née Charles)
Daniel O'Donovan
John Parkinson
Margaret Power (née Cahill)
Gerry Smyth
Ellen Troy (née Maloney)

Contents

Acknowledgements

I would like to thank the following 20 people who in 2003 and 2004 allowed me to record their experiences, memories and stories of the period leading up to, during and shortly after the revolutionary years in Ireland. It's what they said or didn't say, combined with things I subsequently discovered, that led me down particular paths of research culminating in this book. The name in each case is listed in alphabetical order followed by the age they were at the time. Not surprisingly, all of those featured have gone to their eternal rewards since I met them.

George Carpenter (94), Kinsale; Michael Casey (100), Rockmills; Seán Clancy (101), Dublin; George Cooper (92), Dublin; Norman Douglas (93), Belfast; Jack Duff (100), Dublin; Patrick Fitzgerald (100), Dungourney; William Geary (105), New York; Patrick Greene (102), Ballinalee; Patsy Holmes (101), Mallow; Dan Keating (101), Castlemaine; John Kelly (100), Athenry; Anthony McGinley (98), Largnalarkin; Mai McMahon née Grogan (101), Kilrush; Kathleen Noonan née Charles (100), Dublin; Daniel O'Donovan (100), Tralee; John Parkinson (96), Belfast; Margaret Power née Cahill (98), New Jersey; Gerry Smyth (96), Trim; and Ellen Troy née Maloney (102), Mountmellick.

I would also like to express my thanks to the following (in alphabetical order) for allowing the interviews to take place and in some cases for facilitating them:

Margaret Brosnan; Joan Carpenter; Teresa and John Cleary; Cecil Cooper; Dawn DeSantis; Anthony Fitzgerald; Commandant Eddie Fitzgerald; Michael Fitzgerald; Sister Mel Greene; Patricia Holland; Eileen Hulsman; Jack and Eileen Keating; Margaret Kilcommins; Commandant Victor Laing; Sarah Madden; Helen Markett; Rose, Muiris and Máirtín McGinley; Mary McMahon; Allison Murphy; Alice and Marion O'Donovan; Niamh O'Sullivan; Maureen Power; Phyliss Prior; Judge Michael Smith; Vincent Smyth; and Noreen Vaughan.

In addition to some of the above I also express my gratitude to the following for assisting with historical information or photographs or for just pointing me in the right direction:

Brian Anderson; Elizabeth Burke; John Caplice; Cathal Brugha Barracks; Fintan Clancy; Michael Clancy; Noel Cleary; Ken Cooper; Olive Cooper; Cork City Library; Dublin City Library and Archive; Terry Dunne; Helen Ferris; Diarmaid Ferriter; Donal Fitzgerald; Patrick Fleming; Hugh Forrester; William Fraher; Ann-Marie Frehill; Garda Museum; Geraldine, Paddy and Fergal Griffin; Robert Harris; Mary Healy; Jim Herlihy; Sinéad Holland; Ann Kavanagh; Gerard Kelly; Kerry County Library; Kilkenny Archaeological Society; Gearoid Kingston; Matthew Kinsella; Valerie Kinsella; Deirdre Lafferty-McGinley; Laois Local Studies; Matthew Larkin; The *Longford Eye*; Longford Historical Society; Carina Markett; Mark Markett; Philip McConway; David McCullagh; Edel McMahon; Michael McMahon; Military Archives; Patrick J. McNamara; Jacquie Minchinton; Orla Murphy; Gillman Noonan; Eddie O'Donovan; Theresa O'Farrell; Seán O'Sullivan; Dr Alan Parkinson; Tom Parkinson; Bill Power; Paudie Taylor; Joe Troy; Derry Twomey; and Edwina Vaughan.

A sincere word of thanks to the publishers: Gill Books.

A huge thanks to Marie, Bláithín and Iarlaith for their support while I was putting this project together.

Introduction

The Irish Civil War ended on 24 May 1923. Prior to that there was World War I, 1916, the War for Independence and partition of the island. Eighty years on in 2003, I wondered were there many civilians and combatants left from across Ireland who would have experienced these years from 1919 to 1923, their prelude and their aftermath. If so, what memories had they, what was their story, and how did they reflect on those turbulent times? Did the 80 years since the Civil War do anything to quell the bitterness often associated with that conflict and, before that, British rule in all of Ireland? Had attitudes changed in the years that followed?

To find out and to learn more about the 1919–1923 period and its prelude and aftermath, I set about recording elderly people's experiences of life in Ireland leading up to, during and shortly after May 1923. In the first seven months of 2003, I met and recorded interviews with 18 people. Two further interviews were recorded in the United States in July 2004. I wanted to speak to a cross section who would have ideally been in their teens or early twenties during the Civil War. I would fund the project myself and work independently. Interviewees or their families or carers were told in advance of being recorded that I hoped to use the content down the line to make a radio documentary series, a book, or perhaps both, but that even if neither of these ever came to fruition, it would be worth recording what they had to say for the purposes of posterity.

I decided that the year 2023 – which marked the 100th anniversary of the end of the Civil War – was a suitable time for the publication of this book. I may also explore the possibility of getting the accompanying radio documentary series aired at a future date. This has never been broadcast.

This book is for the most part structured around information garnered from those recorded interviews which I conducted with 20 individuals (both Catholic and Protestant), all born on the island of Ireland well in advance of the end of the Civil War in 1923. It is an oral account of the 1919–1923 revolutionary period and its prelude and aftermath based on their experiences and stories of having lived through it. It is what they told me or didn't tell me that led me down particular paths of research. I have adopted a chronological approach to the book that spans 50 years, beginning with the oldest interviewee's birthday in 1899 and ending on the date that the Irish Free State was declared a republic in 1949. While it's the 1919–1923 period that is the subject of particular focus, my belief is that those years can't be taken in isolation. Tensions were brewing in the prelude to them, and tensions were also rife in their aftermath.

Eighty years and more after the end of the Civil War, it was remarkable to come across individuals so receptive and talkative regarding the 1919–1923 period and its prelude and aftermath. Not surprisingly, many had, in advanced age, perhaps forgotten details and stories they might have retained up to some years previous. Perhaps there were other stories and memories they just didn't want to talk about. However, with the passage of time and old acquaintances, many may have felt that incidents they might not have discussed before could now be recorded. Overall, I feel very fortunate to have got the opportunity to meet and interview these extraordinary 20 people.

All those I spoke to were good storytellers and, what's more, were willing to speak. They also had remarkable memories for their ages. What they conveyed to me were events, incidents and stories that had stuck in their minds through the decades. There were, of course, instances where interviewees were reluctant to go into detail on certain aspects, particularly those relating to the Anglo-Irish War or the Civil War. This is totally understandable, and rather than pursue them during interviews, I left them be and moved on to other topics. For me, this occasional reluctance to speak only added to the credibility of the storyteller and gave a sense of the 'genuine' to their accounts. It is often the case that silence or a reluctance to speak can say more than words.

Each person featured is speaking entirely from their own point of view. Personalities played a huge part in the War for Independence and the Civil War. One person's hero was often another person's target for ridicule. This is clear in the instances where certain personalities come in for both praise and attack. All remarks must be taken within the context of the day based on the individual experiences of the interviewees. The odd personal jibe might have been directed also. These are trademarks that go with any war situation. I could have edited them out but decided not to. I was also mindful that some of the views and opinions expressed wouldn't necessarily equate with what other individuals of the period might have encountered or experienced. Those featured had the advantage of 80 years of hindsight, which most from the 1919–1923 period never got.

In terms of research, every effort has been made regarding the veracity of the dates and details provided in the book's chronology. All incidents and stories featured in the book are there because either an interviewee raised or alluded to them or – having researched what they said or omitted – I felt further detail or attention was warranted. In some cases, I have added extra information to provide background and context. The age of the interviewees must be remembered when reading their version of events, but for the most part these are very accurate. I have corrected the occasional mistake in brackets where I felt it was most warranted, but for the most part I have left their versions alone.

An important aspect to point out is that the individuals featured in the book are included because I, and their families or carers, considered them to be up to the task of being interviewed. If I thought their minds were faulty or that what they were talking about was insincere, they would not have featured. The book gives a brief account of goings-on as raised by or pertaining to the interviewees' experiences but is by no means an in-depth or definitive account of the period. The book's aim is to give a flavour of the turbulent times through which the interviewees I spoke to lived. The content of the book is focused more on the militaristic side of things rather than the political, but ordinary, everyday life is a prominent theme too.

I interviewed the vast majority of these individuals knowing only a certain amount about their background and the area from which they hailed. What I did know was that they had a story worth telling. My strategy was to record what they had to say first and to check out the veracity and details of it later. Some said more than others, but I have done my best to investigate all I was told and indeed what I wasn't told. It was often only in the years afterwards, researching what they had said and not said, that I discovered the extent of their involvement in particular events that transpired. I am satisfied that all details contained within the book are true. However, if any are proved incorrect or off the mark, I am open to correction and clarification.

I am extremely grateful to the 20 contributors to this book, because it's well known that the effects of World War I, 1916, loyalism, republicanism, the War for Independence, partition, the Treaty, the Civil War and the years that followed left a mark on Ireland, and that some issues that were sensitive to talk about in 2003 and 2004 are perhaps still sensitive to talk about today.

All of the civilians and combatants featured in this book have since gone on to their eternal rewards, as indeed have some of their offspring, historians and others who were of assistance to me along the way since I started out in 2003. In writing the book I tried to be balanced and impartial and hope this was achieved to some degree. I am grateful to those who provided the photographs associated with the 20 people interviewed that are included in the book - it is their experiences, memories and stories that feature, and I feel it should just be their photos that are included also.

From my point of view, it was a most worthwhile experience to have spoken with these 20 people about the 1919–1923 period and its prelude and aftermath in the year that coincided with and followed the 80th anniversary of the end of the Irish Civil War. Together theirs are the last voices of the Irish Revolution.

Interviewee details

Each name is listed in alphabetical order and is followed by their age at the time they were interviewed. All interviews were recorded in Ireland between January and July 2003, except those with William Geary and Margaret Power (née Cahill), which were recorded in the United States in July 2004.

GEORGE CARPENTER
(94) was born in Cork city in 1908. Growing up, he often came into contact with both the Volunteers and the British military. His father was a member of the Royal Irish Constabulary (RIC).

MICHAEL CASEY
(100) was born in Mitchelstown, Co. Cork, in 1903. He took part in many engagements with the Irish Republican Army (IRA) during the War for Independence and took the anti-Treaty side during the Civil War.

SEÁN CLANCY
(101) was born in Co. Clare in 1901. He joined the East Clare Brigade in 1918 and the Dublin Brigade in 1919. He supported the Treaty and joined the Free State Army in 1922.

GEORGE COOPER
(92) was born in Dublin in 1910. He had connections with the British soldiers as well as with the insurgents of 1916. He witnessed much that occurred in the capital during the troubled times.

NORMAN DOUGLAS
(93) was born in Belfast in 1909. He remembered when the city's industries were booming and was present on the day the Northern Ireland parliament was opened in 1921.

JACK DUFF
(100) was born in Dublin in 1903. In his early teens he worked for the Dublin United Tramways Company and took part in the Civil War as a member of the Free State Army.

PATRICK FITZGERALD
(100) was born in Co. Waterford in 1902. A member of the IRA, he was in a training camp during the Truce but took no part in the subsequent Civil War.

WILLIAM GEARY
(105) was born in Co. Limerick in 1899. Having spent almost a year sailing around the world, in 1921 he joined the IRA and later the Civic Guard (An Garda Síochána).

PATRICK GREENE
(102) was born in
Co. Longford in
1900. He trained as
a teacher in 1918
and spent some
time studying the
Irish language in
West Cork during
the Civil War.

PATSY HOLMES
(101) was born in
Co. Cork in 1902. He
was active with the
IRA around Mallow
and was interned in
Cork Gaol followed
by Ballykinlar
during the conflict
against the British.

DAN KEATING
(101) was born near
Castlemaine,
Co. Kerry, in 1902. A
member of Na
Fianna and later the
IRA, he fought with
the anti-Treaty side
during the Civil War
and was subsequently
captured and
interned.

JOHN KELLY
(100) was born in
Co. Galway in 1902.
He was an active
member of the IRA.
One night in 1921 he
was savagely beaten
and his house was
ransacked by the
Black and Tans.

**ANTHONY
MCGINLEY**
(98) was born in
Co. Donegal in 1905.
He was active with
the 1st Northern
Division during the
War for
Independence and
sided against the
Treaty in 1922.

**MAI MCMAHON
(NÉE GROGAN)**
(101) was born in
west Clare in 1902.
She recalled the
goings-on in her
area leading up to,
during and
following the Civil
War period.

**KATHLEEN
NOONAN
(NÉE CHARLES)**
(100) was born in
north Cork in 1902.
Through her
father's business,
she came into
contact with the
local Volunteers
and was active with
Cumann na mBan
before the Truce.

**DANIEL
O'DONOVAN**
(100) was born in
Bantry in 1903. He
went on to join the
Third (West) Cork
Brigade and served
time as a prisoner
on Spike Island. He
joined the Free
State Army in 1922.

JOHN PARKINSON
(96) was born in
Belfast in 1907.
Raised in the
unionist community,
he saw the *Titanic*
in 1912. He
recounted military
and political
goings-on in the
city both before and
after partition.

**MARGARET
POWER
(NÉE CAHILL)**
(98) was born in
Co. Kerry in 1905.
She acted as a
dispatch carrier for
the IRA during the
War for
Independence and
emigrated after the
Civil War.

GERRY SMYTH
(96) was born in
Co. Meath in 1907.
He recalled many of
the historical
goings-on that
impacted on his
area including
World War I, 1916,
the Anglo-Irish War
and the Civil War.

**ELLEN TROY
(NÉE MALONEY)**
(102) was born in
Portarlington, Co.
Laois, in 1900. She
never knew her
mother and was
raised by relatives.
She evoked the fear
that was instilled
into the people by
the Black and Tans.

Chronology of events

26 July 1914:	**Jack Duff** alludes to Bachelors Walk.
4 August 1914:	Britain enters World War I.
7 May 1915:	The *Lusitania* sinks off the Cork coast.
21 May 1915:	**Seán Clancy**'s cousin is killed.
1 August 1915:	Jeremiah O'Donovan Rossa is buried in Dublin.
9 February 1916:	**Margaret Cahill** celebrates a wedding.
24 April 1916:	The Rising begins in Dublin.
1 July 1916:	The Battle of the Somme takes place.
7 December 1916:	Lloyd George becomes British prime minister.
1 April 1917:	**Patsy Holmes** joins the Irish Volunteers.
10 May 1917:	Joe McGuinness gets elected in South Longford.
11 July 1917:	Éamon de Valera is elected in East Clare.
11 August 1917:	**William Geary**'s friend is killed during the Great War (World War I).
25 September 1917:	Thomas Ashe dies while on hunger strike.
29 September 1917:	Éamon de Valera begins a tour of Co. Clare.
20 February 1918:	**Ellen Maloney** meets Countess Markievicz.
16 April 1918:	**Seán Clancy** joins the Volunteers in east Clare.
2 September 1918:	**Patrick Greene** enrols in St Patrick's College, Drumcondra.
31 October 1918:	Spanish Flu claims the life of **Gerry Smyth**'s sister.
11 November 1918:	World War I ends.
14 December 1918:	Sinn Féin comes to power after a general election in Ireland.

1919

7 January 1919:	**John Parkinson** joins the Boys' Brigade in Belfast.
21 January 1919:	The First Dáil meets and the War for Independence begins.
1 April 1919:	**Seán Clancy** moves to Dublin.
17 June 1919:	**Patsy Holmes** sees Countess Markievicz in Mallow.
29 June 1919:	**Gerry Smyth** receives a prize for prayers.
20 August 1919:	The Volunteers change their name to the Irish Republican Army.
23 August 1919:	**William Geary** receives a Certificate of Proficiency in Radiotelegraphy.
7 September 1919:	An armed party of British soldiers is attacked in Fermoy.
28 September 1919:	**Dan Keating** attends the All-Ireland Football Final in Croke Park.
19 December 1919:	Martin Savage is killed.

1920

2 January 1920:	**Dan Keating** joins the IRA.
9 February 1920:	**William Geary** embarks on a voyage.
23 February 1920:	A 'Curfew' Order comes into effect in Dublin.
3 March 1920:	Frank Shawe-Taylor is murdered in Co. Galway.
25 March 1920:	The Black and Tans arrive in Ireland.
1 April 1920:	**Margaret Cahill** joins Cumann na mBan.

15 May 1920:	**Michael Casey** is active with the IRA.
16 May 1920:	An evacuated RIC barracks at Blackrock, Mallow, is destroyed.
25 May 1920:	Loughgeorge RIC Barracks is destroyed by the IRA.
12 June 1920:	An RIC constable is shot dead between Bantry and Glengarriff.
26 June 1920:	The Belfast *Titanic* Memorial is unveiled.
17 July 1920:	Lieutenant Colonel Smyth is shot dead in the County Club in Cork.
21 July 1920:	Rioting and sectarian strife erupt in Belfast.
4 August 1920:	Brigadier General Crozier becomes commander of the Auxiliaries.
15 August 1920:	A deployment of soldiers guarding a plane is attacked near Kanturk.
20 August 1920:	Curfew is imposed in Kanturk.
31 August 1920:	Curfew is rigidly imposed in Belfast.
3 September 1920:	The printing office of **Kathleen Charles**' father is raided by the military.
8 September 1920:	The 'Specials' are established in six counties of Ulster.
14 September 1920:	A British military convoy is ambushed in west Clare.
20 September 1920:	Kevin Barry is arrested in Dublin.
26 September 1920:	**Patsy Holmes** gets held up by the military.
28 September 1920:	Mallow Barracks is raided for arms.
5 October 1920:	**Patrick Fitzgerald** is by now an IRA man.
8 October 1920:	**George Carpenter** gets caught up in the Barrack Street Ambush.
11 October 1920:	**Patrick Greene**'s lecturer is shot.
14 October 1920:	Seán Treacy is killed.
15 October 1920:	**Norman Douglas** is taken to the pictures in Belfast.
22 October 1920:	**Daniel O'Donovan** participates in the burning of Bantry Police Barracks.
24 October 1920:	**John Kelly** goes into hiding after a publican is murdered.
31 October 1920:	**George Carpenter** attends the funeral of Terence MacSwiney in Cork.
1 November 1920:	Kevin Barry is hanged.
9 November 1920:	Two police are fatally shot at Ballybrack Railway Station.
12 November 1920:	**Michael Casey** meets Dan Breen in Mitchelstown.
21 November 1920:	Bloody Sunday takes place in the capital.
22 November 1920:	**Patsy Holmes** is arrested.
27 November 1920:	**Anthony McGinley** joins the IRA.
28 November 1920:	The Kilmichael Ambush takes place.
7 December 1920:	A postman is held up on his journey with the mails to Bantry.
9 December 1920:	**Patsy Holmes** is transferred to Ballykinlar Internment Camp.

10 December 1920:	The British government declares martial law in specific counties.
11 December 1920:	Cork city is burned by the Auxiliaries.
17 December 1920:	A British military convoy is ambushed at Glenacurrane.
23 December 1920:	The Government of Ireland Act separates northern and southern Ireland.
30 December 1920:	The Auxiliaries arrive in the Bantry area.

JANUARY – JULY 1921

17 January 1921:	Two men are shot dead inside Ballykinlar Internment Camp.
21 January 1921:	**William Geary** returns home having been away at sea.
31 January 1921:	A tragic series of killings takes place in Mallow.
1 February 1921:	Cornelius Murphy is executed in Cork.
4 February 1921:	James Craig becomes leader of the Ulster Unionist Party.
7 February 1921:	**John Kelly** is beaten up by the Black and Tans.
15 February 1921:	The Upton Train Ambush takes place.
8 March 1921:	An RIC man is killed near Kanturk.
10 March 1921:	**Patsy Holmes**' friend is shot dead.
18 March 1921:	The Burgery Ambush takes place.
19 March 1921:	The Crossbarry Ambush takes place.
21 March 1921:	An engagement is carried out at Headford Junction.
22 March 1921:	An ambush at Lispole results in three casualties.
31 March 1921:	A constable is left for dead near Mitchelstown.
11 April 1921:	The Dublin Brigade mounts an attack on the Auxiliaries.
12 April 1921:	An attempt is made to bomb two Crossley tenders in Cork.
18 April 1921:	**Gerry Smyth**'s neighbour ignores soldiers' orders.
21 April 1921:	Dennis O'Loughlin is shot dead in a public house.
23 April 1921:	Two of **Michael Casey**'s comrades are arrested.
3 May 1921:	Crown forces are ambushed at Whitehall.
15 May 1921:	**Seán Clancy** takes part in an ambush of troops crossing Ballybough Bridge.
19 May 1921:	A general election is held in the twenty-six counties.
21 May 1921:	**Daniel O'Donovan** is arrested.
25 May 1921:	The Custom House in Dublin is attacked by the IRA.
1 June 1921:	**Dan Keating** participates in the Castlemaine Ambush.
2 June 1921:	The Mandeville monument in Mitchelstown is tarred.
4 June 1921:	Bombs are thrown at a military party in North Strand.
10 June 1921:	**Daniel O'Donovan** is court-martialled in Bantry.
15 June 1921:	A young woman is shot in Holles Street.
22 June 1921:	The Northern Ireland parliament is officially opened.
8 July 1921:	A truce is announced between the IRA and British forces.
10 July 1921:	**Dan Keating** participates in an engagement at Castleisland.
11 July 1921:	The truce comes into effect.

JULY 1921 – JUNE 1922

14 July 1921:	Éamon de Valera meets David Lloyd George in London.
17 July 1921:	**Michael Casey** encounters drunken British soldiers.
18 September 1921:	The funeral takes place of a man engaged to **John Kelly**'s sister.
10 November 1921:	**Daniel O'Donovan** is released from Spike Island.
12 November 1921:	**Patsy Holmes** rejects potential freedom from Ballykinlar.
15 November 1921:	Tadhg Barry is shot dead inside Ballykinlar Internment Camp.
22 November 1921:	**Michael Casey** is involved in an investigation.
3 December 1921:	**Patrick Greene** meets Johnny Collins whilst teaching in Horseleap.
6 December 1921:	The Treaty is signed in London.
9 December 1921:	**Patsy Holmes** is released from Ballykinlar.
14 December 1921:	Debates on the Treaty commence in the Dáil.
7 January 1922:	The members of the Dáil vote to accept the Treaty.
9 January 1922:	Éamon de Valera resigns his presidency of the Dáil.
13 January 1922:	Major Hallinan is kidnapped.
16 January 1922:	A formal transfer of power takes place at Dublin Castle.
9 February 1922:	A new police force for the Irish Free State is formed.
3 March 1922:	British troops leave Bantry Barracks for England.
15 March 1922:	**Anthony McGinley** joins the Free State Army.
17 March 1922:	Changes are made to the school curriculum.
19 March 1922	Éamon de Valera visits Killarney.
26 March 1922:	Anti-Treaty IRA officers hold an army convention in the Mansion House.
30 March 1922:	The Collins-Craig Pact.
9 April 1922:	The new anti-Treaty IRA executive reassembles.
13 April 1922:	The Four Courts is occupied by the anti-Treaty IRA.
14 April 1922:	**Patrick Greene** arrives in Ballingeary.
23 April 1922:	Michael Collins comes to Kerry.
26 April 1922:	Mick O'Neill is shot dead.
2 May 1922:	**William Geary** joins the Civic Guard (An Garda Síochána).
7 May 1922:	**Jack Duff** joins the Free State Army.
15 May 1922:	The Kildare Mutiny begins.
17 May 1922:	Emily Brown is shot.
22 May 1922:	**Seán Clancy** joins the army.
26 May 1922:	**John Parkinson**'s school is burned down.
1 June 1922:	The Royal Ulster Constabulary (RUC) is established.
2 June 1922:	**George Cooper**'s sister marries a British soldier.
11 June 1922:	Éamon de Valera visits Kanturk.
16 June 1922:	A general election is held in the twenty-six counties.
22 June 1922:	Henry Wilson is shot dead in London.

JUNE 1922 – MAY 1923

28 June 1922:	The Civil War begins.
29 June 1922:	Republicans occupy Mitchelstown Castle.
30 June 1922:	The anti-Treaty garrison in the Four Courts surrenders.
1 July 1922:	**Dan Keating** is part of the IRA that occupies Listowel.
4 July 1922:	Skibbereen is captured by men from the anti-Treaty IRA.
5 July 1922:	The fighting in the centre of Dublin ceases.
7 July 1922:	Fighting breaks out between pro- and anti-Treaty sides in Limerick.
10 July 1922:	The Derry train is raided by republicans operating out of Glenveagh Castle.
13 July 1922:	Michael Collins becomes commander-in-chief of the Free State Army.
17 July 1922:	The Coshla Ambush takes place.
20 July 1922:	Pro-Treaty forces capture Limerick city.
26 July 1922:	**Anthony McGinley** loses a neighbour to the Civil War.
28 July 1922:	**Dan Keating** is interned in Maryborough Gaol (Portlaoise Prison).
29 July 1922:	A contingent of the army which includes **Jack Duff** arrives in Kilkenny.
30 July 1922:	**Mai Grogan**'s neighbour's house gets burned down.
2 August 1922:	Free State troops land in Co. Kerry by sea.
9 August 1922:	**Patrick Greene**'s great friend succumbs to the conflict.
12 August 1922:	Arthur Griffith dies.
13 August 1922:	**Jack Duff** and the army come under fire in Clonmel.
17 August 1922:	**William Geary** travels to the capital for the takeover of Dublin Castle.
22 August 1922:	Michael Collins is shot at Béal na Bláth.
26 August 1922:	**Daniel O'Donovan** joins the Free State Army.
29 August 1922:	Maryborough Gaol (Portlaoise Prison) is burned.
7 September 1922:	**Gerry Smyth**'s cousin is killed.
9 September 1922:	The O'Connor 'Scarteen' brothers are shot dead.
22 September 1922:	**Anthony McGinley** leaves the Free State Army.
1 October 1922:	**William Geary** is promoted in the Civic Guard and transferred.
15 October 1922:	A Special Powers Resolution allowing the death penalty comes into effect.
19 October 1922:	Lloyd George resigns as British prime minister.
12–13 November 1922:	A census of Free State Army personnel is recorded.
14 November 1922:	Garda Henry Phelan is killed.
17 November 1922:	Four republicans are executed in Kilmainham Gaol.
3 December 1922:	An intense battle rages in the Carrick-on-Suir area.
7 December 1922:	Seán Hales TD is killed.
8 December 1922:	Michael Daly dies in Maryborough Gaol (Portlaoise Prison).
10 December 1922:	The *Slievenamon* armoured car is recovered.

21 December 1922:   **Anthony McGinley**'s comrade is killed.
12 January 1923:   A young boy is injured by a Mills bomb.
14 January 1923:   **Margaret Cahill**'s brother is shot.
19 January 1923:   Free State troops are ambushed at Nine-Mile-House.
20 January 1923:   Four republicans are executed in Co. Kerry.
25 January 1923:   Paddy O'Reilly from Youghal is executed.
9 February 1923:   Liam Deasy calls for unconditional surrender by the anti-Treaty side.
22 February 1923:   **Dan Keating** is transferred to Tintown Internment Camp.
25 February 1923:   **Daniel O'Donovan** is transferred with the army to Lismore.
26 February 1923:   Army Headquarters announce that Thomas Gibson has been executed.
28 February 1923:   General Denis Galvin dies by accident.
6 March 1923:   Five members of the Free State Army are killed at Knocknagoshel.
7 March 1923:   The massacres at Ballyseedy and Countess Bridge take place.
12 March 1923:   Five republicans are blown up in Caherciveen.
14 March 1923:   Executions are carried out at Drumboe.
17 March 1923:   Richard Mulcahy, commander-in-chief of the army, visits the Curragh.
6 April 1923:   **Patrick Greene** becomes principal.
7 April 1923:   The Catholic church at the Curragh camp is discovered to be on fire.
10 April 1923:   Liam Lynch is shot in the Knockmealdown Mountains.
27 April 1923:   Frank Aiken issues a command to suspend all offensive operations.
24 May 1923:   The Civil War ends.

MAY 1923 – APRIL 1949

25 May 1923:   Thomas Mackey is shot dead.
27 August 1923:   A general election is held.
9 September 1923:   **Anthony McGinley** is arrested.
3 October 1923:   **Patsy Holmes** appears as a witness in court.
6 October 1923:   **Daniel O'Donovan** is discharged from the army.
10 October 1923:   Garda **William Geary** is transferred to Monaghan Town.
16 October 1923:   The 47th Infantry Battalion is transferred to Wexford.
18 December 1923:   **Dan Keating** is released from the Curragh.
7 February 1924:   Efforts are made to restructure the army.
5 August 1924:   Legislation to award Military Service Pension is passed.
1 October 1924:   **William Geary** is promoted to superintendent.
6 November 1924:   The funeral of Charlie Daly is held.
8 December 1924:   **William Geary** is transferred to Newport.
4 February 1925:   **William Geary** is transferred to Templemore.
6 March 1925:   **Daniel O'Donovan** joins An Garda Síochána.

7 March 1925:	**Anthony McGinley** leaves the country.
16 June 1925:	**Mai Grogan** gets married.
10 February 1926:	**William Geary** assumes Garda duties in Kilrush.
18 April 1926:	The Irish Free State census is taken.
17 May 1926:	**Margaret Cahill** arrives in the United States.
10 July 1927:	Kevin O'Higgins is assassinated.
25 November 1928:	**William Geary** leaves Ireland.
11 June 1929:	Detective Garda Timothy O'Sullivan is killed.
22 July 1929:	The Ardnacrusha hydroelectric power station is opened.
7 March 1931:	**Jack Duff** leaves the army.
9 March 1932:	De Valera comes to power.
28 March 1932:	**John Parkinson** goes to Dublin for the first time.
25 April 1933:	**Dan Keating** is imprisoned in Cork Gaol.
6 September 1934:	**Kathleen Charles** gets married.
5 July 1935:	**George Carpenter** has an extraordinary encounter with Hitler.
August 1936:	**Anthony McGinley** arrives back in Ireland.
27 March 1937:	**Jack Duff** is discharged from the army.
25 April 1938:	The Treaty ports are returned to the Free State.
1 September 1939:	World War II breaks out.
13 September 1939:	**John Kelly** appears in court.
4 August 1940:	**Dan Keating** is arrested.
10 October 1940:	**Seán Clancy** achieves the rank of commandant in the army.
30 April 1945:	World War II ends.
18 April 1949:	The Irish Free State becomes the Republic of Ireland – partition remains.

CHAPTER 1

Born into history, February 1899 – September 1912

28 FEBRUARY 1899

WILLIAM GEARY was one of seven children born in Cloonee Cottage, which was located on a farm on the Ballyagran to Feenagh road in Co. Limerick. Coming from a well-to-do and respected family, his mother had a dowry of not less than £300 when she married his father in 1896.[1]

> My father was Patrick Geary and my mother was Helen Walsh of Newlawn. The farm had ninety-three acres of land, arable land, capable of growing wheat ... When I was old enough and strong enough, I did some work on the farm such as weeding and helping to save the hay and also to clean out the cow houses and hen house. And on the farm we had, we used to keep an average of about twenty-eight cows, not more, usually it could handle about thirty. On average it took about twenty-eight cows. Now to milk those cows, we had a boy and a girl. They were hired in March and they stayed in the bed and board in the house until Christmas Eve. Their pay at that time was about eighteen pounds.[2]

Mary Drum and Michael Hogan worked as farm servants for the Gearys in 1911.[3]

> And in addition to that we had a ploughman and he lived locally and he got about a pound a week. On the farm we had two horses, a pony and a donkey. We had a flock of white-leghorn hens. About a dozen Indian runner ducks, a flock of geese and all of them just ran over the place.
>
> Now I must tell you about Cloonee Cottage. Cloonee Cottage by all was a local mansion compared to the other houses. They were just mud cabins. It was so distinguished it was shown in the ordnance survey map of 1906. It was about a mile behind the village on the south side. Now the house was a two-storey thatched house. On the ground floor there was the old dairy ... Then there was the parlour and there was the hall. Behind the hall door there was a small room – a dining room. Then the kitchen and then there was a large space where they used to store

turf in the old days. There were no locks for the hall door and you had an iron bar and for the kitchen door there was a stick on the wall.

Now the lead-up to the house there was a beautiful double gate and piers and a stile. And then coming up to the house, lead-up to the house, it was about one-hundred-and-fifty yards from the road lined with daffodils. Funny thing, the cows never touched the daffodils. Then when you got close to the house there were two lovely piers with a small wicket gate and a beautiful flower garden in front of the house. I'd say about fifty paces by fifty paces. In that there were the most exotic plants ever you saw. Two horse-chestnut trees and a lilac a holly bush, I'll think of it later, and then there were exotic shrubs. The roses reached to the roof of the house. Now upstairs we had four rooms, four rooms.[4]

The Geary family did not feel isolated in their big house, as there were regular callers, including those described by William as 'mendicants' or 'tinkers'. These could be given a small coin, a bucket of potatoes or perhaps a plate of flour. In the winter months, some neighbours came for milk, which was always given for free.[5]

Now I went to Ballyagran School I'd say at the age of about five. I walked to school every day, winter and summer. In the summer we took off our shoes – glad to do it. There were two schools there – a boy and a girl school. The boys' school had just about thirty-eight students and Mr Daniel Quill was the teacher. He was a wonderful man. He never assaulted us. Well, he never, when he wanted to assault us the canes were never available. For some reason they used to disappear and he'd tell a boy to bring another cane but the canes always happened to disappear.[6]

Irish was prohibited in Ballyagran school. However, the clergy had the power to appoint teachers, and in this case they appointed Daniel Quill, whom William described as a 'wonderful nationalist'.

Now we used come in to school at nine o'clock in the morning but he used require us to come in at eight-thirty to learn Gaelic. Now this is interesting. We were so good or at least his initiative took hold right through the county and every school in the county got into the act of teaching it to them. So consequently, there used be a competition in Limerick in the summertime. Our school was so good we won three times in a row and there was an engraved copper panel certifying to our ability hung in the school. That was the only Irish we got, what we were taught by him. And as I said the national school system was the downfall of the Irish language and culture.[7]

William could remember a lovely summer's day in 1911 when a company of British army infantry in two columns, with a kettle drummer at its head, marched past the school. They were going south to camp that night in nearby Drewscourt.[8]

Ballyagran School, all we had in it was thirty-eight, about thirty-eight pupils, all sizes and the teacher used to handle them all. We had no writing tablets, only a slate and a pencil and most of it, all our education was mental. We had to study poems and we had to learn off all the tables. Now that education, oh yeah, I'll tell you this much, we learned what you call Latin roots such as transportation, transcross and port and carry. Another one was agriculture; agriland and we learned all the poems by heart. Now that education was so good for me it enabled me to pass the examination for a superintendent in the Garda Síochána. The next education and funny thing, we had no books to keep, we had no homework and once we left the school, we were free.[9]

6 JUNE 1900

John Greene and his wife Rose (née Naughton) resided in south Longford in the ancient parish of Rathreagh. On this date their eldest child **PATRICK GREENE** came into the world.[10]

Now the name Rathreagh is nearly forgotten because that little parish is incorporated with two other parishes into the present parish of Legan and the name Rathreagh except on official papers locally is not known. It's forgotten.

John, who was a carpenter by trade, built the family home in the 1890s. All his life he worked locally at Foxhall House, which had been constructed by the Fox family back in the 1700s. The then owner of the house was William Waller Fox, a retired British army officer whose wife was Emma Louisa Fox.[11] They were Church of Ireland and had their own place of worship on the grounds of the Foxhall estate. Perceived to have been well off because they lived in a big house, at this point they were in fact not, as a lot of the money associated with the estate had been gambled away years earlier by a previous owner.[12] Patrick Greene had two brothers and one sister, and his maternal great-grandmother lived to the age of 102.[13]

Well, quite a peaceful countryside. Our house was a ceilí house and every night three or four middle-aged or old fellows came in to ceilí. My father wasn't a young man when he married – he was nearly fifty, upper, nearly fifty. These were all his neighbours and my longest memory is four or five of these people coming in sitting down. He used to read the papers at the weekend. That was the only time; there were no daily papers in those days. And the local breadman came on Saturday, and he brought papers, sold them on his route – the *Longford Leader*, the *Irish Catholic*, the *Weekly Independent*.[14]

These were the days before people had electricity.

Oh, there wasn't a word about electricity. We never heard of it any. The light in towns at that, in most towns that time, some towns had gas but there was no word about electricity at all, not for fifty years afterwards. Here where I live now in 1954 the ESB came. Up to that you had paraffin oil, oil lamps, candles. Some people rarely lit an oil lamp. They sat in the light of the fire and candles because they didn't read. A lot of them were illiterate say eighty, ninety years ago – illiterate or semi-illiterate. I knew a number of men who they could make an attempt to write their name but that was all. They didn't read.[15]

Patrick started in Legan school at the age of six, where the principal was Barney Thompson.[16]

School was the nearest thing to an ice house you could imagine in the wintertime – a big single room and forty or fifty. The school I went to was comparatively good, a good stone building. It still stands, not as a school though – as a private house now. There were two separate schools – boys and girls. Two separate yards where you played and the ancient lady who was principal in the girls' school wouldn't allow the girls to play at the same time as the boys. From half twelve to one, they played from one to half one so that they couldn't mix with the boys. That was the system in those days.[17]

Patrick never heard of any trouble in the area when he was a youngster.

It was much like it is today – a peaceful farming community. The fact that the British were at a barrack in Longford didn't affect the lives of the country people at all. They never thought about it. Longford wasn't the town for our part of the county. Our town was Edgeworthstown and Edgeworthstown and Ballymahon were the principal fair towns. Longford was the northern part of the county and most people round about me didn't go to Longford at all. They went to Edgeworthstown if they had any shopping to do. The breadmen who travelled our country came from Edgeworthstown. We had little contact with the town of Longford. And the fact that there was a police barracks five or six miles from where I went to school, we saw the policemen going by on their bicycles or walking by the school and when we were small we had a certain amount of dread of these men with their uniforms. But then we got to know them and we discovered that they were perfectly harmless individuals just like the people around about us.[18]

20 JUNE 1900

Portarlington, Co. Laois was the home of **ELLEN MALONEY**, born on this date. By now her father, Michael, a native of the county, was a private in the 1st Lancashire Regiment, while her mother, Kate (née Lovely), of Hybla, Monasterevin, lived and worked as a shop assistant in her aunt and uncle's public house on Bracklone Street, Portarlington. Kate's aunt and uncle were named Mary-Ann (born in Co. Kildare) and Michael Duffy (from Portarlington). Ellen's father was an only child and his parents also lived on Bracklone Street.[19]

Ellen's mother and father had married in August 1897 in the town. On the marriage register, Michael is recorded as an 18-year-old carpenter and Kate as a 15-year-old servant; she was, in fact, 14 and pregnant.[20]

> There was one boy older than me and I was born then in the Queen's reign in 1900 ... Me brother died at four months old. I don't know what he died from.[21]

Ellen's brother, John, born in October 1897, died aged 20 days as a result of bronchitis.[22] It was two years later in September 1899 that her father Michael had enlisted in the 3rd South Lancashire Regiment at Liverpool.[23] His army service record is incomplete, but he is documented as a labourer who worked at Odlums Flour Mills in Portarlington. Furthermore, he is recorded as 'single'. There's a chance Michael fought at some stage in the Boer War of 1899–1902 with his then battalion, 1st South Lancashire Regiment, as they were in South Africa throughout the conflict.[24]

31 MARCH 1901

The 1901 Census of Ireland was taken and details for **WILLIAM GEARY**, **PATRICK GREENE** and **ELLEN MALONEY** (the only interviewees born to date) feature. William is in his grandparent's house in Drewscourt East, Ballyagran, Patrick is at home with his parents at Killeen, Foxhall, and 10-month-old Ellen is resident in the public house on Bracklone Street, Portarlington, along with her mother, Kate, and the owners of the public house, Mary-Ann and Michael Duffy (Kate's aunt and uncle). Ellen's father, Michael, was not in the country at the time. From the age of one, however, Ellen would be raised entirely by the Duffys, who themselves had no children.

> I was born in 1900 in the Queen Victoria's reign and I was left. My grandmother reared me, me grand-aunt reared me and she brought me up to do what I was told and when I was young enough I went to the pub and served.[25]

The story goes that Ellen's father was posted to Scotland with the British army. Incidentally, Ellen said she also had an uncle (one of her mother's brothers) living in Scotland at this time.[26] In any event, her mother, Kate, found her husband's absence difficult and (some time after the 1901 Census was taken) moved there to join him, initially it seems leaving their daughter Ellen in the care of one of her siblings in Co. Kildare. However, Ellen's grand-aunt Mary-Ann Duffy, with whom the pair had been residing, wasn't happy about this arrangement:

> She took, she went, me mother brought me to Monasterevin to her sister and me (grand)-aunt went and brought me home and reared me.[27]

Over 102 years later in 2003, Ellen still kept a picture of her mother close to her heart.

That's my mother. I never saw her. She went to Scotland when her husband joined the British army. She went to Scotland to her brother and she died there.[28]

Kate apparently died from cancer while in Scotland (I found no death record), and afterwards her widower, Michael Maloney, returned home to work as a carpenter as well as in the public house on Bracklone Street. Ellen's grand-uncle Michael Duffy, owner of this pub, died in 1908, and Ellen had fond memories of him going to the nearby railway station:

He got barrels, used to bring the porter down from the station.[29]

Ellen's father was back in Portarlington and living with his own parents on the same street by 1911.[30] However, his young daughter, Ellen, never lived with him and remained in the care of her grand-aunt, attending school at the Presentation nuns' convent in Portarlington. One of her teachers was Sister Margaret, and a fire was lit to keep the classroom warm. Ellen made her First Holy Communion in the local church in 1908.

I grew up in Portarlington, made me First Communion, made me First Confession and made me Confirmation in Portarlington.[31]

Indeed, at this young age Ellen would help out in her grand-aunt's pub, often resulting in sore hands from pulling corkscrews, bottling porter and labelling bottles, all before going to school.[32]

7 JULY 1901

SEÁN CLANCY was one of nine children raised on a farm in Earl Hill, Clonlara, Co. Clare. His parents were Michael and Kate (née Ryan), the latter a native of Co. Limerick.[33]

I'd say it probably was very backward, of course. Farmers they had almost to do everything by hand in those far-off days. There was no machinery on the land and it was done by hand. I was born during the hay-saving season and my mother used always tell me that I wasn't a bit welcomed by the men folk because they were working from dawn till dusk on the hay. And it was a wet summer – a bad summer – and suddenly when I arrived, around the time I arrived the weather suddenly changed for the better and they got to work cutting the hay. And it was said, she told me anyhow that they found difficulty in finding somebody to act as godfather when I was brought to the church to be baptised. And there was a story about that. Will I tell you about it?

They had no trouble finding a potential godmother, but the godfather was the problem because they were all so busy saving their hay and all the neighbours and friends. But somebody got the idea that the local school. There was a family there which consisted of a, I don't know what age he was – ten or twelve years of age – a boy and somebody thought of him as the potential godfather. So on their way to the church they called to the school. They knew the principal and of course the youngster was delighted for the day off and he did the job. And I suppose he got a few bob for the purpose.[34]

Seán's godfather was 13-year-old Michael Carmody, whose father was a publican and farmer in O'Brien's Bridge.[35] In terms of politics, Seán's own father was a firm supporter of John Redmond, who had become leader of the re-merged Irish Parliamentary Party in 1900. John Dillon was deputy leader.

Well of course, I at that age, I suppose I hadn't any, I had no interest in the political side of it, the country, but my father he was interested in, he was active actually with the Irish Parliamentary Party. Clare – that part of Clare was represented by Willie Redmond who was a brother of John Redmond's and he represented East Clare in parliament at that time. And my father, there was an election on I think around that time when I was a young fellow and he was active with them, canvassing and so on. And I remember some of the meetings that were held locally and so on but I wouldn't be familiar with the real details of the politics at the time you know.[36]

Emigration was common at this time. Some of Seán's family went to Australia, whereas other people from the locality opted for America. There used be an 'American Wake', which involved all the neighbours and friends meeting up a night or two before the person's departure for a night of singing, dancing, drinking and merriment tinged with sorrow, as the person leaving might never be seen again.[37]

2 JANUARY 1902

The townland of Lisanaul, Castlemaine, Co. Kerry, was the birthplace of **DAN KEATING**, who would be the eldest of nine children. His parents had married a year earlier in Kiltallagh, Castlemaine. Dan's mother was a local girl named Julia Hanifan, whose brother served as a policeman in Dublin but would resign in 1916 to go into the insurance business.[38]

Dan's father, Cornelius, also born locally in 1866, now worked as a farmer but had seen service with the United States Army. Records show that he first enlisted in Springfield, Massachusetts, for a period of five years in 1890. Following this, he re-enlisted in 1895 for another three years at Fort Sheridan, Illinois, and in August 1898 re-enlisted for the same duration again at Fort Grant, Arizona. However, he was discharged in July 1899 at Ciego de Ávila, Cuba, and made his way back to Castlemaine. His character and conduct as a soldier were rated as 'excellent' for the duration of his army service, and going forward Cornelius was the recipient of an American navy pension, having also seen action in the 1898 Spanish-American War.[39]

Well at that time now right up, the Fenians, the United Irishmen and there's no doubt the Moonlighters that they kept the soul of Ireland that time because it must be said that coming up to the world's war we were satisfied with what we got which was very little.[40]

The Fenians first came to light in the 1850s. They were a small, secret, revolutionary body committed to the use of force to establish an independent Irish republic. They were also known as the Irish Republican Brotherhood (IRB), which developed from the Fenians in 1858. Although similar, in reality the two movements were separate.

The United Irishmen were founded in 1791, and their immediate aims were to reform parliament and end religious discrimination. They soon turned to the pursuit of outright Irish independence and attempted a rebellion in 1798, which failed.

'The Moonlighters' was a term used to describe secret societies that were often engaged in night-time activities against landlords. It is believed that they originated in Castleisland in 1879.[41]

29 MARCH 1902

Michael and Bridget Grogan (née Lynch) became the proud parents of a daughter, whom they christened Mary Josephine, although she became known as Mai.[42] They lived in Tullycrine, Kilmurry McMahon, Co. Clare. **MAI GROGAN'S** father's ancestors came originally from Spain and her great-grandfather came from Wexford.

> Well there was nine of us in family, five boys and four girls – tearing away together. That's it ... Well, we always had full and plenty. We had over a hundred acres of land and my father was a great farmer and we always had servants ... Well, we all worked on the farm. It was all milk the cows by hand and there was no such thing as electricity or anything like that ... Oil lamps up on the wall.[43]

Mary Lynch and Stephen Halpin were the names of two people the McMahon's employed as servants.[44]

> Oh, sure there were of plenty people going around. They'd be very glad you to give them, employ them. They'd be looking after the cattle and cows and saving the hay and all them kinds of stuff ... Well, we had a big farm, over a hundred acres at home. We had land in Tullycrine, Carniska and Drumdigus and that was it. But my father was a great man to make out and he was grazing the most of Hickman's hundreds of acres and he had up to one hundred head of cattle there. And it was all work. It was easy to get help them times.[45]

Francis William Gore-Hickman was a wealthy landlord and solicitor of the loyalist persuasion. He owned a lot of property in the county, including the Kilmore estate at Knock, about six miles from Kilrush, on the banks of the Shannon. Its amenities included an extensive wood, 500 acres of land and a fishery.[46] Mai's father paid Hickman so much a year to graze the land; she could remember this landlord's people coming to their house to collect the money.[47]

> Oh, sure walking to school, we weren't far from the school. And we had our teachers – Mrs O'Gorman and Mrs Stullard – and the cane was flying. The cane was, for the least thing you'd get the cane ... I remember one Sunday, Mrs O'Gorman lived near us and I suppose we'd have to stay at home on our turn for to mind the house while the rest of them would go to Mass on a pony and trap. Someone would have to stay at home and mind the young lads anyway and were you at Mass yes or no? The cane was used then, that was it.[48]

Mai remembered there being a better sense of community back then:

> Well the neighbours were always there to help you. They'd be always there if a cow was calving or anything else. They'd be there the neighbours. According to who you were, you'd have your neighbours. That's it ... Oh, the day you'd be cutting turf you'd have many of them in the bog. Oh, there'd be no trouble in having nine or ten men.[49]

2 MAY 1902

A house on Fair Street, Mallow, Co. Cork, was the residence of horse trainer and groom William Holmes and his wife, Bridget (née O'Connor, although her surname is also recorded as Gray). In total their union yielded seven boys and four girls. By 1901, a son Michael had died of measles and a daughter Bridget of convulsions. On this date, their third-youngest child Patsy arrived, whilst his parents resided for a spell in Kilcully. He was the only one of the children born outside of Mallow.[50]

> I was born in Whitechurch, couple of miles outside Cork city. I was christened in Blackpool where Jack Lynch was christened in 1901, 1902.[51]

PATSY HOLMES left school at 12 years of age.[52]

> I had cousins in the old times, my mothers' people – they were old Fenians you know.[53]

19 JUNE 1902

An 18-acre farm in Caherbriskaun, Athenry, Co. Galway, was the setting in which **JOHN KELLY** grew up. His parents were John (Seán Mór) and Julia (née Freeney).[54] John's ancestors came from Cloon outside Galway and were brought to the area originally as herdsmen by the Lamberts, who were landlords.[55] His father and grandfather were also herdsmen on the Castle Lambert estate.[56]

> I know that times weren't very good anyway. It was hard to get money.[57]

John had one brother and three sisters. Michael, Norah and Mary attended

Carnmore School, but John and Aggie went to Carnaun.[58] John, the youngest in the family, was known as 'Mock', which derives from 'mac' – the Irish word for 'son' by which he was often referred to by his father. Everybody would have spelled it and pronounced it as 'Mock'.

> All I can remember, I remember when I was confirmed and I was fourteen years of age when I was confirmed, a big crowd of us, seven or eight of us in the one village and all boys. That's all I can think of now. I was about fourteen years that time or so. Around that age anyway.[59]

Although John liked his teacher in school, there were occasions when she would lose her temper:

> She pulled my ear one time and she hurt me. She was the cause of leaving me deaf. I thought she had the ear taken off me altogether.[60]

John was witness to organised bouts taking place locally between various factions – often for money.

> There used be anger and fight. And even out on fair days of a market day, you'd often see a big fight with country people. Say you were one side and I was the other side and they'd have a bit of a fight.[61]

5 OCTOBER 1902

PATRICK FITZGERALD was born in Dunmoon, about four miles from Tallow in Co. Waterford. His parents, John and Ellen (née Murphy), had six in their family – four boys and two girls. Patrick was the youngest and endured the loss of his oldest sibling, Mary, to tuberculosis just shy of her 15th birthday in 1908.[62] Having grown up on a farm, he remembered there being some big merchants in Tallow, but he used to travel more frequently to Youghal, even though it was further from Dunmoon:

> I knew more about Youghal and it's twelve miles and Tallow's only about four and I knew more about Youghal. People would go most to Youghal that time ... It was fairly good. You had a few corn merchants there you know – people bringing grain there ... The market was down at the quay.[63]

He remarked that 'it was very few who were well off that time'.[64]

23 NOVEMBER 1902

Kanturk, Co. Cork was the birthplace of **KATHLEEN CHARLES**. She had four brothers, and her father was a printer named Webb Gillman Charles who operated out of Egmont Place in the town. He was also a skilled wood engraver.[65]

> Oh yes, all belong to me were Protestants. My father was belonged to very rich people.[66]

In his youth, he had been an extensive traveller, having spent periods in Belgium, Germany and America.[67] Kathleen's mother's name was Mary Helena (née Barr), and she was from Newmarket.[68] Growing up, Kathleen remembered Kanturk as being:

> Very badly off – it was a very small struggling town.[69]

The Charles family lived at the back of the courthouse, which is at the end of Church Street. They could trace their roots in the town back to the 1700s.[70] Kathleen's grandfather William Charles, a retired shoemaker, had been keeper of the courthouse in Kanturk; indeed, the Charles family were responsible for the care of the courthouse over several generations.[71] His wife was Jane Allen. Kathleen's mother's father, John Barr, was a land steward.[72] Kathleen remarked that he was Scottish and that his wife, her grandmother (Eliza Tanner), was from Bandon.

> You know there were no motor cars at that time. I remember the first motor car that came into our town … Well, I was about six. I remember the first car … I just saw it going up the road.[73]

Unusually for the time as a member of the Church of Ireland, Kathleen indicated that she went to a Catholic school.

> Oh, the convent school there – the nuns. I went to school when I was about five and I stayed there until I was seventeen … Seventeen was very old at that time to go to school. They all stopped about twelve, fourteen or anything like that you know. They went out as servant girls.[74]

23 FEBRUARY 1903

DANIEL O'DONOVAN took his first breath in Bantry, Co. Cork.

> It was a small coming town of three thousand of a population and I was reared in the centre of it in the place called the Quay, Bantry. Where I lived in a public house, which my parents had, and there was eleven in family – mother and father – that was thirteen.[75]

Having attended school locally, like many others during this era his education was cut short.

> I went pretty young but I only recollect the latter end of it at about the age of ten. It was the convent school run by the nuns and I was transferred to the boys' national at the age of ten roughly and went as far as class sixth when I left and took up helping the parents at the home, which was a pub in those days. Now gone and all but myself left.[76]

Daniel's father (of the same name) was a fluent Irish speaker from Maultrahane, Leap, and his mother, Mary Anne Tobin, came from Whiddy Island. Their pub was called the Hibernian Bar. In 1911, a relative named Mary-Anne O'Driscoll worked as a barmaid and Mary Murphy was hired as a domestic.[77]

15 MAY 1903

Mitchelstown, Co. Cork, had a new inhabitant in the form of **MICHAEL CASEY**. His parents, Michael and Ellen (née Finn), had four other children, and the family lived on Lower Cork Street. His mother was a native of Bartnahown, Ballyporeen, Co. Tipperary.[78] In 1911, the Casey's had a domestic servant and cook working for them named Hanna O'Brien, aged 35, who couldn't read or write, which was far from unusual at this time.[79]

> My father had a store there, flourmill, bakery, public house, a corn store. You know everything like that. The co-op then finished all that. They formed a big association there.[80]

Michael's father was one of the founders of Mitchelstown Co-op, which was established in June 1919. The co-op's largest shareholder was a man in his eighties called William Downes Webber, who owned Mitchelstown Castle.[81] Michael admitted that although his own family were wealthy, there were parts of the town where:

> There were a share, a share of poverty everywhere at that time.[82]

30 MAY 1903

East James Street, off Lower Baggot Street in Dublin, was the birthplace of **JACK DUFF**. His mother was Catherine (née Donnelly) and his father, John James, was a cab owner.[83] Jack, the eldest, would have two brothers and three sisters.[84]

> Well, when I was young and growing up, our thoughts weren't political in any way that I can remember until? Oh God, I couldn't tell you when we started to take an interest in it. We used to knock around with a couple of lads and we'd go to a picture and play cards and one thing or another like that. Other than that, we done nothing out of the ordinary.[85]

By 1909, the family would reside at No. 3 Baggot Court, Lower Baggot Street, Dublin.[86]

6 FEBRUARY 1905

ANTHONY MCGINLEY was born in Breenagh, Co. Donegal, to Bridget (née McDevitt) and her husband, Michael.[87]

> You go over Roy Hill and down into Glenswilly. It's about eight miles from Letterkenny and I was born there on a farm.[88]

He had an older brother, Michael, and a younger sister, Nora.

> Well, you couldn't say you was well off but I had a happy childhood. We were on a farm just, you know.[89]

Anthony's family tree was steeped in history, and the family were known as the Glenswilly McGinleys. Over the years, they had a reputation for opposing foreign landlords and occupiers whenever possible, and were regarded as great nationalists. Anthony's father, Michael, had three well-known siblings (Peter Toner, Pat and Bridget). The latter wrote many poems depicting the plight of the Irish against the British, including 'The Stubble Moon', 'With a Wreath of Shamrocks' (dedicated to Michael) and 'The Swallow's Return'. Peter Toner was a noted Irish language enthusiast and writer under the pen name Cú Uladh. He helped Patrick Pearse establish St Enda's, and would on on to have sons in the 1916 Rising, while Pat was chairman of the Gaelic League branch in Druimbolg.[90] Anthony's father, Michael – a poet and balladeer – had also been active against the British.

> My father was an old Fenian in England, the time of '67. He wasn't a young man when he got married and he was still alive as far back as '67. He was a member of the Fenian Brotherhood in England.[91]

In 1867, the Fenians had attempted a rising, but it failed miserably. In his early years, Anthony's father had also been connected with the Whiteboy movement, for which he served a term in Lifford Gaol.[92] In 1878, aged 26 and in search of a better life, Michael emigrated to New Zealand on board a steam sail ship named the *Invercargill*. He wrote the poems 'Glenswilly' and 'An Emigrant's Farewell' whilst en route, not knowing if he would ever see Ireland again. He settled in Dunedin, but after two years grew homesick and returned to Donegal. On his return, he helped to initiate the Land League in Glenswilly and went on to join the IRB.[93]

1905 was also the year that Arthur Griffith helped found the Sinn Féin movement. Its aim was to advocate economic nationalism and to re-establish the independence of Ireland. In the north, the Ulster Unionist Council came into existence with the aim of maintaining the union with Britain.[94]

5 NOVEMBER 1905

MARGARET CAHILL was raised on a farm in Ballinasare, Annascaul, Co. Kerry. She was the youngest of the eight surviving children of Michael and Mary (née McDonnell). Four others had died in infancy. Margaret cherished a picture of the house where she grew up with her two brothers and five sisters.[95]

> The lower house there, that was an English house put up for sale and my father was the highest bidder so that's the reason we had it.[96]

Names she remembered from the locality included the Sullivans and the Fitzgeralds. She also remembered the explorer Tom Crean from Annascaul. When she was older, Margaret would also do a bit of travelling herself.

7 JANUARY 1907

JOHN PARKINSON resided with his family at 35 Distillery Street, off the Grosvenor Road in Belfast. He was delivered on this date by the local district nurse, who lived close by on Excise Street. Her name was M. McDowell. John's parents (Frank and Ellen née Boyd) owned four properties plus a shop in the middle of Distillery Street. However, his father also worked as a carpenter for the Harland & Wolff shipbuilding firm. John had two brothers and one sister.[97] His parents stated the family's religious profession as 'Epyscipilian' in the 1911 Census.[98]

> The school I went to was called Saint Philip's National School. That was the school I went to and I signed that on all my exercise books – John Parkinson, Saint Philip's National School.[99]

Hugh Campbell was head teacher of this two-room school, located on Excise Street, close to the Royal Victoria Hospital. There was a large fireplace for which pupils were required to pay 'coal money' or else bring in their own fuel to heat the rooms. Those who brought in such money or fuel could sit near the fire; those who brought nothing had to sit at the back of the room.[100]

> In my days people always seemed to be in work. There was no such a thing as unemployment benefit in those days. I mean people weren't really unemployed … In those days you were either a Catholic or a Protestant but it didn't make very much difference. You just got on with it. The Protestants had their demonstrations of loyalty at the Twelfth of July as they had the other day and the Roman Catholics, they had their day in August and it was accepted. And people just got on with each other and there was no great, no great troubles.[101]

The Catholic demonstrations and parades were organised by the Ancient Order of Hibernians (AOH), which had been founded in 1641. It was the Catholic nationalist counterpart of the Protestant Orange Order and was stronger in the province of Ulster than anywhere else in Ireland.[102]

> The street where I lived in, we were on the Grosvenor Road here in Belfast, which one side of the road was Protestant and the other side of the road was nationalist. But we got on very well together. We'd two public houses on the corner. One was a Protestant owner and one was a Roman Catholic owner and we all got on well together.[103] … There were certain things we knew just that you had to be careful about and not to cause any provocation and we just got on with our lives.[104]

One of John's neighbours was in the Royal Irish Constabulary (RIC):

> In our street it was largely, we were on the Protestant side of the Grosvenor Road but there were a number of Roman Catholic families lived in the street. My mother was very friendly with a particular family; I always remember them called McDermott. The father was a member

of the police force. The original police force in northern Ireland, the original police force in Ireland was the RIC – the Royal Irish Constabulary. And he was a member of it, and my mother and Mrs McDermott were great friends and her daughter and her sons, we all played together.[105]

Mr McDermott was stationed at Springfield Road RIC barracks. Other neighbours included the Gilmores, the Storeys, the Barretts, who owned the Celtic Bar, and Johnny Lynch, the owner of the Distillery Bar.[106]

> Where I lived, my father had lived before me and his parents had lived before him. So we were there in that area for about a hundred years or so and there was never any trouble.[107]

12 JANUARY 1907

National schoolteacher Joseph Smyth and his wife, Lizzie (née Elms), lived in Stackallen, Co. Meath. They had six children, the last of whom they named Gerry, who came along at the start of the year. Mary Gertrude was his oldest sibling and only sister.[108]

> Well my father, my mother, God rest her, my grandmother before her, me, taught in Stackallen School. My grandmother was born in 1835, twelve years before the Famine and my mother died when I was born. My father taught there until 1924 when he retired and my eldest brother took over the job instead. So it runs in the family like wooden legs.[109]

GERRY SMYTH'S mother died aged 33 in March 1907. She had been principal of the girls' school.[110] It was his father, principal of Stackallen National School since 1890, who taught him, and Gerry described him as 'strict but not cruel'.[111] By 1911, Mr Smyth's late wife's mother and brother (also a teacher) were living in the house, together with a domestic servant named Catherine Flood, to help him raise the children.[112]

> Life was very slow in that time. There were no cars. When the first car would come around, we'd run out on the road and somebody would shout, 'Oh, here's a car coming.' We'd go out and take down the number if you could get it and to know but that would be about one car in the month would be the most that you'd get.[113]

23 MAY 1907

WILLIAM GEARY'S father, Patrick, died of pneumonia at the age of 47 years. At his wake, a neighbour named Davy Jordan from Coolagown is supposed to have said that 'he was a good judge of a little bull', which was considered to have been a great compliment.[114]

23 SEPTEMBER 1908

GEORGE CARPENTER was born on this date to William Carpenter from Sligo and his wife Frances (née Harman), who had been raised on a farm in Adrigole, West Cork. They had married seven years previously and now lived in Maymount in Cork city. They went on to have six sons and one daughter.[115]

> We weren't a very wealthy family but Dad had to hold three jobs at a time and then as each one of us reached the age of sixteen we went out to work.[116]

When George was born, his father, William, worked as a store clerk. However, in November 1904 he had been pensioned from the RIC after 28 years' service. His record shows that he had been allocated to the districts of Cork West Riding and Cork East Riding. He had a poor disciplinary record in the force, having been fined on no fewer than five occasions in addition to being admonished and cautioned on two others. He went on to become an insurance agent for the Hearts of Oak in Cork City.[117] One of George's earliest memories was centred on an old piseog (charm, spell, superstition).[118]

> When I was about three years old, I remember I was down in Youghal and we were playing away there and mother had us dressed in skirts and with my other brothers and I asked her why the skirts? ... Why weren't we wearing pants I said? And she said the gypsies would steal boys. But later on I discovered you didn't want any nappies when you had a skirt.[119]

When he was old enough, George attended a school in Christ Church, off the Grand Parade in Cork. Moll Savage and Moll Baker were teachers there.[120]

> I remember my first day in school when we had to do the alphabet up to A, B, C and D and on a sheet of paper and whilst I was doing that, the teacher spotted I was doing it with my left hand. So, she went and consulted with another teacher then and they decided to pin my left hand up behind my back and pin my exercises down on the desk so I could write away then. But when I got up, they had then top hoarding right around the walls and you get chalk and you had to do everything? And when they spotted me doing again with the left hand they turned around and made me write using my right hand instead. But my right hand is really not my master hand. When I'm shooting it's all with the left side – left eye, playing football, rugby and all of my sports, fencing.[121]

Interestingly, his mother had also been a schoolteacher.[122] George looked forward to visits to his grandfather William Harman, especially during the summer months.

> Wonderful type of man – he was the apple of my eye. He was a great tailor, a great man for telling us how to judge the weather and I still remember it. And when you look out, I nearly always know every day

now which way the wind is coming and what's going to happen, etc. And one favourite one of his – if the wind is from the east and a rising moon, you're going to get it good for two weeks. And nearly always that has come true – winter or summer. And I used it when I was going out in the boat, we used watch the weather changing and then we'd go out in the boat and it was lovely outside ... Adrigole was the place where we used live and there was a little pool at the end of the lawn and we used go in there swimming. But it was very cold fresh water. Then we used go out in Adrigole slipway there. There was sand but we were told be careful because there was sand taken by the farmers and they left a hole there and you could dip the hole if you weren't careful.[123]

28 DECEMBER 1909

NORMAN DOUGLAS was the fifth of six sons that resulted from the union of Robert and Elizabeth (née Harper). The family lived in Ravenhill Avenue, East Belfast, in a three-bedroom terraced house. Robert, from Ballynahinch, Co. Down, was a fitter, employed as an assistant foreman in the Sirocco Engineering Works in the city, whilst Belfast native Elizabeth worked in the home.[124] Norman's parents stated their religious profession as Baptist in the 1901 Census and as Presbyterian in the one taken 10 years later.[125]

> Well, what I remember of Belfast at that particular time was as I grew up and was able to get around. It was a playful place, the shipyards were functioning and there were linen mills and that sort of thing and my early childhood was quite happy.[126]

In time, the Douglas family were in a position to afford to relocate to a more substantial four-bedroom terraced house across the street. Norman's father was never unemployed, and their standard of living could be considered to have been good.[127]

> Well, I started school. School business was very much as it is today – it wasn't integrated. There were Catholic schools in Catholic areas and Protestant schools in Protestant areas. And I was, but they were all under the style of national schools in those days. That was up until the Northern Ireland Parliament was founded. I went to one school where there was only a headmaster and one teacher. That was infants and first class and then another school after that. When I finished my schooling, you went from class two to sixth and then you had to leave and go to work.[128]

In February 1910, Edward Carson (a Dubliner) became leader of the Irish Unionist Parliamentary Party.[129]

23 MAY 1910

No. 8 Buckingham Place, Dublin, was the birthplace of **GEORGE COOPER**, the latest addition to the young family of George Samuel and Margaret Ann (née Moore), both natives of the city. His father was a house painter.[130]

> Altogether there were eight of us. There were three boys and five girls ... In fact, it's hard to believe this but I am a descendent from a refugee. My ancestors were French and because they were Protestant they were driven out of France. They were called 'Huguenot'.[131]

George's great-grandfather John Cooper, a cabinetmaker, together with his sons Edward (also a cabinetmaker) and Samuel (an upholsterer and George's grandfather), had been granted Freedom of Dublin in February 1861. Freedom of Dublin was in effect citizenship. Freemen had the right to vote in addition to being exempt from certain tolls and taxes.[132]

> When I was born my dad had a small shop, which he used to sell bread, sweets and all that sort of stuff. And then I asked him years afterwards, how the shop shut up? And what he said was that he had what's called rheumatic fever in those days and my mother was in the shop and seeing in those days there wasn't much money going around and people were coming into the shop with hard stories and my mother was giving out this, that and the other and when it came to paying the bills, the money wasn't there. So that was the end of the shop which meant it was like being bankrupt and you had nothing, so many the time I went around in my bare feet ... And I wasn't the only one. There was plenty things like that and nowadays if you see a whole lot of wood lying at the side of the road or anywhere else, it lies there. But when I was young if you saw even an empty wooden box, you'd bring it home. But things were bad because there was no dole in those days.[133]

By 1916, George and his family would reside in D'Olier Street, which would be followed by a move to Holles Street by 1918. He could recall singing 'We are little Britons' in school.

> I went to the national school in Westland Row facing the railway station, which is the school is gone now. But it was a national school and I was there until I was fourteen.[134]

Meanwhile, **KATHLEEN CHARLES** and many others from Kanturk were amazed by an object in the sky that can only be seen once every 76 years. It first became visible in the north Cork area on this date between 9 and 10 o'clock in the night.[135]

> Did you ever hear of Halley's Comet? ... I only saw it one time ... There were very little talk about it but I remember when it came out first. Everyone in the district was out sitting up on walls and everything watching it. I watched it every night and it would come up from the east

and go right over us like that now and go down the other side and it had a tail as long as? Oh, I suppose a hundred miles and you'd have to wait until that was gone for the ordinary light to come off again – a bluey light. It had a red light like that.[136]

2 APRIL 1911

The 1911 Census of Ireland was taken, and details for all 20 people featured in this book are recorded. All are at home on the night in question. However, while **KATHLEEN CHARLES** is in Church Street, Kanturk, with her parents and brothers, her younger sibling, Webb Charles, is listed as being at her aunt's house in West Cork. Kathleen said that as a child she enjoyed visiting this particular aunt (her father's sister), who ran a business in Clonakilty, 'a fine country town' that she remembered had a British army presence.

> I went a lot down there on holidays. The sea was near us you know and everything. It was lovely.[137]

Kathleen's aunt was Mary Jones (née Charles), originally from Kanturk but by 1911 operating as a postmistress in Rathbarry, Castlefreke, located between Clonakilty and Rosscarbery. She had five children. In 1897, she had married an RIC constable named John Arthur Jones, originally from Co. Kildare. Having served in Cork East Riding and West Riding, he was promoted to sergeant in 1907 whilst based in Kilkenny. He was pensioned there in August 1911.[138]

Kathleen also remembered Castlefreke Castle, which at the time belonged to one of the most powerful land-owning families in Ireland – the Carberys. Part of the castle was destroyed by fire in March 1910, but was rebuilt and had a new wing added within five years.[139]

> I don't know was it malicious or what but we used to take telegrams there from my aunt's house. She had a post office and a shop and we used to be given the telegrams. You know there was no phone that time ... I'd be about eight or nine, very young.[140]

In June 1911, Carson accepted James Craig's invitation to lead the Ulster Unionists. His objective throughout was to preserve the union between Britain and Ireland, believing it to be in the best interests of his fellow countrymen.[141]

2 APRIL 1912

The Belfast shipbuilding firm Harland & Wolff began the construction of the *Titanic* in March 1909. Three years later, and thanks to efforts of over 3,000 employees, the ship was complete. It was built at a cost of nearly $8 million and was said to be unsinkable. On this date, **JOHN PARKINSON** saw the *Titanic* for the third and final time as it left Belfast for Southampton.

> That was the great era of the times then. My father had worked in the shipyard all his life and this was his greatest building the *Titanic*. He

talked about it often and told me all about the great ship and then he took me down on a Sunday afternoon to see it. I saw it before it was launched when it was in the gantry and then about six months after that he took me down again to see it when it was at the finishing wharf. It looked more like a boat then and then I saw it on the second day of April 1912. I remember it as if it was yesterday. I saw it sailing away up Belfast Lough out to Southampton.[142]

John was too young to have known the local people that were on the *Titanic* when it left Belfast that day.

I didn't know any people, actually. I had friends who had gone out to America on ships earlier but they were not on the *Titanic*. I just knew that some of my neighbours on the street had left. They went on it.[143]

Thousands had watched, cheering, waving handkerchiefs, and singing songs such as 'Rule Britannia' as the ship sailed from Belfast. Eight days later, during its maiden voyage to New York, passengers would embark at Southampton, Cherbourg and Cobh before it sailed off across the Atlantic with a total of 2,208 souls aboard. The *Titanic* sank on 15 April with the loss of 1,503 lives. Only 705 passengers were rescued.[144]

My father was actually devastated when he heard the news. Indeed, he just broke down and he cried like a child. I never saw my father crying in my lifetime until then. He was very, very saddened by it all, not only the loss of the ship and the pride in building it but the loss of the lives because a lot of the people who were on the ship were the men who worked with him. His head foreman, his manager and a young apprentice beside him, they were all lost on the ship.[145]

Captain Smyth of the *Titanic* had been to Belfast on a number of occasions. In 1904, he had conducted sea trials of a ship named the *Baltic*, followed by visits in 1911 and 1912 in connection with the *Olympic*. He had also been in Belfast on 2 April 1912 to command the *Titanic's* sea trials and subsequent delivery to Southampton.[146] John deemed it unlikely, however, that his father would have ever seen or met him.

Well, I wouldn't think so, no. No, he wouldn't have. I don't know that he was ever on the *Titanic*. He worked in the joiner shop making the doors and all for the *Titanic*. He worked for the *Titanic*. He wasn't actually on it.[147]

John remembered the reaction to the sinking around Belfast.

The whole city was in gloom and despair and my father was terribly annoyed about it. All the pictures that he had up on the walls – he had lots of pictures of the *Titanic* on the walls. We had a long hall in our house and he had a whole load of pictures up on the wall and of the managers of Harland & Wolff, pictures of them. He took them all down, put them away. He just couldn't bear to look at them afterwards until about six months after the event he came to us one day, to the children. He says, he brought us all together.

See my father was a woodworker and he made us wooden money boxes and we saved up our money for the holidays and he got us to open our money boxes and to give him a donation and he had this subscription list and he wrote down our names on the list and we all gave. I remember giving a silver six pence. That was towards a memorial to the *Titanic*, which was being built in Belfast.[148]

The idea for a memorial came about because the people of Belfast felt a deep connection with the ship, as it had been built there and many of the drowned had been natives of the city. In May 1912, a memorial fund raised over £1,000 towards the endeavour, with contributions from, amongst others, the people of Belfast, Harland & Wolff, White Star Line and the family of its deceased designer, Thomas Andrews. The man entrusted with creating the memorial was Sir Thomas Brock RA, who had been responsible for works such as the statue of Queen Victoria outside Buckingham Palace.[149] It wouldn't be unveiled until eight years later (see 26 June 1920).

II APRIL 1912

The Third Home Rule Bill for Ireland was introduced in the House of Commons. John Redmond of the Irish Parliamentary Party believed that Ireland would shortly have Home Rule. Other nationalist groups weren't so sure, as previous Home Rule bills had been defeated in 1886 and 1893. They were right to be sceptical, because although it was passed in the House of Commons it was rejected in the House of Lords and thus denied. The same thing would happen when the bill was put before both houses the following year.[150] **PATRICK GREENE** in Co. Longford:

Well sure they were hoping to get a parliament of our own. That's all they were hoping for but they were well aware of conditions in the north of Ireland. When I was at school I remember one day in early July we were out in the yard playing and three policemen whom we knew to see passed the school and of course we looked across the wall in curiosity. They had bicycles, they were talking to the teachers, to the master and they had guns on their bicycles, we thought they were guns and they had a helmet hanging on the handlebars. We never saw them wear helmets.

And they were on their way from Abbeyshrule; the barrack would be down to a sergeant and a man at that time. They were on their way to Belfast for the twelfth and they had to cycle from Abbeyshrule into Edgeworthstown the nearest railway station, get on the train, travel five miles up to any junction in the middle of a bog, de-train, wait for a train that went from Mullingar to Cavan. Get on that, change at Cavan, and onto the northern line, probably change at Clones; eventually wind in Belfast to be on guard for the twelfth and probably have their heads hammered with stones or bolts and nuts.

That was the, what went on at that time. And then they came back. Sometimes they came back with black eyes or cuts but they got over it. But every year that happened, a big lot of police from the south were drafted up to the north and the people didn't know at the time, well, Carson's Volunteers hadn't arrived at that time but they didn't know what they were going to do. What was going to happen in the north of Ireland? That there'd be a lot of Protestant MPs from that part of the country when whatever parliament we had in Dublin but it never worked out that way.[151]

The Orange Order was founded in 1795, and two years later, on 12 July 1797, the first Orange procession was held in Belfast to commemorate the Battle of the Boyne. The tradition is an annual event every 12 July since.[152]

28 SEPTEMBER 1912

Over 200,000 male unionists signed the Solemn League and Covenant, which was the brainchild of the Ulster Unionist Council. James Craig stage-managed Covenant Day; it was an act of protest against the Home Rule Bill and a pledge to keep Ulster within the United Kingdom.[153] Over 200,000 female unionists signed the corresponding women's declaration; among them **JOHN PARKINSON'S** mother Ellen in Belfast.

> We had very fixed ideas. See we're Protestant people and we just we always wanted to stay really with Britain. And we were suspicious of the Home Rule Bill and of Ireland becoming all one and we in the north our particular part of the community we were all very solidly in favour of staying with Britain. And we used to go round shouting slogans: 'No Home Rule Here'. We just didn't want it. So, we were against Home Rule.[154]

NORMAN DOUGLAS' father's job as an assistant foreman in the Sirocco Engineering Works often required him to travel to various locations in Ireland and the UK to service machinery. Political tensions were often in the air.

> My father worked in a firm in Belfast here. This is only a memory, only a memory. He was down in Cork doing, with four workmen from this factory in Belfast fixing a boiler or something in some particular and I remember him telling me that they were there only working the one day when the boss came to them and told them that they would have to pack their bags and get out of Cork by, within twenty-four hours and that was in 1912.[155]

Norman maintained they were on the receiving end of a republican threat 'because they came from northern Ireland'.[156]

CHAPTER 2

Conflict at home and abroad, January 1913 – December 1918

13 JANUARY 1913

The Ulster Volunteer Force (UVF) was officially established. Its aim was to resist – by physical force if necessary – Irish Home Rule.[1] James Craig helped organise the UVF, and by mid 1914 about 90,000 men had enlisted province-wide. **JOHN PARKINSON**:

> Yes, I remember it well because my father [Frank] was a member of the Ulster Volunteer Force and I remember seeing him going out, putting his uniform on, his haversack and going out with his rifle out to the parades. He was a member of it.[2]

The UVF engaged in drill and military exercises.

> I saw them. They had marches, inspection day parades and that and I would have gone to see those. They were held at a place – Balmoral Showgrounds here in Belfast and also, they'd march past the Belfast City Hall on occasions.[3]

26 AUGUST 1913

James Larkin, with his union, the Irish Transport and General Workers' Union (ITGWU), attempted to break the anti-union stance of the Dublin United Tramways Company (DUTC) and other businesses in the city. William Martin Murphy, chairman of the DUTC and leader of the Dublin Employers' Association, stated that he and 300 other employers would dismiss any employee in the ITGWU. Larkin called a general strike and the companies responded by closing their businesses and locking the employees out.

In November, the Irish Citizen Army (ICA) was launched by James Connolly, who was working with Larkin to enable the locked-out men to defend themselves in clashes with the police and to combat the demoralising impact of unemployment. However, it was evident by January 1914 that the workers had lost the dispute, and they drifted back to work on the employers' terms.[4]

In the coming years, **JACK DUFF** would go on to work as a clerk for the DUTC.[5] One of **GEORGE COOPER'S** earliest memories concerned the food shortages endured by many Dublin families at the time of the strike.

> Sometimes I do believe I remember 1913 – big strike. Liberty Hall was only a small place at that time before it was bombed in 1916 and I remember going down the steps into Liberty Hall which was into the basement at that time, seeing big sacks of sugar which somebody was dealing out a mug-full to each person. But they were hard times.[6]

It was also around the time of this 1913 strike that George's uncle (his father's brother), John Dutton Cooper, with an address at 33 Lennox Street, Portobello, Dublin, first became acquainted with James Connolly and James Larkin. He had sympathy for the workers and their families, as he encountered many of them through his work as a chemist. He would go on to join the ICA. Interestingly, under religion in the 1901 Census John Cooper had described himself as a 'Free thinker', but by the 1911 Census he had reverted to the Church of Ireland.[7]

25 NOVEMBER 1913

The Irish Volunteer Force (IVF) was established, and over 180,000 would go on to join. Their aim was to safeguard the rights of the Irish people, which events in Ulster and in British politics were threatening. The IVF could also be used as a pressure group to force a just solution to the Irish question.[8] Some months later, Cumann na mBan, the 'League of Women', was formed in 1914 as an auxiliary corps to complement the IVF. As children, **GERRY SMYTH** and his friends used to gather and watch a corps of the Volunteers drilling in Stackallen.

> They had a rook rifle point 22 and we used go down the field. And you know an ordinary griddle for cooking? That was propped on the ground and a target stuck on that and that was what they fired at.[9]

Their playtime was often spent mimicking the Volunteers' drill.

20 MARCH 1914

The British government were concerned about the strength of the UVF in Ulster and wanted to increase the army presence there. At the time, the British army were stationed at the Curragh, Co. Kildare, and were propositioned about going north to march against the unionists and to bring them into line. The reply was that many would rather resign than go, and the event was known as the Curragh Mutiny.[10] In April, the UVF landed arms and ammunition at Larne in Co. Antrim that had come from Germany in two ships. **JOHN PARKINSON'S** father didn't bring his UVF activities home with him.

> No, he very, very seldom spoke about it. All I knew of it was that I saw him coming out with his uniform and coming back in.[11]

NORMAN DOUGLAS said none of his 'friends or relations had any part to play' in the UVF or 'in any of the organisations at all'.[12] It was around this time that **ANTHONY MCGINLEY'S** parents left their farm in Breenagh, Glenswilly, and moved into the liquor trade.

> But sadly, the farm, we had a pretty good farm as farms went on the glen. It was sold in 1914 and my parents went into Tyrone – Strabane – to a public house. And I went to school there for a while and the public house.[13]

Anthony's father, Michael, endured much intimidation from loyalists when he moved to Strabane, but apparently this only served to make him more active in nationalist causes in the town.[14]

Meanwhile in Cork city, **GEORGE CARPENTER** joined the 1st Cork Company of the Boys' Brigade, which was connected to Christ Church, South Main Street.[15] The Boys' Brigade is basically a Protestant organisation aimed at promoting God as well as Christian values amongst boys. There is also a big emphasis on instilling discipline and obedience through sport and other activities.

> The Boys' Brigade for training youths how to be, live a good life and also, we had gymnasium and boxing and other drills, foot drills. And then we had dummy-rifles and when the trouble times broke out, all our rifles, dummy-rifles, were stolen by the IRA. And in fact, we had a few boys that were in the IRA too and they were really good soldiers. And the training we got was real infantry training. We'd have to go out and around fields and field crafts and study streams and how to jump across a stream using sticks, you see? And we used get over quite easily then afterwards. There was some people fell in.[16]

13 APRIL 1914

GEORGE CARPENTER'S brother Herbert Henry was born at their home in Maymount. That night, in advance of the birth, George and his siblings Richard, Willie and Bobby were told by his father that he was taking them to the pictures. They all walked to the Palace, where variety shows were held, but they were denied entry because they hadn't booked. The Dixie Minstrels were performing there that night. The Carpenters then walked down to the South Mall to the Assembly Rooms, where they were admitted. The first picture they watched was about lions and tigers. All through the performance, a lady played the piano. The next film shown was a boxing match between Georges Carpentier from France and Bombardier Billy Wells from England. They had fought each other in June and December of the previous year, both bouts won by Carpentier (the similar sounding name to his own wasn't lost on George). He and his siblings were exhausted when they arrived home, having walked roughly three miles in total that night. On reaching the door, they heard a child screaming and then a nurse came down the stairs holding their new brother. George would go on to meet Georges Carpentier at his bar in Paris in 1957 (see Chapter 9).[17]

In the early part of the twentieth century, many diseases and infections that are rare nowadays were prevalent. George Carpenter had first-hand experience of these later in the year and was treated by a Dr Hegarty.

> Diphtheria and scarlet fever, scarlatina. I got diphtheria and I remember walking down with my mother and father and I was only about five or six and we went to hospital in the District Hospital. It was off the Douglas Road. And I got injections inside there then and I spotted my temperature was a hundred and three at times. And one day, mother brought in biscuits to me. She wasn't allowed in, she had to see me through the window and she gave the nurse biscuits for me and she put them into a cupboard. And that night, the nurse was going along to the cupboard stowing away the biscuits, so when she had gone out, I went out and took them. Brought them to bed with me and my temperature was up to one hundred and three the following morning.[18]

George recovered, but a school friend of his named Tom Daly and his sister weren't so lucky. They both died from scarlatina around the time that he left hospital in 1914.[19] A year earlier, **JOHN PARKINSON** also contracted diphtheria and had to spend a few weeks in Purdysburn Fever Hospital in Belfast.[20]

25 MAY 1914

The Third Home Rule Bill was passed in the House of Commons and did not need to go through the House of Lords this time because of a Parliament Act. For it to become law, all it required was the royal assent. Many nationalists felt that Irish Home Rule was imminent, and **PATRICK GREENE** recalled the atmosphere around his locality in Co. Longford.

> The National Party, the United Irish League, the Irish Nationalist Party. They were all. Our two Members of Parliament were both the same party. There wasn't anything very, they were all looking forward to Home Rule and when Home Rule was granted, 1913 they had celebrations and bonfires and that sort of thing. Then the war started and Home Rule was put on the shelf.[21]

The bill received the royal assent on 18 September 1914, but it was accompanied by an Act simultaneously suspending it for 12 months or until the end of the Great War.[22] This led to many nationalists losing faith in the constitutional path. **JOHN PARKINSON** spoke about loyalist reaction to the Third Home Rule Bill at the time.

> Well of course we treated everything with a lot of suspicion. We just didn't want it. We wanted to be always part of Britain, then the war came on in the year 1914 and it suddenly took over. People were more concerned about the war than they were about Ireland and so more attention was paid to it.[23]

12 JULY 1914

At this time, the headquarters of the Orange Order institution was located in Dublin and there were several Orange halls scattered around the city. However, Fowler Memorial Hall, which was located at No. 10 Rutland Square (now Parnell Square), served as the principal Orange hall for the majority of the city's 2,000 Orangemen, who were all opposed to Home Rule. In 1914, there were eleven lodges based in Fowler Memorial Hall.[24] One of the brethren was George Samuel, father of **GEORGE COOPER**.

> Well believe it or not, in the early days that's when my father was young, they had Orange lodges in Dublin and my father was in those days an Orangeman. And even in those days there was pitched battles. Even in his day there was pitched battles because there's a place on Parnell Square and it was a Freemason hall and my father was in there one day and the next thing what they call a float – a horse-drawn car with stones in it – and there were stones being thrown and my father was on the steps and the heroes in the hall shut the door and left my father and somebody else on the steps when they were young and they had to grapple with the other people. So in those days there was terrible, I mean religious bigotry was terrible in those days. There was a lot of it.[25]

Two Belfast interviewees had childhood memories of orange parades, first **NORMAN DOUGLAS**, who disputed the notion that there was ever much trouble.

> In my early days my dad used take me to see the Twelfth parade but that was the only time on the Twelfth day. There was no lead-ups or anything of that nature that I can remember ... [The parades were] very different to what they are today. There were lovely bands and the marchers were all well-groomed and properly dressed and it was done in great precision. It was really a great sight to behold.[26]

JOHN PARKINSON was also a regular at Twelfth celebrations in the city. Although his father was a member of the UVF and a staunch unionist, displaying the Union Jack from their house on occasions, he was not a member of the Orange Order.[27]

> In those days we always went to see the parades. I never became a member of the Orange Order, but I was always interested in just going to see it. It was always a great spectacle seeing the men all marching, the bands and all playing so the flags waving. It was an occasion.[28]

26 JULY 1914

The Howth gun-running took place when 1,000 members of the IVF marched to Howth to meet a consignment of arms and ammunition coming from Germany in two yachts. British troops tried in vain to intercept the operation and on their return were jeered by crowds. Some members of the crowds threw stones. What happened next was touched upon by **JACK DUFF**.

Our Bloody Sunday would have been away back in 1914 or 1915 when the Sherwood Foresters (King's Own Scottish Borderers) opened fire on a meeting of people in Bachelors Walk in Dublin and opened fire on them.[29]

The King's Own Scottish Borderers opened fire on Bachelors Walk, killing three civilians and wounding many.[30] The dead were Mary Duffy, Patrick Quinn and James Brennan.

4 AUGUST 1914

Britain declared war on Germany and entered World War I. Edward Carson, the unionist leader, and John Redmond, the nationalist leader, worked to persuade their supporters to join the British army and the war effort. They claimed that if they did so, Westminster would have to give in to their political demands. The Irish Volunteer Force split following Redmond's appeal, resulting in 170,000 breaking away and forming the National Volunteers. About 11,000 remained in the Irish Volunteers.[31] **DAN KEATING** discussed reaction to the split in Kerry.

> In the course of time the World War broke out and the British and some Irishmen, they wanted to convert the Volunteer force into the British army ... At that time now when the split came between Redmond's Volunteers and you could say the IRA, the vast majority favoured the IRA and the IRA now were led by among others Austin Stack, Paddy Cahill, John Joe Sheehy, Johnny O'Connor – Farmer's Bridge and John Joe Rice in south Kerry, Jeremiah Riordan in Caherciveen and when they did divide there was very few went with Redmond's Volunteers. They all supported, and it was that way along.[32]

Indeed **JOHN KELLY** in Co. Galway, by now aged 12, claimed to have joined the Irish Volunteers, Derrydonnell Company, in the year 1914. His brother, Michael, was also a member. Their captain was Michael Keane.[33]

In Ulster, many thousands of men from the UVF went on to fight in the war. In all, roughly 200,000 men from the island of Ireland served in the conflict and 40,000 died. **GERRY SMYTH** watched a local corps of the National Volunteers preparing for war in Stackallen, Co. Meath.

> This was before 1916. 1914 you had John Redmond's volunteers. There was probably a corps in every parish and as a child of about five [or] six a group of us used to gather. They used to drill on the crossroads at the school and we used to fall in behind them and do all the drill work and I suppose before I was eight years of age I was able to slope arms and shoulder arms and stand to attention and the lot. Fully trained in military drill and never lost it ...
>
> The man who was drilling them that time, he was a British army reserve which was quite usual in the country and he did all the drilling on Redmond's Volunteers and he was very strict. Even his own brother, he'd shout at him when he'd be drilling them. I remember him getting them to number off do you see. When the line corps line would be lined

up, you'd get number off 1, 2, 3, 4 down the line do you see and his brother happened to be number 11 and he shouted out. 'Number 11, stop the talking' – very strict.[34]

PATSY HOLMES said that the train station in Mallow used to give the departing soldiers a great send-off.

> Now coming up from Queenstown there, the British navy were stationed down there in Haulbowline. Now they were coming up and at every station there was a little – a buffet for to give them all when they'd be passing. They'd all get teas and things there at the buffet in Mallow. There was one in every station. They were going straight to the front after that.[35]

Patsy's father, William, was greenkeeper at Mallow Golf Club, which was located at the 'Carrigeens' near the Convent of Mercy. Incidentally, Patsy's older brother Bill later played professionally and forged out a successful career for himself as a golf coach in the United States.[36] At weekends, Patsy did a bit of caddying and he never forgot four British army officers whom he claimed to have met for the last time in 1915. However, because of the battle he references, there's a possibility that it was the year previous.

> There was four, my brother, now one of my friends was in charge of a golf-links in Mallow – my father. Well, I was too young for it. I was a caddy, but I used go up caddying after school on a Saturday and four officers they used come up from Ballyvonaire. That's Ballyvonaire down near Buttevant you know, a big army post. There was thousands of them there ... but there was four of them used come playing golf every Saturday – Lieutenant Leckett, Captain Orwald, Anderson and Kelly.
>
> Well, I was caddying for the young fellow – Leckett was his name and of course I knew the layout of the course well and he used play a great round there. By God this day I said to him, says I, will you be up on Saturday? ... And he put his hands around me, 'No Patsy,' says he, 'We're all going away Tuesday to Mons.' The war broke out, I never saw him after. Four of them were killed. And I do remember them well going off and the soldiers and they singing when they'd come up from Queenstown and the buffet would be there and the trains waiting and they all going off – poor old devils.[37]

Mons in Belgium had been the location of the first battle between British and German forces on the Western Front. It was fought on 23 August 1914. The British inflicted heavy losses on the Germans despite being heavily outnumbered, but on hearing that their allies the French had retreated from fighting the Germans at Charleroi and would therefore not be in a position to offer them assistance, the British decided to likewise retreat from Mons. To remain on would have left them further exposed to attack, and the Germans had already drafted in re-enforcements. Overall, the British suffered 1,600 casualties and the Germans 5,000. Close to half of the British casualties came from the 4th Middlesex and the 2nd Royal Irish Battalions.[38] Theoretically, the four officers known to Patsy Holmes could have been killed or subsequently died from wounds at any stage of the war, but of the surnames he gave, only a Lieutenant Colin Knox Anderson of the Queen's Own (Royal West Kent Regiment) was killed on the actual day of the Battle of Mons. The 26-year-old was a native of Kent.[39] Whether he was one of the four men Patsy knew from the golf course may never be known.

NORMAN DOUGLAS' older brother Bertie was another who joined up, enlisting aged 19 in Belfast as a private in the Royal Irish Rifles on 14 September 1914.[40] The former clerk seemingly trained at Finner Camp in Co. Donegal prior to being deployed to France with the British Expeditionary Force as a rifleman in October 1915 (see 1 July 1916).[41] **ANTHONY MCGINLEY** was living in Co. Tyrone when the war broke out.

> Well I was only a schoolboy at that time but I remember big recruiting meetings you know in Strabane and there was great excitement altogether. And there was a terrible lot joined the British army and went out to France.[42]

When in April 1915 the poet Tom Kettle of the Royal Dublin Fusiliers visited the town as part of his nationwide tour to encourage enlistment into the British army, Anthony's father Mick challenged him as he spoke from the platform as to why an Irishman should fight for England. The RIC were called to arrest him, but he managed to evade them down a side street.[43] It was shortly afterwards that Anthony made the move back to rural Donegal.

> I never liked the town, I didn't like the public house and I came up the hills here to my uncle and aunt and I never went back, never lived with my parents again.[44]

These were his mother's siblings, Máire and Muiris Mac Daibhid (McDevitt), who lived in Largnalarkin, Ballinamore.[45]

> Because my father and mother do you see lived in a public house in Strabane, sold the farm in 1914 and I left there and come up here to me; this was my grandfather's house, to my uncle and aunt.[46]

His grandfather Anthony McDevitt, known locally as Anton Ned McDevitt, also resided in the house at this time. Regarded as a great storyteller, he died in 1917.[47]

> It was kind of exciting times because that was the start of the Great War and well around here; they worked as they always did on the hills. They put in a bit of a crop and had sheep and cattle and more or less they have the same way of living yet.[48]

Also in the north, **JOHN PARKINSON** had clear recollections of the war's impact on Belfast.

I do remember it quite well 1914–1918. You see I'd be a wee boy of about seven, seven to ten then and I remember seeing all the men going off to war and saw them coming back on leave sometimes, sadly some of them coming back after being wounded. Some of them had their legs amputated and their arms amputated and made it very gruesome and a lot of them. I had a cousin myself of my own who was taken prisoner of war and he was never heard of after that, he was declared missing presumed dead.[49]

John's cousin was named Johnny Boyd. At one stage during the war he returned home to Belfast on leave, bringing with him a spiked German helmet that he had picked up as a souvenir on the French battlefields. Prior to heading back, he allowed John and the other children to try it on. This was the last time they set eyes on him, and his exact date of death is undetermined. Interestingly, his father, Tom Boyd, also served in World War I and survived.[50] John Parkinson's father had a role in the war effort as well.

He was not allowed to join the forces. The workmen that were engaged on important government work were not allowed to join the forces. So my father was registered as a special munitions worker and he worked for the war effort but not in uniform. You weren't allowed to join up if they wanted to use you and use your skills at your trade.[51]

Frank Parkinson had plenty of skills to put to use.

Well, my father was very much involved as in aircraft, as a worker in Harland & Wolff because they were involved in building all the ships, not only passenger ships but battleships, cruisers and all. And he was very much involved in building for the war effort. And then he switched and he started building, helping to build airplanes. I remember him going out to the airplane factory to work in the airplane factory.[52]

GEORGE COOPER'S father, George Samuel, a house painter, would leave Dublin and work in Scotland for a period during the 1914–1918 war.[53] Similarly, these years were tough for **GEORGE CARPENTER'S** family because they were separated. His father, William, went to look after a farm he owned in Leitrim and took three of his sons with him. George remained in Cork and looked forward to going to the train station with his mother to collect the potatoes his father would send down. He continued in the 1st Cork Company of the Boys' Brigade and remarked how some older members of the organisation lied about their age in order to join the British army. Since they already knew how to drill, many of them were sent out to the front quicker than other recruits, with some of them even promoted to officers.[54]

KATHLEEN CHARLES could picture in her mind's eye several men from Kanturk who enlisted. One man in particular ran a bakery and joined up in England; she said he was ultimately shot.[55] **PATRICK FITZGERALD** from Dunmoon remembered that World War I 'put prices soaring'.[56] As a teenager in Bantry during the war years, **DANIEL O'DONOVAN** spent time boxing fish and helping to sell these in various towns in West Cork. In fact, the family had considerable dealings with salted fish and operated a fishing trawler for a period. They also had salmon boats for drift net fishing.[57]

> Well, as for ourselves, my father being a publican was also a fish merchant and he sent his fish chiefly to the Cork and Dublin market and during the war years to Billingsgate, England.[58]

Daniel's father died in 1918, the same year that the conflict would end.

7 MAY 1915

The *Lusitania* sank ten miles off the Old Head of Kinsale after being struck by a German torpedo. The ship was on the last day of its voyage from New York to Liverpool. Nearly 1,200 passengers on board died, including one of the ship's surgeons Dr Joseph Garry, from Shanahea, Kildysart, who was known to **MAI GROGAN**.[59] The man she would later marry, but for now knew as a neighbour, would also have a connection to the disaster.

> Well, I heard about it. I did, I remember it all right. There was a first cousin of my husband's. He was in America and he was flying, coming home because the war was starting in America and it got caught coming into Queenstown was it? They were all lost and that was it. I remember that much of it.[60]

This man's name was Michael Galvin, formerly of Derryshane, Coolmeen, Kilmurry McMahon, who had emigrated to New York in September 1906, aged 22, on board the SS *Baltic*. On 9 May, his brother John had received a letter from him stating that he was embarking on the *Lusitania* at New York with the intention of coming home to Co. Clare. He may have wished to avoid being conscripted into the United States Army in the event of them entering World War I, which they did in 1917. Galvin travelled as a third-class passenger and was a general labourer and unmarried. He and Dr Garry have no known graves.[61] Years later, **GEORGE CARPENTER** came across items from the *Lusitania* that had been washed up in West Cork.

> There was an auction below in Glandore in the castle. The furniture in the castle was being sold and there was three deckchairs there and I bid for them and I was told afterwards that they came off the *Lusitania*. And so when I was told that I relished it more and I kept them carefully and then when I went down to Glandore we took them out and used them as garden seats. They were lovely. I had one then left over (two fell apart) only when I came to Kinsale and I presented that to the museum in Kinsale.[62]

George said he paid 'about a pound each' for the chairs.[63] It was also around the time of the *Lusitania* disaster that Mai Grogan moved away from home for the first time. She would live with her uncle in Derra, just outside Kilrush, and attend the technical school in the town for a year. She was struck by the deprivation in the town compared with the country.

> Kilrush was a nice town that time, a lot of poverty there though that time – a lot of it. You could know it. But Kilrush is not as good as it should be. It's not like Ennis. Ennis is a thriving town. But we had Glynn's Mill in Kilrush and Ryan's Mill and there were several factories there – Doherty's. None of them are there today. We got all our flour and meal from Glynn's in Kilrush.[64]

The move to Kilrush was a big change for Mai. Even though it was relatively close, she had rarely been outside of Kilmurry McMahon before this. Travel was unheard of.

> You had your horse and trap and as for Ennis, you wouldn't see Ennis from the round of the year. But Kilrush only when you want clothes or shoes or something. Kilrush was about seven or eight miles and Ennis was double that. There was no such thing as going to Dublin or anything else in them times.[65]

21 MAY 1915

The life of **SEÁN CLANCY'S** 15-year-old cousin and best friend, Michael Dineen, was cut tragically short. They lived near each other in Earl Hill, Clonlara, and were in the same class at school. The boy was helping his father, who was training a young horse to pull a cart on the public road near Seán's home, when suddenly, as reported in the *Nenagh News*:

> The animal took to flight. The runaway collided with a car, and Dineen was thrown violently, and when attended to by his father, life was found extinct. The driver of the other car was also injured.[66]

This driver of the second pony and trap was an elderly man, but fortunately he recovered. Seán Clancy was among the first to find his cousin's lifeless body on the side of the road near O'Brien's Bridge and was given the job by his own father of fetching the local priest. A cow-house door from Seán's home was used to carry Michael Dineen's body back to his parents' house. Naturally, there was terrible grief, and memories of the incident remained with Seán throughout his life.[67] The boy's parents were Malachy and Bridget Dineen.[68]

1 AUGUST 1915

Jeremiah O'Donovan Rossa, the veteran Fenian leader, was buried in Glasnevin Cemetery, Dublin. **DAN KEATING** from Castlemaine claimed that the funeral was a successful propaganda exercise for the Volunteers.

> The first awakening must be by Patrick Pearse at an oration over O'Donovan Rossa the noted Fenian. He captured the imagination of the people of Ireland, the Volunteers started to grow everywhere.[69]

9 FEBRUARY 1916

MARGARET CAHILL'S family in Ballinasare had a wedding to celebrate, although it's unlikely they all attended.

> Oh yeah, in Mayo, Nell my sister, Nell was a nurse there and she married. Farmer was his name. He was an Englishman that came over and he fell down and he hurt his knee and she took care of him. She was a nurse and they got married. His name was Michael [Patrick] Farmer.[70]

Ellen Cahill and Patrick Farmer, a solicitor's clerk, were married in February 1916 in Ballina.[71] He was actually a native of the town and played football for Ballina Stephenites GAA club.[72] One of his sisters, Maggie, was also a nurse in the local hospital.[73] Ellen Farmer had given birth to at least six children by 1924; a son named Patrick died after 16 days in 1923.[74]

> I went up to visit my sister Nell. She was a nurse there. We were all nurses, all of us and I used to go and visit her in Ballina.[75]

In later years, Margaret would train as a nurse (see 17 May 1926).

24 APRIL 1916

The Easter Rising began in Dublin; it lasted six days (24–29 April). Patrick Pearse proclaimed the Irish Republic to the people of Ireland outside the GPO, and the IRB, together with the Irish Volunteers and the Irish Citizen Army, took part in an armed insurrection. Cumann na mBan also played a part. It failed for a number of reasons, but **DAN KEATING** offered two, which centred around Co. Kerry.

> You had the group in Dublin, and they believed that they'd have a rising against the British, and it must be said first of all the ship that was bringing in the arms came along and there was no one to meet it because the men that had all the information were drowned in Killorglin, which left then they had no information whatever. Casement was captured and shortly after executed.[76]

The ship Dan refers to was the *Aud*. It left Germany on 9 April, destined for the coast of Kerry and carrying arms and ammunition. It had no wireless, but was due to arrive on 20 April and be met by Roger Casement, who was travelling from Germany to Ireland by submarine. The submarine landed, but the *Aud* went to the wrong port. Casement by now had decided against the Rising, but was arrested while waiting. Meanwhile, the *Aud* assumed that there was some change of plan when there was no one there to meet it. Soon the Royal Navy spotted the *Aud* and escorted it to Cobh. Just before getting there, the German captain scuttled his ship and he and the crew jumped into the sea. The arms were no more. Roger Casement was hanged on 3 August.[77]

The drownings Dan mentions occurred on the night of 21 April 1916. Seven men had orders to dismantle a British wireless transmitting set at a wireless training school in Caherciveen and to set up their own transmitter at Ballybard, Tralee, in order to contact the *Aud*. They were unaware that the *Aud* had no radio, so it was a pointless task. In any event, two cars made their way to Caherciveen to take the radio transmitter. They travelled via Killorglin, but eventually the second car lost sight of the first. The driver drove along what he thought was a bridge but in fact was Ballykissane Pier. On realising his error, the car was halfway over the pier, so he shouted a warning to his three companions and bailed. He survived, but his three companions in the car drowned in the River Laune.[78]

> Nevertheless, the rising went on in Dublin and there was bitter fighting for the course of a week and the British actually they had to bring in re-enforcements and they were met in Dun Laoghaire and Mount Street Bridge and they suffered terrible casualties. But they had the guns and the artillery and finally they reduced the GPO in Dublin to a burning inferno and the Volunteers had to surrender. Most of them were captured and they were sent with the exception of the top people in the IRA – a number of them captured, court-martialled and sentenced to death.[79]

In his Military Service Pension file, **JOHN KELLY** wrote that he rendered service with the Derrydonnell Company of Irish Volunteers during the week of the rebellion. On Easter Monday, he did guard duty for Captain Alfred Monahan at 'Costello', Co. Galway; did outpost duty armed with a pike at the Agricultural Station, Athenry, on Tuesday; did outpost duty at Moyode on Wednesday; helped to break up railway lines at Derrydonnell Bridge on Thursday; went to Limepark on Friday; and was demobilised by Liam Mellows on Saturday.[80] Even though he was only six at the time, **GEORGE COOPER** had a clear recollection of events in Dublin.

> Well, we lived so near to it in D'Olier Street. Just off, even today now you can see it, it's called Leinster Market. It's just; you can get into it from the gas company. In fact, the Leinster Market where I lived – I believe it's the gas company have offices there now at the moment. I remember looking out of that window in 1916. Soldiers, a British soldier had come up the market and my father warned him and what he said to them was: 'Be careful because it's hot up there.' Meaning there was plenty of bullets flying around. But evidently one soldier didn't heed the warning. There must have been a sniper just waiting for somebody to put their head out and he was shot. And I remember the woman who lived in the house beside us going down and washing the blood away. And that was in D'Olier Street. Now the archway is still there in D'Olier Street and if you ever stood and looked into the archway, you'll see the window where I stood in 1916.[81]

The gunfire was so intense that the Cooper homestead needed protection from wayward missiles.

So all the shots and all the bullets and then our bedroom looked out to a little alleyway, which looks onto O'Connell Bridge. Seeing how much stray bullets flying around, my father put a mattress off the bed up to that window so that any stray bullets would go into the mattress.[82]

George also witnessed the destruction caused to the capital by the events of Easter week, with some people taking advantage of the situation for their own betterment.

As soon as it finished my father brought me up to the GPO, which was still smouldering and of course it was in ruins and so was O'Connell Street, the Gresham Hotel and all that was flattened and of course Cleary's. I don't know whether Cleary's was there before, and I remember they were in Abbey Street and then they went back to O'Connell Street after that. But all O'Connell Street and I remember my father bringing me out to the laneway, which looked out at the back of our house. And at the corner of Abbey Street was a big shoe place called Mansfield's Shoe Place and as we looked out and it was blazing, it was on fire.

A lot of the boys, the bigger boys from Townsend Street used to come up the market, Leinster market out onto the quays and they were doing looting as much as they could. My two brothers were a little more clever as well as some of the others because when these boys went into the next place called Lemons in O'Connell Street and got boxes of sweets. As soon as they were starting to come down the laneway somebody would hit the box and they'd be all on the ground, so everybody was diving on it. But they were hard times.[83]

JACK DUFF also lived in Dublin at the time of the Rising.

I did indeed. The whole of O'Connell Street was still smouldering and in ruins. Liberty Hall on the Quays was shelled from a gunboat that was moored at the bridge and I understand but I'm not sure that the Liberty Hall was also shelled – not Liberty Hall but the GPO and the other buildings in O'Connell Street were also shelled from that also. But they continued shelling and firing on it until eventually they started with incendiary bombs, incendiary shells and that's what set the place alight.

My clearest memory of the remaining buildings being pulled down. They were a danger, is to see the fire brigade putting big wire ropes around them. Fixing them onto tenders, driving the tenders out and down came the remains of whatever building they were pulling down. So it was a long, long time before things got back in to normal again.[84]

He summed up the significance of the Rising, including the reaction amongst ordinary Dubliners to it.

Leading up to 1916 and after 1916, things seemed to take a complete turn over. Sinn Féin began to be known and Sinn Féin began to be known as the party who was going to clear the British out of Ireland. And they were going to do it by various means that they had started off on their own accord such as boycotts of British goods and burning of British newspapers and other small items like that but there was no real trouble here until the rebellion took place.

And the rebellion of 1916, I believe I would be about thirteen years of age then. It wasn't wholeheartedly supported by the people – not by no means. Because at that period of time in Dublin anyway, an enormous amount of people – men had joined the army the British army and while they were away on service their wives were getting what was known as the ring paper. And the ring paper was a folder and they got paid a separation allowance for their husband being away and each time they got this there was a stamp put into the ring. That's where it got the name of the ring paper. But if anything happened such as their pulling out of it or something like that, the ring paper money was immediately stopped or if they were convicted of any sort of crime in the army or out of it, the money was also stopped. So, it's understandable as to why they weren't very keen on rebellion – they were getting nothing out of it.

So much so that when the prisoners were being marched down the Quays for to be shipped away to British prisons, people of Dublin came out and threw stones at them, threw insulting remarks at them and that continued oh for a long, long time until the IRA and Sinn Féin combined. They decided they were going to take this seriously and put an end to this. That's what brought about the Proclamation of the Republic and the formation of the Irish Republican Army.[85]

The attitude of George Cooper's parents and siblings towards the Rising mirrored that of the majority.

Against it because I was twelve years of age before our government took over. My eldest sister was married to a Welsh soldier and so all the years gone by there were intermarriages and so when it happened there wasn't much sympathy for those people.[86]

This marriage didn't take place until later (see 2 June 1922); however, not everybody in George's wider family circle was against the rebellion.

But of course, I know my uncle was in with them. He was in the Citizen Army, which was Larkin's and Connolly's. I believe my uncle was more on chemicals and I do believe that his job was to help the wounded. And as far as I know, he was one of the stretcher-bearers who carried Connolly out of the burning GPO into Henry Street.[87]

John Dutton Cooper had been attached to the South Circular Road Section of the Irish Citizen Army, having joined in 1915. He went on to attend ambulance lectures by Dr Kathleen Lynn and drilling in Liberty Hall under James Connolly.[88]

During Easter week John Cooper hadn't been mobilised to participate in the actual fighting but was in the GPO from the Tuesday until the Friday, assisting the men by erecting barricades, administrating to the wounded, and bringing up coal from the cellars. It is untrue that he had carried James Connolly out of the burning GPO into Henry Street following the surrender (which occurred on the Saturday), as Cooper had left the burning building with the nurses on the Friday on the orders of Connolly to escort the wounded to Jervis Street Hospital. In fact, it had been on the Thursday when James Connolly was wounded in the lane off Abbey Street that John Cooper had brought the stretcher out to where Connolly lay, though he admitted that it had been two other men who physically carried Connolly back into the GPO, as he had been too heavy for him to lift. Cooper did accompany them back into the GPO, however. John Cooper was subsequently arrested by the British, deported to Wakefield prison followed by Frongoch, and released in August 1916.[89]

In later years Cooper fell on hard times and his health broke down. By 1935, he was an inmate of No. 1 Protestant Hospital (Men), Dublin Union, James Street, which was essentially a workhouse. In 1938, when he got special permission to leave the Dublin Union for a few hours to appear in a group photograph being taken of 1916 veterans in Croke Park, such were his dire circumstances that a small subscription was made up for him before the men dispersed. Subsequent newspaper articles referred to him as a '*Pauper*'.[90]

George's father, George Samuel, never lost contact with his brother who never married and would occasionally visit their home prior to getting ill. However, John Dutton Cooper's involvement in the rebellion resulted in many of his family and friends shunning him, so when he died at the Protestant Rest for the Dying, Camden Row, Dublin on 1 July 1943, not all were willing to attend his funeral. He is buried at Mount Jerome Cemetery in Harold's Cross.[91] George remembered that he enjoyed music but insisted that in terms of politics it would be inaccurate to describe his uncle as a republican.

> No, he was communist. See … Citizen Army is not the IRA. See they're Connolly's men – Jim Larkin's men. Jim Larkin is in O'Connell Street, the big statue and I shook hands with him when my uncle died and at the funeral Jim Larkin came up and I shook hands with Jim Larkin.[92]

In April 1944, Jim Larkin would ask Minister for Defence, Oscar Traynor, to consider the case of John Dutton Cooper, whom he said had actually been in the Dublin Union for 16 years. The expense of paying for his funeral had impacted on the financial circumstances of his three siblings (George Samuel, Mary and Elizabeth), so Larkin asked Traynor if the government would repay the money for burying him and associate his name with the National Graves Association who would foot the bill instead. The minister replied that if Larkin sent him the particulars, he would have them considered.[93]

A second interviewee with a family connection to the events of Easter week was **ANTHONY McGINLEY** in Co. Donegal.

> But they [his parents] were living in a public house in Strabane and 1916 came and a brother of my fathers had a job in Dublin – pension officer and his two sons marched out with Pearse. They were students, two first cousins of ours.[94]

Anthony's uncle Peter Toner McGinley (Cú Uladh), who lived in Drumcondra Road, Dublin, was a noted writer and patriot. He established the *Donegal Christmas Annual* in 1882, and along with James Connolly, Maud Gonne, Arthur Griffith and others was a frequent contributor to the republican periodical *Shan Van Vocht*. He established the first branch of the Gaelic League in Ulster in 1895 and helped establish a branch in Portarlington in 1905. One of his closest friends was Patrick Pearse who opened St Enda's all-Irish school for nationalist boys in 1908. Peter Toner not only helped Pearse to set it up, he also sent 10 of his 12 children to the school.[95] In fact, five of the men executed following the Rising had taught at the school and over 30 St Enda's boys (past and present) had fought in the GPO.[96] These included two of Peter Toner's sons – Eunan and Conor – who were past pupils at the time. They were members of the Rathfarnham Company of the Irish Volunteers and had helped construct homemade bombs in the basement of St Enda's in the period leading up to the Rising. Aware of the likelihood of death, Pearse had sent them home for their father's permission to participate in the Rising, which was granted. They joined him in the GPO on Easter Monday and evacuated with him the following Saturday after the surrender. In fact, Eunan, aged 16, was the youngest fighter in the GPO and was sent to Stafford Jail before Frongoch.[97] Conor was sentenced to 10 years' penal servitude in Frongoch but was released the following Christmas.[98] Anthony would go on to cite the exploits of his cousins as a motivating reason as to why he and his brother would later join the Volunteers, but what was his recollection of the reaction to the events of 1916 in Donegal?

> Well, you see there was a curious reaction. Ireland was so long under England and peace that there was a lot of, well the ones belonging to the Hibernians. That was the Irish society. They made out they would ruin the country with trouble getting up arms. They couldn't see it all. But bit by bit the Sinn Féin party started to take over you see as time went on and naturally a lot of the young people followed the adventure of them rising in arms you know.[99]

It's interesting to note that another set of McGinley brothers from Dublin (unrelated to Anthony) also participated in the Rising. Patrick and Liam fought in the GPO in O'Connell Street and were subsequently incarcerated.[100]

When the rising was in full swing, many families living in Dublin left their homes and didn't return until the fighting had ceased. **GERRY SMYTH** in Stackallen, Co. Meath, received a visit from his cousins.

> When the rebellion broke out, an uncle of mine and his wife and three children they wheeled a pram from Dublin to Malahide. There were no trains you see from the station, no post anything else and they wheeled it to Malahide and came down to Boat Park Station which was the out station from where I was born about two miles or three from us and wheeled the pram from there to us and they lived there with us for over a fortnight until things calmed down in Dublin. He was teaching in Dublin, and they headed back again then.[101]

The most up-to-date research at the time of writing found that in total 504 were killed during the course of Easter Week. Of these deaths, 84 were insurgents, 127 were British military, 17 were police and 276 were civilians.[102] In the region of 2,500 people were wounded. In the aftermath of the Rising, over 3,000 participants and suspected Volunteers from throughout the country were rounded up, and although many were released, some 1,800 were imprisoned or interned in Britain.[103] Among those rounded up was John Kelly's brother, Michael, of the Derrydonnell Company in Co. Galway. He was interned in Frongoch along with his friends Martin Ruane, Tommy Connell and others. Michael Kelly was released in August, whereupon he rejoined the company.[104] John Kelly was not arrested owing to having gone on the run.[105] **MAI GROGAN** remembered the impact of the Rising on her community.

> We had that trouble there too. And we had a lot of our neighbours, they were in the Rising and the O'Donnells near us, but they were most respectable people. They were the head lads in it – O'Donnells of Tullycrine ... Arthur O'Donnell he was. He was a teacher. He was the head of the IRA there and he got jail for a while after it. In the finish he got a school in Ennis and that was it.[106]

Art O'Donnell from Tullycrine was arrested in Kilrush and was commandant of the 7th Clare Battalion of the Irish Volunteers. He hadn't gone to Dublin, but had prepared himself for action in his own area should the need arise. He was sent to Frongoch Internment Camp in Wales and released in July. O'Donnell was related to Con Colbert, who was one of those executed after the Rising.[107] **PATRICK GREENE** in Co. Longford reiterated what was said earlier about the negative reaction to the Rising at the time.

> Most of the farming community, most of the country people, they didn't agree with 1916. Some of them were old enough to remember the Fenian times and there were a couple of my neighbours had been in their youth had been Fenians although they didn't fight any but they didn't approve, in general people didn't approve of going to war with anybody. It wasn't until later on after 1916.[108]

This was partly due to the executions that the British carried out afterwards. Fifteen rebels were executed in May and one in August (Roger Casement). Dan Keating maintained that an entrepreneur named William Martin Murphy seized the chance to exact revenge on one Rising participant who had helped organise a strike against him some years earlier (see 26 August 1913).

> When there was five or six executed the British were satisfied but the *Independent* newspapers led by Murphy at the time were not satisfied. There was one man still living and wounded. That was James Connolly. But there was a demand by the *Independent* newspapers and Murphy that they be tried and executed, which he was. He was actually, he was wounded but he was tied to a chair and executed.[109]

On 10, 11 and 12 May the *Irish Independent* published editorials warning against leniency towards Connolly and MacDiarmada, who were surviving signatories of the Proclamation. It is important to stress that while William Martin Murphy owned the newspaper, the editorials were actually written by the editor – T.R. Harrington.[110] Éamon de Valera was spared and became one of only three commandants (the other two being Thomas Ashe and Thomas Hunter) to avoid execution after the Easter Rising, as Jack Duff went on to explain.[111]

> He took up a position in Boland's Mill and he was a commandant in the Volunteers at that time and he done all his fighting inside of Boland's Mills in Grand Canal Street in Dublin. And when he was arrested, he was sent off to jail along with the rest of them. He was, I'm speaking now of 1916. He was arrested and put into prison. He was court-martialled and sentenced to death along with the remainder of the Volunteer leaders. Now as you know and as the whole world knows the majority of the leaders were all shot. He was one of them that was saved in Dublin. He got a reprieve, and he was out of jail in about two years' time [June 1917].[112]

Thomas Ashe from Co. Kerry had worked as a teacher in Dublin and was leader of the 5th Battalion of the Dublin Brigade. The week of the Easter Rising they learned that many troops were being shifted from Athlone to Dublin and arranged for the cutting of the railway line at Batterstown. The next morning (28 April), the 45 Volunteers came across Ashbourne RIC Barracks, and on capturing two constables, Ashe called on those inside to surrender. They refused and the firing that ensued began the Battle of Ashbourne. Less than an hour later, those RIC surrendered, but backup arrived in the shape of 24 cars of police. Five-and-a-half hours later the entire RIC surrendered, and the Battle of Ashbourne was won. In total, eight RIC, one of their chauffeurs and two Volunteers were killed. One of the RIC casualties was a Sergeant John Shanagher from Navan.[113] Ashe was later arrested, court-martialled, and sentenced to death. Like de Valera, Ashe managed to avoid being executed and the sentence was later commuted to penal servitude for life. He was released in June 1917, however. Gerry Smyth had a vivid memory of hearing that Sergeant Shanager had been killed – he was with his father at the time.

> We were standing on the road near the school ... with another man. And two people came up from Navan – Barber and a friend of his. And there was no papers and they asked him [Barber] was there any news? And he said, 'Oh Sergeant Shanagher was shot on Ashbourne' – this was the Battle of Ashbourne.[114]

The man standing with Gerry and his father was relieved to hear the news.

> And the answer was when he heard that, 'Thanks be to Jesus,' he said. 'He has the number. He took my name for no light on me bike last week.' That was the sympathy he had with the unfortunate man that was shot in Ashbourne. Memory is I never forgot it now and I was only seven or nine.[115]

As a result of the 1916 Rising and its aftermath, nationalist sentiment in Ireland grew like never before. A tide of young men and women would go on to become actively involved in a struggle for a free, independent Ireland. One of those was **SEÁN CLANCY** from Clonlara, who was greatly influenced by the events of Easter Week.

> Well, I tell you, after leaving the national school I went to Limerick. Limerick city was only a few miles from where I lived and I cycled into secondary school and that was about 1916–1919. The Irish rebellion of 1916 happened of course, as you know at that time. But I think that's what attracted me to the political side of the movement. The young people at that time in Clare, I think they forsook the Home Rule people and the country was very much shocked by the way the British government treated those people who took part in the Rising of 1916. They were shocked at the executions and all the internments and so on. And the young people I think straight away they more of less forsook the parliamentary people and supported the Sinn Féin movement from then on.[116]

DANIEL O'DONOVAN described the impact of news of the rising in Bantry.

> Yes, we heard it and we thought it, going by the elders, we thought it a wonderful thing because it was getting a great blow up. And naturally for us it was the thing because we read so much history in school and spoken about it so much that our side was very much on the favour of an Irish freedom.[117]

I JULY 1916

The bloodiest day in the history of the British army takes place during the Great War. It had a profound impact on **JOHN PARKINSON'S** locality in Belfast.

> There were quite a number of people in our street that went out and never came back. There was a terrible battle on the first of July 1916. It was called the Somme – The Battle of the Somme. And the Ulster Division was nearly wiped out that time – a terrible loss of life.[118]

The battle, which lasted until November, saw the British and French forces attempt to break through the German lines along a 25-mile (40-km) front north and south of the River Somme in northern France. On the opening day of this offensive alone, the British suffered nearly 60,000 casualties, including more than 19,000 soldiers who were killed.[119] Over 2,000 of these fatalities came from the 36th Ulster Division.[120]

> That was when there was the Battle of the Somme and there was thousands of Ulster soldiers. The Ulster Battalion went over the top, as they called it, at a place called Thiepval in France and they were slaughtered. There were hundreds killed. I always remember that. We

commemorate it here to this day here in Belfast with remembrance services.[121]

Ultimately the British and French failed to secure a breakthrough. It's estimated that the British army had suffered 420,000 casualties by the end of the battle and the French 200,000, and the Germans had at least 450,000 killed and wounded.[122]

> The sad thing was a lot of them came back maimed. I had one or two friends who came back that lost limbs, lost their legs and their arms. There was a lot of people were blown up by explosions and it was very, very sad. I lived on the Grosvenor Road near the Royal Victoria Hospital and it was used largely for accommodating the soldiers that were brought over to convalesce here in Belfast and I used to see them out on their crutches and in their wheelchairs. It was sad to see it all.[123]

Having enlisted in Belfast at the outbreak of the conflict, **NORMAN DOUGLAS'** older brother Bertie had been deployed to France in 1915. In March of the following year, his family received a letter informing them that – whilst serving with the 14th Battalion, Royal Irish Rifles – he was hospitalised in France as a result of heart disease. His father, Robert, was employed in London at this time.

> My brother fought in World War I. He was gassed at the Somme but he lived. He came home. He was demobbed sometime afterwards because of his problem.[124]

According to his Army Service Record, Bertie Douglas was in France until December 1917. He was then transferred to the Army Service Corps on 1 March 1918, re-posted to the Royal Irish Rifles on 8 April 1918 and transferred to the Royal Army Medical Corps on 6 May 1918. His total army service amounted to 4 years, 322 days, and his character was rated as 'very good'. Bertie Douglas transferred to Class 'Z' Army Reserve on 1 August 1919 and was discharged from the army on demobilisation on 31 March 1920.[125]

> And I knew a man that I worked with opened a business and I worked in his firm for a while and he was a major in the army. He went, he joined up and three or four other friends of mine joined up. Two of them didn't come back of course.[126]

7 DECEMBER 1916

David Lloyd George became British prime minister. He started to release some 600 prisoners jailed for their parts in the Rising. Two of these were Michael Collins and Arthur Griffith. De Valera was released the following June.[127] Participants in the Rising were welcomed home as heroes as public opinion shifted towards supporting independence. **DAN KEATING** reiterated the attitude of the day.

Naturally the executions brought a revulsion of feeling in Ireland and Ireland at that stage was very bitter ... In Kerry now it was over 90 per cent republican, and it remained that way all along up to the conflict.[128]

Running as an independent candidate, Count Plunkett was elected to the constituency of North Roscommon in a by-election held in February 1917. He refused to take his seat at Westminster. He was the father of Joseph Plunkett, who was one of those executed after the Rising.

I APRIL 1917

PATSY HOLMES, who was just shy of his 15th birthday, joined the Mallow Company of the Irish Volunteers.[129] He recalled that recruits were given an important piece of advice.

> The first thing you learn when you join up is – see and don't be seen, hear and don't be heard.[130]

He engaged in a lot of training and drilling that was carried out under the charge of Owen Harold, his commanding officer and vice O/C of the Mallow Battalion.[131] Patsy said that such was the intensity of the drilling that on one occasion some 'fellows ran home and they never came back'.[132]

10 MAY 1917

Joe McGuinness was elected to **PATRICK GREENE**'s constituency of South Longford in a by-election. At the time, he was serving three years in Lewes Gaol for his part in the Rising.[133]

> The 1917, we had an election in Longford and one of the candidates was Joe McGuinness. He had, his people had a draper shop in Longford. They were Roscommon people. He had a shop or two in Dublin. He had a shop in Dorset Street and he was out in 1916. He was interned and the local cry was: 'Put him in to take him out.' People thought if he was a Member of Parliament he'd be released. And the nationalist party put up a very brilliant individual – Joseph Mary Flood, a highly educated young man, a native of Longford.[134]

Initially, the Irish Parliamentary Party had three candidates, but close to the day of the election they all agreed to stand down and let the chairman select one to run as the party's sole candidate. It transpired that he picked Patrick McKenna over Joseph Mary Flood and Hugh Garrahan to contest the election.[135]

> And of course, McGuinness was elected. But I don't think he was released that time or for some time afterwards. He might have been released, rearrested later on. That was the start of Sinn Féin – mostly attracted younger people; very few of the older people had any attraction towards Sinn Féin at all.[136]

Patrick remembered the election well and remarked that even though it was a significant victory, support for McGuinness' party was strongest at the other end of the county. He also knew some men who joined the Volunteers.

> Not a lot, I was only a teenager that time. I knew a man – a working man – was first captain of the Volunteers about 1917 or around that time. He was working for a shilling a day for a neighbouring farmer. And he was proposed at a meeting, and he was appointed, but in a year's time Sinn Féin had become popular and he was demoted and a smart farmer's son became head of the Volunteers. He wound up eventually in the army. I don't know what became of him. I lost all track of him in the thirties because I was gone out of the district at the time when I started work. But he, there wasn't very many. Two fellows who went to school with me were actually flying column men, were engaged in some small scraps. Not as much as North Longford. North Longford was much more given to Sinn Féin than South Longford. But there were a number of fellows in the Volunteers and they were round about and they lifted shotguns if they could get them and in some cases they commandeered bicycles for their use. But there wasn't, there was no scrap, no fight in South Longford.[137]

Patrick was never called upon or approached to join the Volunteers:

> No, I was never a Volunteer at all. My father disapproved of all these things. We wouldn't dream of going against my father at that time. I was never a member of the Volunteers at all.[138]

II JULY 1917

Éamon de Valera (Sinn Féin) was elected to **SEÁN CLANCY'S** constituency of East Clare.

> In my part of Clare there was a general election, no not a general election a by-election. Willie Redmond was killed in the war in France, created a vacancy in Clare and there was some doubt about who the candidate should be. Two or three men were suggested and I think they refused to accept the invitation to attend but then out of the blue came this very strange name that was accepted – name of de Valera. People even couldn't pronounce his name at the time. Most of the voters only the households had votes then. Women had no votes. But some of them hadn't even heard of him even though he was a survivor of 1916.
>
> But the young people including myself supported him and I was only what, sixteen years of age at the time but I supported him. And I was on my bicycle going. There was a lot of open-air meetings in those days and I, myself and a young priest, it was the summer months. Month of June, July and we were on our bicycles going from one place to another attending open-air meetings. So that was the start of my interest in politics I think.[139]

Seán was a student in Limerick at the Munster-Connacht College when he heard the news that de Valera had been elected. The news was delivered by three men, one of whom would be dead in two months.

> I laid eyes on Thomas Ashe once. It was the day after the election that I speak of and myself and other fellow students, we took a day off from school. A half-day off from school that day because the result was expected some time in the afternoon and we were floating around the centre of Limerick hoping we'd get some news and excited about the situation and we spotted a car. Do you know Limerick well? We spotted a car crossing the Sarsfield Bridge. It was then known as the Wesley Bridge from the direction of Ennis and they were flying a tricolour flag on it. And we realised that this was coming from Ennis where the count was taking place and they pulled up at William Street corner in Limerick and they held a small meeting. But they gave the good news anyway that Sinn Féin had won the election in Clare ... Thomas Ashe was in that car and he made a short speech. There was another man who I knew of, he was a Limerick man named Anthony Mackey. He was in that car too and I think there was a third man I didn't know who he was.[140]

A member of the IRB, Anthony Mackey from Castleconnell had been a staunch supporter of Parnell, but in later years threw his lot in with the Sinn Féin leaders. A campaigner and organiser for de Valera during the election, Mackey also served as an energetic member of Limerick County Council.[141]

11 AUGUST 1917

Having enlisted in Cardiff in 1915, the only man that **WILLIAM GEARY** knew from around his area of Co. Limerick that fought in World War I was killed in action.[142]

> We had a boy on the farm by the name of Patrick Sullivan. He was from Clash. And we used to take the milk to Feenagh and I used to go along with him. And he, I don't know if he was drafted or he joined but he died of wounds.[143]

Private Patrick O'Sullivan (Service No. 18937) aged 23 of the 1st Battalion, Royal Irish Fusiliers, was the son of Michael and Kate O'Sullivan of Ballysally, Ballyagran. He had been born at Cappanihane, Co. Limerick, and had formerly served in the Hussars of the Line (Service No. 23683).[144] His remains lie in Brown's Copse Cemetery, Roeux, Pas de Calais, France.[145]

25 SEPTEMBER 1917

Thomas Ashe (who had already served time for his part in the Battle of Ashbourne) had been arrested again in Dublin on 22 August. The British charged him with making a seditious speech in Ballinalee and engaging in illegal drilling. Sentenced to two years imprisonment with hard labour, he died on this

date as a result of being force fed while on hunger strike in Mountjoy Gaol.[146]
SEÁN CLANCY:

> Thomas Ashe, oh, I remember that well. That was the following
> September. The election in Clare was July and again that made a
> wonderful impression on the people. There was great sympathy for
> Thomas Ashe when he died on hunger strike in the Mater Hospital here
> in Dublin and it got great publicity in the newspapers and so on.[147]

The circumstances of Ashe's death served as a further boost to republican
recruitment. He had also been president of the Supreme Council of the IRB. His
graveside oration was delivered by Michael Collins, who had shared the
platform with him in Ballinalee.[148]

29 SEPTEMBER 1917

Éamon de Valera arrived at Ennis railway station to begin a tour of Co. Clare.[149]
In fact, he was a regular visitor to **MAI GROGAN'S** neck of the woods at Tullycrine
in west Clare and used to stay in the area with a man called Simon O'Donnell
(Art O'Donnell's father and brother were both named Simon).[150] Even a field was
permanently named 'de Valera's Field' after he addressed a gathering of over
1,000 people there around the time of his election.[151]

> De Valera came to Tullycrine, very near it but we went around the road.
> It was wintertime. We went around the road to see de Valera and there
> were thousands and thousands of them there all marching. Sure, it was
> a great thing – de Valera to come to Tullycrine. But the Cumann na
> mBan were there marching with them too. But we weren't in the
> Cumann na mBan like more it. No.[152]

On 25 October 1917, de Valera – who was already leader of the Volunteers – was
elected president of the Sinn Féin party.[153] By January 1918, the national
movement had become two-fold in its aim to bring about an independent Irish
republic. Sinn Féin remained the political wing and a reformed IVF became the
military wing. Michael Collins and Cathal Brugha were instrumental in
reforming the Volunteers, which by now had a membership of 100,000. They
were referred to as the army of the Irish Republic (IRA).[154] **ANTHONY MCGINLEY**
recalled the political scene in Donegal at the time.

> Well there was a big split in Irish politics. They had the Ancient Order of
> Hibernians and they were conservative and then Sinn Féin come in and
> the IRA and that meant they'd drive the British out of the country by
> force of arms and there was a big clash between the two political
> parties.[155]

Largely up to this point, the Ancient Order of Hibernians had been the mainstay
of Catholic rights and Irish nationalist principles in Ulster (see 7 January
1907).[156] It drew much of its membership from the Irish Parliamentary Party, but

in the aftermath of 1916, disillusioned with its constitutional approach, most members left to support Sinn Féin or the IRA.

20 FEBRUARY 1918

ELLEN MALONEY'S grand-aunt Mary Ann Duffy died the previous October, and Ellen was by now aged 17. She spoke of a visit to Portarlington by Countess Constance Markievicz who had fought in 1916.[157]

> I remember going to the station to see the Countess Markievicz and Lady John MacBride coming off the train. And she stayed, she stayed at Russell's. There was a big strike there. A timber, and she stood on a big board, and they hooted the horn inside the way she wouldn't be heard. And she brought us to the town hall, down the town ... She shook hands with me.[158]

Since 6 December of the previous year, there had been a lockout at Messrs Russell Brothers' sawmills in Portarlington owing to its management's dissatisfaction with the fact that so many of its employees had become members of the ITGWU, which had started a branch in the town.[159] Russell Brothers issued their workers with the choice of withdrawing membership of the union or being denied work.

Union workers staged a strike that dragged on until a Munitions Tribunal sat in the courthouse on 4 February for the purpose of hearing a complaint brought under Munitions Acts against Messrs Russell Brothers in respect of the dismissal of the men from their employment. At the tribunal, Mr Russell submitted that he had no objection to trade unionism, but characterised the ITGWU as more akin to a 'political organisation'. He claimed the workers were not locked out – they were dismissed.

The tribunal ruled that Messrs Russell Brothers had acted illegally in dismissing workers who were engaged in essential work for the war effort. Among the much-needed items being manufactured at the sawmill were stretcher poles, railway sleepers, boxes and furniture. The company was fined, and these monies went as compensation to the dismissed workers.[160]

When Countess Markievicz visited Portarlington on 20 February, the dispute was still not resolved. As part of an entertainment organised in aid of the victims of the lockout, she addressed workers at the picket lines outside the sawmills, receiving an enthusiastic response, despite attempts by management to drown out her voice by sounding klaxon horns. In the town hall, Markievicz delivered a lecture outlining her experiences during Easter Week, whilst a drama and concert were also performed. In the streets, before and after the entertainment, there were processions headed by the Tullamore and Killenard Pipers' Bands. The visit of Markievicz raised £30 for the workers' fund, but also did much to boost their morale.[161] Markievicz also gave a lecture in Tullamore in aid of the Portarlington workers' lockout fund.[162]

In June 1918, however, a number of the sawmill workers returned to work, having withdrawn from the ITGWU. From the beginning of the strike, the union had paid the men 10 shillings a week strike pay and made up the difference in their wages out of voluntary funds that were subscribed to by branches and sympathisers. The men had been informed by their union that because of a strike in Dublin causing heavy demands on union funds, it was obliged to discontinue their strike pay and so advised them to look for work.[163]

16 APRIL 1918

Conscription had been in force in Britain since 1915, and now with severe losses in World War I, parliament there passed a Military Service Act, which empowered the government to extend conscription to Ireland. John Redmond had died the previous March, so John Dillon, as the new leader of the Irish Parliamentary Party, decided to withdraw from Westminster in protest. A nationwide anti-conscription campaign immediately began in Ireland, and people started to support Sinn Féin and join the Volunteers like never before in defiance.[164] **SEÁN CLANCY** explained how events took shape around Clonlara.

> Well I'll tell you, the following year 1918, there was a crisis in the country. The British government threatened conscription on the young men of the country. They passed an Act of Parliament to enforce conscription on everybody over the age of eighteen. I was only sixteen at the time but there was great resistance to this move on the part of the British government.
>
> And the British, the Irish representatives in Westminster, the Members of Parliament in Westminster from Ireland, they actually left Westminster and came back to Ireland and they never went back to that parliament. But there was a great movement then, the Church and all the political parties; they all joined up to resist this terrible thing – to impose conscription on the country. The young men didn't want it and nobody wanted it.
>
> And I remember there was great resistance organised. The Church took over and novenas were held in the church every evening and after the novenas the young men would fall in outside the church. That's how a company of the Volunteers commenced in my parish and they'd do drill movements. There was an ex-soldier of the British army and he used drill them outside the church and they used have hurleys posing as rifles and do drill with the hurleys. And I think that the young men in particular were very serious about the resistance. I think they'd have resisted very forcibly if it was imposed. Of course, the months and the weeks went on then during that year of 1918 and the war ended in November. But conscription was never imposed anyway. It died out.[165]

It was at this time of crisis or possibly as early as 1917 that Seán joined the Volunteers and served with the Clonlara Company in the East Clare Brigade. Michael Brennan was in overall charge here. Sean's captain was John McCormack.[166]

> Well I used fall in with them. I was only sixteen years of age but I used fall in with the Volunteers, probably the youngest in the company. Oh,

yes, there was another thing then. At that time the powers that be decided that a pledge would be taken by every young man, pledging to God that he'd resist conscription and I remember the words of the pledge – 'I promise with the help of God to resist conscription at every means at my disposal.'

And I remember outside the church on the Sunday before Mass, there were two or three young men with a table and a book. A big book and they got every man, everyone I suppose over eighteen, women didn't count but the men over eighteen were asked to sign this pledge and of course everyone did. But I attended Mass with my father and my father having signed and he asked if I could sign. And one of the men looked at me and he said, 'Ah he's too young.' I was only sixteen; they're supposed to be over eighteen. And apparently there was some bit of a conflab between them and they felt that I wasn't entitled to sign.

And then the parish priest happened to be coming along on his way to Mass and he stopped and signed and somebody said to him, 'What do you think of this young fellow, should we let him sign?' 'Oh, he's a good lad, he's a great fellow,' he said. 'He's going to answer my Mass, let him sign.' And I did sign and I felt very proud that day. I felt I was a young man at last ... We did a good bit of drilling and that kind of thing between then and the end of 1919.[167]

2 SEPTEMBER 1918

PATRICK GREENE enrolled in St Patrick's College, Drumcondra, to train as a primary teacher.[168] Previous to this he had been a monitor, where his duties included asking the children their spellings and tables. In order to attend the college, Patrick had to complete an exam for the King's Scholarship. It was also necessary to get a nomination from the bishop, who was Dr Hoare at the time. This was secured through the parish priest, and Patrick then studied at the college until 1920.[169] Some fellow students included Joseph Dunne of Lisnageeragh, Edgeworthstown, Tom O'Connor, Offaly, and Kit Halpin from Drumlish.[170]

One of Patrick's lecturers at St Patrick's was John Willie Carolan, who occupied the position of Senior Professor of Method. He delivered his lectures in a very charismatic and personal fashion. He spoke from his own notes rather than from books, took his time, and carried out his job in a very effective and interesting style. In addition, Carolan lived up the road from the college, and prominent Sinn Féiners on the run or otherwise were regular visitors to his house.[171]

There was hardly any Irish spoken in the St Patrick's of 1918. There was a Gaeltacht table in the refectory specifically for that purpose, but it was never occupied by more than a dozen people.[172] Patrick remembered the trams and that the capital had its own police force known as the Dublin Metropolitan Police (DMP) at this time.

I was in Dublin. I was in college from 1918 to '20. There was no RIC. The Dublin Police they were parading the streets that time – big, hefty men with big feet – quiet men. Nobody passed any remarks to them. Dublin was quiet that time. Sinn Féin was, the movement was seething underneath at the time. When I left in 1920 sure there was nothing going on anywhere.[173]

31 OCTOBER 1918

The great influenza pandemic (Spanish Flu) had arrived on Ireland's shores the previous May, striking down people of all ages at an alarming rate, but in particular those who were healthy and young.[174] It wouldn't desist until April the following year, in the process claiming over 20,000 souls.[175] One of these was the eldest sibling and only sister of **GERRY SMYTH** in Stackallen – 22-year-old Mary Gertrude – who died on this date.[176] **PATRICK GREENE**, whose friend Joseph Dunne in St Patrick's College also died from it in May 1919, commented that up to this point:[177]

> Measles, whooping cough, a rare outbreak of scarletina; that was all that kids suffered from.[178]

In Cork, every member of **GEORGE CARPENTER'S** family was laid up with Spanish Flu except George himself, so he took on the roles of nurse, chief cook and bottlewasher. He used to boil milk with pepper in it and beef bones with vegetables to make soup. Everyone in his house recovered, but one family living near them suffered the loss of the father, the mother and two sons. Their corpses were laid out wrapped in sheets in the garden before being taken away for burial.[179]

11 NOVEMBER 1918

World War I ended. The impact on **MICHAEL CASEY'S** district was no different from that experienced by any other community throughout Ireland:

> A lot of people from Mitchelstown went out fighting; a lot of them never came back.[180]

Over 400 men from the town enlisted to fight in the Great War, and at least 44 were killed.[181] Michael knew about 20 of the men who returned home and recalled them being traumatised from their experiences.[182] Likewise, **MAI GROGAN** in Tullycrine was conscious of the effect that the conflict had on the population of her locality.

> A lot of people went here from Kilrush but not from the country. And most of them never came back.[183]

At least 476 men from Kilrush fought in the Great War, of which 119 were killed.[184] Closer to Mai's home, Private Martin McMahon from Kilmurry McMahon fought with the 1st Battalion, Irish Guards, and met his end on 10 October 1917. Mai would marry his younger brother Patrick in 1925.[185] Several men that **GEORGE CARPENTER** knew were killed, and he was able to recall another who survived the war only to fall victim to injury on his return.

> I remember one chap was coming back on the boat when the war was over, and he fell through a hawse or a hole in the boat and he broke his thigh. He broke and the doctors were going to operate on him straight away and he wouldn't let them. They put a splint on him and they sent him home with the splint. But he hasn't his legs now because he's dead but he was working in Fords and he became assistant manager at the department there. Then he was sent over to Dagenham. He started in Dagenham then.[186]

In October 1919, a memorial window was erected in Christ Church, Cork. The names of 34 men killed in World War I were inscribed on marble panels in the alcove, 18 of whom were members of the 1st Cork Company of the Boys' Brigade. The other 16 would have attended services at Christ Church sometime before the war.[187] The *Cork Constitution* reported that on the day of the unveiling '[o]ccupying seats in the front centre of the church were the Cork Company Boys' Brigade, and immediately behind them were seated past members, most of them wearing war ribbons.'[188] **PATRICK GREENE** in Co. Longford was also aware of men who either came back or lost their lives to the war.

> Oh, plenty, I knew several of them. Some of them survived. A number of them survived. Our postman, we had him for years until he retired. He joined up. He survived the First World War. A neighbour of mine, a fellow who was at school with me, he not much older than me, he not many years dead, he was in the First World War. We had a local blacksmith in the village here. He was a Sergeant-Farrier in the First World War – never got a scratch, plenty of ex-soldiers.[189]

GERRY SMYTH maintained that some of those that came home to Stackallen afterwards were so traumatised by what they'd been through that it affected them mentally.

> Some of them came back you might say practically raving lunatics. There was a man up the road from us and he arrived home complete with his rifle, uniform, and rifle and with ammunition. And he used to go out and fire shots up the road. He wanted a brother of mine to get on a bicycle and cycle down the road and he'd fire at the brakes at the wheels going by which my brother didn't do ... Do you see he was probably gassed and didn't know where he was? He had an old uncle down the road and he said, 'Oh, he's living too long, sure I'll go down and shoot him.' So you can see some of them they were just completely; they didn't know what they were doing.[190]

When the war ended, Mai Grogan's house received a visit from relatives who had left Kilrush before 1900. They were the offspring of her father's aunt and uncle, who had sold their Tullycrine farm to Mai's grandfather before emigrating. These relatives who had fought in the war were now seeking to rediscover their west Clare roots.

> Well, I had my father's cousins. My grandfather bought the farm where we were in and the Reidy's – my grandmother was Reidy. And there was seven boys and one girl there and their mother died when they were young so I don't know were they not able to make out or not but they all went to Australia. And when the war broke out then, they were conscripted in Australia and they were sent on to France. So they all were only young when they left and they were anxious to see the house where they were born and they called to our place. Mary-Anne was a nurse, she was conscripted too and in France and she came. They all came to see where they were born and that was it.[191]

ELLEN MALONEY'S future husband was Michael Troy, also from Bracklone Street, Portarlington.[192] The pair would attend the annual maypole dances in Killenard and Cloneygowan together, and married in 1925.[193] Aged 29 by 1915 and a shoemaker by trade, Michael joined the 2nd Leinster Regiment at Maryborough (Portlaoise). He suffered a fractured ankle fighting in France in August 1916 and was hospitalised in Rouen. He then served in the Labour Corps, which was a British army unit formed in 1917 for manual and skilled labour on the Western Front and Salonika in Greece. He would be employed as a boot repairer:

> He was a shoemaker in the British army making boots for the wounded soldiers.[194]

In his service record, Michael Troy is described as reliable, intelligent and very capable at his trade, although he was confined to barracks for seven days as punishment, having been found guilty of drunkenness *'whilst on active service'*. This offence was committed eight days after the war ended on 19 November 1918. Michael Troy was demobbed in Nottingham in 1919.[195]

> He was discharged out of the army. He had eight shillings a week to live on ... He came home and worked at home and half a crown for women's pair of shoes.[196]

Ellen remembered a local man by the name of O'Connor being killed in France, whilst 'Michael Downey' was another from Bracklone Street who survived. He went on to work for the Department of Posts and Telegraphs.[197]

GEORGE COOPER lived in No. 26 Holles Street when the war ended, his family having moved from D'Olier Street. He observed that many war veterans returned to Ireland to find that service in the trenches for Britain was not something that rested easy with many people. As a result, they got little recognition in their native country, and George believed that in later years they were practically forgotten about altogether.

> After we got independence there were plenty of ex-servicemen Catholics, plenty of ex-servicemen Protestants. They used to meet on

the 11th of November in O'Connell Street. The Catholic men would go to the Pro-Cathedral in Marlborough Street, the other Protestants would go to Patsy (Saint Patrick's) Cathedral and then after the Mass and after the service they'd meet together and they used go out to the Phoenix Park to have a you know a parade out in the park. And they were allowed to carry their battle flags. But then you see according as we got control, more control, more control here, they were told you can carry your flags but don't unroll them. In other words that in case and then there was a special park – a remembrance park built out in the Phoenix Park for the British soldiers and all that was stopped. The parade and all was stopped.[198]

Political allegiances of the time were often reflected in the games that children used to play. There was a mixture of British and nationalist sympathisers in the terrace in Maymount where **GEORGE CARPENTER** lived in Cork.

Well, we had five RIC and of course we were all very pro-British when we were there as our parents were paid by the British and there was IRA there as well. And one day we decided to make a red, white and blue flag and we put it up on the gas lamp or the gases as we used call it. And we hid and we had water pistols and also a, what's that you call these things that you shoot? ... A peashooter. We used get a peashooter from a weed that's growing out in the country. A long weed and it had a depth of about a half an inch in the centre of it you see and we used get sconies then which are hawthorns – the seed – and we used use these for shooting at each other and so on.[199]

However, it transpired that their efforts had been in vain on the particular day that they put up the Union Jack flag:

No one came out of the house. We were waiting to bombard them with sconies but no one turned up so we took the flag down and put it away.[200]

14 DECEMBER 1918

There was a general election in Ireland. Sinn Féin won 73 seats, Unionists 25, Irish Parliamentary Party 6 and Independent Unionists 1. Sinn Féin stated that its elected members would not sit in Westminster and set about establishing an independent government.[201] **MICHAEL CASEY** noted that from this point forward the balance of power in Mitchelstown and elsewhere was altered dramatically.

A lot of them were loyal to the British you know, a majority nearly that time but the general election in 1918 in December, that finished the whole lot. They got in with a terrible majority. They put out a lot of the big fellows you know – the English. It was a great controlling to the people that time. Things changed a lot.[202]

In his Military Service Pension file, **JOHN KELLY** detailed that over the course of 1918, as a member of the Derrydonnell Company, he had been engaged in training, drilling, anti-conscription work and duties associated with the general election. His commanding officers over the period were James Murray and Bill Freaney.[203]

CHAPTER 3

Striking for freedom, 1919

7 JANUARY 1919

JOHN PARKINSON celebrated his birthday and shortly afterwards became a member of the 44th Belfast Company of the Boys' Brigade, which was attached to Christ Church of Ireland in Durham Street.[1]

> I joined when I was twelve ... It was very, very good. We met in the Church Hall and we did drill. Drill can be interesting you know? Doing formations and there's a drill book that the officer follows and we used have drill competitions between the different companies to make you more skilful at your training and then we also did physical training. We took off our jackets and got into short pants and we did physical training and we did some gymnastic work. We had different things to climb on and jump over ... Then we went to camp in the summertime.[2]

John stayed in the organisation until he was 17, going on to become an officer and later captain of the company.

> Well, it was connected with the church. The company was connected always with a church and it had a Bible class and you attended the Bible class and then there were church parades usually one a month. And then there were other churches had Boys' Brigade companies and we met. We had annual camps together. We had a very famous camp here up in the north of Ireland at a place called Ganaway between Millisle and Ballywalter and that camp was very famous. I can remember Captain Faris from your city – Cork – coming and bringing his boys from Cork several years to that camp. Many a time I think of Captain Faris, he was a lovely man and I got to know Cork boys through the camp and that was held every year and there were a thousand boys attended that camp.[3]

Captain Samuel M. Faris from Cork city had a long association with the organisation. From at least 1916 through to 1925, he served as honorary secretary and treasurer of the Cork Brigade Battalion (comprising local companies of the Boys' Brigade and Church Lads' Brigade). He was attached to the 2nd Cork Company of the Boys' Brigade, which was connected to Trinity Presbyterian Church, Summerhill. He worked as a tea agent.[4] Incidentally, **GEORGE CARPENTER** joined the 2nd Cork Company of the Boys' Brigade in 1923, and besides drilling and indoor sports, he played football in Captain Sammy Faris' garden in Sunday's Well.[5]

When I joined the Boys' Brigade then – the 2nd Boys' Brigade – I was playing soccer with them. The 1st Boys' Brigade was in Christ Church and the 2nd Boys' Brigade was up in Summerhill – just the end of McCurtain Street. That was known as King Street then, opposite the Coliseum [Picture Theatre/Cinema] – the little church there. That's where we used hold our meetings there ... Well, the other chap and myself we used play full back for Boys' Brigade. We used play against other little teams that were around. Terrace teams we'd call them and that was done up in Sunday's Well alongside the river and the ball used go into the water now and again – the river Lee. We used, somebody had to get out and get it.[6]

JOHN PARKINSON knew some members of the Boys' Brigade from the Catholic community.

Well, it was really a Protestant organisation, connected to the Protestant churches although we had a few Roman Catholic boys in our group because they were from what we call 'mixed marriages'. Their fathers and mothers were Protestant and Catholic. So, they joined the Boys' Brigade, they were very welcome.[7] ... The Catholic Church had a Catholic Boys' Brigade too which didn't develop as well as our Boys' Brigade but there was a Catholic Boys' Brigade as well.[8]

The Twelfth parade was an annual event for members of the organisation.

I always went to see the marches and was a member of the Boys' Brigade and I used to, in those days we even walked over to our church hall in our Boys' Brigade uniforms.[9]

In Dublin, **GEORGE COOPER** was also a member, but suffered abuse from some people when wearing his uniform.

When I was young and my sister was young – the two of us, we'd be going down to school or church and of course we'd get called all the time. And then I was in an organisation you may have heard of it – the Boys' Brigade. And when we were passing through a place called Gordon Lane near the cathedral, things were being fired down on top of us, you know? Yes, in fact it was so bad at one year that we couldn't parade. We had to carry our uniform up to the cathedral and dress in the cathedral.[10]

In the course of time, **JOHN PARKINSON** experienced similar tensions in Belfast.

Well, we had to be very careful and you had to be careful and watch not to get into any trouble. And we got orders not to wear our BB uniforms going to the halls because they might have upset a lot of others. So we stopped doing that and we put our BB uniforms in little bags which our mothers got for us and put them on in the halls rather than going to and from.[11]

The Boys' Brigade in Belfast didn't have **NORMAN DOUGLAS** within its ranks.

> No, I was in the Scouts. I wasn't in the Boys' Brigade ... Well, the Scout
> movement was much the same as the Boys' Brigade. It was a voluntary
> organisation and it was just what you'd call a youth club really. We had
> Scoutmasters and there wasn't anything political about them at all. I
> mean the Catholic organisation had Scout troops and from time to time
> we met at jamborees and festivities – Scout festivities.[12]

21 JANUARY 1919

The First Dáil met in the Mansion House in Dublin. Only Sinn Féin members
attended, as those elected from unionism and the Irish Parliamentary Party
declined the invitation. In fact, most of Sinn Féin's elected members were also
absent because they were in jail. Those present in the Dáil declared Ireland a
republic and sought complete separation from Britain. The British
government refused to recognise the Dáil, and this led to the bitter Anglo-
Irish War of 1919–1921. This conflict also became known as the War for
Independence or the Tan War.[13]

　　Coincidentally, on the same day that the First Dáil met, Dan Breen, Seán
Tracy, Seamus Robinson and six (according to Breen) other members of the
Third Tipperary Brigade (without Dáil sanction) took part in an ambush at
Soloheadbeg in which two RIC constables (McDonnell and O'Connell) were
killed.[14] The nine Volunteers became wanted men, with a price of £1,000 on their
heads. This is often cited as the first engagement with the Crown forces since
the Rising of 1916 and as marking the beginning of the actual War for
Independence. It was significant because two policemen were killed, but it was
by no means the first engagement. For example, in April 1918 two Volunteers
had been killed by the RIC when they raided Gortatlea Barracks, Co. Kerry, for
arms. The following July, two RIC men were ambushed at Beal a Ghleanna, Co.
Cork, and their arms were taken, but they recovered from their injuries.[15] Even
as far back as 4 January 1918, there had been a successful action against the
British military in the townland of Meenbanad in west Donegal, when local
volunteers rescued two prisoners bound for Derry on the train without firing a
single shot.[16] **DAN KEATING** reiterated that smaller-scale engagements had been
taking place against the British long before Soloheadbeg.

> The conflict, which was started actually, it was started actually in Fíries
> by Jim Riordan and continued by Dan Breen and Seán Tracy in Tipperary
> and it gained. All the time it was gaining.[17]

On 29 April 1916, Jim Riordan had gone into Fíries for a newspaper to see if there
was any information about what was happening with regard to the Rising in
Dublin. He encountered two RIC officers putting a proclamation on the window
of the post office announcing the introduction of martial law. As he passed
between them, one made to open his holster and the other started to unsling his
carbine. Riordan drew his gun, firing two shots at each, wounding them.[18]

The Volunteers were being trained and they were getting arms. Actually, most of the arms were captured from small patrols of RIC and they took some barracks. It led on anyway to the formation of the flying columns everywhere. Kerry had actually two flying columns, one in north Kerry another in south Kerry.[19]

MICHAEL CASEY summed up initial reaction amongst ordinary people in Mitchelstown to the use of physical force.

> Well, a lot of the people were partly against it you know but they saw when it was going ahead, they had to give in you know to the republicans that time. You see the soldiers' republican army; they had to give in to them.[20]

I APRIL 1919

Having worked for a short time in the City Tannery in Limerick, **SEÁN CLANCY** moved to Dublin in 1919 to take up a different position.[21] This was his first time on a train.

> I left school then and at that time jobs were scarce for school-leavers. They had some kind of a rule that preference was given to young men who had joined the British army during the war and were now being demobilised and they got preference in employment in places like banks and the civil service and all that. So jobs were scarce and apparently I couldn't find a suitable job for myself and the next thing I got made a contact with a cousin of mine in Dublin who was managing a big establishment here in Dublin and he invited me to Dublin to a clerical job and I headed for Dublin. So that was my first entrain to Dublin.[22]

Cabra Park in the north side of the city would be his new place of residence.

> There were a lot of slums of course ... Dublin was really an awful place to live in at that time. There was terrible poverty, a lot of unemployment and all the rest of it. But then of course there were good areas as well and I found digs at one pound a week – full board. And I had a couple of very happy years in Dublin thereafter.[23]

On arrival in the capital, Seán – who had already served in the East Clare Brigade – joined a contingent of the Volunteers attached to Dublin No. 1 Brigade, which was under the command of Paddy O'Daly.[24] His new company is recorded as having had a membership of 126 men by the Truce of 11 July 1921.[25] Another cousin of his was already a member, and parades were held on a weekly basis.

> I got transferred straight away after arrival to a company here in Dublin – B Company of the 2nd Battalion on the north side of Dublin. And early on, of course, there wasn't a lot of activity but in course of time activities

gradually developed and I remained active with the Volunteers from then until the Truce of July the 11th 1921.[26]

Seán described himself as a part-time Volunteer, as he continued to hold down a job. There was, however, a full-time group called the Active Service Unit (ASU) that was always available to Michael Collins or any other person in authority who wanted their help in an operation.[27]

17 JUNE 1919

Constance Markievicz, who had been elected a member of the First Dáil, was tried at Mallow in connection with a speech she made at Newmarket some weeks previous. A huge crowd turned out to see her, including **PATSY HOLMES**.

> I saw the Countess brought into Mallow in 1918. Countess Markievicz, she was in Cork Gaol. It was an aunt of mine gave her a cup of tea but they brought in about five or six hundred police that day with her and there was a squabble. Another one had a flag but she was a grand woman. She was a grand woman and a great woman.[28]

Markievicz was sentenced to four months in Sunday's Well Gaol in Cork, which was also known as Cork City Gaol or the Women's Gaol.[29] June was also the month that de Valera went to the United States as president of the Irish Republic. He sought unsuccessfully to gain US recognition of the Irish Republic, but did manage to raise $5 million in funds. He returned in December 1920.

29 JUNE 1919

On this Sunday, favoured by summer-like weather conditions, **GERRY SMYTH** from Stackallen attended the Meath Feis (Feis na Midhe), which was held at the Showgrounds in Navan. Despite the fact that no train service was available, extremely large crowds travelled to it by road from all parts of the country. The festival, which was formally opened by Eoin MacNeill (president of the Gaelic League), featured competitions in various age categories for Irish music, dance, singing, history and literary subjects, as well as other genres connected with the Irish language and culture. In his speech delivered in English and Irish, MacNeill advised the crowd to learn the language but to do so by not bothering so much about books or grammar, learning it instead as a living tongue. When it came to knowledge of the language, one adjudicator remarked that conversationally the children from Stackallen School were in advance of all competitors. Listed among the prize-winners in the category – 'Prayers for children under 10 years of age' – was Gerry Smyth from Stackallen NS (although he was 12 at the time). In fact, he tied for second prize with Eileen Sheridan and Mollie Scanlon from the Mercy Convent, Navan.[30]

Gerry's prize, which he still had on the day I interviewed him in 2003, was a book published by the *Irish Times* in 1917 entitled *The Sinn Féin Rebellion Handbook, Easter 1916*. It contained lists, pictures and accounts, as well as a collection of articles that ran in the newspaper covering the events of Easter Week.

That's a book that I got. It has enough of these pictures. I think I got it for prayers at a Feis in 1919. I got a prize at a Feis in Navan ... Oh, yes we were very, very Sinn Féin that time. It gives all the lists of every prisoner who was taken after 1916 ... See the hundreds that were shipped over to England? It has the hundreds that were shipped over to England.[31]

Gerry's father, Joseph Smyth, principal of Stackallen National School, had been a member of the Gaelic League since at least 1903.[32]

20 AUGUST 1919

Following a resolution of the first Dáil, the Volunteers changed their name to the Irish Republican Army (IRA).[33] Although they were supposedly under the control of Cathal Brugha, the Dáil Minister for Defence, in practice they acted independently and wanted to be separate from Sinn Féin. Michael Collins held the posts of adjutant-general of the IRA, director of organisation and director of intelligence, and was committed to looking for a solution to the problem of British occupation of Ireland through physical force.[34]

From the age of 16, **PATSY HOLMES** had been working in Lucey's butcher shop in Mallow. In addition to the shop, Lucey's operated a slaughterhouse, and it was during 1919 that Patsy became much more active with the Volunteers/IRA in the town through a man who worked there named Edward Waters.[35] Waters had been instrumental in the formation of the Mallow Company, which by the time of the Truce on 11 July 1921 is recorded as having had between 128 and 137 members.[36] The Mallow Company formed part of the 4th Battalion attached to Cork No. 2 Brigade.[37] By 26 April 1921, however, it was 'G' Company, 5th Battalion, Cork No. 4 Brigade, 1st Southern Division.[38] Essentially, from that period various changes came about as brigades throughout Ireland were formed into divisions, creating a new top tier in terms of IRA structure. The 1st Southern Division would comprise brigades located in Counties Cork, Kerry and Waterford and in west Limerick. Patsy's commanding officers were Patrick Corbett, Tadhg Byrne, John Saunders and Jeremiah Leahy, but he also came into contact with other important figures in North Cork.[39]

There was Moylan, Seán Moylan, Liam Lynch, Meaney, Con Meaney.[40]

Patsy carried dispatches and was involved in raids for arms.[41] On one occasion, after returning from running an errand for the IRA which involved delivering a brown parcel 'to two houses across the bridge', Patsy had to interrupt a brigade meeting being held one night on the grounds of the convent in Mallow to warn those present that the British were making arrests.

But anyhow I was coming up the street at half eight about half eight and this girl stopped me. Callaghan was her name. God rest her she's dead since now. 'Patsy,' says she, 'they're arresting all the boys and the men uptown.' I said, 'Annie, where are they [the British]?' She said, 'Kate Hanlon's.' That was in a public house near the town hall. So they used come out, they used come march, go out with rubber boots on them –

the military. So I had to cross the street to get to the brigade where they were holding the meeting.[42]

Patsy subsequently discovered that plans for the procurement of weapons were among the items on the agenda discussed at the meeting.

> The IRA had no stuff [guns] at the time so they decided they'd go and they'd collect all the farmers' guns. Every farmer that time had three or four. And each one of them had a gun or two of their own. Now them guns were taken. Now my brother was one of the fellows set about it. He was one of the two and one of the leading other men. So they got a good share of them and they were stacked in a place. And there were two brothers that lived in Mallow that were what they call whitesmiths. You often heard of blacksmiths but what do you mean by a whitesmith? Well now, a blacksmith is a man that shoes horses, the whitesmith is a man that makes guns and things. So they got a good share of the guns off of them anyway.[43]

Cumann na mBan was the women's section of the IRA, and Patsy said 'I'd know them in Mallow'. In early 1918, a branch had been formed in Mitchelstown, with some of its first members being Julia Ryan, Lizzie Clifford, Annie Luddy and Babs Walsh.[44] Within a short time, many of the young women in the district had joined up and the benefits of the Cumann na mBan organisation around Mitchelstown were not lost on **MICHAEL CASEY**.

> They were a great help though; women could go places where men couldn't go. They wouldn't be suspicious, so much suspicious carrying messages and things.[45]

JACK DUFF in Dublin said, 'They done an enormous amount of work in carrying guns and carrying ammunition from place to place and things like that.'[46] Cumann na mBan were also active in Kanturk (Cork No. 2 Brigade), with **KATHLEEN CHARLES** claiming to have served with them from 1918 through to 1921. By the Truce, the Kanturk Company was attached to the 4th Battalion, Cork No. 4 Brigade, 1st Southern Division.[47] However, it's likely that Kathleen had become mixed up with the movement earlier than 1918, having begun running errands for the Volunteers almost from their inception in 1913. She may have been as young as 12 when she joined.

> But sure I went through all that. I helped the IRA – the Irish Republican Army – when they were forming. And my father was a printer and of course, everything was suspicious at that time. The English had us in their grip, you know? And we wanted to get out of it – quick too. So I used to see when I was very small, all the boys, men, husbands, wives, husbands, sons, grandchildren – not grandchildren I'd say but older men all going up the road every evening drilling in the fields – learning how to become soldiers and how to use guns. And the British were going around the country in lorries waiting to see an

Irishman to shoot him. You see we wanted to get rid of them and that's how we did it.[48]

Kathleen said her mother, Mary Helena, was also a member, as 'were a lot of women in the town'.[49] They joined having been approved by those in charge:

> Just to get to the heads of it; those that were organising it and running it. It was they were doing the running for the army getting soldiers and that you know.[50]

Kathleen's commanding officer was Ciss Courtney, but when she became ill in 1919 and died in 1920, Annie Sugrue (née Murphy) took over as company captain of the Kanturk branch.[51] Kathleen said that Mary Helena was a member of the Kanturk Company at the same time she was and that they served under the same officers.[52] She insisted that members of the organisation were very dedicated and that although a lot of women were mixed up in it, not all of her friends were involved.

> There was a select few, you know. You had to know who you were talking to and the interest they had and they were very interested.[53]

She insisted that it had to be like this 'because everything was so secret, and your life was in danger'. Kathleen added that her own life was really only in danger once darkness fell:

> If I was going home at night, after dark, I had to go with my hands up – to be recognised, scrutinised and there was some other '-ised'. Have to go up into your own house and the British soldiers would be there.[54]

Nell Cronin of Ballyrushen, Kanturk, was a Cumann na mBan member with a reputation for constantly organising.[55] Alice Hennessy was another within the ranks of the local branch.[56]

> Very hard workers, they were knitting and sewing for the boys and all that sort of thing. Carrying, there was a lot of notes being sent from place to place quietly.[57]

On occasion, Kathleen would carry some of these dispatches.

> You see as I said, I was small. I just handed in and say 'so and so told me'. But I did it at the risk of my life.[58]

Sinn Féin and the IRA regularly placed orders for bills, leaflets or posters in her father's print shop.

> They used to go up our road every evening ... They'd go up our road and all the roads every evening and hide and drill there ... And they ran raffles and all these things you know, to make money. They'd [the

British] never know who printed them. My father would never put his imprint to them.[59]

It was often Kathleen's job to make sure the bills reached their intended destination.

What I did when I was young and very young was the most important part. Where I got the bills delivered to be posted up to say there was a dance or a raffle or something like that would draw in money. The proceeds of these dances and things they were never kept like – the money.[60]

23 AUGUST 1919

WILLIAM GEARY from Ballyagran received a Certificate of Proficiency in Radiotelegraphy, Morse Code, granted by the British Postmaster General.

You know, farmers' sons in Ireland unless they were destined for the Church, law or medicine. They were expected to work on the farm and I did like the others I worked on the farm. Now one day I was out in our field and I was digging out scrubs that were interfering with the grass and my uncle Michael Geary, he had a farm across the road and he came over and he said to me, 'Would you like to join and be a wireless operator? I'll pay your tuition.' I accepted it.

The next thing is they made arrangements for me to go to Caherciveen, Co. Kerry, to the Atlantic Wireless School. Mr Maurice Fitzgerald was the principal. Now to get there I went by pony and trap to Newcastle West Railroad station and from there I took the train. Now I boarded with a Miss O'Reilly who had a boarding house in front of the church and she had two other boarders. They were tailors. Well, I attended classes and in due course, I received a first-class wireless certificate enabling me to operate, to be a wireless operator aboard a British ship.[61]

William was lucky to have been afforded such an opportunity. **MAI GROGAN** recalled the fate that awaited many young people around west Clare at the time.

That was the whole thing long ago – matchmaking and a fortune going with it – money. That was it and when you bring the fortune into a house there was a girl or a boy there waiting for it to go and get married some other place.[62]

Dances were held in a venue locally.

Well, we hadn't much parish halls only the school. The national school that was the hall we had … Was I matchmaking? No, I knew my boyfriend beforehand. He wasn't far from me.[63]

Mai said that when she attended dances in the school women would sit on one side of the hall and men on the other.

> They would and they'd be mixed every way. They wouldn't be all together. That was all that was into it. Oh, the dances were very few and far between them times, very few. They used have dances at the school for to do up the church and that was the biggest part of it. That's it. They used have IRA dances after that then in country houses and the next thing the Black and Tans might arrive and that'll finish it.[64]

Although Mai never attended any of these IRA dances, she was well aware of their purpose.

> Well, to make money sure – 2 and 6 for the dance, half a crown.[65]

7 SEPTEMBER 1919

When an armed party of British soldiers arrived to attend Sunday service at the Wesleyan Church in Fermoy, they heard a whistling sound followed by a call on them to surrender. Over 30 men from the Second Cork Brigade under the command of Liam Lynch were executing their plan to hold them up, take their arms and load the weapons into cars parked nearby. After the soldiers disobeyed the IRA's call and resisted, shots were fired and there was hand-to-hand combat on the road. At one point, Lynch slipped and a soldier went for him with his rifle. This soldier (Private William Jones, 2nd Battalion King's Shropshire Light Infantry) was immediately shot dead, and soon they were all overpowered. The collected arms were piled into one of the cars and the Volunteers made good their escape in the vehicles and on foot. Liam Lynch (wounded) was one of eight Volunteers that travelled in the same car as the captured weapons.[66] Another was the workmate of **PATSY HOLMES** from Lucey's butcher shop in Mallow, referred to earlier in this chapter.

> He was a chap named, called Ned Waters, he came from about five miles from Mallow. He was a butcher in a slaughterhouse, and I was with him, helping him in the slaughterhouse. I wasn't a butcher but I was there helping him. The woman we were working for – her husband got hurted or something and on Saturday morning we would take the meat up to the shop and it would be cut in portions to help the woman. So after that Waters went away ... I was doing other jobs and it was nothing strange to me to see Waters go but anyhow on Monday morning, Waters never returned to work.[67]

Naturally, Patsy knew nothing of the advance plans for the attack in Fermoy, but of Private Jones he insisted it was his friend 'Waters shot him dead ... and only for he shooting that soldier – that Black and Tan, the whole brigade would be captured. The car wouldn't be able to go.'[68]

> So there was an uproar anyway about it and they [the British military] came on. They knew when Waters didn't come back to work, they went

to the shop and he wasn't there at all. I knew he wouldn't be there. And I was there.[69]

Patsy would discover, however, that not every member of the Crown forces in Mallow was keen for Waters to be apprehended.

So there was no account of him. I was going down the street anyway and a sergeant, what's that his name was? Sergeant Leary, he was an RIC sergeant at the time and he called me to one side. 'Patsy,' says he, 'keep your mouth shut.' So I said nothing anyway but I was thinking then that this sergeant, why he came and warned me? So I thought he was having me on, you know, so I went to one of the head intelligence men on the IRA side and I said to him, 'Do you know anything about Leary?' That was the sergeant. 'Oh,' he said, 'I do. He's a great help to us,' he said.[70]

Arrests were made in the days, weeks and months that followed. However, Waters was now on the run and managed to evade capture.[71] In July 1920, five men were released, but three of Waters' comrades from that incident were imprisoned. One of them was Michael Fitzgerald, who was untried and unsentenced.[72]

28 SEPTEMBER 1919

DAN KEATING travelled from Tralee to Croke Park to attend the 1919 All-Ireland Football Final. The final score was Kildare 2-5, Galway 0-1. A crowd of 32,000 watched the game.[73]

That was my first All-Ireland Final. It was between Galway and Kildare. Galway beat Kerry in a replay and they were very firm favourites to win the All-Ireland. And a young Kildare team, some of them under nineteen, destroyed Galway on the day. That was my first All-Ireland. That was football.[74]

This same year back in Clare, **SEÁN CLANCY'S** local hurling club (Clonlara) won the county championship by defeating Scariff.[75] The Gaelic Athletic Association (GAA) had been founded in 1884 for the promotion of Irish games and culture, and **PATRICK GREENE** (who frequently attended Croke Park whilst a student at St Patrick's College) spoke about the game of hurling in Co. Longford during that century when his father played it.[76]

It wasn't very strong here. I had no interest in games. They did hurl in Co. Longford. In this particular parish they had a good hurling team in the 1860s, I believe. I mean somebody told me of an old fellow – that I believe is an old fellow eighty years ago, seventy years ago that he was a good hurler. That he was on a team that won a county championship or something of the sort.

They didn't call it hurling then. They played the game in the '50s when my father was, they called it 'cumans' and the hurley stick was more like a hockey stick. They went to the bog and they found a good strong furze bush with a bent root on it and they dug that out. That was the sort of cuman that they used. The word had gone from 'cuman' to 'cumans' and they made a sort of a ball. They hadn't a sliotar at all. It was they made it with twine if they could – rolled up a ball of twine and they covered it with cloth. They didn't cover it with leather. That was, the game was dying out at that time.[77]

GEORGE CARPENTER played hurling out on the streets of Cork as a youngster.

We would put down markers with our coats and they were the goals. And at that time there was no traffic on the roads – only horse and car. And you could hear a horse and car. You'd have time to pick up your coat and let the horse and car pass. And we used go out to the line then, Bandon line and cut down any ash tree with a bend in it and bring that home and with my father's tools then I was able to make a hockey stick rather than a hurley but it was really good fun.[78]

The sliotar was a combination of cloth with twine.

We used find all the cloth we could find and then we discovered if we made the tongue of the shoe, if we got two shoes we had two tongues and they worked in opposite and we used sew them up and everything.[79]

In Belfast, **JOHN PARKINSON** and his friends played soccer with a 'hanky ball'. This was a homemade ball of newspaper rolled up inside a handkerchief and tied in a knot. On occasion, they had a rubber ball. Soccer was usually played on the streets with the lamp posts used as goalposts. However, they were always on the lookout for police, as football wasn't permitted on most of the streets they played on. John was once caught by an RIC man when trying to get away following a street game. He was brought home to his mother instead of to the police station, getting off with a caution as opposed to a fine, which could be as much as five shillings.[80]

John lived close to Grosvenor Park on Distillery Street, which was home to Distillery Football Club. He remembered Dublin teams such as Shamrock Rovers, Bohemians, Shelbourne and St James's Gate coming to Belfast to play matches.[81] Incidentally, the first international goal scored by Ireland was by a Distillery player, Sam Johnston, against Wales in Wrexham in 1882.[82] Unfortunately, Ireland lost 7-1.

19 DECEMBER 1919

The IRA carried out an ambush in Dublin whereby they hoped to eliminate the Viceroy Lord-Lieutenant French – the King's representative and supreme commander of the British army in Ireland. Lord French, who was returning to Phoenix Park from Roscommon via train, disembarked at Ashtown Station, where he was met by a military escort consisting of three cars. It was customary for him to travel in the second car, so the IRA planned to block the road with a cart after the first car had passed and then take aim at French's car. The fierce gun battle that ensued resulted in some British casualties, but Lord French succeeded in getting away unharmed in the first car. On the Volunteer side, Dan Breen was wounded in the leg and Martin Savage from Sligo was killed.[83]

By February 1920, a poem/ballad entitled 'On Ashtown Road' had been composed in Savage's honour by an unknown author, and it quickly became popular throughout the country. Some of the words were recited by **PATSY HOLMES**, who recalled hearing it in Mallow.[84]

On Ashtown Road

On a cold December day
A motor ploughed its way
Through bullets, slush and hale
On Ashtown Road.

In the car the living tool
Of England's hated rule
And there began the dual
On Ashtown Road.

Martin Savage undismayed
With rifle and hand grenade
Attacked him unafraid
On Ashtown Road.

Till a bullet laid him low
From the fingers of his foe
That's another debt we owe
For Ashtown Road.[85]

CHAPTER 4

A call to arms, 1920

2 JANUARY 1920

It wasn't too long after his birthday that **DAN KEATING** joined Farmer's Bridge 'F' Company, 1st Battalion, Kerry No. 1 Brigade of the IRA, which is recorded as having a membership of 76 men by the truce of 11 July 1921, when it formed part of the 1st Southern Division. Moss Galvin was captain.[1]

> Well, I mean they were there and they were appealing for recruits and everything. You just go, everyone knew who the local commandant was and they went to him and joined up.[2]

At the time, Dan was serving his apprenticeship as a barman in Gerry McSweeney's Bar and Grocery in Castle Street, Tralee, and it was while here that he got talking to a soldier from Liverpool of Irish descent who often came into the bar. He loved ballad singing and got on well with the locals. One day when the discussion turned to acquiring arms, the soldier declared out of the blue that he would sell any man a Lee-Enfield rifle for a pound. Dan took him up on the offer straight away despite his manager Pat Garvey's misgivings and met the soldier early one morning at the back of an old graveyard to complete the transaction. The soldier would report that he was held up and the rifle taken from him.[3] Dan took the rifle to IRA man Johnny O'Connor in Farmer's Bridge, and the two of them presented it to John Duggan, who had an arms dump.

> Well, first of all, I joined the Fianna [Irish National Boy Scouts] in Tralee and I was in them for a number of years. And I graduated from them to the IRA in Farmer's Bridge ... I'd say I was just gone eighteen ... I suppose that would be early 1920.[4]

Despite having acquired the rifle, Dan had no call to it, and in terms of weapons, it was mostly shotguns they had.

> Coming on the end of the campaign I had a rifle.[5]

He didn't worry too much about the possibility of being shot.

> Well, it didn't bother no one that time. When you're young you don't think of it at all. ... I mean there was bullets whistling everywhere but there was never one of them for me anyway.[6]

During the conflict, he would participate in several engagements against the British.

> Oh, well, of course, I was in Castlemaine [see 1 June 1921] and Tralee [31 October 1920] and Castleisland [10 July 1921] you know. Well, the only complete success you'll have to say was Castlemaine.[7]

9 FEBRUARY 1920

Having earned his qualification in Morse code, **WILLIAM GEARY** embarked on a voyage that would last almost a year in total. He was not long out of the Atlantic Wireless School when the opportunity presented itself.

> Now at that particular time, the Marconi Company of London had exclusive rights to supply the equipment and the operators to all British merchant ships. Now I don't know if they got in touch with me or I got in touch with them but in any event, I went to London and they hired me. When I was in London I stayed with people who were from our parish. He was a constable in the London Metropolitan Police. And I got my uniform – white uniform and ducks [white British navy uniforms made from a material called 'cotton duck']. I carried a gold stripe on my arm and they were officer's uniforms.
>
> Well, within a few days, not more than a week, I was sent with another wireless operator – my senior. His name was Charles Kelso (a Scotsman) and we took a train to Newcastle-on-Tyne. From there we went out on the coast to Jarrow and I joined a ship called the *City of Birmingham*, Ellerman City Line, and I was the second operator on board. At the time the ship was loading bunker coal and she was flying the Blue Peter flag ready to sail. Within a few days, we set sail.
>
> On our way down the east coast of England, we stopped at Middlesborough. From Middlesborough, we went to London. From London across to Antwerp, Antwerp back to London and from London we sailed to South Africa, stopping at Cape Town. From Cape Town, we went up the east coast of Africa stopping at East London, Durban, Port Elizabeth, and Portuguese East Africa. We turned around, stopped at all those again, those ports and then returned back to Cape Town. From Cape Town, we sailed the Atlantic to the United States, made a stop at Philadelphia. That was twenty-eight days clear at sea. Our next stop was New York. We stopped about ten or fifteen days.[8]

William remembered seeing trolley cars on Broadway and one day when an aeroplane flew over their ship everybody came out on deck for a look, as planes were such a rarity at the time.

> After that, we hit across the Atlantic past Gibraltar, Mediterranean Sea and on to the Suez Canal. Through the Suez Canal, on to India, to Bombay, Madras, Calcutta. From Calcutta, we sailed to Rangoon in Burma. From Burma, we came back again to Calcutta and from Calcutta

to Colombia Ceylon. From Colombia Ceylon we went to the Gulf of Aden at the south side of the Suez Canal. Sailed through the Suez Canal to London, from London to Liverpool. I signed off the ship in Liverpool after more than eleven months aboard [21 January 1921]. The Captain – James Finisterre – rated my conduct as very good.[9]

The ship's signal was BDS, and the wireless equipment was always shut down at ports.[10]

> The ship was 5,000 tons gross, coal-fired, a tramp steamer. The crew, the European crew was the captain, the mate with four assistants, chief engineer with four assistants, Chips the carpenter, boatswain, two apprentices in training for deck officers, two wireless operators. We were called Sparks, S.P.A.R.K.S. because we operated on the data what were called the Morse System. Then there was a steward. Now all the deckhands and firemen were Lascars (native East Indian sailors), Muslims from Madras and Calcutta. And occasionally to keep them happy they used keep sheep on deck for slaughter.
>
> Now the interesting thing, one of those guys, one of the deckhands was assigned to me and Mr Kelso to take care of us. His duties were shine our buttons, attend us at table, bring us in tea when we were on duty, take care of our linen and in other words handle us. Take care of our uniforms.
>
> Now aboard the ship, even on a passenger ship – the food aboard was excellent. Where I dined was called the saloon and that was exclusively for officers. There was never such a thing as any fun aboard. Everybody was busy working, sleeping and eating. Incidentally, I did six hours on and six hours off.
>
> Now in the dining room, there was the most beautiful silver provided. We had a beautiful napkin. A linen napkin in a cylinder and then there was a written menu for each meal. The food was beyond belief, really wonderful. So I had the rank of an officer aboard.[11]

William reflected on how life on board the ship was good. The work was not hard, there was a great sense of discipline, and they received good pay. Both he and Mr Kelso called the Lascar who attended them 'Joe'. William was the only Irishman aboard.[12]

23 FEBRUARY 1920

A 'Curfew' Order requiring all persons except those provided with a permit to be within doors from midnight until 5 a.m. came into operation in the Dublin Metropolitan Police District. All street lights were turned off from 11.30 p.m. until 6 a.m.[13] British military patrols filed out of the police stations and took up positions on the quays and bridges, while the streets were patrolled by military cyclists.[14]

In July 1920, the curfew hours for Dublin were changed to between the hours of midnight to 3 a.m., and in November they became 10 p.m. to 5 a.m. In early

March 1921, Dublin curfew hours were 9 p.m. to 5 a.m., but later that month they were altered to an 8 p.m. start.[15] **SEÁN CLANCY**:

> Yes, curfew at eight o'clock, which went on until six o'clock in the morning and you had to be indoors at eight o'clock and if you were caught on the streets after that hour, you'd be picked up in a lorry. Maybe an army lorry or a police lorry and taken in for the night and held. I suppose further enquiries would be made about you before they released you. That was common practice.[16]

Curfew caused much resentment and affected a vast number of night workers, as was indicated by the fact that thousands of applications for permits were received by the British authorities.

3 MARCH 1920

Frank Shawe-Taylor (a landlord and rent office agent) of Moor Park, Coshla, Athenry, Co. Galway, was shot dead after being ambushed on his way to Galway Fair in his motor car. His chauffeur, James Barrett, who was slightly wounded, had accompanied him, although he wasn't driving, as this was something Shawe-Taylor frequently liked to do himself. The incident happened after 6 a.m., one mile from his residence and close to Egan's public house in Coshla. A cart had been used to block the road, and upon stopping, Shawe-Taylor directed Barrett to move it. As he sat observing in the car with the engine running, a volley of shots rang out. The attack was carried out by eight or nine men.[17]

In the lead-up to the murder, Sinn Féin leaders in Galway had advocated the redistribution of grazing land from wealthy landowners on the grounds that people were living in poverty, as they were not getting the land they were willing and able to till. Agrarian agitation was carried out on a large scale by local branches of the party. Frank Shawe-Taylor had been born into a family that owned 7,605 acres at Castle Taylor in Ardrahan. In 1892, he had purchased over 1,200 acres of the Castle Lambert estate near Athenry, which included Moor Park House and Castle Lambert House.[18] He had refused to give up any of his grazing land to a series of deputations, and as a result, had been subjected to repeated intimidation. In 1905, he had survived an attempt on his life.[19] By 1911, Shawe-Taylor's residence, Moor Park House, was being used as a temporary RIC station to accommodate 14 men, whilst his other property, Castle Lambert House, was also accommodating six members of the force in a temporary capacity.[20] This suggests that during that period at least he was under constant police protection.

It's reputed that when in January/February 1920 a group of local IRA men – including Michael Kelly (**JOHN KELLY'S** brother), Paddy Kelly, Bill Freaney, Larry Lardner and Christy Daly, and several tenants – visited Shawe-Taylor requesting a portion of his land for distribution amongst surrounding tenants, he refused outright, declaring that if he had to give up any land he would rather give it to ex-British military.[21] It is said locally that the deputation also required the land for a road to enable people to go to Mass.[22]

People around my place there, they were narrow in land a lot of them and they asked the landlord – that Frank Shawe-Taylor. One day after Mass they went down walking to him and they rang the bell and he came out and they told him what they wanted. And he took all the names down then that was there. 'Well,' he said. 'ye can go home now,' he says. 'I won't even give ye even a perch.' And that's all I know now. That was the answer they got. So it was only a couple of weeks after when he was shot down near a public house in Egan's the Coshla. Oh, it would be two hundred yards away from the public house anyway. Some time around three in the morning I suppose. I couldn't tell you about the time now.[23]

Following the murder, letters were sent to other landlords and graziers in the county threatening them with the same fate as Shawe-Taylor unless they gave up their land. As the weeks and months passed, more landowners were killed in the agitation, and some decided to just give in and leave the county. The clergy criticised what they saw as the people's greedy pursuit of land.[24]

Ah, sure he was rotten with land that man. He must have had seven or eight thousand acres of land. Don't mind hundreds. He owned the Castle Lambert round Lisheenkyle, Moor Park, Coshla all them places. This big landlord, he came from Ardrahan. Frank Shawe-Taylor was his name. Oh, a big rich man and he wouldn't give up; he wouldn't give up none of the land. That was the trouble. So wasn't he stubborn enough?[25]

In the meantime, Moor Park House was placed under RIC protection, and in the weeks that followed five men were arrested in connection with the murder – two brothers named Patrick and Michael Kelly from Carranduff and three others from Lisheenkyle, named Martin Ruane, Thomas Holland and Thomas Connell. No one was ever convicted.[26] It's written that Shawe-Taylor was likely shot by members of the South Galway IRA who were involved in the agrarian agitation. Senior members had been amongst the deputation that called to his house asking that he give up his land for redistribution, and others had gone into hiding in Roscrea immediately after his death.[27]

They weren't a quarter of a mile away from where the house was. We were all in the one village – all these houses. These, the people that wanted the land now and they only wanted one hundred acres and he had five or six thousand acres. And that's the answer he made them, to go home that he'll never give ye a perch. So later on he got killed below about five hundred yards or a hundred yards beyond the public house. That's all I can tell you about them now.[28]

Frank Shawe-Taylor's youngest son, Bryan, who was five years old when his father was killed, went on to become a well-known racing driver. His other son, Desmond, who was 13, became a well-known music critic and writer. Frank Shawe-Taylor's only daughter, Vera Cecilia, died in February 1914, aged 11. Her death was attributed to an accident in Ardrahan the previous November involving a runaway pony, in which she was dragged along for a considerable distance.[29] However, suspicions lingered that there may have been more to this than met the eye. In the months surrounding Frank Shawe-Taylor's killing, John Kelly had been taking care of an arms dump on land owned by his future father-in-law (Thomas Creaven). He was also involved in raiding private houses for arms.[30]

25 MARCH 1920

The first Black and Tan recruits arrived in Ireland, and by July of the following year, there would be close to 12,000 in the country. They were composed largely of World War I veterans, employed in the RIC as temporary constables. The Black and Tans acted with the regular RIC and the army as the British government attempted to quash the IRA. **SEÁN CLANCY** explained how the 'Black and Tans' got their name.

> Well, they were a poor type of manhood I think. They were organised mainly from the English cities, and it was shortly of course after the termination of the First World War. There was a lot of unemployment among them and there was a lot of crime amongst them too before they came here. But the first lot of them came about March 1920 and they were trained out in Gormanstown in County Meath. And they were sent out there as they arrived on the boats in Dublin. They were trained and dressed and apparently there was a shortage of uniforms at the time and they appeared eventually in a mixture of RIC and military dress and that's how they got the names of Black and Tans. There was a gang of foxhounds in Tipperary. They called them the Black and Tans. You know that? That's how they got their name after this Black and Tan crowd in Tipperary.[31]

They would commit many atrocities throughout Ireland.

> You'd see them driving through the city at very fast speed. There were places where they were attacked of course. There was one place in the south city; they called it the Dardanelle's because they were hardly a day without attacks. A narrow street, Camden Street and they were attacked there nearly every day and they called it the Dardanelle's and they lost quite a number of men in Dublin in those street ambushes too.[32]

JOHN PARKINSON in Belfast knew some of the Black and Tan recruits personally.

> I remember them. There were some of my neighbours joined up as members of the Black and Tans and I saw them when they were home on leave. They were wild sort of men ... Well, they were wicked. They were wicked. They were going out to try and kill the other sort as they called them and vicious sort of people. I was nearly afraid to look at them ... I just saw them going back and forward. One or two of them lived in my area.[33]

One particular Black and Tan who was stationed in the North Mall had a fearsome reputation in Cork City, and he was a familiar sight to **GEORGE CARPENTER.**

> Well, in the troubled times of course, we had to go to school and we were always told to keep close to the wall and to run as fast as you can as the trouble was really bad and the Black and Tans were a really bad crowd. They'd whip people around town. One fellow by the name of 'Chance'. He had two sets of revolvers. One pair down by his knees like a cowboy, another pair up around his chest. And he one time took a whip off a jaunting car and started driving the people down Patrick's Street but we objected strongly to that. Though my father objected and he went to the head office and head office to people who he had. He was shifted afterwards up to somewhere else but he'd walk into a pub, put the two guns on top of the table, go into the toilet and come out after hours and get all the brandy for himself and charge it all up to the King.[34]

The Black and Tan in question here was known locally as Charlie Chance, but his real name was Stephen Henry Chance. Born in 1892, he was a builder, decorator and ex-soldier from London who, having joined up for service in Ireland in January 1920, was allocated to the district of Cork East Riding the following month. He was based in Shandon RIC station. Within a year, he had been promoted to the rank of a Black and Tan sergeant and went on to give evidence to the Court of Inquiry into the Ballycannon Ambush of March 1921, where six members of 'C' Company, First Battalion, Cork No. 1 Brigade were massacred by a party of Black and Tans and RIC at a farm at Ballycannon, Clogheen, just outside Cork city. He left the country from Gormanstown in March 1922 after the force was disbanded.[35] **NORMAN DOUGLAS** could still picture seeing the Tans in Belfast.

> They were a fearsome crowd and I only encountered them on one occasion. I was coming home through town and six to four tenders came around the corner and just beside the Albert Clock on High Street and these boys got out. They had their guns strapped round their top leg and they just got out, went into one of the streets and started firing – at what I've no idea. The only thing I'm glad of – they didn't come the other way because I wouldn't be here to tell the story today if they had.[36]

ELLEN MALONEY noted a tactic being used by the IRA in Portarlington to restrict the Tans' movement.

> We had to shut the door and stay inside and let them pass through. And they used to dig holes in the road – the IRA – to keep them from travelling and it didn't keep them from travelling. We had to stay inside.[37]

It was often the case that the Black and Tans would search for locals to fill in the holes again. On one occasion, the priest locked Ellen and other parishioners inside the church so that they couldn't get at them.

And the priest wouldn't let us out until they were gone and they moved on to a different town and the priest let us out then – let us go home.[38]

Men she remembered from the IRA included 'Roy Crossin next door and Sheas of Bracklone.'[39] She recalled one woman associated with Cumann na mBan.

I remember Mary Kelly. She went to America and that's all I remember.[40]

This was Mary Kelly of Patrick Street, Portarlington, who emigrated to the Bronx, New York, in March 1922. She served as president of the Portarlington Branch of Cumann na mBan, Leix Brigade until 1921 and was engaged in delivering first aid, organising dances, collecting money and supplying food to an IRA training camp in Ballybrittis, as well as other activities.[41] Ellen said republicans never held meetings in her pub and that her future husband, Michael Troy, did not join the movement after returning from World War I.[42]

I APRIL 1920

This was the month that **MARGARET CAHILL** from Ballinasare became a member of Lispole Cumann na mBan, which was attached to 'C' Lispole Company, 5th Battalion, Kerry No. 1 Brigade. Other members of her family were also actively involved in the movement.[43] Margaret operated primarily as a dispatch carrier.

I used to take the dispatches from Ballinasare to Lispole about seven or eight miles I'd walk. Yeah, and they would take them some other where ... The Fitzgeralds were the ones who gave me the dispatches yeah ... They were very prominent in the IRA – Fitzgeralds. They were very prominent.[44]

Siobhán Fitzgerald of Ardamore, Lispole, was captain of Lispole Cumann na mBan, which is recorded as having had 12 members by 11 July 1921.[45] Her brother James Fitzgerald was O/C of Lispole Company IRA.[46] In addition, siblings Maurice and Bridget Fitzgerald from Minard West, Lispole, were also involved in the movement.[47] Margaret said that she got training before carrying the dispatches and that they 'were told never to read them and all that'. She also delivered food and clothing to IRA men on the run.[48] Many of these men hid out in the mountains.

Because if they were down, they'd be arrested so they went up on the mountains. The most of them were in the mountains ... Oh, I used to know a lot of them – Murphy's and I used see the whole lot but they're all gone I guess, yeah.[49]

Tim Murphy was a member of Lispole Company, whilst his sister Katie was involved with Cumann na mBan.[50] Margaret's brothers, Michael and John, were members of 'C' Lispole Company, 5th Battalion, Kerry No. 1 Brigade IRA, as was Thomas Ashe from Kinard East, Lispole (cousin of Thomas Ashe who had died in 1917).[51] Her commanding officers, in addition to Siobhán Fitzgerald, were

James Fitzgerald O/C Lispole Company, Michael Cahill (her brother) and Thomas Ashe.[52]

> Thomas Ashe, oh, Ashe, Thomas Ashe, I knew the Ashes – all of them. They were very prominent. I went to school with them. There was some of them in my neighbourhood. Ann Ashe – she was my age.[53]

Mary Ashe was another member of Lispole Cumann na mBan.[54] The Cahills had an underground shelter in their backyard where IRA men would meet, were fed and could change clothes.[55] Fortunately, this shelter was never discovered by the Black and Tans, who would come raiding on occasion.

> They came into the house – sure. They'd look under the table [to] see if the guns were there in the dining room.[56]

An incident which she said took place near Ballinasare left a lasting impression on her mind.

> One time I was coming back after taking dispatches and there was cows on the street and off came the Black and Tans and the cows wouldn't move for them so they shot them all. Oh, wasn't that awful? They shot all the cows.[57]

In 1920, Margaret's brother Michael had been one of 16 men selected by James Fitzgerald to serve in a newly formed Active Service Unit for the Lispole Company area. He was expected to be ready at any time of day or night for action against Crown forces.[58] As an extremely active Volunteer, he rarely slept at home, opting instead for hay barns.[59] Margaret recalled her own encounter with the Tans.

> Oh, the Black and Tans were all prisoners really. One of them said to me one time, 'I was in, last week I was in jail for life for killing my wife and today I can kill man, woman and child in Ireland and nothing will happen to me.' He said that to me. And he was, they're all from jails, took them out of jails and put uniforms on their backs and sent them to Ireland. That was terrible, wasn't it? ... It was in a place where we always went dancing every Sunday and he was there and he told me the story about what he did with his wife. Wasn't that awful? How could he do that? They should have arrested him but they didn't. They were all jailbirds, Black and Tans.[60]

It was also in April 1920 that **DANIEL O'DONOVAN** in Bantry joined the IRA. Growing up, he had known people with nationalist sympathies in the town but had also been aware of others with a pro-British outlook, some of whom owned big businesses.

> It was a mixture but it, in later years coming on when the Sinn Féin started, it became more and more national and as time went by it

became more so and like many more young people I fell in line with Sinn Féin and became a Sinn Féiner.[61]

He had a vivid recollection of the day he became a member of the IRA.

Well, I was encouraged by a Volunteer known to me and brought to an outside camp, which was held every Sunday and like others we were sworn in as members of the IRA ... Third Cork Brigade – the Bantry Company. It was only one company in the town of Bantry but it was in the Third Cork Brigade.[62]

His older brother Pat was also a Volunteer, and by 11 July 1921, a figure of 206 is recorded for the membership of what was termed 'A' Company, 5th Battalion, 3rd (West) Cork Brigade, 1st Southern Division. Daniel's O/C was Thomas Ward.[63]

Well, there was quite a lot of names I disrecollect at the moment but the officers was, Ralph Keyes, Mossie Donegan, John Cotter. They were the principals, all officers but my captain was O'Sullivan. I'm trying to think of his Christian name – O'Sullivan. Jimmy Sullivan from Barrack Road, Bantry. He was my captain at the time and the company was fairly big. I suppose about, those known to me would be about fifty.[64]

Drilling was held regularly.

Every Sunday in the wintertime, well not the wintertime, in the summertime and occasional meetings in the winter but chiefly in the summertime. We were notified of where the meeting place would be. In Bantry, it was mainly Wilkinson's Wood, some few miles outside Bantry town. Then we were, I remember on one occasion we were taken to the tennis court in Cove around the strand by Bantry new pier, but it was mainly Wilkinson's Wood.[65]

15 MAY 1920

MICHAEL CASEY turned 17 years of age. He was by now a member of the Mitchelstown Company, which he said belonged to the '3rd Battalion, 2nd Cork Brigade'.[66] By the Truce, it formed part of the 2nd (Castletownroche) Battalion, Cork No. 2 Brigade, 1st Southern Division IRA. He had been involved with the movement since 1919.[67]

I joined the Boy Scouts first, you know. I was about fifteen or that way. Begorra when I saw things were getting a bit hot – I joined ... A couple of more lads asked me that were in it to join even, you know. I just took on, I done a good lot of dispatch riding then on horseback ... I was young you know. I was the youngest I'd say in the whole lot.[68]

Michael had access to these horses through his father, and the IRA badly needed them for delivering dispatches.

I used ride up, ride out with a horse, maybe have a horse and car and pass up the barrack where the Black and Tans were and they never took a bit of notice.[69]

Michael had access to a weapon when in the IRA.

Mostly a shotgun, an odd rifle the odd time. Guns were scarce during the whole trouble. If they had the guns that time that they had later, it would be different.[70]

The Mitchelstown Company were also engaged in acts of destruction aimed at preventing the British military from travelling. This was usually slow, painstaking work.

Only small, very small things, we had no bloody gelignite or anything you know. You'd have to work the pickaxe. We done that at a couple of bridges – it was cruel.[71]

Such activities were carried out after dark.

Oh, at night, at night and to get home then was the trouble ... Ah, everyone would make out their own place and an odd night maybe you mightn't get home at all.[72]

Michael made a lot of friends upon joining the IRA, there being between 82 and 121 men in the company by 11 July 1921.[73] His commanding officers were Liam Kearney, William O'Regan and George Power.[74]

There were Willie Roche – Skeheen and Jack Neill – Skeheen. They were captains anyway and Jerome Hurley was quartermaster, he was something anyway [adjutant]. He was a gentleman – this Jerome Hurley now.[75]

16 MAY 1920

A dwelling house at Blackrock, Mallow, known as Bellevue Cottage, was totally destroyed by fire and explosives. Although evacuated by the time of the attack, it had previously been used as a temporary RIC barracks.[76] The action had been carried out by Tadhg Byrne, John Moloney, **PATSY HOLMES** and several other members of the IRA's Mallow Company.[77] Patsy said that four of his brothers were also involved in the movement but in particular Jim, who was six years his senior.

They were all IRA men. Every one of them called up immediately, never a want in them.[78]

25 MAY 1920

Loughgeorge RIC Barracks in Co. Galway was attacked and destroyed by the IRA. Gelignite was used to blow in one of the gable walls and all of the windows were shattered by rifle and revolver fire.[79] The outer buildings attached to the barracks were burned down. The IRA didn't enter the building and hence no ammunition was seized, resulting in the operation being viewed as somewhat of a failure.[80] There were no police casualties, and the building was evacuated afterwards. **JOHN KELLY** of the Derrydonnell Company assisted in the blocking of roads in preparation for the attack on Loughgeorge Barracks. He had the same role when Moyvilla Barracks was burned the following month, it having already been evacuated by the RIC.[81] In preparation for this, John had participated in a raid for petrol at Athenry Railway Station.[82]

12 JUNE 1920

RIC Constable Thomas King was shot dead halfway between Bantry and Glengarriff, sparking off a tense situation within the district.[83] Nine days later, Constable James Brett was killed outside Bantry when a police patrol on bicycles was ambushed.[84] **DANIEL O'DONOVAN** of the Bantry Company attached to the Third (West) Cork Brigade never participated in attacks on the RIC and added that he was never shot at or wounded during his time in the IRA.

> There was one policeman shot in town at that time and there was another a few miles out of town but there were no military at that time there.[85]

This was followed on 25 June by the murder of Bantry Sinn Féin member Cornelius Crowley. He was killed in his bed by disguised men believed to have been the RIC.[86] Other prominent republicans were also singled out for attack and had their property burned.[87] On 24 August, Constable John McNamara was shot dead in Glengarriff, as was Constable Matthew Haugh in Bantry a day later.[88] Daniel remembered how, to combat the violence, the British sent extra reinforcements of troops to the town. In fact, by the end of August, there were over 600 based in the district.[89]

> Well, the Black and Tans came with the military. Well, the military came first, then the Black and Tans joined them, later on, the Auxiliaries.[90]

26 JUNE 1920

Eight years after the sinking of the famous passenger liner operated by the White Star Line, the Belfast *Titanic* Memorial was unveiled in Donegal Square North. It carried the names of 22 Ulstermen who perished. The names appeared underneath a statue of the goddess Thane, who was looking down, ready to bestow a wreath on a drowned seaman's body that was being carried through the waves by two sea nymphs. There was a significant turnout for the unveiling, which was performed by the Lord-Lieutenant of Ireland, Field Marshall Viscount French. The Royal Irish Constabulary Band provided the music, and among the hymns they performed was 'Nearer My God to Thee'.[91] It was an emotional occasion for everybody present, including **JOHN PARKINSON**.

> If you're here in Belfast, if you go down to the Belfast City Hall just at the east side of the city hall, you'll see that memorial today. That was the memorial that was purchased and given by the citizens of Belfast in memory of the Belfast people. There were about thirty or so who went down with the *Titanic*.[92]

In 1959, the memorial was relocated by Belfast City Council to the grounds of Belfast City Hall to protect it from increased traffic in the city.

> Every time I look at that memorial as I often do at the east side of our Belfast City Hall, I think of the day when I subscribed my money towards it.[93]

17 JULY 1920

Lieutenant Colonel Gerald Bryce Ferguson Smyth – divisional commissioner of the RIC for Munster – was shot dead in the County Club in Cork by the IRA. The reason for his murder originated in Co. Kerry on the 19th of the previous month, as outlined by **DAN KEATING**.

> He was based in Dublin and he decided to do a tour of the country and he went down along anyway and he found himself in Listowel. He addressed the [RIC] garrison and he ordered them that they were to go out in ones and twos at night, take up positions behind hedges and if they heard people coming along the road if they were talking republicanism or anything that they were to be killed. One of the policemen anyway decided that he wouldn't have any of it and he took off his uniform and he said, 'That is yours, it's British,' he said. 'I'm not prepared to murder anyone for you.' The garrison fell in behind him and Smyth had to retire in a hurry.[94]

The story made big headlines, especially in Co. Cork, where an affliction picked up by the Lieutenant Colonel whilst serving in World War I was known to **PATSY HOLMES**.

> Smyth, he had only one arm. He went into Listowel and he told the soldiers inside. He came to give them orders. Jerome O'Mee – he was guard there, threw off his jacket and, 'I'm taking no more orders,' he said, 'from you.' There were three or four others beside him in Listowel. Now you can get that story clarified. Jerome O'Mee was the sergeant's name. I think he became a priest after. And he told them in Listowel he came to issue 'shoot first and ask questions after'.[95]

Lieutenant Colonel Smyth ordered the arrest of Mee, who was one of five constables in Listowel to quit the RIC. He would go on to serve with Sinn Féin and the IRA, whilst it was his colleague Constable Hughes who later joined the priesthood.[96] Smyth had already signed his death warrant in the mind of **DAN KEATING**.

But word travels quick and when he went back to Cork he went to dine in the County Club in Cork. At the time now the County Club was a hotbed of British imperialism – the one thing that you had in Cork. And three men anyway, Michael Murphy, Sandow Donovan and oh, I forget the other fellow. He was a Kerryman anyway. The three of them they decided and they got word from a waiter who was inside in the location of the table and everything. They got on very quickly and they confronted him anyway and told him and they shot him dead in the club.[97]

The six men who fired at Smyth on the South Mall that day were Sandow Donovan, Seán Culhane, Corney Sullivan, J.J. O'Connell, Danny Healy and Seán O'Donoghue.[98] **PATSY HOLMES** heard from a source in later years that Dan (Sandow) Donovan (so-called because of an apparent resemblance to the German bodybuilder Eugen Sandow) had inflicted the most damage on him.[99]

Sandow came in and fired at him. He had only one hand and the fellow sure he went in under a billiard table and Sandow Donovan finished him off there. Oh, he was a right hoor.[100]

Smyth was buried in his native Banbridge, Co. Down, and sectarian riots followed his funeral. **DAN KEATING** summed up the significance of his shooting.

That had a fierce effect on the British too that news could travel so quick – today ordering this thing and the next day killed dead in Cork in the County Club.[101]

A curfew order was imposed on Cork City on 21 July in the wake of the killing of Lieutenant Colonel Smyth, whereby people were not allowed to be on the streets between 10 p.m. and 3 a.m. without a permit. From 6 August, curfew was extended to other parts of Munster.[102]

21 JULY 1920

A Catholic named Francis Finnegan was shot dead by British military in the Kashmir Road district of Belfast.[103] He was the first casualty of what has been termed the 'Belfast Pogrom', which would last until December 1922. Over 80 per cent of the victims would be civilians, as opposed to members of the IRA or British forces. It was mainly fought between Catholics and Protestants and was sectarian in nature.[104]

It was sparked by several factors, including the killing of Lieutenant Colonel Smyth and competition for jobs that saw Catholic workers being expelled from the shipyards, linen mills and engineering works in the city. The rioting and large-scale evictions were remembered by **NORMAN DOUGLAS**:

That was another thing that happened that particular time which is having a backlash really. Protestants were put out of Catholic areas and Catholics were put out of Protestant areas – people who had been living together for ages. And the same thing pertains now because there's what's known as Catholic areas and what's known as Protestant areas to this very day ... 1920 to '21 was the start of the real segregation of communities. It existed to some extent but I think the 1921 when Protestants were having a go at Catholics and Catholics were having a go at Protestants and they were more or less flocking into their particular own areas and that built up this segregation attitude and it still pertains unfortunately.[105]

Originally from Co. Fermanagh, 70-year-old Lukie Clarke ran a spirit grocery on Rosebery Road in East Belfast, close to Norman's house. The retired RIC sergeant and his wife, Mary, who hailed from Co. Westmeath, had seven children.[106] Norman related what happened to him:

Yes, I do remember that. As a matter of fact, round where I lived there was what was known as a spirit grocery. Now those were a sort of set up that you could buy spirits, you could buy a beer, you could buy whiskey, you could buy butter, you could buy sugar, you could buy such and such a thing. And there was this gentleman that I went in different times for my mother for groceries and the Protestants set about him because he was a Roman Catholic. And one particular night I remember they took all his furniture out on the street where the shop was and they burned it and cheered and got on and that was the end of that gentleman. He went to live in some other area of Belfast and I regretted that very much because I was very fond of the same gentleman.[107]

On 22 July 1920, Lukie Clarke was one of many admitted to the Royal Victoria Hospital, close to **JOHN PARKINSON'S** home in Belfast. He had sustained an injury to his head due to an assault.[108]

Oh yes, as I say we lived on the Grosvenor Road and we saw the ambulances going up and down, people being killed and injured. It was terrible.[109]

By the time of his death in March 1926, Lukie Clarke had relocated to the Glen Road in West Belfast.[110] John also knew a family that was put out on the street.

Around where I lived, I saw quite a number of Catholics being put out of their homes. In fact, one was a particular friend of my mother's, and she was very, very annoyed about it. But they were put out and later on they came back and things quietened down. They came back again.[111]

It was such a tense time in the city that a brother of **NORMAN DOUGLAS** had to travel to and from his job at James Mackie & Sons' textile machinery manufacturers on the Springfield Road, always anticipating that he might be set upon.

My eldest brother [John] who worked in a Roman Catholic area in one of the big factories there, he had to have; they nearly all had to have their own homemade mallets with lead in, in case they were attacked. Some of them were attacked but these were handy things to counteract that sort of thing. Because of being based in a Catholic area and coming back home from that they were very often attacked making their way home at night and they had to have these homemade protections which served a useful purpose.[112]

One night when he was returning home from work at the Sirocco Engineering Works, Norman's uncle was set upon by a mob and badly beaten. The 59-year-old was in hospital for three months as a result. Afterwards, the police informed Norman's father, Robert, that their investigations revealed the attackers had got the wrong man and it was him they were after. The Short Strand, which they had to pass through to get to work, was recognised as a volatile area.

4 AUGUST 1920

Brigadier General Frank Percy Crozier assumed the position of commander of the Auxiliary Division of the Royal Irish Constabulary (ADRIC) or Auxiliaries. This newly formed force, numbering roughly 1,500 ex-army officers, was the British government's latest attempt to seek out and eliminate the IRA. By the end of the month, 15 companies were garrisoned in Ireland. In total, there would be 21 companies made up of between 40 and 80 cadets.[113] **DAN KEATING** remembered the arrival of the Auxiliaries to Tralee in November and how attitudes towards their brutality varied.

> Oh well, of course we all saw the Auxiliaries in Tralee when they were burning houses and firing indiscriminately at people and all that you know. They were very arrogant. They were supposed to be first of all invincible and they were under no discipline whatever. At a very early stage the man in charge, General Tudor [Crozier] escaped or at least resigned [in February 1921]. He wasn't prepared to stand over the atrocities that were committed and he resigned. But at the same time, everything they done was condoned by the British and by some of the people in Ireland, notably the bishop of Cork – Dr Coholan [see 1 February 1921].[114]

As the British military presence in Ireland increased, IRA efforts were made to curtail their ability to travel. Operations were frequently carried out at night and Mallow was no exception, as **PATSY HOLMES** – who on one occasion was engaged in scouting while a raid on a train carrying petrol was carried out – explained.[115]

> I'll tell you why you'd be out. Mallow was a depot you know and when they'd come to Mallow – all the oil and things they'd have for Buttevant Station. That's a military station. We'd burn it all. We used take it down the back of the slope and burn it. Petrol and everything fired out. Petrol and anything at all went in there. I had a cousin; I had a far out relation of mine. He was a dispatch man. He was working in the, he was a goods guard, taking a lot of stuff.[116]

Patsy also admitted to having been on the run for a short period during 1920.[117]

> Jesus I was, I had to go on the run sure. I had to go on the run. Five of us slept in an old barn of hay one night and it's a wonder we didn't get our death of cold out of it. It was a long time.[118]

15 AUGUST 1920

A British sentry (Private A.E. Nunn) from the Machine Gun Corps (Infantry) was shot dead when a group of Volunteers led by Jack O'Connell attacked a deployment of soldiers who were guarding a plane near Clonbanin, about four miles from Kanturk. The following day, O'Connell and his friend Paddy Clancy were shot dead at Derrygallon, three miles from Kanturk, by a party of police and soldiers. The pair had been sleeping at O'Connell's house when it was surrounded. They had tried to fight their way out, but some distance from the house were both struck down.[119] **KATHLEEN CHARLES** was deeply saddened by the deaths.

> This man that I used to go to was Jack O'Connell. Now Jack O'Connell and his pal called into their own house one night. They were going through the country you know – hiding. And they just went in to say 'Hello and we're alright' and somebody gave word to them to say that the British soldiers were coming in a lorry and they'd probably call to his house. So off they went out to the yard, the back yard and out through a fence to escape you know. They were both shot there. I knew them very well.[120]

Kathleen didn't attend the funerals but said that her parents may have.

> There's a cross or something put up in the square you know, a memorial to them, those two.[121]

This memorial stone was unveiled on 17 August 1924 in memory of the six local men who died for an Irish republic.[122] Paddy Clancy hailed from Cush near Kilfinane and held positions in the East Limerick Brigade and the North Cork Brigade IRA.[123] Jack O'Connell, O/C of the Kanturk Battalion IRA had been particularly friendly with Kathleen, and she often ran errands for him.[124]

> I did because my father was a printer and the IRA had no money when they're out like that. They were sleeping in hay sheds and piggeries or everywhere. They dare not go near their homes because they were tightly watched. And they were working in shops – inside the counter. And my father used to print posters, we'll say for a dance. And that dance would be known by the public that it was for the money for the boys on the run, you know? And those bills couldn't be seen by the English because whoever had them would be shot. So, I got the job, I was about eight, nine, ten and they were strapped to my waist when they were printed and ready to be posted up – that this dance would be held. And

nobody knew who started the dance, who was getting the money or anything about it. And they said somebody will address the dance during the night and they'd think it was a proper dance.

So the bills for that and to advertise it would be put around my waist and my pinafore put over them. And I'd be sent down to this shop where this fellow was – he was one of the heads of the IRA. And my father said I was to say that I wanted a pair of shoes size eight – men's shoes size eight on approbation. That meant that I could take them home and get them fitted. So I'd bring them back the next day, of course, saying they were too small but they weren't fitted at all you see. They were only an excuse. And that dance would be held and whatever money they'd get, the cap would go round as the man said – collecting from the crowd. And that money would go to feed those boys who are learning to be Irishmen – the IRA. And how to fight and how to get guns and all that and that made them the IRA soldiers.[125]

Whilst Kathleen's family home was potentially open to men on the run, she maintained that harbouring them was a risky business, as the British tended to shoot first and ask questions later:

Now that money went to buy whiskey, cigarettes, tobacco, clothes. They had only wet clothes being out in all the weather and they bought clothes and shoes and boots and everything for them to keep them alive while they were doing that.[126]

Kathleen recalled conveying some of the proceeds raised at the dances to Jack O'Connell.

That's the lad that was shot that I gave the money, the bills to … Yeah, in the shop, ask for a pair of shoes and he'd take me into the back room. He said, 'Where the stock is.' There was no stock there but I'd give him the bills. He'd untie me and take the bills and then they'd paste those up around the country and the town and draw the crowd to the hall. We had a lot of little things to do.[127]

Jack O'Connell had worked in Lucey's Drapery, Market Square, Kanturk, and Paddy Clancy was creamery manager of Allensbridge Co-op near Newmarket. On Sunday 16 August 1970, when another monument was unveiled to these men, **MICHAEL CASEY** was in attendance:

Oh, I met Tom Barry. Tom Barry was born behind in Killorglin, he was reared in Liscarroll (Rosscarbery) and there were a Paddy Brien, Liscarroll. He was a great man the time of the trouble and his brother was shot. They were great friends, but I met him Tom Barry with Paddy Brien at an unveiling behind in Derrygallon. There were two men shot.[128]

Paddy O'Brien belonged to Cork No. 2 Brigade and took part in numerous engagements during the Anglo-Irish War, such as the Rathcoole Ambush (see 26

September 1920). His older brother Dan was executed in Victoria Barracks, Cork, in May 1921.[129] Tom Barry of Cork No. 3 Brigade is perhaps best known for ambushes at Kilmichael and Crossbarry.

> They were unveiling a monument to them there years ago and I was at it and it was there I met Tom Barry and Paddy Brien and I spent about a couple of hours with them and we were brought into a farmer's house and they got tea and things and we traced everything. Tom was a great man and Tom was the son of an RIC man.[130]

The monument, which contains a life-size figure of a Volunteer, was unveiled by Paddy O'Brien, and Tom Barry delivered the oration. About 3,000 people subscribed to the memorial, which also commemorates Daniel Clancy from Kanturk (see 9 December 1921).[131]

20 AUGUST 1920

Owing to recent events, coupled with increased IRA activity in the Kanturk area, the British imposed a curfew on the town. This meant that between the hours of 9 p.m. and 3 a.m. **KATHLEEN CHARLES** and all residents were not permitted to be outside unless they had a permit in writing from the military.[132]

> I remember it well. That you had to be indoors in your own home at a certain time. They'd lay out the time for you ... Stay indoors all night.[133]

She didn't recall her family having to pin a list with the names of everyone sleeping in the house on the front door. 'No, they'd just watch. Soldiers would be all around the streets.' Kathleen insisted the local IRA were aided and supported by her family, who were Protestant. There is a myth in Ireland that Protestants were all pro-British and never suffered abuse at their hands. Kathleen's mother was also in Cumann na mBan, and when it came to the movement, her father 'was a great man for them' also.[134] She indicated, however, that it wasn't the norm for Protestants to be republican back then. 'No, not usual but it has happened.'[135] Kathleen revealed that from a young age she turned against the Protestant religion, although her reasons for doing so were somewhat vague:

> I didn't believe in it the way they were acting about the sacraments. So the day I got married I became a Catholic too [see 6 September 1934].[136]

But there were sectarian and political tensions. Within two years of having finished school, **KATHLEEN CHARLES** took up work as a live-in teacher. She spent part of this in Co. Westmeath, admitting that once she left home she drifted from the political side of things for a while.

> That's where I was teaching – Mullingar. Teaching the two boys for six years ... I was about seventeen at that time.[137]

She was employed by the Aldworth family, and her accommodation was arranged by them. The Aldworth name is synonymous with Newmarket, which lies 9km from Kanturk. At this time, Newmarket Court was principal home to Boer War and World War I veteran Major John Charles Oliver Aldworth and his wife, Lena Stephanie Cecil Collins. The couple had three daughters and one son, named John Richard St Ledger Aldworth, who was born in 1914.[138] The Newmarket Aldworths sent their son up the country for a period, to reside with and be educated together with another boy, who may have been related and whose father was a man of the cloth. John Richard's mother travelled also, and perhaps his sisters. It's possible that Major Aldworth, who remained behind, was looking to get his family out of Co. Cork because of the escalating unrest; likewise, perhaps Kathleen's parents were concerned about her safety also and facilitated her move to Westmeath, which was quieter in terms of hostilities.

> Well, it was real country but it was all these big mansions and a lot of Protestants ... I had a great life there. I was one of the family and they were the real gentry.[139]

Kathleen recalled having to address the woman of the house as Lady Aldworth. There was no sympathy on the part of Mrs Aldworth towards the Irish struggle for independence. Kathleen remarked that it was laid out to her that if she mixed with individuals that she deemed to be undesirables there would be consequences. On one occasion, Kathleen was even ordered not to attend a dance that was being held in the area:

> That was the lady that had me employed – Lady Aldworth. She was a dead [staunch] Protestant and she wouldn't let me mix with Catholics ... There was that about it. The same as is in the north today – snobbery.[140]

Kathleen was in no doubt that had she gone against her employers' wishes she would 'be told go home'.[141] She reflected that likewise back in Kanturk, whilst Catholics and Protestants lived beside each other in the community and generally got on well, 'they were always kept at a distance from each other'.[142] She added that many of the Protestants around Kanturk were loyalists, such as the 'well-off shopkeepers and farmers' and those that lived in 'mansions'.[143] She had fond memories of one of her students in Mullingar.

> But I took on this job with this clergyman; this other clergyman and I educated his two boys. I got the whole care of them. I wasn't to lift my finger only teaching them. So the older boy, he got to know as much as I did and he wanted to go to England and become a clergyman. So he did that and he went to England and he became a clergyman and he wanted to go out into the front where the fighting was – Hitler and those and he got shot dead.[144]

Kathleen is referring to Aldworth's son here. On leaving Ireland, John Richard St Ledger Aldworth of Newmarket Court was educated at Rugby School, Warwickshire, before graduating from St John's College, Oxford, in 1937 with a

Bachelor of Arts degree. He joined the British army and rose to the rank of major in the Royal Ulster Rifles. He was killed in action during World War II in Normandy, France, on 10 June 1944, leaving behind a widow and son.[145]

The 1943 Irish Tourist Association Survey mentions that the Aldworth family ultimately went to live in England during the Anglo-Irish War and that Newmarket Court was occupied by Crown forces.[146] However, Major John Charles Oliver Aldworth continued to reside there also until 1921 or 1922.[147] During the Civil War, the residence was used as a barracks by the Free State Army.[148] It was sold in 1927 following owner Major Aldworth's death the year before.[149]

> A lot of these big houses closed down because nobody would mix with them. They weren't Irish anymore.[150]

In his will, Major John Charles Oliver Aldworth provided for his wife, three daughters and son, but directed 'that any child professing the Catholic religion or becoming or marrying a Catholic should forfeit the right of succession and that any daughter or person inheriting through a daughter should assume the name and arms of Aldworth unless a peer'.[151]

It was during her time as a teacher in Mullingar that Kathleen first laid eyes on a piece of apparatus rare for its day in Ireland.

> One day I was speaking to a lady and she said to me, 'Did you ever hear the wireless?' I kind of looked at her. I said, 'What is that?' 'Come on with me,' she said. At that time, I was teaching in a mansion, two boys which I took on. That was during the trouble times – when the social war and I took on one job and it was as a teacher. I was a Protestant that time, my father and mother were too.[152]

It's possible that it was a gramophone as opposed to a wireless that Kathleen was introduced to in Mullingar. Although radio broadcasts had begun in Britain in 1920, it wasn't until 1926 that 2RN began broadcasting in Ireland, and even then, most radios only had a range of less than 30 miles. The BBC had begun broadcasting in Ulster in 1924. Staying in the midlands, **PATRICK GREENE** from Rathreagh but resident in Ballinalee when interviewed, described the arrival of radio as a wonderful thing even though very few could afford one at that time.

> The first radio around here was in a house in the village. I remember a fellow climbing up on a roof and sticking up an aerial, bringing an aerial across the road to the house. You kept spinning the dial until you got a sound of something or other. If you got music, somebody – you listened to it. You got plenty of foreign stations that time. But you, there were no radios. It took a while before radios; people hadn't money to buy those things.[153]

Even though times were bad and she had what might be considered a good job, it is interesting to note that **KATHLEEN CHARLES** was highly critical of the prospects for women in Ireland during these times.

Women were made servants of, except those with money and businesses. But the general run of women were maids, housemaids and slaves ... They had no say at all. It was all the men, especially the young men. Well, do you see they never had any say in government, even in the English time?[154]

Women had no vote unless they were over 30 years of age and owned property. **MAI GROGAN** in Clare expressed similar sentiments regarding the plight of women.

Well, it was all the home with them and that's the way they were reared. ... I don't think I ever voted when I was young – never.[155]

The woman's place in society was further emphasised when **ELLEN MALONEY** remarked on the kind of characters that frequented her pub in Portarlington.

Every kind only women – women wasn't allowed in. They had to stand outside and bring them out the drink ... It was the rule ... The canal men used to come down and they'd have a sack and they'd get the week's grocery and they'd drink porter till the cows come home.[156]

MAI GROGAN agreed that it was hard for women back then, but pointed out that only very few in those times – including men – could afford the luxury of going to the pub.

Well, it was but sure the women weren't bothered with pubs. The women hadn't the money to be going to the pubs – not at all. The women didn't bother with them things at all that time. Money was unheard of ... There was two pubs down the road from us about a mile away but that's all we knew about them. The pubs, there was no such thing as drink at that time like today, oh, no.[157]

Ellen Maloney chuckled that the price of the pint was only two pence at this time. She had fond memories of the bargees who used deliver the barrels of stout from Dublin as well as some of the local characters like Cliff Kealy, who used to lead the horses that drew the barges along the canal, Mr Brennan, the lock keeper, and Jack Lane, the gardener.[158]

Yeah, ah they were nice men in the pub and they'd drink their fill. And the canal man would come for them and say, 'You should be in Mountmellick now.' And they'd go then with him.[159]

31 AUGUST 1920

When 22 people were killed in the city in just five days, the military authorities rigidly enforced a curfew for the Belfast area between the hours of 10.30 p.m. and 5 a.m., unless persons were furnished with a permit in writing.[160] **NORMAN DOUGLAS** remembered it well:

Yes, indeed I do. A lovely period of time during the summer when you had to be in the house at nine o'clock at night because the caged tenders came along with soldiers with fixed bayonets and guns peering out and they didn't ask any questions. They just shot at you if you happened to be about.[161]

On the first night of curfew, two people were shot dead by military patrols. One was Frederick Saye, whose body was found in Bankmore Street; the other was Private James Ayton Jamieson of the Cameronians (Scottish Rifles) who, whilst on duty in the Linfield Road, was accidentally shot by a comrade.[162] Numerous arrests were made by the military during curfew:

They did make arrests and asked no questions. You were just taken off and that was there was no reason for you being out on the streets when the curfew would be there and that was it.[163]

In Belfast, curfew was to last, with variations in the times, until 1924.[164] **JOHN PARKINSON:**

I remember having to be in for ten o'clock at night and we had army patrols at the corner of our street and the soldiers were in behind sandbags because there was a lot of sniping went on. A lot of people were killed by snipers' bullets. As I told you we lived in one side of, the Protestant side of the Grosvenor Road, and then there was the nationalist side on the other side and there was a lot of sniping went on.[165]

3 SEPTEMBER 1920

The printing office of Webb Gillman Charles in Egmont Place, Kanturk, was raided by a large force of military, who took up positions at the front and rear of the business, stopping all approaches while their search was in progress, which took nearly two hours. The *Evening Echo* reported that the object of the raid was apparently for seditious literature, but nothing was found.[166]

KATHLEEN CHARLES, who was possibly in Westmeath at this time, said her father had received unwanted attention from the British after printing a copy of the 1916 Proclamation.

He did the most forbidden thing that anyone could ever print. His life was at stake and he was caught and a clergyman from another parish came to our clergyman at the time and asked him to intercede for my father and he did and they let him go for this time ... I wasn't there but he would have been shot only for the other clergyman.[167]

Another piece in the *Evening Echo* following the death of Webb Gillman Charles in 1965 referenced the incident.

Possessing a kind and pleasing disposition, he carried on a large business up to his retirement as proprietor of the old Kanturk Printing

Works. Always sympathetic to nationalist activities he had the distinction of printing copies of the 1916 Proclamation which were seized as 'seditious literature' by the military authorities and he would have paid a dire penalty were it not for the intervention of a Protestant clergyman to which church Mr Charles belonged until being received into the Catholic Church with his wife and daughter.[168]

8 SEPTEMBER 1920

A result of the Northern troubles was that a new Special Constabulary or 'Specials' as they became known were established in six counties of Ulster. The Ulster Special Constabulary had over 30,000 members, drawn mostly from the UVF and the Orange Order. Their role was to defend the union against any threat of an Irish republic.[169] **NORMAN DOUGLAS** remembered them well.

> We had Specials of all descriptions – A Specials, B Specials and C Specials. What purpose they served? They were supplemental to the regular police force. But what they really did I have no idea because there was a C Special Company lived or based up the avenue where I lived and they used go out at eleven o'clock at night and came back at eight o'clock in the morning. But what they did in the interim period, I've no idea.[170]

JOHN PARKINSON said they were seen by unionists in a positive light.

> I remember when the Specials were formed and they gave a lot of people more new hope that but they largely worked on the borders more than in the cities. We didn't see a great lot of them. They were more involved in the border counties.[171]

Some men from John's Street joined the Specials and they were looked up to by fellow unionists.

> Oh yes, they had a good respect for them. In fact, they were nearly afraid of them because they were very menacing looking with their guns and aye so you had to be careful.[172]

Staying in Ulster, **ANTHONY MCGINLEY** rarely encountered the Black and Tans around Largnalarkin, Ballinamore.

> The Tans didn't come a big lot around the mountains here. They raided – just only once found them in this house here and weren't too bad. They were poor specimens to look at the most of them and they weren't, well what came around here, they weren't as bad as the name they got down in the south at all.[173]

14 SEPTEMBER 1920

The West Clare Brigade Flying Column assembled at Drumdigus, Kilmurry McMahon, for a prearranged ambush of a British military convoy. A deep trench was dug across the road in the hope of stopping the vehicles, and the column occupied an elevated position on the east and west sides of the road. The military arrived earlier than expected and observed two IRA signalmen running to their positions. They immediately stopped their lorries short of the trench, dismounted, opened fire and began to spread out in an encircling movement. The Volunteers on the west side of the road returned fire and kept the British in action long enough to allow the main body of the column on the east to withdraw to their headquarters at O'Donnell's house in Tullycrine before making off themselves.[174] **MAI GROGAN** recalled the ambush and said that various arrests were made afterwards.

> I remember that well. I was eighteen or twenty that time. I remember them – the Black and Tans. They were down at Hickman's in Kilmore. It was a big estate and they were driving from Knock, Kilmore up to Kilmihil every day and they laid a plot for them about half a mile away from the next road and they cut the road and covered it with something to disguise it anyway and they came on and there was a hill at the back of it. And the IRA were there and they fired at them and they came out of the vans and they followed them and they caught a good deal of them and they gave them the jail. I remember that well ... They cut the trench on the road at Paddy Haugh's and there was a big hill at one side of it[175]

According to Volunteer Martin Chambers, Third Battalion West Clare Brigade, who was there that day:

> The party consisted of about 20 men equipped with rifles, revolvers and shotguns and were assembled at Paddy Haugh's haggard. The trench was cut in the road between Drumdigis Cross and Haugh's house and was large enough to contain a lorry. The top of the trench was covered with netted wire of a very fine mesh over which was put straw and gravel, the whole arrangement being carefully camouflaged so as to prevent detection by anyone driving towards to in a car or lorry.[176]

Dr Bill Shannon, Carthy, McGrath and one other Volunteer were captured; two of them were later released. The military got the trench filled in and resumed their journey with the four prisoners to Kilmore House, Knock. There were no fatalities on either side.[177] Mai Grogan:

> They got jail for years. That was it. Oh, they were all afraid of the Tans. The Tans were a dangerous crowd. They were English and that was it.[178]

The previous month, shots had been fired by several men at five police from Kilrush as they proceeded to Ennis in their motor car at Tullycrine. The police returned fire, but further up their car ran into a hole in the road and came to a standstill. It was reported that none of the parties sustained any injury.[179] Back in July 1920, the agent on the Gore-Hickman property at Kilmore House had been shot by the IRA and seriously wounded. Following this, a party of British military were garrisoned there, only to have been evacuated in August after an IRA ambush.[180] With such activity in the area, it was inevitable that the Black and Tans would darken the doors of the local people.

> Oh, sure enough to look at them sure, they were dangerous. I remember they called to our house one day for there was some fellow shot near us. And I was doing something in the kitchen anyway and whatever I was doing I wouldn't look around to see them anyway. So, they searched the house and we had nothing to do with them, we were a different policy [weren't in the rebel forces]. And we were after bringing home a load of turf from the bog with the horses and cars and the reek of turf was freshly stacked, so they riddled it and knocked it to the ground thinking we had arms that it was no lexing. I remember that well. Oh, them were tough times ... My mother was talking to them and that was it. We were glad to see them out of the house.[181]

Mai also admitted to receiving visits from men mixed up with the West Clare Brigade.

> The IRA coming to our house, they did ... Tullycrine was a hilly country so they'd be on the hills every night and they'd be coming down in the morning to get into bed to sleep for the day. We often had them lads coming in and you had to take them. They'd sleep by the day then and be out by night and that was it ... We took them in. You don't want to be arguing with them. That was it.[182]

Although stories abounded, Mai stressed that she never actually witnessed anyone either from the British side or the Irish side being beaten, killed or shot during the troubles.[183]

20 SEPTEMBER 1920

Kevin Barry (a member of 'H' Company, 1st Battalion, Dublin Brigade IRA and a medical student), aged 18, was arrested after taking part in a raid for arms that led to the death of three British soldiers in Church Street, Dublin.[184] They belonged to the 2nd Battalion Duke of Wellington's (West Riding Regiment). Meanwhile, in addition to intelligence work, the removal of arms dumps, raiding for arms and mails, and assisting in a house-to-house collection for the purchase of arms, **SEÁN CLANCY** became engaged in numerous ambushes of Crown forces in the capital.[185]

> Well, of course from I'd say mid-1920 to the Truce of July 1921, it was very hard to describe it. It was a dangerous period to be living in Dublin. There were ambushes every day on the streets. Military lorries, Crossley tenders with police, army, Black and Tans, Auxiliaries were attacked in

the streets day after day by the Volunteers. Attacked with hand grenades maybe, with revolvers and sometimes rifles, although rifles were very scarce in Dublin. They were all sent to the country. And it was a risky period but thanks be to God I came through it anyway with flying colours.[186]

He was involved in attacks on military convoys in Dorset Street Bridge and Fitzroy Avenue in Drumcondra and from the garden of Bishop's Palace in Drumcondra. Most of his duties were carried out after he finished his day job, so he was particularly active at night and on Sundays.[187] Although in many instances throughout the country they were crying out for recruits to the IRA, not everybody was accepted, as **JACK DUFF** discovered, much to his frustration.

> I will tell you this and I won't go any further. I applied to a man who was a 1916 fighter and was in the Old IRA. I applied through him, he was a neighbour, he lived in 2 and I lived in 3. I applied to him on three or four different occasions and each time I did so he had some sort of a cock and bull story that I couldn't join at this particular time for some particular reason. He always cooked up some sort of a reason why I couldn't join. He told me afterwards the reason why I wasn't accepted in the British army or in the IRA. And I'm not going to tell you the reason because it would involve my father who is dead. Let him rest in peace. I won't tell you that. I have never told it to anybody and I won't tell it to anybody now.[188]

This neighbour was Tom Scully, who lived at 2 Baggot Court, Lower Baggot Street, Dublin. He had been interned after the 1916 Rising and went on to serve in the 3rd Battalion of the Dublin Brigade.[189]

26 SEPTEMBER 1920

PATSY HOLMES was never involved in any ambushes, but on this particular Sunday had been engaged in removing arms from the Mallow Company to the Mourneabbey Company (Brigade headquarters was located at Mourneabbey). Chris McCarthy collected the arms from Ned Spring and Patsy, who had used a common butcher's cart pulled by a pony to transport them. Simultaneously, a detachment of the 17th Lancers (Duke of Cambridge's Own) was mounting a raid on the home of Tadhg Byrne (O/C Mallow Battalion), who happened not to be in the house at the time.[190]

> And the shotguns then, they were brought in to all repaired and after we got across the bridge, across the other side of Mallow Bridge. I can't remember how many guns but they were put into a pony and car. They were covered with hay and straw. And a lad said to me, 'I partly guessed there was something going to happen.' But we got into the car on Sunday morning anyway. We had the guns with us and he – the lad that was with me he was sitting in the front and I was on the right-hand side and that particular morning there was a, the whole place was

surrounded. There was a chap named Byrne – the head man, and they were watching him night and day and they thought they had him in the house when the house was surrounded but he was gone.[191]

As the raid was taking place, the military was on the roadside outside Tadhg Byrne's house.[192]

I drove up to them, we drove up to them and they stopped us and what he said, 'Get on the hell out of here.' We did. The guns were in the car. And myself and the lad we weren't long going away with the pony and car but they were taken from us shortly after.[193]

Writing about this incident many years later, an IRA veteran from Mallow and district maintained that the two boys looked so innocent that they were allowed to pass without being searched. He said that he could well understand how Ned and Patsy felt when they were halted by the military, but that the guns arrived at their destination without incident.[194]

But I often enquired after about what became of them. But there was an ambush brought off in a place called Rathcoole not far from Kanturk and it seems a lot of the guns, the shotguns they had them.[195]

The Rathcoole Ambush occurred later, on 16 June 1921, when 140 members of the Second Cork Brigade under Paddy O'Brien attacked four lorries of Auxiliaries coming from Banteer. The Auxiliaries suffered two fatalities (W.A.H. Boyd and F.E. Shorter), with a number of others badly injured. There was no loss of life inflicted on the IRA. Soon afterwards, the Auxiliaries killed two local men in retaliation. Their names were Michael Dineen and Bernard Moynihan.[196]

28 SEPTEMBER 1920

Mallow Barracks was raided for arms by a group of Volunteers led by Liam Lynch in which Sergeant Gibbs of the 17th Lancers (Duke of Cambridge's Own) was mortally wounded. An attempt to burn the barracks was unsuccessful. Some 200 men drawn from companies that made up the Mallow Battalion had duties in connection with the raid.[197] One of them was **PATSY HOLMES**, who was engaged in scouting while the attack and capture of the barracks was being carried out.[198] The following night, large detachments of troops from barracks elsewhere entered Mallow, intent on venting revenge on the town. Many premises and businesses were set on fire.

Oh, they were great bastards. There was about twenty-thousand of them outside Buttevant in a place called Ballyvonaire and they were below in Fermoy again in a big place.[199]

5 OCTOBER 1920

PATRICK FITZGERALD from Dunmoon, Co. Waterford, turned 18 years of age. The previous month, he had joined the 2nd Battalion, (West) Waterford No. 2 Brigade.[200] There were three companies close by, but he opted for the Kilwatermoy Company, the other two being the Glendine and Tallow Companies. A brother of his joined before him. Patrick recalled being given a warning in advance of being sworn in.

> If you informed or anything you know. Of course, you'd be shot. You were bound by that, not to give anything away. No information or if you did you could be in trouble.[201]

There were 28 members in the company by the Truce of July 1921 (by which time it formed part of the 1st Southern Division), and each was bound by their pledge.[202] Patrick never knew anyone that dared break it. 'They didn't inform now. There was no informers there.'[203]

Men he knew in the IRA besides his older brothers Michael and Thomas included Frank Ryan, the Dunnes, Tom Roche, Pax (Whelan, O/C West Waterford Brigade) and Moss Flanagan. He said Frank Ryan had a butcher's stall and was a great singer. In addition to Pax Whelan and Frank Ryan, Patrick's other commanding officer was Michael Hennessy.[204] He and his two brothers once mobilised to Tallow to take part in an IRA engagement. It was ultimately abandoned, however.

> There was three of us in them. There was two more with me. They're dead and gone though. We were called one night; they were going to attack the soldiers. They would come from Fermoy that time. That's the British army. They didn't come at all.[205]

Names Patrick recalled from Cumann na mBan included Mary Dunne, Liz Roche and Hannie Cunningham or Connaghan. Patrick never had a gun, and most weapons obtained were taken from the RIC. It was mostly shotguns they had, but there was also an odd rifle.

8 OCTOBER 1920

In Cork City shortly before 9 a.m., 15 to 20 IRA men under the command of Commandant Mick Murphy and Captain Tadhg O'Sullivan attacked a military lorry on its way to Elizabeth Fort as it slowed down at the junction of Cove Street and Barrack Street. It being a Friday, the vicinity was packed with people on their way to work and children heading for school. In addition to gunfire, the IRA threw grenades. When one of them entered the lorry, a 17-year-old soldier, Private John Gordon Squibbs from the 2nd Battalion Hampshire Regiment, had his arm blown off when he attempted to throw it out. He died later from shock and loss of blood. In total, the 15-minute ambush resulted in three other soldiers, one IRA man and four civilians being injured. Shortly afterwards, a foreboding engraving was made into the parapet of the nearby South Gate Bridge.[206] This engagement is known as the Barrack Street Ambush, and **GEORGE CARPENTER** happened to get caught up in it. He was saved from potential harm by one of the ambushers.

> When I was going to school (Christ Church, off the Grand Parade) another time, the Black and Tans were in Elizabeth's Fort, which is just a bit up off of Barrack Street. And we had to turn into Barrack Street and just as I was turning, a lorry came down and I was caught from behind by my bag and I was dragged back and when the lorry came level with me I was pushed forward landing on the ground and then there was an explosion and there was another lorry following it and the soldiers jumped out of it and stuck a bayonet up against my throat and said, 'Get up you nipper and go to school.' So, I went to school very fast. But before going to school, I looked around and I don't think I mentioned this in my book (see bibliography) but because it was gruesome. There was a chap's face, half a face clung to the wall of a pawnshop, and it was a real bad sight.
>
> But on the way back from school, there was a lot of people standing around the bridge and of course, I had to see what they were standing there for and they were all reading looking at something. And when I got close enough, I saw the word 'REVENGE' and they say that that was done by a soldier with his bayonet.[207]

One British reprisal came in the form of an attempt to destroy Cork City Hall during the early hours of 9 October, but the prompt arrival of the fire brigade thwarted their efforts somewhat.[208] George recollected that many people living close to where the ambush had taken place sought alternative accommodation for the night.

> They all left that area because they would be burned down you see. And fortunately, they [the soldiers] were all confined to barracks. But we had a lot of people in our gardens – small little gardens. I think we had three small families in the garden until the morning. But fortunately, it was a dry night.[209]

II OCTOBER 1920

Major George Osbert Sterling Smyth, who had requested a transfer back to Ireland from Egypt to avenge the murder of his older brother Lieutenant Colonel Gerald Bryce Ferguson Smyth in July, was himself killed whilst part of a nine-man mixed unit of troops and intelligence men trying to capture two of the most wanted men in the country. Captain A.P. White was also killed. **DAN KEATING** maintained that the younger Smyth was consumed by bitterness.

> There was a man in charge of the Auxiliaries in Dublin and through a tout they located that Seán Treacy and Dan Breen were staying in a house in Drumcondra. This man I think Colonel Smyth was his name raided the house and was killed and a number that was with him and

Treacy and Breen escaped even though Treacy was killed only a fortnight after.[210]

The house they escaped from was the Fernside residence of Professor John Willie Carolan, who was one of **PATRICK GREENE'S** lecturers at St Patrick's College (see 2 September 1918). After Breen and Treacy had made their escape, he was forced to stand facing a wall and was deliberately shot by a British officer. He survived for several days, but ultimately succumbed to his wounds in the Mater Hospital.[211] Dan Breen was badly wounded in the process of making his getaway but managed to reach a safe house. In the weeks to come, he served out a lengthy recuperation period in various safe houses and the Mater Hospital.[212]

14 OCTOBER 1920

Seán Treacy was killed three days after the Drumcondra raid in a shootout in Dublin. A British intelligence officer named Lieutenant Gilbert Arthur Price and two civilians (Joseph Corringham and Patrick Carroll) were also killed during the firing. **SEÁN CLANCY** happened to be outside the particular 'Republican Outfitters' shop on the day, which was located at No. 94.[213]

> Seán Tracey, well he was shot in Talbot Street outside this shop now that was owned by Peadar Clancy. Peadar Clancy and a man named Hunter of Cork. They owned this shop in Talbot Street and of course, it was a great meeting place and that's where Seán Treacy coming out of that shop when he was attacked. They tried to, I suppose they tried to arrest him and maybe shots were fired but he was killed anyway outside the shop ... I never met Seán Treacy.[214]

15 OCTOBER 1920

Winnie Loughran married joiner Joseph Wilson in Great Victoria Street Presbyterian Church in Belfast. She came from a Catholic family that lived on Sunwich Street in the east of the city, and her father, Henry, worked as a butcher.[215] **NORMAN DOUGLAS**, who lived nearby on Ravenhill Avenue, recounted that it was this same year that Winnie took him to the pictures for what was his very first time. They watched Charlie Chaplin at Willowfield Picture House.[216]

> Where I lived we had three or four Catholic families and we had great relationships with them. We played with the children and the first time I had been to the pictures was with a lady of one of the Catholic families. My mother wasn't well and she asked if she could take me to the pictures and more or less get me out off the road. And that was the sort of relationship. We moved in and out of homes. Then we had another family, if my mother was ill or anything like that, I had to call in there coming from school for lunch. We grew up together and in later years we still became great friends.[217]

Willowfield Picture House, Woodstock Road, in east Belfast, had been opened in December 1915 by the Ulster Unionist Party and also served as the local Unionist Club.[218] There is the possibility, however, that it could have been 1918 when Winnie took George to the venue, as in December of that year Charlie Chaplin was referred to at a public meeting of the supporters of Mr. W.J. Stewart, the Democratic Unionist Electors Association candidate for the Ormeau Division. The subject of a report in the *Belfast Newsletter*, this meeting held on Ravenhill Avenue was largely attended.

> Mr. A. McConnell who introduced himself as a 'working man in the division for almost thirty years' said Sir Edward Carson had told them that the day of democracy was at hand. But it was not at hand in Willowfield Hall. They might bring Charlie Chaplin there to amuse the people but that would not serve at election times. (Laughter and applause.) That grand hall had been taken from them – the place where they had learned to shoulder their rifles like men. They were now labelling Mr Stewart as a Home Ruler – Mr Stewart, who had been vice-president of the Unionist Association until last Month![219]

22 OCTOBER 1920

In West Cork, **DANIEL O'DONOVAN**, together with a number of other Volunteers, participated in the burning of Bantry police barracks. Having been evacuated by the RIC some months previously, it was completely destroyed. An unsuccessful attempt to burn it had been made a week previously. The military succeeded, with the aid of the town hose, in preventing the fire from spreading to adjoining buildings. It was burned to prevent it from being occupied by the Auxiliaries.[220]

24 OCTOBER 1920

Publican Tom Egan, in Coshla, Co. Galway, was murdered by four men dressed in police uniforms. He was the father of seven children.[221] It was believed locally that his killing was in retaliation for that of Frank Shawe-Taylor near his pub the previous March, although Egan is reputed not to have been involved in it. The Black and Tans had only arrived in the area a month previously and were being billeted together with RIC in Shawe-Taylor's Moor Park House close to where **JOHN KELLY** lived in Caherbriskaun.[222] John, together with his brother, Michael, and several other men from the Derrydonnell Company, had succeeded in burning Shawe-Taylor's Castle Lambert House the previous month to prevent it from being occupied by Crown forces.[223] On their arrival, the Black and Tans temporarily conveyed Shawe-Taylor's widow, Agnes Mary (a relation of Edward Carson's), and her two children from Moor Park House to Galway for their safety. In the coming months, they dished out many reprisals. They went on the rampage, calling to many homesteads, including **JOHN KELLY'S,** taunting the locals and demanding to know who was behind the killing of Frank Shawe-Taylor.

> But they all got a bad beating all these people. They were all the names now that the landlord took the day they were looking for the land.[224]

John Kelly, who knew Tom Egan and his family well, went into hiding around this time with Michael and a number of others.[225] He said that although the Black and Tans were ruthless, it was the RIC who were really pulling the strings when it came to dishing out maltreatment in the area. He was sure that it was they who told the Black and Tans what to do and to whom.

> But sure the Black and Tans weren't the worst at all. The old police – it's they were doing the harm. Sure the Tan knew nothing ... Sure it's they that were doing the harm. Sure weren't they hunting the police out of this country one time? They weren't hunting them out for nothing either. They got new Garda then instead – later years to come. They were all English police; the old police and they weren't too good either ... As I said the Black and Tan wasn't the worst, the old peelers – the old police. It wasn't the Tan, only just what he was told to do.[226]

It has been alleged that the RIC at Moor Park had been responsible for the murder of Tom Egan, although no one was ever charged. **PATSY HOLMES** and a friend of his discovered that RIC intelligence around the Mallow area was extremely sharp following an occasion when they had been delivering dispatches.

> He was Flynn. He lived seven miles away. He lived at a place called Killavullen. Well, I knew he'd be the next man that would probably handle the dispatch so I met him after and I said it to him. 'I did,' said he. 'I left Killavullen,' said he, 'and I walked the railway line from that to Fermoy which is about seven miles.' He delivered the goods anyway and he came back and he told me that when he came back the sergeant in the village said to him, 'Jim,' he said, 'you were in Fermoy yesterday and you walked the line,' he said, 'and you came back today.'[227]

MARGARET CAHILL in Kerry was approaching her 15th birthday at this juncture, but even her young age didn't save her from the suspicions of the police.

> I was arrested one time, but they let me go ... We were in Annascaul and they thought I was doing something wrong and they arrested me but they let me go right away.[228]

31 OCTOBER 1920

The funeral of Terence MacSwiney took place in Cork. Since 11 August, there had been a hunger strike in Cork Gaol involving over 60 prisoners, the majority of whom, having been detained without charge, trial or conviction, demanded political status or release. Three men would die on the strike, the first being Michael Fitzgerald from Fermoy on 17 October. He had gone without food for 67 days. Untried, he had been a member of the Second Cork Brigade (see 7 September 1919).[229] Joseph Murphy, also untried, died in Cork Gaol after 76 days on hunger strike on 25 October. He was a member of 'H' Company, Second Battalion, First Cork Brigade.[230] Earlier the same day, Terence MacSwiney, the

Lord Mayor of Cork, died after 74 days on hunger strike in Brixton Prison in London. He was officer in command of the First Cork Brigade and had succeeded Tomás MacCurtain as Lord Mayor after he was murdered the previous March.

MacSwiney was arrested in Cork City Hall on 12 August and conveyed to Cork Gaol, where he and ten other prisoners joined the hunger strike that had started the previous day. Unlike most of the other prisoners, MacSwiney was tried on 16 August and had a two-year jail sentence imposed on him. He was transferred to Brixton Prison on 17 August, where he continued his protest, whilst within days the majority of the remaining hunger strikers in Cork Gaol were either released or transferred to other British prisons, where they received orders from home to abandon their strikes. This left just 11 men (including Fitzgerald and Murphy) still on strike in Cork Gaol at the start of September. Like the aforementioned, MacSwiney continued his hunger strike to the very end and his body arrived home for burial on 31 October.[231]

GEORGE CARPENTER was on the South Mall with his mother Frances and a nurse named Lou Mitchell on the day that MacSwiney's body was carried through the streets of Cork.[232] They were witnesses to an incident that caused quite a stir.

> When MacSwiney went up to the, I'm trying to think of the name of the place, up to the cathedral, he was refused entry there. So, they had to bring him all the way down to the City Hall. And I was with my mother on the South Mall and there was another nurse with us. And when they were coming up there was a sound like a machine gun and everybody ran up the other end of the Mall and dropped everything they had in their hands like umbrellas or walking sticks. And the nurse went out and gathered up a couple of umbrellas.
>
> And what it was, there was a toilet there – a corrugated iron toilet – and some fellow had run a stick across the toilet so 'DI-DI-DI' a sound like a machine gun and that's what frightened the people. In the morning we came up, a policeman came up actually. Then he [MacSwiney] was brought into the City Hall. That's before it was burned down.[233]

George was of the opinion that MacSwiney lay in state in the City Hall because the Church regarded death by hunger strike as suicide and wouldn't allow his remains into the cathedral. However, before arriving back in Cork, MacSwiney's body had lain in state in Southwark Cathedral in England. On his return, the City Hall in Cork was chosen as the most logical and suitable place to accommodate his remains. It was where his office as mayor had been, it had also been the location of his arrest, and it was large enough to accommodate the throngs of people that would file past his coffin. It was also a suitable place for a show of strength by the Volunteers.

> Oh, there was a huge crowd but I didn't go in at all. But most people did. Mother went in but I didn't.[234]

Having lain in state overnight in the City Hall, his body was removed to the North Cathedral for Requiem Mass. Following a request from Arthur Griffith, acting president of the Irish Republic who gave the graveside oration, the hunger strike in Cork Gaol ended on 12 November, by which time there were nine men in frail condition still on the protest.[235]

MacSwiney's funeral sparked considerable IRA activity throughout the country that night. When the Longford IRA shot dead RIC District Inspector Philip St John Howlett Kelleher in the Greville Arms Hotel in Granard and Constable Peter Cooney the following day on his way from Ballinalee to Granard, reprisals were expected. On the night of 3 November, 11 lorries of mixed British forces entered Granard and set over 14 business premises on fire.[236] When in the early hours of 4 November the same lorries headed for Ballinalee to carry out more revenge attacks, they were ambushed by the IRA under Seán MacEoin and forced to retreat. The village was saved, and the engagement became known as the Battle of Ballinalee. Some of those who participated were known to **PATRICK GREENE** from Rathreagh, over 20km away from Ballinalee.

> They took over a house in the village here. They had a pitched battle in Ballinalee – MacEoin. There was a DI shot in Granard and several lorryloads of Auxiliaries and Tans came down from Gormanstown the next day and they burnt half the town. But on their way back, they came to Ballinalee and they were attacked and some of them were shot, some of them. They cleared out of the place anyway. There was nobody in the Volunteer side injured. That was the local battle. I knew fellows, who were there that night, several of them. I knew MacEoin himself – Conway. Conway was high rank in the army afterwards. Conway was a very young fellow at the time and several others (Seamus Conway became a colonel in the Free State Army).[237]

GERRY SMYTH in Stackallen saw the British military vehicles both before and after the fighting that took place on 3 and 4 November.

> I remember the famous Battle of Ballinalee where Seán MacEoin was the hero. I remember seeing the lorries of Black and Tans going by from Gormanstown and around and after the thing I could see them going back and they all smashed up after it.[238]

DAN KEATING disclosed that on the same date as MacSwiney's funeral and the shooting of RIC District Inspector Kelleher in Granard, he had been in Tralee on November Eve for an attack on British forces, but that no enemy showed themselves where he had been positioned. He said that on the same night, two Black and Tans had been killed by the Strand Street Company and were never seen again.[239] An account by Dan's comrade Johnny O'Connor provides more information.

> Late in October, the Brigade O/C Paddy Cahill, asked for volunteers from the company to participate in an attack on enemy forces in Tralee which

had been fixed for 31st October 1920. With four other men, I was selected from among the men who volunteered and on the night fixed for the attack, reported to John Joe Sheehy at the sports field, Tralee – now Austin Stack Park. Sheehy had a short time previously been promoted to Acting Battalion O/C Tralee Battalion.

The three local companies in the town – Boherbee, Rock Street and Strand Street – were mobilised that night. I was allocated a position at Edward Street with members of Boherbee Company. I had a rifle; one or two others also had rifles; the others had shotguns. John Joe Sheehy was in charge of the section to which I was attached. His instructions were to open fire any time after 9.30 p.m. on any enemy personnel in our vicinity. It so happened that no enemy appeared in our position that night. A section under Paddy Paul Fitzgerald did, however, capture two Tans that night; these two Tans were later taken outside the town, shot dead and buried where they fell. This same section later in the night opened fire on a Tan patrol, wounding two of them. I went to Castleisland on the following day, which was the 1st November.[240]

The dead police were Constables Ernest Bright and Patrick Waters. For the next nine days, Tralee was subjected to a reign of terror by the Black and Tans and Auxiliaries, and two men named John Conway and Tommy Wall were shot dead.[241] Many of the most active Volunteers got out of the town for the week, where Dan recalled a strict curfew was imposed:

> Oh, Christ yes, that had to be when you'd go to bed at night your list of the people that were sleeping in the house. That was during the Tan war, oh yeah.[242]

The unionist outrage at the thought of members of the RIC and the British forces being killed on such a large scale throughout the country was not lost on **JOHN PARKINSON** in Belfast.

> That caused a lot of trouble and then of course the attitude here was to go out and shoot somebody in their place and there were quite a number of people shot. Living as I did on the Grosvenor Road, I often saw the ambulances rushing up to our Royal Victoria Hospital with the casualties.[243]

1 NOVEMBER 1920

Kevin Barry was hanged in Dublin, and **SEÁN CLANCY** was in the city at the time.

> I was but there was great sympathy of course for Kevin Barry. He was so young. He was only eighteen and there were all kinds of efforts made to the powers that be to reprieve him, but it was no use. He was just hanged on the 1st of November 1920.[244]

Another with vivid memories of that day was **JACK DUFF**.

I was working in the Dublin United Tramway Company at the time and practically the whole city stopped. The whole city practically stopped work on that day and there was hundreds gathered outside the Mountjoy Gaol. Gathered outside the Mountjoy Gaol and they said prayers for the repose of his soul at the gaol gates.[245]

9 NOVEMBER 1920

Constable Turner was killed outright and Constable Woods was fatally wounded as they sat in a carriage on board the 8 p.m. Tralee to Killarney train when it halted at Ballybrack Railway Station. The shots had been fired from the platform by a number of men.[246] This incident was to impact **PATSY HOLMES**, who at this time – in addition to helping out in Lucey's butcher shop – worked for a cattle dealer named John Clancy, who hailed from Kanturk, near Mallow. He told the story of how he was instructed by Clancy to drive 38 cattle a distance of 44 miles within hours of the killings at Ballybrack. Curfew between 9 p.m. and 3 a.m. had been imposed on Mallow since 2 October.[247]

> During curfew didn't I tell you I was working for this man Clancy and we went to Killarney Fair. He had to buy thirty or forty heifers. And when he had the heifers bought, we went to the station to load them to send them to Mallow. There was plenty wagons there but no engine. Now I'll tell you why they didn't have them ... There was two soldiers killed in Ballybrack that night and they were afraid the same thing was going to happen them and be shot and they made off. They left and took the trains and left the wagons. But anyhow he said to me, it was two o'clock in the day anyway and no wagons but, 'You'll have to walk them.' It was forty-four mile from Mallow this time.[248]

Patsy commenced his journey, and at 6.50 p.m. on 10 November he arrived at the village of Rathmore. Having made arrangements to sleep the night in Hassett's public house, he was permitted by the owner to leave the cattle overnight in a field close to the premises. Early the following morning, he set about resuming his journey.

> Not a soul around. You'd see no one but I saw a tallish man coming down the street ... He came down near me and he had an English accent. He said, 'Can I help you?' I said, 'You can.'[249]

The affable stranger assisted Patsy in getting the cattle out of the field and back onto the road.

> He came up to the top of the village with me. It was then I discovered he was a Black and Tan. Be Jesus I didn't know and he came up through the village with me, shook hands with me and all. Jesus says I; how did I escape at all? But by God, I was mad to get rid of him anyway but I did in the finish and I started away for Mallow – thirty-eight miles.[250]

En route, Patsy (who never drank alcohol) stopped at another public house and once again put the cattle into a field nearby, having been given permission to do so.

> I went in for a drink, a bottle of lemonade or something and who arrived only a lorry with Black and Tans and Auxiliaries ... When they had enough drank, they broke everything what was inside and they told her [the owner] de Valera would pay for it. But I kept stumm. I kept silent anyway. I didn't even open my mouth at all and all bad luck to them anyway. Eventually, they stood out, pulled out and they fired shots. They blew mortar off the house everywhere and the old cattle went half cracked but I got them all.[251]

Patsy arrived at Mallow on 11 November in advance of the curfew being at 9 p.m.

> I landed with all the cattle. There wasn't a prouder man in sight. And after that Lord Kenmare, do you see Killarney was a famous stop but Lord Kenmare ... He got liberty to hold a fair for two hours. So that was my last journey through the Black and Tans. They were a great lot of hoors though.[252]

Lord Kenmare (Valentine Charles Browne) was a Catholic peer whose Kenmare estate extended over 10,000 acres, including the Lakes of Killarney.[253] As well as being a director of Messrs A. Guinness, Son and Co. Ltd. since the company was formed in 1886, he was also a director of the Great Southern and Western Railway Company.[254] On 16 November 1920, he expressed *'sympathy with the relatives and friends of the two members of the RIC who were foully murdered near Ballybrack'* and deplored that *'such a terrible crime should sully the fair name of the Killarney district.'*[255] On a separate occasion, Patsy Holmes had used his position as a cattle drover to carry dispatches from Cahir to Tipperary town.[256]

12 NOVEMBER 1920

MICHAEL CASEY met one of Ireland's most wanted men in Mitchelstown.

> I had a bit of a touch with Dan Breen. Did you ever hear? Dan Breen the time, there were a thousand pound on his head – dead or alive and he walked up the middle of the road in Mitchelstown at eight o'clock in the morning on the 12th of November 1920. And do you know how he walked up? A thousand pounds on his head was a lot that time. There was a fair in Mitchelstown. There were droves of cattle coming into the fair. He was dressed with an old shabby coat and, you know with a farmer from around, Kilbehenny I think – Luddy was his name. But he was helping him by the way coming in and he. Once he came to the Square he just dropped off and went into Ryan's pub. Everything was fixed for him you know.
> But I happened to be over there, that night and I was brought into the room where he was. And he was very cautious you know – afraid. But he

was behind the door. If the door opened, he was kind of covered but there were a low table there about that high and a chair on top of that and he was sitting there. If any Tans or anything came in, he'd have the first of them you know. They'd fire low. They wouldn't be firing up that way. They'd be firing low to hit him. But I left him anyway and he hung around for about a week, but he didn't stay there all the time. He went up to Mulberry and he slept at Powers another night and he changed around. But he was never killed and he'd be hanged if he was caught. But he wouldn't be caught alive. He'd fight.[257]

According to *Guy's Postal Directory for Cork City and County 1914*, one of the days set aside for Market in Mitchelstown was indeed 12 November, and whilst I do not doubt that Michael Casey met Dan Breen, it is possible that the date he provides for their encounter is incorrect. In his autobiography, *My Fight for Irish Freedom*, Dan Breen claims to have been between Dublin and Wicklow at this time, recuperating from wounds incurred the night of the Drumcondra raid (see 11 October 1920). He went on to write that once fit enough to commence lengthy travel, he didn't arrive in south Tipperary until a few days before Christmas 1920 and spent most of the remainder of the Tan War in that vicinity.[258] Once there, he could easily have crossed into neighbouring Mitchelstown and met, amongst others, Michael Casey. Historian Bill Power records an incident that happened during the Black and Tan times whilst Breen was staying in the area.

> Breen and Willie Ryan were hiding in Bartie Power's home at 6 Brigown Cottages, when the daughter of a next-door neighbour, who was returning home late from a rendezvous with her boyfriend, disturbed Power's Irish terrier. A Black and Tan patrol was attracted by the commotion. They shot the dog, but fortunately for everyone inside, they did not bother to search the house. [259]

It's also possible, however, that Michael's encounter with Breen occurred much earlier, in 1919. Breen wrote that within a very short time of the Soloheadbeg Ambush, he – together with Treacy and Hogan – crossed the border into Co. Cork.

> We decided to go on to Mitchelstown which is situated at the extreme end of the Galties. We spent a night in O'Brien's of Ballagh, and while we were there a peculiar thing occurred. We were sleeping in a room upstairs when strange voices aroused us. We looked out and saw several peelers entering the house. At once we got ready for a fight, expecting to see them mounting the stairs at any moment. But they did not come up. In a few minutes, they made their departure. It was only when they had gone that we learned that the object of their visit was to ascertain if the owner of the house had paid the licence for his dogs.
>
> Eventually, we reached Mitchelstown where we met Christy Ryan who welcomed us and gave us the shelter of his house. While we were there we saw eight armed policemen pass by the door. They were

guarding a little packet of blasting powder. Evidently, the Soloheadbeg Ambush had taught them to take no chances; they now had quadrupled the escort.[260]

An account penned by a Mitchelstown volunteer in *Rebel Cork's Fighting Story 1916-1921* states that Breen, Hogan and Treacy arrived at Mick O'Sullivan's house in Mulberry two nights after the Soloheadbeg Ambush. As his house was under RIC surveillance, he promptly escorted them to Christy Ryan's house in New Square, as he figured that no one would suspect such badly wanted men to be hiding out in one of the busiest establishments in the town. They remained there for a week before Patsy Walsh conveyed them by horse and trap to Pat McGuire's house in Carrigturk, Ballylanders, where they remained for a further period.[261] Although Breen makes no mention of it in his book, Mick O'Sullivan himself claimed that Breen, Hogan and Treacy visited him in May 1919 soon after Hogan was rescued at Knocklong Station.

> As my home was being raided regularly at this time, I felt it was not safe to allow them to stay so I took them to Christy Ryans, The Square, Mitchelstown where they remained for about ten days. It was a lucky move as, early next day, my home was raided. I was not sleeping at home at that time.[262]

Incidentally, Michael Casey said he didn't know Seán Treacy but remembered Breen as 'a bold man, a daring man, always out to kill'.[263]

21 NOVEMBER 1920

Bloody Sunday took place when 19 British Crown forces personnel were awoken and shot by Michael Collins' 'Squad'.[264] Fourteen of these were killed outright, one died later and four were wounded. Eleven of the dead had been British intelligence agents. Collins obtained information on these men from his network of spies, one of these being David Neligan, who operated out of Dublin Castle.

JACK DUFF, who resided at No. 3 Baggot Court, Lower Baggot Street, maintained that his mother, Catherine, had witnessed one of the killings by the Squad that morning.[265] Captain W.E. Newbury had been shot at No. 92 Baggot Street Lower and Captain George T. Baggally shot at No. 119 Baggot Street Lower. Members of the Squad had also called to No. 54 Baggot Street Lower, but it was a mistake, as there were no British intelligence officers in residence.[266]

In the afternoon, Black and Tans and Auxiliaries shot at a crowd in Croke Park attending a Dublin Tipperary football match. They killed 14 and wounded many.[267] **SEÁN CLANCY** wasn't far from the ground at the time the slaughter was being carried out.

> I heard the shooting in Croke Park. But that was a terrible affair altogether. It was a terrible day in Dublin. You had the shootings - the Bloody Sunday shootings that morning in Dublin and then you had the

shootings in Croke Park in the afternoon. So it was tit-for-tat if you like.[268]

Three men who had been captured the night before – Dick McKee, Peadar Clancy and Conor Clune – were later killed in Dublin Castle in retaliation. Clancy and Clune were from Clare, but the latter had not been a member of the Volunteers.

> I knew Peadar Clancy – a namesake of my mine. I'm from Clare but no relation. I knew Peadar Clancy. He had a shop in Talbot Street here in Dublin. He was of course murdered on Bloody Sunday. He was arrested that morning and he was one of the people who had planned to take part in the Sunday morning shootings. But himself and a man named Dick McKee – he was leader of the Dublin Brigade – they were arrested and Conor Clune third man and they were taken to Dublin Castle as prisoners and they were shot in the garden. All three were shot dead in the garden.[269]

Seán was subsequently part of an association that did its bit to commemorate Peadar Clancy's name.

> We had an organisation of Clare people here in Dublin. Ah, this is twenty or maybe more years ago and somebody here in Dublin at a meeting suggested that Peadar Clancy being a famous man from my own county, that we should honour him in some shape or form. And I don't know – couldn't tell you who suggested it. That 'why not get a portrait, a good portrait and present it to the school where he was educated in County Clare – a place called Cranny?' And we did that.
>
> The portrait was made and it was decided then to get in touch with the school in a place called Cranny in west Clare and the parish priest who was manager of the school. I forget his name now, he was approached for permission for to hang the picture in the school and he refused. He maintained that it would make a wrong impression on youngsters, the manner in which he was killed and that it might not appeal to them. So he refused anyhow.
>
> So we then decided, the inter-party government at the time was in power, led by John A. Costello and he was approached and Dick Mulcahy was Minister for Education in that government and he was approached and asked if he could do something about it. So he made an approach to the Bishop of Killaloe who was Dr Fogarty. Did you ever hear of that man's name – a very well-known man? And apparently, he got in touch with the parish priest and made him change his mind and the picture was presented to the school and I presume it's still hanging there, I couldn't tell you that.[270]

The portrait was the work of Belfast artist Padraig H. Marrinan, whose father was from Cooraclare. It was presented to Cranny National School in 1951 and still hangs proudly in the hallway.[271]

In the aftermath of Bloody Sunday, **GEORGE COOPER** in Dublin had reason to suspect that the IRA were concerned about the intentions of a particular girl who was in a position to identify some of the gunmen in Collins' Squad.

> But if you remember there was, I think a Bloody Sunday in Croke Park. What led up to that was eight British soldiers or officers were shot dead in their bed in Mount Street. We lived in 26 [Holles Street], 27 that family went to the same school as I did and I'm not sure of the circumstances, but I think one of the girls of that family was working in that house at the time and I think she recognised some of the fellows who did it. Because as far as things worked out, she must have squealed because next thing was an armoured car had come to that house and whisked her away. About a day or so afterwards my mother used to go into their house and talk to her mother and when she went into the house and went up the stairs there was a fellow (IRA) with a revolver and he said, 'Mrs Cooper, we have nothing against you or your family but if we get her we'll blow the head off her' ... Her name was Stapleton.[272]

Nellie Stapleton worked as a maid at 22 Lower Mount Street, where two British agents that the Squad had orders to eliminate were located.[273] Two men from the Squad, together with six men from 'E' Company of the 2nd Battalion proceeded to the address, with the intention of shooting Lieutenant Henry Angliss and Lieutenant Charles Ratsch Peel. They knocked on the door and a maid (reputedly to have been Nellie Stapleton) admitted them. The IRA left two men inside the door to ensure that nobody could enter or leave the house, while the remainder proceeded upstairs to two rooms, the numbers of which they had already ascertained.

Angliss was shot dead, but Peel remained uninjured when he barricaded himself in his room. Meanwhile, two women (again, one was reputed to have been Nellie Stapleton), on hearing the shots, shouted from an upper window to a party of Auxiliaries passing by outside the house. The Auxiliaries immediately tried to gain admission. Shots were fired, and ultimately seven members of the IRA managed to get away in the confusion. One, named Frank Teeling, was hit, and they had to leave him behind.[274]

In January 1921, Teeling and three others (William Conway, Daniel Healy and Edward Potter) were charged at a Field General Court Martial with the killing of Angliss. The case against Healy was put back for a separate trial. The *Irish Independent* reported that the young maid (not named, but believed to have been Nellie Stapleton) was the principal witness for the prosecution. She identified Teeling, Potter and Conway as having participated in the raid. She knew none of them before the morning of the shooting and they were all strangers to her. She said she had gone to Dublin Castle a fortnight previously to make a statement before the prisoners and laid eyes on Teeling. Previous to this, she had identified him at the Bridewell. Before Christmas, she had pointed out Potter at a line-up at Wellington Barracks. She had also identified Conway at the Bridewell.[275] Teeling was sentenced to death but managed to escape from Kilmainham Gaol in February 1921, along with Simon Donnelly (Vice-Commandant, 3rd Battalion,

Dublin Brigade IRA) and Ernie O'Malley.[276] The death sentences of Conway and Potter were commuted to penal servitude, while Healy was eventually acquitted.

22 NOVEMBER 1920

In the aftermath of the IRA's raid on Mallow Barracks, it was routine for large numbers of suspected Volunteers in the area to be rounded up by Crown forces such as on this date, when many of those arrested were described in the press as 'mere boys'.[277] **PATSY HOLMES**, who lived on Fair Street, was amongst their ranks.[278] He said he had just returned from driving cattle in Tipperary and that the military had 'shot the door' at 4.30 a.m. to gain access to his house. Some of them then 'charged up the stairs'.[279]

> I was arrested in 1920 after the raid on Mallow barracks ... And I'd probably be eighteen years at the time.[280]

Patsy, whose brother John (aged 14) was also in the house at the time, remembered the words of the British officer in charge of the party that arrested him.

> He said, 'If you try to escape, my brother,' he said, 'is a crack shot. Plop flop,' he said, 'and you're a corpse.' So, I didn't escape and there was a place where I could have escaped. It would be about forty yards or more from my home door but it was too near to chance it. So a hunger strike was on in Cork at the time and I was working with a butcher in Mallow.[281]

Patsy was in no doubt as to why he had been rounded up and sent to jail.

> Well, you see what happened was, they knew I knew all about Waters ... They knew I was with Waters all the time. And he was staying in a little house down the town with two old ladies – well, I knew that. That's what they knew.[282]

Patsy was friends and worked with Edward (Ned) Waters in Lucey's butcher shop in Mallow, and Ned had been on the run since the attack on the British soldiers at the Wesleyan Church in Fermoy the previous September.[283] His infamy was growing, as the British now added the raid on Mallow Barracks (in which he had also participated) to his rap sheet, so he went into hiding.[284] Such was their desire to apprehend him that in December as many as three lorries of military raided his home, albeit unsuccessfully.[285] Informers were plentiful and, in any event, they would have figured that since they worked together and were good friends, Patsy would possibly have known his whereabouts. More than likely, they saw Patsy as a Volunteer also. Either way, they interned him in Cork County Gaol (on the present-day site of University College Cork) after a brief interrogation at Victoria Barracks (present-day Collins Barracks).

> But the night I went into Cork Gaol, it was a big old room I was fired into and I heard the door opening and this fellow came in and he had a grand grey suit on him. It was like a bank clerk. So he was there. I didn't

> open my mouth to him. So after a bit, 'I tell you,' he says, 'my name is
> Tadhg Crowley.' He was from Rathmore. He was a merchant, they
> arrested him.[286]

Patsy was adamant that this man was Tadhg Crowley from Rathmore, but it
may have been Kerry County Councillor and Volunteer Fred Crowley who was
arrested by the military in the village on 3 November along with his brother
Eddie. Having been confined to Killarney Police Barracks, Tadhg Crowley was
conveyed to Cork and his brother was released.[287] Originally from Gurteen in
Cork, Fred Crowley's family had relocated to Rathmore in his youth. He had
obtained a Diploma in Textile Manufacture at Leeds University, and his late
father had worked as a woollen manufacturer. In later years, Crowley became a
TD.[288] In any event, Patsy's arrival in the gaol would have coincided with the
aftermath of the hunger strike for political status or release that had begun on 11
August and which claimed the lives of two men in the gaol and one in Brixton
Prison. It ultimately ended on 12 November.

Patsy noted the bleak atmosphere in the prison when he entered. Prison
chaplain Rev. Father Fitzgerald and assistant chaplain Rev. Canon Thomas
Duggan, as well as other clergy and nuns, were regular visitors to the nine
republicans, who were in a weak state physically, having just come off the
strike.[289] The prison governor was Joseph King.[290]

> There was a hunger strike there, and Mickey Fitz. now was one of men in
> Fermoy that died, he died on hunger strike and Willie (Joseph) Murphy. So I
> was coming in one evening in the jail – the old jail now – and one of the
> nuns called me. 'Patsy,' says she, 'don't make much noise there's a couple of
> the boys very bad.' They were the lads that were on hunger strike.[291]

It would appear that 18-year-old Patsy did not adhere to the nun's request and
that incarceration coupled with goings-on within the prison were taking their
toll on him. On becoming a bit too loud for their liking, the authorities
attempted to quieten him.

> So I was taken upstairs again anyway, where the cell was, and shortly
> afterwards the warder came. He said, 'I must take you downstairs Patsy,'
> he said. 'Ok,' I said, decent man he was, he was a Kilkenny man. I'm
> talking about the warder now; he was a Kilkenny man and one of them
> played there with Kilkenny. He was a very decent man but I went in.
> When I went down below, there was two men in the cell, and I said to
> one of them, 'You've a bit of room here,' I said but I wasn't to know. 'Oh,'
> says he, 'this is a condemned cell.' I said, 'This is a condemned.' 'It is,'
> says he. One of them was from Millstreet. So I said to myself, I said
> nothing quite frankly. I said nothing. So I was there for a while when
> John Comerford the warder, he said, 'Come on Patsy,' he said, 'I'm taking
> you back up again.' Now, they probably put me in the, in the cell to
> frighten me or something you know.[292]

In the following days, things settled down within the prison and Patsy had little option but to adapt as best he could to his new surroundings. He remarked that it was possible to meet 'every kind of a fellow' in the jail, including those who just didn't want to be homeless.

> There was one old lad there above in Cork Gaol, he wasn't a political prisoner but he was a prisoner. He wanted to be put to jail anyway for the winter.[293]

Food items the prisoners were given included either boiled or preserved eggs. Patsy recalled them being distributed from a bucket by a man named Hogan, who was accompanied by a warder named John Comerford from Kilkenny. On one occasion, when Patsy pointed out that the inside of his egg was coloured green, a convicted criminal joked that 'all the old hens in Ireland are all turning Sinn Féiner. They're laying the eggs green, white and yellow'.[294]

John Comerford was an ex-serviceman employed as a temporary prison guard in Cork Gaol, and his already dangerous job had been even more perilous during the hunger strike. The suffering and death of prisoners had a profound effect on the gaol staff, and some took it upon themselves to apply for transfers.[295] They also feared IRA reprisals. On 10 October, after finishing duty, John Comerford and a regular warder named Thomas Griffin were held up a distance from the gaol by at least six men with revolvers. Comerford was made to face a wall for a quarter of an hour with a pistol at his back before being instructed to go home by a certain route, whilst escorted. Thomas Griffin was kidnapped and held until 19 November, when the strike had concluded. It was reported in the press that he had been detained for 'having made frequent attempts to persuade hunger strikers to take food', while another account claimed 'he was not friendly to the I.R.A. prisoners who were on hunger strike in that jail'. Both Comerford and Griffin were married men.[296]

27 NOVEMBER 1920

The *Donegal News* reported that the inspector-general of the RIC had lodged a claim for £100 for a quantity of furniture burned at Fintown Barracks.[297] Some weeks previously, an attempt had been made by the IRA to burn the barracks, but the garrison inside was alerted to the sound of slates being removed from the roof and opened fire. A half-hour gun battle ensued before the IRA withdrew, unscathed. The next day, the RIC abandoned the barracks and it was burned.[298]

November 1920 is one of the dates provided by **ANTHONY MCGINLEY** for when he joined the Fintown Company, 3rd Battalion, Donegal No. 3 Brigade.[299] Inducted into Fintown Company by Mick McGeehan (Company O/C in 1920) and Eddie Ward, his commanding officers were John Houston, Patrick McHugh, John Herron, John Wright (Company O/C in 1921) and Con Quinn.[300] He claimed service in the neighbouring districts of Edenfinfreagh, Glenties, Ballinamore, Fintown, Glenfin and Ardara during the Tan War and was also considered to have served in Letterbrick.[301]

Well, I joined the local company at the age of fifteen. I was the youngest in it. That's around here. You see it was brought up in companies. You had companies, battalions, brigades and divisions more or less all over Ireland. We belonged to the 1st Northern Division here in Donegal. And I was the youngest in the company because I had two first cousins fought in 1916. They marched out. They were living in, born in Dublin and they were pupils of Pearse and they marched out with Pearse and of course then all their relations here in Donegal all became Sinn Féiners. You see.[302]

By March 1921, the 1st Northern Division consisted of Co. Donegal, part of west Co. Derry (including Derry City), part of west Tyrone (including Strabane) and a section of northern Fermanagh. There were four brigades in the division. Much of Donegal's countryside was poverty-stricken, and it suffered from high migratory labour to Scotland at certain times of the year.[303] As a result, the 1st Northern Division was deprived of many potential volunteers.

Donegal or the north was a bit slower than the south getting into action, you know? But the most of them did and you must know that there was far more loyalists – the Protestants – living in the north than there was in the south and they had to go very carefully. Aye, they had to go very carefully. But yeah, it was pretty amateurish, but they done the best they could and we set up Sinn Féin courts and you were out at night, you were raiding ones that had shotguns that wasn't in the movement at all you know. Ah, careful people and then into, well in the hills here then the Crossley tenders used to come tearing in and in every glen there was always ones watching out.[304]

Anthony knew nobody associated with the Orange Order in his locality.

Well, not in the hills here you see. There were no Protestants lived in the hills but when you went down the valley started to go into the good lands, they were a majority there. And is yet. And of course, they took it by force and we, our forefathers was driven and fell back in these hills.[305]

Being young and living in a remote area high in the hills, Anthony admitted to seeing little military action during the Tan War. Most of his activities with the company were done after dark across the local districts.

First thing we done, we went out and we raided for arms and we had to get shotguns and arms in houses raiding at night. And there wasn't a big lot of real, there was not a big lot of fighting here, but you kept the things going and set up Sinn Féin courts and all this you see … The way the like of me was, I had to be here with my uncle (Muiris Mac Daibhid) and we had to make a living on the farm and you had to put down crops. My uncle was very near-sighted, so I worked the horses. The horse you know, I had to work very hard to try and put down as much crop as you could and ah, but I was out at night often and you know in stuff and raiding arms and all that … We had shotguns first and then there were some rifles but every man didn't have a rifle you know. But there was some in the company.[306]

Joe Sweeney took over from Frank Carney of Derry as O/C of the 1st Northern Division in May 1921. Originally from Burtonport, Sweeney had attended St Enda's in Dublin and was engaged in bomb-making in the school's basement, along with Anthony's two cousins (Eunan and Conor McGinley), before the Rising. He was based in the GPO during the fighting and was afterwards interned. Some in the Fintown Company were veterans of World War I.

> There was a certain amount around here came back and some of them joined the IRA and damn good men they were. Paddy Kelly of Ballinamore out there, a very quiet fellow. He was all through and he was captured and he was a prisoner of war in Germany and he came back and he was one of the best Volunteers we had around here. Aye. Of course, he knew his stuff you know.[307]

Anthony's only brother, Michael, likewise became involved in the Fintown Company, by now having returned from Strabane, where he had also been active. Neither of the McGinley's names appear on a list of those involved in the burning of Fintown RIC Barracks.[308] However, the names of those who may have been engaged in blocking roads or scouting are seldom featured on lists.

> Oh, my brother who was two years older than me, he drilled the company here.[309]

In 1920, Michael McGinley served as 2nd Lieutenant, and Dan Doherty was 1st Lieutenant.[310]

> My brother in Strabane, he started the scouts – Sinn Féin scouts. Very much underground because Tyrone in the north, it was very English. You had a police force there and all. But they drilled and eventually got arms and then they as they got up joined the Volunteers.[311]

A number of operations against the Crown forces took place in Co. Donegal, and Anthony was adamant that his company, positioned in the southwest, did their best during the whole trouble. At the same time, however, he resented that they weren't in a position to do more.

> That was one thing that Donegal or the north nearly generally had a fairly bad record. We had no leaders. We had bad leaders. It was just local fellows that done any, there were no, leaders were no damn good … There was not. A few good men in the south made all the difference … Oh well, Charlie Daly was from Kerry and he was arrested then. They had been out. They were good leaders. Daly was a great, great man. He was a gentle type of a man you know, a real gentleman but dedicated.[312]

Daly was a native of Firies and had been sent north by GHQ in September 1920 to organise the IRA in Tyrone, although he did cross into Donegal also. He was arrested in January 1921 and imprisoned for three months in Dublin but went north again following his release. He was appointed O/C of the 2nd Northern Division, which covered Tyrone and south Derry, in May.[313]

> Charlie Daly was sent up here to form the columns to take the weight away from Kerry in the south because they were getting it too hard from the Tans. And there was nothing right doing in Donegal or around the north only an odd thing to take the weight and they did come up. And they put them into shape and they attacked barracks and all the rest of it.[314]

It's possible, however, that Anthony McGinley was involved in more IRA operations than he discussed with me on the day I met him. In his Military Service Pension file, he states that he joined the Fintown Company, 3rd Battalion, 3rd Donegal Brigade in July 1919 or April 1920 (both dates given) under the command of Michael McGeehan, Daniel Doherty, Edward Ward, PJ McHugh and John Wright. Anthony claims that during the Anglo-Irish War, he took part in raids for arms, carrying dispatches, drilling, the destruction of a railway line, the destruction of telegraph and telephone lines, the burning of Tievelough RIC Barracks, the burning of Fintown RIC Barracks, the burning of Ardara RIC Barracks, trenching roads, the holding up of a train at Ballinamore Railway Station and the taking of mails, the arrest of a spy in Ballinamore, an attack on Glenties RIC Barracks in April 1921, and raiding for arms in Fintown and Ballinamore in May.[315]

28 NOVEMBER 1920

The Kilmichael Ambush took place when a contingent of 18 Auxiliaries left their barracks in Macroom and were intercepted by the Third (West) Cork Brigade Flying Column under Tom Barry. Sixteen Auxiliaries were killed during the engagement. Lieutenant C.J. Guthrie escaped, but was subsequently captured, executed and buried in a bog. The only Auxiliary to survive was Lieutenant H.F. Forde. Three IRA were killed as a result of the ambush: Pat Deasy, Michael McCarthy and Jim O'Sullivan.[316] **GEORGE CARPENTER** witnessed the funeral procession of the 16 Auxiliaries as it passed through Cork City on 2 December. Businesses had been ordered to close as a mark of respect, and there were many onlookers.[317]

> That was the ambush in Kilmichael and before that, the British made an order that no funeral can be longer than so many yards and because a funeral, if there was an IRA man shot, the funeral was fairly long you see and they didn't like the idea of that. And then they had to keep themselves then to that distance also. I remember they had ten or eleven gun carriages or other types of lorries to carry the coffins.[318]

The bodies in these coffins were those of Auxiliaries F.W. Crake, W.T Barnes, C.D.W. Bayley, L.D. Bradshaw, J.C. Gleave, P.N. Graham, W. Hooper Jones, F.

Hugo, A.G. Jones, E.W.H. Lucas, W.A. Pallister, H.O. Pearson, F. Taylor, C.H. Wainwright, B. Webster and A.F. Poole.[319]

> And I was standing outside the cinema in Washington Street and there was an officer – a Black and Tan. He was bodyguard to the, walking alongside the hearse and there was a man had a bowler hat on him and he took the bowler hat off and put it under the wheel of the lorry. And another thing they used do, if you had your hands in your pockets, they'd come behind you and rip your hands down and your trousers would rip down the side.[320]

The remains of the 16 Auxiliaries killed at Kilmichael were carried back to England for burial. First, they were taken from Custom House Quay in the city on board the S.S. *Thistle* to Haulbowline and then transferred to the destroyer *Undine*, which landed them at Milford Haven.[321] However, many members of the Crown forces were buried in Cork down through the years. It must be remembered that a lot of these were Irishmen. According to George, a British military funeral was an interesting spectacle to see.

> Yes, there'd be a lot of people turn up for these funerals, all kinds of funerals and one thing that if there was an army funeral, they had a band and they used play all the tunes that are necessary for a funeral. And one day we followed them right out to a graveyard in – we used call it, oh out in Tory Top Lane – the Platonic Gardens we used call it. Platonic Gardens it was known as. Platonic Gardens and they used walk up with everything in black, draped in black and drums and the men with the reverse rifles and when the funeral was over they used come outside, take off all the black and start marching away with la–la–la–la–la–la. And it always amazed me to hear a funeral going up with the slow music and then suddenly changing in five minutes – bang and off again.[322]

The Platonic Gardens (as George called it) is the present-day St Joseph's Cemetery in Ballyphehane and was known as the Botanic Gardens. In 1830, Father Theobald Mathew purchased the Botanic Gardens of the Royal Cork Institution and used it as a cemetery for the poor as well as a place where Catholics could be buried with full religious rites.[323] St Josephs, which is still in use today, contains the headstones of, amongst others, 18 men who died whilst serving in the British forces during World War I, and a further 5 who died between 1919 and 1920.[324]

7 DECEMBER 1920

The postman was held up on his return journey with the mails to Bantry from Durrus post office and his bicycle taken from him. He then had to walk to Bantry with the mails, which were not interfered with. The same postman had already been held up some months previously along the same route and his bicycle appropriated.[325]

DANIEL O'DONOVAN of the Third (West) Cork Brigade said bicycles were one of the principal mechanisms used by the IRA of the district to deliver dispatches, whereby the note might be hidden by the rider in the hollow of the handlebars. Sometimes it might be carried in the hand, wrapped around a stone, so it could be quickly dropped or thrown into the ditch or sea if, for example, the cyclist got alerted on enquiring from a passer-by that Crown forces might be approaching. However, Daniel said an older man on a bicycle was much more likely to be stopped and searched than a boy of 17 such as he was at this juncture. He was never involved in any ambushes.

> No. There were very, very few of my age were in ambushes but they were in blocking roads such as blowing, I was engaged in the blowing up of Storer's Mill (Bridge) just outside Bantry town and a few other things apart from occasional dispatches, deliver dispatches.[326]

Delivering a dispatch often involved Daniel cycling seven or eight miles, which on occasion took him as far as Durrus. One time, as he attempted to cycle over a partially blown bridge near Durrus, he fell 10 feet below it. The bicycle was damaged and he received minor injuries. On a separate occasion, Daniel travelled to Whiddy Island to collect money for guns. He was also engaged in intelligence work.[327]

Storer's Mill was a crushing mill for barytes (a mineral used in the production of pottery and paint). However, Storer's Mill had never been blown up by the IRA. Instead, Daniel O'Donovan and a number of others, including his brother Pat, had been involved in the destruction of a bridge on the road to Drimoleague, which was known locally as Storer's Bridge. Twice targeted, it was partially destroyed by explosives on the second attempt, along with some other bridges in the district such as Coomhola Bridge over the river at Mill Little. These bridges were destroyed in February and March 1921 to curtail the movement of British Crossley tenders as well as other military vehicles.[328] Throughout the whole trouble, Daniel was never armed.

> No, I never carried a weapon. We weren't allowed. They were too dangerous in those days. The weapons were only used when required and they were all kept in safe places. But we were drilled in weapons and I know on one occasion some six M.L. rifles taken from a destroyer at Bantry pier during the trouble. We were shown all about them and one thing or another. But outside that they were kept very much in the dark except when required.[329]

The M.L. rifles that Daniel refers to were taken on Sunday 16 November 1919, when men from the Third (West) Cork Brigade, led by Moss Donegan, sneaked on board a British navy vessel anchored at Bantry and made away with a sizeable amount of arms and ammunition.[330] An M.L. (Motor Launch) was a small, high-speed military vessel designed for harbour defence and submarine chasing.

So disturbance and destruction were prevalent in much of West Cork and elsewhere in the county, as **GEORGE CARPENTER** discovered first-hand when travelling to visit his mother's people, who lived on a farm in West Cork.

> Oh, there were a lot of ambushes around the place, bridges blown up, railway tracks blown up. And we used go that time, we used go down to my grandfather's down in Adrigole and we went by train from Cork. And the train stopped along the line somewhere and then we had to walk about two hundred yards along the track and get in again. And we landed in Bandon anyway about an hour late and then we caught the Princess Beara, which was a boat there from Bantry over to Glengarriff and we were met there by my grandfather. There was two of us only at the time and my mother and he. My grandfather had a sidecar and we sat up on the sidecar and we drove then from there from Glengarriff to Adrigole to the house.[331]

9 DECEMBER 1920

Having been marched to a vessel docked at the city quay in Cork Harbour along with 250 other prisoners, **PATSY HOLMES** was transferred from Cork County Gaol to Ballykinlar Internment Camp in Co. Down.

> We left ... Cork at half past four on Thursday morning and ... I didn't know where I was going no more than anyone else. On Saturday morning we landed at Harland & Wolff in Belfast. We went up through that place there outside Wexford and ... we were taken by boat ... and it was a cabin boat. It was a gunboat; there were four guns in all. She was the *Heather* ... So we went by boat and the name of the boat was the *Heather*. We got there ... in Belfast Station and so we were taken out and re-handcuffed again. And I was handcuffed to a very old man, he was seventy-four at the time and I was seventeen ... and he was an athlete and a fairly good athlete. But he was an Irish speaker; he was from Ring in County Kerry [Waterford]. I learned a lot of Irish from him. Dan Fraher was his name. Dan Fraher, an old, he was a great athlete. He was from Waterford. After walking about three miles anyway we arrived, oh what's the place called? Tullymurry I think it was. We were taken into the camp – Ballykinlar Camp. And it was a few days I think before Christmas or a week. So, I stayed there until the following Christmas.[332]

He had clear recollections of other internees staying there at the time.

> There was a writer there at that time by the name of Walsh – Louis Walsh ... There were very prominent men there. The man that wrote 'The Soldier's Song' was there, ah, what's his name — Peadar Kearney. He wrote 'The Soldiers Song'. He was an uncle of Brendan Behan's. There was McGrath, Joe McGrath, himself and Dick Duggan they formed the Irish sweepstakes, and Noel Lemass was there. There were very prominent men there, north and south in Ballykinlar.[333]

Louis J. Walsh was a solicitor from Maghera, Co. Derry. Following a period of confinement in Derry Gaol, he entered Ballykinlar Camp on 5 January 1921 and was released on 9 May 1921.[334] He wrote several books and plays, and upon his release published '*On My Keeping' and in Theirs: A record of experiences 'on the run', in Derry Gaol, and in Ballykinlar Internment Camp*. In later years, he went on to become a district judge in Letterkenny.[335] Peadar Kearney was arrested in November 1920 and interned in Ballykinlar until December 1921.[336] Fred Crowley, who may have been the man in the suit that Patsy met in Cork Gaol, was also transferred to Ballykinlar Internment Camp.[337]

> There was gallant men, able men, gallant men, Bandon men: Barney Driscoll, Jack Fitzgerald – Kilbrittain, Mick O'Neill – Bandon, Coneen Crowley. They're all West Corkmen every one of them. Moss Donegan from Bantry, a very prominent man.[338]

Moss Donegan was arrested along with Ralph Keyes, Cornelius O'Sullivan and Seán Cotter (all comrades of **DANIEL O'DONOVAN**) on 29 November 1920. They were then detained in the military barracks in Bantry for a week.[339] Michael O'Neill and Jack Fitzgerald, both natives of Kilbrittain, were arrested on 19 October 1920.[340] The Auxiliaries arrested Coneen Crowley (also from Kilbrittain) on 21 November 1920 after incriminating documents were found on him.[341] Barney O'Driscoll (a former O/C of Skibbereen Battalion) was arrested and jailed when the British military raided an IRA training camp at Glandore on 13 August 1920.[342]

> There were four men there, they were on hunger strike. They done sixty days. They were Jim Lalor, Kilkenny, Tom Nolan Kilkenny, Tom Treacy, Kilkenny, the Corkman I can't think … Paddy Sullivan. Paddy was thirty days on hunger strike.[343]

Lalor, Nolan and Treacy had also served two periods of imprisonment in Cork Gaol. They were there for 10 days in April 1920 before being shipped to Belfast Gaol and Wormwood Scrubs, where they joined a hunger strike amongst republican prisoners for their release, which was in progress during May. They were released before that month was over but were arrested again on 23 November. They arrived in Cork Gaol for the second time on 8 December and only remained there one night before being transferred to Co. Down.[344]

Ballykinlar Camp had been established originally as a summer training ground for British troops in the Belfast district. It was only used for a few months in the year, during which time the men lived under canvas. When World War I broke out, huts were erected capable of holding about a thousand men, and some of the battalions of the Ulster Division received their training there before setting off for France.[345] When Patsy arrived at Ballykinlar, it initially consisted of one camp holding 38 huts. In early January 1921, a second camp was opened containing the same number of huts.

There were about 25 men in each hut, and Patsy stayed in Hut No. 19 in Camp No. 1 where, according to him, they were known as 'C-Company'.[346] In the camp, a company comprised ten huts and their occupants, to which a line captain amongst the internees was appointed. The line captain was held responsible for the discipline of his line, ensuring that the huts were kept clean and that the hut leaders carried out the duties imposed on them and their hutsmen, both by their own IRA commandant and by the military.

Patsy was detained in the same hut as Louis J. Walsh, who listed every man staying there and described general camp conditions in his book.

> Our Camp consisted of four lines of huts with chapel, cook-house and dining halls, hospital, etc., in the centre. Pat MacCartan, Tom Larkin, John Bonner, Owen Gallagher and myself were sent to Hut 19 C Line. There were twenty other men in the hut already from Cork, Tipperary and Kilkenny, and our five made the full complement of twenty-five. The huts were zinc buildings; our beds were composed of two wooden trestles about eight inches high with three boards laid on top, on which we placed our bedding, consisting of a mattress and bolster packed with coarse straw and four army blankets; and the other furniture comprised a long table, three or four forms, some shelving, a few buckets, etc., and a stove.
>
> I was very lucky in my hut, as my fellow-hutsmen were men with whom it was a pleasure to live. Some of them such as Paddy Sullivan, the 'hut leader', Jim Lalor, Tom Treacy, Tom Nolan and Jack Fitzgerald had had a fairly extensive acquaintance with British prisons and had been through 'hunger strikes' and such episodes, and most of the others had been very active figures in the national movement in one way or another. One of the most striking figures in the hut was Pat Rohan, County Councillor of Ballina (Tipperary), a man of very great ability and high ideals, whose constructive mind would be a most valuable asset in any normally governed country. I shall always be inclined to forgive Sir Hamar Greenwood portion of the score I have against him, in as much as, when it was deemed necessary in the interests of law and order in Ireland to lock me inside a barbed wire cage, he had me housed with men of such high character and kindliness as my friends, William Cleary, John Creed, Mick Dowling, Bill Condon, Jer. Mulvey, Paddy Guerin and Bill Sheehy, not to speak of my own Ulster comrades and the 'Young Guard', consisting of Paddy Holmes, J. Keating, J. Egan, Jim Sharman, Andy Callaghan, Mick and Nick Murphy. [347]

When Patsy arrived in Ballykinlar, the conditions in the camp were not good. The food was utterly inadequate. There was no canteen, and the internees were not allowed to receive parcels. However, they set up an internee council led by their commandant Patrick Colgan, which succeeded in forcing the military authorities to make concessions. Louis J. Walsh wrote:

> The British Commandant, Colonel Little, seemed really anxious to do the best he could for us and exerted himself, I am convinced, to secure for us every right to which as prisoners of war we were entitled by

international usage. But he was hampered all the time by orders and limitations of his authority from the military G.H.Q. and Dublin Castle.[348]

Louis J. Walsh also dedicated a chapter in his book to 'Some Camp Notables' amongst the internees. He described how Barney O'Driscoll from Skibbereen, in addition to being a humourist, had a very short temper and an awful command of explosive language. The beard he wore evoked a certain biblical character in the mind of one young inmate.

> My friend, Paddy Holmes, had evidently been the victim of Barney's wrath at a parcel distribution, for one night he remarked as we sat round our stove:
> 'Wouldn't that Barney O'Driscoll mind you of Judas, although I never saw the man?'
> The conversation took another turn, and about half an hour later we were discussing cinema pictures. Suddenly Paddy broke in on the discourse with the exclamation:
> 'I knowed I saw him somewhere!'
> 'Saw who?' we inquired, in amazement at Paddy's sudden outburst.
> 'Saw Judas Iscariot,' he responded, 'I saw him in the pictures of the Passion Play at Mallow.'[349]

Inside the camp, internees established their own government, military, courts, post office and even currency in the form of tokens, as real money was prohibited lest attempts be made to bribe British officers. Besides drilling, which was eventually prohibited, internees attended such classes as Irish, history, dancing and music. They also played sport, with GAA matches between different huts taking place. Patsy referred to an occasion when they picked a team of internees to represent Munster to play against another province represented by other internees. The Munster team comprised '14 Kerrymen and one West Corkman – Moss Donegan'.[350]

Interestingly internees also produced a typed newspaper entitled *Ná Bac Leis*, which consisted of various articles, gardening notes, GAA notes, verses and editorials. A second newspaper entitled The *Barbed Wire* was handwritten, and internees in Camp No. 2 established a library to which they donated books.[351] Inmates were not permitted visitors, but they could send and receive letters or parcels. These were frequently opened by the British, especially if they contained food. Patsy recalled being able to see the mountains of Mourne in the background, maintaining that conditions overall in the camp were not too harsh.

> Well now, they gave us what they had. What they got they gave us. It was all right. There was a loaf of bread now between four of us and then you'd get stuff but they done their best. Now I wouldn't like to come against them at all – the British I'm talking about. Because I needn't tell you when it's a couple of thousand men, it's very hard to save them.[352]

However, they could never become too complacent when it came to their British handlers (the Duke of Cornwall's Light Infantry and the King's Royal Rifles), as Louis J. Walsh wrote.[353]

> On the whole, the senior officers with whom we came in contact were all right and comported themselves as soldiers and gentlemen, but some of the juniors were awful bounders and thorough cads.[354]

Pasty Holmes mentioned a Black and Tan from Cooley who used to come to the camp whom he dismissed as a 'right hoor'.[355]

10 DECEMBER 1920

The British government declared martial law in the counties of Cork, Kerry, Limerick and Tipperary, whereby the whole administration of the law was given to the military.[356] By the end of the month, martial law was also extended to Clare, Waterford, Kilkenny and Wexford. Since February, curfew had been imposed on many cities, towns and districts throughout the country, but from now on it was more rigorously imposed, especially in areas under martial law. **GEORGE CARPENTER**, living in Maymount, Cork, resented being forced to stay indoors during these times.

> Curfew was terrible ... You had to be indoors so you couldn't take part in any sports or anything these times. And one person near us was looking out the window and a soldier saw her and brought her down and put her into the lorry and away with her down to the barracks. They weren't even allowed look out the window. It was terrible.[357]

On one particular occasion, George's home was ransacked by the British army.

> We used have a raid now and again, our house used be raided because Dad was known to carry a revolver. My father had, well, he was allowed one on account of being an ex-RIC man but he left the RIC about 1913 [1904] so he wasn't actually in the troubled times at all [see 23 September 1908]. But so there was a raid one time made in the house by the British army and mother caught the revolver, Dad's revolver and pushed it down inside her blouse you see and she was very slim built so it wasn't noticeable and they searched through the whole house and turned it upside down and went away then. And mother fainted so I remember bringing her over the cup of tea and water to her face. She soon came round.
>
> But at that time, we had to have a blanket – wet and keep it very wet and hang it up inside of the door. And the idea of that, if there was a shot fired through the door, the blanket would hold the bullet from coming forward. And also, behind the door we had to have the names of all the people who are resident and their ages, typed out if possible and I think everybody had to have that.[358]

GEORGE COOPER pointed out that in many instances it wasn't the case that the Black and Tans and British soldiers respected loyalists who lived in Ireland, as often 'they didn't know' and 'had no way of knowing' who was pro-British or not.[359] In many situations, they simply didn't care; hence there were raids on pro-British households such as the Carpenters and others. In Mitchelstown, the restrictions of curfew meant that since August people had been prohibited from being out of doors between the hours of 9 p.m. and 3 a.m.[360] In May 1921, this was relaxed to between the hours of 10 p.m. and 3 a.m.[361] In June 1921, it was changed to a 10.30 p.m. curfew start; however, none of the times appear to have deterred **MICHAEL CASEY**.[362]

> Well, you couldn't be out after ten o'clock in the evening until six in the morning. But I often went out and all the boys went out in a quiet way you know. I used go up past the church and in Mitchelstown and there's a by-road there. I could go where I liked. We used be outside in a farm we had behind out in Ballynamona, out a couple of miles from Mitchelstown and we'd be training there in the wintertime. We couldn't go in the summer you know; you'd be seen after curfew. But we'd come back in any time we liked then.[363]

PATRICK GREENE pointed out that Co. Longford and the midlands didn't experience curfew.[364] However, the Crown forces were a familiar sight to **GERRY SMYTH** in Stackallen.

> British military were stationed in Navan and I used to polish my father's shoes on a Saturday night for Sunday and I was sitting at the window with no electrical light of course. I had a candle in the window and I looked up. I could see a British soldier with a rifle on the ready and he looking in at me. So came in and raided the whole house. There was nobody in it only myself and a young maid; searched the whole place.[365]

11 DECEMBER 1920

On this night, Cork City was burned by K Company of the Auxiliaries in reprisal for an earlier ambush carried out against them by the IRA at Dillon's Cross, near their headquarters at Victoria Barracks. Twelve Auxiliaries were wounded, and one, named Chapman, died shortly afterwards. In reprisal, they set fire to shops and houses in many areas of the city, including Dillon's Cross, Patrick Street and Winthrop Street. Buildings such as Carnegie Library and the City Hall were destroyed, and locals were shot and wounded. The British government would later pay £3 million in compensation to the people of Cork for the damage.[366]

At this time, **GEORGE CARPENTER'S** family were living in Maymount but were preparing to take up residence on the other side of the city (Patrick's Hill). He was in bed and woken up by the shouting and screaming outside their house. The sky was red with flames. Several families that had fled the scene were put up in the Carpenters' garden that night. The next day, George's father couldn't get transport to carry their belongings to their new house. The family carried what they could by hand and had to pass through Patrick Street along the way. He remembered there being utter chaos and destruction. There was widespread looting from burned-out shops. The fire brigade was still trying to put out the flames, aided by the police. Bystanders cheered when the fire chief, Captain Hudson, got a ladder and rescued a howling cat from the top of a surviving wall at the corner of Princes Street. Overhead wires from the trams were alive on the ground and a danger to anyone who might go near them. Most of the streets leading into Patrick Street were blocked off by police for safety reasons, as unsteady structures were expected to fall.[367] Not long after the Carpenters had completed their move, George had an encounter with the British military whilst on his way home from choir practice with some friends.

> Oh, top of Patrick's Hill. We changed residence then up to Patrick's Hill. It was just on when the Truce was coming up and it was on Christmastime. And there were soldiers there and they were drunk, standing on top of Audley Terrace and they were firing shots at Shandon Steeple and trying to make the fish go around. There's a fish and it's still there. And they weren't worried where the bullets landed and then they turned around to us when we came and they, come on see, shouting at us, 'Come on, sing "God Save the King"'. So we sang 'God Save the King' and we went home then.[368]

17 DECEMBER 1920

A British military convoy travelling in two lorries was ambushed at Glenacurrane between Mitchelstown and Anglesboro. It was a combined operation carried out by the Mitchelstown Company and flying columns from the Castletownroche Battalion (Second Cork Brigade) and the East Limerick Brigade. Two soldiers from the 1st Battalion Lincolnshire Regiment (Sergeant L. Ellis and Private J. Minchin) were killed and three wounded. Arms were also seized.[369] There's no account of **MICHAEL CASEY** having taken part in this engagement, but he had been busy beforehand.[370]

> I was collecting guns then. Before an ambush at Glenacurrane – that's below in Mitchelstown. There was one man outside, about a mile outside the town and no one would go to him for his gun. They were afraid of him. So I volunteered to go with that someone would come with me. So we went myself and a man by the name of Bulman – Davey Bulman. He went to America after. But anyway, we went into the man's house and we told him what we wanted. He was the grandest man you ever saw and they were all afraid of him ... Oh, he had the gun outside in a big hedge and he'd canvas around it and galvaniser around the canvas and he went up on this old double ditch and pulled down the whole lot of it and opened it for us and gave us the gun.[371]

Davey Bulman lived at Upper Cork Street, Mitchelstown (see 12 August 1922).[372] In addition to the acquiring of arms, the months leading up to the Glenacurrane Ambush had been characterised by such activities as mail hold-ups, seizures of petrol and attempted ambushes that didn't come off primarily because of the non-arrival of Crown forces.[373]

> We were notified one night now, to meet at the poorhouse in Mitchelstown ... at the back of the gate at a quarter to eight. That was quarter of an hour before curfew. So we, there were about twenty-five or thirty of us there and we went into this old building. It was a fine building. There wasn't a thing there that we could sit on for the night. We had nowhere to rest. So one of the boys said, 'There were outside in the front winds of hay made,' says he, and 'wouldn't ye go out and bring in plenty hay and put it around in a ball and lie down?' So we did and we slept there.
>
> But we were called in the morning. We didn't know what we were there for, but we were called in the morning and we lined up and we in single file and in towards Mitchelstown. It's only a small bit outside Mitchelstown now that place and we went to the creamery, to a small creamery – Newmarket Dairy Company. And when we went into the yard, it was then we knew what we were on for.
>
> But we were given two two-gallon tins of petrol each and we'd to carry that two miles. We went in, we came out of the yard, went into the field with the, went into the side of it. We went up to the church, the back of the church and we crossed a couple of more fields and down to Fanaghan's Well. Did you ever hear of Fanaghan's Well?
>
> And we went out to Ballynamona and there were a lios [a circular prehistoric structure] there and we dumped all the petrol there. There were no petrol pumps that time and the creamery had to get all their petrol in tins. So we didn't hear any more about the petrol or what became of it.[374]

Newmarket Dairy Company had a creamery located on the Clonmel Road, Mitchelstown.

23 DECEMBER 1920

Having been passed by the Houses of Commons and Lords, the Government of Ireland Act (Fourth Home Rule Bill) received the royal assent. It provided for two Home Rule states – Northern Ireland and Southern Ireland.[375] Their creation was a compromise produced by the British government because of the demand by nationalists for Home Rule and that of unionists against it. Elections to both houses of parliament would take place in May, and they were scheduled to convene in June. Many commentators regard the Government of Ireland Act as having heralded the birth of Northern Ireland as a separate and individual state. Nationalists vehemently opposed the Government of Ireland Act. **NORMAN DOUGLAS** spoke about the reaction to it in the north at the time.

> Well, of course, the separation caused a lot of antagonism on the Catholic side and that spilled over into the Protestant side too. Catholics became known as Catholics and Protestants became known

as Protestants and it spoiled a lot of relationships I would say, the very fact of that. But having said that I mean I had, my family were associated, had Catholic friends and they were great, great friends and were friends for many, many times. And in where I lived there were as I say, there were several Catholic families and next door to one of them was a Salvation Army family and they were in and out of each other's house. Even during the troubles that was and there was that faction just who wanted trouble and they had trouble and they caused trouble on both sides[376]

30 DECEMBER 1920

The *Cork Examiner* reported that over 150 Auxiliaries arrived in Bantry on 22 December and by 30 December had commandeered the Eccles Hotel, Glengarriff, as their headquarters.[377] However, in his book *Brother Against Brother*, Liam Deasy provides a lower figure, there being a half-company of 50 Auxiliaries in Glengarriff.[378] Whatever the exact number, on New Year's Day (a Saturday) they and the military conducted a swoop of the area, arresting over 40 young Sinn Féiners. They took them away in lorries to their headquarters for questioning, with most of them being released again later. In addition, the Auxiliaries made thorough searches of the whole outlying district that weekend.[379] In a short space of time, they would make themselves known to **DANIEL O'DONOVAN**.

> Well, the Auxiliaries came along to a place called Glengarriff and I remember on one occasion being arrested by them and interrogated and released again [see 19 March 1921].[380]

Of the Black and Tans, **PATRICK FITZGERALD** said they never came up his way in Dunmoon, but he remembered people had to have the names and ages of every person in their house written down and pinned onto the back of the door. Sometimes, the soldiers came and everyone knew that if they caught anyone on the run hiding in the house there'd be trouble. According to Patrick, his family home wasn't big enough to hold anyone on the run, but he did recall a man called 'Brown' from Tallow being sought by the British at the time (this was John Brown from the Tallow Company who had gone on the run).[381]

Interestingly, Patrick did reveal that on one occasion his family housed a British soldier who had turned deserter. He had joined the British army and 'when he got the holidays he didn't go back at all'. He just arrived through the door. The British army shot fellows like that, but this man lived because 'they never followed him up much'. Patrick said that this deserter was 'a bloody saucy lad but a coward then' named Jack Bolstone. Perhaps this was during World War I, but Patrick added that this man even attempted to join the IRA but got little hearing.[382]

CHAPTER 5
Fighting and talking, January – July 1921

17 JANUARY 1921

On the stroke of midday, two men from the Moate district of Co. Westmeath were killed inside Ballykinlar, Camp No. 1. They were Patrick Sloane and Joseph Tormey. Sloane was a blacksmith and had been married only four days when he was arrested eight weeks previously. Tormey worked as an agricultural labourer and his brother had served in the Great War.[1] Their demise was witnessed by **PATSY HOLMES**.

> The morning McGrath issued a notice – every man say a rosary, there were two men shot dead. I saw the two of them, the two of them shot dead with the one bullet inside in Ballykinlar Camp.[2]

There were five raised sentry boxes overlooking Ballykinlar Internment Camp, one at each of the four corners and one additional one at the point where Camp No. 1 joined Camp No. 2. An armed sentry occupied each of these sentry boxes day and night.[3] The initial British line was that a sentry had opened fire on one of the men for refusing to obey an order four times. The bullet, however, passed through the intended target and struck the second man, who also died.[4] Internee Fred Crowley ran for the camp doctor as soon as it happened, but when the doctor arrived both were dead.[5]

Louis J. Walsh wrote that this incident occurred within days of Camp No. 2 being opened. A portion of this camp adjoined Camp No. 1 and was only separated from it by a barbed wire fence. Along this fence on the Camp No. 1 side was a macadamised road, which internees used as a promenade. The men in both camps got into the habit of talking to each other through the fence, and whilst initially, the military made no objection, they had ordered the men not to approach to within an arm's reach of the fence. If they did so, sentries would order them back. In the beginning, this was done in a good-natured sort of way; but over time, they noticed the sentries getting rather aggressive, to the point that the sound of gunshots became commonplace, so much so that Commandant Patrick Colgan in Camp No. 1 had complained to the British commandant, but the latter dismissed any notion that the shots were fired to hit.[6]

Patsy Holmes explained that McGrath had 'issued a notice' prior to the shootings because news had filtered through to the internees in Ballykinlar that an execution or executions would be carried out in Cork.

In the morning Joe McGrath issued a statement and he said, 'Everyman,' he said, 'in this compound must say a rosary today to try and get the boys in Cork Gaol reprieved.' They wanted to say a rosary for them.[7]

The man due to be executed was Joseph Murphy, who was charged with killing Private Squibbs during the Barrack Street Ambush in October.[8] Louis J. Walsh pointed out the irony of the situation.

> On Sunday evening, the 16th January, we learned that a prisoner was going to be executed in Cork Gaol the following morning. We had a special Rosary for him that evening in the Church and special prayers for him at Mass the following morning. Amongst those who offered up their prayers for him on that morning were Patrick Sloan and Joseph Tormey; but all unknown to themselves; it was at their own Requiem they were assisting. For the prisoner in Cork was reprieved, and before the sun had set they themselves had fallen to a British bullet. [9]

When the solitary shot rang out at noon, Walsh, who was in his hut, took no notice. However, word soon reached him that two men had been killed. He immediately rushed to the scene near Hut 11 to discover that practically the whole camp had gathered there, and many were on their knees saying the rosary. Three days later, the bodies were removed from Ballykinlar, having been carried to the gates by their comrades. The men in both camps stood to attention as the remains were being driven back to their homes for burial.[10]

Colgan and the internee's council demanded an inquest into the shooting and immediately got the wheels in motion. They wrote letters intended for parties such as the victims' families, solicitors and senior republicans within Sinn Féin and the IRA. At the same time, the military set about hushing up the whole affair by issuing a report to the *Belfast Telegraph* implying that the sentry had fired to prevent one of the men who had ventured too close to the wire from escaping. They also withheld the letters destined for individuals on the outside, including the victims' families, and finally refused the internees' demand for an inquest, declaring they would hold a military inquiry instead. The internees were adamant that neither Sloane nor Tormey had been near the wire when shot and were not engaging in any escape bid.[11]

The finding of the Military Court of Inquiry was issued in an official report by Dublin Castle and published in the Irish daily papers on 9 February 1921.

> The Court found Joe Tormey and Patrick Sloan died from shock and haemorrhage caused by gunshot wounds inflicted by a sentry in the execution of his duty, and was a case of justifiable homicide.
>
> Every facility was extended to any of the internees who desired to give evidence before the Court, but none availed themselves of the opportunity.
>
> Upon the enquiry as to how one shot killed the two prisoners, it was stated that the bullet passed through the base of the head of Joe Tormey and then pierced the throat of Patrick Sloane, who was behind the former.[12]

The internees found this outcome totally unsatisfactory. However, the British government shared the view of the inquiry.

> In the House of Commons last evening Mr. McVeagh asked whether any action had been taken in the case of the soldier who shot two interned prisoners at Ballykinlar Camp.
> 'SIR H. GREENWOOD: A Military Court of Inquiry, held in lieu of an inquest, found that no blame attached to the soldier who fired in the execution of his duty. No action of a disciplinary character is, therefore, called for, and none has been taken.'[13]

This, however, was far from the end of the matter as far as the internees were concerned, and they proceeded to hold their own inquiry. Their report concluded that the shooting of Sloane and Tormey was an act of deliberate murder and that they had been over six feet away from the wire when shot and had not broken any military regulations.[14] When Joe McGrath presented the internees' version of the shooting to the British commandant, he insisted that the sentry was telling the truth and would face no further action.[15]

Not surprisingly, relations between the internees and the camp authorities deteriorated dramatically. The former maintained their campaign for an inquest, and the British responded by arresting the ringleaders, including Commandant Colgan, who they stated were obstructing them from their running of the camp. The internees' council then issued various orders, including that all inmates were to refuse to answer their names either at roll call or otherwise. Line captains and others were instructed not to cooperate with British instructions when it came to running the camp. The military O/C then withdrew all the internees' privileges and letters, and parcels were cut off. Furthermore, the offices of commandant and vice-commandant within the camp were abolished. Aggressive raids and searches by soldiers on huts also commenced. Attempts between the internees' council and camp authorities to broker a resolution ended in failure, until peace was eventually restored through the mediation of, amongst others, Joe McGrath. It was agreed that upon his release Colgan would go to Camp No. 2 and that the offices of commandant and vice-commandant would be restored, as would internees' privileges, with the promise that some of them would be extended. They also secured other concessions, and generally the inmates strengthened their position. In the aftermath, Joe McGrath was elected the new commandant in Camp No. 1.[16]

As a postscript to the Sloane and Tormey affair, it's worth reading the brief telegram sent by the British to Patrick Sloane's young widow in Moate, which she received 24 hours after his death.

> Regret to inform you Patrick Sloane died yesterday from gunshot wounds. Wire if you desire to remove the body for burial. Otherwise funeral Thursday afternoon at Tyrella. Military inquest being held tomorrow. [17]

It's written that the sentry who shot Sloan and Tormey was Rifleman Murfitt.[18]

21 JANUARY 1921

Having completed eleven months' service, **WILLIAM GEARY** signed off the SS *City of Birmingham* in Liverpool and returned home to Cloonee Cottage. Along with his younger brother Thomas, he joined Ballyagran 'F' Company, 3rd Battalion, West Limerick Brigade, which had roughly 72 recruits by the Truce of 11 July 1921. By then it formed part of the 1st Southern Division.[19] William's name was omitted from the membership list gathered in 1935, which was probably deliberate because of how his reputation was later tarnished (see 25 November 1928).

> You must remember that I was off to sea and when I came back, I help to work on the farm. Now there was very little IRA activity around Ballyagran but everybody was a Volunteer, every able-bodied man and I used to drill them. What we used were broomsticks. At least learn how to salute, how to form fours and what else, yeah, that's about it.[20]

He wasn't aware of anybody from the Ballyagran area that was killed during the Tan War.

> No. My captain was John Bresnihan and when I wanted to join the Garda Síochána I got a letter from him and that was it. But there was none that I knew from neighbouring active service.[21]

It wasn't long before William had an encounter with the occupying forces.

> While I was at home one day, it was on a Sunday in fact, I was at a funeral and we went to the graveyard in Shanavoha. And after the deceased was buried, we went to a local pub and everyone was maybe ten or fifteen cars. And right then who came along but the local military – the army. They lined us up outside the road outside in the street and one of them, we had to put our hands up and because I didn't put my hands up one of the soldiers gave me a punch in the jaw. After that we were marched down the road and we were all interviewed by an officer and of course when they used come to Ballyagran – the Black and Tans. They'd come into the saloon. They'd put a grenade on the counter while they were drinking, they didn't pay all the time. [22]

31 JANUARY 1921

News would eventually filter through to **PATSY HOLMES** in Ballykinlar that a tragic series of killings had taken place in his hometown of Mallow.

> Inspector King was coming from the railway station with his wife and the boys shot the woman. They shot the Inspector King's wife in place of himself. And the Tans were stationed down the road about a hundred yards from Mallow Railway Station and they ran amok and ran up and they killed four fellows. They killed Harry and young Bennett, Mullane. They killed four of them anyway.[23]

Shortly after 10 p.m., RIC County Inspector, Captain William H. King, was fired at by members of the local company near Mallow Railway Station as he walked with his wife Alice Mary. He was slightly wounded, and she died hours later from injuries received. Visibility was very bad on that particular night as a result of heavy drizzle, and Leo Callaghan, who participated in the attack, claimed that their target had been a party of Black and Tans that usually came to Mallow Railway Station each night to take their post to the night mail train. He and his comrades lay in wait, and when they saw a party of three approaching, they opened fire.[24] Ned Waters also participated.[25] Cumann na mBan member Siobhán Lankford later wrote:

> Nobody regretted Mrs King's death more than the men involved. There was no intention to ambush Capt. King himself – the target was unruly and savage subordinates. The town's sympathy went out to the man who had lost his devoted wife in the fortunes of war. The attacking party numbered seven men – five on the embankment and two on the railway bridge. They moved quickly out.[26]

Soon after the attack, the Black and Tans and Auxiliaries emerged from the nearby military barracks intent on revenge. They fired indiscriminately at every man they saw, including many who were working at the railway station at the time. The result was that many were wounded and three were killed – Denis Bennett, Patrick Devitt and Daniel O'Mullane. Harry Martin was seriously injured but recovered.[27] He died four years later.

Although Mrs King's death has been attributed to the IRA, there is another account that disputes this. Historian Jim Copps wrote about it in the *Mallow Field Club Journal* in 1984.

> District Inspector King and his wife were walking up the footpath on the Railway Station Hill on their way to dinner at The Royal Hotel. A stack of coal was piled on the railway embankment opposite the footpath. One of the Auxiliaries who was billeted at Broadview had taken cover behind the coal, nobody knew, not even his comrades anything concerning his devilish plan, which was to shoot the Inspector. The marksman had excellent cover, took aim; missed his target and shot Mrs King. The date of those barbaric deeds was 31 January 1921.
>
> This story was told to me by a brother of a man who was shot that night. I quote his words, 'District Inspector King was a just and fair-minded man, popular and trusted by all who knew him, but a strict disciplinarian. The Auxiliaries were billeted at Broadview a few hundred yards from the station. A train from Cork to Mallow arrived each night between 7 and 8 p.m. (the train time may not be accurate). Among its passengers were some ladies of ill repute who came to keep rendezvous with the Auxiliaries. A train left Mallow for Cork two hours later. The behaviour of his men was told to Inspector King who was not amused, particularly when he heard that this was a regular occurrence. The Inspector confined the Auxiliaries to billet during the hours of seven

and nine o'clock. His order was disobeyed and he was made aware of this. The Inspector made a surprise raid on Broadview and found some of the culprits absent. He took more severe steps in view of this subordination. This angered them more. One of the number made plans to shoot Inspector King. ... Both the Black and Tans and Auxiliaries believed that Mrs King was shot by Republican Forces. The murderer kept his secret well. The case was discussed in the House of Commons. The Inspector refused any financial compensation for the loss of his wife. Alice King is buried in Gould's Hill Cemetery. The Inspector left Mallow, a broken man. [28]

It is said that shortly before he left Ireland, the guilty Auxiliary got drunk in a local pub and spilled the beans.[29]

I FEBRUARY 1921

The first official execution under martial law took place when Captain Cornelius Murphy of the Millstreet Battalion, Cork No. 2 Brigade, was executed in Cork. He was a native of Ballydaly near Rathmore. He was arrested on 4 January, charged with possession of a loaded revolver at his court martial in Victoria Barracks on 17 January, and sentenced to death.[30] In late February, April and May, further executions took place in Cork. Elsewhere, one of those to be hanged in Mountjoy Gaol was an ex-Ballykinlar internee who had been convicted of involvement in the Bloody Sunday killings the previous November. Thomas Whelan arrived in the camp on 3 December 1920, was transferred to Belfast and then Dublin on 22 December, was found guilty and hanged on 14 March 1921.[31] By July, a total of 24 men would be executed by the British, including Kevin Barry, who was executed the previous winter.

PATSY HOLMES and his comrades in Ballykinlar had prayed for all these men, and there was huge disappointment, anger and grief when the executions were carried out. Rosaries had been said in the hope of a reprieve and to pray for their souls. Thus, religion was strong in the prison, and Patsy had fond memories of one particular priest from Co. Antrim who used to visit the camp.[32]

> Father McLister was the man, was in our hut. And I, the first morning I went to him he said to me, 'You're a comparatively very young man,' says he. 'Well, I am Father,' says I. 'What age are you?' 'Well,' I said, 'about eighteen.' 'Where do you come from?' he said. I said, 'Down south, in a town called Mallow in the County Cork.' 'I know it,' says he. Now he was the priest that was up in County Down. There was a public house in Mallow and he met the owner of it and he was on holidays in Youghal. Father McLister, he was a grand man.[33]

Louis J. Walsh wrote that their devotion helped a lot of internees get through the monotony of life in the camp.

> The mass of the prisoners led lives of great piety in Ballykinlar. The prisoners' chaplain, Father McLister, was most attentive to our spiritual

needs and was much beloved by everybody. We had Mass every morning and the Blessed Sacrament always in the Camp. The rosary was said in the huts every night, and many of the huts perhaps all of them were in time formally consecrated to the Sacred Heart.[34]

Of course, being a priest wasn't a safeguard against internment, as staunch republican Father Thomas Burbage of Geashill, Co. Offaly, discovered when he was arrested on 15 January 1921 and shortly afterwards conveyed to Ballykinlar.[35] He went on to become chaplain for Camp No. 2, leaving Father McLister (who was up to this point between both camps) to attend to Camp No. 1.[36] For the most part, members of the clergy were held in high esteem throughout Ireland at this time. According to **MAI GROGAN** in Co. Clare:

> Oh, there were respect for the priest that time. They wouldn't answer the priest that time. They were all afraid of the priest, not like today. There's a difference in them.[37]

Her local priest never shied away from condemning the violence that went on between the British and the IRA.

> Oh, they used give it off the altar. We had a priest in Kilmurry; he was Father Hayes from the Lissycasey side. Oh, he'd give it out about the, condemn any windows that would be broken or anything else. You'd hear about it on the altar the following Sunday. Our windows were broke and I remember the piers at the gate at the road were knocked. You can say it was our next-door neighbours that done it. That's it.[38]

Mai asserted that these particular neighbours had been members of the IRA. Father Patrick Hayes was curate of Kilmurry McMahon from 1915 to 1928 and was renowned as a very brave man who often reprimanded the Black and Tans and Auxiliaries face to face for their behaviour in the locality.[39]

> Ah, sure the priest would be condemning all them things long ago. All they wanted was peace and quietness but when you're up against some people, they'll show you the law. That's it.[40]

DAN KEATING for his part was critical of the attitude of the clergy. Although there were three curates at St John's Church in Tralee who were outspokenly sympathetic to the republicans, he felt that a lot of them tended to back whatever was the establishment of the day.[41] He described a priest from Cork named Doctor Coholan as being 'opposed to the [IRA] movement from the word go'.[42] Dan's assessment goes back to December 1920, when Doctor Coholan had issued a decree threatening anyone within the diocese of Cork who was involved in IRA activity with ex-communication from the Church.[43]

4 FEBRUARY 1921

James Craig succeeded Edward Carson as leader of the Ulster Unionist Party. Carson was later appointed Lord of Appeal in Ordinary and took a life peerage as Baron Carson of Duncairn.[44] Years later, **NORMAN DOUGLAS** would come face to face with Craig (who, from 1927, was known as Viscount Craigavon).

> As a matter of fact, I was in company of Craigavon at one occasion. We were doing singing at a function and he was on the Shankill Road and he was in the chair. So I had a shake hands from him but beyond that. But I did know, I did know a lot of the Northern Ireland parliament officers ... I shook hands with Craigavon yes on that particular night and it was just a passing shake hands. How much he enjoyed the programme and so on – that sort of thing. But beyond that I, but I never met Carson – no.[45]

Craig's face was also a familiar sight to **JOHN PARKINSON**.

> I remember seeing Sir James Craig very much and see we lived in Distillery Street. It was called Distillery Street because there was a distillery in it and the distillery was called the Dunville – Dunville's, Dunville's Whiskey. You've heard of Dunville's Whiskey. Well, Sir James Craig was one of the directors of Dunville's so some of the board meetings were held up in the offices in Dunville's offices in Distillery Street. And I'd have seen him driving up occasionally to the meetings in his big Rolls Royce or big motorcar. A very important looking man he was ... All the loyalist people were devoted to him.[46]

Edward Carson was also a figure whom John recognised.

> Carson too, I remember seeing Carson speaking at one or two meetings. My father was a great man for Lord Carson. We had a photograph of him hanging up on our hall.[47]

7 FEBRUARY 1921

Having slept away from home for most of the time since Tom Egan's murder in October, **JOHN KELLY** and his brother, Michael, made the fateful decision to spend a night in Caherbriskaun. John's mother, Julia, had died in 1919, so his sister Aggie and father, John, were also in the house at the time.[48] The family were about to experience first-hand the terror and tactics used by the Black and Tans.[49]

> By God, I tell you. I never will forget them either. They have me sick today thinking about them. Black and Tans, oh sure they were all murderers – killed the people. Faith I got my share of them and my brother and four or five more in the same village the one night. A big lorry full of them, about three o'clock in the morning, that's the Black and Tans now.[50]

John recounted what they did to him.

> Oh, sure they dragged me out. Sure I was pulled out of the bed. We.were in the one bed the two of us – myself and the brother as they do. And my sister in another bed and my father in another bed and man he drew me up by the two legs and drew a few kicks on me. And pulled me out the door and there was a tank of water just outside the door and threw me down the tank of water – two or three of them. And brought my brother out in another place further out – another stable and they crushed him and got on with them. And that's all now like, you know. One of the first ones – I got it in the mouth. They cracked my teeth too that time and a kick in the side and a kick here and a kick there. Oh, they were right savages now. They were right bad.[51]

The tank that the Black and Tans threw John into was used for storing rainwater. Before throwing him in, they pinned him up against the wall of the tank, questioning him about the killing of Frank Shawe-Taylor whilst at the same time threatening to shoot him and his brother. They also questioned him about another man, and about several others that were on the run, but John told them he knew nothing. Shots were fired over his head.[52] He was kept for roughly over an hour in the tank of freezing water in nothing but his nightshirt. They then pulled him out and threw him inside the door of the kitchen, ordering him not to leave the house until daylight. Michael was also thrown into the tank. John said he and Michael afterwards went into his father's bed, whilst his sister Aggie frantically tried to warm them both up using hot lids and warm sheets.[53]

> They didn't leave a bit of fowl in the house and a brand new bicycle ... Ah, the accordion; they even took the alarm clock that was on the dresser. And I was learning how to play the accordion – trying to. It was gone the next morning and it all melted with the rain.[54]

John (who was 18 at the time), even remembered the tune he was trying to learn on the accordion – 'Maggie in the Wood'.

> A big lorry full of them. The lorry and they didn't leave us a damn bit of fowl that time. They bagged all the fowl – hens, about thirty, forty or fifty hens maybe – ducks. Bagged them and my brand-new bicycle. My heart was near broke after it ... Oh I was sorry for the bicycle and all the fowl taken away. We couldn't eat an egg for our breakfast that morning.[55]

John explained that the Black and Tans also visited nearby farmhouses.

> They done five houses the one night. They were all neighbours ... They belted them, same as everyone – kicked them around ... All farmers. But all these people now, we were all living in the village. You could say they were all within half a mile of one another.[56]

In the darkness of night, the Tans' Crossly tender departed from one house to the next; some travelled ahead on foot. Neighbours of John's on the receiving end of beatings that night included Martin Ruane, Jack Grealish and Tommy Connell, who was hit over the head with a shovel.[57] The local doctor (Dr Gannon of Oranmore) was busy in the weeks that followed.[58]

> He went around every three or four days to see all these people that was being beaten – beaten up. All these people the Tans beat that night he used go around treating them. Yerra that was a long time ago, I was lame as an old duck. All my sides and everything were hurted. Here I am with my neck now and a pain in my neck and it's from it, it came.[59]

John recalled that the Black and Tan most responsible for his beating was foul-mouthed:

> Oh sure I don't know in the name of God. He might call you something funny. The man said 'You f-er you' or something. Excuse me, it's a curse anyway, now. 'You f-er you.' How well I can think of that.[60]

Following their ordeal, John and Michael were laid up for a number of months, with the result that neither was able to work on the family farm.[61]

> We had to live in a dugout the year before that ... We were out in a dugout for four weeks sleeping underground – five or six of us. And we were only two weeks home when the Tans came after. You'd think someone must tell them that we were home.[62]

John explained that they had to live in a dugout because of fear.

> We were afraid. It was all over a big landlord that was shot there one time – Frank Shawe-Taylor. It was all over that – all over land.[63]

The dugout was located 'away out in the mountains entirely in a wild place [Ruane's mountain]'.

> And we had a big hole down the ground like a house and we had the blankets and sheets and everything. They were all in it. We'd go out there once it would get dark on a winter's night. We were four weeks sleeping out in the dugout. Oh, it was a big heap of straw, we used lie in it at nighttime, making fun and sport and laughing. Oh, stop it. That's the story now.[64]

Others in the dugout included John's brother (Michael Kelly), Martin Ruane, Paddy Kelly and Bill Freaney, who was engaged to John's sister Aggie.[65] John Kelly's recollection was that he and his neighbours were assaulted by the Tans in January 1921. However, the date of 7 February 1921 comes from Martin Ruane's Military Service Pension file, which contains documentation detailing injuries sustained by him at Caherbriskaun, Athenry, at the hands of Crown forces that night.[66]

Claimant was sleeping at his brother's house when same was raided by above. He was taken from his bed and brought out into the yard where shots were fired over him, and they threatened to shoot him as some of the party said that they recognised him as being in ambushes at the time. He was then struck on the head with a shovel and knocked down. He was also struck with a cart axle which knocked him unconscious and was left lying in the yard until his brother carried him into the house later.[67]

Martin Ruane and Michael Kelly were extremely active members of the IRA and participated in numerous operations. Both men's names are recorded among the 41 members of the Derrydonnell Company, 1st Battalion, Galway No. 1 Brigade (Mid Galway), 1st Western Division for the period up to the Truce of 11 July 1921. John Kelly's name is also listed, but he appeared reluctant to go into specifics regarding his involvement when I spoke to him in 2003. Perhaps aspects of it were too painful to speak about, but he too appears to have been very active and was often armed with a shotgun.[68] His commanding officers included Michael Newell, Brian Molloy and Michael Keane. Michael Freaney of the Derrydonnell Company wrote of John Kelly that he carried out '[a]ll duties assigned to him'.[69] He was approaching 19 years of age when beaten up by the Tans, and I asked him if, apart from that night, he ever saw any violence or ambushes.[70]

> No, I didn't. I wasn't near them at all but sure they'd be going without me. I was too young to be out in them places. I'd be kept away from them with the old crowd.[71]

15 FEBRUARY 1921

Men from Cork No. 3 Brigade IRA planned to open fire on a party of British troops travelling on the Cork to Bantry train when it reached Upton Station. These soldiers usually occupied one carriage. However, unbeknownst to the IRA, additional troops had boarded the train at an earlier stop at Kinsale Junction and mixed among civilian passengers rather than also occupying a carriage of their own. Through misadventure, IRA scouts failed to board the train and attempted warnings didn't reach the awaiting ambushers in time, so when firing commenced, they were vastly outnumbered. In addition to IRA losses, this engagement resulted in nine civilians being killed besides others wounded. Six British soldiers sustained injuries.[72]

The dead IRA were Batt Falvey, John Phelan and Patrick O'Sullivan. The names of the civilians were James Byrne, John Spiers, Thomas Perrott, Charles Penrose Johnston, William Finn, William Donoghue, May Hall, John Sisk and Richard Arthur.[73] **DANIEL O'DONOVAN** saw the ambushed train when it eventually arrived at Bantry, and the memory of the blood-stained carriages was to stay with him for life.[74]

8 MARCH 1921

KATHLEEN CHARLES, who may or may not have been still teaching in Mullingar by this date, spoke of a British fatality not far from her home.

> I remember a British soldier being shot somewhere around Kanturk and going away in his coffin in the train from Kanturk.[75]

There are a number of possibilities as to whom Kathleen was referring to, but it's likely to have been one of the following three. On this date, men from the Kanturk Battalion of the Second Cork Brigade ambushed an RIC patrol at Father Murphy's Bridge three miles from the town. One RIC man was killed. He was 22-year-old Nicholas Somers from Co. Wexford. On 11 October 1920, a soldier named E.W. Cowan from Manchester had been shot a mile outside Kanturk on the road to Newmarket.[76] It is also possible that she was referring to the sentry that died the previous August when Jack O'Connell had led a group against the soldiers guarding a plane. He was a native of Chesterfield, England, and was named Albert Edward Nunn.[77]

10 MARCH 1921

Weather conditions were foggy when, in the early morning, staff belonging to Cork No. 2 Brigade were almost surrounded and attacked by a large force of British soldiers at Nadd in north Cork. In February, Liam Lynch moved brigade headquarters to Nadd because of increased British activity around the Lombardstown area. However, acting on a tip from an informer, the British on this date set about encircling the Volunteers, who were scattered in farmhouses around the district. Fortunately, an intelligence report received by Lynch the day before meant that most of the IRA were alerted and got away, while others obstructed roads to foil the British efforts.

In one instance, however, before any warning arrived, **PATSY HOLMES'** friend Edward (Ned) Waters (see 7 September 1919), who had been attached to Mallow Company, was one of five Volunteers sleeping in a safe house called Herlihys when British forces suddenly entered and caught them by surprise. They were ordered out through the yard and into a field. Two of the Volunteers managed to escape in the fog, but Waters and two others (David Herlihy and Michael Kiely) were shot dead. A fourth man (Edmond Twomey) was also killed that day when fired on by a British patrol.[78] Shortly afterwards, the informer who gave them away was identified as William Shields, a member of the Kanturk Column who had previously served in the British army. He fled and was never seen in Ireland again.[79]

> I was in jail and poor Waters was out and I was inside in the jail and never knew he was dead.[80]

Patsy found out about Waters' death through a newspaper in Ballykinlar Camp.

18 MARCH 1921

PATRICK FITZGERALD, from Dunmoon, Co. Waterford, often ran dispatches without knowing what was inside of them. Some of these he brought to a man in Youghal. He revealed that on one occasion he 'did an outpost for Plunkett'. Patrick said that this Plunkett was 'a brother to that man that was shot in Easter Week, was he Count Plunkett?' He was staying in a very quiet place where there was a hut opposite a house and a stream running between them. According to Patrick, Plunkett 'was the man that was living in that house. I know.' [81]

This is very interesting because in 1921 George Plunkett (known as 'the Count') came to Waterford to try to reactivate the West Waterford Brigade. Apparently, it was felt by Collins and others in Dublin that they weren't as active as they could have been. He toured around, carried out inspections and met with senior IRA officers in charge of the area. Plunkett would go on to participate in the Burgery Ambush, which took place on the night of 18 March and the morning of 19 March 1921. The district referred to as the Burgery is situated two miles from Dungarvan.

The IRA had assembled there to attack a force of military travelling in a motorcar and lorry heading towards Dungarvan. They succeeded in taking prisoner a Captain Thomas, four soldiers and an RIC man named Sergeant Hickey. They were all later released unharmed except for Sergeant Hickey, who was sentenced to death and executed. The IRA returned to their base. George Plunkett felt that guns and ammunition had probably been discarded by uncaptured Crown forces in their effort to escape, and insisted that a group return and collect them. He and several others went back but came under heavy fire from the British military as they crossed an open field. Two of the IRA, John Fitzgerald and Pat Keating, were killed. In the crossfire, an RIC constable named Sydney Robert Redman was hit by the IRA and later died from his wounds.

In the aftermath of the Burgery Ambush, Dungarvan and the surrounding district witnessed some deplorable acts committed by the Crown forces. Premises were ransacked and burned, and civilians were beaten and killed. [82]

19 MARCH 1921

Men from the Third (West) Cork Brigade Flying Column under Commandant Tom Barry attacked and smashed an encircling force of British military and police at Crossbarry. At the time, the column was operating at a strength of 104 men. They were outnumbered at 10:1, but at the end of the battle, according to one account, there were at least 39 British soldiers dead and 47 wounded, as against 3 IRA men dead and 2 seriously wounded. [83] Other accounts claim British casualties were overstated and that 10 had been killed and 3 wounded. [84] Whatever the truth, Crown forces dead included Privates S. Steward, W. Wilkins, J. Crafer, S. Cawley, Acting Sergeant E. Watts and Lieutenant G. Hotblack, all of the Essex Regiment. Also killed were Privates C. Martin, W. Gray and H. Baker, who acted as drivers, and Constable A. Kenward of the Black and Tans. [85] An 11th man, Private A. Tower of the Essex Regiment, died in 1923 from wounds received that day. [86]

From the start of the battle, Flor Begley, the brigade piper, played martial airs on his bagpipes, which inspired the IRA volunteers. **DANIEL O'DONOVAN** remarked that engagements like Crossbarry and the earlier one at Kilmichael were a great boost to the morale of those fighting against the British in West Cork.

> There was a great jeer up. We thought in our time hearing about them and the columns being so successful and I happened to know a few in the column at the time and they were heroes to us then.[87]

The IRA killed at Crossbarry were Con Daly, Jeremiah O'Leary and Peter Monaghan. Comrades present on the day such as Tom Barry, Tommy Kelleher, Liam Deasy and others lived to tell the tale:

> Well, I knew all those to see and by repute but I never saw any of them during my time.[88]

DAN KEATING emphasised the effect of Flor Begley's pipes on the day. In his view, not only did they rally the Volunteers to glory, they demoralised and frightened those attempting to encircle them. At this time, the total British military presence in Co. Cork was over 12,500 men.[89] Dan summed up the significance of Crossbarry.

> It was the most complete victory that was achieved by the IRA in the whole campaign. After some time anyway the British counterpart in Cork, he demanded that if they were to defeat the IRA he wanted 30,000 troops in Cork plus field guns and armour cars. The British were in no position to supply all that at the time. Times were bad in Britain after the war. Actually, some of the people in Britain were starving at the time. They just couldn't do it and they decided anyway after some time, they started throwing out feelers and all that anyway. It must be said that Crossbarry was the cause of bringing about the Truce you had in Ireland.[90]

On 19 March, Brigade Commandant Charlie Hurley was also shot by British forces. He had sustained an injury after taking part in the ambush at Upton Railway Station in February and was convalescing at a house near Crossbarry when it was surrounded by the British on the morning of the ambush.[91] Liam Deasy replaced Hurley as brigade commander, thus becoming the third man to occupy this role. Incidentally, it was also in the month of the Crossbarry Ambush that the Auxiliaries made themselves known to Daniel O'Donovan in Bantry.[92]

> No, I didn't know any Black and Tans at the time I was there, only the Auxiliaries. And I was arrested by the Auxiliaries on one occasion and brought to their barracks which was the Eccles Hotel, Glengarriff and after interrogation was released again.[93]

Interestingly, he pointed out that the Auxiliaries who arrested and questioned him were not brutal.

> No, the Auxiliaries they seemed gentlemanly from what I know of them.[94]

This assessment of the Auxiliaries may be at odds with what one might have expected to be told, but it is backed up by his comrade Ted O'Sullivan from Bantry, V/C Cork No. 5 Brigade.

> The Auxiliaries in Glengarriff were not bad. They rounded [up people] to fill in trenches. There were huge round-ups from Beara to Furious Pier. Then [Royal Navy] sloops brought troops to the Kenmare River but they were not bad like the Essex [regiment].[95]

Daniel's arrest occurred one Sunday after Mass in Bantry when he was part of a congregation held up and searched by the Auxiliaries. Having been found in possession of a Volunteer drill book that had been issued at the time, he was conveyed to the Eccles Hotel, questioned and subsequently released from custody that evening. Upon the arrival of the Auxiliaries in the district, such occurrences were common. However, Daniel's name was now known to them, which meant he had to tread more carefully, though he denied that this necessitated having to go on the run.

> No, I wasn't on the run because I wasn't suspected of anything until I was arrested. And that was after going to the bank looking for the bicycles, which someone gave my name, someone who saw me and gave my name.[96]

He is referring here to his second arrest, which occurred on 21 May 1921. He wouldn't get off as lightly this time.

21 MARCH 1921

The largest engagement in Kerry during the War for Independence took place at Headford Junction. **DAN KEATING** (not a participant) described what happened.

> Danny Allman was in charge of the IRA. He had about thirty men there to meet a patrol coming from Kenmare that went to Killarney once a week.[97]

Thirty British soldiers were due to change trains at Headford Junction and join the Mallow to Tralee train for Killarney. The IRA reached the platform shortly before the train they were on was due to arrive. They took up positions on both sides of the railway station, but the train arrived earlier than expected and Volunteers Allman, O'Connor and Healy hid in the platform toilet. In the meantime, the soldiers and some civilians started disembarking the train.

> It was unfortunate that the train came in ahead of time and Allman and Coffey they were trapped in the toilet and the next thing the British army went in. Some of them went into the toilet and they [the IRA] shot

them and the conflict started there before they wanted it to start. They had almost all the soldiers accounted for. There was about four remaining under the engine of the train still holding out when another contingent of soldiers arrived almost unnoticed on top of them.[98]

These extra soldiers of the same regiment were passengers on board the approaching Mallow to Tralee train, and on seeing them the IRA started to retreat.

They were very lucky to get away with only two casualties. They admitted, the British admitted there was eight killed and four or five wounded but it must be said that it wasn't a success because the following day when they met again and they pooled everything and there was only three rounds of ammunition per man left. It was very inadequate anyway.[99]

The IRA dead were Dan Allman and Jim Bailey. The eight British fatalities were all members of the 1st Battalion Royal Fusiliers: C.E. Adams, G. Brundish, E.A. Chandler, A. George, F.G. West, F.E. Woods, G.E.L. Young and C.R. Greenwood.[100] Three civilians (John Breen, Michael Cagney and Patrick O'Donoghue) were also killed and a number of others wounded after they got caught up in the gunfire during the engagement at Headford Junction.[101]

22 MARCH 1921

A police patrol in a lorry travelled from Dingle to Annascaul at least once a week, and preparations were made to ambush them at Lispole. However, through information received beforehand, they became aware of the IRA positions and instead arrived with reinforcements of up to four lorries. Rather than driving into the ambush position, they stopped their vehicles a distance away and attempted to outflank their would-be attackers by foot.[102] Because of this prior knowledge, **DAN KEATING** (not a participant) was adamant that the operation wasn't a success.

It must be said that Lispole from an IRA point of view was a disaster. They [IRA] had been lying in wait for a couple of days and the Black and Tans in Dingle were aware of their position and they came in behind them with a fall of ground behind them and the attack started anyway. There was bitter fighting for the better part of half an hour and the Volunteers started to retreat anyway.[103]

At this point, Thomas Ashe was wounded, and together with seven of his comrades took cover in a sunken stream. Trapped, they were almost encircled, but a contingent of troops, overestimating their numbers, suddenly retreated on hearing bluff calls in the distance from the IRA men in the stream for them to surrender.[104] Elsewhere, Thomas Hawley, already wounded by machine-gun fire during the heat of battle, was captured along with four other IRA men by Crown forces that had come up behind them unexpectedly from the rear.[105] Several of these Volunteers were rescued almost immediately by their comrades, however.

There was two of them captured and were being led away by two Black and Tans when Tadhg Brosnan of Castlegregory saw what was happening and he came around, another man and himself again and he, when they were facing him, he ordered them to put their hands up. They did, he captured them the two of them and he freed the two men then – Jack Moran and Lar. He freed them two anyway and one of the Black and Tans said to him, 'Are you going to kill us Paddy?' He said, 'No, we're not going to do that.' He said, 'You didn't kill any prisoners we're not doing the same,' and the British actually – the soldier – he repeated that after to the press.[106]

The engagement lasted about three hours, and according to one account, it only ended due to confusion when a whistle blown by an IRA man was mistaken by the police and military as a signal from their own commander to withdraw. Apparently, on hearing it they immediately abandoned their remaining prisoners, hurried back into their lorries and sped off back towards Dingle, leaving some of their ammunition behind. Another version attributes the British withdrawal to a fear that they were being outflanked by other IRA volunteers.[107]

But when they counted everything, they had lost three men, Hawley from Tralee, Ashe and Kennedy [Fitzgerald]. Three of them killed. The British had a number of casualties all right, seven or eight but it must be said that at the end of the road that as far as the IRA, they captured nothing, and it must be said that it was a disaster.[108]

Maurice Fitzgerald from Minard West, Lispole, had been killed when a comrade's shotgun accidentally discharged before the ambush began whilst waiting for the British to arrive.[109] His sister Bridget of Lispole Cumann na mBan, with two other women, helped prepare his body for burial that night.[110] Siobhán Fitzgerald, Captain of Lispole Cumann na mBan, as well as other members of the branch, assisted the men who fought in the Lispole Ambush both before and afterwards in terms of providing food, shelter and first aid, and in storing weapons.[111] Thomas Ashe from Kinard East, Lispole, died the following day from wounds inflicted during the fight at Lispole.

Both Maurice Fitzgerald and Thomas Ashe belonged to 'C' Company, 5th Battalion, Kerry No. 1 Brigade, and would have been known to **MARGARET CAHILL**, whose brother Michael had also participated in the engagement. He had been armed with a shotgun but got no chance to use it, having been surrounded by the Black and Tans. Michael Cahill and several of his comrades ultimately escaped into a glen and got away.[112] The third fatality that occurred as a result of the ambush at Lispole was Thomas Hawley. He was nursed for six weeks until succumbing to his injuries on 2 May.

31 MARCH 1921

Michael Cusack & Sons operated a number of businesses on Lower Cork Street, Mitchelstown, including a hardware shop.[113] It was here that **MICHAEL CASEY'S** great friend, who served as adjutant of the Mitchelstown Company, worked during the trouble.[114] Reflecting on those times in 2003, Michael touched on an IRA operation that took place on this particular date.

> I knew a man now Hurley from West Cork. He worked in Mitchelstown during the trouble and he was in the republicans. But anyway, he was in a hardware shop but he was a grand lad – Jerome Hurley. And he's from West Cork. I don't exactly know where, but he finished up in Dublin and I called. He had a shop in at the back of Cleary's – a hardware shop. You know Cleary's?
>
> In at the back of that so I met him off one day and he was delighted. He was delighted. So I called again another time and he had a private house out a bit from Dublin. Not very far out you know but I went out there one night and the first thing he said to me – says he, 'Have you a place to stay?' 'Oh, I have,' said I. 'Everything's all right.' I went up to the sales or something there but he was a great man.
>
> He was in the IRA and Cusacks in Mitchelstown and I don't know whether I should tell you this but he used be going in late at night and he had to be very careful. But there were a girl working next door and she was going with a Black and Tan and says he, 'She should be shot.' He was afraid of his life of her.[115]

Michael pointed out, however, that the girl was not shot, as 'things worked out all right'.[116] She may have been spared, but an attempt was made on the life of her suitor Constable Griffin, who would travel from Ballyporeen to meet her once or twice a week. Two Volunteers from Mitchelstown Company named Perrott and Skinner were detailed to carry out the job and caught up with him when he cycled to Mitchelstown in plain clothes to have teeth extracted on 31 March 1921. He was found two miles outside the town, on the road and in critical condition, after being shot in the back of the head. Having been removed to Mitchelstown Barracks followed by the military hospital in Fermoy, he somehow survived. Afterwards, whenever prisoners were brought to Fermoy, he would be summoned to try to identify his attackers.[117]

11 APRIL 1921

Some weeks earlier, the London & North Western Hotel located on the north side of the River Liffey at the North Wall in Dublin had been occupied by Q Company of the Auxiliaries, among whose objectives it was to examine boats, detect suspects entering and exiting the country, and intercept any arms being imported for republicans.[118] On this date, shortly before 8 a.m., the hotel was attacked by members of the IRA's 'E' Company and 2nd Battalion, Dublin Brigade, under the command of Tom Ennis. They had advanced up the quay by mingling with dockers proceeding to their work on the ships. Suddenly they broke ranks, took up positions and fired on the hotel. Others took aim from adjacent rooftops and from behind barrels along the quayside. It was reported that bombs, acid and petrol were also hurled through the windows.[119] A fierce battle ensued, with some of the Auxiliaries still dressed in pyjamas, having come off duty from the night before. After 20 minutes, the IRA withdrew and scattered in several directions, pursued by small groups of Auxiliaries. On crossing the canal and the entrances to the docks, they cut off communication by raising the swing bridges.[120] In terms of casualties, two civilians were wounded and an Auxiliary sentry named Gerald Alfred Body was shot in the leg but survived. IRA man Peter Freyne, aged 18, was shot in the head and died in hospital. His brother Frank also participated in the attack, as did **SEÁN CLANCY**, who said he lost 'some very good friends' in the war against the British.[121]

12 APRIL 1921

On this Tuesday, shortly after 10 a.m., an attempt was made by Cork No. 1 Brigade to bomb two Crossley tenders loaded with police on Washington Street near the courthouse. Shots were also fired. One bomb was thrown across the street between the vehicles and exploded near the kerbstone on the other side. The occupants escaped injury and returned fire. Some civilians were injured by the bullets coupled with the bomb blast. One, William Kenefick, would die from his wounds the following day.[122] An account by Patrick A. Murray, 1st Battalion, Cork No. 1 Brigade notes that some of the bombs thrown failed to go off.[123]

The use of bombs was a common feature of the IRA campaign in Cork City, according to **GEORGE CARPENTER**, who would have been over 12 years of age at this time. He insisted that on one occasion he had unintentionally aided in the destruction of a military lorry in the vicinity of the courthouse.

> Yes, well that happened. One day I was just finishing school and was coming out with my knapsack and one of our ex-Boys' Brigade chaps, he was an officer in the IRA and he had a can of petrol and he asked me would I bring it up outside the back of Dwyer's [a large clothing manufacturing business based on Washington Street]. So I caught hold of it and away with me. It was a very heavy can of petrol. It was a two-gallon tin and by the time I got to Dwyer's, I was really tired. Then he undid the cap and he asked me to carry it over towards the courthouse. And outside the courthouse there was a Tan lorry there and when we got level with it he took the can from me, threw it into the lorry and there was another fellow standing by that had a lighting role of twine, roll of paper and he threw that in and up. There was a bang. Everything blew up.[124]

The three scattered, but George was caught by a soldier oblivious to the fact that the schoolboy in front of him had unknowingly participated in the attack. On being asked which way one of the two IRA men had run, George replied that he didn't know, and he was let free. The lorry was burned out.[125]

18 APRIL 1921

GERRY SMYTH had an interesting story about an incident that he claimed happened on this date in Stackallen.

> When the war was on British military were going round camping and a contingent of them camped near us and sent out scouts. Do you see the roads were all barricaded? Every road leading to the place was barricaded and there came a rap to the door one night, actually on the 18th of April in 1921. A rap at the door and my father went out and there were soldiers outside it. And they said that they wanted a barricade, put up a barricade on the road. And he said, 'Well I'm a teacher,' he said. 'I've nothing here to barricade it.' So, across the road from us there was an old mowing machine with a long single shaft and they pulled it out on the road as a barrier.
>
> Now that time as kids we used to shout at people to 'halt'. That was a regular thing do you know? People going home at night from the pub or somewhere else you'd say 'halt' do you know? And this man was coming from playing cards and they, the soldiers were outside at the barricade with my father and saw this man coming down the road and they shouted 'halt' and he didn't pass any remarks and they opened fire over his head.[126]

The same man was unharmed, and in the morning Gerry went out and collected the bullet cartridges off the road. He kept them for the rest of his life, thus ensuring that he never forgot the date.

> That's a cartridge of one of the bullets fired at him. Bullets were two a penny. Kids in school would have them in their pockets including myself and we used to pull the lead out of them and empty them and blow them up then and bang them. How we weren't all shot I don't know. It was a regular thing. A kid would have three or four bullets in his pocket when he'd come to school ... I found that bullet – the cartridge on the road. There were about a dozen of these on the road in the morning when I went out and I collected them do you know? And I gave one to that man's widow that was fired on since and I don't know what became of the rest of them. Other people got them do you know? But that's a genuine relic of that.[127]

21 APRIL 1921

Temporary Constable Dennis O'Loughlin, Auxiliary Division RIC – an ex-serviceman who is said to have worked locally as a cook – was shot dead in Knightly's public house, Tralee, by the IRA. As a reprisal, the military burned down the pub.[128] **DAN KEATING** maintained he had no option but to go on the run immediately with two comrades (Tommy 'Nuts' O'Connor and Percy Hanafin), as local gossip suggested they might have been responsible for or facilitated the men that killed him.[129] Dan didn't confirm or deny involvement, but Tommy O'Driscoll is named in the Military Archives Witness Statements as one of the shooters.[130] Indeed, a possible reference to Dan and his comrades was featured in the press two days later.

> The bartender had his back towards the centre of the shop from which the shots came. It is however stated three young men were seen turning away from the centre of the shop and walking coolly away.[131]

Safe houses around Firies would be Dan's home for the next few months. Before the month was through, **SEÁN CLANCY** readied himself for an attempted raid on Trinity College Dublin to capture rifles. However, as outlined by Lieutenant William James Stapleton of 'B' Company, 2nd Battalion, Dublin Brigade, the mission was aborted. [132]

> There was a British Officers' Training Corps (Cadets) for students at Trinity College, and it was said that they had arms for training. The Dublin Brigade O/C, Oscar Traynor, decided that these arms should be captured. The Squad were asked to co-operate. I remember meeting Oscar and members of the Squad, the Brigade Council and the Dublin Battalions at the Plaza Hotel. At this time I was recognised as No. 1 or crack motor-driver, together with Pat McCrae, and Oscar instructed me to obtain a car and bring it to the rear of Trinity College in Lincoln Place at about six-thirty in the evening. He gave me a general outline of what was to take place such as members of the Squad and Volunteers were to approach the training quarters in Trinity College, which were near the Lincoln Place gate, and there raid the hall and capture the guns. My job was to have a car at the Lincoln Place gate at six-thirty to take the guns, and any members of the raiding party that I could, to one of the Battalion dumps off North Great Charles Street. I remember distinctly it was left to my own discretion how I was to get the car, or where I was to get it, and I felt a thrill of pride that such confidence was placed in me. We had cars in our dumps but there was no time to go for one of them as I believe the meeting took place about six o'clock in the Plaza. I had one member of the Squad with me. It may have been Vincent Byrne – I am not quite sure. He and I walked down Cavendish Row towards the Rotunda and on the way down I decided that the type of car I'd require should be a van. I was fortunate in meeting a *Freeman's Journal* van near the Rotunda and we stepped out on the road, held our hands up and stopped it. We quietly took the driver out and told him to clear off. I turned the car and drove it over to Trinity College gate at Lincoln Place. I waited there about twenty minutes and some members of the raiding party came out to me – I forget who – and said 'The job is off.' I am not quite sure why the job was called off. I have an idea that the training hall or gymnasium was locked, barred and bolted and our men were unable to open it. I drove the car away and I think I parked it in some side street and cleared off.[133]

23 APRIL 1921

MICHAEL CASEY and all available Volunteers from Mitchelstown Company were notified to report to Ballygiblin Church at 9 p.m. on this Saturday night to partake in the destruction of Ballygiblin Bridge.[134]

> We were often out at night busting up bridges you know and we were outside in Ballygiblin. It's three miles outside Mitchelstown. We were about, there were about fifty of us there. We were going to break down a bridge and a couple of the fellows didn't turn up. We were to be there at nine o'clock. We were there. We had a donkey and car with pickaxes and crowbars and everything like that but those two fellows were caught with a lorry of soldiers coming from Clonmel to Mitchelstown and on to the camps. So they saw those two fellows and curfew was on. They held them up and searched them and they had arms and they had a dispatch that [said] *'Parade on at Ballygiblin chapel at nine o'clock.'* So they were arrested anyway and they were sentenced to death.[135]

On being caught around Quinlan's boreen, the pair had also been in possession of bicycles, which were banned at this juncture.[136] Tried by court-martial on 3 May on a charge of having been found in possession of arms, they were found guilty and sentenced to death.[137] Their case, which went on to receive major coverage in the press, was brought before the highest court in the jurisdiction – the House of Lords – which reached the decision to stop the executions.[138]

> But anyway, there was a solicitor in Mitchelstown by the name of Skinner [James G.] and they were sentenced to death but he got thousands of signatures and sent them to England and they were reprieved. And there were about thirty more with them that were reprieved again.[139]

Michael said the two that were caught were 'Paddy Clifford and Mick Sullivan'. The *Freeman's Journal* reported the release of these men and over 80 others who were detained in Cork County Gaol on 13 January 1922.

> They comprised 32 convicted men, 21 under sentence of death (unconfirmed), 20 with other unconfirmed sentences and 13 untried men. Those under sentence of death included two men named O'Sullivan and Clifford from Mitchelstown, who were sentenced by a military court in Cork but on appeal the Master of Rolls, it will be recalled, gave a decision which created a sensation in legal and military circles – that military courts at the time had no legal powers and consequently could not pass sentence of death.
>
> Prior to this it will also be recalled that a number of men had been executed in Cork Barracks on conviction by similar courts. Some slight delay occurred before the second batch of 53 were released; but the crowd waited patiently and cheered and cheered again as the men came out.[140]

When Clifford and O'Sullivan had failed to turn up at the effort to knock Ballygiblin Bridge, Michael and the assembled Volunteers quickly realised that the military was onto them and therefore would inevitably attempt to encircle Ballygiblin church. The pickaxes, crowbars and shovels were immediately thrown over the ditch, while the donkey owned by Jack Neill in Skeheen ran off on being hit a slap.[141] The volunteers could hear the faint sound of military lorries approaching as they scattered through the fields. Not daring to risk going home, they opted instead to stay in safe houses until they deemed it safe to leave.

> The night of Ballygiblin, I had to stop in a farmer's house. Sit at the fire all night and the windows were well covered not to have any light be seen.[142]

3 MAY 1921

Bombs and bullets were showered on two military lorries proceeding towards Dublin city near the Thatch, Whitehall, and a fierce fight of roughly six minutes duration ensued. The attack was made from a fence on the right-hand side of the road that was barricaded with stones. Although carts had been used as obstructions by the attackers, the lorries containing Royal Army Service Corps employees and soldiers ultimately got away. The only fatality was a little Irish terrier, found shot dead on the road.[143] **SEÁN CLANCY** was involved in an ambush of Crown forces at Whitehall, and although no date was given, this may well have been it.[144] The action was summed up by participant Lieutenant William James Stapleton.

> Tommy Ennis, Officer Commanding, 2nd Battalion, Dublin Brigade planned an ambush on a number of military tenders which were in the habit of coming from Collinstown to the GPO each morning to collect workmen. The ambush was planned to take place on the bend of the road at Whitehall which would be now approximately, as far as I can remember, a halfmile above the present Whitehall Garda Station. Selected Volunteers from a number of Companies of the Battalion were nominated with Volunteer members of the Squad, myself, I think Tommy Keogh and Vincent Byrne and two others. The party took up positions behind the wall of a large private house at the bend of the road nearest the city. There was a large wooden gate leading on to the road and behind this gate the party arranged a heavy country cart with which it was intended to barricade the road. On the opposite side of the road, inside an open entrance to some other houses, I took charge of four men each of us armed with, in addition to revolvers, rifles. The idea was to cut off the retreat of the enemy or to hold off re-enforcements from Collinstown direction. The cart in the passage behind the gateway on one side of the road would, on the opening of the gates, only require a gentle push to roll right across the road as the roadway was somewhat below the level of the house grounds. Eventually two tenders appeared and passed my position without incident, but apparently the main party

on the other side of the road were too anxious about the barricading of the road and pushed the cart out somewhat too soon, with the result that the tender pulled up a considerable distance before reaching the barricade in time to reverse and turn back and drive it into the gateway where there was cover, and behind which we were lying in wait. We were taken by surprise. We opened fire but the whole thing was so unexpected that I am afraid our aim was not very accurate as I don't think we inflicted any casualties on the party. I took my party across country and over rivers etc. and we eventually came out on Botanic Road. From there we continued to our dumps. The main party cleared off in the direction of Fairview and got away without any losses of equipment. I well remember being rather reluctant to meet Tommy Ennis because we had failed so badly. Our attacking party had numbered about sixteen or eighteen in all.[145]

15 MAY 1921

SEÁN CLANCY took part in the Sunday morning ambush of troops proceeding in lorries from Collinstown to Dublin as they crossed Ballybough Bridge in the direction of Clonliffe Road, Drumcondra. Although few civilians were in the vicinity at the time, loud explosions followed by rifle and revolver fire could be heard as the rebels took aim and the British responded in kind. The windows in several houses nearby were shattered. In the aftermath, two wounded men were attended to in hospital, one of whom was IRA Volunteer Brian McSweeney. There were no casualties to Crown forces.[146] On another occasion, Seán was involved in the bombing of a military lorry in Ballybough.

> Well, I was in a number of scraps here in the city and of course we were badly armed. Usually there might be only half a dozen of us in an attack. And we'd be badly armed. We might have only two or three weapons, revolvers, we had no rifles but each of us would likely have a hand grenade and in those days especially in the winter months we used wear trench coats as they call them and you wouldn't be noticed with a hand grenade in a trench coat. And we'd hang around street corners and the first military lorry or police lorry to come along we let fly and of course we dare not run for our lives I suppose in fear and dread and we'd possibly get away. Maybe there were cases where some of our friends and comrades didn't get away but by the time they'd get off the lorry and start shooting anyhow we'd be gone. And I remember a great old friend of mine, down it was in Ballybough. He delayed a little too long. He dropped the grenade and apparently couldn't pull the pin out of it and then he tried to pick it up but he delayed for those few seconds too long and he was wounded in the head but he escaped and got away.[147]

Seán also participated in a raid on Amiens Street train station and in an abortive attack on a Ford car on Botanic Road.[148]

19 MAY 1921

A general election was held in the twenty-six counties under the terms of the Government of Ireland Act (1920). The result was Sinn Féin 124 seats and unionists 4 seats. The 124 Sinn Féin MPs wanted nothing to do with any Home Rule parliament and regarded themselves as TDs of the Second Dáil, refusing to take the Oath of Allegiance to the British Crown.

On 24 May, a general election was also held in the six counties, under the terms of the same Act. Nationalists, despite their opposition to the election, still ran candidates. The result was unionists 40 seats, nationalists 6 seats and Sinn Féin 6 seats. James Craig, the leader of the Unionist Party, was elected prime minister and only unionists took their seats.[149]

In the run-up to the election, **JOHN PARKINSON** saw and heard Éamon de Valera of Sinn Féin speak at an election meeting on the spare ground in Hamill Street, near Christ Church in West Belfast.[150]

> There were huge crowds there. There were big demonstrations there and you had to be very careful that you weren't picked out as being not one of them. But I just happened to be there and I got a chance to hear him and see him.[151]

In 1918, de Valera had been defeated by Joe Devlin of the Nationalist Party in this constituency, but this time around both had agreed to a pact in which nationalists would not stand against Sinn Féiners to limit any unionist whitewash. De Valera was elected in the Down constituency.[152]

21 MAY 1921

On this Saturday night, **DANIEL O'DONOVAN** was arrested for a second time in Bantry, on this occasion by soldiers from the King's Own Regiment (Liverpool).[153] The background is as follows. Three weeks earlier on 30 April, the following notice had appeared in various publications, including the *Cork County Eagle and Munster Advertiser.*

> Colonel Commandant H.W. Higginson, Military Governor Cork has prohibited as from the 22nd inst. The use of bicycles, for any purpose whatsoever in the following union and rural districts:- Castletown, Bantry, Schull, Skibbereen, Clonakilty, Bandon, Dunmanway, Macroom, Kinsale and Youghal owing to the continuance of murders, attacks on the crown forces and the destruction of roads and other communications and whereas, it is known that members and supporters of the IRA make use of bicycles for communication purposes and for movement from one area to another.[154]

In the lead-up to this notice, the Auxiliaries had been seizing bicycles in raids, but in the weeks that followed they stepped up their operation, set about collecting as many bicycles as possible, including those used by shops and businesses. In Bantry, all bicycles seized were stored at their headquarters in

Glengarriff, and anyone caught trying to break the order was severely dealt with.[155] Recognising that the loss of bicycles would somewhat hinder their campaign, the Third (West) Cork Brigade Council held a meeting culminating in an order that on 10 May all available bicycles in their brigade area were to be collected and safely dumped. An exception was made for bicycles whose owners could be relied upon not to let them fall into enemy hands. On that single day, 3,000 volunteers took part in the operation, and for the most part, it was successful, although two Volunteers were shot when interrupted by the British.[156] It was intelligence gathered pointing to Daniel O'Donovan's participation in this operation that led to his arrest 11 days later. His brother Pat was also arrested.

> At that particular time, we were, all bicycles and matters of conveyance that were available to us were taken up by the Auxiliaries. All bicycles chiefly, which we were in need of for dispatch riding to outside places. However anyway in the course, later on after sometime later when we were very short of bicycles, we started to search for those of who were left bicycles mainly for the colour, ah, were observed of at the time and when we went for to look for those bicycles in the course of one such thing my name was given and I was later arrested by the military who were stationed in Bantry.[157]

The *Southern Star* newspaper carried news of his arrest exactly one week later on 28 May 1921.

> The curfew patrol displayed unusual activity on Saturday night. Coming from the barracks sharp at the hour of curfew they searched several houses including that of Mrs. O'Donovan, Hibernian Bar. Two of Mrs. O'Donovan's sons were arrested and are still detained. Also three bicycles which were found at the premises were taken by the military to the barrack.[158]

Ted O'Sullivan V/C Cork No. 5 Brigade said troops from the King's Own Liverpool Regiment stationed in Bantry never ill-treated prisoners. However, that is not true in this particular instance.[159] The soldiers who were accommodated at the workhouse subjected Daniel to a beating and mock execution during questioning that they carried out in a wood located close to Bantry House. After demanding information from him, which he refused to give, a Lieutenant Smyth held a gun to his head and told him to say his prayers. Soldiers standing behind Daniel were ordered to move aside as he closed his eyes expecting to be shot. Instead, however, Daniel was knocked off his feet after being punched hard in the face by a sergeant (he suspected it was the sergeant, as this was a big man capable of delivering such a blow). The force of the assault opened Daniel's lip, leaving a lifelong mark. He would be detained by the soldiers until discovering his fate on 10 June. Pat O'Donovan was released after a week.[160]

25 MAY 1921

The Dublin Brigade of the IRA occupied and burned the Custom House in the city in an attempt to cripple British administration in Ireland. Over 160 volunteers were involved in the operation, which resulted in the deaths of 5 of them and the capture of up to 80. Amongst those killed were two of **SEÁN CLANCY'S** best friends – they were brothers attached to the 2nd Battalion of the Dublin Brigade named Patrick and Stephen O'Reilly.[161] The other IRA men were Dan Head, Eddie Dorins and Sean Doyle.[162] Four civilians (Francis Davis, Patrick Lawless, James Connolly and John Byrne) were also among the dead.[163] Five Auxiliaries were reported wounded. It appears that Seán Clancy was not directly involved on the day, although some of his comrades from 'B' Company, 2nd Battalion, Dublin No. 1 Brigade had been. He wrote that:

> Regarding service from 1st April 1921 to 11th July 1921, Captain (Thomas) Kilcoyne was Company Captain until he was captured in the Custom House on 25th May 1922. Captain (Stephen) Murphy then took charge of the Company.[164]

1 JUNE 1921

A 12-man cycling patrol consisting of three RIC and nine Black and Tans was ambushed by the IRA at Ballymacandy between Castlemaine and Milltown.[165] Five of the police were killed. **DAN KEATING** participated in the engagement and afterwards helped take wounded IRA man Jerry Myles part of the way to O'Brien's of Derry na Feena for medical treatment.[166] Myles was fortunate to survive.

> I was a Volunteer and we were active around Farmer's Bridge and we had been active in Tralee and other places. The next big ambush came in Castlemaine on the first of June. It was a beautiful day. I remember it like yesterday and twelve Black and Tans cycled to Tralee to collect their pay and the pay of the garrison they left in the barracks behind them. They were spotted going at half past ten in the morning and it was arranged that they'd be met on coming back and an ambush was arranged just outside Castlemaine on the road to Milltown. At the outset there was only four rifles there but there was a lot of shotguns. The first man to arrive was Jackie Brosnan from Farranfore. He was another rifle and a welcome addition. He had been active in Headford Junction before that.
>
> In the course of a half an hour ten men well armed with rifles arrived for a hut [hideout] in over Keel. They were all Tralee men. Among them was Dan Jeffers, Mick McMahon, Den Kane, Michael O'Leary, Nap Daly, Joe Sugrue, Big Dan Sullivan from the Loch, Donnacha Donoghue, Jerry Myles and Unkey Connor from Boherbee. Also arrived and they were posted in an out guard – Johnny Connor from Farmer's Bridge, Mossy Galvin, Johnny Connor, Paddy Connor.
>
> At that time they [IRA] were well spread out because going into town now they [RIC and nine Black and Tans] were paced about, oh, anything

maybe twenty yards apart. But coming home anyway they had some drink taken and they had some drink in Castlemaine and they came along in a bunch and they [IRA] got the signal. It started anyway and most of them were destroyed in the first five minutes. Some of them held out for a bit. One of them got in through a laneway and he shot Jerry Myles from Tralee and he was wounded badly. But Dan Mulvihill from Castlemaine spotted him and he shot him dead.

The couple that was left anyway surrendered. They [IRA] captured all the equipment including twelve rifles, some revolvers, all their ammunition, which was a lot and twelve bicycles. They made the wounded prisoners comfortable and the local women came out and they dressed them up and everyone escaped. The ambush must be said was a complete success. They captured everything and it was a serious dent in the morale of the troops in Killorglin.[167]

An account of the ambush provided by participant and former Clann na Poblachta TD Johnny O'Connor sheds more light on Dan Keating's involvement that day. O'Connor died in a car accident at Ballyduff on the Castleisland side of Headley's Bridge in December 1955.[168]

Around this time we received information that Tadhg Brosnan, Battalion O/C., Castlegregory Battalion, and Tom O'Connor, Battalion O/C., Killorglin Battalion, both in Kerry No. 1 Brigade area, were planning an attack on a cycle patrol of RIC who travelled from Killorglin through Castlemaine to Tralee and back once or twice a week. They requested the assistance of a few of our men on the battalion column. Moss Galvin, Dan Keating and I volunteered to assist and some days later met Brosnan and O'Connor near Milltown. We were informed that the patrol had passed through Castlemaine on their way to Tralee that morning and that it was intended to ambush them on their way back that day.

With members of the Castlegregory and Killorglin battalion as well as members of the Kerry No. 1 Brigade Flying Column, we took up positions on one side of the road between Castlemaine and Milltown in extended formation. In all, we had about 45 men most of whom were armed with rifles, the others had shotguns. Brosnan and O'Connor were jointly in charge.

After a while we were informed that the patrol had arrived back in Castlemaine and had gone into a public house there. We waited and eventually saw them cycle into the ambush position. When they were well within the position, O'Connor gave the order 'Open fire'. We fired a couple of rounds each; there was no reply. Seven RIC were shot dead. Two others, who made up the patrol, managed to escape. When we crossed the ditch we collected seven rifles and a number of revolvers as well as a sum of about £150 and a number of important dispatches on the officer in charge of the patrol. This attack took place on 1st June 1921.[169]

The dead were District Inspector Michael F. McCaughy, Sergeant James Collery, Constable John Quirk, Constable Joseph Cooney and Constable Joseph S. McCormack.[170]

2 JUNE 1921

John Mandeville (1849–1888) had been a nephew of the co-founder of Fenianism (Colonel John O'Mahony) and a champion of tenants' rights. A resident of Clonkilla, Mitchelstown, he had led the Mitchelstown tenants' 'Plan of Campaign' against Anna – Countess of Kingston – in 1886 and, following the Mitchelstown Massacre of 1887, had served two months' penal servitude in Tullamore Gaol for calling on tenants to resist eviction at a national league meeting. Mandeville was refused political status as a prisoner and died a short time after his release in 1888.

On 9 September 1906, William O'Brien MP had come to Mitchelstown to unveil the Mandeville monument in Newmarket Square in front of a crowd of 20,000 people, which included a three-year-old **MICHAEL CASEY**.[171] After curfew hours, on the night of 2 June 1921, in an act aimed at provoking the IRA, the Black and Tans set their sights on the monument.

> There were a monument in Mitchelstown to John Mandeville. Well, they came out one night and they brought buckets of tar and tarred every bit of it and the monument, the base of it and all. Did you ever see that monument? … The County Council had to clean it and a big job they had on it. It was desperate … It wasn't nice and it was never brought back the same.[172]

They also painted it red, white and blue and engaged in other acts of desecration around the town, such as painting slogans and Union Jacks on the premises of leading merchants and republicans. Inscriptions were also painted on the shops and footpaths such as 'Come out and Fight', 'Up King William' and 'Down with the Rebels'. The RIC were reported as not being on curfew duty that night.[173] Michael remarked that the Black and Tans never destroyed anything belonging to his family.

ANTHONY MCGINLEY, attached to the Fintown Company, explained how people in the district were usually alerted to the Black and Tans' presence, when I enquired as to whether there had been curfew in the area, as had been the situation in other parts of the county:

> No, there wasn't around here but you didn't know when the lorries come along the roads, but we didn't give a damn. We kept to the hills and you see.[174]

He described it as being akin to being 'more or less on the run'.[175]

> You worked every day on the farm surely but you were out at night and you were raiding for arms and other things. And you took to the hills and when you would hear the sounds of, the Crossly tenders had a

sound that you could tell besides any other. They had an engine you could know it anywhere. It was a dead giveaway. So, if you were on the lane or on the road you got off the road you see and you hid in and all that. Aye. I suppose it was a pretty dangerous exciting time but when you're only young you didn't mind. Aye.[176]

Either before the Truce or at the end of July 1921, the 3rd Battalion to which Fintown Company was attached was divided up and a 4th Battalion formed out of part of the 3rd Battalion area. This was done because the 3rd Battalion area was considered too large and scattered. Fintown Company then formed part of this newly formed 4th Battalion. There was a difference of opinion as to when exactly this 4th Battalion was established, so as a result Volunteers such as Anthony who had served with Fintown Company prior to the Truce were considered to have served with both the 3rd and 4th Battalions. Fintown Company, 3rd & 4th Battalions, 3rd Donegal Brigade, 1st Northern Division had a strength of 49 at the time of the Truce.[177]

4 JUNE 1921

According to his Military Service Pension file, **SEÁN CLANCY** participated in an ambush that took place at the 'bridge on North Strand'.[178] No specifics are provided, but several engagements took place at Newcomen Bridge, North Strand. On this date, at least three bombs were thrown at a military party travelling in a Ford car when they reached the top of the bridge. Some of the missiles exploded on the road, injuring a considerable number of persons. The military car dashed into Talbot Street before pulling up. Crown forces were soon on the scene and searched pedestrians, but no arrests were made. At least 10 individuals were treated in hospital for wounds, and a 12-year-old boy named Joseph Hanratty was killed. He had been crossing the bridge to make a purchase in a shop in the North Strand.[179] Some months earlier, on 1 February 1921, a bomb had been thrown at a military lorry containing about 15 soldiers on Newcomen Bridge, North Strand. It fell short of its target, exploding with a deafening crash that shook nearby houses. Shots were exchanged by both sides, apparently without either sustaining casualties. So far as could be ascertained, no members of the public had been injured on this occasion.[180]

> Well, yes, of course once I was a member. I was involved of course. I came safely through the whole thing and then the Truce came then in July in 1921.[181]

For this same month, **JOHN KELLY** claimed in his Military Service Pension file that he was engaged in cutting telegraph poles and participated in a raid on the Agricultural Station, Athenry, in which a sum of money was procured for arms.[182] A battery box and ammunition were also seized. John and his comrades were spotted by the Black and Tans who followed them, however. Fortunately for them they managed to evade capture. John recalled being armed with a shotgun but being unable to use it, as he was carrying the items that had been seized. His brother, Michael, also participated in this operation.[183]

10 JUNE 1921

Having been arrested and detained on May 21, **DANIEL O'DONOVAN** was tried by Summary Court in Bantry for the offence of having a bicycle contrary to Martial Law.[184]

> And after about three weeks [I] was tried by military court martial and sentenced to six months most of which was spent in Spike Island. After which I was released in late 1920 [1921], about September or October and remained of course, at that time the organisation had taken a big part in Volunteers and of course I rejoined and continued as previous until peace was settled.[185]

His sentencing appeared in two articles in an issue of the *Southern Star* newspaper dated 18 June 1921.[186] Interestingly, the Cork County Gaol General Register records the date of his sentencing as 10 June, whilst the first *Southern Star* article identifies it as 15 June in addition to inaccurately reporting a three-month prison term.[187]

> Six men were brought from the Drimoleague district under heavy escort on Sunday and were removed to Cork on Monday morning. The boy Daniel O'Donovan, sentenced at a military court on Wednesday to three months imprisonment was taken with them. He appeared to be suffering from a cold and the effects of a recent operation. His brother Pat requested to be allowed take his place but of course the request could not be granted.[188]

The second *Southern Star* article contained more accurate information regarding the sentence:

> A young man named Donovan, son of a shopkeeper resident in Bantry, has had a courtmartial sentence of six months passed on him in respect of a charge, as alleged, of unlawfully commandeering a bicycle.[189]

Daniel went into further detail concerning the background to his arrest.

> In a raid by our own party I was engaged in visiting the local bank. We were to pick up oil or to pick up bicycles. All our bicycles had been commandeered with the result that of the few we heard that were left bicycles, we went to collect them and one of them was the local bank for a bicycle belong to the manager.[190]

He is referring here to the Bantry branch of the Provincial Bank of Ireland Ltd, managed at the time by Mr William Cecil Ringwood.[191] It was located only a stone's throw from the pub where Daniel lived at the quay.

> But having got there he had taken it asunder and we had to leave it. While in a hotel nearby, there was another party took a bicycle that they found belong to a gentleman that was staying in the hotel and later on I

was arrested by the British military, at my own home and brought to the barrack with a brother of mine and kept there for three weeks when I was tried and had a court martial. Tried by two officers and a soldier as a witness who gave evidence that I was. He saw me take a bicycle from a hotel, cycling off from a hotel, which was belong to a border and later after three weeks I was court-martialled. As I say the soldier giving evidence and I was sentenced to six months most of this I spent in Spike Island.[192]

Under sentence from 13 June, Daniel was initially held in Cork County Gaol before being transferred to Spike Island, Cobh, on 22 June. His sentence was due to expire on 9 December 1921, and the earliest date he could be released was 10 November.[193]

15 JUNE 1921

GEORGE COOPER recalled the following incident as having taken place over the weeks or months following Kevin Barry's execution.

The Black and Tans came into where we were living in Holles Street at that time and they ransacked the place. You see in those days there was no radios, there was no televisions so the boys and girls in the tenement houses would congregate on the steps of those houses and just talk. And then somebody would cop on and here's the Tans and everybody would disappear out of their way. I lived in 26. Number 25 – they were open hall doors and they were singing Kevin Barry and they opened the door and fired a shot and one girl was shot in the back in those days.[194]

George didn't witness the actual shooting, 'but we knew the girl and we heard the shots you know'. Regretfully, I never asked George her name, but as reported in the *Freeman's Journal*, a shooting did occur on Sunday 15 June 1921.

At 10.30 last night a girl, aged about 22 years, was carried by a number of people to Holles Street Hospital, suffering from a bullet wound in the foot. It is believed she was standing at her doorstep in Holles Street shortly before the curfew hour, when a shot was fired, which struck her. She was detained in the hospital. No explanation has been forthcoming of the occurrence.[195]

Incidentally, the ballad 'Kevin Barry' was being sung from very soon after his execution in November 1920. In January 1922, a journalist wrote that *'no one knows who wrote it or who fitted the words to it. But from lip to lip the song has passed until, through all the length and breadth of Ireland, there is scarcely one boy or girl who didn't sing it.'*[196]

22 JUNE 1921

King George V came to Belfast City Hall to officially open the Northern Ireland parliament and made a speech in which he appealed for peace in Ireland. This occasion marked significant memories for three of the interviewees, the first being **JOHN PARKINSON**, who played an active role in proceedings and got a 'very good view' of the King:[197]

> I was there as a member of the Boys' Brigade. We formed a guard of honour and I was part of the guard of honour ... There were huge crowds from everywhere. Terrific, terrific crowds of people there from all over the country – even from abroad.[198]

On Upper Ann Street, **NORMAN DOUGLAS** was one of those in attendance in the crowd.

> My dad took me to see the King and Queen – King George V and Queen Mary –coming but it was a lost cause so far as I was concerned. Because the police were all six-foot high and the military were interspersed with them and I had to peer around the side of the policemen to get a look at what was happening. But it was so very well guarded. It was really as a young lad of what was it – twelve years of age? It was a spectacular thing so far as I was concerned.[199]

Meanwhile, 50km away from where all of this was taking place, **PATSY HOLMES** and some of his fellow internees in Ballykinlar watched their possible escape route fall through.

> I dug a tunnel there ... I'll tell you what happened there ... What happened was, to get material to hold it up, but there was a lot of it bordered/stacked. There was an old Jew man there – a military man and he was always on the phone so we stole any amount of the standards. And we had it studied out for good resistance and there used be a Crossly tender or two pass every day, and they knew the weight of the Crossly tender. Another lad, Lalor, he was an engineer, he knew it sure I was only digging it. And it resisted a lot of pressure but what happened was the King came to open the English parliament. And previous to that it was Crossley tenders would be passing with A-Specials in it. You could have over sixteen stone. And the King came to Belfast to open the Northern Ireland parliament and they had a double big load of, lorry load of soldiers and when they came to this place it fell in – that particular part. We never anticipated there'd be a lorry of soldiers you know, and that's what happened, it fell through.[200]

Patsy was of the view that even if they had escaped through the tunnel they would have been quickly recaptured.

> Would we have escaped? Well about it, I'd say not because we were in a hostile country. And it was over the mountains, you could see the

mountains of Mourne over there and there was a little house on the hill and they had it pin-pointed but when they'd get to that house they were, you were surrounded then anyway you go. Then the military, you couldn't fight your way through it.[201]

Escape attempts by means of tunnelling were as common in Ballykinlar as they have been in almost every prison since time began. In early October 1921, the British discovered two tunnels at an advanced stage in Camp No. 2 and once again foiled any attempted escape by internees.[202] When Maurice Donnegan and Paddy Colgan did manage to get out disguised as British Tommies, they were apprehended near Gormanstown and returned to Ballykinlar for six weeks' solitary confinement. They were subsequently sentenced to six months' hard labour in Belfast Gaol.[203]

On 22 June 1921, **DANIEL O'DONOVAN** was transferred from Cork County Gaol to Spike Island by vessel from the quay in Cork. For 38 years prior to 1885, when it ceased to be used as such, Spike Island was the chief depot for detaining convicts before they were deported to various convict settlements such as Australia. Afterwards, it was used purely as a military post, with its strongly fortified military complex known as Fort Westmoreland housing various garrisons. From 19 February 1921, the island was again used by the British as both a prison and an internment camp for republicans and was run by soldiers from the Cameron Highlanders.[204] The Union Jack could be seen flying in the breeze.

When Daniel arrived on Spike Island, the prisoners' compound consisted of 14 bomb-proof arched buildings running in parallel, referred to as huts. The exercise yard was about 80 yards long by 30 yards wide.[205] The internees' compound consisted of 'A' Block – a two-storey cut limestone building containing 22 cells (again referred to as huts) and 'B' Block (25 wooden huts on a lawn).[206] Conditions were for the most part poor, with prisoners and internees living in cramped, cold, damp accommodation and surviving on food that was often inedible. As a consequence, protests and strikes were frequent. On 31 May, internee Patrick White from Meelick had been shot dead by a sentry named Private Whitehead from the King's Own Scottish Borderers.[207] The internees played hurling every day in the barrack square, but were forbidden to touch the barbed wire. On this particular day, the ball went into the wire, and White was shot whist he attempted to retrieve the ball.[208]

> Well, there were two camps in Spike Island, one for the internees and one for the hard labour, convicted prisoners. I was a convicted prisoner and there was from three to four hundred in my camp and there were from six to seven hundred in the internee camp. We were separated except at Mass on a Sunday. There was a wire barricade separating us. But beyond that we didn't meet them. We were never in touch except shouting to one another before or after Mass for the few minutes we were there.[209]

Prisoners like Daniel who had been sentenced to hard labour were forced to pick oakum, which consisted of teasing the fibres from old ropes. They were also forced to dig a trench at the back of a huge moat nearby, but eventually the prisoners organised themselves and refused to work for the camp authorities. They and the internees elected their own camp commandants and officers and would not accept any order from the British that wasn't approved by them.[210] There was very little interference with the prisoners' camp from the authorities apart from the general rules imposed by the British. The camp was entirely run by the prisoners themselves. One difference between both camps was that smoking was not permitted in the prisoners' camp. They were largely dependent on internees passing them cigarettes at Mass on Sundays.[211]

> Well, we were allowed; we did our own cooking. We had our own cookers. We were supplied pretty well; reasonably well in plain good food and got the change of desserts or a thing like that – well, not desserts but meat and sufficient tea and bread. So we weren't bad in that respect and we were allowed mix but we were all in huts and there'd be about twenty to twenty-five in each hut and there were something like twenty-four huts so the most of them were filled. But they mightn't be even in number. But there must be anything from around the four hundred above or below during my time there conveyed, contained in the whole camp – in that particular part of the camp.[212]

He met some very famous republicans in jail, but two names in particular stuck in his mind:

> Well, the only ones I really remember well who would have a name were … Well, our first commandant, Sinn Féin commandant in charge of us was Jerry Ryan of Thurles and Seán Hayes of Cork city … And there were about roughly four to five hundred in the camp – prisoners. We looked after ourselves, supplied with all the stuff by the British military, did our own cooking, our own washing, our own cleaning up etc. and were reasonably well treated.[213]

Seán Hayes had a Cork city address when arrested but was a native of Glandore. Elected a Sinn Féin TD for West Cork in the First Dáil (1919–1921), he had been transferred from Cork County Gaol to Spike Island on the same date as Daniel.[214] The former *Southern Star* editor was a member of the Volunteers and was among those arrested on 18 April 1921 in a raid on the Cork District Lunatic Asylum, of which he was a member of the management committee. Having been found guilty by a summary court at Cork Military Barracks of having given a false name and of consorting with rebels, he was sentenced to six months' hard labour on Spike Island.[215] This was not a new experience for Hayes, who had previously served prison terms in 1916, 1919 and 1920. He was released on 11 August 1921 and died in 1928.[216]

Jerry Ryan of Moycarkey near Thurles was commandant of the 1st battalion, 2nd (Mid) Tipperary Brigade. He was captured by the RIC in Thurles on 26 January 1921 following an ambush in Poynstown and severely interrogated at their barracks. He was then conveyed to Limerick Military Barracks and tried by military court martial on a charge of carrying out an attack on Littleton RIC Barracks some months previous. Having been found guilty, he was sentenced to 15 years of penal servitude. After serving one month of this sentence in Limerick Gaol and a further two weeks in Cork Gaol, he was sent in May 1921 to Spike Island.[217] He was elected O/C of the prisoners in August, replacing Seán Twomey. Ryan was transferred to Kilkenny Gaol in October, but before the month was over, he and 46 other prisoners had managed to escape through a tunnel.[218] Jerry Ryan went on to become O/C of Free State forces in mid Tipperary, with headquarters in Templemore, during the Civil War, and led a column of troops on Golden in July 1922. In 1937 he became a TD.[219] Jerry Ryan died in 1960.

Seán Moylan TD, Con Conroy and Michael Murphy were also amongst the convicted prisoners and would have been detained in the same compound as Daniel.[220] A well-known internee there at time was Johnny Collins (brother of Michael), who was arrested on 16 April, and the family home at Woodfield, Clonakilty, was burned.[221] He was sent to Spike Island internee camp.

> No, I never met him. I'm not sure if he was there in my time. I didn't know him anyhow. And like that, I only knew those in my own billet to any extent and the few around. Even with such a crowd you never got, you mightn't meet some of them in your full term there because you were confined chiefly to your own quarter or your own hut and you knew those in the hut joining you or a few like that who would extend around.[222]

It's worth noting that on 29 April, three convicted prisoners – Seán MacSwiney, Tomás Malone and Con Twomey – had made the only known escape from Spike Island during the War for Independence.[223] The following November, seven internees managed to escape, amongst them Henry O'Mahony of Passage West, who acted as O/C of the internee camp, and Bill Quirke, who was Vice O/C.[224]

8 JULY 1921

It had been clear to Lloyd George for months that efforts had to be explored to reach a settlement. Having made contact with de Valera, a truce was announced between the IRA and the British forces in Ireland, to begin three days later. However, in those three days at least 61 people from both sides of the conflict were killed (22 of these in Belfast). Although many in the IRA and British forces had no prior knowledge that a truce was imminent, **DAN KEATING** said that there had been murmurings in the lead-up.[225]

> Everything went by and in the meantime, there was fears went out about a truce. They were going on for some time. There was a truce called.[226]

10 JULY 1921

Forty IRA men were divided into three sections and positioned in various buildings and landmarks for an attack on a night curfew patrol in Castleisland,

Co. Kerry. It turned out to be a disastrous attack from an IRA point of view. **DAN KEATING**, who participated, offered the following reason as to why this engagement was planned and carried out only hours in advance of the Truce.

> The night before, the South Kerry Brigade which comprised Castleisland, Firies and Ballymacelligot, they decided to attack the troops. They were very arrogant these troops now and they were going through the streets at night taunting the people. So they decided anyway they'd ambush them and a big ambush was prepared for Castleisland.[227]

When the patrol left their barracks, not all the IRA were prepared or in position, so when one section commenced firing before everyone else, the lull gave the patrol enough time to scatter and take cover so as to return fire. There was utter confusion, as some of the patrol had sought cover in buildings very close to where IRA men were located, resulting in several finding themselves hemmed in. In time, most of the IRA managed to withdraw, but two found themselves trapped in the town. It was decided to return to attempt a rescue effort, but this was aborted when they met the two men retreating as they neared Castleisland.[228]

> Again, they were very badly placed when it started. The patrol came out all right as usual but they left another crowd inside who knew the positions of the ambush and they just had them nearly surrounded when Ned McCarthy and Johnny Connor from Farmer's Bridge spotted what was taking place and they took them on. But in the meantime, they lost three great men.[229]

Their names were Jack Flynn, Jack Prendiville and Dick Shanahan.[230] In addition, there were four soldiers from the Loyal North Lancashire Regiment killed in Castleisland that night: Sergeant Davis and Privates Rankin, Ross and Kelly.[231]

11 JULY 1921

The Truce came into effect at noon, but in the hours leading up to it, the IRA in Mitchelstown also carried out one last attack on the British military. **MICHAEL CASEY** participated in this engagement against soldiers from the King's Own Yorkshire Light Infantry, which took place at the junction of Lower Cork Street with Clonmel Road, where there was a public water supply.[232]

> There were a few ambushes around the town. The last ambush was on the what – the 10th of July 1921. Soldiers had a barracks in Mitchelstown and they'd go down there for water and they were ambushed below alongside the creamery and their guns were taken from them and things like that.[233]

Captain Willie Roche arranged the ambush, and around 25 Volunteers participated, including P.J. Luddy and Jack O'Neill.[234] Michael outlined his own role in the engagement.

That ambush now that morning at the fountain in Mitchelstown, I was, I took part in that ... Yerra it wasn't much of a, you know it wasn't much of an ambush. There were only seven or eight soldiers there. They only went down for a load of water down to the fountain. And I happened to be above near the railway station, meself and two lads by the names of Dunnes and we were firing across at the barrack. That when the first shot would go off, we'd have to, there was one gateway out of the barracks and to fire an odd shot right across, you know, to keep them inside for fear they'd have re-enforcements below, they'd be captured.[235]

The fountain was located at the opposite end of the town and well away from both the military barracks and the Black and Tan barracks. The weather was dry and the water supply to the military barracks was prone to failing, so about 12 soldiers regularly had to walk to the fountain in extended order, escorting a water wagon. The IRA arranged for three volunteers to cover each barracks whilst others took up positions in the creamery yard opposite the fountain, on nearby rooftops and on the street. At 9 a.m., the soldiers arrived at the fountain and some of the attacking party charged from the creamery, calling on them to surrender.[236] Some ran away, whilst others responded by grabbing their rifles and firing. A few managed to take cover behind a low wall before eventually fleeing towards their barracks. Three soldiers and two IRA men (Leo B. Skinner and Billy Gallaghue) were wounded in the ambush. The IRA also only managed to capture two rifles. At the other end of town, having succeeded in holding both barracks for long enough, Michael and his comrades got away quickly before the arrival of armoured cars from Kilworth camp.[237] The ambushers kept a low profile in the days following this engagement.

I remember after the Truce there were a good lot of us brought out about two miles outside Mitchelstown and we weren't supposed to go home into the town for a week. But I had friends about a mile from it then and I used go there to sleep at night. And three or four would be ordered around to farmers for our dinner and we used get a great meal of bacon and cabbage.[238]

The War for Independence of January 1919 to July 1921 was at an end. Although a resumption of the guerrilla campaign was expected, that didn't really materialise. In terms of overall fatalities, the most recent research – which looked at figures from January 1917 to December 1921 – arrived at a total of 2,346 killed in Ireland, although more have come to light since its publication. Of these, 491 were IRA, 919 were civilian, 523 were police and 413 were British military.[239] Many hundreds of others were wounded, and 6,000 republican prisoners and internees were in jail (including **PATSY HOLMES** and **DANIEL O'DONOVAN**).[240] Although the British government had in excess of 80,000 well-armed Crown forces personnel in Ireland at this time, no more than 15,000 IRA Volunteers had taken an active part in the war. They had been supported by 3,000 members of Cumann na mBan.[241]

CHAPTER 6

An uneasy peace,
July 1921 – June 1922

14 JULY 1921

Éamon de Valera and David Lloyd George held the first of four July meetings in London to conduct preliminary negotiations for the Treaty.[1] De Valera wanted a 32-county republic, but this was too much for Lloyd George. De Valera then proposed that Ireland have an external association with the British Empire rather than being a fully-fledged member.[2] **JACK DUFF** contended that 'de Valera went over with a delegation and come back with nothing'.[3]

Deadlock ensued, but following an exchange of letters between the two, back in Ireland de Valera accepted Lloyd George's formal invitation to negotiate a settlement and sent delegates to a conference in London commencing on 11 October.[4] There were six in the delegation, which was headed by Arthur Griffith and included Michael Collins. Having been released from internment, Joe McGrath went to London as the Irish delegation's accountant. He had been **PATSY HOLMES'** former commandant in Ballykinlar Camp No. 1. De Valera opted not to go himself, believing that by remaining in Ireland he could best maintain his position as head of state and guard against any hasty decisions by the delegates by acting as a final court of appeal. There were to be seven in the British delegation, including Lloyd George and Winston Churchill.[5] Patsy questioned de Valera's decision not to go to London as part of the Irish delegation.

> I'll tell you one thing. I wouldn't like to hear any man saying one word against Collins. I wouldn't listen to him, because Collins had everything at heart but with all de Valera's education he could go there as an interpreter. He could play a part in it anyway ... They were two different type of men you see. Collins was a soldier and a fighter. De Valera, well now. I tell you they were two different type of man but it was very hard for two different type of men agree.[6]

17 JULY 1921

Even though a truce was in effect, there were breaches whereby some members of the IRA and Crown forces engaged each other militarily over the next few months, often resulting in casualties. Indeed, **DAN KEATING'S** friend Percy Hanafin from Tralee, with whom he had gone on the run in April, would die of wounds received in an engagement with Black and Tans in January 1922. In other instances, civilians and suspected spies who might have cooperated with the British against the IRA were singled out for attention. What follows from **MICHAEL CASEY** concerning his encounter with three drunken British soldiers before they would leave Ireland in 1922 was minor, in that no one was killed, but it does demonstrate the underlying tensions that existed during the Truce.

> I was a bit far away from the Kilworth Camp when they were leaving but I remember the Truce came on the 11th of July 1921 of a Monday morning at twelve o'clock and the Sunday after was the 17th of July. And there was a man called to me in Mitchelstown, I was living in Mitchelstown of course but says he, 'Will you come for a cycle?' 'I will,' says I, because we weren't on a bicycle for two years you know. You couldn't have them out. But anyway, we drove out to a pub just down here there, you came up, oh, you didn't the road is closed but the Punch and Bar. We came out there on to Glanworth and from Glanworth to Molly Barry's Cross. That's on the main Dublin road from Cork – Cork to Dublin. We turned left back towards Mitchelstown again – back home. But there were a hotel above at the Blue Dragon they call it now. It was belong to O'Briens.
>
> So we went in there for a bottle of lemonade or something and there wasn't a sin or soul there only two oldish men. Bill Allen and Éamon Brien was their names. And there were three soldiers inside, three British soldiers. They shouldn't have been out. They were all confined to barracks all the soldiers for a long time after the Truce. But those three soldiers came out of Moore Park. You know where Moore Park is – the high wall? They came out over a high wall, came up a mile of ground up the fields and into the hotel and they were inside when we went in.
>
> And the next thing they started blagarding the two old men. So the man that was with me anyway, he went at them straight away. I helped take them on with him. We beat the three of them out the door and cross the road and they lay down the bloody dyke in the road and we battered hell out of them and left them there and hopped on our bicycles and home into Mitchelstown – three miles. I'm telling you, it was a dangerous thing to do … six days after the Truce.[7]

In the months to come, many IRA training camps were set up as members engaged in drilling and military exercises in the countryside. Tours of inspection also took place, and **SEÁN CLANCY** described it as a 'very active period'.

> We established camps, training camps. First of all each company had its training camp, then the battalion and finally officers, potential officers. There was a special course of them. I had one of them you see.[8]

Seán took part in training camps in Dublin at Kilbarrack, Artane, Kilmore and Coolock.[9] **JOHN KELLY** was engaged in drilling and collecting funds.[10] Some Volunteers were deployed to keep law and order in their localities as Sinn Féin established its own police force. In fact, both Seán Clancy and Michael Casey went on to serve with what was termed the Republican Police, as did **MARGARET CAHILL'S** brother Michael in Ballinasare, Annascaul.[11]

During the Truce, **PATRICK FITZGERALD'S** IRA unit did a lot of drilling, marching and forming fours in a field near Dunmoon, Co. Waterford. They were preparing should there be a resumption of the conflict in the event that the settlement talks beginning in October would come to nothing:

> I was in Kilcalf. That's about five miles away from our home. I was there for a week. There was so many picked you know for if the Treaty broke down. They'd be the first to face the battle. They'd be the first called. That was the meaning of that ... All the company wasn't called at all – only so many out of every company. They'd be the first in the, if that broke down that should face the trouble.[12]

As to whether his company expected the talks to break down, the reply was that 'sure anyone didn't know'. One thing he was sure of, though, was that as a man living during the trouble times 'you should be in while the fighting was on'. Patrick had little time for men who tried to join the IRA during the Truce. [13]

18 SEPTEMBER 1921

The funeral was held of IRA man Bill Freaney (also spelled Freeney) from Derrydonnell, Athenry, who had been engaged to **JOHN KELLY'S** sister Aggie. The previous October, some days after publican Tom Egan had been murdered, Freaney had sympathised with his widow and declared his intention with the IRA to blow the Black and Tans and RIC out of Moor Park house where they were billeted. Mrs Egan managed to dissuade him, however.[14]

On the night of 30 June 1921, with the help of Martin Ruane, Jack Mahon and six others, he set his sights on burning the Galway County Cricket & Tennis Pavilion near the railway station in Athenry, it being a place frequented by many with British sympathies.[15] The building was doused in petrol, but the fire was started accidentally while three were still inside. The force of an explosion blew out Ruane and Mahon, but Freaney got trapped in the cellar and burned to death. When his charred remains were initially discovered, no one could identify them and some assumed them to be the remains of a tramp that had burned the place accidently whilst lighting a cigarette. Medical experts couldn't even determine if it was a male or a female corpse. However, arson was confirmed when a bicycle was found parked outside the pavilion and three empty petrol tins were discovered in the ruins.[16]

Fearing that identifying him could lead to reprisals against his family by the Black and Tans, the IRA decided not to tell the family that the body was that of their son. Freaney was subsequently buried as an 'unknown soldier' in St Mary's cemetery, Athenry. It wasn't until the Truce had come into effect that his body was exhumed and buried with full military honours at Willmount cemetery.[17] Tom Egan's daughter Nora relayed the story many years later.

> Well, they went to the pavilion in Athenry and they sprinkled the petrol. The Lord have mercy on Bill Freaney he was down in the cellar and the

lads overhead gave the 'all clear'. They shouted 'Is everyone out?' and they thought they were and the next thing they lit it from one end and the whole place went up. Martin Ruane and Jack Mahon were on the upper floor and they told me the story after they doing it. Hadn't they the great confidence in me that they would tell me their story but there was no informer in our house. The end of the story was anyhow, 'What did ye do lads?' I said. Do you know what they did? They went down on their knees upstairs and said an Act of Contrition. And we were prepared they said to 'meet our God' when another explosion came and blew out a window and Martin Ruane and Jack Mahon landed on the ground. Nobody knew how – they knew it but they didn't say anything about it that Bill Freaney was burned.

And Bill Freaney was engaged to Mock's [John Kelly's nickname] sister Aggie Kelly. I remember she was a lovely girl but anyway it went on until June. That was six months. They got the charred remains of a human being in the building, didn't know who it was and they put it in a little box – there were big biscuit boxes at the time – and interred it in the grounds of St Mary's Church in the square in Athenry. So it went on for six months until a truce was called. Bill Freaney was then exhumed. They could do it then you see as the Tans couldn't interfere then you know. I remember the Sunday well. It was after last Mass in Athenry – half eleven Mass. I'd be fourteen now. I was at Mass and they put the little box into a full-length coffin and I can see Mick O'Grady there and the two horses and the hearse and I couldn't say how many men were outside and they had the green, white and gold [flag] and black armbands and they all marched to Willmount to bury him there.[18]

In his Military Service Pension file, John Kelly claimed to have been one of those involved in the burning of the Galway County Cricket & Tennis Pavilion when Bill Freaney was killed. He added that 'the best friend I had got burned that night'.[19] In 1924, John Kelly's sister Aggie emigrated to Melrose, Massachusetts, on board the SS *Carmania*, which sailed from Cobh. Her passage was paid by Norah Mahon, her sister, who resided at Foster Street, Melrose. She had married in the United States in 1909. Aggie married John Fay (originally from Peterswell, Gort) in New York in 1929 and gave birth to a son. By 1950, however, the couple had separated. Aggie returned home to Athenry for a 10-week holiday in 1956 and died in New York in 1968.[20]

10 NOVEMBER 1921

Having served five months of his six-month sentence, **DANIEL O'DONOVAN** was released from Spike Island on the earliest possible release date. He returned to a rapturous reception in Bantry on 16 November, and this was reported in the *Southern Star* newspaper.

Mr. Daniel O'Donovan, The Square, Bantry arrived home apparently in the best of form on Wednesday after a term spent in jail and internment. He met a good many of the Bantry internees in Cork and Spike Island and reported all in good health and spirits although the conditions in the latter place were such as would test the endurance of the strongest. His youthful friends showed their joy at his return by a bonfire and tar-barrel display on the quay wall on Wednesday evening and he had other evidence of the general pleasure felt at his safe return to home and friends.[21]

In the days and weeks following the Truce, there was initially a far more relaxed atmosphere in the camps, with both tried and untried men believing they would be released imminently because de Valera would surely insist on such during his meetings with Lloyd George over preliminary negotiations. An indicator of this relaxed atmosphere occurred when the convicted prisoners were allowed to bathe in the sea, though under heavy armed guard.[22]

> Well, we were hoping for the best and we didn't mind so much the delay. As I said, say we were pretty well treated and we were free to mix with one another and free to write and read as required so I have no complaints as regards that.[23]

However, with August almost over, complaints did arise and on the 28th of that month, 20 convicted prisoners began a hunger strike following a refusal by the authorities to comply with various demands that included release. The internees had also been deliberating about going on hunger strike themselves, but this action by the prisoners hastened matters somewhat. They decided to put the question to a vote, which resulted in 450 men out of the 473 opting in favour of the action. Most of the remaining 23 consisted of hospital patients and the unfit. The internees immediately demanded of the governor their unconditional release, on the grounds that the English government had neither the legal nor moral right to hold them by force. Should their demand not be granted, they would join the strike at 6 p.m. on 30 August.[24] Their demand was ignored, and by that date every able-bodied man on the island, both tried and untried, was on hunger strike. At the time, Commandant Tom Barry, in his capacity as IRA Chief Liaison Officer for the Martial Law Area, had the job of investigating the hunger strike. He went to Cobh with the purpose of travelling to meet the prisoners, but was denied permission to do so by the governor.[25] By 2 September, however, largely due to outside influence, the hunger strike was over 'as a result of certain circumstances brought to the attention of the internees'. The prisoners, however, maintained their right to be liberated.[26]

Thus, a tense situation existed between the prisoners and authorities on the island, culminating in another brief strike in late September over what inmates described as intolerable conditions. They complained of being assaulted by guards and of being deprived of rations, so wrecked their huts and bored through their hut walls in protest. The military responded in kind.[27] Discourse between inmates often turned to the progress of the treaty negotiations in London, but Daniel O'Donovan recalled being told very little about how things were progressing in this regard. The senior men in the prison only told him odds and ends.

> Well, I'd only hear it from those in more authority and we never heard as youngsters. I was one of the youngest and we never heard how their information was got. It was kept from us I suppose. But we didn't hear. But it was coming in I'm sure, probably the clergyman or those bringing any commodities to the island from the grocers or one thing or another.[28]

There was a chapel on the island, and Father Edward J. Fitzgerald was clergyman to the prisoners and internees.[29] As well as saying Mass and hearing confessions, he managed to smuggle in and out many IRA messages. He had also aided the escape of Tomás Malone and two of his comrades the previous April.[30] Father John Callanan also served as Spike Island chaplain.[31]

> Well, I only saw the clergyman once a week and that was on the island and I was never speaking to him myself but he seemed a nice gentleman as far as I could see. Because being one of the youngest, we didn't hear what those in authority would hear, or probably wouldn't be told. But that everything was going well outside. You'd hear those things but nothing more.[32]

By mid October, Spike prisoners and internees had reached the end of their tether. The *Cork Examiner* dated 19 October 1921 reported serious disturbances taking place, with internees demolishing much of what was known as Block A and Block B as well as setting fire to furniture, personal possessions and beds. Loud cheering coming from the island could also be heard at Cobh, while some internees had to be taken to hospital with injuries. The outbreak was caused by *'disaffection among the untried prisoners at succeeding releases of others of their class, while they were continued in captivity'*. The men were also protesting against the prison conditions and had issues with the food, which they described as unfit for human consumption. They complained that sickness and disease had become rampant. The authorities responded in vain by blocking parcels from the outside, dishing out beatings and putting the ringleaders in irons. One internee was even shot in the foot and left untreated for over an hour afterwards.[33] The disturbance eased off after a few days, but the destruction caused to the compounds made living conditions even more uncomfortable for the men. What little clothes they had were damp and torn, whilst their huts were left without windows, doors, and in some cases, roofs. The chapel was also damaged, and the authorities turned it into a makeshift jail. Sanitation was non-existent.[34] In the words of Jerry Ryan:

> There were quite a number of IRA prisoners in Spike Island at the time and we soon made the place uninhabitable. During the Truce period we received a visit from the late Michael Staines, then Chief Liaison Officer, and, as a result of his visit we were transferred.[35]

In the aftermath of the destruction, it was decided that Spike Island was no longer suitable for the purpose of incarceration, and by the end of November preparations were made for the release or transfer of prisoners and internees.[36] Consequently, some five hundred convicted prisoners and internees were removed from the island on 19 November and taken by train from Cobh to Maryborough (Portlaoise) and Kilkenny Gaols, accompanied by three hundred Cameron Highlanders.[37]

Daniel O'Donovan didn't mention the various protests, riots or hunger strikes on Spike Island during my interview with him, although to be fair I hadn't asked him about them. In any event, Daniel remained in the movement upon his release and took part in some intense drilling practice.

> Yes, I continued in the IRA and even went to an outer camp. There was a camp in such all the members were trained for a week or a fortnight; I'm not sure which. We were billeted in farmhouses about three miles from Bantry town.[38]

12 NOVEMBER 1921

Batches of men were being freed on parole from internment in Ballykinlar Camp, and on this evening hundreds of friends and relatives gathered in the vicinity of Amiens Street terminus in Dublin awaiting the arrival of the 9.30 p.m. train from the north, which it was believed contained more than a hundred released men. Most in the crowd were disappointed, however, when they discovered that only ten former internees were on board the train.[39]

PATSY HOLMES said that one day in 1921 an offer was presented that would have made it possible for some of the internees in Ballykinlar to go home but that would have involved signing a certain form. Apparently, a prison officer came around with a bunch of forms telling the men that he could guarantee their release within days if they signed one. The form was a pledge swearing true faithful allegiance to the King and a commitment not to get involved with the republican organisation upon release. Patsy recalled it being discussed and that Peadar Kearney was against any man signing, much to the consternation of another internee who belonged to some evangelistic organisation and had been arrested by mistake some months previous.

> Now to sign that, you were released in two days. But there was a fellow named Kearney, he was after going through the war and he was up in the back and there was an old man there. The old man started off at him, 'I'm belong to no army,' says he, 'only the army of God.' 'Well,' says Kearney, 'you're a long way from your barracks here.' You had that kind going on there. There were good men and I'm telling you they were good men.[40]

According to Louis J. Walsh:

> The military sent to Ballykinlar quite a number of men who could hardly have been described as Sinn Féiners at all.[41]

Patsy Holmes recalling two internees in particular, pointing out that the camp was centred in a predominantly loyalist area.

Alongside of it, Downpatrick and Tullymurry and the County Down and all that, they were a tough old crowd … The strangest thing about it; there were two – Georgie Goodman now and another fellow. They were two Protestants. There were only two of them in there.[42]

George Goodman with an address at 15 Quadrant Street, Belfast, was interned in Camp No. 1 along with his brother Joseph.[43] The Goodman's were actually Catholic, but some of their immediate family may have had pro-British leanings, as their parents had been married in a Church of Ireland ceremony in Darkley, South Armagh, in 1887. By the 1901 Census, both parents are listed as Catholics.[44] In March 1920, George Goodman, aged 18, was charged with having fired a revolver during disturbances at a match between Celtic and Glentoran held at Cliftonville football grounds on St Patrick's Day. It was the prosecution's argument that George Goodman (a Celtic supporter) had intended to kill RIC Sergeant Michael Lavelle, who had been grazed in the throat by a bullet. Two other men had also been wounded by shots allegedly fired by Goodman, although he protested his innocence. Goodman's father, Thomas, aged 63 at the time of the trial, had served in the Royal Irish Fusiliers for 27 years and had volunteered for service at the outbreak of World War I. Having been wounded in action, he had been a patient in the UVF hospital until a week before his son's trial.[45] In addition, one of George Goodman's brothers, Francis Pasteur, had been killed in the war at the age of 17 in 1915.[46] Sentencing was delayed until George Goodman underwent an independent medical and physical examination.[47] Following this, the judge acquitted him of firing intentionally at Sergeant Lavelle, but found him guilty of firing shots indiscriminately and recklessly during the disturbances at the football match, which had an attendance of nearly 10,000 fans. Taking into account his father's military service and that this was apparently completely out of character, George Goodman (although referred to as Joseph in press reports concerning his sentencing) was imprisoned for eight months with hard labour.[48] Shortly after his release, George was rearrested and sent to Ballykinlar Internment Camp along with his older brother Joseph.

Interestingly, **ANTHONY MCGINLEY'S** cousin Conor McGinley had also been interned in Ballykinlar. He was released on 2 November 1921 and returned home to Dublin.[49] **MAI GROGAN'S** neighbour Art O'Donnell from Tullycrine was another internee there, and he was released a month later.[50]

15 NOVEMBER 1921

Corkman Tadhg Barry was shot dead inside Camp No. 2, Ballykinlar Internment Camp. The incident ironically took place 40 yards from the British commandant's office in which a joint Irish–British commission had been sitting to investigate complaints of maltreatment of Irish political prisoners in jails and internment camps.[51] Commandant Michael Staines TD was chief liaison officer representing Irish prisoners. The shooting was witnessed by **PATSY HOLMES** from Camp No. 1:

Well now, Tadhg Barry that day, they were going out on parole going home. They'd have to go back again and whatever happened they fired and they killed poor Tadhg.[52]

Barry came from Blarney Street in Cork and had been a well-known figure in public life. He had been a prominent official in trade union circles and a member of the Volunteers, and was also elected alderman of Cork Corporation. He was involved in several other bodies, including the GAA. Barry had been transported to Ballykinlar on board the *Heather* following his arrest at Cork Courthouse the previous January.[53] As a group of internees being released on parole were boarding lorries to take them to Tullymurry railway station, their comrades in the camp began waving and cheering them off. Tadhg Barry was standing on an upturned bucket in order to see over a galvanised fence and was amongst those waving when a sentry in a sentry box about 20 yards away shouted at him to get down and get back. Suddenly, as Barry was in the act of doing so, a shot rang out and he fell to the ground.[54] His fellow internee Father Burbage was on hand to give the Last Rites. Barry's remains were brought to the morgue and the men in Camp No. 1 were given permission to appoint a guard of honour to watch over them during the night.[55] An 18-year-old sentry named Barrett was arrested in connection with Barry's death, although there were suspicions that another soldier was responsible, as recalled by internee Hugh Gribben.[56]

> It was alleged that a military sergeant named Forde from Waterford, entered one of the sentry boxes, following which a shot was fired and Tadhg Barry fell, shot dead.[57]

The press at the time reported that this shooting again caused a lot of indignation amongst the internees, and one man who helped maintain restraint in the camp was Father McLister.[58] At the inquest, it was stated that the sentry thought Barry was in the process of attempting to escape, but many internees argued that there was not the slightest suggestion in his movements to warrant such a belief.[59] In 1956, close to the site of the camp, Ballykinlar's current GAA pitch was opened and named Memorial Park, Ballykinlar, in memory of Alderman Tadhg Barry.[60] Internee Thomas Treacy from Kilkenny, who stayed in Hut 19 in Camp No. 1 with Patsy Holmes, remembered how:

> Some very sad things occurred in the camp. Some prisoners died, some were shot and some lost their reason and became mentally afflicted. One fine young IRA man became insane and tried to run up the barbed wire fence near a sentry box in broad daylight. He would have been shot only Barney O'Driscoll roared at the sentry that the man was mad. He was brought by the military to Dundrum Asylum. Considering all the times the prisoners were fired on it was a miracle that there were not more fatal consequences.[61]

22 NOVEMBER 1921

In his capacity as a member of the Republican Police in Mitchelstown, **MICHAEL CASEY** related to historian Bill Power how he was one of six volunteer recruits involved in an investigation into who was stealing whiskey from the mill in Bank Place. They set a trap, watched the mill and caught the culprits Tim Coughlan (an ex-RIC man who owned a public house) and Mick Pigott, a jobber. Coughlan was arrested and brought to Robinsons in Kildrum, who were known to be sympathetic to the IRA. Coughlan was held there in a corn store for a short period of time. Michael recalled guarding him on the day of Mrs Finn's funeral in Pollardstown.[62] Ellen Finn from Pollardstown died on 22 November 1921.[63]

As related to historian Allison Murphy, it was also on this date in Belfast that **NORMAN DOUGLAS** witnessed two loyalist gunmen running out of a pub at the corner of Pottinger Street having shot the man behind the counter, a Catholic. Norman and his mother were crossing from Cherryvale Street onto the Beersbridge Road when they heard the shots ring out.[64] According to the press, this incident occurred at about 8.30 p.m., and five or six men were involved. They entered the spirit grocery premises of Patrick Malone and held him up. Their demands being refused, one of them shot him in the chest. It was reported that the raiders then marched from the premises – which was in a predominantly unionist locality – with 'amazing indifference'. Malone was removed to the Mater Hospital, where he died.[65]

JOHN PARKINSON often travelled on the Belfast tramcars during this period, which on occasion would come under attack.

> People had to travel very carefully. The tramcars, it was a common practice you lied down on the floors in the tramcars when you were passing certain streets in case you'd get hit with a sniper's bullet.[66]

NORMAN DOUGLAS also remembered them.

> Well, going and coming it was always a dangerous thing because the trams were open at the front and back end and you never knew just, there were areas were nationalist and areas which were Protestant and from time to time they fired at one another and trams became involved in that situation in travel.[67]

On one occasion, Norman was on the trams when they came under attack.

> My mother and I were in town at a meeting and we were coming home and at Short Strand and the Ravenhill Road they were firing across and we were all told to lie on our tummies in the tram until it got past that particular area. But that was the only occasion.[68]

John Parkinson said that it was quite common during this time for various explosive devices to be thrown directly at the trams.

> They threw bombs. Not so much on the Grosvenor Road, it was more sniping but down in the city centre there were several cases of bombs

being thrown into the tramcars. There was one very bad case where men coming home from the shipyard, what they call a workman's car, workman's tramcar from the Queen's Island. They threw a bomb into the tramcar and there were several men killed. Then the next day in the shipyard they took it out on the Roman Catholics and they drowned some of them in the River Lagan.[69]

Two tramcar bombings in particular made world headlines. On 22 November 1921, three Protestant shipyard workers were killed in Corporation Street when IRA men from the Third Northern Division bombed their tramcar. The dead were William Cairnduff, James Rodgers and Robert Nesbitt. Two days later, a similar action resulted in the deaths of four shipyard workers as their tram passed through Royal Avenue in the city. Their names were Richard Graham, Jeremiah Fleming, Robert Johnston and Thomas Rodgers. Many people were also injured in these attacks.[70] In June 1922, John O'Hare of Thompson Street drowned after being seized by a loyalist mob and thrown over the Albert Bridge into the River Lagan. He was a hotel porter.[71]

3 DECEMBER 1921

Johnny Collins arrived back in Clonakilty after almost eight months incarceration on Spike Island followed by a spell at the military hospital, Victoria Barracks, which he had been transferred to for treatment some weeks earlier. No charge had been preferred against him.[72] His wife, Kate, had passed away in February, leaving him eight children to look after. She had been in bad health for some time.[73]

Having qualified the previous year from St Patrick's College, Drumcondra – where he destroyed all his books on leaving in a ceremonial book burning – **PATRICK GREENE** had met Johnny Collins some days prior to his return to Clonakilty whilst teaching on the Offaly/Westmeath border.[74]

> I had a job as a substitute in 1921. A fellow who, a place called Horseleap, it's between Moate and Killbeggan, he was interned in Ballykinlar [Joe Boyle] and I did sub for eleven months there.[75] And in the village of Horseleap there was a namesake of your own – a woman named Hurley. She was married to Jim Maloney who had been a full private in the British army. He was a Westmeath man himself and she had a sister who was married to John Collins – Mick Collins' brother. And she, Collins' wife died and two of her children, two girls, Mai and Kit were living with their aunt in the village in Horseleap. And they were going to the girls' school in the village. Now they were they could be about nine and ten or ten and eleven, that was their age at the time.
>
> So in November '21, Collins had been interned in Spike Island and in November he was released and he came to Horseleap to where his two daughters were. Now I met him there and he informed me bluntly that without Irish there was no chance of getting a school. The poor man thought that Irish would be the national language in a few years' time

and he advised me to go to the Gaeltacht. So I knew nothing about the Gaeltacht. I didn't know any Irish, I hadn't a word of Irish, never heard it spoken and he gave me an address in Ballingeary and he said to write to that address and say he told me which I did and I was invited to come along.[76]

The address Patrick was given was that of Tadhg Twomey, who ran a post office and shop in Ballingeary.[77] He and his brother Liam were members of the Ballingeary Company, Cork No. 1 Brigade IRA, and had participated in numerous engagements, including the ambush at Beal a Ghleanna in 1918 (see 21 January 1919). They lived just over a mile from Ballingeary in Tuairín Dubh with their parents, Johnny and Máiréad.[78] But what kind of a man was Michael Collins' brother – Johnny?

> I didn't know very much about him. He came and he was only a very short time there. He went back; he went back to Cork with his children. He went somewhere. I don't know where he went. I think he went to Dublin. I met one of his daughters – Mary. I met her years afterwards in Lough Derg of all places. I never met Kit. I think she only died two years ago. She's the mother of Mary Banotti and her sister [Nora Owen]. They're both in politics. I don't know if Mary the elder ever married at all. I never met Collins afterwards.[79]

Having married in 1934, Mary Pierse (née Collins) died in Listowel in March 1992 in her 83rd year.[80] Her younger sister, Kitty O'Mahony (née Collins), married in 1937 and died in Dublin in January 1997, aged 86.[81]

6 DECEMBER 1921

Negotiations having taken place from October to December, the Treaty was signed in London. The main points of it were:

- A republic had not been achieved. Instead, Ireland would have Dominion status within the British Empire and the twenty-six counties would be called the Irish Free State.

- All members of the Dáil would be required to swear an oath of allegiance to the English King.

- The Crown representative in Ireland would be the governor general.

- Britain retained three Irish ports, which became known as the Treaty Ports, for defence purposes – Berehaven, Spike Island and Lough Swilly.

- The government of the six counties of Ulster, which were still partitioned, would have a year and a day to decide whether or not to come into the Irish Free State, and if they decided not to, then a Boundary Commission would draw up a border between the two jurisdictions in accordance with the wishes of the inhabitants.

On their return to Ireland, the negotiators attended a cabinet meeting in which de Valera denounced the terms. However, when put to a vote, the Treaty was approved by four votes to three. De Valera then announced it would be put before the Dáil. Almost as soon as the terms of the Treaty became public, two of the interviewees decided to side with the majority view in their brigades and to reject it. First of all, **MICHAEL CASEY** from Mitchelstown, who maintained that in the finish the Treaty was a rushed effort and that the Irish delegation had been conned into accepting it:

> Well, I think that Winston Churchill, when the boys went over Michael Collins and the rest of them went over that Churchill frightened them. He told them that if they wouldn't sign that he'd declare war immediately, and they were anxious to come back, put it to the people but they wouldn't be allowed … They [the British] were all bad.[82]

Reflecting on whether de Valera should have gone to London with Michael Collins and the others to negotiate, Michael maintained that he should have, 'but why he didn't go I don't know'.

The vast majority of republicans in Kerry had no hearing for the Treaty, perceiving it as a surrender of their principal of an all-Ireland republic free of the British regime. **DAN KEATING** was no exception.

> Collins knew he was wrong and said so. And he said, he said when he signed the Treaty he said that, he turned to the next man and he said, 'I surely signed my death warrant,' he said you know. He knew he was wrong. But then again, the man that was in charge of that delegation to London – oh God – anyway he wasn't renowned for any bravery and he'd – Arthur Griffith was his name and he'd settle for anything you know.[83]

Arthur Griffith, a moderate republican, had believed the Treaty was a noble compromise and had been prepared to sign it even if the other members of the delegation weren't. **GEORGE COOPER** in Dublin remembered the signing of the Treaty for a reason other than politics. He had a neighbour called Donnelly who lived above them in their tenement in Holles Street.

> And I used to wait on a Friday morning, a Friday afternoon at the hall door and when this man Donnelly would come in, he used to give me a penny. And then some time afterwards there was another man who used to go up to Donnelly's and I heard it was Donnelly's brother. And he was to be executed on the day that the Treaty was signed – so he was let off.[84]

John Donnelly of 26 Holles Street was a member of 'B' Company, 3rd Battalion, Dublin Brigade IRA. On 21 May 1921, he was charged with murdering Auxiliary Cadets Francis Joseph Farrell and Bernard James Leonard Beard the previous

March during the course of an ambush on Great Brunswick Street. The IRA had attacked two Crossley tenders and an armoured car with revolvers and grenades. David Kelly of Sinn Féin and IRA Volunteers Leo Patrick Fitzgerald and Bernard O'Hanlon lost their lives, as did three bystanders – Stephen Clarke, Thomas Asquith and Mary Francis Morgan. John Donnelly suffered bullet wounds and was captured and taken to hospital. His comrade Tom Traynor was also captured and taken prisoner. He was sentenced to death and hanged in April 1921. Tried by general court martial, Donnelly was sentenced to death with no recommendation for mercy. Imprisoned in Mountjoy whilst awaiting execution, he was about to be transferred to the condemned cell when the Truce came. The British authorities declared they would not release John Donnelly until the Treaty had been ratified by both governments. It was after Christmas, coming into the New Year, when he was released.[85]

9 DECEMBER 1921

In the lead-up to 1922, the British began releasing prisoners and internees from the jails, as they hoped such a move would generate support for the Treaty.[86] It's estimated that altogether 6,000 republicans were incarcerated, including **PATSY HOLMES**, who was released from Ballykinlar Internment Camp on this date along with 1,700 others who were interned there.[87]

> When we came out, Mick O'Neill was one of the men I was handcuffed to. He was a big able man and when they came out he went to some house around Bandon to get a gun or something that was in there and a Black and Tan shot him dead [see 26 April 1922].[88]

Patsy's journey home started out with jubilation, but was to encounter hostility and end in tragedy. The internees were out of bed since 6 a.m. and were marched from the camp to the nearest station, at Tullybridge, where they connected to the Great Northern Railway.[89] Their luggage was taken in military lorries. There was plenty of cheering at the station, with crowds having lined the route waving greetings to the internees. There were also plenty of newspaper reporters asking the men what they made of the Treaty. Patsy maintained that at this stage:

> We didn't know what with the Treaty. When de Valera was there and Collins, you wouldn't know what to expect. Now funny thing the majority of the fellows thought it only an old matter of forms. It would be all over. Sure we didn't know what was going on.[90]

There were three special trains organised to take the men home. One conveyed men mostly from Ulster and the second and third were packed with internees from the south, the west and Dublin. All internees had to travel to Dublin before making their way to their own counties.[91] Sinn Féin flags flew from the windows of most carriages, and Patsy boarded the special train conveying the southern contingent, as did a released internee named Declan Hurton.

He had a coat made out of a military blanket but we kept together anyway. We came to Dundalk. There was a small bit of trouble in some part of the north but it isn't worth talking about.[92]

When Patsy's train had reached Newcastle, the liberated men disembarked for a time and were given tea, cigarettes and fruit by a large crowd of well-wishers. It was a different story at Katesbridge, as loyalists flung stones and nuts at the train. Shots were also fired and carriage windows were broken. Four ex-internees were slightly wounded. One of them was Jack (John) Fitzgerald from Kilbrittain, who was hit by flying glass.[93] At Banbridge, the train was again attacked. At 3 p.m., it arrived at Amiens Street Station (present-day Connolly Station) in Dublin to deafening noise, as hundreds had gathered to greet the released men.[94] Some of the men from Munster got off, but most – including Patsy and his friend – did not alight, travelling on instead to Kingsbridge Station (present-day Heuston Station), from where they continued their journey south.[95]

> But I came anyway myself and poor Declan. Hurton was his name. We were talking away about everything and there was banners under each train to let them know the prisoners were on board the train. And I came to Thurles Station with him.[96]

There are two accounts pertaining to the status of the train with regards to what happened once it reached Thurles. While there is no dispute that bombs were hurled at it, one account claims it happened while the train was still in motion, whilst the other account – which is supported by Patsy – claims it had already stopped, with some passengers having disembarked and others such as himself standing outside more or less stretching their legs before continuing the journey south.

> And there was an old woman. She had sandwiches or something but I got off the train and I crossed over to her ... There was a loud explosion and it was behind my back and I saw two or three men helping this man, helping him on and who was it but poor Declan. He was from Ardmore – Declan Hurton. He died four days after.[97]

According to the *Cork Examiner*, the train was still in motion when the incident happened. It reported that at 7 p.m., as the train carrying the ex-internees approached the bridge at the entrance to Thurles Station, the bombs were thrown at it under the cover of fog. Either way, the brazen act directed at those on board was carried out with little regard for the large crowd of well-wishers that had gathered to greet the liberated men. The attack led to several civilians and ex-internees being wounded, including Declan Hurton (prisoner no. 792) from Ardmore, who was removed from the train and treated at the scene by a local doctor.[98] After a delay, the train resumed its journey to Cork and a distraught Patsy got off at Mallow.

News travelled quickly, and two men from the Third Tipperary Brigade went to Thurles to investigate the incident. They noted that the town was in complete darkness – '*not a light shone in a house*' – and a sense of terror reigned. Acting on information that a bomb had been thrown by an RIC Sergeant Enright, who was based locally, they went to the RIC barracks to demand answers. Those inside refused to open the door to them, however, as recounted by John Sharkey.

> Seeking accommodation for the night we knocked at the hotels and at some likely houses but nowhere did we get an answer to our knocking. Eventually [we] went to the railway station and got shelter for the night from a signal-man in the signal-man's cabin. Next day we returned to Clonmel. The investigation of this incident probably fizzled out as the RIC were disbanded shortly afterwards. At any rate I have an idea that Sergeant Enright was shot dead at a coursing which he attended somewhere in North Tipperary within a few weeks of the bombing incident at Thurles Railway Station.[99]

Sergeant Thomas Enright of Thurles RIC Station was killed on the street in Kilmallock, Co. Limerick, while there to attend a coursing meeting on 14 December 1921.[100] As for Declan Hurton, he was conveyed to the North Infirmary in Cork, where he died on 16 December. Patsy claimed that he had no further involvement with the IRA after his release. However, for a spell during the remainder of the Truce period he was engaged in training under the command of Patrick Corbett.[101]

> I came out anyway and I took no part in anything else only to get my job back. And I came back and the man I was working with he was a cattle dealer. And his brother was one of the first men to die. What was his name? He died in Spike Island – Dan Clancy. It was Dan was his name.[102]

Dan Clancy of the Kanturk IRA had died in Cork Military Hospital on 11 November 1921 following an operation for appendicitis. Having been arrested the previous April together with his brother who was subsequently released, he was interned on Spike Island. Clancy was taken ill in late October during the protest for freedom and removed to Cork Military Hospital, his condition likely not helped by having to exist in a demolished hut during terrible wintry weather. He had also been shot in the foot by a British soldier. Two operations within ten days failed to save his life.[103] Patsy's employer was John Clancy, for whom he had already worked prior to his arrest. He said that a lot of his work for Clancy was carried out in a neighbouring county.

> He was a cattle dealer and I stayed with him when I came out. I was in Tipperary for a long time ... I was in Tipperary all nearly during the Civil War.[104]

Patsy reflected on the four men he had befriended only for them to have been killed since he had last set foot in Co. Cork (his former work colleague Edward Waters had also been killed since he was away).

I did know a lot of them. I knew them. Poor old devils and poor old Tadhg Barry. They were going out on parole that night and a bodyguard to him and at 2 o'clock I saw his face changing. The poor devil. He was gone altogether and the other two lads again before him – Sloane and Tormey. One bullet killed the two of them. It hit Sloane there look and caught Tormey here. Two of them died. I saw him just gave one kick out of him. I did and then the poor devil at Thurles that night. Poor old Declan. Poor old devil. I did, I saw the four of them die. I did, I saw them dead too.[105]

In addition to Sloane, Tormey and Barry being shot, five other internees had died as a result of maltreatment and illnesses within Ballykinlar Internment Camp: Patrick O'Toole, Maurice Galvin, John O'Sullivan, Maurice Quinn and Edward Landers.[106]

14 DECEMBER 1921

Debates on the Treaty commenced in the Dáil. De Valera was furious and condemned its terms, whilst Collins argued for its acceptance. De Valera put forward what became known as Document No. 2 as an alternative. It contained no oath or governor general and put forward a proposal whereby Ireland would have a loose connection with Britain by means of an 'External Association' and the King would be recognised as head of that association.[107]

It was during these debates that **SEÁN CLANCY** went home to Clonlara for Christmas and made up his mind on the Treaty after a discussion with a neighbour who happened to be an old Fenian named Johnny Hickey.[108]

Well, I suppose we were all young and inexperienced and we were all hoping that we'd get our Irish republic, there's no doubt about that. That's what all the propaganda was about and of course the negotiations went on for a long time and eventually it was decided to send negotiators to London and there was a big disappointment that de Valera decided not to go to London and there were five others, Griffith, Collins and three or four others went. And we were expecting great things but there was a certain disappointment we didn't get more.

I remember see; they had the vote on the Treaty in Dáil Éireann. It was adjourned just before Christmas. The Treaty was signed on the 6th of December and the debate went on then up to I think Christmas Eve. And it was postponed then until January before the vote was taken. But I went home that Christmas on holidays and I was more or less against the Treaty. I thought we should have got more out of it. And I remember meeting an old neighbour on my way home from Mass and he said to me, 'What do you think, what do they above in Dublin?' – they always refer to Dublin as 'above in Dublin'. 'What do they think above in Dublin about this treaty?'

'Well,' I said, 'there's a certain amount of disappointment,' I said, 'but at the same time I said there's a lot of good things in it.' 'And what are the good things that you can see?' he said. 'Well,' I said, 'we're going to have our own army, we're going to have our own police force. They're two great things anyway,' I said. 'And what about the things that you don't like?' 'Well,' I said, 'our country's being partitioned,' I said, and there was a second thing too. There was some other factor that I said I didn't like in it. Partition of the country was the main thing. So he, we discussed it anyhow and he convinced me that that the Treaty should be accepted.

That he said, 'It's a stepping,' oh, yes, he used the words 'stepping stone'. He said, 'It's a stepping stone.' Oh, he put it to me this way. He said, 'Look,' he said, 'if you want to cross a river, a fast-flowing river and there was a torrent in it. And you felt that if you tried to jump across that river or stream that you might fail and be swept away. But further, a few hundred yards further down that river there was stepping-stones, and you knew about those stepping stones, what would you do? Would you take a chance and jump across the river or would you go down and cross stepping stones?' 'Oh, by God,' I said, 'I'd take the stepping stones.' Well, see that's he, and he was a knowledgeable old fellow and he said, 'That's the position we're in with this Treaty,' he said. 'They're stepping stones and we should accept the stepping stone policy.' And mind you he convinced me.[109]

Seán said he couldn't remember whether he had formulated a time frame in his mind as to how long it might take the stepping stones to work but that 'to make a long story short anyhow I decided that I'd support the Treaty'.[110]

7 JANUARY 1922

Members of the Dáil voted to support the action of the Irish delegation in signing the Treaty with Lloyd George and his ministers. The result was 64 to 57.[111] It would be put to the people in a general election in June. Partition was perhaps not the most contentious issue regarding the Treaty in the Dáil debates. However, it's a myth to suggest that it wasn't mentioned or debated. The Government of Ireland Act of 1920 had in essence already partitioned the country, but it was anticipated by many that the future Boundary Commission would deliver the six counties. That said, many republicans on the ground, particularly in Ulster, weren't so sure, and did voice their concerns and opposition to partition in any guise, no matter what the duration of its existence might be. The other major issues of contention regarding the Treaty were the oath of allegiance to the King and the fact that Ireland had not become a republic but remained within the British Empire. **JACK DUFF** felt the Dáil had made the right decision in accepting the Treaty.

I'll tell you what I thought of it. I thought then of it as something that Collins had brought back and if it was good enough for him, it would be good enough for me.[112]

DANIEL O'DONOVAN, who was not long out of jail at the time, explained his reason for supporting it.

> Well, the fact is, being young I didn't understand the whole thing but listening to those who were in more authority and higher up I was pleased to hear it. Otherwise, I was glad that it [the conflict] was all over.[113]

Although northern unionists objected to the idea of any Boundary Commission, **JOHN PARKINSON** in Belfast described the outcome of the Treaty negotiations as being broadly favourable to them and commented on the sense of relief felt when the southern government had accepted the terms. Unionists hoped to be free of nationalist leaders in the south such as Collins and de Valera.

> Well, the people just didn't want them. That was just it all. We wanted to live our lives and we wanted to be closer to Britain. We didn't want to be caught up in, we always refer to the south as the Free State. Some people still call it that yet. It was called the Free State.[114]

9 JANUARY 1922

Éamon de Valera resigned his presidency of the Dáil and Arthur Griffith replaced him. The next day, claiming that the Republic was being undermined, de Valera led his followers out of Dáil Éireann.[115] Four days later in the Mansion House, Dublin, a Provisional Government was elected with Collins as chairperson. De Valera and his supporters refused to attend, although they did return to the Dáil in February without explicitly accepting the parliament's decision on the Treaty.[116] **SEÁN CLANCY** offered his opinion on Éamon de Valera's actions up to this point.

> Well, I admired de Valera in the beginning of course. He represented my part of Clare and he represented the government of the country for a long time but I think he made some great mistakes. First of all, he should have gone to London with the negotiators. He had already gone to London, met Lloyd George the British prime minister and he knew from his visits to London what it was possible to get out of the negotiations. He must have known and he was accused at the time of having known it and made up his mind that he wouldn't go to negotiate further. In other words he'd throw the onus over on others and in other words to get them to do the dirty work. And then when they came back with the Treaty, he let them down. He refused to support them. I think that was a terrible weakness on his part and that's what led to the Civil War and there was only one man that could stop the Civil War and prevent it from happening and it was de Valera and he did nothing to try to stop it.[117]

JACK DUFF held a similar view.

He was a power-crazed man who if he didn't have the upper hand and didn't have the reins of power in his hands, he didn't want to have anything to do with it, absolutely nothing.[118]

ANTHONY MCGINLEY agreed that de Valera made a bad decision not to go to London to negotiate the Treaty with the rest of the delegation.[119] It must be pointed out that the vast majority of those in Cumann na mBan rejected the Treaty, including Annie Sugrue – company captain of the Kanturk branch. **KATHLEEN CHARLES** had no involvement with the organisation after July 1921.[120] **PATSY HOLMES** disliked the Treaty terms, since a republic hadn't been delivered, but was of the view that although 'it broke his heart' to sign it, 'Collins must have had an idea in his head' on how to take it forward.[121] In his book *Michael Collins – A Biography*, Tim Pat Coogan wrote of Collins' ambivalence.

> Viewed from the Unionist standpoint Michael Collins, in the last months of his life, could be regarded as the supreme practitioner of this policy. Janus-faced he stood in Dáil Éireann, arguing fiercely for the Treaty and the establishment of law and order in a democratic, independent Irish State, while at the same time he acted with the vigour, intent, and methodology of any chief of staff of the provisional IRA to wreck the other state enshrined in that treaty, 'Ulster'. He told northern IRA men that although the Treaty might appear to be the 'outward expression of Partition ... Partition would never be recognised even though it might mean the smashing of the Treaty.' [122]

Coogan cites how pro-Treaty figures like Seán Hales and Eoin O'Duffy were also indicating more to come, suggesting they were privy to Collins' intentions.[123] Coogan contends that Collins' 'stepping stone' was to be a jumping-off point for raids, kidnappings and gunrunning into the north.

Again, Patsy Holmes spoke about being with men who knew Collins, and how in his view and theirs, Collins was planning something.[124] In fact, on 7 February 1922, after a meeting with Craig, Collins wrote a three-page document to one of Patsy's closest friends from Ballykinlar – none other than Louis J. Walsh. Collins was replying to an earlier letter from the Derry republican, and in it outlined his opposition to the partition of Ireland, conveying his belief that it would end in the long term, as ties would increase between north and south.

> I am no lover of partition, no matter what form it appears ... It would be far better to fix our minds for a time on a united Ireland for this course will not leave minorities which would be impossible to govern. [125]

In February 2003, this letter by Collins was sold at auction for €28,000.[126]

13 JANUARY 1922

The Russian Revolution had inspired some workers across Europe to become more radical. From 1919, what became known as 'workers' soviets' were established in Co. Limerick and quickly spread to neighbouring counties. They usually manifested during unresolved labour disputes between employees and employers. The theory behind a workers' soviet was that industry should be run by the workers, for the workers, with the profits shared by the workers. To do this, they would seize factories or land from the owner, occupy them and usually hoist a red flag signalling their intentions.

An unresolved pay dispute had erupted at a flourmill at Quartertown, which is about a mile from **PATSY HOLMES'** hometown of Mallow. It resulted in a strike and in workers (some of whom were members of the Transport Workers' Union) being locked out by the owner – Major Tom D. Hallinan & Sons – for refusing to accept reduced wages.

> That wasn't political now at all. It was just there was trouble between the workmen and this old major. He owned a mill and the boys kidnapped him anyway and they took him away down to Killmallock or somewhere.[127]

On this date, Major Hallinan was kidnapped and his motor car taken by a number of masked strikers. He was then conveyed to a hut at Bulgaden near Killmallock. In retaliation, during a branch meeting the next day, Michael Lenihan, Secretary of the Mallow branch of the Transport Workers' Union, was kidnapped by the IRA and taken away in a lorry. Both men were found unharmed following an extensive search operation and were back home within three days.[128] The major lived at 'The Hermitage' within a short distance of the mill, so his associates, concerned for his future safety, went about getting him some IRA protection.[129]

> So they came up to meet and they asked would any two fellows volunteer to mind him … 'I will,' says I, 'I might get a few quid off them.' He had a mill in Mallow so the two of us [Patsy and his friend Murphy] decided we'd stay with him and … We used be there at night and go out if we heard anything – no fear of him.[130]

When arranged talks between the mill workers and Hallinan's representatives failed to reach a resolution, the employees' period without a wage appeared to be extending. They soon found themselves locked out for over three weeks, with their Dublin-based Transport Workers' Executive refusing to give them lockout pay. Matters came to a head on 25 January when Major Hallinan's employees formed themselves into a workers' council, seized control of the mill and set about running production themselves 'for the public good'. The IRA warned the strikers against any damaging or looting and placed armed guards by the mills. The workers responded by placing their own guards.

The whole affair made big headlines at the time, with Liam Lynch and Michael Collins getting involved at the behest of Cork employers who wanted the mills restored to their rightful owner. Collins and the Provisional Government arranged to end what they described as 'the unauthorised action of certain persons in taking over the mills', and on 8 February the workers evacuated after being advised to do so by the IRA. The workers issued a statement saying they understood the IRA position but felt stabbed in the back by the lax support they had received from the executive of the ITGWU. The mill was handed back to Major Hallinan & Sons, and by 27 February the dispute was settled, with the men returning to work.[131]

> But anyhow they settled the strike and he [Hallinan] said to me, 'Paddy,' says he, 'do you want a job?' 'I do not, Major,' says I, but I said, 'What about my man – Murphy – whose the fellow with me?' He was a hard man. 'Alright,' says he. Murphy spent fifty years with him. He got a job but I was minding the old major that time. He was Hallinan. They owned a couple of mills through the country – Hallinan's Mills and they had one in Rathcormac and one in Mallow. But they had a dispute with the workmen but they had to use this password to get in at night. He lived outside Mallow. Oh, I had two nice guns, with a barrel on top of the timber you know. The old RIC had them years ago. Oh, I often bought plenty guns. I used do a lot of shooting myself.[132]

16 JANUARY 1922

A formal transfer of power took place when the King's representative in Ireland, the Viceroy Lord-Lieutenant Edward Talbot FitzAlan, handed over Dublin Castle to Michael Collins, head of the Provisional Government. Lord FitzAlan had taken over from Lord French as Viceroy in May 1921. **SEÁN CLANCY** was on guard duty for the occasion.

> I was. I was connected with what they call the Republican Police at the time and apparently the powers that be, they knew that the seat of government was being handed over. It was the first thing that was handed over by the British – Dublin Castle and the powers that be decided that Collins, he was head of the government at the time and he was going in to take over the thing officially and apparently they felt that he should get protection in case that some busybodies might attack him you see. So I was one of the number of people detailed to go to the castle. We were armed, again we had our trench coats and I suppose the guns weren't noticeable, but we were there hanging around. Place was full of British army, bands a playing, flags were flying, etc. and there was a lot of uncertainty that Collins was a bit late you see arriving.
>
> But eventually he arrived in an old L.S.E. taxi and he was alone in the car too. So as he alighted from the taxi I noticed a British official in morning dress approaching him – tall well-built man, morning dress, watch chain across his breast. And as he arrived, as Collins was alighting from the taxi, he said to him, 'Mr. Collins,' he said, 'you're seven minutes late.' He was looking at his watch at this time. 'You're seven minutes late and you've kept the Lord-Lieutenant waiting.' Lord-Lieutenant, remember was head of the government. So, Collins half smiled and looked at him, 'Yerra,' he said, 'you people are here seven hundred years, what bloody difference will seven minutes make now that you're

leaving,' he said. So end of story, it's not recorded what the answer of the official was.[133]

In fact, seven other ministers of the Provisional Government had accompanied Collins on this historic day and had arrived in two other taxis at the same time as him. One of these was Joe McGrath – Minister for Labour.[134] This date heralded the official start of the Provisional Government, but the Free State was not due to come into existence until 6 December. Almost immediately, plans were made for the evacuation of British troops, many of whom would leave on a phased basis, although they would not be completely withdrawn from the south until December. Plans were also made for the disbandment of the Black and Tans, Auxiliaries and RIC. The first unit of a new army was also established in January 1922. It was called the Dublin Guard and was drawn from Active Service Units of the Dublin Brigade and members of the Squad. This unit took over on 31 January and established its general headquarters (GHQ) at Beggars Bush Barracks, Dublin, which was among the first barracks handed over by the British.[135]

9 FEBRUARY 1922

A meeting was held at the Gresham Hotel, Dublin, to establish a police force to replace the RIC, which was being disbanded. Among those present were Michael Collins, Richard Mulcahy and Michael Staines, who acted as chairman. The wheels were put in motion, and on 21 February a selection of IRA Volunteers who had fought in the Tan War and who had been recommended by their superior officers presented themselves to Staines at a temporary depot at the Royal Dublin Society Showgrounds, Ballsbridge, as the first candidates. On 27 February, this new police force was named the Civic Guard (later An Garda Síochána), and Michael Staines was appointed its first commissioner on 10 March. Initially, it would be an armed police force, and in April Staines transferred his headquarters from Ballsbridge to the Artillery Barracks in Kildare town.[136] The DMP (Dublin Metropolitan Police), which was not disbanded, remained in the capital. **GEORGE CARPENTER** in Cork touched on reaction to the Civic Guard from amongst RIC men that he encountered through his father's association with them.

> A lot of the RIC stayed on and joined up with the new force, which I think was a great thing to do. And some of them went away, not very many. There was no one in our terrace left it. So it was interesting.[137]

3 MARCH 1922

A large number of British troops left Bantry Barracks for England. Many were in civilian dress and a large amount of baggage was transferred with them.[138] They had been busily engaged in packing up and leaving the town since January.[139] Much of what they didn't take with them, such as corrugated iron, barbed wire, timber and blankets, was auctioned off by J.J. Roycroft, Auctioneer and Valuer on 21 and 22 March.[140] **DANIEL O'DONOVAN** would assist in occupying the vacated military barracks in the town.[141]

When I came out I think the barracks was taken over shortly after by the republicans.[142]

PATRICK GREENE maintained that in the Rathreagh area there was no big fuss about the British leaving.

Well, nobody, Co. Longford nobody passed a bit of remarks on it. They were going. That was that. British troops marched out of Longford and nobody bothered.[143]

ANTHONY MCGINLEY in Co. Donegal observed notable signs of their evacuation, including 'their flag coming down here and there', such as from the top of barracks.[144] While this made some of those he knew happy, others pointing to the border and Lough Swilly weren't content while 'even one yard of our country left was still under Britain'.[145]

In some areas, the Provisional Government and IRA members who opposed the Treaty jostled with each other to take over these vacated RIC and British army barracks. By 5 March in Limerick, the anti-Treaty IRA had started to arrest pro-Treaty officers, occupy buildings in the city and take over British army posts. GHQ sent down a contingent of pro-Treaty IRA under Michael Brennan, who also attempted to take over barracks and salvage what was seen as the key military position, which commanded the River Shannon. It looked as if both sides would come into conflict, but a compromise was sorted out through the mediation of amongst others Liam Lynch, Michael Brennan and Donnacha O'Hannigan.[146] Resident in Ballyagran, Co. Limerick, at this time, **WILLIAM GEARY** relayed reaction to the Treaty amongst his IRA unit.

Well, I believe that they were in favour of it, of the Treaty. I think they were because I don't think there was much, as I said there was relatively little activity there so I think they, and anyway I think Michael Collins did the best he could because it's now well known that the IRA were exhausted. They had no equipment and a lack of equipment; a lack of ammunition and they were more or less tired of it. And then they were threatened, as you know with outright war by Lloyd George. So I think he did the best he could.[147]

Ballyagran Company had a strength of 72 at the time of the Truce. The membership recorded for 1 July 1922 is 44, including its captain, John Bresnihan.[148] On a general note, men whose names appear on IRA lists for the date of 1 July 1922 are for the most part considered to have taken up arms against the Free State government during the ensuing Civil War unless otherwise stated. There are, for example, sometimes annotations next to a name signifying that someone may have left the IRA, gone neutral in the Civil War or joined the Free State Army.

However, IRA company lists for 1 July 1922 often include the names of men who didn't appear on the list dated 11 July 1921. In some cases, these are men who had fought against the British as members of different IRA units during the Tan War and transferred to others during the Civil War. In other cases,

IRA lists for 1 July 1922 might include the names of men who had not fought at all between 1919 and 1921 (Truce recruits). In other words, while the numerical membership of particular companies recorded for 11 July 1921 and 1 July 1922 might appear broadly similar in certain instances, it doesn't necessarily signify that particular companies were made up of the same personnel on both dates. In some brigade areas, reorganisation and restructuring also took place.

15 MARCH 1922

Since the Truce came into effect, **ANTHONY MCGINLEY** had been taking care of arms, drilling, training, raiding for poitín and enforcing Republican Court decrees. On this date, however, he went with some men he knew and joined the Free State Army, enlisting as a private at Glenties.[149] He is recorded as having been 18 and a labourer. His army number was 57361.[150] Anthony served with 'B' Company, 1st Northern Division, and he was based mostly at Drumboe Castle. He signed a document to serve for six months and he bore arms. His commanding officers were Joseph Sweeney and Joseph McLoughlin. Anthony claimed to have had republican views and IRA sympathies throughout his membership of the army.[151]

   Anthony was very young, having in fact just turned 17 when he joined the pro-Treaty forces, and it may have been a decision he regretted. It wasn't spoken about when I met him in 2003. When I asked if he had been for or against the Treaty, he replied, 'Oh, we were against it, that's why I was arrested' (see 9 September 1923).[152] His father, brother and many others he knew were opposed to the Treaty, with little hearing for any stepping stones analogy.

> Oh, they didn't fall for it at all. They knew right away that Collins was compromised. Aye and you see God the young fellows on the farms that never had a gun in their hands, when they did take up a gun in all they – it was all or nothing. There was no such thing as a divided country, England get out that was it you see. That's what kept the Civil War going. And anyone that had that idea it was out, no grip at all in this country.[153]

He did know others who supported it, however.

> Oh yes, a hell of a lot of them. Sure my first cousin was a terrible leader in the Treaty – Joe McGinley of Letterkenny. He was a doctor of course – a big shot.[154]

Dr Joseph Patrick McGinley was the son of Anthony's uncle Pat (see 6 February 1905). He graduated from Queen's University Belfast in 1916 and ran a practice in Letterkenny. He was a member of the Volunteers and as a TD had argued for the Treaty during the Dáil debates of December and January. Dr Joseph Patrick McGinley had also been on the committee that established the Civic Guard in February.[155] Anthony's uncle P.T. McGinley (Cú Uladh) in Dublin went anti-Treaty.[156] Comrades attached to Fintown Company were also divided over the Treaty.

Ah, well you see it was just a split, a big split. There was a lot and there it was aye that was Volunteers together even it got down to brothers. Men would think it I suppose genuinely enough that it was a very good bargain and the other man he not at all – England get out that's all's to it.[157]

Fintown Company, 3rd & 4th Battalions, 3rd Donegal Brigade, 1st Northern Division had a strength of 49 at the time of the Truce. The membership recorded for 1 July 1922 is 51, including Anthony McGinley and his brother Michael.[158] Clearly in the case of the former, this is somewhat inaccurate, although he did join the anti-Treaty IRA later (see 22 September 1922). There is no record of Michael ever having joined the Free State Army.[159] Anthony knew of Protestants who were opposed to both the IRA and the Free State Army.

They were very loyal and they hated the movement but the orders was, the orders was in the IRA and in the army, not to interfere with them any way at all, no matter what they said or done. Aye.[160]

It was also on 15 March that Éamon de Valera formed an anti-Treaty party called Cumann na Poblachta (League of the Republic).

17 MARCH 1922

From St Patrick's Day 1922, the Irish education system was officially structured in a way that reflected the country's unique culture as opposed to that of England. Irish was introduced into the national school curriculum as a compulsory subject and was taught for at least two hours a day. Both Catholic and Protestant schools taught Irish. **GEORGE COOPER** in Dublin:

I remember when Irish was being introduced to the schools. That at that time it was not compulsory. There was a letter delivered to each parent asking them did they mind or would they allow the child to be taught Irish but that all changed.[161]

At the National Programme Conference of this same year, it was agreed that if a majority of parents objected to their children being taught Irish as a compulsory subject, then their wishes would be respected, but this never became government policy in practice.[162] From his encounter with Johnny Collins, **PATRICK GREENE** in south Longford believed that many revolutionaries had unrealistic hopes for the native language should independence ever be achieved.

Well, of course they had the mistaken idea that they were going to revive Irish in areas like this where it was dead for over a hundred years. And it just died out slowly. English took over. I say that there wasn't, there might have been Irish spoken around here maybe in the early 1800s. I did meet an old man who said that, ah, he was an old man eighty years ago and he said his father and mother spoke Irish when they didn't want the children to know what they were saying. That was the only

Irish that was left. He didn't know a word. I met one old woman who had, she was taught her prayers in Irish. Now she would have been born in the 1850s or '60s but she had them forgotten. She had a little bit of the 'Hail Mary' left that was all.[163]

In Cork, **GEORGE CARPENTER**, who would have been 13 years old at this point, enjoyed school, but was reminded of the loss of one particular subject, which he regretted very much, when I asked if his family would have been staunchly unionist.

Well, staunchly, not too staunchly. We still loved Ireland and we were told that we'd have to get on in Ireland, as it was our country and so on. And we had a good schooling but the unfortunate part about it. When the country changed, we had science class and science was stopped and it was very unfair to us because we had every type of equipment that was necessary for teaching science including the scales. And you couldn't touch the weight from the scales. You went out and used the forceps and we used make all our own temperature tubes you know with, put mercury into them to mark them up the side. We used make our own.[164]

Emphasis in primary schools, for example, was placed on the Irish language, history and culture. Science was omitted as a compulsory subject and became optional. This was also the case in many secondary schools.[165]

19 MARCH 1922

From March and April onward there were many open-air meetings around the country as Collins, de Valera and others tried to sell their particular take on the Treaty to the public. I asked **WILLIAM GEARY** if there were many of these open-air meetings held in Limerick city.

I do not know. Don't forget that I was twenty miles away from Limerick city. Our parish Ballyagran was on the border of County Cork. In fact we were, our land was only three fields away from the Cork border.[166]

On 19 March, de Valera spoke in Killarney and later in Tralee. He encountered no hostile opposition from the crowd on either occasion. **DAN KEATING** reiterated the atmosphere in the county at the time.

At the outset, with very few exceptions, the IRA stood by the anti-Treaty forces.[167]

26 MARCH 1922

Richard Mulcahy was Minister for Defence in the Dáil and had been confident that the IRA would remain loyal to the Provisional Government. His thinking was that IRA Volunteers would now join the new army of the Irish Free State. However, anti-Treaty IRA officers held an army convention in the Mansion House on this date and appointed an executive to be its supreme authority. Two days later, they issued a statement declaring that Mulcahy had no control over the IRA and called for an end to recruitment for the new Free State Army. Pro-Treaty IRA officers regarded this as an attempt to set up a military dictatorship, and a split occurred in the ranks of the IRA, dividing it into pro- and anti-Treaty sides.[168] They were sometimes known as 'Regulars' (pro-Treaty) and 'Irregulars' (anti-Treaty), although these terms were coined by the former. Both factions considered themselves republicans, although the term became more associated with the anti-Treaty side.

MICHAEL CASEY described the split as having 'ruined everything' but pointed out that it was a clear choice for him whom to support. He went on to say that neither he nor the majority of his comrades around Mitchelstown could accept the Treaty because 'it wasn't good enough at all'.[169] He and the men he knew were expecting a republic. Consequently, between 91 and 127 men are recorded as belonging to the anti-Treaty Mitchelstown Company for 1 July 1922. At the time of the Truce, it had a membership of between 82 and 121. The company now formed part of the 4th Battalion (Glanworth), Cork No. 2 Brigade.[170] **DANIEL O'DONOVAN** in Bantry also reached an important decision at this point.

> Well, the way it was, I had no part after the peace after the – what will I call it – the terms of peace were made. And after a while then when the split came, well, I took the side of Collins and so did my brother and the parties generally were split evenly half and half.[171]

He stressed that family loyalties and friendships were also important factors in shaping whether people accepted or rejected the Treaty.

> Well, it was chiefly those that were better known to me that I took the side of because I had lost all connection with them [the IRA] when the peace was set up. But a brother of mine did, he remained on as an officer until the split. Then he took the side of the Free State while the parties in general were split halfway and I followed the brother.[172]

Over the coming weeks and months, 47 men from the Bantry Company of the IRA, which had a membership of 206 on the date of the Truce, would join the Free State Army. Those who chose the anti-Treaty IRA side numbered 121. They formed part of the 4th Battalion, Cork No. 5 Brigade.[173]

> Well, we thought they were entitled to their own view but I think the way it was with all at that time on both sides, they followed the leader and if your leader was such or if someone belong to you was in one side, you followed him above the other. And as regards side, they didn't seem to matter so much at that particular time when the split came but we'd have much dearly loved if the peace had continued and that they had all continued to the end – that there was no split.[174]

At the time of the Treaty, Michael Collins emphasised that it was a stepping stone, maintaining that there could be an all-island republic eventually. Daniel O'Donovan was in agreement.

Well, I considered such could happen and probably the six counties mightn't be here today if the split didn't come because there might have been a settlement made at a later date. But the split made it more difficult to fall in with the north especially with those that remained separated from the movement at the time.[175]

Likewise, **JACK DUFF** supported the Treaty.

When the split came, I went with the pro-Treaty party – Collins and the rest of his men – and I fought with them and for that I have no apology to make from anybody. And I would do the same again tomorrow if I was fit and I was able to do it.[176]

26 March 1922 was also the date that Michael Collins visited Dungarvan, Co. Waterford, for a pro-Treaty meeting, and **PATRICK FITZGERALD** was in attendance to hear him speak from the back of a lorry that was being used as a platform. 'There's a big square in Dungarvan. It was there they had the truck.'[177] Along with Collins on the vehicle, he remembered a Dr White and a man named Brennock. According to Patrick, they came from Lismore and Cappoquin. He said a man named Wall from near Cappoquin was also on the truck. There was a big crowd, and Patrick recalled having a good view. 'I could hear them better that time than I could now.'[178] Many anti-Treaty people in the crowd started to shout and jeer when Collins and a man from Cappoquin got up to speak. Patrick thought the man from Cappoquin owned a meat stall. He also heard a priest that day retort that 'anyone of them that was shouting wasn't in an ambush at all'.[179]

Newspapers reported that trenches had been dug and trees knocked to keep Collins' motor party, which included Mr Kenny and Mr Milroy, out of Dungarvan that day, but they arrived shortly before 6.30 p.m. Collins was due to speak in the square from the back of this lorry, which had been obtained from a local firm. Patrick Fitzgerald was spot on regarding those on it with him, as they included Michael Brennock, Chairman of Dungarvan Urban District Council, Fathers Conway, Gleeson, Flavin and Rea, a woman and four journalists. Other people due to speak included Dr White, Mayor of Waterford, who arrived later. A crowd of over two thousand had assembled to hear them.[180]

What Patrick neglected to mention, however, was that as Mr Brennock was opening the speeches, the lorry began to move. Three young IRA men had jumped into the front seats and proceeded to drive it away at high speed through the crowd and over Bridge Street. People looked on in amazement, with some giving chase and others firing shots at the driver. One of those on the back of the moving vehicle then produced a revolver, broke the back window, and pointed it at the driver's head, ordering him to stop or he'd shoot. The driver and his two companions responded by jumping out with the lorry still going. It went over a bridge and was eventually halted on hitting an embankment, which led to several of those in the back being thrown off onto the road.[181]

Collins and the other speakers gathered themselves together before going back into Dungarvan and addressing their supporters from the balcony of the

Devonshire Arms Hotel. They continued to be heckled and jeered by a portion of the crowd regarding the Treaty and the ongoing atrocities against Catholics in the north. A shot was also fired. Collins asked the hecklers where they were 'when nine Black and Tans were holding Dungarvan'. 'They were under their beds,' someone else shouted. Rev. J. Rea, CC Abbeyside asked how many of the hecklers 'were in the Burgery Ambush'. Another man accused them of being 'post-Treaty republicans'. Collins referred briefly to what had happened regarding the lorry. The men who drove it away had never held up a Black and Tan, or if they did, what they had done that day was unworthy of them and he was sorry for them, he said. By this stage, Dr White had arrived and joined Collins and the other speakers on the balcony. Mr Seán Milroy also addressed the crowd.[182]

30 MARCH 1922

Having already met in January, James Craig and Michael Collins agreed to what became known as the Collins–Craig Pact. Its overall aim was to promote some kind of cooperation between northern and southern Ireland. It wasn't long before the pact broke down, partly due to the growing level of violence all over the north coupled with both leaders' apparent inability to deliver on what they had agreed. For example, Collins had apparently been unable to secure an end to IRA activities in the north and Craig had apparently failed to get expelled Catholic workers from the shipyards reinstated.[183] **PATRICK GREENE** remembered the attitude of the people he knew at the time towards having two parliaments in Ireland.

> Older people thought it was only a temporary thing. Craig himself said it could only be temporary and a country the size of Ireland couldn't remain divided for so long but of course at the same time he didn't want to have anything to, at that time you see a good strong majority in the north of Ireland and they had all the wealth and as the saying is, 'they had the ball at their foot'. And they could do what they liked. And they were England's faithful garrison at that time and England didn't want to disturb them.[184]

One account has it that between July 1920 and June 1922, as a result of the civil unrest and ongoing sectarian clashes between nationalist and loyalist groups, there were 455 people killed in Belfast (267 Catholics, 185 Protestants and 3 unascertained). Over 2,000 were wounded.[185] **JOHN PARKINSON**:

> There was a lot of scuffles and trouble here in the city – riots and that. As I told you, I lived in a mixed area in Belfast and it was very, very, very, very uneasy feeling for everybody, and there was a lot of bombs went off – explosions.[186]

Members of the British military were also shot, and **NORMAN DOUGLAS** had a vague recollection of one particular incident.

The only incident that I can recall was we had a Scottish Regiment based in some part of Belfast and one of the officers was shot dead on a Saturday night right in the heart of the city. And the story went that the soldiers of the regiment went on the rampage but what the rampage really involved I've no recollection at all.[187]

This was Lieutenant Edward S. Bruce of the Seaforth Highlanders, who had been shot dead on Friday 10 March in Albert Street. Dressed in civilian clothes at the time, he had been on his way to the War Hospital on the Grosvenor Road. Both loyalist and nationalist sides accused the other of killing him as great military activity occurred in its aftermath.[188]

Security along the border between the north and the Free State was very strict, and **ANTHONY MCGINLEY** remembered hearing talk of it.

Well, in the beginning surely, they were very particular. They sized you up terribly well and you could be searched if they had any suspicion at all.[189]

He said there were nationalist people who left the six counties to live in Donegal, but that 'a lot of them left the country altogether'. There were also loyalists from the county that travelled in the other direction, to take up residence outside of the Irish Free State.

There was a certain amount, not a big exodus but aye there was a brave crowd cleared out aye.[190]

John Parkinson echoed this.

Yes, there was a lot of movement. A lot of people came back again and a lot left. There was a lot of movement, yeah.[191]

GEORGE COOPER said his family in Dublin were not anxious about living as Protestants in the nationalist-dominated Irish Free State.

We weren't afraid you know what I mean. Well, we seen the numbers going down because as soon as the British soldiers went around well of course there was thousands gone you know, and their wives and their families were gone. That's the only thing you know. But we weren't afraid for to stay in the country or anything like that.[192]

He did point out, however, that some southern Protestants felt abandoned by the British at this time.

We were so-called loyalists in those days because we were living under the British rule for so long but then when it suited them, they just went off and anybody who was a loyalist could have been the target for to be killed. So, they didn't care.[193]

9 APRIL 1922

The new anti-Treaty IRA executive reassembled in the Mansion House and appointed a seven-strong army council with Liam Lynch as chief of staff.[194] Lynch did not want a Civil War and made strenuous efforts to maintain peace and avoid confrontation with former comrades. The hardline opponents of the Treaty sidelined de Valera and distrusted his alternative idea of external association. He was also criticised by pro-Treaty supporters for making inflammatory speeches. **DAN KEATING** was never a great fan of de Valera and believed that many republicans of the time held reservations about his character, including one particular high-profile figure that for years had a hostile relationship with Michael Collins.

> Well, de Valera was never seen with a gun after 1916. And while he captured the imagination of the public a lot of the older men that knew didn't regard him. Notably I suppose Cathal Brugha. Cathal Brugha never wanted him, he never liked him or he never liked Arthur Griffith. He always regarded Griffith as a rat, which he was of course.[195]

Brugha and de Valera were in fact close, and in a speech back on 7 January during the Dáil Treaty debates, Brugha had supported de Valera's Document No. 2 concept. In the same speech, he had dismissed Griffith as having won the war for England, singling him and Collins out as having been the weakest members of the Irish delegation to London.[196] On 26 April, he would accuse the pair of being British agents.[197]

13 APRIL 1922

The anti-Treaty IRA commanded by Rory O'Connor took over the Four Courts (the seat of legal administration) and other buildings in Dublin. They demanded the delay of the general election and the disbandment of the New Civic Guard, and declared that they refused to recognise the Provisional Government. In the weeks to come, **GEORGE COOPER** may have caught a glimpse of what some of those occupying the Four Courts were doing inside.

> In 1922 I was twelve years of age. I was doing messages during my summer holidays. I was working for a place called Domigan's, which is opposite the Four Courts when I was sent out with a message. I went over and I would see these fellows in civvie clothes drilling in the Four Courts before it went up.[198]

Initially, de Valera didn't agree with the behaviour of the anti-Treaty IRA, but later issued a statement requesting support for them. He then reported to his old battalion to enlist as a private.[199] Liam Lynch was also reluctant to give the occupation of the Four Courts his 100 per cent backing. Those inside had locked him out at this point, as they didn't view him as being extreme enough when he went against a motion calling for a resumption of the war with Britain. He didn't want a further split amongst the anti-Treaty faction.[200] Michael Collins, like Lynch, was anxious to avoid hostilities, and despite pressure from the British, he decided not to act against those in the Four Courts for the moment.

14 APRIL 1922

About this date (Good Friday), **PATRICK GREENE** arrived in Ballingeary in the late afternoon, having got a lift in a truck from Macroom Station. He remembered being awestricken by the beautiful mountains on the journey as the man driving the truck called out their names to him. The Co. Longford native had never seen real mountains before.[201] Patrick would go on to work on Johnny Twomey's farm in Tuairín Dubh and attend Coláiste na Mumhan, which had been established in 1903 by the Gaelic League as the first college for training teachers in Irish. Whilst in the area, Patrick would be addressed by his name in Irish – Pádraig Mac Gréine.

> From Easter till September I worked on the land there, picked up whatever Irish I could, went to the college. It opened, it ran for two months that year – July and August – and got a certificate.[202]

Some of the teachers at the college at the time included Tadhg Ó Scanláin, Eibhlín Ní Chroinín, Pádraig Ó Suibhne and Conchúr Ó Muineacháin.[203]

> The first thing I noticed in Ballingeary, the first Sunday I was at Mass that nobody was wearing a collar and tie. Most farmers went to Mass and they had a white shirt on with no collar and no tie. I got used to that though. I became the same myself. You had maybe, there might be a handful of people, local shopkeeper maybe or local teachers; they'd have a collar and tie on them but the ordinary man – a white shirt on a Sunday.[204]

The Irish language was thriving in the region.

> There was no English spoken in the house where I stayed. Irish was the everyday language of the people in the house and for most of the people or oldish or middle-aged people around about. Oh, *tá malairt scéil ann anois* [it's the opposite story there now]. You wouldn't hear, you'd rarely hear any Irish down there now.[205]

When Patrick arrived, a contingent of the British military were still present in the area but were in the process of preparing to leave.

> I remember on one occasion a British officer. He came in and he was giving out and the *bean an tí* never spoke a word of English to him and he had to walk away. He couldn't do anything about it.[206]

He observed how many of the local people made a living.

> Every Wednesday the people travelled down from the mountain down to the butter market – horse and cart, a slatted floor cart. We had

nothing like it here in the midlands, long heel sticks and the man sat in the front, the woman sat back. She had her big rolls of butter sitting in bases down in the butter market in the village. That was their way of living as well as sheep. Sheep weren't worth very much that time. They all had sheep on the mountain.[207]

In an article contained in the *Ballingeary Historical Society Journal 2000*, Patrick said he had been aware that he was in an area where there had been much activity during the Troubles of 1919–1921. There was a feeling when he came of things not being the same – a sort of a boil needing lancing. People were objecting to the Treaty but there weren't many rows about it. There was a meeting of local people in Twomey's, Tuairín Dubh, around a week after he arrived that was attended by Seán O'Hegarty, who travelled in a car from Cork. He had originally come to Ballingeary in 1914, after being served with an order by the British under the Defence Against the Realm Act to reside outside of Cork city. Returning to Ballingeary in 1916, he took charge of the local company at the time of the Rising in Dublin.[208] O'Hegarty later served as O/C of Cork No. 1 Brigade IRA. Patrick recalled a big talking session in the parlour at the meeting, where the crowd affirmed that they wouldn't accept the Treaty. Although also opposed to the Treaty himself, O'Hegarty said he'd never lift a gun against a fellow Irishman, and he left Ballingeary vowing to remain neutral in the event of a Civil War.[209] He subsequently attempted to mediate between the two sides. Patrick Greene never noticed the IRA training or drilling:

> No. I never saw them. They might be out parading the roads but I wouldn't have been out at night. I'd have my head stuck in a book.[210]

23 APRIL 1922

Collins spoke in Killarney on 22 April and in Tralee on the following day.[211] Roads were blocked and pro-Treaty supporters were prevented from entering the towns, but Collins still went on to address gatherings in both places. **DAN KEATING** recalled the period well.

> Collins even came to Tralee on a recruiting mission and he got twenty-four hours to leave with his troops and he did at the time but he did recruit a number particularly a couple from Kenmare which included the O'Connor brothers.[212]

Having originally come from the townland of Scarteen, Tom and John O'Connor were known as the O'Connor 'Scarteens'.[213]

> A number of Tralee men joined the Free State Army including Éamon Horan from Tralee, Cronin from Currans, Tom Slattery from Tralee, Bill Clifford from Tralee, Bailey from Tralee and Mulally from Tralee. There was a number of these they were known as the 'Dandy Six' because they dressed very well. But it must be said in fairness to the people that joined the army in Tralee they were not known to commit any atrocities

> and the man in charge, Brigadier Murphy who was in charge of the IRA
> in Kerry, he demanded that they be transferred some other where as
> they were only doing himself harm.[214]

By August, General W.R.E. Murphy, originally from Co. Wexford, would be O/C
of Free State forces in Kerry. He was constantly lobbying Richard Mulcahy to
commit additional troops to the county.[215]

> It must be said that there was a couple in Castleisland who were very
> different to them and they done immense harm to the IRA until they
> were got at.[216]

Humphrey Murphy was O/C of Kerry No. 1 Brigade IRA. Dan remembered the
day that he firmly aligned himself with the anti-Treaty forces rather than those
of the opposite persuasion. In fact, all three IRA brigades in Kerry were anti-
Treaty.[217]

> Well, all Kerry. Our unit in Farmer's Bridge were lined up and they were
> told that if any man wanted to join the anti-Treaty men he could. The
> fallout, there was no fallout in Farmer's Bridge, even though one man
> did join the army after but it was never known that he done any damage
> at all, this same man.[218]

Seventy-four men are listed as belonging to the anti-Treaty Farmer's Bridge 'F'
Company, 1st Battalion, Kerry No. 1 Brigade for 1 July 1922. When the Truce
occurred, the membership was 76.[219]

26 APRIL 1922

A former internee whom **PATSY HOLMES** had befriended in Ballykinlar Camp No.
1 was killed on a loyalist-owned farm at Ballygroman about ten miles from
Bandon.[220]

> And then you had Mick O'Neill. Mick was from [Kilbrittain], poor Mick
> was shot in Hornibrook's house.[221]

One account has it that O'Neill and three comrades had gone there in the early
hours to commandeer a car for IRA business but found it immobilised, with the
magneto missing. On knocking at the house door to get it, they were refused
admittance, but on entering through a window instead, O'Neill was shot as he
made his way up the stairs.[222] At the time, O'Neill, of the 1st Battalion, was
deputy commandant of the 3rd Cork Brigade.[223] Later that morning, Thomas
Hornibrook, his son Sam and son-in-law Herbert Woods (who admitted firing),
were driven away from Ballygroman house by a group of IRA men and never
seen again. The property was burned some time afterwards. Over the next four
nights, 10 local Protestants were shot in their homes in what became known as
the Dunmanway Massacre. Michael O'Neill's shooting may have been a catalyst,
but the killings may also have been in reprisal for Protestant attacks on

Catholics in the north. The names of the dead were Francis Fitzmaurice, David Gray, James Buttimer, John Chinnery, Robert Howe, Alexander Gerald McKinley, John Buttimer, James Greenfield, Robert Nagle and John Bradfield.[224]

It was around this time in Co. Galway that, with the RIC disbanded and the Black and Tans gone, Agnes Mary, widow of Frank Shawe-Taylor (killed over two years previously), was feeling ever more vulnerable in Moor Park House, Coshla. Ironically, she took the step of requesting that the local IRA protect her and her servants whilst sleeping there. Accordingly, **JOHN KELLY'S** brother Michael and Matt Ruane were detailed to guard her there at night.[225] In April 1922, she and her two sons were awarded £15,000 in compensation for her husband's death by Mr Justice Moore on an appeal from a decision of the recorder of Galway dismissing the application made under the Malicious Injuries Act 1919. It was submitted that the case came under the Act in 1920.[226]

Despite the IRA protection, Mrs Shaw-Taylor claimed she nevertheless remained the subject of intimidation, and so on the advice of friends left the property to take up residence near Dublin. By May 1922, Moor Park House was empty except for the presence of a servant.[227] Early one morning in June 1922, it was occupied by the anti-Treaty IRA, whose forces included John Kelly's brother Michael. He was engaged in taking arms, blocking roads and carrying out all orders from his officers.[228]

KATHLEEN CHARLES, having taught for a period in Mullingar but by now back in her native Kanturk, was fortunate, as between April and June 1922 the Mullingar area also experienced a sharp increase in violence, intimidation and destruction of property against Protestants. Again, the reasons are complex, but some were carried out in response to loyalist attacks on Catholics in the north. Several mansions in the area were targeted and burned.[229]

2 MAY 1922

After it was suggested to him by a neighbour, **WILLIAM GEARY** made up his mind to join the Civic Guard (An Garda Síochána).

> I was home you know after coming out as a wireless operator and one day, now wait till I tell you this much. In Ballyagran, Cloonee it was a mansion but we had no electrical lighting and we had no pump or nothing. Now we had to get the water. We had to go about a field away to a place called Ellen's Well. So one day somebody told me to go down and get a bucket of water so I went down to the well. It was at the end of the field at the corner of the field near the road and Jim Walsh and his wife Ellen lived there. But all the other people around the neighbourhood used get their water there too – never failing. It was in the early spring of 1919, no 1922. Yeah, 1922.
>
> And James, he had a garden there about half an acre and he was digging it for early potatoes, and I went over and talked to him. I was no hurry anyway and we got talking. Now James knew me from when I was a child. In fact, he never actually worked in the place but he used to dig drains on what they call patchwork, paid by the length of the drain

he dug. And he said to me, 'Why don't you join the Garda Síochána?' I thought it a good idea. I never thought much about it before.

Now to join the Garda Síochána all you needed was, you had to be five feet nine, you had to be a member of the IRA and you had to have a letter from your local parish priest. So I got a letter from my parish priest John Cannon Reeves and I got a letter from my captain John Bresnihan and I made application to the Garda Síochána. And I joined the Garda Síochána on the 2nd of May 1922, Newbridge, Co. Kildare … To get there I took a bicycle from Ballyagran … I rode a bicycle from the house to Charleville and then took the train from Charleville to Newbridge.[230]

William recalled there being men from almost every county in Ireland eager to join the Civic Guard.

In fact, the man after me, my number was 938 and the man after me was a man by the name of Tom Curran. He was from Kerry and two men from Clare, all over.[231]

In fact, the force had a strength of about 1,500 members by the middle of May, and 28 per cent of these came from the counties of Clare, Galway and Limerick.[232]

7 MAY 1922

Having already served with a group connected to the army called the Reserve, **JACK DUFF** quit his job as a clerk with the Dublin United Tramways Company (DUTC) and joined the Free State forces on what he described as a full-time basis. He enlisted at 3rd Battalion HQ, Brunswick Street, Dublin, under the classification of a Reserve.[233]

I wanted to join the army because I wanted to be a soldier. That was the one and only reason. I was interested in military affairs at the time and I just wanted to be a soldier. And I joined the army on the 7th of May 1922.[234]

This date is in all likelihood accurate, although it's worth noting that the Military Census taken in late 1922 actually records his date of attestation as being one month later on 7 June, and to add further confusion his service record gives 14 July as his date of enlistment.[235] The dates of army enlistments are problematic, as it depended on how quickly the pay office was notified of new recruits. Inaccuracies and omissions in files were commonplace, especially once the Civil War started, as administration struggled to catch up with the situation on the ground.[236]

However, the date one joined the army was important in terms of classification. For example, it would transpire that any man who enlisted after 28 June 1922 came within the terms of the Government Reserve Scheme and was classed as a Volunteer Reserve. A quota was allotted to each area, and when this was filled, recruiting ceased. The term of service for such men was six months. However, depending on the Civil War situation, service could either be cut short or renewed for a further six-month period.[237] These terms and conditions did not apply to men who were attested into the regular army before 28 June 1922.

In any event, Jack would be based at Wellington Barracks, which had been taken over a short time previously. He was familiar with the barracks from his time in the reserves, as he and his comrades used to meet at Leonard's Corner and march in there to do their training. Interestingly, it was his neighbour Tom Scully, who had denied him membership of the IRA during the 1919–1921 campaign, that conducted the training for the reserves before Jack joined the army full-time. Scully had himself joined the army following the split.[238] Rifles were borrowed from the Dublin Guard and Scully would teach Jack and the others how to load, unload, aim and fire them. They also did foot drill roughly three nights a week.[239]

Ironically, Tom Scully had been eager to bring Jack and others from the reserve into the Free State Army full-time. Jack was working for the DUTC, but when Scully put the proposition to him, he accepted right away. He and the other new recruits used to sleep at home but would be in the barracks all day.[240] Jack's home was at No. 3 Baggot Court, Lower Baggot Street. They did not have army uniforms at this point.

At the time, when someone such as Jack joined the army that hadn't previously been in the IRA, they were referred to as a 'Truce Recruit'. A similar tag was placed on new recruits to the anti-Treaty forces. To reiterate, from this point forward many companies that declared themselves anti-Treaty were made up of certain personnel that hadn't previously been members of the IRA during the recent conflict, or if they had been, had transferred from other companies. Therefore, if IRA membership figures for 1 July 1922 appear broadly similar to those recorded for the date of the Truce a year earlier, it is sometimes because men that declared themselves neutral or pro-Treaty were replaced by this influx.

15 MAY 1922

Many ex-RIC members who joined the new Civic Guard were given positions of high authority by Commissioner Michael Staines. Michael Collins had supported their appointments, maintaining that these particular RIC men had put their own lives at risk to play an undercover role for the republicans during the War for Independence. This information, however, was not common knowledge to the new recruits at headquarters in Kildare town. They had no issue with ex-RIC members joining the new force, but did object to them being given commissions within it.[241] For example, they noticed that ex-RIC occupied virtually every rank above that of sergeant. This rested uneasy with the recruits, who had fought against them in the IRA up to the Truce. They didn't want to be governed, trained or ordered around by men who, in their view, were trying to model the new force on the old one, which they detested.[242]

Things came to a head on 15 May, after it was announced that five more RIC men had been promoted. Some recruits formed a committee and sent a written ultimatum to Staines demanding the removal from high rank of former members of the RIC. Staines summoned a parade, read out the names of the signatories and ordered them to fall out. Then he asked for those loyal to him to stand on the other side, but only a handful of the 1,500 moved. The event became known as the Kildare Mutiny, and Staines headed for Dublin to inform the government of the situation. The committee had assured him that they were loyal to the Provisional Government and were not going to join the anti-Treaty forces. They were adamant, however, that their demand be met. Although this happened at the depot in Kildare town, it did spill over into Newbridge military barracks, which was also being used as a training depot for the Civic Guard. **WILLIAM GEARY** was based there and recalled that during the mutiny some members of the force were brandishing guns in a menacing fashion.

> When I joined the Garda Síochána in 1922, there was talk of a rebellion in the place. I found no evidence whatsoever. It seemed perfectly serene to me. I was paid regularly; the food was good and I spent most of my time roaming around the barracks checking it out because it was an artillery barracks – British artillery. And I used go look at the stables and the rest of it. The only thing that happened was there was a big meeting in the parade ground and certain guys denounced the Irish government for giving jobs to members of the Royal Irish Constabulary, to the detriment of IRA men. And with me up there, some of them just come off the field and some of them had their guns. You know, they had their guns.[243]

The government regarded the recruits in Kildare and Newbridge as mutineers and adopted a policy of isolation and deprivation.[244] Pay was cut and supplies were halted. Kildare depot was home to a large arsenal of weapons, and Staines feared that it might find its way into the arms of the anti-Treaty forces. Free State troops were sent from Dublin to collect the arms, but the mutineers denied them access. Staines was given a similar reception when he visited in early June. The mutineers decided to run the depot like nothing had happened and appointed a new commissioner. Armed sentries were also placed on patrol. Staines set up a rival headquarters in Dublin, and for a two-month period the Civic Guard was divided into two rival groups, both accepting new recruits. Attempts at reconciliation between the recruits' committee and the Provisional Government always broke down, and Collins visited Kildare on a number of occasions. On 17 June, the small anti-Treaty element within Kildare left the barracks and met up with Rory O'Connor – commanding officer of the Four Courts garrison – and a number of his comrades. They returned and facilitated O'Connor and his men to enter Kildare barracks in a number of lorries in order to take all the weapons. They then sped back to the Four Courts.[245]

This incident was the catalyst that saw Collins agree terms with the mutineers to bring the saga to an end. He outlined that an enquiry would be set up to look at the causes of their discontent; they would be paid the money owed to them and in the meantime all men were to be suspended.[246] The Kildare Mutiny had lasted for six weeks, and existing without money or supplies had demoralised many of the recruits. Pay arrived three days after the weapons were taken, and the recruits started drinking and enjoying themselves whilst armed. The following comes directly from memoirs, typed and signed by William Geary, and concern his experiences in Newbridge Barracks around the time of the Mutiny.

> One day, a company of recruits (me included), led by a Sergeant Kierce a Clareman, marched out of the barracks, through the town for about two miles into the country, a good training exercise. Most of the time I spent exploring the barracks, formerly occupied by a British Artillery Regiment. No lectures or drill. There was one very distressing occurrence. Two recruits, McKenna and Liddy from County Leitrim, inseparable, out on the town one evening after curfew, in attempting to scale the wire fence, McKenna's revolver discharged accidentally, the bullets hitting Liddy in the stomach killing him. I still have the pair in my mind's eye, but apart from the accident that is all I know. [247]

The *Cork Examiner* reports that just before midnight on 20 June Liddy received a bullet wound to the heart close to the centre of Main Street in Newbridge. A second member of the force was injured in the head. A large number of members of the Civic Guard and of the public were on the streets at the time, as it was race week at the Curragh. Local IRA members rushed to the scene after some shooting was heard to find Liddy bleeding profusely. They conveyed him to a local doctor, but he died shortly afterwards in hospital.[248]

While these details differ somewhat from William's account, there is no doubt that both recruits involved in the incident were from Co. Leitrim. Their names and numbers were Farrell Liddy (463) and Michael McKenna (466). Both men had been off duty but in a licensed premises in Newbridge after breaking curfew in the barracks. Two other men named Quinn and Macken had also broken curfew.[249] The publican described them as being in a 'partly jolly' but sober state on leaving. McKenna claimed that just before midnight, whilst on their way back to the barracks, he saw what appeared to be suspicious groups of men and drew his revolver from his pocket. It went off suddenly, fatally injuring his friend. The verdict at the subsequent inquest was that Liddy died from '*shock and haemorrhage caused by a gunshot wound accidently fired by Michael McKenna.*'[250] Assistant Commissioner Brennan reported that his comrades had no money to pay the funeral expenses owing to the non-payment of wages during the mutiny.[251] Liddy was buried in his native Leitrim.[252]

In the weeks after the mutiny, the recruits remained in the Kildare and Newbridge depots. They had been paid but were suspended from duty. The enquiry began work on 13 July and made a number of recommendations. One of these was that politicians should not serve in the force. As a result, Michael Staines TD tendered his resignation as commissioner of the Civic Guard and would leave office on 18 August. It was also largely because of the mutiny that the Civic Guard were to become an unarmed police force. Most suspended recruits were accepted back into the force, although the issue pertaining to high-rank RIC men, which had been at the centre of the mutiny, was barely addressed. Most of them kept their positions, but in the years afterwards, few ex-RIC men were recruited into the force. The enquiry concluded that the issue of high-rank RIC men was largely a red herring devised by anti-Treaty sympathisers within the Civic Guard to throw the force into turmoil in order to assist their agenda. They based this on the fact that during the mutiny ex-RIC members were given positions of high rank when they ran Kildare barracks on their terms.[253]

17 MAY 1922

An unfortunate neighbour of **JOHN PARKINSON'S** in Belfast found herself on the receiving end of some bullets that passed through the front window of her home. She was trimming a hat at the time.

> I knew one girl in particular called Brown and she was hit by a sniper's bullet in the spine and she was paralysed and had to live the rest of her life and go about in a wheelchair. I always remember that very sad case.[254]

This was 21-year-old Emily Brown of No. 172 on the Grosvenor Road, who was hit in the abdomen and leg by shots fired from McDonnell Street towards the Grosvenor Road at 9.40 p.m. She was taken to the Royal Victoria Hospital. Her brothers, Billy and Jim, were good friend of John's.[255] Emily Brown's shooting occurred on the worst day of firing the city had seen for many months, with many civilians being targeted by both loyalists and republicans. Some of the casualties from other districts on the day included Robert Dudgeon (19), 34 Westland Street, and Nellie McMullan (28), 8 Keegan Street, who were killed, while Maggie Hanley (23), 24 Lagan Street, Eddie Barrow (28), and Ernest Callender, 3 Fairview Street, were wounded.[256]

22 MAY 1922

SEÁN CLANCY joined the Free State Army in Portobello Barracks, Rathmines, becoming part of the staff in the Accounts & Records Unit. The unit also looked after enlistments. Portobello Barracks was part of the 2nd Eastern Division Eastern Command. The officer commanding Seán's unit was Commandant Colgan, while the area commander was Commandant-General Ennis. Seán, whose army number was 31968, remarked that he encountered no hostility from friends or family upon taking this action to join.[257]

> No, no, my family went pro-Treaty at home of course and most of my friends did too. So that there was no, in Clare especially, there were no prejudice or no bitterness – not much anyhow as regards the Treaty.[258]

Seán joined the army from 'B' Company, 2nd Battalion, Dublin No. 1 Brigade, which had a membership of 126 at the onset of the Truce the previous July. Just 21 joined the anti-Treaty IRA, whilst 61 joined the army.[259]

Regarding his own particular take on the political situation, **PATRICK FITZGERALD** in Dunmoon said that as 'soon as the Treaty was signed, that finished me with it'.[260] He left the IRA and took no part in anything else, declaring that the impending Civil War 'was no help to take the country into anything good'. He thought Michael Collins was 'a great man' and that Éamon de Valera 'made a bad job of it', as 'he divided the people [and] then you had a Civil War'. He recalled some of his IRA comrades in the Kilwatermoy Company being divided as regards the Treaty: 'Some thought it would do harm, more thought it would do good.' In fact, there were nine men from the company who took the anti-Treaty side in July 1922, by which time the Kilwatermoy Company was in the 5th Battalion, Cork No. 2 Brigade, 1st Southern Division.[261] There had been 28 members in the company by the Truce of July 1921.[262] Patrick regretted that a republic hadn't been achieved, but supported the agreement, maintaining that it gave the country more than it had before. He said he never considered joining the Free State Army.[263]

26 MAY 1922

JOHN PARKINSON was affected by the sectarian troubles when his school was burned down by the IRA. It had already been attacked on two previous occasions, but this time bombs were used, the first exploding at roughly 8 p.m. to ensure total destruction.[264] John, who had transferred to the school aged 12 in 1919, watched it burn from the front door of his house in Distillery Street.[265]

> One of the things I had to be careful about, very careful about, I finished my schooling in a school called the Belfast Boys' Model School and my sister she also went to the Girls' Model School. It was a special school and it was actually based in the lower part of the Falls Road in Divis Street and we lived on the Grosvenor Road. And my sister and I had to walk from the Grosvenor Road over to Divis Street to that school each day and we had to get, the police were at the corners and all just watching that there was no interference. But it was a very risky business.[266]

This was down to sectarian tensions.

> As Protestants, the school was an all, well it wasn't all Protestant. One of my teachers was a Roman Catholic – a man I can remember well called O'Sullivan but there were some Roman Catholics went to it but not many. It was largely Protestant.[267]

It was a tough school where pupils were expected to work hard; there was also liberal use of the cane. The headmaster was nicknamed 'Waxy' Haslett because of his distinctive moustache, while other teachers included Mr Neilly from Newtownards and Mr Young. One of John's classmates was Ivan Graham, who lived in the Donegall Road area of the city.[268]

> It was a well-known school and it was situated right in the heart of the Falls Road.[269]

With the school building burned, alternative accommodation for its pupils was acquired on the Cliftonville Road in Belfast. John wanted to work rather than attend school, and his father agreed providing he continued his studies at night school. So, at the age of 15 he started work as a message boy in the offices of the shipbuilding firm Harland & Wolff.[270] His apprenticeship as a joiner could not begin until he was 16.

> Well, my father as I told you worked in the shipyard as a joiner and I wanted to do the same as my Dad and I went and I worked in the shipyard as a joiner, served my apprenticeship for five years and then I stayed on for another five years. Then I qualified, went to the technical college in the evenings and I qualified and I became a teacher and I left the shipyard and went into technical college and served as a teacher for thirty-something years until I retired.[271]

John's father, Frank, passed away in November 1923.[272]

I JUNE 1922

The Royal Ulster Constabulary (RUC) officially came into existence. **NORMAN DOUGLAS** remembered seeing them for the first time around Belfast.

> They carried guns and they patrolled in tenders as caged tops just the same as the military too. But it was a very dangerous sort of livelihood for the RUC at that particular time because the troubles were at their height and they were launched into it with the British army. And my recollection was that there were a lot of casualties and a lot of shootings and nonsense going on which was a very unfortunate time for a young person like me anyhow.[273]

The RUC had a strength of 3,000 officers across the six counties and was backed up by the Ulster Special Constabulary, which had already existed as a volunteer body of part-time auxiliary police since September 1920. The Ulster Special Constabulary also had its own command, administrative and training structure distinct from the RUC. The headquarters of the RUC was established at Atlantic Buildings, Waring Street, Belfast, and Charles Wickham was appointed the force's first inspector general. In the period from 1 June 1922 to 31 December 1923, 10 members of the Ulster Special Constabulary were killed (comprising six by IRA action, the rest by a mixture of mistake or accident). The first incident of a member of the RUC being killed by the IRA was not until 1933. The RUC member was a Catholic from Co. Tipperary named John Ryan.[274]

2 JUNE 1922

GEORGE COOPER'S eldest sister, Harriet Maud Victoria, married Corporal Baden Percy Lawrence of the 2nd Battalion, Welsh Regiment, in a Dublin registry office. The couple's residence at the time of marriage was recorded as No. 36 Holles Street.[275] The Cooper family lived in No. 26. George said that although his were perceived to have been a loyalist family, they enjoyed a good relationship with most of their neighbours. Certain things, however, were not tolerated.

But previously you were saying about people in Holles Street you know and there were a lot of republicans, IRA men we knew. I mean you could tell who they were you know. And as I say we had connections with the British soldiers, my sister was married to one and sometimes on the 11th of November we'd hang a flag out and there were a lot of people tried to burn it at that time. But we knew, but the only thing was that we were accepted.[276]

11 JUNE 1922

Having arrived by motor car, Éamon de Valera was one of a number of speakers to address a large crowd in the square in Kanturk ahead of the forthcoming general election.[277] However, this was not his first visit to the town. In late August 1921, preparations had been made in Co. Cork for a tour of inspection by President de Valera where he came to visit some of the ambush sites and to inspect IRA companies. The tour began in Cork city and took in 20 centres, including Kanturk.[278] Even earlier, following his election as president of the Sinn Féin party and leader of the Volunteers in 1917, he had ventured to Cork on a tour. Therefore, it was probably on one of these occasions that Cumann na mBan members **KATHLEEN CHARLES** and her mother met him.

De Valera came to town one day and out in a field he was inspecting a battalion of IRA. And we were told to meet him there in the field and present him with a bunch of flowers – my mother and I.[279]

16 JUNE 1922

A general election was held in the twenty-six counties to act as a referendum on the Treaty. The Irish people voted on whether to accept or reject the decision of Dáil Éireann. From 128 seats in total, pro-Treaty Sinn Féin got 58; anti-Treaty Sinn Féin 36; Labour Party 17; Farmers' Party 7; and Independents 10.[280] The people had voted in favour and the pro-Treaty side felt they had a clear mandate, as **SEÁN CLANCY** explained.

The proof is there of course at elections that took place after the Treaty. Dublin gave a vast majority I think to the pro-Treaty government, so did most of the counties of Ireland so that there was no justification for the Civil War. It was the most unnecessary war that was ever fought I think. Because they have no justification for it and it should never have happened.[281]

Militant republicans felt that with democratic avenues explored, the only course open to them was a resort to arms. **JACK DUFF** commented on the choice they decided to take.

Well, the only charitable thing you can say about them is that they acted according to, they acted according to the dictates of their own conscience and they done what they considered to be right, in the same way as we considered ourselves to be doing right on the other side.[282]

At this stage, **DAN KEATING** was part of an IRA unit – which included Tommy Barton from Ballyroe and Paddy Buckley (ex-RIC) – that had occupied Ballymullen Barracks in Tralee in order to secure it for anti-Treaty forces.[283] He was prepared to take up arms against the Treaty.

> Well, of course we were against it. Kerry was against it at all times, all of them. The south were very much against it. It was accepted in the Dublin and the midlands you know and they had the majority of course you know. And there's no doubt, you need only look at what's happening today, it was a disaster you know. And at the time they had only to hold out for another bit and they'd get the whole lot of it [a republic] because after Crossbarry the British wanted to get out and they wanted to make peace someway in the world.[284]

He dismissed the pro-Treaty argument that the Treaty was a stepping stone, as under its terms part of the north in addition to three ports based in the south were in the hands of the British.

> Well, I mean the stepping stone as they called it now. That was very, I don't know, the people that said it, I don't think they believed it you know. Because what they done in effect was that you handed over part of your country to a foreign country.[285]

Both sides felt that they were absolutely in the right, and the issue of whether to accept or reject the Treaty became so divisive that in many cases families found themselves at odds with each other.

22 JUNE 1922

Sir Henry Wilson was shot dead in London by the IRA. He had been chief of the Imperial General Staff until February 1922, after which he had acted as military adviser to the Northern Ireland government. He came from Currygran near Ballinalee in Co. Longford, and at the time of his death was a Conservative MP for North Down.[286] **PATRICK GREENE**, resident in Ballinalee when interviewed, knew an old farmer locally named Micky Callaghan who maintained that before he gained notoriety for his hardline unionism at this time, Henry Wilson was regarded as a gentleman and that it was his brother Jimmy who was the more disliked of the two of them.[287]

> Henry Wilson was a native of this parish. Sir Henry Wilson – chief of the General Staff, First World War.[288]

Wilson's murder outraged the British public, and Lloyd George came to the conclusion that the anti-Treaty IRA garrison in the Four Courts had ordered it, as they had declared their intention to attack British forces in the north so as to restart the war. He demanded that either the Provisional Government take action against the IRA or he would. The Provisional Government claimed it would not attack the Four Courts because of a British threat, and it wasn't until

Free State Deputy Chief of Staff J.J. Ginger O'Connell was abducted on 26 June by a Four Courts garrison that Collins decided to take action. He saw little option if the government was to carry out its duties, having been elected by the people. O'Connell had been abducted in reprisal for the imprisonment of IRA man Leo Henderson by the army.[289]

CHAPTER 7
A terrible war,
June 1922 – May 1923

28 JUNE 1922

Shortly after 4 a.m., and using artillery supplied by the British, pro-Treaty troops directed fire at the Four Courts after those inside refused to evacuate and surrender. The Civil War was under way in a military sense, although outbreaks of trouble had been commonplace since the vote in the Dáil on 7 January to accept the Treaty. **SEÁN CLANCY**, who was based in Portobello Barracks, did not participate in the attack on the Four Courts, but **JACK DUFF**, who was based in Wellington Barracks, did.

The night before the attack, he was in company headquarters in Great Brunswick Street with four other army men – Hancock, Birch, Tom Scully and Paddy Conlon – in what was an old British army recruitment office under the charge of Conlon. After catching some sleep in the recruitment office, they walked a few doors away to a garage known as Thompson's Garage, which contained a Lancia armoured car. There, Jack and Birch were ordered to get in.[1] They drove to Winetavern Street, where Jack observed that the guns were already in position to attack the Four Courts. When the bombardment started, Jack, Birch and other soldiers were positioned down near the end of Winetavern Street. Their job was to shoot at the windows of the Four Courts so that their comrades manning the larger guns would be covered by their fire.[2] Jack was armed with a Lee-Enfield rifle. There was also a Lewis machine gun, but Jack didn't know how to use it.[3]

Regarding the whole Four Courts manoeuvre, opinion was divided among army members and pro-Treaty individuals whom Jack knew at the time. 'Some said it was the right thing to do; others said it wasn't.'[4] When I asked him how well he knew Emmet Dalton, who was the army's director of operations, the answer was: 'Heard of him, never met him.'[5]

29 JUNE 1922

Liam Lynch set up headquarters in Limerick and took over as chief of staff of united anti-Treaty forces after they patched up their differences. He called on all anti-Treaty forces to rally against those of the Free State. The same day, republicans occupied Mitchelstown Castle – the largest Gothic house in Ireland – when shortly after 6 p.m. about 60 men led by Commandant P.J. Luddy entered the premises and ordered the castle's Anglo-Irish owner, William Downes Webber (see 15 May 1903), his niece Edith Webber, nephew Arthur

Webber, some guests and the servants to leave immediately.[6] The family refused, however, because of the hour of the evening, leaving instead the following day to be put up by friends. They spent that night gathering up personal possessions and storing others away, as Luddy would only allow them to leave with small items rather than furniture or paintings.

Over the next few days, the republicans got to work digging trenches, laying mines and erecting barbed wire around key parts of the estate. They also placed sentries at all gates and entrances. Furniture and other objects from the castle were used to block the windows and bar entry to the castle grounds. Webber's car was also commandeered for Luddy's use, and the republicans flew a flag from the castle tower. Webber family members were allowed to visit the castle on a number of occasions, though not without prior written permission from Luddy.[7] In the weeks to come, massive looting took place and, as the Civil War progressed, the number of republicans in the castle increased. Reports at the time suggested that at the height of the occupation there were over 2,000 anti-Treaty IRA in the castle, but **MICHAEL CASEY**, who claimed he 'took only very little' part in the Civil War, refuted this.[8]

> I was inside in the castle in Mitchelstown, you know. I'd go in there during the day maybe and things like that.[9]

Michael said he 'did nothing at all only fool around' when inside the castle.[10]

> There were a big crowd there you know. They were saying there were thousands there but a fellow came here to me. Says I, there were only hundreds there, says I. A couple of hundred you know. Couple of hundred was a big crowd inside in a house, in a castle or anywhere.[11]

Michael was slow to give much information away but conceded that the occupation could be summed up as a protest against the Treaty. Elsewhere in Mitchelstown, republicans occupied the old RIC barracks, the workhouse and the military barracks.

30 JUNE 1922

The anti-Treaty garrison surrendered, and Rory O'Connor and Ernie O'Malley led 180 survivors out of the burning Four Courts. They were arrested and taken to Mountjoy Gaol as well as other jails around the city. In addition to civilian fatalities, three anti-Treaty IRA Volunteers had been killed and eight wounded in the battle for the Four Courts. Seven members of the army were killed and over seventy wounded, largely as a result of mines that exploded and the storming of the building.[12] Some of the republicans had managed to evade capture and went off to join comrades who had occupied other buildings in the capital. **JACK DUFF** and his army colleagues were soon on their trail.

> I fought at the Four Courts. After the Four Courts I went on night-post in Dublin. I returned to Griffith Barracks, what we know now as Griffith Barracks, it was Wellington Barracks then, up on the South Circular

Road there. And the army was being formed up there in Dublin. The army was being formed in one of the barracks up there to be formed up and ... I done guards and patrol duties around the city.[13]

Jack was sent with a number of others from Wellington Barracks to Beggars Bush Barracks, where Commandant Tom Ennis was O/C of Intelligence. He ordered those who lived in the vicinity and knew the capital well to go out, keep their ear to the ground, eye up any unusual activity and search for any other buildings that might be occupied by anti-Treaty forces. They ventured out dressed in civvies. Jack, who lived in Baggot Court, was assigned a district he knew well, taking him down the canal, into Percy Place, Haddington Road and Baggot Street into Fitzwilliam Place. When he had it all monitored, he reported back to Commandant Ennis. Within a short time, he found himself back at Wellington Barracks, where he observed 'red raw recruits' being brought into the army, most of whom had never handled a weapon in their lives. When two companies named Dublin No. 1 and Dublin No. 2 were hastily assembled, he was made a corporal and assigned to Dublin No. 1 on the basis that he had already amassed more experience than many within their ranks.[14]

> On the day following the Four Courts being shelled I went to the Curragh Camp. I was sent to the Curragh Camp. It wasn't a question of I went there, I was sent there. I was sent to the Curragh Camp. There we got a uniform – full uniform out.[15]

Spending roughly two days on the Curragh with his comrades, Jack was placed on guard duty at a place called the Eastern Expense Stores, located down at the very far end of the camp. He didn't know where the name originated from except that it was a huge store full of materials the British had left behind.[16]

1 JULY 1922

Listowel and Skibbereen were the only two posts in south Munster in pro-Treaty hands. Kerry No. 1 and No. 2 Brigades joined forces and attacked the Free State soldiers billeted in a workhouse in Listowel. They killed a Private Edward Sheehy before the ultimate surrender of the remainder of the soldiers on 1 July.[17] **DAN KEATING** had left Ballymullan Barracks with a number of others and was part of the anti-Treaty IRA that occupied Listowel before moving on to Limerick.

> Well, during the Civil War we happened to be based in Tralee and when the trouble broke out the IRA, they took over Listowel, which was occupied by the Free State Army under Tom Kennelly. Kennelly you'd have to say was a good Irishman and he didn't want any bloodshed between two different sides in the trouble. And on our way up anyway every place they captured. They [IRA] captured Listowel and right into Limerick, they got into Limerick.[18]

MARGARET CAHILL from Ballinasare wrote that she continued to serve as a member of Lispole Cumann na mBan attached to 'C' Company, 5th Battalion,

Kerry No. 1 Brigade right through until 1923, having joined in 1920.[19] The membership list for Lispole branch, which records the names of 12 women as having served up to the date of the Truce, lists only 4 members as having stood by the anti-Treaty forces from 1 July 1922. Margaret's name is among those crossed out, but many of these membership lists are of dubious reliability. For example, the name of Bridget Fitzgerald (sister of Maurice Fitzgerald who was killed in the Lispole Ambush of 22 March 1921) is also crossed out for Civil War service, even though she was also active with Lispole Cumann na mBan until 1923, having joined in 1918.[20] Incidentally, Siobhán Fitzgerald, Captain of Lispole Cumann na mBan, and her brother James, O/C Lispole Company IRA, both went anti-Treaty, as did Margaret Cahill's brother Michael.[21]

4 JULY 1922

Skibbereen was captured by men from Cork No. 3 Brigade. They were led by Commandant Gibbs Ross, and the republicans were to control the town for one month before retreating. Staying in Co. Cork, **PATRICK GREENE** discussed Ballingeary and the people who visited the area both before and after the start of the Civil War.

> Ballingeary was full of curious people at that time. All sorts of people came and went there. You never know who you met. You met some of the higher executives of the IRA. The Civil War was on the boil at the time, it was just starting and the house I stayed in they were anti-Treaty. But at that time being anti-Treaty didn't mean affect their friendship for people. The week after Easter Mrs Tom Clarke and her boys, two boys I think and her sister came on a visit there and they left and the week they left John Collins' sister, Mrs Powell, came with a cousin and they stayed there. And you met various sorts of people there. I remember the, oh, what was her? Lord Listowel's sister calling there one day – an old lady riding a bicycle with a big long skirt and a bonnet and cape. The honourable Albina Broderick, she was a friend to the people, the house I stayed in.[22]

Albina Broderick was a sister to William St John Broderick, who was the 1st Earl of Midleton and leader of the southern unionists. Politically, they couldn't have been further apart, as she herself was a committed republican and Gaelicised her name to Gobnait Ní Bruadair.[23]

> When the Civil War started the place was a regular barracks. All-important people from Cork city who were anti-Treaty were out there – businessmen, doctors, Paddy O'Keeffe who was a great friend of mine afterwards – secretary to the GAA park in Cork called after him 'Páirc Uí Chaoimh'. His wife, his children I knew them all down the years. It was a conglomeration of various forms of idealism and they all mixed together and they were on the best of terms. They didn't quarrel.[24]

Liam Lynch was another who used also visit Ballyvourney/Ballingeary.

No, never saw Lynch but all the Cork, the Cork people who came out, they all stayed in Tuairín Dubh. We all, men there who were going to the college, we all slept outside in a loft outside known as the Lochta Fada – it held six beds. And during the Civil War it could be full of boxes of Mills bombs or ammunition or rifles or machine guns and all that sort of thing. The following year that was all gone. The place, the Civil War was over although the feelings were still running high.[25]

Patrick claimed never to have been a member of the volunteers (see 4 February 1917). Interestingly, though he is listed as a member of anti-Treaty Ballingeary No. 4 Section, D Company, 8th Battalion, Cork No. 1 Brigade on the Military Archives IRA Membership Series for 1 July 1922, he is also recorded as having been a member of the company up to 11 July 1921. There is obviously a mistake here, however, as he only came to Ballingeary in Easter the following year. The lists were drawn up in 1935 so must be taken with a grain of salt, but perhaps he did serve or was perceived to have served with the local anti-Treaty IRA for the few months he was in the area, as many of his friends and associates were in it. Incidentally, one set of figures points to Ballingeary 'D' Company, 8th Battalion, Cork No. 1 Brigade, 1st Southern Division as having 126 members on the date of the Truce and a strength of 125 when it went anti-Treaty.[26]

5 JULY 1922

The fighting in the centre of Dublin lasted until this date. Republicans had been dislodged from other buildings they had occupied around the capital, including the Granville Hotel, where Éamon de Valera and Cathal Brugha were based. De Valera managed to escape, but Brugha was cut down by rifle fire as he emerged from the burning Granville Hotel refusing to surrender.[27] He died in hospital two days later on 7 July. **JACK DUFF**, by now back in the capital following his stint at the Curragh Camp, admitted that some great men were lost.

> I don't know how you'd describe Cathal Brugha but he certainly was a very brave man and died with a revolver in each hand in O'Connell Street fighting during the Civil War. That's as much as I know about Cathal Brugha.[28]

At some stage during the conflict in Dublin, **GEORGE COOPER** got caught up in the action.

> In 1922 I was delivering some messages for a shop called Tierney's, which sold cups and saucers. I went up to a bakery called Kennedy's bakery, which at that time was near St Pat's Cathedral. It also was near; it's still there – Ivy Flats, which is facing the cathedral. I had dropped in my message into the bakery, crossed the road, going up the side of the flats there was a big iron gate, it's still there and about six fellows came out, shouted at me, I don't know what they said even to this day but they were standing beside me ... They were standing beside me with revolvers firing at a Free State car, which had come down the hill from

Christ Church and when it went by the gap they were firing. They must have shouted at me to sit, to lie down but I don't know what they said. I was still standing there but evidently they didn't fire back because I'm still here.[29]

7 JULY 1922

Despite earlier attempts by Liam Lynch (anti-Treaty), Michael Brennan (pro-Treaty) and others to avert clashes, fighting broke out between the two sides in Limerick. **DAN KEATING** was amongst the republican contingent in the city at the time.[30]

> When we got into Limerick there was a truce arranged between the Brennans and Liam Lynch and some of the Kerrymen that was in charge there. All the men that made this arrangement were IRB members and they didn't want a split in it. But it went on for a week or more you know and there was no trouble whatever but finally anyway Mulcahy and Collins. They sent four hundred Dublin Guards, two armoured cars and two field guns to Limerick. They were in charge of a fellow MacManus. Someone said one time he was an ex-British officer and he done what he was told. He demanded and they turned the guns anyway on the barracks (Strand Barracks) and it was very hot there for the better part of a week.[31]

The IRB had split over the Treaty. Its supreme council was in favour, but many rank-and-file members, particularly in Munster, were opposed.[32] They argued that the Treaty went against everything that the IRB and the 1916 Rising had stood for. Thomas Ashe had served as president, and following his death that position passed to Michael Collins. Dan Keating and **ANTHONY MCGINLEY** maintained that, once captured, IRB members within the ranks of the anti-Treaty forces were severely dealt with by those of the Free State during the Civil War. Co. Mayo native Commandant-General Dermot MacManus had fought in Gallipoli during World War I, and at the battle of the Four Courts just ended; he repudiated the Truce made with the anti-Treaty IRA in Limerick, intending to secure the city for the army.[33]

10 JULY 1922

Glenveagh Castle in north-west Donegal was taken over at the start of April and was now occupied by a mixture of republicans, including those from Donegal, the six counties and from the 1st Southern Division led by Seán Lehane (O/C 1st Northern Division) and his second in command Charlie Daly (O/C 2nd Northern Division). Their intention had been to combine and fight the unionist government in the six counties, which they commenced, launching almost daily attacks from the Donegal border. Initially in Donegal the pro- and anti-Treaty IRA worked together in operating this 'northern offensive', believing that a civil war could be averted in the south.

When this turned out not to be the case, republicans found themselves having to change focus and contend with over 2,000 Free State troops in the county under Joe Sweeney. Initially, they hoped that anti-Treaty and pro-Treaty forces in the county could combine and continue to fight the north; however, the commencement of Free State attacks on republican positions ended such hopes, prompting them to respond in kind.[34] Efforts to avert civil war in Donegal having failed, defensive operations were put in place should Glenveagh Castle come under attack, and the republicans proceeded to use it as their headquarters. **ANTHONY MCGINLEY** said his brother was amongst the republican forces in the castle.

> Daly was a wonderful man. I never really was talking to him. My brother Mickey, my brother Mickey fought under him. He was working in Letterkenny and he went away with him. Went out in Glenveagh. They took over Glenveagh Castle and he had a lot of the local men of course under him.[35]

On this date, a contingent left the castle and set off in motor cars bound for Churchill Railway Station, which was nine miles away. They raided the train from Derry and took a large supply of foodstuffs back to the castle.[36] The press reported that, previous to this, republicans drove to a number of farmhouses in the Churchill and Termon districts. Here they conscripted about 11 young women whom they brought with them to the castle to act as domestic servants for them (these women may also have gone of their own free will). They were also accused of having blown up Gweebarra Bridge, which was a quarter of a mile long and connected the main roads for traffic in west Donegal.[37]

It was also on 10 July that five Free State soldiers were ambushed at Drumkeen, resulting in the deaths of two of them. They were Privates Jack Sweeney and Charles McGinley. Two others were captured. All five were travelling from Drumboe Castle to Letterkenny in a Ford car when fire was opened on them. The ambush had been carried out by a column of about 18 men from Glenveagh Castle, led by Charlie Daly.[38] Reinforcements were at once obtained from Drumboe Castle, but the troops at this juncture could find no trace of the ambushers.[39]

13 JULY 1922

Michael Collins resigned as chairman of the Provisional Government, was given the rank of general and became commander-in-chief of the army. He also became chairman of the War Council. He set out to win and end the war. At the start of July, anti-Treaty forces technically outnumbered those of the army, but the government undertook a massive recruitment campaign. Soon it had over 50,000 armed soldiers within its ranks.[40] They also borrowed war materials from Britain. The republicans could not compete with this.

Owing to the army's increase in personnel and weaponry, anti-Treaty IRA in west Donegal knew that their occupation of Glenveagh Castle was under threat. By 18 July, many had abandoned the castle and gone home, but about 300 others broke up into small groups and scattered into the remote hills and mountains. They took to operating in the form of roving flying columns, carrying out attacks on the Free State forces and obstructing roads and railway lines where possible.[41] **ANTHONY MCGINLEY**:

> Glenveagh Castle was attacked when the Civil War broke out and my brother, Charlie Daly fell back in the hills and my brother Mickey was one of his men.[42]

Many of these republicans, however, weren't native to the county and didn't know the area well. They depended on local sympathisers or volunteers for food and shelter, to act as guides through the mountains and to run errands for them. Anthony stated in his Military Service Pension file that '[d]uring the time I was in the Free State Army I handed out all the ammunition I could to the IRA'. He provided the names of Mick McGeehan and Patrick Timoney, who were the IRA leaders in the area at the time, as witnesses of this.[43]

17 JULY 1922

By this date, **JOHN KELLY** of the Derrydonnell Company was engaged in assisting an anti-Treaty IRA column based at Moor Park House under the command of a Mr Brennan and Captain Jim Duggan. John collected food for the column and procured milk. He also assisted in blocking roads, guarding prisoners and transporting arms.[44] On 17 July, John Kelly's brother, Michael, also occupying Moor Park House, participated in the Coshla Ambush. The latter wrote:

> I was armed with a rifle which I used during the attack. One of the enemy was killed and others captured and taken prisoner on that occasion.[45]

The army maintained that as the funeral party of a Private Patrick Greaney (killed two days previously) was travelling from Gort to Galway, they were obstructed by a wall sprawled across the road at Coshla, Athenry. As they instructed some men standing by Egan's public house to remove the stones, shots rang out from both sides of the road. Battalion Commandant Rooney of the Free State forces was shot dead and a number of troops who had been accompanying the remains of Private Greaney were captured and taken prisoner. When the remainder of the funeral party reached Galway with news of what had occurred, eight lorries were obtained and headed for Moor Park, which had been occupied by the anti-Treaty IRA since June. When they reached Moor Park, 12 occupants emerged with their hands up, surrendered and declared that they had nothing to do with the Coshla Ambush. The Free State soldiers who had been taken prisoner during the ambush were released unharmed. A number of the occupants who had denied involvement in the ambush were later identified as having been present. Quantities of bombs and ammunition were apparently found at Moor Park when it was searched.[46]

The anti-Treaty IRA issued a report with their version of events, maintaining that at Coshla the funeral party, which consisted of four motor cars occupied by Free State troops, met a motor car in the charge of one of their transport drivers.

At the time, their car was positioned on the roadside to let the funeral pass, with the driver saluting the corpse. The funeral party then proceeded to stop; some Free State troops got out of their cars and placed the IRA's driver under arrest. They also made him clear the barricades under threat of shooting, even though he maintained they could easily have driven past it. As the IRA's driver was clearing the stones he shouted 'Up the Republic', resulting in him again being threatened with shooting. The Free State soldiers then took the IRA's car and driver, proceeding to move in the direction of Galway, when members of the anti-Treaty IRA, who were undercover during this time, decided to rescue their motor car and driver (now their prisoner). They opened fire, and after a short fight the Free State forces surrendered, although others ran away. The IRA claimed they captured all their men, arms and ammunition and would not have interfered with the funeral party in any way were it not for the aggressive way in which the Free State Army had acted in arresting their driver. The anti-Treaty IRA claimed that among the funeral party was a clergyman, who could bear out the facts as relayed in their statement.[47]

I asked John Kelly, who would have been 20 years of age at the time of the Coshla Ambush, if he remembered anything about the Civil War.

> No, no they used have ambushes here and there but I'd be far away from them ambushes. I wouldn't be let go far myself. I would be too young … Sure I suppose I heard talk about it and that's all. Yerra what news I had, I forget all them things now.[48]

That said, John Kelly is listed among the 36 members of the Derrydonnell Company, 5th Battalion, 2nd (South-West Galway) Brigade, 1st Western Division IRA for the date 1 July 1922. This company had 41 members on the date of the Truce, during which it was reorganised.[49] John, however, claimed not to have been fighting or involved in ambushes of Free State troops.[50] In any event, his brother, Michael Kelly, managed to evade capture for now and continued to serve with the republican forces.[51] John continued to assist them in any way he could. He recalled IRA men on the family farm in Caherbriskaun around the time they abandoned Moor Park House.

> Oh, often out in the barn. They slept all night there – a crowd of them, guns and all rifles. They were stationed below in Moor Park in that man's big house now – Shawe-Taylor's big house. That's when they were leaving up across to my place they came about a mile cross-country. By God whoever shut the barn door in the morning he nearly dropped dead to see all the army. There was guns and all thrown here and there thrown around in sleep, taking a rest for themselves.[52]

20 JULY 1922

Pro-Treaty forces captured Limerick city following an intense battle.[53] This forced the anti-Treaty IRA to withdraw to positions at Kilmallock, Bruree and Newcastle West. Here again they encountered stiff opposition from the army and required all the manpower they could muster to help hold their positions.

In the lead-up, **DAN KEATING** had been dispatched to Co. Tipperary to bring back extra republican re-enforcements.

> There was a column up in Tipperary, outside Thurles that, they were inactive Kerrymen. They were in charge of Jerry Myles from Tralee. I was sent from Limerick to instruct them they were to come down to Killmallock to help hold the line there.[54]

After being billeted in the Templemore area with a group from Cork, Dan and a number of others arrived at Two Mile Borris, which is located between Thurles and Littleton.[55]

> And when I went up there, there was a scout anyway taking us to the barrack anyway and he walked us into a place where we had no chance against a Free State crowd that were based in Thurles.[56]

Dan named this scout that led them into a trap as Anthony Maher, who had been with the Cork column. A gun battle ensued and there were a number of casualties.[57] Dan and his comrades were subsequently held in Thurles Barracks for at least two days. He claimed not to have been interrogated or asked for any information.

> I was captured in Thurles at that time and after a couple of days, we were conveyed to Portlaoise Prison [then known as Maryborough Gaol]. We spent roughly eight or nine months there before we were transferred to the Curragh.[58]

Although no exact date is provided, Civil War Internment Records list Dan's place of arrest as Templemore. It's the same for his comrade Jerry Myles.[59] However, the testimony of Denis Quille from Listowel, also arrested in the county, may provide a clue. Following the fall of Listowel, he had gone to Tralee with a column commanded by Myles that had subsequently gone on to Co. Tipperary. His column's orders were to operate with other columns around Thurles. Quille maintained that on or about 14 July, he and his comrades were surrounded and eventually captured in Rahealty (6km from Thurles and 15km from Templemore) by a large force of soldiers from Thurles under the charge of Colonel Jerry Ryan (O/C of Free State forces in Mid-Tipperary and Daniel O'Donovan's former commandant on Spike Island).[60] In fact, a total of 54 anti-Treaty IRA men were captured, all believed to have been from Co. Kerry. Another 20 were captured later the same day, principally from Cork and Kerry, so Keating may well have been among them.[61] According to Quille:

> We were fighting around a farmhouse. Seán Kennedy, an ex-Guardsman got the Lewis gun into action, but it jammed. A F/S lieutenant, Furlong from Enniscorthy was killed (at Ballyduff, Thurles on July 14th). We were captured later on, taken, twenty-five to thirty of us, to Thurles. We were a week there in some old mill. Afterwards, we were in the Town Hall. Jerry Ryan was good to us. When we were first captured, the ex-

Connaught Rangers were ... who had been a week with us. They were inclined to beat us up in the farmyard where [there] were fourteen of us and Jerry Ryan came in. He said, 'If ye were in the same position as these men, cornered in, I wouldn't let ye fire a shot. So there'll be no beating up of these men.' Jerry's sister was accidently killed by a F/S officer at the Funeral of Furlong, the F/S lieutenant, the next day. We were seven days in Thurles. Then seven days in Templemore. Then we were taken to Maryborough. [62]

Jerry Ryan's sister Margaret had been fatally wounded on 15 July 1922 as the remains of Sergeant-Major Furlong were being put into the hearse in Thurles for removal to Enniscorthy. While placing a floral tribute on the coffin, she was shot through the side by a soldier's revolver, which accidentally discharged as he took it from the case. She succumbed to her wounds later in a Dublin hospital.[63]

26 JULY 1922

A friend of **ANTHONY MCGINLEY'S** became a casualty of the conflict. He was a native of Largnalarkin, Ballinamore, where Anthony had lived with his aunt Máire and uncle Muiris Mac Daibhid.

Unfortunately, anyone around here, the few that did get killed, it was later on in the Civil War – got killed in the Free State Army. There was a fellow next door, a neighbour, there was that house over there – Scanlan. He was a soldier in the Free State Army and he, they were ambushed by the, and he was killed. That was about all around here, I think. I think it was all near here anyway.[64]

This was Private James Scanlan, who prior to joining the army had worked in Doogan's bar in Glenties, where he bottled stout.[65] He and his brother John had served in the Fintown Company of the IRA with Anthony and his own brother, Michael, during the Tan War.[66] Scanlan had attested for army service on 8 May and was attached to Glenties Barracks, No. 3 Brigade, 1st Northern Division.[67] Shortly after 10 p.m. on 26 July, he was one of about 50 Free State troops who had split up into small groups to search for republicans (including Charlie Daly and Seán Lehane) in the Glen of Glenties. IRA men were being billeted in three houses off the road, with turf reeks and bog holes all around. They had sentries on watch, and when they saw the soldiers a gun battle commenced.

One account reads that sometime later, when the firing had died down, Scanlan's group went to surround some republicans whom they had spotted on the move. As they attempted to close in on them, they were attacked by another group of republicans, and both he and another soldier named Alfie Devine (22) from Derry were shot dead.[68] However, the press at the time reported that they had been shot on the hill by a man dressed in a long black coat and black waterproof leggings who was accompanied by a red setter dog. On first seeing him, the group of soldiers mistook him for a priest and ordered him to halt, proclaiming themselves to be 'Dáil troops'. The figure in black paused for a while before throwing himself to the ground, pulling a gun from his coat and firing. The soldiers returned fire, but Scanlan and Devine were killed. Their man then escaped into the night using the turf reeks for cover.[69]

As it turned out, the man they had mistaken for a priest was Glencolmcille republican Donncha MacNelis, who had become separated from Daly and his comrades during the earlier firing. The republicans denied the Free State reports in the press, which accused them of dressing as priests to mislead their enemies. The dog had begun following MacNelis whilst on the run in the county and he couldn't shake it.[70]

28 JULY 1922

After periods of detention in Thurles and Templemore, **DAN KEATING** (prisoner number 9274), Jerry Myles and Denis Quille, along with numerous others, all entered Maryborough Gaol (Portlaoise).[71] Quille recounted that Seán (Jack) Twomey was the governor and that Joe Griffin from Tralee was O/C of republican prisoners following his capture in Skerries on 31 July.

> Twomey was then in charge of Maryborough and we were the first unit into the place before the 1st of August. Then Joe Griffith and others came along. Joe Griffith was put in charge of us. We smashed all our doors with locks in the first night. A big crowd had come in from Dublin, and there were about eight hundred in all.[72]

Dan reflected on the men he encountered in Portlaoise and later in the Curragh.

> Well, of course you met them from all counties in jail. In Portlaoise now there was some very famous fellows in there at the time. There were the Bradys of Laois. These Bradys, they were famous IRA men and famous GAA men as well – Lar and Tom. Both of them were about six feet four. You'd have to say they were grand men.[73]

Having been arrested in September 1922, Thomas Brady was imprisoned in Portlaoise until February 1923. He was then transferred to Tintown Camp until January 1924, followed by incarceration in Hare Park Camp up to being released in June 1924. His brother Laurence managed to evade capture throughout the Civil War, so Dan didn't meet him.[74]

> And then again you had Tom Malone. Tom Malone now, better known in the south as Seán Forde. During the Tan War he was based in south Tipperary and Limerick and he did some great work there no doubt. He was an IRB man as well. Himself and his brother Séamus, they came from Tyrrellspass in Westmeath. And people often said you know about Westmeath that there was no republicans in Westmeath but that isn't true at all. There was some great men in Westmeath, none better than the Malones I'd say.[75]

Tom Malone had been captured in a back yard in Nenagh on 7 August after being surrounded by Free State soldiers commanded by Jack Ayres. When Ayres phoned Dick Mulcahy to inform him, the message came back: '*Hold him. He is the most dangerous man in Munster.*'[76]

> But there was a number of others. I just can't recall the names. They were a grand crowd to meet. You had a grand crowd from Dundalk and Drogheda. The Lawlesses now, they were a law onto themselves, Johnny Greene, Cooney, Pat Fitzsimons and oh, some others from Dundalk. They were great and you had a lot of men from Clare there as well. The Considines now they were famous in Clare and other fellows too from West Clare now. You had them from almost every county.[77]

It was also on this date that Glenveagh Castle was captured by the army after the building was approached from four points and no republican opposition was encountered along the way. The *Irish Times* reported that eight men and a Derry girl who identified herself with the recent activities of the anti-Treaty IRA were caught inside. They also seized a quantity of ammunition as well as foodstuffs that had been looted from trains at Churchill. The same day, the army arrested 24 republicans who were thought to have fled the castle shortly before they approached. Ten more men found in lorries with red crosses painted on the sides of them were also arrested, and the majority of those taken prisoner hailed from Cork and Kerry.[78] **ANTHONY MCGINLEY** was mindful of a particular man who had avoided arrest at this stage but was still in the county. He was a native of Scart near Bantry and had been commandant of the Schull Battalion, 3rd (West) Cork Brigade, during the Tan War.[79]

> There was Corkmen here during the Civil War and my, Seán Lehane, very well known. He's a Corkman. He had more of them with him. He had a flying column here and my brother was in it, fought under Lehane ... But my brother was a barman and he had to leave and he was on the hills and he was in Lehane's column. Aye.[80]

Lehane had been sent to Donegal by Liam Lynch during the spring to act as O/C of the First Northern Division and to build up forces on the border.[81] In fact, one of his deputies was Moss Donegan from Bantry.[82] Glenveagh Castle had become the headquarters of the Donegal anti-Treaty IRA and they were referred to in the county as the 'Red Army'. They used lorries identified with red crosses painted on the sides of them and they even produced a war news bulletin called the *Tirconnaill Bulletin*. One of the men responsible for its production was D.J. Donovan, and he was one of those arrested in the castle.[83] Once the castle had been captured, the army occupied it as a barracks.

Soon after abandoning Glenveagh Castle, Seán Lehane and Charlie Daly had separated, commanding small IRA units (consisting mostly of southerners) in different parts of the county. They found life on the run very tough, and Daly described the county as being so poor that it was often impossible to get something to eat from locals. In addition, many natives and indeed men in his column turned traitor and informer. Safe houses weren't exactly plentiful, and Lehane was critical of the poor support they had received from many of the Donegal people. With some in the columns deserting and others captured, the remainder were left completely outnumbered by Free State forces, so much so that in late October 1922 Seán Lehane in the east was ordered by the IRA leadership to leave Donegal and withdraw his men. Instead, he was to focus on trying to revitalise Wexford. Lehane sent a dispatch to inform Daly (who at this time was with a column in the west of the county) and ordered him and his men to head towards Drumkeen to reunite with him for the purpose of making evacuation arrangements.[84]

29 JULY 1922

Over this weekend, **JACK DUFF** arrived with a contingent of the Free State Army into Kilkenny. It was shortly after returning from the Curragh Camp and undertaking successful operations to subdue the fighting in Dublin that they had been instructed that they would be going there.[85]

> We returned to Griffith Barracks again, where we got weapons – rifles and ammunition.[86]

Two or three Leyland lorries were driven in, each containing chest upon chest of Lee-Enfield rifles. The soldiers were all lined up on the square and armed, many for the first time.[87]

> Shortly after that, a day or two after that, two companies that had been formed up in Dublin known as Dublin No. 1 and Dublin No. 2 were shifted to Kilkenny.[88]

Jack and his comrades boarded lorries that took them to a special train bound for Kilkenny. On arrival, they were lined up, given blankets and mattresses, marched to the riding school, which was being used as a barracks, and told to do the best they could. It was whilst in Kilkenny that Jack got his first ever army pay cheque, which amounted to £3. Next a priest visited the soldiers and told them that they were going on a dangerous job and that they could avail of confession beforehand in the riding school if they so desired. They also got absolution out in the barracks square before boarding onto lorries once again on 1 August.[89]

> We remained in Kilkenny for a day; two days maybe and then started the push on into Tipperary. I went with Dublin No. 1.[90]

The vehicles could only get them as far as Callan, where they remained overnight, because beyond that the roads, railway lines and bridges were all blocked, blown or mined. They set off on foot in the morning, going cross country and experiencing torrential rain as they went. Wearing only tunics and breeches, they cursed the fact that they weren't supplied with overcoats.[91]

Jack explained that the fighting was only now starting in the country. It had ceased in Dublin, and the anti-Treaty IRA were now retreating back into the country. As they retreated, he and his comrades pursued them. The army's objective was to keep them on the move and intern as many as they captured. If it came to a fight, then the soldiers were not going to fire over the republicans' heads.[92] By 3 August, Jack and the army would reach Carrick-on-Suir, having fought their way through Callan, Windgap and Nine-Mile-House. They would rest in Carrick-on-Suir for a few days before setting off on their advance on Clonmel early on 8 August.[93]

30 JULY 1922

MAI GROGAN had earlier (29 March 1902 and 14 September 1920) referred to the Gore-Hickman family and Kilmore House. The Gore-Hickmans were Anglo-Irish gentry and Kilmore House was a large 18th century, two-storey house over a basement. It had 24 rooms and was located in the townland of Kilmore, one mile from the village of Knock, Kilmurry McMahon, Co. Clare.[94] Francis William Gore-Hickman, who died in 1917, was succeeded by his son of the same name.[95] Both had been landlords with a tough reputation, and Mai could remember numerous people having been evicted from the land over the years.

> Oh, there was, plenty of them for not paying the rates. Plenty of them and Hickman, he was a Protestant. He lived a few miles away from us. Oh he, several he evicted. Several of them and took up the land and that was it. The rent was small but at the same time they weren't able to pay it. Times were bad.[96]

On this date, the anti-Treaty IRA of the district (following a period of occupation) were responsible for the burning of Kilmore House. The property was looted and animals driven out beforehand. In April, F.W. Gore-Hickman had been served with a notice signed by Frank Barrett, 1st Western Division IRA, to leave the residence for good; the treatment of the Catholic population in the north by Orange gunmen was cited in the notice. In reality, though, the Gore-Hickman family had by this stage all but withdrawn from Kilmore, already citing extreme levels of violence and intimidation against them. The house had often come under attack previously, and the Gore-Hickmans soon vacated the area permanently, leaving the property an open commonage. They were compensated in 1925 and the land later divided among the farmers of the locality.[97] Mai said the smaller farmers got 10 acres for free, and there were walls built on the land to divide it.[98]

> We gave up a farm of land in Carniska and we got a divide of the land in Kilmore and that's it.[99]

Another of the late Francis William's sons, Thomas O'Brien Gore-Hickman, was an ex-army officer who had served as an RIC district inspector during the Tan War, having been appointed to the force in 1919.[100] He had been based in Mohill, Co. Leitrim, but fled for England after the Selton Hill Ambush of March 1921 in which a patrol he led was responsible for the deaths of six IRA men. He returned to Ireland briefly after the Truce, but emigrated to Alberta, Canada, following the disbandment of the RIC.[101]

Mai said her family supported the Free State side during the Civil War and didn't look favourably upon the local republicans.

> Oh, sure we had them too. There was a certain crowd around it but we were a different crowd, we didn't mix much with them and that was it. But they'd be going around and that was it ... My father was the other side and we were only growing up and you had to take his side. They weren't all de Valeras that time ... The Free State and republicans and that was it.[102]

She remembered her father telling her and her siblings to 'keep clear' of the republicans.[103]

2 AUGUST 1922

In his Military Service Pension file, **ANTHONY MCGINLEY** revealed little about his activities with the Free State Army, except that he was at the capture of a column at Drumkeen whilst under fire and was engaged in several roundups.[104] On this date, an IRA column was captured with their arms and ammunition whilst billeting near Drumkeen, by troops stationed at Letterkenny. The fighting had lasted for over two hours before 13 of them were rounded up and taken prisoner, with 7 escaping.[105]

Meanwhile, when as many as 250 of Kerry's most effective anti-Treaty IRA men, including the now captured **DAN KEATING**, had been off fighting in Co. Limerick, a large number of Free State troops landed in Kerry by sea. About 450 soldiers on board SS *Lady Wicklow* docked in Fenit and would go on to capture Tralee in a very short space of time.

> There was a very large contingent of Dublin Guards sent to Tralee in charge of Commandant Daly who was one of the notorious twelve apostles of Michael Collins in Dublin. He was a great soldier, no one could take it away from him, it was just he was the wrong side; actually his brother was a republican. He demanded anyway that all these be transferred and that, Murphy did, and they sent a very large contingent of Dublin Guards to Kerry.[106]

Brigadier Paddy O'Daly, O/C of the Dublin Guard, was also well known to **SEÁN CLANCY** (see 1 April 1919). **DAN KEATING** maintained that General W.R.E. Murphy, O/C of Free State forces in Kerry, kept seeking to have these and additional troops dispatched to the county.

> These comprised of very large, more than average amount of ex-British soldiers who had seen the troubles in France in the later stages of the war. It was a very well-known fact that at that stage of the war the British wanted no prisoners, they wanted dead men. It wasn't an order but it was a hint. Oh, that was gladly accepted by some of the soldiers at the time and there's no doubt they murdered Germans wholesale when they caught them and other prisoners as well. These were stationed in Tralee anyway.[107]

One of Michael Collins' most effective intelligence officers during the war of 1919–1921, by now an army commandant, was also on board SS *Lady Wicklow*.[108]

> There was a fellow in Tralee, Neligan now – a west Limerick man. He had been the spy in the castle during the Tan War and oh, he was absolutely ruthless. He was actually the man that picked out the men that were to be killed in Ballyseedy [see 7 March 1923].[109]

Although these Free State troops managed to capture Tralee with little opposition, they did have some casualties inflicted on them by the IRA. On 5 August, SS *Lady Wicklow* arrived back in Dublin carrying the bodies of nine soldiers, mostly from the Dublin Guard, who had died in the advance on the town and hinterland. They were escorted by troops to Portobello Barracks, where they were received by Michael Collins and other senior army officials. Two days later, a Requiem Mass was held there for them.[110] **SEÁN CLANCY**, who was serving with the army in Portobello Barracks at this time, saw the nine bodies laid out in the gymnasium prior to their funerals in Glasnevin. He lamented that over the years there hasn't been much said about these men, some of whom he knew personally.[111] Private Edward Byrne was killed in Spa (between Tralee and Fenit), and the following were killed in Tralee: Private John Kenny, Private Patrick Harding, Private Thomas J. Larkin, Corporal Michael Farrell (2nd Eastern Division), Private Patrick Desmond O'Reilly, Private Patrick O'Connor, Sergeant Fred Gillespie and Corporal William David Carson.[112]

9 AUGUST 1922

A good friend of **PATRICK GREENE'S** was killed in Rochestown, Co. Cork. Ian Graeme Baun (Scottie) McKenzie-Kennedy had come to Ireland from Scotland with his mother and possibly his sister around 1916 and was 23 years old when he died. His mother had decided to leave to ensure he avoided enlistment for World War I, as it had already claimed the lives of two family members who Patrick claimed had joined the Norfolk Regiment.[113] McKenzie-Kennedy and his mother lived first in Killarney with the Honourable Albina Broderick, the latter subsequently taking up residence in a Killarney hotel.[114] He was a proud Scot and over time also developed a love of Irish culture, going on to become a member of the Irish Literary Society.[115]

Already fluent in Scots Gaelic, around 1918 McKenzie-Kennedy moved to Ballingeary to learn the Irish language. During the Anglo-Irish War he served with the Ballingeary-based 'D' Company, 8th Battalion of Cork No. 1 Brigade, and became a highly respected volunteer, so much so that in early 1921 he was sent to England to buy arms and returned with 11 revolvers.[116] McKenzie-Kennedy's mother appealed to him to return to Scotland but he refused, taking instead the anti-Treaty side in the Civil War.

One evening, Scottie invited Patrick to come along with him to test some gunpowder he had made. Patrick was unable to attend, having been asked by Liam Twomey to saddle a horse and ride it on the road because his father was going to Macroom the next day and the horse hadn't been on the road for a while. When he was riding back, Patrick heard a loud boom. He arrived to find Scottie's hands were all black marks and that his eyebrows were burned. Scottie was fortunate he hadn't been killed.[117] Had Patrick not been detailed to ride the horse, he might have indulged the Scot and suffered the same fate. Patrick spoke of a permanent memorial to Scottie in the Ballingeary area.

> There is a monument just beyond Tuairín Dubh to two fellows, one fellow escaped from Tuairín and got across the River Lee to the mountains and some Black and Tan took a pot shot at him and killed him. I think he was Criostóir Ó Luasaigh. The other fellow was a Scotsman – 'Scottie' McKenzie-Kennedy – whose father and brother were officers in the British army – shame to say.[118]

His unfortunate friend used to refer to him as 'Longford' because there were so many 'Pádraigs' around Ballingeary at the time.

> A big tall six-footer – I knew Scottie well. And he went east as they say there to prevent the Free State troops landing in Cork with a lot of other people and he was one of the first people to be shot. And according to his genealogy he was the last male descendent of Robert the Bruce. And as Father Twohig [a historian] says in his history of that event – 'He lost his life fighting for a cause that wasn't his own.' And he was a great character – big six-footer. His father and brother were killed early on in the '14–'18 war and he was the only male of the family left.[119]

According to one source, Ian Graeme Baun McKenzie-Kennedy's father had been killed in a tribal clash on the North West Indian frontier.[120] The people of Ballingeary had tried to stop him departing for Cork, but undeterred, together with a number of others he left with his rifle and bicycle early one morning.[121] Having travelled from Dublin by sea, Major-General Emmet Dalton and 450 Free State troops landed at Passage West on 8 August with the intention of capturing Cork city. They would do so within three days following some fierce fighting.

Ian Graeme Baun McKenzie-Kennedy was killed following a shoot-out against these soldiers at Belmont Cottage in Rochestown, along with a comrade named James Moloney. They and a third man, Frank O'Donoghue, had been inside covering the evacuation of fellow republicans from a broken-down lorry. Apparently they kept firing from the cottage until their bullets expired.[122] Then, according to Free State sources, McKenzie-Kennedy and Moloney were shot down as they dashed from the side door.[123] There is a republican account stating that McKenzie-Kennedy jumped up to re-attack across a roadway at Rochestown but was hit by a stream of tracer bullets from a machine gun.[124] Other republicans claimed the pair were shot with their hands up whilst in the process of surrendering, and that 12 Free State soldiers had been killed and 15 injured by the 3 men. Frank O'Donoghue was taken prisoner.[125] Years later, Emmet Dalton, who had led the seaborne landing at Passage West, paid tribute to the courage of McKenzie-Kennedy: *'He wouldn't give in, wouldn't surrender so he died ... I salute bravery wherever I see it.'* [126]

Free State soldiers killed at Rochestown and Passage West between 8 and 9 August included Privates James Madden, Christopher O'Toole, Henry Quinn, James Gavigan, Patrick Maguire, William Nevin, Gerald McKenna, Frederick McKenna, John Curley and Michael Collins, as well as Sergeant Patrick Perry.[127] Jeremiah Hourigan, Christopher Olden and Daniel McCarthy of the anti-Treaty IRA were also fatally shot in Rochestown over 8 and 9 August.[128]

Patrick Greene also refers to Criostóir Ó Luasaigh (Christopher Lucey). On 10 November 1920, the Auxiliaries raided Ballingeary and the 22-year-old was shot dead. He was Section Commander, 'B' Company, 1st Battalion, Cork City. He had been on the run in the area, and on spotting the approaching lorries, hurried to Twomey's house in Tuairín Dubh to warn his companions inside. They had already left, and as he ran from the rear of the house, he came under heavy gunfire.[129]

Free State forces, including **JACK DUFF**, also entered Clonmel on 9 August 1922. They did so close to midnight, as the republicans retreated. The army had made the journey from Carrick-on-Suir, but owing to the difficulties experienced on the roads and having to make several detours, it took them the most of two days to reach Clonmel. The anti-Treaty IRA had damaged the railway line, making it impossible for trains to enter the town and leaving it isolated. Also, food supplies had been running low since June, and republicans are reported to have been taking goods off traders without paying for them.[130]

> It took us nine days to get from Kilkenny into Clonmel. Now if you know the distance it will give you some idea of what we were up against the whole way through. Both from the weather, which teemed rain practically all of the time and fighting our way through. And worse, worse, much worse than all, we were out with a body of men who knew as much about a rifle as a newborn baby up in the Coombe Hospital today. They were armed in Griffith Barracks with rifles and ammunition without being given one hour's training in the use of the weapons that they were going out to fight with. And you were in more danger sometimes than the fellows behind your back than you were of the fellows in front and the best and safest way to lead them in that time was to lead from the rear, not from the front.
>
> It's on record from Tommy Ryan – a Tipperary fighter, he was with No. 1 at the time. A number, he came out in front of No. 1 and tried to get the bloody eejits to stop from firing their rifles because he said you wouldn't have a round of ammunition by the time you got to Clonmel if you didn't go out and stop them. Once they learned to use the bloody, once they learned to put a round of ammunition into the breech, pull the trigger and eject the empty case and put another one in, that was the sub-limit of their and by Christ they done it everywhere and everywhere that they could and at nothing. If they saw a cat on a tin roof, on a roof by God they'd have a shot at it.
>
> It's only men like myself who went out and experienced all these things and that know about all these things. They were all bloody stupid, the whole lot of them. Our people were mad. I think myself that the

army authorities, Dick Mulcahy, Mick Collins and the remainder of them, were under the opinion that if they [the IRA] saw a whole big crowd of green-clad soldiers coming up against them that they'd turn and run – they didn't. The soldiers they would have seen coming up in front of them hadn't the foggiest idea of what they were doing or what they were using or anything else about it.[131]

Once the army entered Clonmel, they found that the military barracks, police barracks and other buildings in the town were blazing. Bridges and roads were also mined and damaged. Many of the locals were overjoyed to see the army arrive as they proceeded to be billeted in the town hall and numerous other buildings around the town. Some townspeople offered their homes as billets. Hearns Hotel was made headquarters for the command, and that's where Jack Duff – who was put in charge of the guard with another soldier – was billeted. He recalled that he used to hang around with a soldier named Gormley and that they got no breakfast on the morning after their arrival. This was remedied when a woman who owned a small confectionery shop took them in and fed them. Soon the army got organised and Dublin No. 1 Company took over the technical school, whilst the grammar school was taken over by Dublin No. 2. A guard was also put on the 'brick house' on the Cashel Road. It was called the 'brick house' because it was one of the few brick houses in the district, as the majority were of thatch. Barricades were also erected. The borstal institution was taken over by Dublin No. 1, and for a time Dublin No. 2 used the church for billets.

Names from the army in Clonmel at this time that Jack remembered included Jim Fitzgerald from Belfast, who was in charge of Dublin No. 1; Harry Kelly from Irishtown, who was in charge of Dublin No. 2 and was O/C in charge of anti-Treaty prisoners that were held in the borstal; Commandant Tommy Ryan and Commandant Jimmy Skehan from Tipperary; Dwyer; Dominic Mackey, who was in charge of the Kildare Unit; Lieutenant Connolly from Tipperary; Ger Heaslip; Commandant McCarthy; Commandant John T. Prout; Paddy O'Connor; McRory from the north; and a Captain Dunne who loved doing drill. There was also an ex-British army officer named McCarthy who in later years was a quartermaster in the Army School of Music.

In the course of time, the army formed battalions. Dublin No. 1 – to which Jack belonged – and Dublin No. 2 were merged into what became known as the 64th Infantry Battalion, initially commanded by Ned McGrath from Co. Tipperary. A man named Myers was his adjutant. Tommy Ryan from Co. Tipperary later got charge of this 64th Infantry Battalion to which Jack was attached.[132]

> I was stationed in Clonmel. That's where I finished up after the town was taken over.[133]

Some of the families in Clonmel etched on his mind included the Howards who lived in a big house in Queen Street near the crossroads that led to the railway station. One rainy night when he was on sentry duty, the hall door was left open so that he and his comrades could shelter inside. They were invited in for tea and returned many times after that. There was also a shop owned by a lady called Hall who had been in the United States. She used to allow the children in behind the counter to take their own sweets once they had paid. There was a house owned by a tailor named Mitchell, who did a good trade in altering the army's new uniforms, and opposite the barracks was a pub owned by a man named Tobin who also ran a guesthouse.[134]

12 AUGUST 1922

Arthur Griffith, President of Dáil Eireann, died from a brain haemorrhage in a private hospital in Dublin. Michael Collins, who was on a tour of inspection in Munster, turned for Dublin upon hearing the news. He would go on to march at the head of the funeral procession to Glasnevin Cemetery.[135] **SEÁN CLANCY** also marched that day; in fact, Griffith's funeral on Wednesday 16 August was watched by thousands, including **GEORGE COOPER**, who had a particularly good vantage point.[136]

> Yes, well when we heard about Arthur Griffith, the school that we went to was facing Western Row Station so we got permission and we were able to go up onto the first floor and we watched Arthur Griffith's funeral first of all. And it was a big funeral – fire brigade and all these different things were in procession. And then the following week it was Michael Collins. So we saw them coming down Western Row.[137]

JACK DUFF had great respect for Arthur Griffith.

> There's no doubt about it, Arthur Griffith spent his lifetime trying to free this country and to better things in it. And he died. They say he died of pneumonia or pleurisy or something in hospital. Take that with a grain of salt. It's hard to know now what he died of.[138]

Cork city was by now captured by pro-Treaty forces, and this was also the date on which Mitchelstown Castle was burned by the IRA. Under the orders of Commandant P.J. Luddy, petrol was doused around the building, and once it was set alight the republican garrison pulled out, with many going back to their homes. In the weeks prior to and following the burning, the castle's contents were looted not only by republicans but also by locals. The republican line was that the castle was burned to prevent it being occupied by the Free State Army and used as a barracks, but Luddy also said that it was done to avenge centuries of landlordism and English occupation in the area. The burning further helped to hide the massive looting that was carried out.[139]

 MICHAEL CASEY was one of the republican garrison in the castle on this date and took part in the burning. He told historian Bill Power that although it was a shame to do it and some of his comrades privately disagreed with it, orders had to be obeyed and carried out. He described it as a grand place with enormous rooms which, if still standing, could be an international hotel or something of great benefit to the Mitchelstown area.[140] He admitted that there was widescale looting of furniture, silver and paintings. A quantity of this remained in houses locally, but a lot of it travelled further afield. Michael maintained that as far as he was aware the men who burned the castle took nothing for themselves.[141]

In the lead-up to the burning, republicans also set ablaze the old RIC barracks, the workhouse and the military barracks in the town. The Free State Army entered Mitchelstown on 15 August and occupied alternative buildings as well as a small surviving portion of the castle. In the weeks following their arrival, Michael was one of a number of republicans arrested, in his case by a man known to him who had joined the pro-Treaty forces at Kilmallock in May.[142]

> Well, I was arrested one night in Mitchelstown, by a friend of mine that was in the Free State Army. And he brought me up to the place where they had the barrack in the college in Mitchelstown. A man by the name of Davey Bulman – he was the man that went to collect the gun from that man long ago you know [see 17 December 1920]. And I gave out like bloody hell to them and they let me go though.[143]

Davey Bulman emigrated to New York in May 1925 on board the *Adriatic*, which sailed from Cobh. He later found work as a bus driver.[144] William Downes Webber, who owned Mitchelstown Castle, deeply lamented the loss of his home and left the country to live in Exmouth, England. In 1923, his nephew Arthur Webber, on behalf of his uncle, lodged a claim for £147,910 in damages against the Free State under the Damage to Property Compensation Act of 1923.[145] Legal proceedings dragged on, and in the meantime William Downes Webber died at the age of 89 in February 1924; he was buried in the demesne graveyard close to the castle ruins.[146] In 1989, Michael Casey described him to Bill Power as a fairly stout, whiskered man who would ride through the town with his companion in the mornings. He added that he kept to his own kind and did not make friends with anyone.[147]

In 1926, Webber's heir, Wentworth Alexander King-Harman, received an initial sum of £41,500 (with conditions attached) from the Free State government, but he was far from happy.[148] With no plans to rebuild Mitchelstown Castle, one-third of the demesne land was sold, and in 1928 King-Harman advertised the sale of the stones used in the castle's construction for building purposes.[149] In the 1930s, the Land Commission compulsorily purchased the remainder of the demesne and divided it into farms (one of which was secured by P.J. Luddy).[150] Additional land was sold to Mitchelstown Co-op, whilst a golf course and town park were also developed. When King-Harman died in 1949, there was barely a trace of the castle left.[151]

Eighty-one years after the burning in 2003, I found Michael Casey somewhat reluctant to talk about the Mitchelstown Castle saga. In his book *White Knights, Dark Earls – The Rise and Fall of an Anglo-Irish Dynasty*, local man Bill Power wrote of how, for a variety of reasons, the burning and looting of the castle were followed by a silence that endured for decades.[152]

13 AUGUST 1922

On their first Sunday after arriving in Clonmel, members of the Free State Army, including **JACK DUFF**, were paraded down Gladstone Street for Mass at SS Peter and Paul's Church. They were led by Captain Dunne and a playing band. All of a sudden, republicans on the hills overlooking the town opened fire on them with a machine gun. Some of the soldiers, being raw recruits, just dropped their rifles and ran.[153] Jack was of the view that the army officers should have had more sense and that the fault lay with them. They were fired on the second occasion they went to Mass also.[154] The press reported that one soldier named Grainger was wounded in the hand and three civilians injured. There could easily have been more casualties, as the street was crowded with people on their way to the church at the time.[155] A republican prisoner named Michael Condon, who was being held by the army in the town hall, began cheering following the shooting. After refusing to draw his head from the window, he was shot dead by a guard. The subsequent inquest into his death fell through.[156] At times during our interview, Jack became uncomfortable when speaking about these troubled times.

> The War for Independence and the Civil War are two things that I don't like speaking about and I'd prefer if you wouldn't ask me questions on it. It was a bad time, a terrible time, a shocking time for this country.[157]

Many years later, Aodogán O'Rahilly, who served with the anti-Treaty forces in Co. Tipperary, gave his recollection of the attack on the army parade.

> A group of lads asked me would I drive them to the mountain overlooking Clonmel. These were Jim Nugent's machine-gun squad – 'Buddy' Donoghue, Sean Hayes and Dick Dalton. There was a big parade organised by the Free State to celebrate the freeing of Clonmel from these Republicans! No one bothered to recall that it was these same Republicans who had fought the Black and Tans and were responsible for the departure of all the British after all those centuries.
>
> The parade was headed by several hundred Free State soldiers and when they came into view we opened fire. We were a long way off and I don't think any of them were hurt but they surely cleared off the street in double-quick time. It did not take them long to find out from where the firing was coming, and they then proceeded to return the fire and we could hear the bullets whistling over our heads. But the old soldiers, and there were several of them, including Jim Nugent and Jack Killeen, who had been through the Great War, said you need never worry about the bullet whose whistle you hear.[158]

17 AUGUST 1922

As part of the Treaty arrangements, the police quarters at Dublin Castle were handed over to the Civic Guard. In advance, together with over three hundred recruits, **WILLIAM GEARY** travelled by special train from Newbridge, Co. Kildare, to Kingsbridge Station in Dublin. On arrival, they were met by a contingent of the force from the city.

> I believe in all there was about 482 if I remember. I read that somewhere. We went by train to Dublin - Kingsbridge Station and we got off at the station. We marched from there up the quays to Dublin Castle. We were in no uniform, we were just civilian clothes, we had no arms and we stood outside the barrack, outside the castle and the British army marched out and we marched in and took our control of the barrack, of the castle.[159]

The inspector-general of the RIC and the commissioner of the Dublin Metropolitan Police had their headquarters in Dublin Castle. It was from there that the RIC was controlled, but it was a detachment of the King's Shropshire Light Infantry under the command of Mayor Torin that William saw march out when he arrived at 1.30 p.m. This was because at 8 a.m. that morning the RIC had vacated the castle and left the job of handing it over to the army. A few of them did wait around in plain clothes, however, intermingled with a small crowd who had come to witness the takeover. Dublin Castle would be the Civic Guard's new permanent headquarters.[160]

> I do not know who led the group up in the railway station, I mean Kingsbridge Station up to the castle. Except I know that it was Michael Staines. He was the Commissioner of the Garda Síochána. Some said Michael Collins was there, I do not know. In fact I do not know who actually led us up to the castle.[161]

It was Commissioner Michael Staines together with Chief Superintendent McCarthy that led about 380 members of the new police force through the castle gates to take it over. Amongst the spectators at proceedings were Chief Superintendent Murphy and Superintendent Campbell of the DMP. Although William Geary claims that some thought Michael Collins was present, he was not. He also mentions that he himself wasn't wearing a uniform on the day. This was because there had been a mistake in the delivery of the uniforms, and as a result only 60 or 70 Civic Guards were wearing them. It's also interesting to note that from this day on the DMP were to wear a new badge.[162] They would continue to operate in Dublin and would be provided with their own depot in Kevin Street. On 9 September, Michael Staines left his position as Garda Commissioner and Eoin O'Duffy replaced him.

> Now while I was in the castle as a member of the Garda, I was expected to do sentry duty and I did sentry duty on the castle towers armed with a Lee-Enfield rifle. I was up there at night ... Every night there was rifle fire all over the city. I don't know to whom they were blasting but I was not under any particular danger because we were protected by what you call an embrasure, you know. And they could be firing at the castle but I do not know. You must remember the war was on at the time. I was, I did that several times.[163]

22 AUGUST 1922

Michael Collins was shot at Béal na Bláth. He had left Dublin two days earlier with the intention of carrying out a tour of inspection, seizing some republican funds, establishing peace contacts and calling to his native place.[164] On route, he paid a visit to Portlaoise (Maryborough) Prison in the midlands, where **DAN KEATING** was being held at the time. There are conflicting accounts of what transpired.

> On his way down to the south, he was killed on the same journey, he called to the jail and he asked to see Tom Malone and Malone anyway was escorted out to the governor's office and he met him there. And Collins anyway put a proposition to him. He started off by telling him he had a proposition he couldn't refuse. But he said that in the event of he going out with him and joining the Free State Army, he'd make him O/C of the First Southern Division. Malone promptly refused and he said, 'If you have nothing else to offer only that,' he said, 'our interview is finished.' Collins was very bitter about it. On his way out he told Twomey that he'd have to paint the top of the wall of the jail white and he said, 'If a fly perched on it, shoot the fly,' he said. Twomey told that after.[165]

Malone's own account of their meeting has it that Collins visited him on the earlier trip south that preceded the death of Arthur Griffith (see 12 August 1922). He asked him to attend a meeting with senior anti -and pro-Treaty personnel to help end the Civil War. Apparently, Malone agreed to some sort of cooperation and Collins' last words to Jack Twomey were, 'That's fine, the three Toms [Barry, Hales and Malone] will fix it.' He then urged him to look after Malone, speaking about arrangements for his release.[166]

Next Collins travelled to Limerick and on to Mallow, which had been captured by Free State troops six days previously.[167] Amongst those who had gathered to greet him or see him was **PATSY HOLMES**.

> I saw him but I wasn't talking to him. The night before he was killed, he was in Mallow [20 August] ... I saw him leaving. It was a motor car or a lorry he had and he went to the hotel in Mallow – Moran's Hotel. One of the men that was in the trouble, during the whole trouble, one of the best men in the north Cork was Dinny Galvin – General Dinny Galvin. He was from a place called Derrinagree outside Cork. He was with Collins' side, with the Free State side ... Well now, Galvin was above in the hotel and near the station and Collins went up to meet him. Well, he was one of his generals [see 28 February 1923].[168]

After Mallow, Collins' next port of call was Cork city, from where he set off shortly after 6 a.m. on 22 August for a tour of West Cork. He died at about 8 p.m. that night after his convoy engaged an ambush party of six. Tom Kelleher was present, but Tom Hales (who had been released from jail following the Truce) was the anti-Treaty IRA commander in charge of the ambush party. Liam Deasy was also in the vicinity at the time, but arrived on the scene later on, firing a few shots at Collins' convoy before they moved off.[169] Rumours have persisted over the years that a group of IRA men from Kerry who were retreating from the battle at Cork also took part in the ambush. The name most often associated with them is Michael O'Donoghue from Glenflesk, and these could be the men that **PATRICK GREENE** was referring to when discussing reaction to the news in Ballingeary the night Collins was killed.[170]

> Well, of course that was a pure fluke. We never knew anything about it. Every night there was a scríocht in the coláiste and I was there at the scríocht and landlord of the house Liam Twomey was along with me and four armed men came into the hall. The Civil War was on at the time. Four armed men came into the hall and they sat with their backs to the stage and he knew one of them – a Kerryman. So he went up to talk to him and he came back to me and he said, 'Collins is shot was shot today,' and he says, 'My mother won't like that.' And she was anti-Treaty but Collins was her friend and that. He had different opinions, but they didn't lose their friendship by differing opinion in politics.[171]

Patrick insisted that at this juncture not even these four men who relayed the news and may even have been present at Béal na Bláth were exactly sure of the circumstances of Collins' death.

> But sure nobody knew how it happened. Nobody knew. These four fellows from Kerry, they were on the retreat from the battle at Cork, do you see? The Free State troops landed at Cork and a big crowd of them were ex-British soldiers and they knew more about firearms than the poor Volunteers, than the volunteers had. These fellows were retreating back, crossing the country back to Kerry keeping off roads and they didn't know anything about Collins being in Macroom that weekend. It's thought he was in Macroom to meet Liam Lynch but he didn't turn up and de Valera was in Gougane that time and he didn't turn up either or Collins didn't see him.
>
>   But these fellows came upon the ambush and they hid. Dropped down behind a ditch and one fellow fired a shot and the other fellow struck down the rifle and told him to keep quiet. They thought they were looking for them you see – the troops they saw. But eventually a man fell. They didn't know who he was. He fell on the road and he was bundled up and the whole lot drove away. It was only later it was discovered that it was Collins was shot. How he was shot, never a post mortem on him – why he was shot?[172]

DAN KEATING was adamant that there were never any of his fellow county men at Béal na Bláth that night (incidentally, Tom Barry was in jail at this time; in what follows he is referring to Hales or Kelleher).

> That wouldn't be true at all. The man, I'll tell you there was a big ambush laid on the day. Now, Tom Barry [Hales] had over a hundred men there

but coming on evening they disbanded you know and they left a small section. They'd be what you'd call the guard to know if there was any round-up coming and they were in charge of Tommy Kelleher [Hales] you know. And six men he had with him now. One of them six went out and he shot Collins.

You know Collins, Collins could have got away. When they ran in and when the firing started, the man that was with him – Dalton. He said, 'Drive on, drive on.' 'No,' says Collins. Collins had some drink taken. Collins had no will fight in him. Got out and stood in the middle of the road you know. It was madness. There was no Kerryman there that time ... I mean you need have no doubt that is certainly not true.[173]

However, Denis 'Sonny' O'Neill, brother of **PATSY HOLMES'** friend Mick, shot at Hornibrook's house in April, had been among the ambush party. Although he didn't divulge the name, Patsy remembered a discussion he had in later years with an ex-Ballykinlar internee from Kilbrittain, who knew the O'Neills and Michael Collins well, about who might have fired the fatal shot. 'Coneen Crowley said it was this fellow shot him. He shot him anyway.'[174]

At this stage of the Civil War, Coneen Crowley was fighting with the anti-Treaty forces in Co. Donegal.[175] In 1957, he was awarded substantial damages, costs and an apology in a libel action he took against Beaverbook Newspapers Ltd., Fleet Street, London, over an article in the *Sunday Express*, purported to have been written by Rex Taylor, which he successfully argued defamed him. Crowley took exception to the following words, which he claimed had damaged his credit and reputation, bringing him into hatred, ridicule and contempt.

Lastly the court of inquiry, without, I would say any evidence, stated Collins' death was an accident, killed by a ricocheting bullet fired from a distance of 600 to 800 yards by Con Crowley of Kilbrittain.[176]

In 1958, it was a less successful outcome for Coneen Crowley when he was awarded damages of a halfpenny with no order as to costs, in a slander action he took against a Kilbrittain man over a reputed allegation that he had fired the shot that killed Collins.[177] Whatever the speculation, gossip, rumours or innuendo that persist against numerous men to this day, Patsy maintained that it was a 'mistake to shoot' Collins and that 'who shot him is a mystery'. [178]

John McPeake had been the Scottish machine gunner in Collins' convoy that day. In the course of the ambush, the ammunition belt was misfed and the Vickers machine gun in the *Slievenamon* armoured car jammed. This lull in firing gave some of the ambushers an opportunity to retreat. Collins saw them from the ditch where he had been firing and took cover at the back of the armoured car to take aim at them. Then he walked onto the road to get a better view and was hit.

One man who was in Béal na Bláth the morning of 22 August was Éamon de Valera. He had stayed in a house quite close to the ambush site the night before, but had no hand, act or part in its planning or execution. In fact, he was well beyond Fermoy when it took place that evening. He had no authority one way or the other, as at no time did he rank as a military leader during the Civil War.[179] His political influence was considerable, however, and at various stages during the war he had attempted to use this to try to bring the fighting to an end. But Lynch and others decided that his efforts should not be encouraged.[180] I wondered if, privately, **JACK DUFF** suspected de Valera of involvement.

> I don't think he would have gone as far as that. I would never think that. I know he done a lot of things. He didn't do a lot of things he should have done, he done a lot of things he shouldn't have done. He was responsible entirely for the Civil War. As soon as the vote in Dáil Eireann was defeated he said he'd get up and walk out. Himself and those that followed him got up and walked out instead of walking out and forming up his Fianna Fáil party and go out and get in and fight his case diplomatically in the Dáil Éireann.
>
> He went out and he gathered all the hard cases he could find – the anti-Treatyite fellows he could find – and armed them with some of the arms that fell into the wrong hands when the British were leaving here and he fought then to destroy the Dáil that had been set up by the people of Ireland here by the use of force of arms. That's, that was all wrong. He should have never; he should have never done that and those that followed him in any sense or form were equally as bad as what he was.
>
> And years afterwards and years afterwards, when the man was almost on the edge of death, he was at some function or at something or another and he had the guts to stand up and say that what he done in 1922 was wrong. He stood up and he said that and you've got to give credit where credit is due. It takes a strong man who has fought so hard against the treaty that Collins brought back. He done so much to destroy that treaty – it took courage for to stand up and say he was wrong and he did do that and for that you have to give him credit.[181]

To date, I have been unable to pinpoint any 'function' or 'something or another' where Éamon de Valera is meant to have said that what he did in 1922 was wrong. Although the wording 'what he done in 1922 was wrong' is possibly open to various interpretations, Jack Duff seemed to be indicating that it was in relation to any responsibility he may have felt he had for the outbreak of the Civil War. In 2022, I emailed historians Diarmaid Ferriter and David McCullagh, both authors of books on de Valera, to get their take on it and enquire if, over the course of their extensive research, they came across any stories, reports or accounts of him towards the end of his life (or earlier) standing up (or sitting down) and saying that what he did in 1922, in any guise, was wrong. Ferriter replied:

> That's an interesting query. There is no documented record that I am aware of that suggests de Valera made any such admission and I think it highly unlikely; indeed, from the archival material I've looked at, quite the opposite is the case; even as an old man in the 1960s he still clung to a righteousness about the decisions he made in 1922. If he had stood up

at a function and said what's claimed in that interview it would have been a big deal and big news and there would be a record of it.[182]

McCullagh responded:

> Doesn't ring a bell I'm afraid – in fact, what I've learned of what he said at various points in his life suggests he would have said quite the reverse in public. He was quite insistent on trying to convince anyone unfortunate enough to come within range that he had acted entirely correctly in 1921–23 – in fact, the persistence of this suggests to me a guilty conscience, but I know of no occasion when he said any such thing. [183]

On the subject of Michael Collins, Jack Duff said he never knew him personally, but that the moment of hearing of his death was etched on his mind.

> I saw him at a distance, only at a distance. I never had any meeting; I never had any talk with him or never had any personal experience of him ... I well remember the day he was shot. I well remember it. I was in Clonmel and on guard at the railway station at Clonmel, when news came through that Michael Collins was being shot. And I can assure you, it took a lot to keep the men under control or Cork would have been levelled – surely would. To say that a man like Michael Collins would go into his own county and be shot by his own countrymen. It's a terrible, terrible thought. One of the best men ever this country produced was Michael Collins and if I was a Corkman I'd hang my head with shame every time his name would be mentioned.[184]

DANIEL O'DONOVAN, who was living in West Cork at the time, also remembered hearing the news.

> It came as a great shock but it was on the day following his shooting. He was to have come to Bantry and got as far as Skibbereen when he turned back. It got too late, turned back. The main road was blocked on the road to Cork and he had to turn back and take a byroad through Béal na Bláth where he was ambushed by the republicans.[185]

He summed up the feeling amongst those he knew.

> Well, they were shocked and surprised to hear it. He was to have come to Bantry from Skibbereen but as I say the road being blocked to Bantry, he couldn't get there ... Did I know Collins? No, I didn't know him personally. I never met the man because he spent all his time in Dublin and we heard quite a lot about him because his aide-de-camp was O'Reilly and he was a Bantry man ... No, I never saw him [Collins] but I knew O'Reilly to see all right.[186]

Daniel, who would join the army imminently, had this to say of the men who had shot at Collins:

Well, the way it was, they were so mixed up. I suppose if Dev came in the sight of our rifles we wouldn't realise what we're doing and we might have done the same.[187]

Daniel mentions Collins' aide, Joe O'Reilly. Collins and O'Reilly had known each other in London, fought in 1916 and had been imprisoned in Frongoch and Stafford together. After their release, Collins bumped into O'Reilly in Dublin and offered him a job as his assistant, where he played an integral part in his intelligence network.[188] O'Reilly went on to become a colonel in the army during the Civil War. Also serving in the army at the time of his shooting was **SEÁN CLANCY**, who encountered Collins on occasion, as the Accounts & Records office where he was based lay adjacent to the block occupied by Collins as commander-in-chief of the army.

Ah, well I wouldn't see a lot of him you know but I met him a couple of times and when I entered the army I was on his staff in Portobello Barracks. So I'd meet him in the mornings, I'd salute him – 'Morning sir' – and he'd salute back and that was that.[189]

Reaction to his death in the capital was immense.

I was of course in Portobello Barracks at that time, serving officer but it was a terrible shock, great shock to most people and in Dublin especially because he was so well known and he spent most of his years after coming back from London and taking part in Easter Week, all those years were spent in Dublin and he'd a lot of safe houses where he lived. He was, I remember he was on the run for two years I suppose before the Truce and he was. He had so many houses where he was welcome that he evaded arrest and they had ten thousand on his head at the time and he escaped all through those couple of years. Nobody ever gave him away.[190]

DAN KEATING was in Portlaoise Prison when news came through that Collins had been shot.

We heard it. Twomey the governor told Jerry Myles and brought him in the paper. We all knew that it happened and everyone then. A lot of people you know sorry for him, more of them knew that he. At this time now, a lot of people and particularly Cork people now, they'd always like to try and save something for Collins but at the time Collins was killed, he was a very confirmed Free Stater and a very bitter man. Unfortunately he knew he was wrong [regarding the Treaty] you see and that didn't help him at all.[191]

Dan admitted that Collins had done a lot of good work during the War for Independence but wasn't a fan of his after that.

Well, there was a certain lot of sympathy. Collins had done so much you know, there was bound to be sympathy for him in places you know.[192]

He was critical of people from the rebel county who, as he saw it, looked up to Collins just because he was born there and didn't realise how bitter he was at the time.

> Well, at the time a lot of the older people deplored it but we were young and at the time Michael Collins was shot, there's no doubt he was a very bitter Free Stater. Some people, especially Cork people would like to hold out something for Michael Collins but Michael Collins was not in Cork. The only peace he wanted to make there was unconditional surrender. I think nobody at the time that knew anything could quibble with that.[193]

Whilst differing with Collins politically, **MICHAEL CASEY** from Mitchelstown had a lot of respect for him.

> Collins was a great man though. He was the best man of them all. Above in Dublin he got all the information out of Dublin Castle however he was getting it out.[194]

ANTHONY MCGINLEY in Donegal never laid eyes on him.

> No, never, we never seen Collins at all. There were several strangers came around. They were officers but they never said who they were you know.[195]

JOHN PARKINSON in Belfast would have been 15, but called to mind reaction amongst the unionist community.

> Well, I do remember it. There was a lot of feeling about it. Of course we weren't altogether really sorry about it but we were concerned that it might start something worse and we'd rather it hadn't have happened at all.[196]

Collins' funeral took place in Dublin on 28 August. An emotional Jack Duff spoke about his remains leaving the county of his birth.

> He was brought from Cork by river [sea] up to Dublin and he was given an escort. And I'm told; I don't know how true it is? That a British naval gunship was stationed somewhere in Cork harbour and as the boat carrying the body of Collins passed by, the crew turned out. Ah, forget about it.[197]

Seán Clancy was amongst the estimated half a million people that turned out in the capital to show their respects.

> I marched in the funeral, I marched with my battalion but we never got as far as Glasnevin cemetery. The funeral was from the Pro-Cathedral in Dublin. And we were in one street there near the Pro-Cathedral but by the time we got started I think the funeral had, the head of the funeral had reached Glasnevin. So we never entered the cemetery that day.[198]

WILLIAM GEARY was stationed in Dublin with the Civic Guard at the time.

> I say it was a tragedy that Michael Collins was assassinated, killed, shameful – too bad. He was a noble man dedicated to his country.[199]

In 2003 Seán Clancy was proud to admit that for him the bitterness surrounding the shooting didn't last forever and that in later years he befriended one of the men who had taken aim at Collins' convoy that day.

> In the Civil War too some of my best friends went anti-Treaty. I went pro-Treaty and there was a lot of bitterness but I think we made it all up – the survivors made it up afterwards. We became great friends. Incidentally I became very good friends with a man from Bandon. Did you ever hear of him down there – Liam Deasy? He was a great friend of mine. That's another story, I'll tell you about it if you'd like [see 9 February 1923].[200]

Richard Mulcahy became Collins' successor as commander-in-chief of the army. **PATRICK GREENE** never got the opportunity to speak to Johnny Collins after his younger brother was shot.

> No never. I called on him once in Dublin. He was living in Dublin and I called on him once and he was away down the country but I never saw him.[201]

26 AUGUST 1922

The shooting of Collins drove many men who supported him into the Free State Army. **DANIEL O'DONOVAN** was no exception, having been attested for service on this date along with his older brother Denis. Another older brother, Pat, was already a member since May. There were different categories of enlistment into the army. Daniel was classed as a Volunteer Reserve, having joined after 28 June and signed up for an initial period of six months' membership. He would serve at Bantry under O/C Michael C. Connolly in the Cork No. 5 Corps, Southern Division, South West Cork Command.[202] The town had been in the hands of Free State forces since the middle of the month.[203]

> It would be about two months after, about a month to two months after the split. After the dividing forces and I followed those from my own quarter, as was the general case then. You followed your own officer and you followed those that lived around you that were mixed in the movement.[204]

Training was minimal.

> Well, you got little or no training except showing you how to use the rifles to do if necessary and this was already known to us. So all we did was we were billeted in houses around the town.[205]

The Government Reserve Scheme provided that all men should be drafted to the Curragh Camp for a short period of intensive training prior to being posted to the Commands as required. However, it was usually found necessary to place a number of recruits on active service at once.[206] Once his enlistment period of six months in the army as a Volunteer Reserve was to expire in early 1923, Daniel had the option of re-enlisting for the same duration again if his service was required.[207] Providing his character was deemed 'good', the decision whether or not to do so would be his.

29 AUGUST 1922

Bantry had come under attack on a regular basis in recent days, prompting the *Irish Times* to describe it as a *'Town in a State of Terror'*. At around 5 p.m. on this date, anti-Treaty IRA began sniping at various Free State targets from the heights overlooking the town. Shots were immediately exchanged by troops who were billeted in houses around the town. There was a loud explosion at 10 p.m, and at 1.30 a.m. an estimated 400 republicans attacked Free State posts in an attempt to capture them for themselves. They had also dug some tunnels to assist their efforts. The sound of rifle and machine-gun fire was kept up continually for over 24 hours.[208] **DANIEL O'DONOVAN** remembered the day well when I enquired as to whether he and his comrades ever came under fire from republicans when in the army.

> Yes, in Bantry, we did, close fire, very close fire in such that there was one on the Free State side killed and five on the republican side. They made it, it was they, the republicans attacked the town and the Fine Gael [army] were all in billets of five or six according to the size of the place generally. Except in a couple of hotels, there'd be maybe up to twelve or twenty.[209]

The fighting resulted in the deaths of IRA men Commandant Gibbs Ross (who was shot while leading an attack on the post office), Patrick Cooney, Donal McCarthy and Michael Crowley. There were a number of wounded IRA men also, and these factors led to the republicans retreating towards Kealkil. Total army casualties amounted to one dead (Captain Jack Hourihan who fought at Kilmichael) and two wounded. Hourihan suffered a fatal gunshot wound to the head whilst defending his position in a building in the square.[210]

It was also on this date that republican prisoners, including **DAN KEATING**, set Portlaoise Prison (Maryborough Gaol) on fire.

> Well, Portlaoise now the conditions there of course, they weren't good. And the food wasn't good. And the republican crowd anyway in 1923 [1922], they burned the jail. And after a time, the police fired at them out in the yard and there was one man killed and a couple wounded and they were hounded back into the cells again. They had to endure then, they had to sleep on the floor then for about six months before they, we were conveyed to the Curragh. But the food, the food was always bad in Mountjoy [Portlaoise]. You could smell it, you could smell the whatever kind of butter they used have you could smell it coming in the gate.[211]

The fire was started at 3 p.m. as a protest against jail conditions after an ultimatum demanding political treatment was ignored. Also, inmates were frustrated that an escape tunnel had been discovered by prison authorities the day before, resulting in enforced disciplinary measures. They had intended to go on hunger strike, but instead prisoners used bedding; furniture, clothes and personal effects to set the top tier of cells alight. The jail had four tiers of cells in its two wings, and they continued burning each one until the ground floor was reached.[212] Prisoners then emerged in a throng into the exercise yard, some of them trying to obstruct the efforts of the Free State Army and prison guards to extinguish the fire. They were assisted by comrades on the outside, as the Maryborough waterworks were raided by armed men and put out of action.

As the water pressure was deficient, Jack Twomey, the governor, ordered about 60 prison staff to tackle the fire as best they could whilst he contacted the Dublin Fire Brigade. It has also been alleged that some in authority made efforts to block certain prisoners from leaving the building. There were almost 700 prisoners in the compound, with utter pandemonium ensuing.

> Hickey was shot in the yard in Portlaoise Gaol. That was the day of the fire.[213]

With many republicans disobeying orders, more hindering efforts to extinguish the fire, and others looking for an opportunity to escape, prison guards opened fire and apparently fired 19 shots in total. Five prisoners were hit, including 21-year-old Patrick Hickey from Inchicore, Dublin, who was shot in the thigh in the exercise yard. They all subsequently received hospital treatment. Their wounds were described as superficial at a later inquest that was told Hickey was expected to be fine but that his health took a dramatic turn some hours later, resulting in his death. The inquest heard that he was in bad health upon entering the prison and that fright in addition to his wound was a factor in his death.

The Dublin Fire Brigade arrived at 8 p.m. with their engine and remained on duty until noon the following day. Although considerable damage was done to the prison, it would have been a lot worse had it not been a very rainy day.[214]

7 SEPTEMBER 1922

This was a date that **GERRY SMYTH** and his family were never to forget. It came to light as he spoke about men in his locality that took the pro-Treaty side.

> Oh, there'd be quite a number of them joined the Free State Army afterwards including a first cousin of mine. He was shot in an attack on the Athboy Barracks. He was at his sister's wedding in '22 in September and he went back. You know they had no uniform or the like of that. They had to go after taking over the barracks from the Black and Tans and the barracks was attacked that night and he was shot dead. His sister was on her honeymoon in Dublin. There was no post, no telephone – she didn't even know he was dead until she got back.[215]

On 4 September, Joseph Smyth, from Etholstown, Balrath Burry, Kells, had attended the wedding of his sister Elizabeth (a schoolteacher) to farmer Thomas Smyth in Moynalty church.[216] Having been attested for army service on 1 July, he entered Athboy Barracks by special request at the outbreak of hostilities.[217] Three days after the wedding, in a well-planned attack at 4.30 a.m., up to 50 republicans laid siege to the barracks. They blocked off roads leading into the town, and some positioned themselves in buildings close to and overlooking their target. It was their intention to drive the soldiers out and occupy the barracks themselves. After detonating a bomb, which blew the shutters off the windows, they commenced rifle fire. When the attack started, many of the soldiers inside were in bed, but by 6.30 a.m. they were on top and the anti-Treaty IRA retreated. Twenty-five-year-old Private Joseph Smyth was the only casualty. He had been hit by a bullet under the heart.[218] The recipient of a large funeral, he was interred in St Colmcille's Cemetery, Navan Road, Kells, on 10 September. Giving it extensive coverage, the *Meath Chronicle* published a list of the chief mourners that included the name of Gerry Smyth and his siblings among the cousins.[219]

> That was the one we say talk least about. No, because memories are, they don't fade and we still remember them. Ah, it was a bitter struggle where brothers against brother. Absolutely, places, shops were boycotted; people were beaten up, shot. I remember the Treaty. It was Treaty and anti-Treaty that time and a couple of lorry loads of the anti-Treaty came down and collared ordinary, including two of my brothers and marched them onto wreck a, blow up a bridge near Slane. I think a lorryload of Free State soldiers came down a hill near them and they just, somebody shouted 'Take cover' and everybody ran. They were out there all night then. They were afraid to come out because they might be picked off.[220]

9 SEPTEMBER 1922

Brigadier-General Tom O'Connor 'Scarteen' and his brother Captain John O'Connor 'Scarteen', both of the Free State Army, were killed in their home on Main Street, Kenmare, by the anti-Treaty IRA as they attacked and retook the town, which had been in the hands of the pro-Treaty forces since August (see 23 April 1922). **DAN KEATING**, by this point in jail, claimed they were shot by 'Sailor' Dan Healy and Con Looney (the latter would die in Killorglin on 27 September).[221]

> When Kenmare was taken by the IRA after the Truce the two O'Connors were killed and there was feeling against them but the two IRA men that raided the house where they were, they had no option whatever. It was a case of kill or be killed.[222]

At the time, the O'Connor 'Scarteens' house was effectively being used as an army command headquarters, although there were no guards controlling entry to the building. Relatives claimed John was shot as he descended the stairwell to investigate the commotion caused by the entrance of IRA men, and that Tom was dragged from his bed and shot in the head. Republicans claimed they were shot after ignoring a call to put their hands up and instead reached for their guns. It would take until December for Kenmare to come back under Free State control.[223]

It was also on 9 September 1922 that a new government was formed when the Third Dáil chose W.T. Cosgrave as President and Kevin O'Higgins as Minister for Home Affairs. Cosgrave merged the Provisional Government with that of the Dáil in preparation for 6 December 1922, the day that the Irish Free State would become a reality.[224] **JACK DUFF** spoke about the enormity of the job facing the new government as regards ruling the country in the midst of a Civil War.

> Of course it was a hard job; of course it was a hard job. The country was in ruins. Trains were derailed, rails pulled up, roads were mined and trenches dug all over them. Huge trees and huge rocks and everything else was thrown on the roadside and thrown along the road. You never knew where you moved a rock, you see a rock like that lying on the road, you never knew but when you picked up that rock it was the means of setting off a hand grenade that gave you seven minutes between you and eternity. Of course it was difficult.
>
> Then they had to turn around and where were they going to get money to run the country? The country was already millions upon millions in debt over, due to the destruction that had been carried out and when the government was voted into power, the Cumann na nGaedheal government, that was Billy Cosgrave and Collins and the rest of them they sat down to it and they done what they had to do even though a lot of it was very, very severe measures but they done what they had to do and credit must be given to them for doing that.[225]

By the end of the war, 291 railway bridges and three viaducts would be damaged or destroyed.[226] **DANIEL O'DONOVAN** reflected on the carnage in the country at the time.

> Well, it took years for some things to be cleared up. The main roads were cleared up rather quickly considering or byways made do the job semi ... Well, I was only concerned locally regards my own town and I know the main bridge for the train to Cork – the railway bridge was blown up and it remained so for some years. In fact, the railway was closed down eventually. Then the roads, there were bypasses made to continue temporary, but things were in a bad way for a while.[227]

The anti-Treaty IRA had blown up the viaduct at Mallow on 9 August and this had the effect of cutting off an important transport link between Dublin and the south. This impinged on **PATRICK GREENE** when he was leaving Ballingeary and Tuairín Dubh to head back to Co. Longford.

> When I was leaving Cork in September '22, I had to come to Dublin by boat. There was no railway. The viaduct at where – Mallow had been blown up and the only way to get to Dublin was by boat from Cork

harbour. And you were pretty well searched when you came in from West Cork that time. Everything belonging to you was searched to see had you any ammunition or guns or revolvers with you.[228]

It has been written that the blowing up of the viaduct at Mallow had been personally sanctioned by de Valera, but **PATSY HOLMES**, who took no part in the Civil War, regretted it very much.[229]

> Childers was there the night they broke up the bridge, all them fellows were there around … I didn't agree with them blowing up the one in Mallow, I thought it was a mistake.[230]

Erskine Childers had been chief secretary to the Irish delegation in London during the Treaty negotiations but was opposed to its eventual terms. He sided with the anti-Treaty IRA during the Civil War and was in charge of the republicans' publicity department, editing the anti-Treaty newspaper *Poblacht na h-Éireann Southern Edition*. He was blamed by the pro-Treaty side for having been responsible for the destruction of the viaduct, allegedly going so far as to bring in engineers from Krupp's (a German factory) to assist in its demolition.[231] Childers subsequently wrote a letter to the *Irish Independent* insisting '[t]hat there is not a word of truth in any of the reports about me which I have seen printed in the daily press during the last six weeks'.[232] For a short period in September 1922, Childers relocated to Walsh's of Tuairín Dubh near Ballingeary, where **PATRICK GREENE** had left plenty of friends behind of the anti-Treaty persuasion, who were prepared to keep the fight going.

> I was out of Cork when the Free State troops advanced into West Cork. They were in Macroom but they couldn't go any further west for the bridges were down and there was big opposition in the mountains that time. The boys had plenty of rifles and plenty of ammunition and it took them some time, maybe a few months before they got into the mountains or got in around Gougane Barra where the *Slievenamon* was hidden [see 10 December 1922].[233]

According to **MAI GROGAN** in Tullycrine:

> Oh, there'd be bridges blown every place. There was a bridge near us. We used to go to Mass every Sunday – that bridge was blown up. You couldn't bring any horse or trap over it. Walk it or if you went to go on a funeral then, you'd have to go back the road and down the Carrowniska road and when you'd go to Clonderlaw the bridge was torn up again. Bohyodaun Bridge then near us was torn up too. So, it was all that.[234]

GERRY SMYTH in Stackallen experienced similar goings-on.

> I remember the roads being ripped up. Riding a bicycle and get off it and climb down into the ditch and river and climb the far side. The bridges were all blown all over the country. I remember that quite well.[235]

22 SEPTEMBER 1922

ANTHONY MCGINLEY left the Free State Army after six months' service. He claimed that he resigned on 28 September, whereas they recorded that he deserted a week earlier on the 22nd.[236] Anthony got no discharge papers and immediately joined the anti-Treaty IRA. He remained active until the end of the conflict, during which time his commanding officers included Con Quinn, Alf McCallion, Donncha MacNelis and Frank O'Donnell. Appointed company captain, Anthony was engaged in carrying dispatches, trenching roads, destroying railway and communication lines, and transferring and caring for arms and ammunition. He also carried out raids for arms and on the homes of those suspected of spying. Anthony harboured IRA men on the run and acted as a guard and guide for them. He specified that he reorganised republican forces in his native district and operated mainly around Fintown, Ballinamore, Glenfin and Glenties.[237]

1 OCTOBER 1922

WILLIAM GEARY was promoted in the Civic Guard and transferred up north close to the border.

> Sometime in September, many of us, probably as many as possible were assembled in a very large room. We were given dictation by Superintendent Muldoon. Within a short time later I was called over to the office and I was given an acting inspector's uniform. The first time ever I put on a uniform. In other words, I was made an acting inspector as a result of my whatever, in other words I probably did well in the dictation. One word did fool me though – habiliments. I didn't know that word – habiliments. You know what that is? Clothing and I probably spelt it wrong.
>
> Within a few days I was sent with twenty-two men and a sergeant, Sergeant Conboy (ex-RIC) to Clones, Co. Monaghan by train. We got to Clones, I was there about a few days and six of us with me, we were sent down to Ballybay. Everything we needed – bedding, clothing, furniture, kitchen utensils, etc. were put in a truck and we went down to Ballybay. We took over the RIC barrack, which was vacant. And mind you I had no books. But anyway we started with our patrols and regular routine.[238]

A cook was hired and a daybook was also maintained.

> The first case I had in Ballybay was a case of infanticide. A Protestant girl poor thing, she was alleged to have had an illegitimate child and she dumped the child into a slough, which was really a, we used to call it in Limerick a dyke and the child was drowned. Well, I had as I told you no instruction so I went to the local coroner and I got from him a book on the law and I read – spent the whole night reading all about inquests. Next day we had an inquest, the doctor was called and there was a verdict of murder brought in. Then later on she was brought before the district court.[239]

The woman at the centre of this case was Mary Anne Tate of Corryhagan, and she was actually arrested together with her mother Eliza by the Ballybay Civic Guard in connection with the baby boy's death on 29 September 1922. Doctors maintained he had been strangled, but the women insisted he had been born dead. When the pair appeared in court in Ballybay in early November 1922, they were admitted to bail in £500 and sureties of £250 each in each case.[240]

> And long after my leaving Ballybay, when I was in Carrickmacross, the case was tried in the Central Criminal Court in Dublin. She came before a sympathetic judge. She was let out on her own recognisance. I felt sorry for the poor girl.[241]

The Civil War wasn't as bad in Co. Monaghan as in certain other parts of the country.

> No, the people up in the north, they were very law-abiding people – every one of them. A lot of Protestants there and the Protestants were models of deportment and they minded their own business. Mind you some of them were very wealthy, well-to-do but they were law-abiding people.[242]

15 OCTOBER 1922

A Special Powers Resolution, allowing the army to hold military courts and enforce the death penalty on prisoners for offences, including the unauthorised possession of arms, came into effect after Cosgrave had succeeded in getting Dáil approval. However, some army commanders were opposed to executions and resisted their implementation. These included Brigadier Hoolan in Nenagh and General W.R.E. Murphy in Kerry.[243]

SEÁN CLANCY was of the opinion that in the course of the next few months the threat of execution could have been one of the factors that changed militant republican mindsets and might have contributed to bringing about the end of the Civil War.

> Well, of course the government was in power and they were elected by the people and there was a huge organisation there trying to destroy that government and destroy the people and the property of the people and they had to take drastic methods I suppose. It was I suppose it hurt the members of the government more than anyone else that they had to execute people but I suppose it had to be done and it certainly ended the Civil War.[244]

However, **JACK DUFF** disagreed with any notion that executions might have hastened the end of the fighting, maintaining that the other side just came too late to the realisation that they had no prospect of victory.

> They didn't stop the Civil War. The executions didn't stop the Civil War. The executions were carried out by a government that was empowered to govern the country by the people of Ireland and if they didn't do what

the people of Ireland wanted them to do, then there was no use of them being there at all. But it wasn't the executions that stopped the Civil War, definitely not.[245]

So with the Special Powers Resolution making illegal possession of arms punishable by death, **PATSY HOLMES** was reminded of his own dilemma concerning his weapon.

> I was a bodyguard to the old major [see 13 January 1922]. I had two of them. I think one of them was a Smith & Wesson and the other a shot 45. But when the Free Staters came into town they came to where I lived down the street and there was a fellow with them from Youghal and there was more of them. And some one of them came back that night for to shoot myself and me brother and we weren't there. But I had two guns and I said I'd better plant those. I said, because they'd come back. So I went up about half a mile from where I lived now and there was a big field and there were three or four ash trees there and I buried the two of them at the bottom of one of them. Jesus when I went up in the morning, they were gone; a fellow snaring rabbits. But there was a girl attached to the intelligence and didn't he give them to his sister and I went up and I got them after. It was only two miles away.[246]

Patsy pointed out that he had these guns for shooting game and not because he was active in the Civil War.

> I took no part in the Civil War nor never agreed with it. The only part I took was the shifting of the guns but for political ideas – I have none. I couldn't understand it.[247]

There's no reason to doubt him. However, he is listed as one of between 137 and 144 men attached to the anti-Treaty Mallow 'G' Company, 5th Battalion, 4th Cork Brigade on 1 July 1922.

> I never took no act or part nor didn't agree one way or another with the Civil War. I did not.[248]

The Mallow Company, which had a strength of between 128 and 137 men on the date of the Truce, now had an increased membership prepared to take up arms against the Treaty.[249]

> The woman now that I was saying her brother found the two revolvers she was belong to Cumann na mBan. She was on the head intelligence. She was, Jones was her name. Jones and there was a girl in the post office then again Ms Barrett and there was a Creedon girl. She was there. She wrote a big book.[250]

Lily Jones was company captain of Cumann na mBan in Mallow.[251] Siobhán Creedon had been an official and Annie Barrett a telephonist at Mallow Post

Office during the War for Independence. They had passed on a lot of coded information, which the British were transmitting via the telegraph system to the Volunteers.[252] *The Hope and the Sadness: Personal Recollections of Troubled Times in Ireland* by Siobhán Lankford (née Creedon) was published in 1980.

19 OCTOBER 1922

David Lloyd George resigned as British prime minister and never again held ministerial office.[253] **MICHAEL CASEY** dismissed him as a 'devil', maintaining that his government was to blame for much of the Civil War in Ireland.

> England were the cause of a lot of it. They gave them guns and everything to the Free State Army and gave them men.[254]

Recruits had come from the British army, which at the time was downsizing. Some soldiers that had been demobbed in England were even brought over to Ireland by ferry, collected in lorries and driven to Beggars Bush Barracks to be recruited into the Free State Army. Tom Barry said that although some of them may have been decent men originally driven by hardship to join the British army, others were violently anti-Irish and had done things against the republican movement during the Tan War.[255]

12–13 NOVEMBER 1922

A census of Free State Army personnel took place to give an indication of its strength and membership. It records that at midnight **JACK DUFF** was still serving with Dublin No. 1 Company in Clonmel as part of the 2nd Southern Division, **DANIEL O'DONOVAN** in his native Bantry with Cork No. 5 Corps, Southern Division, South West Cork Command, and **SEÁN CLANCY** in Portobello Barracks, 2nd Eastern Division Eastern Command with the Army Pay Corps Department.[256] Before the conclusion of the month, however, the latter, who admitted that the Civil War didn't affect him very much, would be on the move.[257]

> Well, I was here for the attack on the Four Courts and I was here for a couple of months afterwards I suppose and there was some fighting going on in Dublin at that time – ambushes, attacks and some of our soldiers were shot and we were attacked in the streets. But then I decided that I'd prefer to be in the country than in the city and I asked to be transferred down to my own part of the country and I was transferred down to Ennis and I was there for a few months and it was; Clare was fairly quiet as far as the Civil War was concerned.[258]

Twenty-two republicans, thirteen Free State soldiers and four civilians were killed in Co. Clare during the Civil War.[259] Based out of Ennis, Seán worked as a payment officer in temporary barracks around the county until February 1923, and this took him to places like Crusheen, Miltown Malby, Kilrush, Kilkee, Corofin and Ennistymon. His commanding officer was Commandant Walle and the area commander was Major-General Brennan.[260]

Clare, the bulk of Clare went pro-Treaty. I'm talking about the Volunteers themselves now. East Clare, there were three Brigades in Clare – East Clare, West Clare and Mid Clare. East Clare went almost completely pro-Treaty. The Brennans, did you ever hear of the Brennans of Clare? The Brennan family – they were in charge there. West Clare was also pro-Treaty but Mid Clare, it was commanded by a family, the Barrett family. They were from Ennis and they were anti-Treaty and they had a lot of followers in that part of Clare. But taking Clare as a whole, I'd say the vast majority of them were pro-Treaty.[261]

On the date of the Truce, the Clonlara Company, 2nd Battalion, East Clare Brigade, which Seán had joined during World War I, had a membership of 57. At the outbreak of the Civil War, it had 18 members.[262]

14 NOVEMBER 1922

Garda Henry Phelan (1347) was shot dead in Mullinahone, Co. Tipperary. He had been stationed in Callan, Co. Kilkenny, where the Civic Guard had opened a barracks the previous month. Phelan had been involved in an initiative to start a hurling team in Callan to raise morale and had cycled to neighbouring Mullinahone along with two colleagues on a recreation trip, one of the objectives of their visit being to purchase a sliotar. Shortly after 3.30 p.m., they stopped off at a public house for refreshments, when Phelan was shot by one of three men who entered.[263] One theory is that he was mistaken for one of his brothers who had served in the RIC. Another is that the gunman (who was unaware that they were an unarmed force) let his revolver off by accident whilst demanding arms from the Civic Guards. In any event, the 21-year-old Laois native was the only member of the force to be killed by republicans during the Civil War, although others were injured in numerous attacks on barracks and patrols.[264]

However, in an incident reminiscent of what had happened to Farrell Liddy in June, another member of the force lost his life when he was accidentally shot by a colleague on 20 September in Ship Street Barracks, Dublin. He was 19-year-old Charles Eastwood (Civic Guard 1017), and his colleague was Leo Herde (Civic Guard 1498).[265] On 5 October, Civic Guard James Greenan also died in Ship Street Barracks after his revolver went off accidentally.[266] **WILLIAM GEARY** did not personally know any of the gardaí that were injured or killed during the Civil War apart from Liddy before the conflict started. 'I had no experience of that.'[267]

17 NOVEMBER 1922

The first authorised executions under the Army Special Powers Resolution were carried out by firing squad in Kilmainham Gaol. The four to die were Dubliners Peter Cassidy, James Fisher, John Gaffney and Richard Twohig. By war's end, 83 prisoners would endure execution (77 of these were claimed as republican dead, 4 were shot for armed robbery and 2 were shot summarily). Over 125 further prisoners would be killed in the custody of the Free State.[268]

MICHAEL CASEY in Mitchelstown was of the opinion that the executions were 'very wrong',[269] while **ANTHONY MCGINLEY** maintained that they only served to create republican martyrs when carried out in Donegal.

> I knew of them you know and some of their people but the ones that was executed here in the county, they were mostly southerners from Kerry that came up here to lead. They were sent up, ordered up by their companies to take the weight off the south, off Kerry. It was getting it too hard and they were no good fighting here in the north until they came up. [He is referring here to the Drumboe executions, see 14 March 1923].[270]

In response, Liam Lynch issued an order identifying categories of individuals in favour of the Army Special Powers Resolution to be shot on sight, including TDs, senators and army personnel.[271] Having been arrested by pro-Treaty troops in Co. Wicklow on 10 November, Erskine Childers was executed on 24 November.

3 DECEMBER 1922

An intense gun battle raged for more than three hours in the Carrick-on-Suir area between a republican column and one from the Free State Army. The latter, which had occupied the town since 3 August, were engaged in combing the mountainous districts on the eastern and south-eastern slopes of Slievenamon, when they were attacked by the anti-Treaty IRA in the Glenbower-Kilcash area. Ultimately, two republicans (Patrick Bennett and E. Butler) were killed and three Free State soldiers wounded in the fighting.[272]

JACK DUFF was acquainted with an army company commander and Cashel native named Tom Taylor who was in charge in Carrickbeg, which is a suburb of Carrick-on-Suir situated on the south side of the River Suir. In 1992, Jack described him to Commandant Peter Young as a 'bloody mad man' who would fire at stones on the road with his revolver as they'd be going along. One day as he was coming through the barracks, Taylor invited him to accompany him and two others dressed in civvies on a ride in a tender out into the countryside. They were armed with rifles and ammunition. They eventually pulled up at the boreen to a house which Taylor described as having been very friendly during the Tan trouble. He hoped to have a chat and a cup of tea, but hadn't knowledge as to whether the house had gone pro-Treaty, anti-Treaty or neutral in the current conflict.

As they approached the house on foot, he advised Jack to hop around the back for safety's sake while he went in. Jack did as he was told, and on reaching the back of the house came upon a thatcher on a ladder busy at his work. Coming from Dublin and having never seen it being done before, Jack stopped to watch, engaging him in conversation while he waited for a sign from Taylor. All of a sudden, he saw a civvie walking across the yard of the house carrying a revolver.[273]

Thinking he was probably one of their own, Jack paid no heed to him and kept on talking to the thatcher. The next thing, Tom Taylor came around like a hurricane, with a gun in his hand, asking where he went, shouting that the man Jack had seen was Seamus Robinson.[274] Jack reflected that had the thatcher not been there and distracted him somewhat, there's a chance himself and Robinson might have encountered each other head-on whilst fully armed. There's no way of knowing what the outcome might have been for either man. Jack thanked God that he hadn't pulled the trigger on Seamus Robinson, as he regarded him as one of the best men that ever handled a gun for Ireland against the Black and Tans. He said he would never have forgiven himself.[275]

Republican Seamus Robinson, who described himself as having been 'on the run' from January 1916 to 1924 except for a break during the Truce, managed to evade capture for the duration of the Civil War.[276] Prior to the present conflict, he had taken part in Easter Week, Soloheadbeg and the attack on Lord French besides other actions against the British. Before the Civil War started, he had been part of the republican force that occupied the Four Courts.

As for Tom Taylor, he disembarked in New York on 7 September 1924, having boarded a ship named SS *America* at Cobh. It was his intention to stay for six months and return home. He next arrived in New York on 23 December 1926 aboard a ship called SS *President Roosevelt*, which again left from Cobh. This time he intended to stay permanently.[277] In the weeks leading up to this voyage, however, he was one of three men arrested and charged with firing into the dwelling house of a man living in Upper Friar Street, Cashel. They were all discharged, as there was insufficient evidence to warrant putting them on trial.[278] In February 1942, whilst residing in Miami-Dade, Florida as an employee of the Bayshore Company, Tom Taylor was drafted into the US Army to serve during World War II.[279] According to a relative I contacted, he died in Miami on 6 February 1962 of natural causes.[280]

7 DECEMBER 1922

Seán Hales TD (a brother of Tom Hales) from Knocknacurra, Ballinadee, was shot dead in Dublin by anti-Treaty forces. His colleague Pádraic Ó Máille TD was wounded. The pair were leaving the Ormond Hotel at the time.[281] Hales hadn't voted for the Army Special Powers Resolution, whereas Ó Máille had. The previous day, the Irish Free State had come into being and they had sworn an oath of allegiance to the King at Leinster House along with other members of the government. As expected, the six-county administration in the north had opted out of the Irish Free State.[282]

DANIEL O'DONOVAN knew Seán Hales 'only by repute', but did know his friend John L. O'Sullivan from Clonakilty, whom Hales had selected to take charge of his advance guard in the Free State Army.[283] Hales had been O/C of the Free State troops in Bandon, and with O'Sullivan had managed to capture many West Cork towns during the Civil War. O'Sullivan, himself a future TD, had been interned on Spike Island and Maryborough Gaol during the Tan War.[284] **SEÁN CLANCY** talked about Hales' shooting and the government's response afterwards.

> Well, of course a lot of tit-for-tat. I suppose in every Civil War you have ugly incidents happening and they were plentiful I suppose during our

civil war too. For instance, now did you ever hear of Seán Hales, he represented West Cork in the Dáil? He was shot on his way to Leinster House. He was a TD and he was shot getting on his car outside a hotel here and that was an awful thing for a member of Dáil Éireann elected by the people to be shot. Well, the following day the government apparently decided to have retaliation and they picked out four prisoners who had been taken in the Four Courts and executed them. It was a terrible thing to happen. But it was one of the incidents that was so regrettable that it's only in a civil war it could happen. So that was an incident where it was tit-for-tat and one side was nearly as bad as the other maybe.[285]

Rory O'Connor, Dick Barrett, Liam Mellows and Joe McKelvey were taken from their cells in Mountjoy Gaol and executed on 8 December. Each man came from a different province and they were members of the IRB.[286] Rory O'Connor had actually been best man at Kevin O'Higgins' wedding, but that didn't prevent him from consenting to his execution. He did shed tears over it in the Dáil afterwards, however.[287]

8 DECEMBER 1922

The death of a prisoner named Michael Daly from Kinsale in Maryborough Gaol (Portlaoise) was the subject of an inquest held by Dr Thomas O'Higgins (father of Kevin O'Higgins), County Coroner, in the boardroom of the Laois County Infirmary. Commandant Jack Twomey, military governor of the prison, said the deceased was received into his custody in August and died in the prison hospital on 7 December. Dr McElhinny, senior medical officer of the prison, said that the deceased suffered from heart disease and had been transferred to the hospital on 5 December for treatment for tonsillitis. Surgeon probationer J. Morkan concurred, and the verdict of the inquest was that Michael Daly died as a result of syncope from heart failure, pre-existing, and tonsillitis.[288]

Although only a select few knew about the plan, in the run-up to Christmas 1922 republican prisoners in Portlaoise attempted to bribe Jack Twomey into giving the gaol over to them. Private Joseph Bergin, a military policeman, brought in £200 that had been supplied by three priests and two lay people. However, Twomey was said to have 'funked it at the last moment'. Had the plan worked, Tom Malone's idea was – with the assistance of outside aid – to rush out the armoured car and then take over Portlaoise military barracks as well.[289] **DAN KEATING** had a bit of time for Jack Twomey, who apparently had a good education behind him.

> Twomey actually came out of college with a degree in engineering. There was nothing doing for him at the time, he joined the Free State Army. But he was very unsuitable for the Free State Army because Twomey didn't want any trouble with anyone.[290]

Although a member of the pro-Treaty forces, the sympathies of Private Joseph

Bergin from Camross lay firmly with the republicans, and he seemed to go out of his way to aid them. He would ultimately pay the price for this treachery with his life (see 18 December 1923).[291]

10 DECEMBER 1922

A big sweep of the Ballingeary/Ballyvourney/Gougane Barra district led to the discovery of the *Slievenamon* armoured car, which had been captured from Free State troops stationed at Bandon Barracks on 2 December, when John McPeake defected to the republican side, taking it with him.[292] He had been perturbed on witnessing the maltreatment of two republican prisoners in Free State custody (one was shot dead and the other wounded), but he was also getting a hard time from fellow soldiers over the machine gun jamming at Béal na Bláth. In any event, disillusioned, he accepted the anti-Treaty IRA's offer of a secret return to his native Scotland in exchange for the armoured car. On the run, McPeake spent Christmas 1922 in Ballingeary before being smuggled to Glasgow. In June 1923, he was arrested there, escorted back to Ireland, and in the finish sentenced to a six-year sentence in Portlaoise Prison.[293]

When in republican hands, the *Slievenamon* had been used in attacks around the Ballyvourney/Macroom area before a tip-off led to Free State troops discovering it hidden under straw and furze at a farm near Gougane Barra, with its tyres damaged and machine gun removed.[294] **PATRICK GREENE** had left Ballingeary in September 1922, but returned for visits in 1923, 1924, 1926, and then not until the 1950s, from which point he became a regular visitor there again down through the decades.[295] He heard accounts of the *Slievenamon* armoured car having being found by the soldiers.

> So they discovered it anyway, they, your man had dismantled portions of the engine and ran away. They left it and the engine couldn't be started. So they commandeered horses anyway, they could get them and they pulled it out and it's above in the Curragh.[296]

Initially, the armoured car was brought back in triumph to their barracks in Macroom. However, Patrick was informed that one soldier may have tried to steal from the farm on which it was located:

> This man he referred to the discovery of it and he referred to the troops as 'the staters'. But he had a good word to say for them. He said an officer came back after to the house, after they discovered it. They had to get horses to pull it away. The driver had left the engine so they couldn't be started and a young officer came back to the house and he said that one of the men, he threw a wad of money on the table, took this money, he said, 'We're not thieves or robbers.' He threw the money on the table. It belonged to one of the men in the house who wasn't there when the soldiers came.[297]

21 DECEMBER 1922

In Co. Donegal, Francis Moy of Glashagh Beg, Cloghan, died from a gunshot wound at nearby Glassagh. The coroner recorded that there was no evidence of how the wound was inflicted. Moy was a 22-year-old native Irish speaker who worked as a farmer.[298] A book published in 2022 and written by Brian Anderson contains a quote attributed to **ANTHONY MCGINLEY** from Fintown, which lies close to Cloghan and Glassagh, claiming that both he and Francis Moy had joined the IRA in the 3rd Battalion area in 1920.[299]

The IRA membership rolls for the district only list Moy as having been '[k]illed in active service'. His older brother Patrick, however, is listed as having been a member of Letterbrick Company and of participating in the destruction of a railway bridge at Cloghan in May 1921.[300] Anthony McGinley would have been six weeks shy of his 18th birthday when Francis Moy was killed, and according to the quote attributed to him in the book, in December 1922 a company in which he (Anthony) was captain were raiding for arms on both sides of the River Finn upper section. A revolver was taken during one of the raids which was assumed to be empty, but while handling it a Volunteer accidentally shot Francis Moy.[301]

12 JANUARY 1923

Just as they were frequent amongst those engaged in the military conflict, accidents with ammunition were also commonplace amongst ordinary members of the public. **GEORGE COOPER** in Dublin was familiar with one such incident.

> I used to go to a meeting at the top of Westland Row, which was for boys and girls on a Tuesday night and during the meeting there was an announcement. There was two brothers named McCurdy that lived in Ringsend and there's a big bus station down in Ringsend and they were going along and they saw this thing on the roadway and they picked it up and blew two fingers off one of them. It was a hand-grenade lying on the side of the road.[302]

Whilst there's no mention of his brother, the *Freeman's Journal* reported that 10-year-old George McCurdy, Pigeon House Road, Ringsend, began amusing himself in the afternoon by kicking around a Mills bomb he had found while passing through Ringsend Park on his way to school. Fearing it would be taken from him by his teacher, he hid the missile until after school hours, when he proceeded to play with it as a football. Not surprisingly, the pin was knocked out of the bomb and the resulting explosion wounded him in both legs. He was removed to Sir Patrick Dun's Hospital and was reported to be 'going well'.[303]

14 JANUARY 1923

MARGARET CAHILL'S older brother Michael (anti-Treaty IRA) received a bullet wound to the head, for which he received hospital treatment.[304] Unable to recall the details of how it came about, she said that he survived, although the effects of the shooting left their toll on him and he never returned to full health.

Oh, I don't know how it happened really. He was out, he used to go outdoors and that's what happened to him alone ... Yeah. He was shot yeah.[305]

Michael Cahill had been captured by members of the Free State Army in a billet near Annascaul in Co. Kerry. Shortly afterwards, while in custody at the barracks in Annascaul, he was taken out into the yard by a Lieutenant Griffin, who wanted to extract information from him. On being savagely beaten, Cahill was then shot in the head at close range by Griffin. Attended to by a doctor for a severe scalp wound, Cahill received medical attention in hospitals at Annascaul and Dingle from 14 January until 8 February. He was later interned in the Curragh and released in December 1923.[306]

19 JANUARY 1923

JACK DUFF remarked that he saw much fighting whilst in south Tipperary and had a rough time facing Dan Breen, who had taken the anti-Treaty side. On this occasion, he was part of a column of Free State troops that had left Clonmel on searching operations but were ambushed at the village of Nine-Mile-House. They were going along when shots rang out at them all of a sudden from a raise of ground. Jack's captain – a Tipperary man named Tom Halpin – was wounded in the leg.[307] Another soldier, Private Joseph Foster, was killed.[308] The encounter was recalled by Dan Breen.

> On January 19th, a large column of Free State troops advancing through the hilly country around Sliabh na mBan, came into conflict with another Republican column operating in that area. The Free State troops were engaged in extensive – and be it said, intensive – searching operations, and having left Mullinahone, were proceeding towards Nine-Mile-House searching and raiding as they went. They were advancing on foot in extended formation along the road, preceded by two armoured Lancia cars and followed by the lorries which had conveyed them from Clonmel, when, on approaching a house with the intention of raiding and searching it, they were fired on by a small group of Republican troops who were billeted in the house. After a brief exchange of shots the Republicans withdrew through the fields to the rear of the house until they reached the main column which had taken up positions commanding the road on the Clonmel side of Nine-Mile-House. Here a barricade had been erected and here the column maintained its positions in the face of intense rifle and machine-gun fire until nightfall. The column then made an orderly withdrawal under cover of darkness without suffering the loss of a single man. The Free State forces, who had one killed and one (Vice-Commandant Tom Halpin) wounded, made no attempt to follow up the column. Evidently, they had seen enough fighting for one day; climbing into their lorries they returned post haste to Clonmel.[309]

Jack remembered that Nine-Mile-House had a fierce reputation. In advance of this day and afterwards, he and his army comrades on the ground were told by their own people on the radio that they'd never get through it because of its mined roads, felled trees and barricades a plenty.[310]

20 JANUARY 1923

A feature of the war was that many anti-Treaty IRA members abandoned safe houses in favour of sleeping in dugouts or out in the open because of the threat posed by informers. **DAN KEATING** knew of two such men who had been caught following betrayal by same and were executed at Ballymullen Barracks, Tralee, on this date. Major-General Paddy O'Daly had recently taken over from General W.R.E. Murphy who, having refrained from executions, was removed from his command in Kerry and promoted under army restructuring.[311]

> There was in all seventy-seven altogether executed you know including seven in Kerry. Actually two of these men that were executed in Kerry be Jack Clifford and Mick Brosnan. They were captured in a dugout, out beyond the top of Ballymacelligott anyway, very quiet place. They were given away by a fellow that was with them the night before – Griffin. When they were captured now, they had no arms but the man in charge took the magazine out, the soldier's rifle and made them shoulder the rifle without a magazine now and they were executed as well. They were supposed to have arms. In all there were seven men executed.[312]

Clifford and Brosnan had been sheltering in a camouflaged dugout in a hayshed at Caher when a man called Griffin, from Keel, whom they had met in a Tralee pub, informed on them. They had naively invited him back for the night on his telling them he had no place to sleep. When they awoke in the morning, he was gone, soon to be replaced by the army. Jack Clifford and Mick Brosnan were executed along with James Daly and James Hanlon. Kept waiting for a considerable time in the barracks yard beforehand, as Captain Edward Flood (the officer in charge) was still in bed, they tried out their coffins for size as the firing squad looked on, most of whom were young and crying. One of the prisoners died of heart failure before a volley was fired; the other three were not killed cleanly.[313]

As January 1923 came to a close, 55 republicans had been executed. Liam Lynch issued an order that Free State senators should be shot and their homes burned by way of reprisal. Kevin O'Higgins, angry and frustrated at the ongoing violence still being perpetrated against the Free State, proposed to General Richard Mulcahy that those captured in arms should now instead be summarily shot on the spot without being taken prisoner.[314] Mulcahy rejected this, however. When it came to executions, **DANIEL O'DONOVAN** said:

> Well, of course I didn't like them but knew little about them. And the way it was I wouldn't be in the army only to self-protection at that particular time. But naturally hearing all the deprivation that was caused during the split it was sad news and although we became, we

were vital enemies at the time we learned to become friends in later years.[315]

Three more anti-Treaty IRA men were executed in Tralee on 25 April: Edward Greaney, Reginald Hathaway and James McEnery.[316] I wondered if **DAN KEATING** had ever feared being executed whilst in Maryborough Gaol.

> No, no we weren't, no that time. At that time, it wasn't as bad that time. It got very ruthless very shortly after you know. It must be said now that when Collins was killed, the rest of them were gone amok. Mulcahy was, Mulcahy now was a notorious murderer you know. He had a very able lieutenant then – Ernest Blythe – who you heard of. Actually, he was manager of the [Abbey] theatre in Dublin for some years after. Should have been shot and was on a short list.[317]

In February 1923, Dr Thomas O'Higgins, the father of Kevin O'Higgins, had been killed by the IRA in his home in Stradbally, Co. Laois, in reprisal for his son's role in initiating and overseeing the execution policy.[318]

25 JANUARY 1923

Anti-Treaty IRA man Paddy O'Reilly from Youghal was executed in Ballybricken Military Barracks in Waterford. In the lead-up, over 2,000 signatures were collected in Youghal and the surrounding district in an attempt to get a reprieve.[319] **PATRICK FITZGERALD** from Dunmoon, who took no part in the Civil War, pondered on whether he may have met O'Reilly, but ultimately concluded that he 'didn't know much about him'.[320] Michael Fitzgerald, also from Youghal, was executed along with O'Reilly; the friends were members of Cork No. 1 Brigade. Patrick exclaimed that over the course of the Anglo-Irish War and the Civil War:

> I had more trouble with the Free State soldiers than I had with the Black and Tans.[321]

One day he went to Knockanore to get beer for a man when the army came and annoyed him. He recalled a man by the name of Barry from Dungourney being a captain in the army.[322]

9 FEBRUARY 1923

The Free State government published a document signed by Liam Deasy, IRA deputy chief of staff, a republican executive member and former adjutant and brigade commander of the Third (West) Cork Brigade who had been captured the previous month at Tincurry, Cahir, calling for unconditional surrender by the anti-Treaty side.[323] **SEÁN CLANCY**, who became great friends with him in later years, gave his version of the story.

> Well, Liam Deasy of course, he was. First of all West Cork, I suppose it was one of our best areas in the War of Independence. It was the best,

there's no doubt about it and Liam Deasy was very prominent in it. His brother was killed in Kilmichael and he himself, he didn't take part in Kilmichael but in Crossbarry, I suppose you often heard of it. He took part in that took a leading part in it.

But later on then as the Civil War progressed and his side was losing badly, he was captured with arms and this is towards the end of the Civil War in 1923. He was captured and he was tried by court martial, and he was sentenced to death and he was to be shot the following morning. And he expressed a wish to the officers who were in control of him down in, this happened now in Clonmel, Tipperary. And he expressed a wish to see the commander-in-chief of the army who was Dick Mulcahy.

And apparently, they got in touch with Dick Mulcahy in Dublin and Mulcahy said 'Yes' he'd see him and anyway they arranged to bring him to Dublin in an armoured car during the night. And he was brought into the presence of Mulcahy in the early hours the following morning and his purpose he said was to admit that his side was beaten in the Civil War and that it was his view that there shouldn't be any more damage inflicted on the country. And that he was prepared to appeal to his comrades in arms to call off the Civil War. And as a result of that interview, he was reprieved and of course the execution was called off and he was kept for some months in prison but he was released. But the funny side of it then when he was released then his own side court-martialled him for cowardice and he was, that was appealed also. So he was a free man, lived afterwards for many years.[324]

Disillusionment with the Civil War had prompted Deasy to seek an end to hostilities prior to being caught, but his arrest intervened. He maintained that on being informed of his death sentence he requested a stay of execution to enable him to get in touch with fellow members of the Volunteer executive, with a view to urging the cessation of the war. Free State Army GHQ in Dublin responded with an ultimatum that this would only be granted if he signed an unconditional surrender. After much consideration, he agreed to these terms and a few days later was conveyed to Dublin, where he was given facilities to send out full details of his action and a covering note of explanation.[325] The government offered an amnesty to all who would comply within 10 days. However, his statement was rejected by Lynch and de Valera (who by this stage had regained influence with the republican leadership). [326]

JACK DUFF was actually barrack orderly sergeant in Clonmel at the time of Deasy's detention in the borstal. He recollected to Commandant Peter Young that it was a close call, as in readiness for his execution the coffin had been prepared, the grave dug and the firing party selected. There was a guard put on his cell under the charge of Larry Dowd from Dublin. Among the senior army men to speak to Deasy in his cell was General John T. Prout, and they were in there with him for ages.[327]

Liam Deasy was imprisoned in Arbour Hill and transferred to Mountjoy in March. Here he was reunited with two friends who had been captured two months earlier – Seán Lehane, who had been in Donegal, and Jack Fitzgerald.[328]

9 February 1923 was also the date that Acting Inspector **WILLIAM GEARY** was transferred to Carrickmacross, where he took up duty as a district officer. Prior to leaving his old posting, he went to have his fortune told and couldn't have imagined at the time how accurate the reading would turn out to be.

> Well, I was only five months in the Garda Síochána up in Ballybay and one night with a Garda and myself; we rode, his name was Cohen coincidentally. He was a Galway man incidentally. And he and I rode out in the country, a wet night too to have our fortunes told. And the woman looked at my cards. And she told me, 'You're going to wear another uniform.' Now I didn't pay her. There was no fee, no nothing. I didn't know what to make of that. Now the remarkable thing is this: twenty years to the day, I was in the army, the United States Army Air Force, Long Beach California – the same month, probably the same day and not alone that – the last three digits of my army number were 938. The same number I had in the Garda. Could you believe that [see 30 April 1945]?[329]

In Carrickmacross, members of the Civic Guard (An Garda Síochána) occupied a private house until the Free State Army vacated the former RIC barracks. Commissioner Eoin O'Duffy was a native of Co. Monaghan. One Sunday, he came to the house to find William in bed with a cold. He proceeded to ask the sergeant many questions, including whether his colleague had been seen by a doctor. William felt O'Duffy suspected him of drinking.[330]

22 FEBRUARY 1923

DAN KEATING was amongst a contingent of over 200 republicans, which included Jerry Myles and Denis Quille, transferred from Maryborough Gaol to Tintown Internment Camp on the Curragh.[331] The name originated from the fact that the inmates were housed in wooden huts clad in corrugated iron in a series of camps known as Tintown Nos. 1, 2 and 3. Tintown No. 1 opened in early 1923; Tintown No. 2 and No. 3 were opened shortly afterwards. There was a fourth camp that had been built earlier known as Hare Park. There were between 20 and 36 men per hut.[332]

Dan Keating, like Denis Quille, maintained that he was held in Tintown No. 2, although existing records place the pair and Jerry Myles in Tintown Camp A.[333] They may have been moved. In any event, Tintown No. 2 accommodated 2,000 men. They cooked their own food, and to pass the time attended education classes and engaged in physical exercise. Many Gaelic footballers were interned there and matches between huts were apparently legendary.

> Bill Landers now, he was, he headed out very late in the time. He was captured you know, he was interned too. He was in the Curragh and then again Joe Barrett who captained the Kerry team. He won six All-Irelands in the same position you know, he was there.[334]

Father Fogarty, Father Dunne and Father Hughes attended to the men's spiritual needs, although the latter denied confession, seeing as the men refused to give an undertaking that they would not take up arms.[335] Commandant-General Seán Boylan from Meath was military governor at the Curragh when Dan entered. Previous to this appointment, he had been O/C of the 1st Eastern Division of the Free State Army stationed at Trim, having been O/C of the Meath Brigade of the IRA in the earlier conflict against the British.[336] Dan Keating told historian and writer Uinseann MacEoin in the mid 1990s, however, that it was Boylan's second in command, McCormack, who made all the decisions – a real bad type who forced prisoners to dig a trench around the camp by prodding them with a bayonet.[337] McCormack was a native of Kilcock.[338] The trench was apparently dug to prevent further escapes by tunnel after a successful breakout by prisoners in Tintown No. 1 and subsequent tunnels discovered in Tintown No. 2.[339] The Curragh Camp was surrounded with heavy rows of barbed wire, with sentry posts on platforms at intervals.[340] The regime there was tough, as recounted by Denis Quille in 1948.

> Boylan was the F/S officer in charge for a time. Éamon Enwright (from Tralee) was our O/C. He was very sincere. We had smashed up something and the F/S wanted him to sign over the prisoners' money to pay for it, but he refused. They took him to the Glass House (punishment block in the Curragh Camp), hung him up by his wrists and beat him. I think his arm was broken. Then they shunted him to the 'Joy as the hunger strike was about to start. He was there for about 6 months.[341]

Another in the Curragh was **JOHN KELLY'S** brother, Michael, who had been on the run since abandoning Moor Park House in July. He was captured by Free State forces near Athenry in January 1923 and interned first in Galway Gaol and then in Tintown No. 3. He was released seven months later.[342] John Kelly served with the anti-Treaty IRA until March 1923. Although not arrested, he was on the run for a little while before going home to Cahirbriskaun.[343]

Incidentally, in March 1923 Agnes Mary Shawe-Taylor had filed a claim alleging that several valuable articles of furniture and farm implements had disappeared from Moor Park between the months of May to September 1922 when she had been deprived of using it as her residence. She also alleged there had been damage done to the property, animals killed and other looting carried out, although the house had not been burned. In 1924, a judge would grant her a decree for £818 and report a decree for £380.[344] In April 1923, she would auction off the contents of Castle Taylor in Ardrahan, where her late husband originally came from, and move to England permanently.[345] In 1926, the Castle Lambert estate on which Moor Park House was located was sold to the Land Commission and divided up among local families. Michael Kelly was among those to obtain land there, building a house around 1932.[346]

25 FEBRUARY 1923

DANIEL O'DONOVAN'S six-month enlistment period as a Volunteer Reserve in the army expired on this date. He had been attached to Cork No. 5 Corps, Southern Division, South West Cork Command in Bantry. He took up the option of re-enlisting for a further six-month stint and was transferred to the 40th Infantry Battalion headquartered at Fermoy, definitely being there from at least the 28th day of the following month.[347] He served under Commandant Aston.[348] The anti-Treaty forces had lost possession of Fermoy on 11 August, although most of Daniel's duties with the army were carried out some 26km away in Co. Waterford. He spoke about the transfer, touching upon his subsequent discharge from the Free State forces, which occurred six months later in October.

> Later when shifted, a new company coming in, we were taken to Lismore in Waterford. And shortly after when six months were completed, I left the army and came home and had no mix-up with it after that.[349]

In terms of military activities and engagements during his time based in West Waterford with the army, Daniel said it was relatively quiet during the Civil War.

> We were in none, only confined to barracks chiefly. That was the general run except make a short run out now and again in a Crossley tender. But we done nothing chiefly beyond holding the barracks until the things quietened down and peace was made. When I mention the barracks, our barracks in Lismore was the castle, known as the castle, the big mansion there.[350]

The army had captured Waterford city on 23 July, and a month later (21 August 1922) a contingent left Fermoy for Tallow in the west of the county. Apart from the bridge on the way into town being blown and the police barracks burned, they entered without encountering any republican opposition. The main body of the army then moved on to Lismore. On hearing of their impending arrival, the anti-Treaty IRA made a hasty retreat from the town, including Lismore Castle (seat of the Duke of Devonshire), which they had occupied for three weeks. On entering the building, the army found oil doused everywhere. Apparently, the IRA had retreated so rapidly that they didn't have time to set it alight. There were reports that as the army were coming in the front door the IRA were leaving through the back.[351]

The army proceeded to occupy Lismore Castle as a barracks and they also imprisoned republicans there.[352] Daniel O'Donovan and his comrades had to be constantly on alert, as the IRA would fire shots sporadically at Free State soldiers acting as sentries at the castle as well as at other posts throughout the town.[353] Others fell victim to accidents. For example, Sergeant Major Thomas Murray was killed in the castle on 27 September, the result of an accident involving a Thompson gun.[354] A second soldier died there following the accidental discharge of a comrade's rifle on 9 October 1922. He was Myles Broughton from Wicklow.[355] On 15 December 1922, Private Laurence Galvin (25988) from the 40th Infantry Battalion had been accidentally shot and killed at the new barracks, Fermoy, by a Private Leary.[356] **JACK DUFF** maintained that such inadvertent deaths were commonplace, when I enquired if he lost many close friends to violence during the Civil War.

Well, yes, we lost some, not a terrible lot and I'll say this without fear of contradiction, that there was more killed in the army through accident, through ignorance of the weapons that were carried, than what was actually killed in combat. And I'd stand over that with anybody.[357]

Army casualties known to him included a Dublin man by the name of Private Joseph Foster, who was killed at the fight at Nine-Mile-House in January, and Corporal John Kelly from Clonmel, who was killed on the day they entered Clonmel in August.[358] In his book *The Forgotten Fallen*, James Langton lists 177 army personnel who died in accidental shootings and explosions during the Civil War. He lists a further 32 who died in other accidental circumstances during the conflict.[359]

Incidentally, February 1923 was also the month that **SEÁN CLANCY** was transferred from Ennis to Gort with the Army Pay Corps. He would serve there with the 28th Infantry Battalion under Commandant O'Donnell until September.[360]

26 FEBRUARY 1923

An official communiqué issued by army headquarters announced that Thomas Gibson from Cloneygowan, Co. Offaly, had been executed in Portlaoise (Maryborough) on this date.[361] However, letters written by Gibson on the eve of meeting his fate, his death record, and other documentation from Military Archives indicate that he in fact faced the firing squad two days earlier, on 24 February. They also point to him being shot in Portlaoise (Maryborough) Barracks as opposed to the prison, where two earlier executions had been carried out.[362] Portlaoise Barracks is located 1.4km from the prison.

Thomas Gibson had joined the Free State Army the previous October, but he deserted to connect up with the Leix IRA.[363] He was court-martialled in Roscrea on 18 January and charged with treachery. He was found guilty of having left Portlaoise (Maryborough) Barracks on 19 November 1922 (two days after the Free State government's execution of republicans began) whilst on active service in the army and taking with him five rifles and one grenade cup. He was absent until 10 January, when he was arrested in a safe house with two prominent figures from the Leix IRA (Frank Dunne and Thomas Dunne), all in possession of arms at the time.[364] The court sentenced him to death by firing squad. **DAN KEATING** alluded to Thomas Gibson when commenting on how inmates in Portlaoise had got information regarding the war on the outside.

> Well, there was always some new fellow coming in you know that would be captured and he'd have all the latest for you. Actually, during that time there was three men executed in the jail there. The last one that was executed there – Tommy Gibson. He was from? Oh, I forget the name now in Leix anyhow. Oh, he was a grand fellow and he was executed anyway and the firing squad they didn't do a good job and the PA [Póilíní Airm/Military Police] went up and he fired four shots into him and killed him.[365]

The two men executed in Portlaoise Prison prior to Gibson (executed in the barracks) were Patrick Geraghty from Westmeath and Joseph Byrne from Offaly, on 27 January 1923. Both had been attached to the 3rd Battalion, Offaly No. 1 Brigade. *The Kingdom* newspaper carried an article on 11 October 2007 in which Dan claimed to have witnessed Thomas Gibson's grim demise.

> I was in Portlaoise at the time and was sick in hospital. I was looking out the window when this man was being executed. There were five men in the firing squad. He was only wounded and a man went up and fired two shots into his head.[366]

Previous to this, in 2006, historian Martin (Bob) O'Dwyer wrote that:

> Dan Keating from Tralee, Co. Kerry, a man of 104 years related to me his memories of the Civil War and how he happened to be in Portlaoise prison hospital where he witnessed from his room window the execution of Thomas Gibson by firing squad.[367]

However, the precise location of this hospital changes later.

> Thomas Gibson's death was witnessed by Dan Keating, Kerry (still living at 104 years of age). Dan was a patient in the military hospital and from his bedroom window he saw the execution taking place.[368]

This is obviously problematic, as it's recorded that Dan had been transferred out of Portlaoise Prison for the Curragh on 22 February 1923, which was two days before Gibson's execution on the 24th. Also, the execution was carried out in the barracks. However, in light of the army's misleading statement regarding Gibson's death, perhaps dates should be taken with a grain of salt.[369] Also, if Dan was sick in hospital, his transfer could well have been delayed until his heath improved. He would have recognised and known Gibson as a soldier or prisoner in Portlaoise, and his version of events is further supported by historian Michael Rafter.

> His execution is reputed to have been a poorly carried out affair. After being hit by a volley of shots from the firing squad, Gibson got to his feet and then received the 'coup de grace' from a revolver fired by an officer at close range.[370]

There is also the more likely possibility, however, that what Dan may have witnessed from the prison hospital was the execution of one of the men in the prison prior to Thomas Gibson. According to John McCoy from Co. Armagh who was imprisoned there at the time:

> They shot Geraghty and two others in Maryborough and one of our fellows saw him. Some of the lads saw him the night before he was shot. Some lads in hospital wing they met these lads. Some of our men saw them being shot. They were taken into Maryborough the night before; a priest brought in, then shot in the morning.[371]

When contacted in 2023, historian Philip McConway, who has researched Civil War executions, replied that he uncovered no information confirming that Thomas Gibson's execution was botched and didn't believe that Dan Keating could have witnessed his execution in the barracks from the prison's hospital wing. He also replied that it seemed to be an anomaly that Keating could have been at the barracks at the time instead of in the prison's hospital wing.[372] Earlier, in The *Midland Tribune*, with reference to the executions of Geraghty and Byrne, McConway wrote that:

> While Geraghty was 'shot out and out', Byrne had to be shot a second time as the first volley of shots was not fatal. He stumbled and fell, got up, and was on his knees crying for his mother when at point-blank range he was shot in the back of the head.[373]

Although most likely down to nerves and distress, the Free State firing squads seem to have failed to initially kill their targets on more than one occasion, so it's possible that both Byrne and Gibson were not cleanly executed. Many in the firing squads would have been uncomfortable with the execution policy, and the fact that blanks as well as live rounds were used would have been of little comfort to them. In the opinion of Philip McConway:

> There were no premeditated 'botched' executions to prolong the pain and agony of victims. Firing squads were composed of hardened and experienced men; ex-British Army soldiers serving in the National Army were often favoured. Where possible the firing squads were composed of outsiders drawn from other counties. It was highly unlikely that any members of the firing squad would have personally known the victims. Where the first volley from the firing squad was not fatal the commanding officer would 'finish off' the victim with shots to the head or heart. There was minimum suffering. Chaplains were usually present and, occasionally, medical doctors to establish the victim was dead (Erskine Childers insisted a doctor was present for his execution). In my view there was nothing markedly different or exceptional with the Irish Civil War official executions from other wartime executions around the world. The Irish executions were relatively humane compared to many ghastly methods employed in other conflicts. Of course this is not to ignore the numerous unauthorised or extrajudicial killings by National Army troops, especially the CID [Criminal Investigation Department].[374]

Father Thomas Burbage, from Geashill, near Cloneygowan, who had been interned in Ballykinlar with **PATSY HOLMES**, openly denounced the Free State executions and particularly that of Thomas Gibson. He maintained that Gibson was 'unbalanced in mind, and that his mother had been a patient in Maryboro [Portlaoise] Lunatic Asylum'. He went on to declare that his execution 'shocked and disgusted everyone who knew him' and that 'practically the entire parish' had signed 'a solemn protest' against the executions.'[375] Thomas Gibson was a veteran of the First World War.[376]

28 FEBRUARY 1923

General Denis Galvin, O/C 38th Battalion, commanding the Mallow area, died from injuries caused by the accidental explosion of a bomb whilst engaged in testing it. The accident happened on 20 February in Mallow Barracks, and even though he had his right forearm amputated, it was thought he would survive. It was not to be, and he died in the Cork Mercy Hospital.[377] **PATSY HOLMES** met someone with inside knowledge of the mishap.

> And a chap was telling me what happened. They were after getting a new bomb. I didn't see one of them but it seems it was an egg-bomb. And when you get an egg-bomb you keep the lever down on it. But this was an egg-bomb they were tipping in the wall and Galvin was trying it out and it hit the wall and it killed him. Galvin killed himself that night. I never heard of one of them.[378]

Galvin's body was conveyed to Mallow church and afterwards interred at Dromtariffe burial ground near Derrinagree.[379]

6 MARCH 1923

Near Knocknagoshel, Co. Kerry, five members of the Free State Army were killed after being lured to a bomb by the anti-Treaty IRA. Another soldier, Private Joseph O'Brien, lost both his legs in the explosion. Since joining the army in December, local man Lieutenant Paddy 'Pats' O'Connor had been a continuous thorn in the side of the Castleisland IRA, picking up many of them on night raids on safe houses. He had had a particular grievance with the republicans, as some months earlier they had held his father captive, accusing him of being a Free State informer. They had also stolen from him.[380] **DAN KEATING:**

> There was a Commandant, O'Connor was his name. Captain O'Connor in Castleisland and he was very active and he was very well aware of the places where the IRA was in his home place of Knocknagoshel. He had done a lot of damage and they decided anyway he'd have to be killed. They placed a mine anyway in a field and sent in word to the barracks in Castleisland with details of where the mine was. O'Connor who knew the field and the area well and five or six others went out anyway to capture what they thought was a dump and anyone that would be in it and the mine exploded. There was five of them killed, two of the squad belong to Commandant Daly – Stapleton and Dunne.[381]

Those killed were Lieutenant O'Connor, Captain Michael Dunne and Captain Joseph Stapleton, in addition to Private Michael Galvin and Private Laurence O'Connor.[382]

7 MARCH 1923

Eight republican prisoners taken from Ballymullen Barracks in Tralee died after being blown up by the army. A ninth man, Stephen Fuller, miraculously survived, afterwards receiving shelter and medical treatment in numerous safe houses. One of those killed was Paddy Buckley (ex-RIC) from Castleisland, who along with **DAN KEATING** had been amongst the anti-Treaty IRA that occupied Ballymullen Barracks before the Civil War started.

> They selected nine men from Tralee and they sent them out. They had a mine placed around a tree in Ballyseedy. They took them out and they tied them to the mine and they retreated then. They exploded the mine and they fired shots into them as well. But one of them – Stephen Fuller was blown straight into the river. And he waded along the river for nearly one hundred yards because he couldn't, and he made his way anyway up to a house in Ashill. Curran's was the name of the house. They dressed him there and they conveyed him to Dailaig's of Knockall. And he was dressed again and taken to a safe house. The British [Free State Army] sent out nine coffins but there was only eight corpses and after a couple of days they started to put out a story that Fuller was mad and that they left him go which was untrue of course. Fuller was able to tell the true story.[383]

The eight killed were John Daly, Michael O'Connell, Patrick Buckley, George O'Shea, Tim Twomey, Patrick Hartnett, James Walsh and John O'Connor.[384] **DANIEL O'DONOVAN**, who deplored the unlawful actions of both sides at this time, described the incidents at Knocknagoshel and Ballyseedy as 'both faults'.

> Firstly I believe it was a trap was laid for the Irish military in a blind arms dump. But when they went there it was a trap with a rifle sticking out of a portion of the dump. When it was pulled out it pulled the string of the bomb, which blew up six as far as I can hear – six officers. And then the military or the army in Tralee then apparently to get revenge. They had prisoners at the time and they took out eight [nine] of the prisoners to Ballyseedy.[385]

On one occasion many years later, he made acquaintance with Stephen Fuller (a future TD).

> I met him afterwards; had a shake hands with him. But he continued a lame leg up to his death. And a very nice man to meet.[386]

The same day as the Ballyseedy massacre, the army in Killarney took five prisoners from the jail there to Countess Bridge, an isolated location between the town and Killcummin.[387] It was their intention that none of these republicans should come back alive. **DAN KEATING**:

> They took up with five men in Killarney again. They arranged them around a stone wall where there was a mine and they decided to kill them anyway. And they retreated and they opened fire and one of them [republicans] anyway jumped over the fence and got away and escaped and was able to tell the story again.[388]

The survivor was Tadhg Coffey, who amid the chaos, explosions and gunfire, made a run for it into the wood.[389] The four dead were Jer Donoghue, Stephen Buckley, Daniel Donoghue and Tim Murphy.[390]

12 MARCH 1923

The trouble continued when five more republicans were blown up by the army over a landmine close to Caherciveen. Their names were Daniel Shea, John Sugrue, William Riordan, Eugene Dwyer and Michael Courtney. This time they were shot in the legs beforehand to make sure none would escape.[391]

DAN KEATING:

> They [army] went to Caherciveen and there were five men who were captured at a wake of a person that was dead the night before and they had them in a barrack. Well, not a barrack, in a kind of a lock-up place [Bahagh's Workhouse – then in use as a temporary detention centre]. It was a barrack all right in the outskirts anyway and they sent out a contingent from Tralee to murder them. The man that was in charge happened to be not there at the time and they went in and they got the key and demanded it anyway from who was in charge there and they took it. Anyway, they murdered the whole five. There was no one to tell the story there, only a man that had been a soldier [Lieutenant McCarthy] there and he told. The whole truth came out and there was naturally revulsion of feeling in Kerry.[392]

These and other incidents in the county became known as 'the Tragedies of Kerry', and Dan said that the atrocities left a lasting sense of bitterness in the minds of the people. He went on to reflect on former comrades whose lives were claimed by the 1919–1923 wars.

> Oh God, no doubt about it, I had some great friends that were killed you know. The local parish here now, the next parish to us, Ballymacelligott – a small rural parish, there was twelve men in the two troubles killed in that ... Oh, I knew them well.[393]

Ballymacelligott formed part of 7th Battalion, Kerry No. 1 Brigade, IRA. Its Roll of Honour reads: James Baily (1921), Denis Broderick (1921), Michael Brosnan (1923), John Browne (1918), Robert Browne (1921), John Flynn (1921), Patrick Herlihy (1920), Richard Laide (1919), John Leen (1920), John McMahon (1920), John Reidy (1921) and Maurice Reidy (1920).[394]

14 MARCH 1923

In the early morning, four republican prisoners were taken from their cells in Drumboe Castle, Stranorlar, Co. Donegal, and marched to an improvised firing range in the woods, where they were shot by Free State forces. **ANTHONY MCGINLEY'S** voice was tinged with sorrow whilst recounting the incident.

> Well, three was from Kerry – Charlie Daly, Tom Sullivan and Daniel Enright and then Seán Larkin who was an older man than them because he was an old IRB man and he was from Derry.[395]

DAN KEATING gave a background to the story.

> Charlie Daly, he just lived down the fields there. Charlie Daly was sent up by Collins to re-enforce the IRA up in Donegal and there was in the course of time anyway Collins died. One of the men kept up Paddy Clifford came home and there was two men from Listowel and Charlie Daly and Seán Larkin a Donegal [Derry] man. They had been over four months in prison when they were taken out and executed. Charlie Daly was an IRB man you know and when the Free State Army captured an IRB man well you could say they killed him in plain language.[396]

Daly had been active with Larkin in the 2nd Northern Division, which covered most of Derry and Tyrone during the War for Independence. During the Truce, they drilled their volunteers and had been amongst the first to reject the terms of the Treaty once they became known. Enright and O'Sullivan were part of a large contingent of Kerrymen that had gone to Donegal in April 1922 after an appeal by Daly (whilst back home) for Volunteers to take up arms against the 'Orange Specials' in Ulster.[397] When Daly's best efforts to avert civil war ended in failure, all four men became active in Donegal against pro-Treaty forces. Dan Keating's friend Patrick Clifford had also gone to Donegal with Daly but had been captured and interned the previous July.[398]

On the night of 2 November 1922, whilst on route to Drumkeen to meet Seán Lehane and his column, Daly, Larkin, Enright and O'Sullivan had been amongst a small column of men captured in two cottages at Meenabul, Dunlewey, in the Errigal Mountains. They had been betrayed by an informer. It appears they had been taken by surprise, as some were in bed and others seated around the fire at the time. The four republicans were taken to army headquarters at Falcarragh and later imprisoned in Drumboe Castle. They were court-martialled on 18 January and sentenced to death after being found guilty of having had a large quantity of arms and ammunition in their possession 'without proper authority' at the time of their arrest.[399] No date was set for their execution, so they were returned to their cells in Drumboe Castle, the army's headquarters in north-west Donegal. In his book *Dr. McGinley and His Times*, Niall Mac Fhionnghaile states that on one occasion Seán Lehane had been captured and incarcerated there but managed to escape.[400] On the other hand, Hugh Gallagher, from Pennyburn, Derry, had no such luck. He was shot and subsequently died whilst attempting to escape in December 1922.[401]

On 10 March 1923, when a Captain Cannon was killed in an army barracks at Cresslough, Co. Donegal, an order was despatched from Free State GHQ in Dublin to execute the four condemned men as a reprisal. The anti-Treaty IRA always denied carrying out this attack. Goings-on in Kerry may also have hastened the demise of the three condemned Kerrymen.

It fell to Commandant General Joe Sweeney to make arrangements for the executions. He hand-picked the firing squad but took no pleasure in the task, as he had been friendly with Daly before the outbreak of hostilities. He had even sought a meeting with him and Lehane in early July at which he proposed that southerners in Donegal would be allowed to leave with their arms, providing they evacuated all their positions, disbanded their garrisons, returned home and wouldn't fight elsewhere. Daly and Lehane, however, would not agree to this, with the former in particular not prepared to give up on Donegal just yet.[402]

Sweeney for his part didn't attend the executions because he disagreed with them, but at the same time he was of the view that orders had to be carried out. Minutes before being shot, the four men could have saved themselves by agreeing to sign a document promising not to use arms against the new Free State government, but they refused. Once dead, they were buried in Drumboe Woods on the grounds of the castle. In 1924, their bodies were among the 77 disinterred by the Free State and removed to Athlone Military Barracks, to be eventually received and reinterred by their loved ones in their home counties.[403]

ANTHONY MCGINLEY admitted that when he had sheltered men, delivered dispatches and acted as a guide through the mountains for republicans on the run during the Civil War, it was generally the case that their identities were unknown to him. He was quite confident, however, of having come into contact with at least one, if not all, of the four executed men, and that they had even stayed at his house – at Largnalarkin, Ballinamore – at points during the six-week period between his leaving the Free State Army and their arrest. Indeed, soon after evacuating Glenveagh Castle in mid July, a column under Charlie Daly and another under Seán Lehane (between them consisting of roughly 25 men) were in the Fintown area, where they established a temporary base. On 22 July, they carried out a raid on a mail car travelling from Ballybofey to Fintown, in an attempt to obtain information on Free State forces. They failed to discover anything of significance, but confiscated a large quantity of stamps bound for Fintown Post Office.[404]

> They were around here and indeed they were in this house too, you know, stopped on different nights. They were from Kerry and one from Derry – Larkin.[405]

Anthony revealed a further connection to the story in that his father, Michael (a poet and balladeer), had actually heard the shots of the firing squad on the day the executions were carried out. Aged 71 at the time and a committed republican, he was by then living in Ballybofey near Stranorlar, having moved back to his native county from Strabane. He was so deeply moved by the circumstances of the four men that he composed a well-known ballad in their honour entitled *The Drumboe Martyrs*, which was recited by Anthony on the day of our meeting:

The Drumboe Martyrs
by Michael McGinley

'Twas the feast of St. Patrick
By the dawn of the day;
The hills of Tirconaill
Stood sombre and grey;
When the first light of morning
Illumined the sky,
Four brave Irish soldiers
Were led forth to die.

Three left their loved homes
In Kerry's green vales,
And one came from Derry
To fight for the Gaels.
But instead of true friends,
They met traitors and foe,
And uncoffined were laid
In the woods of Drumboe.

Four Republican soldiers
Were dragged from their cells
Where for months they had suffered
Wild torments like hell's.
No mercy they asked
From their pitiless foe,
And no mercy was shown
By the thugs at Drumboe.

The church bells rang out
In the clear morning air
To summon the faithful
To penance and prayer,
When a crash from the woodlands
Struck terror and woe
'Twas the death-knell of Daly,
Shot dead at Drumboe.

Let Tirconaill ne'er boast
Of her honour and fame;
All the waters of Finn
Could not wash out her shame;
But while the Finn and the Swilly
Continue to flow,
That stain will remain on
The woods of Drumboe.[406]

17 MARCH 1923

Richard Mulcahy, commander-in-chief of the army, was at the Curragh Camp to review three battalions of troops. The troops were the Cadet Officers Battalion under Colonel Byrne, the 29th Infantry Battalion under Commandant Stevenson and a Reserve Battalion under Commandant Moriarty. The troops were drawn up in close columns of companies on the open plain in front of the camp, and when Mulcahy arrived he was given a general salute. After inspecting the parade, he addressed the troops, while a large number of other soldiers and civilians looked on from outside the cordon.[407]

JACK DUFF, who by now had been promoted to sergeant, was present on the Curragh that day, having been sent from Clonmel by his superior Commandant Tommy Ryan to undertake a course of training.[408] Two other soldiers had been sent along with him. It was the first course of training ever held on the Curragh, and Jack remembered Mulcahy reviewing and inspecting them 'all out on a big field'.[409] When I enquired as to whether he knew Mulcahy well and, if so, what kind of a man he was, Jack replied: 'Never knew the man in my life until I heard of him.[410] During the course of his address, Mulcahy proclaimed that this was the first Saint Patrick's Day ever that the Curragh of Kildare was in the hands of the Irish army.[411] One wonders what **DAN KEATING** and the internees made of it all.

6 APRIL 1923

It was reported that Mr Thomas O'Reilly, who for 42 years had served as principal teacher in Lislea National School, Ballinalee, Co. Longford, had retired on pension.[412] His successor would be **PATRICK GREENE**. Interestingly, it was the same school where his great-grandfather (Peter Naughton) had worked in his capacity as the first national schoolteacher in the parish.[413]

> I started as a monitor in 1914 and did four years until 1918, then went to training and I didn't get a permanent job until 1923. I got a couple of jobs as sub. 1923 I came here [Ballinalee] and I stayed here until '58 when my school became a one-teacher school and I left it in '58 and went nineteen miles away to Coole in Co. Westmeath and finished there in '65.[414]

There had been over 8,000 national schools on the island of Ireland in 1916; by 1923 there were 5,686 such schools in the Irish Free State.[415] Patrick recalled class sizes when he started out.

> Oh, sure it was different. It could be nine or ten. You had classes grouped together for certain subjects. Third and fourth were together, then fifth, sixth, seventh. They were the seniors. They were together but they were still separate classes. Say for arithmetic each class had a different programme. But for reading, recitation that sort of thing classes third, fourth, fifth, sixth and seventh. The sixth and seventh were the same English readers, same Irish books, third and fourth the same.[416]

In contrast, 1923 was the year that **NORMAN DOUGLAS** left school and started work in John Bell's Photographers in Garfield Street in Belfast. He had been eager to learn the trade of developing and printing, but was forced to leave the job after getting heatstroke due to the fact that the premises, and most of his work, were under glass. After vacating this post, he went to work for R.J. Allam and Son, livestock auctioneers in the city.[417] A short time later, he went into an industry in which he would work for close to 50 years.

> I worked in the wholesale drapery and I spent my whole time in the wholesale drapery in two different firms. I was twenty-one years in one firm and about twenty-six in the other and that was my soul. And during that time of business the predominant number of customers I would say, pretty near the predominant number of customers were Roman Catholic and I had lots of friends and good friends in business and we got on so well. Business was business and there was nothing political about anything that happened with the odd exception of course.[418]

7 APRIL 1923

At 3 a.m. on this Saturday, St Brigid's Catholic chapel at the Curragh Camp was discovered to be in flames. The building was constructed partly of wood, topped with a tarred roof. It included a portion of the first chapel built there in 1856, shortly after the Crimean War. Despite the best efforts of the fire brigade together with available military personnel that included **JACK DUFF**, it burned to the ground in a short space of time.[419] St. Paul's Protestant church, which had been closed for some time, became the new St Brigid's until 1948.[420]

At the start of the Civil War, Keane Barracks on the Curragh Camp was occupied by men referred to as 'refugees' who it is believed drew army pay and rations but took no part in the conflict. In fact, they were men from the 2nd Northern Division of the IRA who were using the Curragh Camp to the full knowledge of Michael Collins to train for an armed invasion of the six counties planned for the late summer of 1922. Arrangements were also made for weapons to be sent north. The Civil War, the death of Collins and other factors were detrimental to the endeavour, and these men were subsequently offered membership of the Free State Army. Some in the 2nd Northern Division joined and others felt misled, while the remainder were disbanded on 31 March 1923.[421] There were rumours that it was some of these disgruntled men that had been responsible for setting the church on fire.[422]

Jack Duff made his way back to Clonmel following the burning to learn that troops were to be engaged in column duty in the south Tipperary area, with a particular focus on the mountains, as intelligence reports had indicated the presence of republican leaders in the region.

10 APRIL 1923

Liam Lynch, the anti-Treaty IRA chief of staff, was shot in the Knockmealdown Mountains, Co. Tipperary after being spotted by a contingent of Free State troops under the command of Lieutenant Laurence Clancy. Altogether, there had been over 1,000 soldiers stretched out across the south Tipperary and Waterford region engaged in search operations for republican leaders known to have been in the area.[423] **JACK DUFF**, who had been part of Lieutenant Clancy's search party on the mountains that day, recalled that these troops had come up from Waterford, Clonmel, Clogheen and elsewhere, with the intention of entirely surrounding the area in which these republicans were supposed to be, resulting in them being completely closed in.[424]

He told Commandant Peter Young that the army were scattered all over the mountain, so a Lieutenant Connolly fired one round into the air to attract their attention and gather them all up together again. As soon as he fired the round, away up in the distance a group of men in civvies were seen to run, and fire was opened immediately.[425] Liam Lynch was hit and Jack saw him fall.

Lynch's republican comrades tried to carry him with them up the mountain, but he finally ordered them to leave him behind and make good their escape. When Jack and the soldiers got to where Lynch lay wounded on the ground, somebody called out that it was de Valera, as he resembled him very much. On hearing this, the man identified himself as Liam Lynch.[426]

It was clear to Jack and everyone else that Lynch was in a bad way. His recollection was that he looked like a goner from the word 'go', as there was blood everywhere and he appeared to have lost every drop of blood that he had. At this point Jack had no idea who Liam Lynch was until being told by Lieutenant Clancy, and even then he knew nothing about what position he held in the republicans or anything else about him.[427] The troops brought Lynch down from the Knockmealdowns on a makeshift stretcher of rifles and coats, and once they reached the bottom they commandeered a hay float. He was then taken to a public house in Newcastle, his wounds dressed and an ambulance sent for.[428]

When Jack and the soldiers had brought Lynch down from the mountains, he thanked them all for the way they had treated him and the kind way in which they had done the best they could to make him comfortable under the circumstances. The last Jack saw of Lynch was when he was lying on a chair that he and the others had made up for him. Jack stated that he showed no signs of pulling together at all, as he appeared to have had no life, no energy, no movement in him at all. When another man was then detailed to look after him, Jack's and the other troops' time with Lynch was finished, so they packed off to look for his comrades, who were after getting away on the mountain.[429]

Liam Lynch was carried by ambulance to St Joseph's Hospital, Clonmel, where he died hours later from his wounds. His body was then brought to St Joseph's church in the town, where it was laid out and Mass was held.[430] Prior to his death, Lynch had been attending meetings to decide whether or not to end the Civil War, but no definite decision had been reached. **DAN KEATING** 'never met Liam Lynch' but pointed out that the he 'was an IRB man'.[431] He summed up his determined republican attitude at an IRA executive meeting held over three days in Co. Waterford, beginning on 24 March.[432]

> The Corkmen were there and the Corkmen, they felt they couldn't hold out any longer. You could understand that with one exception and that was Liam Lynch. He was ready to continue and so was John Joe Rice the Brigadier of South Kerry. He still had a very active column and was prepared to fight on.[433]

Both **PATSY HOLMES** and Michael Casey encountered Lynch and regarded him as a great patriot. Patsy saw Lynch more than spoke to him in his capacity as Commandant of Cork No. 2 Brigade, recalling that Lynch had been present at the meeting held on the grounds of Mallow convent which Patsy had interrupted to warn them that the British were making arrests (see 20 August 1919). He got news of Liam Lynch's death when visiting an ex-Ballykinlar internee from Co. Tipperary who had been chief of the prisoners' camp police.[434]

> I was in Carrick-on-Suir the night he was killed. He was killed in the Knockmealdown Mountains outside Mitchelstown and I went to see a chap named Tommy Hickey. Tom was a good man too.[435]

MICHAEL CASEY often spotted Lynch around the locality and was acquainted with members of his family. In fact, Lynch's body was brought from St Joseph's church, Clonmel, to Mitchelstown church before being laid to rest in Kilcrumper cemetery outside Fermoy, beside his old comrade Michael Fitzgerald.[436]

> I knew Liam Lynch terribly well. Liam Lynch was a clerk inside in Mitchelstown in O'Neill's Hardware in Baldwin Street and I often went into him, maybe sent down for a pound of nails or a little thing or another. But that's how I knew him well and he was reared only three or four miles below Mitchelstown and I knew all his people belong to him. I knew his brothers well … He was shot in the Knockmealdowns … I heard it that day … I knew a lot of them, terrible lot of them. There were some lived within a mile of Mitchelstown – very near Mitchelstown. I knew them all nearly. He came from Ballylanders [Anglesboro]. That was a few mile down. But I knew them all.[437]

He described Liam Lynch as 'a determined man' and 'a great man', but pointed out that he was never active with him while in the IRA.[438] Though Lynch had travelled to Dublin on occasions between 1920 and 1922, **SEÁN CLANCY** said he never met him.[439]

27 APRIL 1923

Following a meeting of anti-Treaty IRA military leaders held in Poulacapple, Frank Aiken, the newly elected chief-of-staff, issued a command that all offensive operations should be suspended from noon on Monday 30 April.[440] **DAN KEATING** explained what happened.

> There was feelings in the IRA in almost every county in Ireland. The IRA they were, well they were gone. There was nothing left but they held a meeting in Tipperary and it was decided that the conflict would be called off and that they'd dump their arms.[441]

ANTHONY MCGINLEY was adamant that nothing more could have been done.

> We tried to keep the fight going but sure we hadn't a chance. All the bloody corner boys in the town that never was in anything, they were all

in the Free State Army. Well-armed and all. They were crawling all over the country, you couldn't move. But it was very much underground. We tried to keep it – the republic going but we couldn't.[442]

Eighty years later in 2003, he didn't have a good word to say about the army during the Civil War, despite having been a member himself for six months.

Oh, they were a bunch of hooligans. Do you see there was a lot in the Free State Army that never was in anything? But Lord here the army got up a good pay, three good meals a day and all the bloody bums and corner boys of all the wee towns was in the army and they would shoot their mother. Why wouldn't they? They were getting well paid and well fed for the first time in their life.[443]

This was also the date that the Cumann na nGaedheal party was formally launched, having been fashioned from the pro-Treaty wing of Sinn Féin, which had been running the country since the split.[444] Before the Civil War was officially over, tragedy was to darken the McGinley's door. Anthony's first cousin Eunan McGinley, who had participated in the Rising aged 16, was fatally injured when his motorcycle collided with a military lorry near Balbriggan on 11 May 1923. The driver, J. Murphy, Gormanstown, brought him to the nearest hospital in the lorry, but he passed away a short time later. The inquest that followed exonerated the driver and ruled that the incident had been an accident. At the time, Eunan was employed by the Free State as a local government department auditor, whilst his father P.T. McGinley (Cú Uladh) was president of the Gaelic League. P.T. McGinley stated at the inquest that after the collision his dying son had told him that he had been travelling on his own side of the road at a normal rate of speed.[445]

In a letter to the *Derry Journal* in July 1924, Anthony McGinley's father, Michael, made it known in no uncertain terms what he thought of his nephew's death. He was engaged in a letter-writing spat at the time with 'SAOIRSEANACH', who had written that *'the occurrance was a pure accident'*.[446]

I say now deliberately that it was what is now far too well known in Ireland – premeditated accident. Hundreds of the same kind have happened in Ireland for the past two years. Unfortunately we have got used to them. He ['SAOIRSEANACH'] makes great capital out of young MacGinley being an auditor for the Free State. Why, MacGinley was an auditor before the Partition Government was born, and 'twas well known to all the Free Staters of Dublin and their satellites how thoroughly he detested the Free State and everything connected with it. That's the reason he sleeps today beside his compatriots in Glasnevin.[447]

The mother of Patrick Pearse, who rejected the Treaty, was among those present at his funeral, as was his cousin Dr McGinley TD, who supported it.[448] Incidentally, Eunan's brother Conor worked as an architect in Dublin and was anti-Treaty.[449]

24 MAY 1923

Frank Aiken issued a proclamation to the anti-Treaty IRA ordering the dumping of arms (that they be hidden in arms dumps). Lynch's death enabled Éamon de Valera to reassert some control and he also issued a message endorsing this act.[450] The Irish Civil War ended. Exact casualty figures vary, but in the region of 1,500 people died. Some 800 were Free State troops, some 400 were IRA and some 300 were civilians.[451] Over 12,000 prisoners and internees were in jail, including **DAN KEATING**, who would be released by the end of the year. **MICHAEL CASEY** explained what he and the republicans he knew around Mitchelstown did with their guns.

> We had to give up them guns; we had no call to them guns. The headquarters there had collected all them guns.[452]

At conflict's end, many of his friends were in jail and 'a lot of them went away to America and everywhere ... never came back'.[453] Having made up his mind to leave the IRA at this point, Michael maintained that the Civil War was: 'Shocking. It was a pity it ever happened.'[454]

CHAPTER 8

Picking up the pieces, May 1923 – April 1949

25 MAY 1923

A friend and former comrade of **PATRICK FITZGERALD'S** was killed by the Free State Army. Thomas Mackey, from Fountain, Moore Hill, Tallow, had joined the Kilwatermoy Company during the Anglo-Irish War and taken the anti-Treaty side afterwards.[1] Even though the Civil War was meant to have been over, he was killed near his home at a place called the Green Road after being surprised by a detachment of Free State troops in a motor vehicle. He is buried in Knockanore.[2] According to Patrick Fitzgerald:

> There was a very bad Free State soldier in Tallow. He was an officer. It was he shot Mackey for no reason or no proof at all.[3]

He explained that Mackey had been on the run and 'was going along the road and there was a branch road coming into that and he went up there'. He was then shot by the soldier, who took aim from behind a white fence. Patrick was of the opinion that Mackey could have avoided his fate and that his decision:

> To walk along the public road – a very foolish thing to do. Oh, there was bad men in the Free State Army.[4]

In 1937, a limestone cross was erected at the place where Mackey fell at Sapperton Crossroads.[5]

27 AUGUST 1923

A general election was held in which Cumann na nGaedheal obtained 63 seats and anti-Treaty Sinn Féin got 44.[6] In the lead-up, Éamonn de Valera, a candidate in Co. Clare, had been arrested in Ennis under the Public Safety Act as he was about to make a speech. A tense atmosphere existed at **GERRY SMYTH'S** local polling station in Stackallen.

> I remember an election, general election, I think it was 1923 and my father was presiding officer in the school. This shows you now the awful part of the Civil War and a lorryload of de Valera's crowd pulled up and came in and got the school register of electors and the first fellow came up and said he was a certain man from the area who was dead.

And the personating agent, there was only one personating agent in the room and he was for the Treaty and he said to my father 'Swear him' and the man took the Bible from my father and he held the Bible in one hand and pulled out a point 45 Webley revolver and held it in the other and swore he was the dead man, absolutely there and then.

So when he went out my father said, 'Listen,' he says 'we'll let them all vote,' he says 'because they'll all want to perjure themselves and I don't want it on my conscience.' So they let the whole lot of them vote and when they finished voting got the register and picked up all the rest and went in and my brother went in 'name please,' 'James Moran' – he was the parish priest he was on holidays and we counteracted the whole vote of the anti-Treaty crowd.[7]

Those elected in the Meath constituency were E.J. Duggan (Cumann na nGaedheal), P.J. Mulvanny (Farmers' Party) and David Hall (Labour). J.J. O'Kelly (Republican) was fourth.[8] Despite his imprisonment, de Valera topped the poll in Clare. He was released in July 1924, going on to found Fianna Fáil on 23 March 1926. Many who had fought on the anti-Treaty side during the Civil War would support his party; others would not. Fianna Fáil took the oath of allegiance and their seats in the Dáil in 1927.

9 SEPTEMBER 1923

A week following this date, the *Donegal News* contained a brief notice that within the county national troops had arrested T. MacGinley, Ballybofey, C. Quinn, Fintown, and J. Nagle, Boherlahan.[9] Although it gives Ballybofey (23km away), where his father, Michael, lived as his address, T. MacGinley, Ballybofey, was in fact **ANTHONY (TONY) MCGINLEY** who resided at Largnalarkin, Ballinamore, with his aunt Máire and his uncle Muiris Mac Daibhid. When asked by soldiers, he may just have given his father's name and address as his point of contact. The *Donegal Democrat* confirmed that it was Anthony.

> On the night after the declaration of the poll for Donegal two houses were raided in the Fintown district, and arrests made included two of the Republican personating officers who acted in the booths on Monday, the 27th of August. One of the arrested men is Connell Quinn taken at his father's house at Fintown. The other is Anthony E. McGinley (Tony) son of Michael McGinley, Ballybofey, taken at the house of his uncle, Maurice McDevitt, of Largnalarkin, Fintown. Up to the present no charge has been preferred against either prisoner.[10]

Michael McGinley would have been well known to the army for his opposition to the Treaty and Free State government, which he had expressed openly with great fervour on platforms when campaigning ahead of the recent general election. The previous month at Drumkeen Crossroads and Stranorlar, for example, he had outlined the Sinn Féin policy and appealed to the electors to vote Sinn Féin and save the country from '*the degradation of the so-called Free State'.* [11] The *Sinn Féin* newspaper detailed where the arrested men were taken.

> Two of the Sinn Féin personating agents in Tirconaill were arrested on Sunday night (September 9th) on account of election work. There are rumours of other arrests. The two arrested are Mr. A. McGinley, a nephew of P.T. McGinley (Cú Uladh), and Mr. Quinn, from near Fintown. Mr. McGinley's father gave much assistance as a speaker at the election. Both prisoners are at Drumboe Castle. [12]

This particular election work wasn't mentioned when Anthony went into the details of what occurred that night. During the course of our interview, however, he did remark that elections at this time were 'one-sided' and that the Free State would use the Gardaí against the republicans for 'anything at all'. He also said the Gardaí were used during elections to 'summons' and 'harass' them.

> I was arrested of course, me and another fellow. Sure it was nearly all over then but there was Civil War. We, I was sleeping in that room that I'm sleeping in now and Jesus the door, do you see, was always on the latch because there was men on the run and I was leading them through the hills and keeping them in this house here. Some of them from the south of Ireland and they were wanting.
>
> So they got information. There was always informers you know around Ireland and they got information because when they came in that night, the door was on the latch because we didn't know when a man would come and he'd be kept here for a week or so and I would take him to some other safe house do you know. That's the way they done it. I would take them to another safe house. You couldn't take them to every house you know because there was some of them was on the Free State side. And they got information that they were stopping here and that I was leading them.
>
> In fact, they burst in the door and they didn't have to burst it in because it used to be on the latch because men that was on the run would come and slip in you see. And by chance there was no one here that night and they pulled me out when I was getting out of bed. Oh, there was a strong smell of drink off them and the officer, I never found out who he was? And I was getting out of bed in there in that room. And they were rooms a bunch of them in it you see. There was more outside at the window and weren't they well informed. Outside at that time there was five windows and you see two of them going into the sitting room. I was sleeping in there in that room that I sleep in now. You see in there. And that was the third window when you turn in at the back if you come down the lane – the third window.
>
> A nice calm night and I never heard any lorry coming. I suppose they'd knocked off the engine. But the next thing I heard the sound of the steps coming down and then and by God I got suspicious right away because if there was someone coming had a bicycle and I was a young

fellow at the time and the like of me often would be called to go for the priest for someone who was ill do you see, and they would be coming fast. Jesus, fairly steady step come over the back and made me suspicious so I had my eyes open and the next thing and weren't they well informed. My window was the third over and they passed the other two and there was a part of it down. It was a very close night and the first thing I seen the rifle coming in. There was a good moon. You could see, I seen the uniform covering me in the bed. Isn't it a wonder?[13]

Anthony said it was members of the Free State Army as opposed to Gardaí that arrested him and Con Quinn that night.

There was another fellow in Fintown. They took me up and they stopped in Hightown and Fintown, they arrested him. His mother put up a wild fight. She was a very cross woman. She was reading in the papers where there was ones arrested and they were got along the road dead, they shot them in the back – and that was true. And she was sure. And my aunt Mary raised hell here in the kitchen. She caught a hold of me and she was refusing to let me go. She was reading in the paper too. She figured they'd shoot me out along the road. You see. There was a wild scene here in the kitchen.[14]

Con Quinn's mother was Rose Quinn née McDevitt.[15] Interestingly, Anthony claimed to have known at least one of his captors – he happened to be a brother of the man in command of Free State forces in the county.

Barney Sweeney was the man that was in charge of the arrest of me that night. Barney Sweeney – a no good son of a bitch. His brother Joe was a gentleman you see but he was a bad hoor.[16]

Anthony recalled that at the time of his arrest 'most of the struggle was over nearly'. In fact, the food they got to eat in jail wasn't too bad.

Me and a fellow from Fintown – Con Quinn ... We didn't give a damn once we went down to Drumboe. Didn't give a damn. We were in a cell near the, down in the cellars was the kitchen and some of the cells. And there was a bunch in that kitchen, a bunch of bums that didn't give a damn. We were fed with stuff that we never got at home – the best. They didn't give a damn.[17]

The pair were interned until November in Drumboe Castle, surroundings Anthony knew well from the six months he served in the army.[18]

Oh, me and Con Quinn, no we weren't in too long. They told us to get out.

Anthony claimed that the night he was arrested he was offered £200 or a bullet in the back to betray Donncha MacNelis (see 26 July 1922).[19]

They wanted information, you see? They put me out there in the street and a guy the first thing he done is he hit me a clip in the jaw and then he had the revolver. He was the sergeant or an officer and he stuck it in my chest and started asking me information about men on the run.[20]

Anthony asserted that they got no leads from him and that in any event he knew nothing. Con (Connell) Quinn of Hightown, Fintown, had previously been arrested in July 1922 and interned in Glenties Barracks. However, he was released two months later suffering from a serious medical illness.[21] Once recovered, he rejoined his local IRA company, going on to remain highly active for the remainder of the Civil War.[22] Drumboe Castle was evacuated by Free State troops in 1924.[23]

3 OCTOBER 1923

At a special court held in Mallow, cattle dealer and drover **PATSY HOLMES** appeared as a witness. He was giving evidence in a case against a Denis Horan, who gave his address as 1 Camden Quay, Cork, and who was charged with having stolen seven cattle from a Mr Cornelius Crowley. Evidence was given by Crowley that while attending Mallow Fair he observed certain cattle being offered for sale. He identified them as his own, which he had on his land at Ballyvolane, Cork. When he questioned the men who were selling them to a cattle dealer named English from Co. Tipperary, they ran away. Civic Guard McDonagh stated that while returning to barracks from Mallow South Station, he found the accused lying asleep on the side of the road. After being unable to give a satisfactory account of himself, he was taken to the barracks. Patsy stated that he saw the accused in charge of the seven cattle at Mallow Fair, endeavouring to sell them. Horan was remanded in custody to the next district court.[24] When Mallow District Court sat on 13 November, Patsy again appeared as a witness.[25] The accused was ultimately convicted.[26]

In January 1924, however, there was a further development in the case when a man named Cornelius Jones, who was working in Bachelor's Quay, Cork, was arrested by the Civic Guard and charged with also being connected with the stealing of the seven cattle.[27] When he stood trial before a jury at Cork Quarter Sessions held in City Court in May 1924, he pleaded not guilty to the charge of stealing the animals. In a second count he was charged with receiving. His solicitor stated he had already been in custody for 10 weeks. Patsy Holmes was among those to give evidence against him. Jones was found guilty on the first count by the jury and sentenced to six months imprisonment with hard labour. It transpired that this was his second conviction for the larceny of cattle, having been previously sentenced to four months in 1917.[28]

6 OCTOBER 1923

Time having expired on his second stint of six months' membership, **DANIEL O'DONOVAN** was discharged from the army at Fermoy and returned to Bantry. He had held the rank of private and his number was VR25320 (Volunteer

Reserve). His details were recorded as 5 foot 10 inches in height with fair hair and grey eyes. His character was noted as 'very good'. Daniel had served for a total of one year and forty-two days in the army.[29]

> Well, I found that I felt safer. The time I joined the army you had to do one or the other to feel safe. So that I felt that the thing was practically over and safer and I left the army. I didn't intend the army as a place to take up a job in life.[30]

When he had left Bantry in February, Daniel knew men who had joined the Free State Army and the anti-Treaty IRA but also 'a number who didn't take any part' in the Civil War. He was aware, however, that men might since have adopted a particular stance since he had gone away, whilst others could have switched sides.

> But we wouldn't know. We were separated. First of all to, at least I was first of all from Bantry to Lismore and after that, after coming out I remained out of the movement until joining the Garda about nearly two years later in 25 [see 6 March 1925].[31]

Coincidentally, a few days after Daniel left the army, a prisoner named Morrissey, who was in the custody of the military at Lismore Castle, managed to escape.[32]

10 OCTOBER 1923

District Officer **WILLIAM GEARY** was transferred from Carrickmacross to Monaghan town. Four days later, a hunger strike broke out in Mountjoy Gaol in protest over the lack of republican releases taking place and the poor jail conditions that existed. Prisoners demanded their immediate and unconditional release.[33] The strike quickly spread to other jails and internment camps, including Tintown on the Curragh, where **DAN KEATING** was being held, although 300 prisoners had been released from there days before.[34] Soon roughly 8,000 republicans were on hunger strike nationally.[35] Figures for Tintown Nos. 1, 2 and 3 amounted to 3,390 participants and Hare Park 100 participants. Of these, 1,300 were internees.[36]

The strike was hard to manage, with some men being released or transferred and large defections in the early stages.[37] By 28 October, the number that had gone off the hunger strike in Tintown was 1,360. The governor of the camp was handed a written note by one of the internees on behalf of others, informing him that it was terminated.[38] However, 1,200 men at Tintown did remain on hunger strike, with some 5,000 still on it around the country by the end of the month.[39] Come 20 November, however, the numbers participating nationally had dramatically reduced to a figure of 338, which included 27 in Tintown No. 2 and 41 in Tintown No. 3.[40] This was largely down to prisoner releases taking place, although mainly of men not on the strike. At this point there were 6,834 men incarcerated nationally, reduced from 11,316 in July.[41]

Republican leaders including Tom Derrig visited the hunger strikers on the Curragh, Hare Park and elsewhere, directing them to finish their protest despite the fact that its objective of immediate and unconditional release for all prisoners and internees hadn't been achieved. This culminated in the strike ending for most on 23 November.[42] Dan Keating told Uinseann MacEoin that although every prisoner thought they should join it, not all of them could stand being on hunger strike. Jim Hurley of Clonakilty and Seán O'Connor were two men on the strike in the Curragh that he could vividly remember. Hurley was 42 days on the protest, and when it was called off he sat up and ate half a loaf of bread, which according to Dan he should not have done.[43] Although the government did not give in to the hunger strike, it did start the gradual release of prisoners within weeks of its ending.

16 OCTOBER 1923

The 47th Infantry Battalion of the Free State Army was transferred from Kilkenny Barracks to Wexford; **JACK DUFF**, who was stationed in Clonmel with the 64th Infantry Battalion would be amongst their ranks.[44] In the lead-up, he had been part of an army escort accompanying an accounts officer out of Clonmel to the different posts around the command where army garrisons had been located. Their job was to collect bills and monies due to them for billeting. He was seven or eight days on that job and Commandant Swan was the name of the pay officer.

On arrival back at the barracks in Clonmel after midnight, Jack was instructed to see Adjutant Myers. On doing so, he was informed that the 64th Infantry Battalion, to which Jack was attached, was to be disbanded, and that he and the rest of the men would be off to Wexford in the morning. This 64th Infantry Battalion at the time consisted of 11 corporals and 100 men. Jack was a sergeant.

Some hours later, Jack and the men were all sent down to the railway station in Clonmel to board a special train to Kilkenny and then on to Wexford. They would join the 47th Infantry Battalion, newly transferred from Kilkenny to Wexford Barracks. This battalion was headed by Commandant Jim O'Hanrahan.[45] Despite setting off on their journey early from Clonmel, it was evening before they arrived at their destination and all the men were eager to head out on the town.[46]

18 DECEMBER 1923

DAN KEATING was released from Tintown Internment Camp on the Curragh. His own recollection was that it occurred in March 1924; however, this is the date on record.[47] His comrade Denis Quille was released a day earlier, but Jerry Myles (marked dangerous) was held until 24 April.[48]

> Well, in the Civil War I spent actually nineteen months in jail that time ... We were all nearly left out in the course of a couple of months you know in '24 and the thing was to get a job then. There was no work in Ireland at the time very much you know.[49]

During Dan's period of internment on the Curragh since February, at least five internees had died on its grounds: Daniel Downey, Frank O'Keeffe, Matthew

Ginnity, Dick Hume and Joseph Whitty. A sixth man, Joseph Lacey, would die on Christmas Eve. In addition, the body of Military Policeman Private Joseph Bergin had been found in the canal at Milltown, Kildare, on 14 December. Suspected of spying as well as carrying messages in and out of the Curragh Camp for republican prisoners, he was 'dealt' with by several members of a unit attached to the Free State's intelligence department. The Laois native, who had previously served in Maryborough Gaol, was shot six times in the head. Prisoner John McCoy said: *'Bergin would take anything out. He was talking too much about it.'* In 1925, an ex-intelligence officer in the Free State Army named Captain James Murray was found guilty of Bergin's murder and sentenced to hang, although on appeal his sentence was commuted to penal servitude for life. Charges against two other army men were dropped. Murray died in Portlaoise Prison in 1929.[50]

> Well, the night I came out of prison I got a job driving a bread van in Tralee and I was in that for, oh well a year and a half. I got a job then as an insurance agent with the Prudential Insurance in Limerick. I never liked the job and times were bad anyway and I decided anyway I left that, and I went back what I was trained at. I went back to the bar and I went to Dublin.[51]

Dan had no intention of leaving the IRA.

> Oh, I was actually a member for all years after, never lost touch now with them and gave them every help I could always all along. I mean my house was always open to the IRA.[52]

He disagreed with any notion that the Irish Civil War was a waste of time.

> I wouldn't subscribe to that view at all. You had to take a stand. After all anyone that's honest and they won't stand up to be counted – Ireland should have one parliament for Ireland you know … Well of course the purpose of the Civil War. It was inflicted, it should never have taken place but then again you got selfish men that was prepared to accept that [the Treaty] and to accept the money that went with it you know. No doubt about that.[53]

7 FEBRUARY 1924

JACK DUFF, who had been serving as a Reserve (a different category to Daniel O'Donovan), re-enlisted in the army.[54] There had been 52,000 soldiers and 3,000 officers in the army at the end of 1923.[55] Now, with the trouble over, GHQ sought to restructure it for peacetime and drastically reduce the number of personnel to 18,000. Plans for large-scale demobilisations were objected to by some officers, culminating in the so-called 'army mutiny' of March 1924, which ended when the mutineers were eventually forced out.[56] Demobilisation continued unabated, culminating in some army personnel who had already enlisted in 1922 being required to re-enlist.

Jack told Commandant Peter Young that in 1922 the army had recruited any young fellow so long as he could hold a rifle. In 1924, however, when they started the demobilisation process, men were weeded out by categorisation. Examples included those with no service in the 1919–1921 war, those who were illiterate, and those with some bad character against them. Jack maintained such reasons were used to put soldiers out of the force.

To remain in the army, one had to pass courses and written examinations. Jack recalled serving in Clones and doing an exam in Dundalk. He remembered a man with dark skin named Washington, who was a sergeant from the transport division, sitting next to him during the exam. As this man was just sitting there looking at his paper, the officer came down and asked him whether he was going to commence his examination. Washington replied 'No' because he couldn't write. Jack said this man couldn't even write 'nil' on the paper when asked to do so. This was an examination for non-commissioned officers (NCOs). Those who were deemed fit to be NCOs were put on a list, whereas those deemed not fit were given the option of reverting to the rank of private, being transferred to another unit or taking whatever money was coming to them up to the end of their present service and going out. A lot of them got a lump sum equivalent to what they would have got if they had stayed in the army until the end of their service; some stayed in the army, whereas others took the money and later rejoined the army. There were men, of course, that just blew the lump sum.[57] Jack Duff was among those to successfully re-enlist, and on doing so resumed service with the 47th Infantry Battalion until being transferred to the 20th Infantry Battalion in May 1924.[58]

In September 1923, **SEÁN CLANCY** had returned to Ennis from Gort, continuing to serve as a pay officer, this time with the 12th Infantry Battalion, until January 1924.[59] From there he was moved to Tipperary town and then Limerick.[60] In March 1924, he was sent from Limerick to pay the troops stationed across Co. Kerry. There had been much change in the army there over the course of the demobilisation process, with many officers gone and units having been disbanded. Seán arrived in Ballymullen Barracks, Tralee, in a saloon car accompanied by a driver and two soldiers armed with rifles. Having army authority to write cheques and draw money from the banks, he travelled the county for three weeks paying garrisons in such locations as Listowel, Kenmare, Killarney, Caherciveen and Valentia Island. At the time, significant elements in Co. Kerry were still very much against the government and the army, so Seán was prepared for the possibility of being attacked. In fact, on more than one occasion during his three weeks, shots were fired on him and his men from a distance by republicans, but they emerged unscathed.[61] Having paid the troops, he returned to Limerick. Seán was commissioned as a Lieutenant on 1 October 1924, being among those retained in service in the army.[62]

5 AUGUST 1924

The Irish Free State government passed legislation to award Military Service Pensions to those who could prove that they had rendered service in relevant forces such as the Irish Volunteers during the period from the 1916 Rising to the start of the Civil War in 1922. Crucially, eligible applicants also had to have served in the Free State Army during the Civil War of 1922–1923. This meant that members of Cumann na mBan, neutrals during the Civil War, and those who had fought on the anti-Treaty IRA side during the conflict were excluded until 1934, when the pension system was overhauled.

The board of assessors and the various referees who operated the pension system between 1924 and 1958 applied different and often contradictory criteria. The 1924 board of assessors expected applicants to prove that they had taken part in an 'act of war'. During the 1930s, the referees looked for proof of having 'taken part in at least one major operation'. By the 1940s, 'actual fighting service' was not a prerequisite, and in the 1950s a much more liberal interpretation of service was applied. Between 1924 and 1958, there were 80,000 applications for Military Service Pensions, of which 18,186 were successful, while 68,896 service medals were awarded.[63]

PATSY HOLMES, who had spent a year in Ballykinlar Internment Camp, was among the thousands to apply. In 1957, having had his application re-examined on oath at the Courthouse, Mallow, he was refused a pension.[64]

> Well, I'll tell you now about the pension. I looked for a medal and a lad said to me, 'I can't give you a medal,' says he. That's all right but anyway the other fellow said to me, says he, 'Were you ever,' says he to me, 'in a major engagement?' 'Now,' says I, 'I couldn't be in two places at the one time.' But he was from Dublin. So I came out and one of our own fellows says, 'How did you get on?' Says I, 'Would you believe it,' says I, 'a shilling he offered me.' 'Oh Christ, come on back in.' 'I'm going back no more,' says I. I went back no more. 'Oh Jesus,' says he.
>
> The fellow told me after I was a terrible fool that I didn't take it. It's about £50 a week now. It was a brother of mine borrowed a suit of clothes for me. Like, I had nothing. I hadn't it at all. And Clancy [his employer] and all them fellows went mad. And one fellow locked up left about £40,000 and he was never out day or night. But no, said I, never bother them again with it. Nor I never bothered with it after. Nor if they came out today and gave it to me, I wouldn't take it and I'm going to tell you, I might see a lot more than some of the fellows that got it at all.[65]

His service having been certified, Patsy was issued with a medal in September 1969.[66] He wasn't the only IRA veteran of the 1919–1921 troubles interviewed for this book who applied for a medal or the pension. In total, nine IRA and two Cumann na mBan veterans were interviewed; several of them applied for a medal or the pension and were successful, whilst others weren't. There were some that didn't apply at all and refused to do so.

1 OCTOBER 1924

Garda Inspector **WILLIAM GEARY** was promoted to the rank of superintendent. Transfers were frequent in the early days of the force.

Well, I'll come to something. I was promoted an inspector along the way. And in 1924 October 1st I was promoted to superintendent in Carrickmacross and that year I was supposed to, I was ordered to have a car. I bought a Ford car – a Ford touring car. I paid for it in cash and then I was transferred up to Monaghan town [10 October 1923]. I remained there some time and then my next transfer was to Dublin to the depot [13 October 1924]. I was in charge of, I had a company there. That's very interesting. One day in rotation, mind you the depot was operated like an army barrack. There were sentries set out. Now when you'd be an officer of the day, one of the superintendents, you had to see that the sentries were set out – you had to. You'd inspect them at night, see as the food was cooked properly and you had to lead the parade down the church on Sundays down to the quays – church parade they called it.[67]

Commissioner O'Duffy used to join the men in the officer's mess to play cards at night. William played against him a few times but always lost and gave it up.[68]

6 NOVEMBER 1924

The body of Charlie Daly, who had been executed in Drumboe in March 1923, was reinterred in the burial ground in Kiltallagh near Castlemaine, Co. Kerry. His remains and those of Larkin, Enright and O'Sullivan had been buried in Drumboe Woods on the grounds of the castle, but in 1924 theirs were among the 77 corpses disinterred by the Free State and removed to Athlone Military Barracks to be eventually received and reinterred by their loved ones in their home counties.[69] On Thursday 6 November, **DAN KEATING** was amongst the impressive turnout that came to pay their last respects to Charlie Daly, a man he knew.[70] Such republican funerals weren't always straightforward affairs, however.

> Oh, we were all excommunicated. Yes, firmly excommunicated you know. But in a very short time there was no place worse than the parish where I lived here. You had a man, a parish priest here Father Brennan and he belonged to the Árd Comhairle of Fine Gael (Cumann na nGaedheal) or at the time you know, and oh, he was very bitter. And actually, we held a collection for the IRA one time and he went to take, we had a bucket you know and he went to take it off of us, and he assaulted one of them Pat Hurley. And sometime after that the Free State government they decided they'd release the bodies of the seventy-seven people that were executed to be buried in their home place. Some were buried in republican plots and all that.[71]

Father Patrick Joseph Brennan, a native of Caherciveen and a firm Cumann na nGaedheal supporter, had been appointed as parish priest of Castlemaine in June 1922.[72] Dan recounted that on the day of Charlie Daly's funeral, he locked the church gates and door, denying the remains entry to the building. Consequently, Daly's body was then taken to the chapel in Firies, which was in an outside parish

7km away, to be received by the priest there. When the funeral party returned later the same day to have Daly interred in the family plot in Kiltallagh graveyard, Father Brennan still had the gates locked. This was an outrage in the eyes of the people, so a group took it upon themselves to lift up the gates from the hinges and throw them aside. Charlie Daly was then buried, and a man said the rosary over his grave.[73] The remains of Daniel Enright and Tim O'Sullivan, also executed at Drumboe, were laid to rest in their native Listowel.

On 29 October, when the body of Seán Larkin from Belagherty, Magherafelt, was being conveyed from Athlone for burial to his native county, it passed through Ballybofey and on to Stranorlar, where the cortege made a halt at the main gate of the Drumboe grounds. Here **ANTHONY McGINLEY'S** father, Michael, of Ballybofey, presided at a ceremony in which Seán McMenamin, a well-known Tirconaill writer and Gaelic teacher, recited the rosary, and Joseph O'Grianna delivered a brief oration.[74]

On 17 March of the following year, Michael McGinley also presided at a celebration held in Stranorlar to mark the second anniversary of the four men's deaths.[75] Interestingly, three days earlier, Father P. Brennan had said Mass for the repose of the soul of Charlie Daly at Kiltallagh church. It was exactly two years to the day after his execution. There was a large congregation present, including relatives, friends and comrades of the deceased. Afterwards, a wreath was placed on the grave, which is situated in the churchyard.[76]

8 DECEMBER 1924

Superintendent **WILLIAM GEARY** was transferred to Munster.

> From the depot I was sent to Newport, Co. Tipperary. I remained there about a few months but anyway there was rumours that there was poitín-making up in the hills and one time we organised, we travelled over the mountains to the other side of it. We found nothing.[77]

This was a period when poitín-making was a common activity throughout the country, especially in Gaeltacht areas.[78]

4 FEBRUARY 1925

WILLIAM GEARY'S next posting after having served as a garda superintendent in Newport would earn him the wrath of the IRA after he successfully investigated one of their operations.

> I was transferred to Templemore and Templemore was very quiet although we had a big bank robbery there – £28,000 stolen. Four guys came in armed just as the bank was closing and got away in a motor car. We convicted one man. One of the sergeants there, Sergeant Gallagher, a born detective and interestingly enough he kept a diary, I didn't know of it but he overheard a statement where a certain man said, he said, 'I'll cut my ears off if I don't get Gallagher fired and Geary reduced,' because we got one man convicted.[79]

The robbery occurred at 2.45 p.m. on 24 March 1925, when three armed men entered the Bank of Ireland premises at Roscrea, held up staff and got away with £10,617 in a hired chauffeur-driven motor car.[80] By 10 April, three men from Thurles had been arrested and charged. Interestingly, they were all ex-members of the Free State Army.[81] In November, only Michael O'Brien was convicted following a trial at the Central Criminal Court in Dublin, largely as a result of the wholesale intimidation of witnesses and the non-cooperation of the bank officials. He was sentenced to seven years' penal servitude.[82] All informers, witnesses and investigators associated with the conviction were considered to be in mortal danger from here on in.

6 MARCH 1925

DANIEL O'DONOVAN joined An Garda Síochána. His references when he applied were Reverend M. Murphy, Shanakiel, Bantry and by now Superintendent Michael C. Connolly (ex-Bantry IRA and Free State Army).[83] Having been accepted, Daniel was one of around 35 recruits called to the Phoenix Park Depot in Dublin to undergo the course of training to become a member of the force.[84] The depot at this point was being used as a combined headquarters and training centre.[85] The Civic Guard had been officially renamed An Garda Síochána in August 1923, and in April 1925 would merge with the DMP to form one police service.[86] Daniel O'Donovan recalled leaving Bantry for the capital.

> I came by bus. The train service was knocked down due to the damage done to the railway. And I got the bus to the city, Cork city and by train from Cork city to Dublin where I joined the Garda at the depot – Phoenix Park.[87]

At this time, small numbers of recruits were being admitted to the depot regularly – almost on a weekly basis. Daniel was one of a total of 780 recruits taken in 1925. The average training period was 12 to 16 weeks, but the actual time would depend to a large degree on how long a member took to achieve the required standard.[88]

> Well, there were no other jobs available, all businesses were closed down the most of the businesses were closed down and I was just the age for the Garda and I felt it was one of the best things that I could take up at that particular time and give them a trial and if I didn't like them I could leave them when things got better. But as it was, there were all young lads like myself in the job at the time and I felt quite happy and remained on for the full duration from which I drew a pension that I'm enjoying now.[89]

When Daniel joined the Gardaí, Eoin O'Duffy was the commissioner.

> Yes, O'Duffy was the commissioner. I joined exactly three years after the thing was commenced, the army or the Gardaí were commenced, in '25, March '25 and I served for the full term.[90]

He didn't know O'Duffy in any personal capacity.

> Well, I didn't, I saw him but as regards meeting no. But I saw him because I served under him for six months in the depot ... He seemed nice as far as we were concerned then and gave us every encouragement.[91]

Disputes over land were frequent in society at this time. There was also a big problem in relation to alcohol.

> I'd say there was in the country but of course we were all confined to towns for a good while, maybe for a year or two. And there was a fair share of poitín. I heard all about it because there was no discipline as regards drink at that time. The pubs could be open at any hour and so forth like that. It was only when there was any danger of break-up that the pubs closed and the Gardaí came into being and they brought the law back again as far as pubs and other things were concerned.[92]

Daniel, whose Garda number was 6638, had postings in the Divisions of Sligo/Leitrim, Tipperary and Kerry.

> I was first transferred to Sligo and after spending five to six years in Sligo I was transferred to Cashel. And after spending under two years to Cashel I went to Carrick-on-Suir and served for seven or eight years in Carrick-on-Suir. When I got married and then I was transferred from Carrick-on-Suir to Thurles.[93]

Most of his service was conducted in Tralee, where he was transferred upon marriage in 1942. Daniel retired in 1968.[94]

7 MARCH 1925

ANTHONY McGINLEY boarded a ship named SS *Columbia* and set sail from Moville, Co. Donegal, for pastures new.[95] On the ship's passenger list he is recorded amongst the passengers sailing from Derry as a labourer whose last permanent residence was Ballybofey. His father, Michael McGinley, Ballybofey, is named as his nearest relative or friend in the country from whence he came. Anthony came before an immigration officer on 17 March, who recorded that he intended to stay with his cousin Joseph McDevitt, who had also paid his passage.[96] But prior to this, had he stayed on in the IRA after the Civil War?

> No, I didn't. I done what a terrible, as they says now, many young men of twenty – emigrated.[97]

He would head for the United States.

> Oh, sure Jesus they were crowding, I was booked for nearly eighteen months before I got away, that will show you the crowd that was going ... Oh, there was a whole lot got out. There in the 1920s there was

the biggest influx since the Famine of young men and girls too and every bit as bitter as the Famine.[98]

It's estimated that in the 1920s in the region of 220,000 people left the Irish Free State for the United States.[99] Anthony insisted that a very high proportion of them were republicans who had opposed the Treaty.

> Men that had fought the British and here they want an Irish republic and the split was on and they fought in the split and they were thrown into jail and some of them was killed and what was left was gone, headed for the States and a terrible bitterness. Years later in a pub in California or New York you could go in and you could hear them men, 'I'll never stand in that damn country, they're bloody traitors' – very bitter. Aye.[100]

It would transpire later in 1925 that the Boundary Commission would leave the border between north and south virtually unchanged and ultimately served only to cement it. Con Quinn of Hightown, Fintown, with whom Anthony had been arrested in 1923, had also emigrated. In March 1924, he left Belfast on board SS *Regina* for Halifax, Nova Scotia, with the intention of permanently settling in Canada.[101] However, in 1926 he went stateside, married in 1930 and remained over 40 years there.[102] He became a prominent member of the trade union movement, making occasional visits home to Fintown from Detroit.[103]

In addition, Anthony's brother, Michael, would end his days in San Francisco.[104] Records show that he sailed to New York from Derry, aged 23, on board SS *Cameronia* on 24 April 1927. He is listed as a farm labourer from Ballybofey, and again his father, Michael, is named as his nearest relative or friend in the country from whence he came. His passage was also paid by a cousin with whom he would be initially staying, Ms Ellen McDevitt, 358 East 139th Street, New York.[105] In 1970, Michael died unexpectedly at his residence in San Francisco having spent over 40 years in the country.[106] Michael McGinley Senior of Glenfin Street, Ballybofey, died aged 88 in 1940.[107]

It's worth mentioning that Anthony's sister was Nora Harkin (1910–2012), the lifelong republican socialist. She was a close friend and companion to fellow socialist, revolutionary, trade unionist and writer Peadar O'Donnell, who lived with her in Dublin for the last six years of his life. Her first encounter with him was as a 10-year-old when she cycled from Ballybofey to Letterkenny to deliver an urgent note to him from her father concerning a local woman whose cow had been seized when she fell into debt. The result was that O'Donnell sorted it and the cow was returned.[108]

In any event, her older brother Anthony McGinley's stay in America was eventful to say the least, and there's a good account of it in *Dr. McGinley and His Times* by Niall Mac Fhionnghaile (Niall McGinley, son of Dr Joseph Patrick McGinley).[109]

Anthony's first port of call was New York. Whilst there, he stayed in the Bronx with his one-time neighbours and cousins the McDevitts, just like his brother would. In fact, Anthony is recorded as living with them in the New York

State Census taken on 1 June 1925.[110] He initially secured a job laying pipes with a gas company, but later got more money working for the Con Edison company. His third job was on the docks, loading and unloading freight. At this he befriended a man from Clare named Johnny Nevin, who had booked on the *Titanic* in 1912 but missed the voyage. Anthony's next job was as a keeper in a mental hospital on Long Island. He recalled that a lot of inmates were ex-boxers. One day, Anthony went swimming with some friends in Lake Success. None of them were good swimmers and Anthony almost met his maker when he got into difficulty in deep water. Fortunately, he was rescued by a man who had spotted him just in time.

In Long Island he met a Scot named Eddie Miller from Ayrshire who owned a motorbike. The two men used it to travel across America and headed west. Money was tight, so they avoided paying for accommodation whenever possible. They asked a sheriff in Indiana if they could stay in his jail for the night, and when he saw that Anthony was Irish he was more than happy to oblige. One slept in a cell and the other on the guard's sofa.

The road was completely under water in Illinois, because the Mississippi had flooded. However, there was a large ridge that was well above the water, so they borrowed a nearby boat to transfer the motorbike to the ridge. Suddenly three men noticed Anthony and Eddie making off with their boat and gave chase. It took some time to convince them that they were only borrowing it. The water was really deep on the other side of the ridge because a dam had burst. However, they walked until they reached a ranch, where two brothers put them up for the night. It was in their house that Anthony listened to the Jack Dempsey versus Gene Tunney fight on the radio. That was on 23 September 1926. The next day, the two brothers took the travellers and their bike across the flood in a rowboat. When they got to Oklahoma, they decided to put the bike in a garage and take the train.

They ventured south to Fort Worth and witnessed first-hand the racial segregation there. Ku Klux Klan signs were everywhere, and Anthony was chastised by a Texan for allowing a Black woman carrying a heavy basket to disembark the train before him.

They next travelled to the oilfields in what was termed 'Wild West Country'. They slept in huts that contained 30 men each – most carrying six-shooters. A Baptist caretaker looked after them. This man had fought the Native Americans in his youth and was full of stories of how he had once seen Bob Ford, who had shot Jessie James, and then Red Kelly, who had shot Bob Ford. All the men on the oilfields found Anthony particularly interesting, because he was the only one who practised his religion. Only one or two of them had ever even been inside a church.

Anthony and Eddie spent two years working in Texas and then set out for California, where the Donegal man would see out the remainder of his time in America. The Great Depression of 1929–1939 was very evident in this state, as it was elsewhere, but he survived by doing part-time jobs. The 1930 Census of the United States taken in April records him as being employed as a laundry worker.[111]

Anthony's time in America also coincided with Prohibition (1920–1933), but he remembered alcohol being easily available, as backhanders to those in authority were the order of the day. He encountered a lot of homeless people, and one particular morning, whilst waiting at a railway terminus near San Francisco, he noticed how many of them kept warm during the night – they would lie on the warm cinders that had been dumped from the engines along the railway line.

16 JUNE 1925

MAI GROGAN from Tullycrine married Patrick McMahon from Drumdigis, Kilmurry, and from this day forward she was known as Mai McMahon. He worked on his family's farm, but the couple soon ended up taking over his parents' other business.[112]

> We had a shop in Kilmurry when I got married, all them are gone today. There's no great business at all in Kilrush today. The creameries was up here and they were making butter and buying eggs and everything else, all that is gone.[113]

The McMahon's grocery and hardware shop was located beside the church in Kilmurry McMahon, and Mai served from behind the counter there for over 50 years. Money was scarce during these times, and many customers got their goods 'on tick'. She and her husband could be waiting weeks or months for the money, but a trust existed between them and the people, resulting in payment usually being handed over in the finish.[114] According to Co. Clare native **SEÁN CLANCY**:

> It's hard to imagine the poverty that was there we'll say seventy or eighty years ago here in Dublin and everywhere else and the emigration and everything else. There was no future for people in those far-off days.[115]

10 FEBRUARY 1926

Garda Superintendent **WILLIAM GEARY** was transferred again in what would transpire to be his last posting.

> From Templemore I was sent down to Kilrush and that was on the 10th of February 1926. Now Kilrush at the time was rather disturbed, a lot of arson – rife. Now I do not know whether it was done by militias or what but anyway thanks to the good police duty of a sergeant named O'Malley, we convicted the son of one farmer for burning his own hay. That more or less stopped it but you see they were compensated when maliciously done. They got compensated when the hay got burned down. Well as I said in the beginning it was very disturbed but we in the Garda, we more or less kept aloof from the people. Now I didn't send out a signal that every man expects to do his duty but it was understood that every man do his duty and we did. They were on duty twenty-four hours a day and I supported them to the best of my ability. In fact, we were extremely successful in court. The secret was when we had a

criminal case I used bring all the witnesses into my office, take statements; take out everything, then there was no surprise in court.[116]

With Kilrush as the district headquarters, there were Garda barracks at Carrigaholt, Kilkee, Doonbeg, Kilmihill, Killadysert, Labasheeda and Knock. The total number of sergeants and gardaí was about 50.[117]

18 APRIL 1926

The first census of the population of the Irish Free State was taken. It transpired that since the 1911 Census there had been a 33 per cent decline (107,000) in the Protestant population of the twenty-six counties that became the Irish Free State. Catholic numbers remained almost static.[118] Much of this occurred as a result of voluntary or involuntary emigration during the turbulent 1919–1923 years, but there were many other factors, such as the impact of World War I, British withdrawal, and even deaths attributed to the 1918 influenza. **PATRICK GREENE** touched upon Protestant decline around Ballinalee where by now he resided.

I mean this area here; the Protestant population is gone down. Where you're sitting now, in a mile round about you to the north here, there was over thirty Protestant families seventy years ago [1933] and they're all gone. They just died out. They didn't marry and they died out. There's just one, two of them left out of all that number. They weren't shot, they weren't; I don't know of any Protestant, I didn't know of any Protestant that was chased out of Co. Longford during the trouble.

They all got on well enough with their neighbours but they were intermarried for generations and they reached a stage where they just didn't marry. There were three or four families when I was going to school, there were three or four Protestant families sending their children to our school. At one time there'd have been eight or nine Protestant lads in our school, Protestant girls – two or three in the girls' school. We always thought they had a better time than we had because they got out at 12 o'clock. They had an hour's recreation every day while we had only a half hour.

But we went to school together, we were in and out of their houses and were on the best of terms with them. But then you see they, they dawdled along, the men, two or three men in a house that didn't marry and that sort of thing.[119]

Incidentally, the Foxhall estate, where Patrick's father, John Greene, had worked all his life, was acquired by the Land Commission and the big house demolished in 1946. Much of the land had already been sold in the 1920s by its then owners.[120] **GEORGE COOPER**, whose sister had married a Welsh soldier in 1922, cited the withdrawal after the Treaty of many of those connected to the British forces in Ireland as one of the main factors.

Well, you see why, you see there are a lot of churches being shut up here now right, all over the country because there were British soldiers all over the country. And through over, all the years there was intermarriage and then when the British soldiers withdrew to England, then their wives and children went with them. But we didn't because we were here and that was it.[121]

NORMAN DOUGLAS in Belfast wasn't surprised that the Protestant population in the south declined.

I think that was more or less a foregone conclusion that that would happen. Now I think there could have been a certain amount of coercion involved as well. Maybe Protestant businesses weren't supported just because of the fact of the set-up and I think the Protestant population in the south by reason of that gradually diminished from a fair percentage to what it is today possibly a minimal.[122]*

In the decades to come, there were also instances whereby Protestants converted to Catholicism, as had **KATHLEEN CHARLES** by the time of her marriage to a Catholic in 1934 (see 6 September 1934). Mixed marriages between Catholics and Protestants were also a factor in Protestant decline. In 1938, when **GEORGE CARPENTER** married Catholic Joan O'Kelly, he agreed beforehand to a marriage in her church and that any children would be brought up in the Roman Catholic faith. The difficulty in getting married in Ireland, however, was that he would have to be a Roman Catholic also, which he refused to become. The alternative was to get married in England. The couple looked into this and found they would have to obtain a Letter of Freedom from Joan's parish priest. This was secured without any bother. The parish priest in Clapham, London, where the ceremony took place, was highly amused that George and Joan had to travel to England to get married. [123]

A census was also taken in the north in April 1926; it revealed that Protestants made up 66.3 per cent of the population, while Catholics accounted for 33.5 per cent.[124]

17 MAY 1926

MARGARET CAHILL arrived in New York on board SS *Scythia*, having emigrated from Ballinasare. Her port of departure was Cobh, and her occupation is listed as a 'domestic' on the passenger record. Her final destination would be the city of Holyoke in Hampden County, Massachusetts, to reside with her older sister, Bridie Cahill, at 984 Dwight Street.[125] Margaret moved to Boston in 1928, where she trained as a nurse at a school located at 222 Newbury Street. She graduated in 1931, going on to spend over 40 years in the profession.[126]

I don't know, I just left, I shouldn't have but I did. I went by boat. There was no such thing as a plane then ... I went back to Ireland a lot but lately I can't go back.[127]

Some of her friends also left Ireland.

There was quite a few of them and we'd all get together. They're all gone now.[128]

Margaret's comrade Bridget Fitzgerald, from Minard West, emigrated to Chicago in 1928, returning after five years to subsequently live in Ventry.[129] In fact, of the 257 recorded west Kerry Cumann na mBan members, 106 were overseas by the 1930s.[130] Margaret Cahill's father died in 1930, followed by his widow, Mary, in 1931.[131] Back in July 1924, her brother Michael Cahill, a farmer in Ballinasare, Co. Kerry, had been adjudicated bankrupt in the Cork Local Bankruptcy Court and a farm he owned was sold.[132] Although the eldest son, he cited his activities, imprisonment and head wound (occasional memory loss) as reasons why his father's farm would ultimately be inherited by his younger brother. His sister Kate Cahill claimed that between 1923 and 1926 the family farm was laid waste and that she had to feed the family at this time. Conditions at home were therefore a factor in Margaret emigrating. By 1936, Michael Cahill had been unemployed for four years, couldn't afford shoes or clothes, and was living in a run-down old house in Kilmurry, Minard East, Annascaul, with only an old overcoat and blanket for cover at night.[133] He died in 1975.[134]

When I asked **MAI MCMAHON (NÉE GROGAN)** in 2003 if many of her neighbours in Tullycrine got jailed during the troubles and later emigrated, it was evident from her answer that having supported the Free State side during the Civil War, she still harboured a certain bitterness towards those who had fought on the republican side, some of whom had left Ireland for America during the 1920s.

> A few of them did but not many, not many in the country. They didn't get the jail there but when the war was over, the most of them hit for America. They found out how foolish they were in the war and they all hit for America and that's it. And they had to keep quiet in America. There was no more about the IRA then ... You can't take over America. You could be doing them things here in Ireland but America is a different country altogether.

She had her own view on why so many who had opposed the Treaty ended up in America.

> Poor – they got nothing out of the IRA army. They got nothing out of that. They had to go and look out for themselves then. They went and they never came back, the most of them. When you go to America you have to go and look for a job or else you'll sleep in the street. You have to watch yourself ...
>
> Oh, we know a lot of them that went and they never came back – never. And they used to say, my husband used to say, 'If they hadn't the price, if they could walk it, they'd walk it home.' America wasn't all riches all the time, not at all. If you went to America for years and years and you brought home five hundred pounds, that time you'd be counted very, very well-off. America wasn't that well-off at all. You had to work hard in America.

Mai visited the United States on three separate occasions. She also had siblings who went there, one of whom she never saw again:

> Well, I had a brother Pat that went to America but he wasn't long there until he died anyway. That's it.

Her younger brother, Patrick, emigrated to New York aged 22 on board SS *Laconia*, which departed from Cobh in June 1926. He had been working as a farmer at home in Tullycrine and it was his mother who paid his passage. He stayed with his sister, Miss D. Grogan, initially in Prospect Place, Brooklyn. Patrick found work as a longshoreman (a docker who loads and unloads ships), but died, unmarried, in Manhattan in July 1929 from complications arising from a hernia operation.[135]

10 JULY 1927

Kevin O'Higgins, then Minister for Justice, was assassinated on his way to Mass in Booterstown. On being brought home mortally wounded, he told his wife that he forgave his assailants, and he died almost five hours later.[136] To republicans like **DAN KEATING**, he had always been a particular hate figure over his hardline approach towards executions during the Civil War, which had not been forgotten.

> Kevin O'Higgins was going around the country at the time and he was a very arrogant man and in the course of a speech in Mullinavat in Kilkenny, some man asked him about executions and he said, 'If we have to,' he says 'we'll execute seventy-seven more.' It was decided that was enough and there was three men in Dublin decided that they'd do a job on him and they did. They shot him on a Sunday morning coming from Mass, out in just in the outskirts of Dublin, in the south side of Dublin.[137]

In January 1925, O'Higgins had been speaking at a public meeting in Sligo when somebody interrupted and asked, 'What about the seventy-seven executions?' to which O'Higgins replied that he stood over them and seven hundred and seventy-seven more if they were necessary.[138] Nobody was ever convicted in connection with his killing, but the three men believed to have been involved were Bill Gannon, Archie Doyle and Tim Coughlan.[139]

25 NOVEMBER 1928

Feeling he had little choice, **WILLIAM GEARY** left Ireland, destined for America.

> I had to. Well, things went along very good in Kilrush. I found the people in Kilrush, there was some affinity between me and them. I enjoyed it there. The people were very nice. As I say I enjoyed Kilrush very much and then on the 16th of June 1928, I was ordered to report to the chief superintendent in Ennis in uniform at ten o'clock. Well, I got, I had a car as you know – John McGlynn was my driver. McGlynn he

was from Co. Mayo and I got there on time. Well, when I went into the office there was some small talk and about ten minutes later the superintendent and I we walked down the street to the Old Ground Hotel in Ennis, up a back stairs. At the top of the stairs he bent over and he said to me, 'Your life is ruined, you'd better tell the truth.' Now I'm not sure whether he said you'd better tell the truth or your life is ruined? I'll not swear on that.

Anyway, we went into the room – remember I was in uniform. Do you know who was there? The Commissioner of the Garda Síochána Eoin O'Duffy, Deputy Commissioner Éamon Coogan and Chief Superintendent Neligan. I saluted. The commissioner told me to sit down. He opened the conversation by saying, 'Mr Geary, Mr Geary, we have evidence that you took a bribe for information from the republicans.'

I was shocked. I blushed. I thought it was; could that happen? There's no truth to that – no. I denied it. I denied it. I was never even offered a bribe. Then they asked me many questions. In fact, they offered me if I was to cooperate they'd be lenient in that case. After that Chief Superintendent Neligan, he was a Limerick man, we went into the adjoining room. I wept. He knew my family. I told him, I says you ought to know I'd never do a thing like that.

That afternoon we returned back to Kilrush in the chief superintendent's car. They searched my office. They went to the bank and he searched my digs. That evening I was suspended from duty, then and there with orders to report to the depot the following Monday. The only thing that happened in the depot was this. There was a good friend of mine when I was in Templemore by the name of Michael O'Higgins – a superintendent. He was from Thurles and he came to see me. Why, I do not know. But anyway, he had seen Neligan. He said to me, 'Neligan told me you're going to be booted out of the force, booted out of the force.'[140]

Neligan was a well-known figure, having been a spy for Michael Collins in Dublin Castle.

Yeah, he was. So as it grew on there was no enquiry or nothing and I was dismissed from the force on the 25th of June 1928. All I got was a week's pay. I was a traitor. I went home around Cloonee. I did nothing in particular in Cloonee only all I did is about go to Mass. I didn't know where I was going. So I left the country and I emigrated to the United States at the end of November 1928. I sailed to New York on the SS *Baltic* and arrived in New York on the 5th of December 1928.[141]

William departed Ireland from Cobh.[142] The passenger list records his occupation as 'wireless operator' and his final destination as being Chicago, where he would reside with a friend named Mr Frank at 1373 Chicago Avenue.[143] The 1930 US Census records him as working as an electrician in Manhattan.[144]

Years later, it is believed that the West Clare IRA Battalion headed by T.J. Ryan had originally wanted to kill William Geary because he was too effective against them. William was also convinced that a plan to murder him had backfired and wrote about it in his memoirs.

> In 1928, in Kilrush, one day while I was in the barracks, my landlady sent a message that there was a visitor waiting to see me. When I arrived at the digs, there was a lovely young lady, very handsomely attired waiting, whom I had never seen before. I thought she might have some information for me. To be polite, I asked Miss Green to provide tea. The visitor sat opposite me at the dining room table. There was small talk, but nothing appertaining to police work, and after about twenty minutes she indicated that she was to leave. I escorted her to the door, and never saw her again … She was a decoy to lure me into the country on a date, where I would be an easy target for execution. It may be asked why I did not have a date with her? She did not appeal to me, and perhaps I felt something sinister about her.[145]

The then IRA chief of staff was Seán MacBride, and allegedly it was he who decided on another course of action. It was decided to mislead the Garda authorities into thinking that Geary was associated with them, through a series of dispatches. The IRA suspected at the time that the Gardaí were intercepting their dispatches, and they were correct. MacBride later left the IRA for the constitutional path and entered Dáil Éireann in 1947. He went on to become active in the campaign for human rights and won the Nobel Peace Prize in 1974, followed by the Lenin Peace Prize in 1977. I asked William Geary had he ever written to him for assistance in clearing his name. William replied, 'No.' In the course of his campaign, he did, however, make various appeals to Dave Neligan, but he found him unhelpful. Incidentally, previous to William leaving Ireland, his brother Thomas had emigrated to Sydney, where he married Anna Helena Parsons in 1929.[146] They went on to have three children.[147]

II JUNE 1929

Detective Garda Timothy O'Sullivan, a native of Skibbereen, became the ninth member of An Garda Síochána to be killed in the line of duty. An officer in the Special Branch, he had been transferred to Kilmihill, roughly 10 miles from Kilrush, in December 1928, where he had been particularly active in questioning those he suspected of involvement in anti-government activities, much to the ire of local republicans.[148]

When a booby trap was laid for his colleague Detective Garda John O'Driscoll based at Knock station, whom the IRA also loathed, it was Detective O'Sullivan who, on inspecting the device at Tullycrine, was ultimately killed. Still working in the insurance business in Limerick and into Clare, **DAN KEATING** was among those subsequently arrested and held for a while in Limerick Gaol in connection with the crime, for which no one was ever charged. He told Uinseann MacEoin, however, that he had nothing to do with it. The people the Gardaí were really after but could pin nothing on were T.J. Ryan, Mike Huxley, Martin Calligan and Martin White. He added that in the years before Fianna Fáil was elected in 1932, there was always trouble in west Clare.[149]

The killing of Detective Garda Timothy O'Sullivan demonstrates that **WILLIAM GEARY** wasn't the only member of the force the IRA wanted rid of in the district in which **MAI MCMAHON** resided.

22 JULY 1929

The Ardnacrusha hydroelectric power station was opened, the largest in the world at the time. Three years earlier, the sod had been turned for the country's first modern sugar factory at Strawhall, Carlow. **SEÁN CLANCY** maintained that these were two great achievements.

> Well, I think that the government did a good job after the Civil War. For instance, they started the Shannon scheme, which was a major effort, a very courageous effort at the time. And it was described by de Valera and his government afterwards as a white elephant. I think it's anything but a white elephant. I think they described that and some other enterprise as the two white elephants that they took over, yes, the Shannon Scheme and the Beet Factories. They're anything but white elephants. They're most successful.[150]

In a statement made in the Senate on 22 March 1932, Seán MacEntee of Fianna Fáil said: 'The Shannon Scheme, the Dairy Disposals Board, the Drumm Battery and the Beet Sugar Factory were as precious a collection of white elephants as ever drove their unfortunate owners to the verge of insolvency.'[151] Seán Clancy continued to serve in the army, reaching the rank of captain in May 1930.[152]

7 MARCH 1931

After nine years' full-time service with the army, **JACK DUFF** transferred to the Reserve. Essentially, the Army Reserve was a part-time component of the defence forces comprising volunteers who participated in training in their spare time. Most were engaged in full-time civilian employment.

As a full-time soldier since his re-enlistment in 1924, Jack had been attached to the 20th Infantry Battalion until 1927 (also the year he married), followed by service with the 7th and 2nd Battalions until 7 March 1931. His full-time army career had included postings in Dublin, Clonmel, Wexford, Clones, Dundalk, Kilkenny and Gorey.[153]

> I was a sergeant. I was promoted in 1922 and I held my rank until I came out.[154]

The date of Jack's transfer to the Reserve is recorded as 8 March 1931.[155] He would work in another job, but continued his links with the army through serving with Reserve battalions in Dublin.[156]

I held my rank for six years on reserve. I could have gone on to company sergeant but I was quite happy the way I was and I asked to leave me the way I was.[157]

Jack had enjoyed army life, but felt the employment terms and conditions of a full-time soldier at the time he transferred were not favourable to a married man such as himself with two young children. He was finding it very hard to live on his pay of 34 shillings and 6 pence per week after deductions. Also, the army operated a three-year attestment cycle. The way it worked was that at the end of three years soldiers were given the option of staying on or going out on reserve. Those who decided to stay on started off the following day under the same terms and conditions as men who were only after joining the army for the first time. Service already incurred meant nothing. There was also no such thing as a pension or marriage allowance.[158]

Prior to joining the army in 1922, Jack had been employed as a clerk in the Dublin United Tramways Company. Twelve months before leaving the army as a full-time soldier, he met with the manager of the DUTC, explained his position, and asked if he would give him a job if he came out of the army the following year. The answer was 'Yes.' Jack went back to the army, completed his twelve months and then started as a tram driver in the DUTC.[159] Ironically, the pension scheme came into the army shortly after he had left.

9 MARCH 1932

The first Fianna Fáil government led by de Valera took office. They didn't have a majority, but had the support of the Labour Party; de Valera would spend 21 of the following 27 years in government.[160] When **SEÁN CLANCY** was asked by historian Benjamin Grob-Fitzgibbon what the army's view of de Valera's election victory was, he replied that they had fought a civil war 10 years previously to establish the wishes of the people, and now the people had spoken. The people wanted a change of government and they got just that. He and his army comrades had taken an oath of allegiance to the country to serve whatever government the people elected. There was no question of them not serving de Valera.[161] **JACK DUFF** noted that:

> After things began to settle down and get normal and de Valera and his crowd went into Dáil Éireann, he went into Dáil Éireann in 19–, I think it was 1932 and from that on, things seemed to be steady enough.[162]

The opposition formed Fine Gael in 1933. De Valera released republican prisoners and tolerated the IRA initially; however, he banned them in 1936 as they would not give up their arms.[163] **DAN KEATING** was critical of de Valera's hardline stance towards republicans.

> De Valera down through the years from when he decided and got a majority of one or two that was prepared to accept the Oath of Allegiance and go into the Dáil, from the word go he was undermining the IRA.[164]

Dan was jailed for republican activity on a few occasions during de Valera's terms in office.

> I was in Arbour Hill in 1933 and I was in Limerick Gaol [1929]. I was in Mountjoy [1935] and Arbour Hill [1935].[165]

28 MARCH 1932

JOHN PARKINSON of the 44th Company of the Belfast Boys' Brigade ventured to the Irish Free State for the first time for the annual representative match between the Belfast and Dublin Old Boys' Football Leagues. In the 1920s, past members of the Boys' Brigade organisation had formed the Old Boys' Union (OBU) to also cater for their interests, which included soccer.[166] On this date, the best players from the Belfast Battalion OBU played the best from the Dublin Battalion OBU in a soccer match in Crumlin.[167] OBU soccer was considered to be of a high standard.

> Well, of course, I had my first reactions to going to Dublin was with the Boys' Brigade football team. I was a member of the committee in Belfast at that time, that organised the match and we went down to the south, year about. One year we went to Dublin, the next year Dublin came up here and that was my first impressions and I stayed with a family. I always remember their surname was Watt, and Robert Watt – one of the sons stayed in my house for the weekend. We boarded some of the boys from Dublin and when we went down then, we were boarded down there and we made warm friends in that way.[168]

William Watts of the 8th Dublin Company (St Michan's and St Paul's churches) was on the Dublin OBU team that day. John Parkinson wasn't selected for Belfast OBU, who won 0-3.[169] Similarly, Robert Watts, young brother of William, wasn't selected for Dublin OBU, but regularly played for the 8th Company. The previous year, Belfast OBU and Dublin OBU had played a match at Cliftonville on Easter Monday. On that occasion, both Watts brothers played for Dublin; again, John Parkinson wasn't selected. The game finished 2-2.[170]

The Wattses lived on Oxmantown Road, Arran Quay, in Dublin.[171] Robert later relocated to Clontarf, going on to serve as chairman and then president of the United Churches Football League, which was formed in 1949.[172]

> We liked them, they had a different accent and, but we liked them and we enjoyed going there and we enjoyed having them up here.[173]

25 APRIL 1933

DAN KEATING was imprisoned for a short period of time in Cork Gaol.

> At the time now, you had this force, they were Duffy's force you know [the Blueshirts]. De Valera was there and you had the land war [land annuities dispute/Economic War] at the time. There was a man in Castleisland was supposed to have a number of rifles – which he had but the IRA raided the house and they were satisfied there was nothing

there but they did take a shotgun belong to him and they brought it. The shotgun was lying in Johnny O'Connor's house inside the door in Farmer's Bridge and the police raided it and found the shotgun. They arrested him and they arrested Mick Kennedy who was a local also who had raided Cahill and they tried them in Tralee.[174]

Johnny O'Connor, who had been awaiting trial since January 1933 on charges of 'larceny of' and 'unlawful possession of' firearms, was indicted on 25 April before Judge McElligott in Tralee Courthouse. [175]

All the Volunteers in Tralee and Farmer's Bridge they went in and the courthouse was packed to the door. Johnny O'Connor and Mick Kennedy were arraigned before Judge McElligott. Johnny O'Connor declared that they refused to recognise the authority of that court at the time on any charge and there was pandemonium, and everyone clapped. McElligott was fuming but there was very little he could do. The IRA was nearly in charge you know of the courthouse. But he pointed out and he said, 'Bring that man up there. He's the leader.'

He pointed down and the guards, there was another man from Farmer's Bridge that the guards never liked – Gerry Lynch. They went down and they put their hand on him. He said, 'That's not the man,' he said. 'I want the man with the pin-striped suit.' That was me. He took me up anyway and he said I was guilty of gross contempt of court and he sentenced me to three months. I said, 'You can make it six if you like. I'll do the same again.' And he did.[176]

It was reported that Dan was sentenced to three months for cheering O'Connor, who was remanded in custody until 6 July. When both were being taken from the court to the barracks, a large crowd surrounded the escort and fought with it. The windows of the Garda car were broken with stones.[177] The pair were sent to Cork Gaol, where on 26 April O'Connor went on hunger strike in protest against his treatment.[178] Meanwhile, three or four hundred people accompanied by a pipers' band demonstrated outside the jail.[179]

But during the course of the day anyway there was a number of the Fianna Fáil crowd at the time, Johnny O'Connor was a noted figure always and they were afraid Johnny O'Connor had too much influence on them and they decided anyway that he'd have to be released. And the two of us, we were only in Cork. Johnny O'Connor went on hunger strike the night he went in and he ordered me to remain. There was a warder there that was bringing in and out information you know, and he was ordering me to stay there so that I could get the particular information. We were released anyway after about, I think we were only inside about less than three weeks.[180]

On 1 May, on the recommendation of Judge McElligott, who had incarcerated them, both men were released. Dan insisted they were looked after very well in jail:

Oh, we were treated royally because the Cumann na mBan in Cork. There was enough of grub coming up that would feed the whole prison ... There was one man in particular – Pat Owens. The man had only six months to do as a warder. His time was up and the poor man was in an awful fright during the whole thing that something would happen that would deprive him. I met him after. He was a grand old soul.[181]

When Dan and Johnny O'Connor arrived back in Tralee by train, they were greeted by exploding railway fog signals and a large, cheering crowd accompanied by a band. They were then placed in a motor car and driven through the town.[182]

6 SEPTEMBER 1934

KATHLEEN CHARLES got married; her groom was a salesman from the Banner County (Co. Clare).[183] The couple would live in what was once the prison governor's residence on the grounds of the old courthouse and prison, at the end of Church Street in Kanturk. Her parents operated their printing business across the river at Egmont Place.[184] Details of the nuptials were printed in the *Cork Examiner*.

A very pretty wedding was solemnised in the Church of the Immaculate Conception, Kanturk when Miss K. Charles, only daughter of Mr and Mrs WG Charles, Egmont Place, Kanturk, was married to Mr. Andrew Noonan, son of Mr. P. Noonan, ex-N.T. of Caherhurley, Tulla, Co. Clare. Rev. John Roche. C.C., Kanturk, officiated, and celebrated Nuptial Mass. The Papal Blessing was also given. The bride, who was attended by Miss Eily Lehane, Kanturk, as bridesmaid, was given away by her father. The bridegroom had as his best man his brother, Mr. Frank Noonan. The bride wore a gown of white crepe-de-chene, and carried a bouquet of white asters. After the Church ceremonies, a reception was held at the bride's home.[185]

I asked Kathleen if her husband had been active in the Civil War or the troubles that preceded it.

Oh, he was an IRA man too but he wasn't fighting. He was at Michael Collins' funeral as a, you know, one of the fellows that marches beside the coffin.[186]

Andrew Noonan joined the volunteers in Tuamgraney, Co. Clare, in 1917. Michael Brennan was his senior officer. Later, during the Tan War, he got a job on a farm in Clonlara, joining the volunteers there immediately after the Truce. His senior officer there was John McCormack, who had also been **SEÁN CLANCY'S** captain when he had joined the Clonlara Company in 1917. Noonan drilled with them until December 1921. During his time in the IRA, Andrew Noonan saw plenty of dangerous service, but wasn't involved in any ambushes against the British, so perhaps that's what Kathleen was hinting at when she said 'he wasn't fighting'.[187]

However, he was fighting on joining the Free State Army in February 1922, being stationed first in Ennis. Having fought through Clare, Limerick, Kerry, Cork, Galway, Mayo, Tipperary and Waterford, Andrew Noonan was demobilised on 14 November 1923 at the rank of corporal.[188]

5 JULY 1935

GEORGE CARPENTER sailed to Germany, where he would have an extraordinary encounter with the man responsible for starting World War II. On this date, the North German Lloyd liner *Columbus* arrived at Cobh, and after landing 210 passengers from New York, took on board 75 members of the Boys' Brigade from Cork and Dublin. The Cork section, which included George amongst its ranks, was under the command of Captain Samuel M. Faris, whilst those from Dublin were in the charge of Captain J.F. Warren and others. Over the course of 15 days, the party were to visit to Wangerooge in the East Frisian Islands as well as Bremen, Hamburg and Berlin.[189] The Boys' Brigade party were ultimately the guests of the Hitler Youth and would stay at various barracks, houses and hostels associated with their organisation whilst visiting those cities.[190]

> Well, I was an officer in the Boys' Brigade then and I was invited to go with them to Germany. And we were going over to an island – Wangerooge Island. So, we travelled by liner from Cobh over to it and then we got off at Hamburg and we went from Hamburg out of the island by tender and we stayed a week there and we used have parading and all. We weren't allowed wear our uniform, which was a very small uniform. It's only a pillbox hat and a white haversack over your shoulder and down around your waist and a belt over our ordinary clothes. So it was; it wasn't what you'd call a uniform. It was just the handy things, the belts and the hat, that's all.[191]

Once the Nazis came to power in 1933, the only such uniform allowed was that of the Hitler Youth. Boys wore the swastika armband along with brown hats and shirts, a black neckerchief and shorts, a brown jacket, a belt, white or grey socks and marching shoes. A dark blue winter uniform was introduced in 1934. Those in the League of German Girls wore uniforms consisting of a blue skirt, brown jacket, black neckerchief and a white blouse.[192]

> We travelled from there then to Hamburg and then Hamburg to Berlin. We were met by the British ambassador and he brought us over to the Reichstag and that was the time that the van der Lubbe was caught burning down the Reichstag and afterwards I met the man that was supposed to have caught him and I got his signature on a card and then we discovered afterwards when the whole war was over that he didn't do it at all.[193]

Marinus van der Lubbe was a Dutch communist who was tried, convicted, and executed by the Nazis in 1934 for setting fire to the German Reichstag government building in February 1933. The caretaker who caught him gave George his autograph on the back of a picture of the Reichstag, which was partially burned down when George saw it.[194] The German government granted van der Lubbe a posthumous pardon in 2008.[195]

> And then we went over to the chancellery then and we had lunch and then in came Hitler and he sat at the top of the table. And that's how, he spoke and it was translated by the ambassador to us then.[196]

Once Hitler had finished his speech, it was Captain Faris from Cork who replied to him on behalf of the 75-strong Boys' Brigade. In the course of his few words, which were translated for Hitler by the British ambassador, Captain Faris touched on the fact that the Boys' Brigade hadn't been allowed to wear their uniforms, which he proceeded to describe for Hitler. George said Hitler's reaction was one of surprise and that he responded to Faris by saying that if he had known their uniform was as described, he would have allowed them to wear it. Everybody in the room then got to their feet as Hitler prepared to leave.[197]

> When he was leaving then, he came up. We were just gathered around the door and I put my hand out – shook hands and he did this [Nazi salute] afterwards immediately afterwards. So that was the way I met Hitler.[198]

George added that Hitler said nothing, attributing it to the fact that 'he couldn't speak English'. Looking back, he regretted shaking Hitler's hand, but at the time there was no way of anyone knowing what he would be accountable for in the war to come. When George had visited Germany, there seemed to have been a perception that the Führer 'did an awful lot that time for the youth, and he was admired for it'.[199]

After dining with Hitler, the Boys' Brigade were taken to Tempelhof Airport in Berlin, where they were escorted around the hangars. Here Hermann Goering's private plane was pointed out to them.[200] On 20 July, the Hamburg American Line steamer *Deutschland* docked at Cobh, with George and the Boys' Brigade having sailed on board.[201] It had been an eventful tour of Germany for the group.

AUGUST 1936

ANTHONY MCGINLEY decided to leave California and travel across America by bus to New York. After a five-day journey, he boarded a ship bound for Moville in his native Donegal. It had been quite an adventure that had resulted in him being away for over a decade.

> Me, I was eleven years and five months to be exact.[202]

He arrived home at the height of the Economic War with Britain (1932–1938), and in certain border regions a thriving industry had developed.

Christ, it was all smuggling. It was cat altogether. Everything was smuggled because along with smuggling and getting it they were glad to be doing it – disloyal to the, you know, to the old system.[203]

He recalled that there was no end to what was being smuggled:

Oh, everything, anything at all – clothes and everything that could be got.[204]

His recollection was that it started nearly straight away after partition, but denied ever being involved in it.

It did, aye, and it gathered momentum it did. It was going strong. They weren't able to keep it down at all ... I never was in the smuggling game at all but it was a great game. But we handled, we got the stuff and got it cheaper surely aye ... You see I went away like a lot of them and I was only, still only, I don't think I was twenty when I went away. And all the smuggling was going on and it was still going when I came back indeed you know. Aye.[205]

In the years following the Treaty, the Irish Free State kept its link with sterling, but cross-border smuggling did go on. It was mainly centred on goods such as livestock, bread, butter, sugar, tea, alcohol, cigarettes and clothes, and would have reached its height during the Economic War (1932–1938) and World War II (1939–1945). During the Economic War, the British government had imposed a duty of 20 per cent on imports of Irish butter, eggs, poultry, cream, game and live animals, whilst the Irish government placed a similar tariff on British coal, cement, sugar, steel, etc. Irish people suffered great hardship, with the price of essential commodities such as tea soaring in price.[206] The Economic War also prevented the legal traffic of products across the border, while World War II prevented Ireland from acquiring certain commodities from the international market.

Smuggling developed into a thriving industry, with dealers pitting their wits against the excise men on both sides of the border. Sometimes money didn't even change hands, with supplies that were hard to come by on one side of the border being exchanged for goods that were in plentiful supply on the other side. It must be remembered that from its inception the Irish Free State was to be completely responsible for its own economic future and that partition had separated it from the north-east region, which was the most industrial part of Ireland. As a result, there were often big price differences on opposite sides of the border as well as tariffs on goods.[207]

27 MARCH 1937

His time with the Army Reserve expired, **JACK DUFF** was discharged from duty. For six years he had dedicated a month's service annually to the Army Volunteer Reserve, being attached to the 6th, 8th, 1st and 2nd Reserve Battalions in Dublin. His number was VR18631; he was recorded as being 5 foot 8 inches in height with dark brown hair and blue eyes. His character was described as 'very good'.[208] He continued to drive trams and buses for the DUTC.

This was also the year that **MICHAEL CASEY** from Mitchelstown settled down to a life in agriculture by purchasing Rockmills House in Kildorrery. He would reside there for the rest of his life.

> I was always went farming then. I'd a taste for it so I bought this place then in 1937, when things were very bad ... This was burned. It was burned during the trouble. There were Protestants living here and it was burned ... By the IRA, I think about the 1st of May 1921.[209]

Michael remembered when the house was burned, but 'had nothing to do with it'.[210] He asserted that it was a local crowd of IRA men that were responsible, adding that he knew a few of them. Rockmills House dates back to the late 1700s, and over the years was occupied by the Aldworth, St Leger Aldworth, Harmer Bond and Deane Oliver families.[211] Rockmills was actually one of three loyalist houses in the area burned that night. On 4 May, the homes of six men in the locality accused of being active supporters of armed rebels were destroyed by the British military in retaliation.[212] Between the years 1919 and 1923, up to 300 'big houses' owned by Protestants were burned to the ground.[213]

25 APRIL 1938

The Anglo-Irish Agreement was signed, through which the three Treaty ports were returned to the control of the Irish Free State. **MICHAEL CASEY** claimed that Éamon de Valera deserved credit for this.

> Oh God, I think he was a great man. When they kept the ports and Spike Island, didn't they. He got them back. That was no settlement to have them in charge of the ports of Ireland and Spike Island, it wasn't on at all.[214]

However, **JACK DUFF** lamented that a state ceremony he used to participate in was interfered with. It centred around an annual parade to a cenotaph designed by George Atkinson, which was erected on Leinster Lawn on 13 August 1923 to commemorate the first anniversary of the deaths of Arthur Griffith and Michael Collins. The unveiling of the cenotaph saw the beginning of the Bóthar Buadh (Road to Victory) march by the army, which was essentially a celebration of the Free State defeat of the republicans in the Civil War.

> Oh, up to the time that de Valera came into power. De Valera stopped that. That was termed the 'Road to Victory' and de Valera done away with that. I think that was one of the first things he done away with. We used to march – the army and the air force the whole lot. We used to march through the city and there was a cenotaph in Merrion Square outside the government buildings and we used to pay homage to that as they pass by they saluted us and on that statue was Mick Collins in the centre, Kevin Higgins on, oh, what did they say the other fellow – Griffith on the left.[215]

The cenotaph was a 40-foot cross, containing plaster medallions of both Griffith and Collins. Following his death, a medallion of Kevin O'Higgins was added in 1928. The structure was made of plaster and wood, and on becoming dilapidated was dismantled in 1939 by de Valera, with the agreement of Fine Gael. A new design was produced in 1940, but it was put on the back burner during World War II. When Costello became Taoiseach in 1948, a new design by Raymond McGrath was agreed on and a replacement 60-foot granite obelisk was erected in 1950. It stands today on Leinster Lawn.[216] **PATRICK GREENE** met Éamon de Valera on one occasion.

> Well, of course de Valera was a person; you had two slants of people – people who thought he was a humbug and people who swore by him. That was it. People who thought he was very ambivalent and people who had great belief in everything he said. And then people, the opposition of course had no use for him. I met de Valera once years and years ago. He wasn't in power at the time and I met himself and his wife at a céilí in Dublin one night. A Corkman was a great friend of his introduced me to him and I remember her more than I remember him. She was a lovely woman. He wasn't a very gabby individual. He didn't say very much. At the time of course he wasn't in power at the time.[217]

I SEPTEMBER 1939

World War II began when Germany invaded Poland. Two days later, Britain, France, Australia and New Zealand declared war on the Nazis. In Ireland, the north took an active part in the conflict while the south adopted a policy of neutrality (although a sizeable contingent did enlist in the British armed forces).

When the war broke out, **JOHN PARKINSON** was teaching woodwork to unemployed teenagers at a government training centre in Alfred Street, Belfast. However, this was closed down, and to help with the war effort, his students worked in factories such as Harland & Wolff and Shorts aircraft factory. John himself worked in metal as well as wood construction, so was employed at Shorts to work on the production of Stirling and Halifax bombers as well as Sunderland flying boats.[218]

> In my very early days there wasn't so much poverty but later on round about when the war broke out, round just about the war years, 'the hungry forties' they called it, 1940, there was a lot of poverty and that.[219]

John and **NORMAN DOUGLAS** would experience rationing, blackout orders and the horror of the German Blitz of Belfast in April 1941, which resulted in hundreds of casualties. The south of Ireland also endured bombing by Germany, such as at North Strand, Dublin, in May of the same year, which also resulted in casualties.

In the Free State in 1940, the Dáil Minister for Defence, Oscar Traynor, introduced the Defence Forces Temporary Provisions Bill. A feature of this was the establishment of a Local Defence Force (LDF) made up of thousands of volunteers all over the country.[220] **SEÁN CLANCY**, who supported de Valera's neutral stance, noted that this was the period when people from both sides of the Civil War split mixed together and helped each other out for the good of the country. There was great cooperation between them. Some old friends whom Seán hadn't met since the days of the Civil War joined either the regular army or the LDF.[221]

One of the volunteers in what was termed the LSF (Local Security Force) was **GERRY SMYTH**, by then living at Dunsany Crossroads in Meath, who served as a district staff officer. His role was to recruit ordinary members and set up a district group. They helped the Gardaí with transport, traffic control, first aid and food supplies. He also had to watch for parachutists and was trained in recognising different planes flying overhead in order to identify which countries they were from. On patrol the night of the Dublin North Strand bombings, he went straight up to the capital to offer assistance. It stuck in his mind that a bomb had hit the middle of the road at Newcommon Bridge and created a crater right in the middle of the street.[222]

GEORGE COOPER in Dublin was a member of the LDF. On one occasion, whilst going to Donnybrook for a drill session, he was approaching Herbert Park when he spotted something on the road wrapped in a shawl. On investigation it turned out to be a baby that was still alive. George brought it to the local Garda station and would subsequently receive a medal for his actions.[223]

JACK DUFF too joined the LDF, remaining on until it was disbanded. He later joined An Fórsa Cosanta Áitiúil (the FCA, established in 1946). He recalled that when the war came they took the Dublin buses off the road and put the trams back on again.[224] A fourth volunteer with the LDF was **GEORGE CARPENTER**, who provided a detailed account of his activities in Cork during the period.

> World War II was extraordinary because a lot of my friends, there were some older than me went off and joined up in World War II in England. And when we came to the middle of it, the LDF was formed and I joined up straight away in the LDF. And we had a line made to stand to attention in a line and everybody was asked, we were all asked for any experience of drilling or anything do you see? So a few of the boys stood out that were in the '14–'18 war and, 'Anybody else?' I said I belonged to the Boys' Brigade and there was a bit of a titter – the Boys' Brigade like the Girl Guides or what have you. And so the officer said, 'If you're all in the Boys' Brigade I need you to come around here.' Then he put me in charge of drilling then. I was made officer in charge of drilling. I went from that onto two weeks of in charge of explosives. I was a destructive engineer – not a constructive one. I learnt how to use explosives and I had to train all my troops to enforce eight sections around Co. Cork. And take so many qualified numbers of them so they could handle explosives carefully. I used say to them – your first mistake is your last one. I remember that.[225]

George explained that during World War II 'we were always expecting somebody to raid us and we were prepared to put up a fight as much as we could'.[226] Rationing was also in place.

We got cards for that, for tea and butter and bread. And they were all rationed. And no such thing as meat and then we used get tea – black market tea.[227]

PATRICK GREENE in Ballinalee, who had married in 1935, remembered the Emergency (World War II state of emergency) years well.

Well, I was married in World War II, living here in World War II, and it was a tough time. It didn't impact that much on country people. They had to till more. At that time you see, seventy years ago, most, this was an area of small farmers and they were to a great extent self-sufficient as far as food is concerned. They grew a lot of potatoes, oats, they fed pigs, if they could afford to they killed a pig ... Then they had the local mill down the road – oat and meal. They had a couple of cows, they had milk, they had their own butter, they had their own potatoes and vegetables in the garden ... They had eggs in the summertime when the hens were laying. Some of them fed turkeys for the Christmas market. Some of them fed geese for the Christmas market and if they could afford they kept one for themselves for Christmas day.[228]

13 SEPTEMBER 1939

Having married in 1937, **JOHN KELLY** inherited his parent's place in Caherbriskaun, Athenry, going on to spend his days 'just working on the farm – the land, working on the land, that's all'.[229] But land was always a contentious issue in the Athenry district, and especially so when the big estates were being redistributed after being purchased by the Land Commission. In a slightly farcical case held in the District Court there on this date, District Justice Cahill declared that 'intimidation is a cowardly form of crime' as he dismissed charges of same against John Kelly and his friend Martin Ruane, who lived at Castle Lambert.

In August, the pair had been returning from a fair in Athenry in a horse and cart along with two others when they spotted Michael Farrell and his brother in the process of rebuilding walls, which had been knocked maliciously on the land of Thomas Curran, Athenry, some time previous and for which Curran had been awarded £50 compensation to have them rebuilt.

Farrell, who admitted his nickname was 'Fenian', took exception and started swinging his shovel when John Kelly said in passing, 'Good man, Fenian Farrell, you have the wall finished.' He also claimed to have been called a nasty name and threatened to take Kelly and Ruane to court. Apparently, Farrell had heard that the wall had been knocked maliciously and that there was a notice posted up on the lands stating that the man who would rebuild them would be shot.

Farrell's brother next picked up stones, and together with his sibling who was holding the shovel, ran towards the horse and cart, both men in an angry state. They claimed that in a heated exchange of words with Kelly and Ruane on the topic of land, they were accused of desiring a portion of the acres they were then working on, and reference was made to men having been shot for land in the past. Farrell said he replied to this by stating that such means were not the way to get land. The upshot was that Michael Farrell took John Kelly and Martin Ruane to court on a charge of intimidating him while he was engaged in the building of a wall. The defendants, who admitted having taken drink on the day of the fair, denied it was ever their intention to intimidate Farrell.

In his summation, the Justice said Farrell had properly replied to the remarks about getting land by the gun – that was not the way to get land, because if it was the method, then the biggest blackguard and bully would get land. The state, he said, gives land to the most deserving and those most entitled to it.[230] He said the defendants did not appear to him to be the type of men who would do anything wrong and he had thus come to the conclusion that in this instance Farrell had not been intimidated. He therefore dismissed the case against John Kelly of Caherbriskaun and Martin Ruane of Castle Lambert.[231]

4 AUGUST 1940

Eighteen years after being arrested in Co. Tipperary during the Civil War, **DAN KEATING** was apprehended there again during World War II and interned for four years and a day. He had returned from London in April, having been part of the IRA's 1939–1940 bombing campaign of England in which seven people were killed: Albert Ross, Donald Campbell, Elsie Ansell, John Corbett Arnott, Rex Gentle, James Clay and Gwilym Rowlands.[232]

> It was remarkable that in after years, in 1940, I happened to be based again in Tipperary and I was captured again just outside Clonmel – Ardfinnan, in a house – Carrigan's. It was a famous republican house, and we were captured, we were given away. We were captured the day of the Munster Final and again conveyed, conveyed again to Mountjoy Gaol again. But from we were very, we weren't very long there that time, we were conveyed right away to the Curragh.[233]

The Munster Hurling Final that year was contested between Cork and Limerick, with the latter coming out on top during the replay, held in Thurles on the day of Dan's arrest, when he was surrounded within a house owned by Tipperary IRA man, Ned Carrigan, himself already arrested.[234] It got a brief mention within the pages in *The Nationalist* newspaper.

> A young man, Daniel Keating, said to be a native of Kerry, was arrested near Clonmel by detectives under the Emergency Powers Act.[235]

Known and suspected republicans were interned on both sides of the border during World War II, as both governments feared they would collude with Nazi Germany against them and Britain. The Emergency Powers Act, passed by the Dáil in 1939, had given sweeping powers to the neutral Free State government, including censorship of the press, control of the economy, and internment. Gerald Boland was Minister for Justice from 1939 to 1948, whilst during these years Seán MacEntee served first as Minister for Industry and Commerce and later Minister for Local Government and Public Health. Dan didn't have a good word to say about either of them.

Well, I'll tell you, leading up then, de Valera when he got a majority, he got very arrogant and he had one obsession in life was to finish the IRA for all time. He appointed a number of men around him; Boland was one, MacEntee was another. It must be said that there was never a dirtier rat born than MacEntee. From the word go he was rotten. Dev got very arrogant anyway and the war came. At all times Dev was pro-British in the war, while the majority of Irish people early on they were pro-German. There's no doubt about that. One of his chief men Boland after, at the outset now Boland was pro-German but Dev soon corrected him and he used him for all he was worth for all time after, you know. In the early stages of the war anyway the IRA were still very active and training.[236]

Regarding Irish support for the Germans, **SEÁN CLANCY** didn't think Hitler had much in this country at all. He told Benjamin Grob-Fitzgibbon that any support the Germans might have had would have been quite small. A bigger concern for him was that when America entered the war they might have forced the British to invade Ireland. Neutral Ireland would have resisted any country that might have tried to invade, whether it was the British, Germans or Americans.[237]

Separate internment camps were established on the Curragh for both Allied and German personnel.[238] According to Seán, the British internees were treated in a more friendly way than the Germans. Some of them were even sent back, whereas the Germans were not sent back until the war was over.[239] Upwards of 1,500 prisoners passed through the Curragh Camp during World War II, although peak numbers held at any time never exceeded 550. In addition, the IRA shot dead five gardaí between 1940 and 1944, and de Valera's government executed six members of the IRA.[240] Seán maintained de Valera 'was following in the footsteps of the previous government, which he had condemned. He carried out the very same methods. He executed them.' [241]

The dead gardaí were Detective John Roche, Detective Richard Hyland, Detective Sergeant Patrick McKeown, Detective Sergeant Denis O'Brien and Detective George Mordaunt. The executed IRA men were Patrick McGrath, Thomas Harte, Richard Goss, George Plant, Maurice O'Neill and Charlie Kerins.[242]

In the north, a total of 827 internment orders were made during the war, with men being held mainly in Derry Gaol and Crumlin Road Gaol in Belfast.[243] Four RUC members and two Specials were killed by the IRA, resulting in one of its members, Tom Williams, being executed.[244] The dead RUC were Constables Patrick Murphy, Thomas Forbes, James Laird and Patrick McCarthy. The Specials were Constables Samuel Hamilton and James Lyons.[245]

10 OCTOBER 1940

SEÁN CLANCY achieved the rank of commandant in the army. During the Emergency, he was instrumental in forming the new 18th Infantry Battalion as second-in-command to Major 'Jed' O'Dwyer, a renowned army show jumper.[246] They engaged in a lot of field training, especially during the summer months, and were based mainly in Counties Meath and Cavan. Much of their focus was on marching and fitness parades, as well as other military exercises.[247] Seán recalled that before the war there were only about 8,000 in the regular army, but by the end of the conflict membership had increased to close to 60,000.[248] **NORMAN DOUGLAS** from Belfast spent a memorable time 'down south' during the war.

> I found the people very friendly. There was no question of are you a Protestant or are you a Catholic or anything of that nature. We moved about comfortably, enjoyed every time I went down. I was in Dublin, spent my honeymoon in Dublin [1943].[249]

30 APRIL 1945

World War II effectively came to an end after Adolf Hitler committed suicide in his bunker in Berlin. More than 3,600 from the south of Ireland and almost 3,900 from the north died while serving in the British, Commonwealth and Dominion forces during the conflict. It is estimated that in the British army alone there may have been as many as 100,000 men and women from the north and south of Ireland serving.[250] Some of the returning soldiers were friends of **GEORGE CARPENTER** in Cork.

> I don't remember any that were killed at all. I can't, but I knew a lot of them that came back and some were shell-shocked. Others had wounds that they, small wounds on their bodies but that was all.[251]

On 4 March 1946, George received his commission as Lieutenant in the FCA, which had taken over from the LDF. It was signed by Sean T. O'Ceallaigh, Éamon de Valera and Oscar Traynor.[252]

> I enjoyed that because there were about eight of us. We were given our bars as we call them and made a lieutenant. Then in 1944 I was qualified as a lieutenant, then I was sub, became a full lieutenant and it's nice looking at it because Dev's, de Valera's signature is on it and Oscar Traynor another one and oh, he was president for a while. I can't think of his name [Sean T. Ó Ceallaigh] but I have the certificate up hanging up on the wall.[253]

New York resident **WILLIAM GEARY** had been drafted to serve in the United States forces during World War II. His army number was 1243938. Having been sworn in at Governor's Island in August 1942 and allotted two weeks to get his affairs in order, he reported to Camp Upton on Long Island. After undergoing a series of IQ tests, William was then ordered to Nashville, followed by Long Beach, California, to learn the basics of army finance. On graduating from the military school, he was assigned to Memphis to serve in the United States Army Air Force, Air Transport Command Finance. He was promoted to corporal and then sergeant in charge of pay roll at the base. Among those he paid were airmen who ferried planes to Africa for use in the war effort. William was not involved in any combat, never flew and only held a gun when collecting bags of money in an army jeep from the depot. He was honourably discharged from the United States Army when the war ended.[254]

18 APRIL 1949

The Irish Free State was declared a republic and free from British interference when the Republic of Ireland Act was formally inaugurated – partition remains. In the coming years, large-scale loyalist and republican violence would erupt in the north and impact on the likes of **NORMAN DOUGLAS** living in Belfast.

> In the later troubles in 1969 when the civil rights march started all the business and yes, I was bombed out of three different places by the IRA for no reason. We just happened to be in the wrong area at the wrong time and they planted bombs in a garage, which was just opposite where I worked. My, our building was and when the bomb went off of course our building was affected. The roof was off and all that sort of nonsense. And we were out day after day, after day, after day with bomb scares so it wasn't a very pleasant set up.[255]

He shared his hopes for the future.

> I would love to see a peaceful Ireland that we wouldn't have politicians who are fighting for and people who are fighting just to achieve another piece of ground. If the Free State or Éire or whoever you'd like to call them would abide by the fact that Northern Ireland exists and the people – the Roman Catholic fraction in Northern Ireland would abide by the fact that they're under British rule and let's get on with our lives, it would be a great future for everyone ... I've always had a leaning towards royalty and even when I was a child it wasn't instilled in me in my family, it wasn't instilled in me in the school but I've always had a British outlook.[256]

JOHN PARKINSON admitted to getting irritated when people spoke of the Troubles just going back to 1969, as he could vividly recall the community disorders of the 1920s as well as those of the 1930s. The incident that distressed him most was 'Bloody Friday' in 1972, when nine people were killed and many injured by multiple bombs that exploded all over Belfast. He was in the Oxford Street area when a bomb went off, and he saw a blanket being put over someone's remains. One of his pupils was also blown up by a bomb on the Antrim Road.[257]

> We just hope that things will work out and we'll stay together by being part of the British community.[258]

For **GEORGE COOPER** in Dublin, the south has come a long way since the days of the War for Independence and the Civil War, when in his experience blatant sectarianism was more evident.

Well, we have progressed. Now I'm a member of the Church of Ireland right and I think that leading from that time onwards, we had more protection, as you weren't harassed so much ... When you think that the first president of Ireland was a Protestant, which was Douglas Hyde [1938–1945] and many more have succeeded him so the point is that we are equal.[259]

For their part, **JACK DUFF** and **SEÁN CLANCY** maintained that in the end de Valera and most of the anti-Treaty IRA seemed to accept the terms of the Treaty they had initially fought against. Jack said that de Valera just changed the name of the oath to 'empty formula',[260] whilst Seán pointed to the fact that de Valera was 'in power for a long, long time and failed to get a united Ireland'.[261] They suggested that Collins got more than anyone else could have got during the negotiations. **DANIEL O'DONOVAN** acknowledged that:

We got split up and contact and friendship was parted due to the side we took but in later years when things died down most of us became friends again.[262]

Seán Clancy would continue to soldier until retiring on age grounds on 7 July 1959 (his birthday).[263]

I spent my whole life almost in the army. I was nearly forty years serving. I served in most parts of the country. I enjoyed serving too. I'm nearly forty years retired now. I'm over forty years retired now. I'm longer retired now than I was serving.[264]

His army career incorporated periods in Dublin, Gort, Limerick, Tipperary, Castlebar, Mullingar, Clare and elsewhere. He reached the rank of lieutenant colonel on 5 February 1954.[265]

A lieutenant colonel was my rank. My last appointment was officer commanding the 5th Battalion here in Dublin.[266]

Looking back, **MICHAEL CASEY** summed up the difference between the War for Independence and the Civil War in terms of friendships. He maintained that in the first he 'only made friends' and that in the second 'a lot of them went away'.[267] In 2003, he acknowledged that there was still bitterness around pertaining to the Civil War and that 'it will be there for another 100 years'.[268] Also citing the 'terrible bitterness', **ANTHONY MCGINLEY** said that many who wrote about the Civil War in recent years 'hadn't a real idea at all about it'.[269] Speaking about the decades after 1923, **DAN KEATING** was adamant that 'for a long number of years it was on the cards' that you could have a united Ireland.[270] However, in 2003 he expressed the view that 'it is further away now than it has ever been before'.[271] He maintained that 'politics in Ireland is rotten' and that the politicians will do nothing about it.[272] **DANIEL O'DONOVAN** was more optimistic.

The meeting of both sides – I'd say they'll come together. They'll come together in the end with a new generation. Not with the present. That they'll come together and the border will be done away with because they'll come to some terms with England and with those living within the six counties. I think that will be the grand finish.[273]

In 2003, **PATRICK GREENE** was of the view that:

It's the last little bit of a colonial power, legal ground that England owns – the six counties. It will last for possibly another twenty or thirty years until the Protestants become a minority. What will happen in the interim I don't know.[274]

JACK DUFF felt that 80 years later the bitterness caused by the Civil War was still evident in Irish society.

Very much so but the place where it is most prominent of all is in Dáil Éireann. I think the 1916 fight is still going on there.[275]

Dan Keating had the same views in 2003 as he did 80 years previously.

The exact same. There's nothing will ever come from Ireland; two parliaments will never be acceptable in Ireland.[276]

Interestingly, he revealed that he had never been across the border.

No, never in the north but I was in jail with a lot of fellows from the north, yerra they were grand fellows too. Harry White, you heard of him didn't you? Did you read his book? Get that in the library, his book because Jesus he throws a lot of light on it.[277]

Harry White was born in 1916 on Blackwater Street off the Grosvenor Road in Belfast, close to where John Parkinson lived. He went on to join the IRA and served numerous prison sentences as well as a period of internment in the Curragh during World War II. His book entitled *Harry* by Uinseann MacEoin was published in 1985.

There were many regions and many people in Ireland who were comparatively unaffected by military activity during the Civil War (and indeed the War for Independence). For those who were, it was a traumatic experience, and silence would endure for decades. **PATSY HOLMES** from Mallow alluded to two men with strong political ideals that he met in Ballykinlar. Both survived the conflict after taking opposite sides, but died not too long afterwards.

I knew Lemass. Noel Lemass was in the camp and he was shot in the Dublin/Wicklow Mountains shortly afterward.[278]

Lemass had taken the anti-Treaty side and in 1923, shortly after the Civil War, was abducted and killed in a manner similar to Joseph Bergin. His brother Seán later went on to become Taoiseach. It's worth noting that Seán Lemass, who had been a member of Collins' Squad, spent a year in Ballykinlar, having been arrested in December 1920. He stayed in Camp No. 1, Hut No. 26, but Patsy was adamant that it was Noel he knew.[279]

> Paddy Hogan, he was the first Minister for Agriculture.[280]

Paddy Hogan went on to become Minister for Agriculture in 1922 under the Cumann na nGaedheal government. He died as a result of a car accident in 1936. For his part, Patsy Holmes probably summed up the 1922–1923 conflict best of all.

> It was the most unfortunate day that ever reigned when the Civil War broke out. It should never have occurred; there was no need of it, a difference of opinion. That could be remedied by headstrong men, headstrong men.[281]

CHAPTER 9
The interviewees

It's worth reiterating that 20 interviews were recorded for this book. Eighteen of these were recorded in the first seven months of 2003 across Ireland to coincide with the 80th anniversary of the ending of the Civil War. Two further interviews were recorded in the United States in July 2004. The names of the interviewees, their ages at the time they were recorded, and a brief synopsis of what they went on to do in later life are provided below. The 1919–1923 revolutionary period, its prelude and its aftermath made up only a small portion of their very long lives.

GEORGE CARPENTER (94 when interviewed on 7 January 2003) was born on 23 September 1908. He married Joan O'Kelly in 1938 and the couple had four children. During World War II he served in the LDF and also worked in the hotel and entertainment industry, running the Club Hotel in Glenbrook just outside Cork city. He was an avid sportsman and represented Ireland as a fencer in two Olympic Games – Helsinki (1952) and Rome (1960). He also took part in the World Fencing Championships in Paris in 1957, where he met Georges Carpentier. At home, he and Joan were regular winners of the Irish Fencing Championship throughout those years, and he also found enjoyment teaching fencing to others. He ended his days in Kinsale, going to his eternal rest on 13 August 2005.[1]

MICHAEL CASEY (100 when interviewed on 7 June 2003) was born in Mitchelstown on 15 May 1903. He married Ciss Young from Kilworth in 1937 (the same year that he bought Rockmills House) and they went on to have a daughter named Noreen. Michael's great passion in life was horses, and he was a founder member of Kildorrery Point-to-Point. One of his proudest achievements occurred in 1948, when he bred a mare called 'Golden Glen', which won six races at five meetings, including the Lightweight and Heavyweight at Newmarket. He was also chairman for almost 20 years of Kildorrery races. Michael died on the 2 February 2004.[2]

SEÁN CLANCY (101 when interviewed on 2 April 2003) was born in Clonlara on the 7 July 1901. He joined the army in 1922, and he took part in the army guard of honour during High Mass at the Eucharistic Congress in the Phoenix Park on 26 June 1932. He was a founding chairman of Scoil Uí Chonaill GAA Club and a founding vice-president of Glasnevin Musical Society. Seán married Agnes Creagh in 1926 and they had four sons and a daughter. He rose to the rank of lieutenant colonel in 1954 and retired on age grounds in 1959. In 2006, he attended the 90th Anniversary Commemoration of the Easter Rising in Dublin, but passed away months later on 17 September in Newtownpark House Nursing Home in Blackrock. He had been in his 106th year.

GEORGE COOPER (92 when interviewed on 3 April 2003) was born in Buckingham Place in Dublin on 23 May 1910. George started work as an apprentice in the printing trade at a very young age and worked his way up from being a 'reader's boy' to the post of supervisor in Smurfits, a well-known Dublin firm. He retired at the age of 72. Having married Elizabeth Blackmore in 1935, he was the loving father of three children. Religion was always important to George, and he could remember hearing Richard Hudson Pope (a children's evangelist) speak on the text in 1923 when at the age of 13 he attended the Tuesday 'boys' and girls' night' in the Merrion Hall, Dublin. Over the years, George and his family regularly attended Sunday services in that venue from their home in Balbriggan. He died in Mayo General Hospital on 9 November 2009 in his 100th year.[3]

NORMAN DOUGLAS (93 when interviewed on 14 and 22 July 2003) was born in east Belfast on 28 December 1909. He worked in the wholesale drapery industry and married Gretta McCausland in 1943. The couple honeymooned in Dublin and went on to have two children. Gretta died in 1974, and six years later Norman remarried. From this union with Gertie Foster he gained three stepsons and a stepdaughter, but unfortunately his second wife died in 1987. Norman always had a keen interest in music and sang in a barbershop quartet. He also sang for BBC Radio and once shared a stage with the tenor Josef Locke. On one occasion, when the future British prime minister Clement Attlee came to Belfast for a local Labour party conference, Norman was instructed by his boss to drive him on a tour of the Antrim coast. Norman passed away on 12 July 2010, having lived on the Cregagh Road in Belfast.[4]

JACK DUFF (100 when interviewed on 25 June 2003) was born in Dublin on 30 May 1903. Having joined the army in 1922, he subsequently left it in 1931 and returned to his previous employer, the Dublin United Tramways Company, with whom he worked as a tram and bus driver for 37 years until retiring in 1968. He claimed to have driven every bus in Dublin before finishing up on the number 83.[5] Jack married Kathleen Weafer in 1927, was father to four daughters and resided on the Cashel Road in Crumlin.[6] He was recognised as a pillar of the community and was involved in his local drama group in Perrystown for many years. As a former tram driver, he was invited to be a special guest on the first Luas when it ran in Dublin in 2004. He died on 9 September 2006.

PATRICK FITZGERALD (100 when interviewed on 7 June 2003) was born in Dunmoon, Tallow, Co. Waterford, on 5 October 1902. He lived his life farming and breaking horses at home. He kept in touch with former comrades, and they often reminisced about the olden days. Patrick donated his Centenarian Bounty from the President of Ireland towards the purchase of the historic Dromana papers of the Fitzgerald family, which are housed at UCC. Before I took my leave of him, he commented on how one thing made his blood boil, and that was the number of Irish people who in later years claimed an IRA pension despite not being entitled to it. If he was making the rules, 'anyone that wasn't in before the Truce wouldn't be entitled to no pension'. A pipe smoker to the end, Patrick, who never married, spent his final years in Glendonagh Nursing Home, Dungourney, passing away on 19 October 2003.[7]

WILLIAM GEARY (105 when interviewed on 15 July 2004) was born in Ballyagran on 28 February 1899. He worked for the Con Edison electrical company in New York (just like Anthony McGinley) and served in the United States Army Air Corps during World War II. In 1943, whilst serving, he married Roscommon native Margaret Shryane and they had two daughters. He kept his dismissal from An Garda Síochána a secret from all his employers and always feared the possibility of exposure. Owing to this, he had to proceed in a quiet manner, and it wasn't until after his retirement from Con Edison in 1967 that he pursued the case with vigour. The end result was that his name was cleared in 1999 when the Irish government completely exonerated him following a 71-year battle.

At his home in Bayside, New York, I asked William if he had ever been back to Ireland since the day he left in 1928, to which he replied 'Never'. If he had made the journey back to Ballyagran, one of the first things he'd have done would have been 'to visit my father's and my mother's grave in Newtown Shandrum'. However, going back was not an option for William until his name had been cleared, and it was regretful that it hadn't happened years earlier when his health might have been up to making the trip.

> I was ashamed. You see I didn't tell you at the beginning but we were, had the biggest farm, the most productive farm in the parish of Ballyagran ... So I was disgraced. There was more expected of me than that. So I couldn't go back.[8]

He claimed to have forgiven those in the IRA who stitched him up in 1928, as well as those in the Gardaí and in government who could have done more to assist him during his campaign to clear his name in the early years. I wondered if he was at peace with what happened.

> Yes, long ago. I felt they just did their duty but of course I say that with some reservations because any third-rate attorney, solicitor would have seen that there was no case against me. Of course, now in retrospect I know that there wasn't. At the time I didn't know what evidence they [Gardaí and Irish government] had but all they had were actually copies of, no dispatches from the IRA implicating me that I took a bribe from them. And that was the only evidence they had, not a single scrap otherwise. And besides I had plenty money; I had £300 at the time so there was really no motive for me and that as a policeman the first thing you look for is a motive in a crime.[9]

William passed away on the 14 October 2004.

PATRICK GREENE (Pádraig Mac Gréine) (102 when interviewed on 4 March 2003) was born in Rathreagh, Co. Longford, on 6 June 1900. He qualified as a primary teacher and in 1935 married Helena Sullivan (herself a secondary teacher). The couple had six children. He was a lover of the Irish language and carried out Trojan work for the Irish Folklore Commission, collecting stories and songs. He also did much for the preservation of Cant (a form of Irish spoken by Travellers), and received an honorary Master of Arts Degree from NUI Galway in 2003 in recognition of his contribution to Irish education. A deeply religious man, he retired from teaching in 1965 and resided in Ballinalee until he left this world on 22 February 2007.[10]

PATSY HOLMES (101 when interviewed on 13 June 2003) was born in Whitechurch on 2 May 1902. He lived in Mallow and worked as a butcher, cattle drover and dealer. He travelled the highways and byways of Ireland, but after just one pint of alcohol, opted to remain a life-long Pioneer. Patsy married Hannah McCarthy in 1949 and they resided at David's Terrace in the town. The couple had no children, and when she died in 1960, he moved back to Fair Street.[11] For many years, Patsy was guest of honour at several Old IRA Annual Commemoration Ceremonies, which were held throughout Co. Cork, and in May 2003 he fittingly gave the graveside oration at the commemoration for his friend and comrade Edward Waters in Kilshannig, Newberry, who had been killed in 1921. Patsy lived the last few years of his life at Nazareth House, Mallow, and died on 20 April 2005.[12]

DAN KEATING (101 when interviewed on 13 January and 14 April 2003) was born in Lisnanaul, Castlemaine, on the 2 January 1902. A dedicated and active republican all his life, he was imprisoned on a number of occasions in the years after the Civil War. His great passion was Gaelic Games, and he calculated that he had attended 154 All-Ireland Finals in both football and hurling during his lifetime. In 1944 he married Mary Dollie Fleming from Co. Waterford. The couple had no children. Dan was a barman and spent many years working in the Comet Bar on the Swords Road in Dublin. In 1977, his wife having died, he retired and returned to Co. Kerry to settle in Ballygamboon. Dan was reunited with former comrades on 2 October 2007.

JOHN KELLY (100 when interviewed on 24 May 2003) was born on 19 June 1902, and lived all his life in Caherbriskaun, Athenry. In 1937 he married Ellen Creaven. They worked as farmers and went on to have 12 children. Sadly, Ellen died at the age of 57 in May 1971. John travelled to the United States to visit family on no fewer than 12 different occasions and also visited Lourdes in France. He enjoyed music and singing as well as dancing, and took a keen interest in the history of his local area. In later life, John enjoyed the company of not only his own children and friends but also his 43 grandchildren and 21 great-grandchildren.[13] He died on the 17 April 2005.

ANTHONY MCGINLEY (98 when interviewed on 27 May 2003) was born on 6 February 1905. On returning from America, he resumed residence at his aunt and uncle's house in Largnalarkin, Ballinamore, where he worked the farm and also took a job with the Electricity Board. In 1948, he married Rose McGee, with whom he had two sons. Greatly influenced by the stories, folklore and family history told to him by his father and by his grandfather Anton Ned McDevitt among others, his knowledge of local history was regarded as unsurpassed. He became the chief folklorist, seanchaí and historian of Glenswilly and featured in a 1997 New Zealand televison documentary about two newly discovered ballads written by his father whilst en route there. He passed away on 1 December 2003.[14]

MAI McMAHON (NÉE GROGAN) (101 when interviewed on 22 June 2003) was born on 29 March 1902 in Tullycrine. She went on to marry Patrick McMahon from Church View, Kilmurry McMahon, in 1925, with whom she reared a family of five sons and four daughters. The McMahons ran a grocery and hardware business. In later years, she lived in Kilrush with her daughter Mary, where they operated a knitwear store on Vandeleur Street. With Spanish ancestry, travel was in the veins, with Mai visiting America three times during her life; the last time aged 99 for her nephew's graduation as a lawyer. There is a history of longevity in the family, with Mai's mother living to the age of 93. Mai died on 7 March 2006, just short of her 104th birthday.[15]

KATHLEEN NOONAN (NÉE CHARLES) (100 when interviewed on 28 May 2003) was born in Kanturk on 23 November 1902. Raised in a Church of Ireland family, she converted to Catholicism and married Andrew Noonan in 1934. They would go on to have a son and a daughter. Kathleen was involved in many organisations in the town, including the Local Development Association, the Handicapped Association, the North Cork Agricultural Show and the local ISPCC. She was also the first woman to form a camogie club in Kanturk. Kathleen lived out the last few years of her life in the Baggot Street Community Hospital in Dublin, and passed away on the 22 January 2006, aged 103.[16]

DANIEL O'DONOVAN (100 when interviewed on 1 July 2003) was born in Bantry on 23 February 1903 and after the troubles became a member of An Garda Síochána. He was on duty at the Phoenix Park in 1932 for the Eucharistic Congress and in 1963 for President Kennedy's visits to Cork and Limerick. Daniel married Alice Maher from Cashel in 1942, and they had four children. He retired in 1968 after 43 years in the force, but remained active as a member of the Garda Síochána Retired Members Association in Tralee. Although Daniel had lived and served in Tralee for many years, he was anxious that when referred to in the book he be identified as a West Corkman, as he never forgot his roots. Daniel passed away on the 28 July 2006.[17]

JOHN PARKINSON (96 when interviewed on 14 and 22 July 2003) was born in Belfast on 7 January 1907. He spent 10 years as an apprentice and a joiner in the shipyards of Harland & Wolff before qualifying as a teacher. His area of expertise was woodwork. John married Jean Dickson in 1939, and they had four children. He retired officially from teaching in 1972 but carried on the profession for another 15 years. John's favourite sport was soccer, and he wrote match reports for various newspapers for nearly 60 years. He also had a great interest in history, and up until his death was President of the Ulster Titanic Society. John passed away on the 1 March 2006, having lived at Flush Park, Belfast.[18]

MARGARET POWER (NÉE CAHILL) (98 when interviewed on 9 July 2004) was born in Ballinasare on 5 November 1905. She emigrated to America in 1926 and trained as a nurse in Boston. In 1933, Margaret married a man from Bantry named John Power, whom she met in the city, and they moved to New Jersey. The couple had a son and a daughter, living for periods in Carteret and Woodbridge before eventually settling in Clark in 1961. Margaret was a licensed practical nurse at St. Elizabeth Hospital in Elizabeth, Rahway, and in JFK Medical Center, Edison, for 40 years before retiring. A deeply religious woman, she was also a member of the American Irish Association, Woodbridge, where she served as historian. Margaret died on 17 December 2005.[19]

GERRY SMYTH (96 when interviewed on 26 June 2003) was born in Stackallen on 12 January 1907. He trained as a primary teacher, becoming principal of Dunshaughlin National School in 1932. Gerry married Lucy Peppard, of the same profession, in 1934, and the couple went on to raise a family of eight children. During World War II, Gerry served with the LSF and upon retirement from teaching in 1972 moved to Trim. He was a founding member of Muintir na Tire and a member of the Knights of Columbanus. Gerry always maintained an active lifestyle, and in 2003 at the age of 96 won gold medals in walking events at both the European Senior Games in Belgium and the World Senior Games in Utah, America. He resided at Saint Elizabeth's Nursing Home in Athboy prior to his calling aged 104 on 20 May 2011.[20]

ELLEN TROY (NÉE MALONEY) (102 when interviewed on 15 June 2003) was born in Portarlington on 20 June 1900. She married Michael Troy in 1925 and moved into a house across the road from her late grand-aunt's pub on Bracklone Street. The couple enjoyed some great outings together, such as going to the pictures, working on the bog and watching football matches. Although they took over the running of the pub, Michael still worked as a shoemaker.[21] Ellen gave birth to a son named Thomas, who went on to work for Odlum's Flour Mills in the town. Sadly, he predeceased her in 1999, as did her husband, Michael, in 1947. Ellen had an interest in history and was associated with the Peoples' Museum in Portarlington.[22] She also enjoyed growing vegetables. Ellen lived out her final days in St Vincent's Hospital in Mountmellick and died on 30 August 2006.

Endnotes

CHAPTER I

1   *Jottings and Recollections of William Geary, New York* – 14th June 1974.
2   Tom Hurley interview with William Geary recorded 15 July 2004.
3   1911 Census.
4   Tom Hurley interview with William Geary recorded 15 July 2004.
5   *Jottings and Recollections of William Geary, New York* – 14th June 1974.
6   Tom Hurley interview with William Geary recorded 15 July 2004.
7   Tom Hurley interview with William Geary recorded 15 July 2004.
8   *Jottings and Recollections of William Geary, New York* – 14th June 1974.
9   Tom Hurley interview with William Geary recorded 15 July 2004.
10 1901 & 1911 Censuses ; www.irishgenealogy.ie.
11 1901 Census.
12 The *Longford Leader*, 21 December 2000.
13 The *Longford News*, 2000.
14 Tom Hurley interview with Patrick Greene recorded 4 March 2003.
15 Tom Hurley interview with Patrick Greene recorded 4 March 2003.
16 The *Longford Leader*, 29 December 2000.
17 Tom Hurley interview with Patrick Greene recorded 4 March 2003.
18 Tom Hurley interview with Patrick Greene recorded 4 March 2003.
19 1901 & 1911 Censuses.
20 1901 Census; www.irishgenealogy.ie.
21 Tom Hurley interview with Ellen Troy née Maloney recorded 15 June 2003.
22 www.irishgenealogy.ie.
23 www.findmypast.ie.
24 https://www.nam.ac.uk/explore/south-lancashire-regiment-prince-waless-volunteers.
25 Tom Hurley interview with Ellen Troy née Maloney recorded 15 June 2003.
26 The *Laois Nationalist*, 4 July 2003; www.irishgenealogy.ie.
27 Tom Hurley interview with Ellen Troy née Maloney recorded 15 June 2003.
28 Tom Hurley interview with Ellen Troy née Maloney recorded 15 June 2003.
29 Tom Hurley interview with Ellen Troy née Maloney recorded 15 June 2003.
30 www.irishgenealogy.ie; 1911 Census.
31 Tom Hurley interview with Ellen Troy née Maloney recorded 15 June 2003.
32 The *Laois Nationalist*, 4 July 2003.
33 1911 Census; www.irishgenealogy.ie.
34 Tom Hurley interview with Seán Clancy recorded 2 April 2003.
35 1901 Census; www.irishgenealogy.ie.
36 Tom Hurley interview with Seán Clancy recorded 2 April 2003.
37 Grob-Fitzgibbon, Benjamin. *The Irish Experience During the Second World War: An Oral History.* Irish Academic Press, Dublin, 2004, p. 95.
38 MacEoin, Uinseann. *The IRA in the Twilight Years 1923-1948.* Argenta Publications, Dublin, 1997, p. 617; www.irishgenealogy.ie.
39 MacEoin, Uinseann. *The IRA in the Twilight Years 1923-1948.* Argenta Publications, Dublin, 1997. p. 617; www.irishgenealogy.ie.

40 Tom Hurley interview with Dan Keating recorded 13 January 2003.

41 'The Elections of 1885 and 1886 – Movements for Political and Social reform 1870–1914', *Case Studies in Irish History*, no. 4, National Library of Ireland, 2005, p. 12.

42 1911 Census; www.irishgenealogy.ie.

43 Tom Hurley interview with Mai McMahon née Grogan recorded 22 June 2003.

44 1901 & 1911 Censuses.

45 Tom Hurley interview with Mai McMahon née Grogan recorded 22 June 2003.

46 The *Cork Examiner*, 9 May 1925.

47 The *Clare Champion*, 5 April 2002.

48 Tom Hurley interview with Mai McMahon née Grogan recorded 22 June 2003.

49 Tom Hurley interview with Mai McMahon née Grogan recorded 22 June 2003.

50 1901 & 1911 Censuses; www.irishgenealogy.ie.

51 Tom Hurley interview with Patsy Holmes recorded 13 June 2003.

52 *The Corkman*, 15 January 1988.

53 Tom Hurley interview with Patsy Holmes recorded 13 June 2003.

54 www.irishgenealogy.ie.

55 The Castle Lambert Tape, http://homepage.eircom.net/~oreganathenry/oreganathenry/index.html?history/social/castlelamberttape%205.html.

56 https://athenry.org/record/the-history-of-castle-lambert-and-lisheenkyle-262/.

57 Tom Hurley interview with John Kelly recorded 24 May 2003.

58 https://athenry.org/record/the-history-of-castle-lambert-and-lisheenkyle-262/.

59 Tom Hurley interview with John Kelly recorded 24 May 2003.

60 Tom Hurley interview with John Kelly recorded 24 May 2003.

61 Tom Hurley interview with John Kelly recorded 24 May 2003.

62 1901 & 1911 Censuses; www.irishgenealogy.ie.

63 Tom Hurley interview with Patrick Fitzgerald recorded 7 June 2003.

64 Tom Hurley interview with Patrick Fitzgerald recorded 7 June 2003.

65 *The Corkman*, 22 July 1988.

66 Tom Hurley interview with Kathleen Noonan née Charles recorded 28 May 2003.

67 The *Evening Echo*, 18 February 1965.

68 1911 Census; www.irishgenealogy.ie.

69 Tom Hurley interview with Kathleen Noonan née Charles recorded 28 May 2003.

70 *The Corkman*, 29 November 2002.

71 *The Corkman*, 17 May 1991.

72 1901 & 1911 Censuses; www.irishgenealogy.ie.

73 Tom Hurley interview with Kathleen Noonan née Charles recorded 28 May 2003.

74 Tom Hurley interview with Kathleen Noonan née Charles recorded 28 May 2003.

75 Tom Hurley interview with Daniel O'Donovan recorded 1 July 2003.

76 Tom Hurley interview with Daniel O'Donovan recorded 1 July 2003.

77 1911 Census.

78 1911 Census; www.irishgenealogy.ie.

79 1911 Census.

80 Tom Hurley interview with Michael Casey recorded 7 June 2003.

81 Power, Bill. *White Knights, Dark Earls – The Rise and Fall of an Anglo-Irish Dynasty*. Collins Press, Cork, 2000, pp. 216–217.

82 Tom Hurley interview with Michael Casey recorded 7 June 2003.

83 1911 Census; www.irishgenealogy.ie.

84 1911 Census; www.irishgenealogy.ie.

85 Tom Hurley interview with Jack Duff recorded 25 June 2003.

86 Military Archives, Abstract of Service, John Duff; www.irishgenealogy.ie.

87 1911 Census.

88 Tom Hurley interview with Anthony McGinley recorded 27 May 2003.

89 Tom Hurley interview with Anthony McGinley recorded 27 May 2003.

90 Mac Fhionnghaile, Niall. *Dr. McGinley and His Times*. An Crann, Letterkenny, 1985, pp. 1–3; www.mcginleyclan.org.

91 Tom Hurley interview with Anthony McGinley recorded 27 May 2003.

92 The *Donegal Democrat*, 14 September 1940.

93 Mac Fhionnghaile, Niall. *Dr McGinley and His Times*. An Crann, Letterkenny, 1985, pp. 1–2; www.mcginleyclan.org.

94 Tierney, Mark. *Ireland Since 1870*. CJ Fallon, Dublin, 1988, p. 96.

95 *The Kerryman*, 5 January 2006; 1911 Census.

96 Tom Hurley interview with Margaret Power née Cahill recorded 9 July 2004.

97 Parkinson, John. *A Belfastman's Tale*. Minprint Ltd, Belfast, 2003, p. 1–2; www.irishgenealogy.ie.

98 1911 Census.

99 Tom Hurley interview with John Parkinson recorded 22 July 2003.

100 Parkinson, John. *A Belfastman's Tale*. Minprint Ltd, Belfast, 2003, p. 9.

101 Tom Hurley interview with John Parkinson recorded 14 July 2003.

102 Tierney, Mark. *Ireland Since 1870*. CJ Fallon, Dublin, 1988, p. 100.

103 Tom Hurley interview with John Parkinson recorded 14 July 2003.

104 Tom Hurley interview with John Parkinson recorded 22 July 2003.

105 Tom Hurley interview with John Parkinson recorded 22 July 2003.

106 Parkinson, John. *A Belfastman's Tale*. Minprint Ltd, Belfast, 2003, p. 17.

107 Tom Hurley interview with John Parkinson recorded 22 July 2003.

108 1901 & 1911 Censuses; www.irishgenealogy.ie

109 Tom Hurley interview with Gerry Smyth recorded 26 June 2003.

110 www.irishgenealogy.ie; the *Meath Chronicle*, 26 November 1932.

111 The *Meath Chronicle*, 26 November 1932. Tom Hurley interview with Gerry Smyth recorded 26 June 2003.

112 1911 Census.

113 Tom Hurley interview with Gerry Smyth recorded 26 June 2003.

114 *Jottings and Recollections of William Geary, New York – 14th June 1974*.

115 1911 Census; Jim Herlihy, Royal Irish Constabulary Register Extract – Public Records Office, Kew, Richmond, Surrey, England; www.irishgenealogy.ie.

116 Tom Hurley interview with George Carpenter recorded 7 January 2003.

117 Carpenter, George. *The Life & Times of Cork's George Carpenter*. Innisfree Press, Kinsale, 2002, p. 6; Jim Herlihy, Royal Irish Constabulary Register Extract – Public Records Office, Kew, Richmond, Surrey, England.

118 Teanglann.ie, https://www.teanglann.ie/en/fgb/piseog.

119 Tom Hurley interview with George Carpenter recorded 7 January 2003.

120 Carpenter, George. *The Life & Times of Cork's George Carpenter*. Innisfree Press, Kinsale, 2002, p. 3.

121 Tom Hurley interview with George Carpenter recorded 7 January 2003.

122 www.irishgenealogy.ie.

123 Tom Hurley interview with George Carpenter recorded 7 January 2003.

124 Murphy, Allison. *When Dublin Was the Capital – Northern Life Remembered*. Belcouver Press, Belfast, 2000, p. 17; www.irishgenealogy.ie.

125 1901 & 1911 Censuses.

126 Tom Hurley interview with Norman Douglas recorded 22 July 2003.

127 Murphy, Allison. *When Dublin Was the Capital – Northern Life Remembered*. Belcouver Press, Belfast, 2000, p. 17.

128 Tom Hurley interview with Norman Douglas recorded 22 July 2003.

129   Boylan, Henry. *A Dictionary of Irish Biography*. Gill & Macmillan, Dublin, 1998.
130   1911 Census; www.irishgenealogy.ie.
131   Tom Hurley interview with George Cooper recorded 3 April 2003.
132   The *Fingal Independent*, 8 February 2006; https://databases.dublincity.ie/freemen/ viewdoc.php?searchid=25139&source=integration; 1841–1864 Freedom Roll book, Dublin City Library and Archive.
133   Tom Hurley interview with George Cooper recorded 3 April 2003.
134   Tom Hurley interview with George Cooper recorded 3 April 2003.
135   The *Irish Times*, 26 May 1910.
136   Tom Hurley interview with Kathleen Noonan née Charles recorded 28 May 2003.
137   Tom Hurley interview with Kathleen Noonan née Charles recorded 28 May 2003.
138   1901 & 1911 Censuses; www.irishgenealogy.ie; www.findmypast.ie.
139   The *Skibbereen Eagle*, 5 March 1910; the *Irish Times* 12 March 1910.
140   Tom Hurley interview with Kathleen Noonan née Charles recorded 28 May 2003.
141   www.bbc.co.uk/history.
142   Tom Hurley interview with John Parkinson recorded 14 July 2003.
143   Tom Hurley interview with John Parkinson recorded 14 July 2003.
144   Murphy, Allison. *When Dublin Was the Capital – Northern Life Remembered*. Belcouver Press, Belfast, 2000.
145   Tom Hurley interview with John Parkinson recorded 14 July 2003.
146   Cooper, G.J. *Titanic Captain: The Life of Edward John Smyth*. The History Press, Gloucestershire, 2012, pp. 110, 138, 161.
147   Tom Hurley interview with John Parkinson recorded 14 July 2003.
148   Tom Hurley interview with John Parkinson recorded 14 July 2003.
149   www.titanic-titanic.com.
150   Tierney, Mark. *Ireland Since 1870*. CJ Fallon, Dublin, 1988, p. 98.
151   Tom Hurley interview with Patrick Greene recorded 4 March 2003.
152   Tierney, Mark. *Ireland Since 1870*. CJ Fallon, Dublin, 1988, p. 87.
153   Tierney, Mark. *Ireland Since 1870*. CJ Fallon, Dublin, 1988, p. 99.
154   Tom Hurley interview with John Parkinson recorded 14 July 2003.
155   Tom Hurley interview with Norman Douglas recorded 22 July 2003.
156   Tom Hurley interview with Norman Douglas recorded 22 July 2003.

CHAPTER 2

1   Tierney, Mark. *Ireland Since 1870*. CJ Fallon, Dublin, 1988, p. 101; Boylan, Henry. *A Dictionary of Irish Biography*, Gill & Macmillan, Dublin, 1998.
2   Tom Hurley interview with John Parkinson recorded 22 July 2003.
3   Tom Hurley interview with John Parkinson recorded 22 July 2003.
4   Tierney, Mark. *Ireland Since 1870*. CJ Fallon, Dublin, 1988, pp. 144–151.
5   Military Archives, Abstract of Service, John Duff.
6   Tom Hurley interview with George Cooper recorded 3 April 2003.
7   www.census.nationalarchives.ie; O'Mahony, Sean. *Frongoch – University of Revolution*. FDR Teoranta, Dublin, 1987, p. 177; Membership Roll of the Irish Citizen Army compiled by Dr Ann Matthews at www.communistpartyofireland.ie & www. irishgenealogy.ie.
8   Tierney, Mark. *Ireland Since 1870*. CJ Fallon, Dublin, 1988, p. 157.
9   Tom Hurley interview with Gerry Smyth recorded 26 June 2003.
10   Tierney, Mark. *Ireland Since 1870*. CJ Fallon, Dublin, 1988, p. 102.
11   Tom Hurley interview with John Parkinson recorded 22 July 2003.
12   Tom Hurley interview with Norman Douglas recorded 22 July 2003.

13 Tom Hurley interview with Anthony McGinley recorded 27 May 2003.

14 www.mcginleyclan.org.

15 Carpenter, George. _The Life & Times of Cork's George Carpenter_. Innisfree Press, Kinsale, 2002, p. 19; _Guy's City and County Cork Almanac and Directory for 1916_, p. 118; _Guy's City and County Cork Almanac and Directory for 1921_, p. 113.

16 Tom Hurley interview with George Carpenter recorded 7 January 2003.

17 Carpenter, George. _The Life & Times of Cork's George Carpenter_. Innisfree Press, Kinsale, 2002, p. 4; www.irishgenealogy.ie.

18 Tom Hurley interview with George Carpenter recorded 7 January 2003.

19 Carpenter, George. _The Life & Times of Cork's George Carpenter_. Innisfree Press, Kinsale, 2002, pp. 13–14.

20 Parkinson, John. _A Belfastman's Tale_. Minprint Ltd, Belfast, 2003, p. 4.

21 Tom Hurley interview with Patrick Greene recorded 4 March 2003.

22 Tierney, Mark. _Ireland Since 1870_. CJ Fallon, Dublin, 1988, p. 98.

23 Tom Hurley interview with John Parkinson recorded 22 July 2003.

24 http://www.historyireland.com/volume-22/dublins-loyal-volunteers/; http://www.dublin1313.com/site/lodge-history/; The _Belfast Newsletter_, 11 April 2012.

25 Tom Hurley interview with George Cooper recorded 3 April 2003.

26 Tom Hurley interview with Norman Douglas recorded 22 July 2003.

27 Parkinson, John. _A Belfastman's Tale_. Minprint Ltd, Belfast, 2003, p. 16.

28 Tom Hurley interview with John Parkinson recorded 14 July 2003.

29 Tom Hurley interview with Jack Duff recorded 25 June 2003.

30 Tierney, Mark. _Ireland Since 1870_. CJ Fallon, Dublin, 1988, p. 161.

31 Tierney, Mark. _Ireland Since 1870_. CJ Fallon, Dublin, 1988, pp. 162–163.

32 Tom Hurley interview with Dan Keating recorded 13 January 2003.

33 Military Archives, Military Service Pensions Collection, John Kelly; Military Archives Military Service Pensions Collection, Michael Kelly.

34 Tom Hurley interview with Gerry Smyth recorded 26 June 2003.

35 Tom Hurley interview with Patsy Holmes recorded 13 June 2003.

36 _The Corkman_, 7 October 1977; the _Mallow Field Club Journal 1985_.

37 Tom Hurley interview with Patsy Holmes recorded 13 June 2003.

38 www.1914-1918.net & www.firstworldwar.com.

39 https://livesofthefirstworldwar.iwm.org.uk/lifestory/47070 & www.cwgc.org.

40 www.findmypast.ie.

41 Murphy, Allison. _When Dublin Was the Capital – Northern Life Remembered_. Belcouver Press, Belfast, 2000, p. 113.

42 Tom Hurley interview with Anthony McGinley recorded 27 May 2003.

43 The _Donegal News_, 27 February 2004; the _Ulster Herald_, 24 April 1915.

44 Tom Hurley interview with Anthony McGinley recorded 27 May 2003.

45 www.census.nationalarchives.ie; the _Donegal News_, 30 July 1955.

46 Tom Hurley interview with Anthony McGinley recorded 27 May 2003.

47 www.irishgenealogy.ie; 1911 Census.

48 Tom Hurley interview with Anthony McGinley recorded 27 May 2003.

49 Tom Hurley interview with John Parkinson recorded 22 July 2003.

50 Parkinson, John. _A Belfastman's Tale_. Minprint Ltd, Belfast, 2003, p. 16; email dated 25/2/2023 from Dr Alan Parkinson; email dated 26/2/23 from Tom Parkinson.

51 Tom Hurley interview with John Parkinson recorded 14 July 2003.

52 Tom Hurley interview with John Parkinson recorded 22 July 2003.

53 Tom Hurley interview with George Cooper recorded 3 April 2003.

54 Carpenter, George. _The Life & Times of Cork's George Carpenter_. Innisfree Press, Kinsale, 2002, p. 19.

55 Tom Hurley interview with Kathleen Noonan née Charles recorded 28 May 2003.

56 Tom Hurley interview with Patrick Fitzgerald recorded 7 June 2003.

57 The *Southern Star*, 26 August 2006.

58 Tom Hurley interview with Daniel O'Donovan recorded 1 July 2003.

59 The *Clare Champion*, 5 April 2002; the *Freeman's Journal*, 10 May 1915; the *Cork Examiner*, 10 May 1915.

60 Tom Hurley interview with Mai McMahon née Grogan recorded 22 June 2003.

61 www.libertyellisfoundation.org; the *Freeman's Journal*, 8 November 1919.

62 Tom Hurley interview with George Carpenter recorded 7 January 2003.

63 Tom Hurley interview with George Carpenter recorded 7 January 2003.

64 Tom Hurley interview with Mai McMahon née Grogan recorded 22 June 2003.

65 Tom Hurley interview with Mai McMahon née Grogan recorded 22 June 2003.

66 The *Nenagh News*, 29 May 1915.

67 Tom Hurley notes written post interview with Seán Clancy 2 April 2003.

68 The *Nenagh News*, 29 May 1915; www.census.nationalarchives.ie; www.ancestry.com; www.irishgenealogy.ie.

69 Tom Hurley interview with Dan Keating recorded 13 January 2003.

70 Tom Hurley interview with Margaret Power née Cahill recorded 9 July 2004.

71 www.irishgenealogy.ie.

72 The *Western People*, 5 July 1958.

73 1911 Census; www.irishgenealogy.ie.

74 www.irishgenealogy.ie; The *Ballina Herald*, 10 October 1953.

75 Tom Hurley interview with Margaret Power née Cahill recorded 9 July 2004.

76 Tom Hurley interview with Dan Keating recorded 13 January 2003.

77 Tierney, Mark. *Ireland Since 1870*. CJ Fallon, Dublin, 1988, p. 179.

78 Breen, Dan. *My Fight for Irish Freedom*. Anvil Books, Dublin, 1981, p. 44; Dwyer, T. Ryle. *Tans, Terror and Trouble – Kerry's Real Fighting Story*. Mercier Press, Cork, 2001, pp. 82–83.

79 Tom Hurley interview with Dan Keating recorded 13 January 2003.

80 Military Archives, Military Service Pensions Collection, John Kelly.

81 Tom Hurley interview with George Cooper recorded 3 April 2003.

82 Tom Hurley interview with George Cooper recorded 3 April 2003.

83 Tom Hurley interview with George Cooper recorded 3 April 2003.

84 Tom Hurley interview with Jack Duff recorded 25 June 2003.

85 Tom Hurley interview with Jack Duff recorded 25 June 2003.

86 Tom Hurley interview with George Cooper recorded 3 April 2003.

87 Tom Hurley interview with George Cooper recorded 3 April 2003.

88 Military Archives, Military Service Pensions Collection, John Dutton Cooper.

89 Military Archives, Military Service Pensions Collection, John Dutton Cooper.

90 The *Irish Press*, 25 October 1938; the *Limerick Leader*, 2 November 1938; the *Kilkenny People*, 5 November 1938; the *Irish Independent*, 10 April 1939.

91 The *Fingal Independent*, 8 February 2006.

92 Tom Hurley interview with George Cooper recorded 3 April 2003.

93 The *Irish Press*, 27 April 1944; Military Archives, Military Service Pensions Collection, John Dutton Cooper.

94 Tom Hurley interview with Anthony McGinley recorded 27 May 2003.

95 www.mcginleyclan.org.

96 Sisson, Elaine. *Pearse's Patriots: St Endas's and the Cult of Boyhood*. Cork University Press, Cork, 2004, p. 156.

97 The *Donegal News*, 1 August 1970; www.generalmichaelcollins.com.

98 www.mcginleyclan.org; the *Irish Press*, 14 April 1975.

99 Tom Hurley interview with Anthony McGinley recorded 27 May 2003.

100 O'Connor, John. *The 1916 Proclamation*. Anvil Books, Dublin, 1986, p. 63; www.mcginleyclan.org.

101 Tom Hurley interview with Gerry Smyth recorded 26 June 2003.

102 O'Halpin, Eunan & Ó Corráin, Daithí. *The Dead of the Irish Revolution*. Yale University Press, New Haven, 2020, p. 543.

103 O'Connor, John. *The 1916 Proclamation*. Anvil Books, Dublin, 1986, p. 54; Tierney, Mark. *Ireland Since 1870*. CJ Fallon, Dublin, 1988, pp. 190–193.

104 Military Archives, Military Service Pensions Collection, Michael Kelly; O'Mahony, Sean. *Frongoch – University of Revolution*. FDR Teoranta, Dublin, 1987, pp. 196–198.

105 Military Archives, Military Service Pensions Collection, John Kelly.

106 Tom Hurley interview with Mai McMahon née Grogan recorded 22 June 2003.

107 https://web.archive.org/web/20180307101742/http://markhams-of-derryguiha.com/; BMH.WS1322, Art O'Donnell.

108 Tom Hurley interview with Patrick Greene recorded 4 March 2003.

109 Tom Hurley interview with Dan Keating recorded 13 January 2003.

110 Nevin, Donal. *James Connolly – A Full Life*. Gill & MacMillian Ltd, Dublin, 2005, p. 670.

111 Dwyer, T. Ryle. *Tans, Terror and Trouble – Kerry's Real Fighting Story*. Mercier Press, Cork, 2001, p. 116.

112 Tom Hurley interview with Jack Duff recorded 25 June 2003.

113 Coogan, Oliver. *Politics and War in Meath 1913–23*. Folens & Co. Ltd, Dublin, 1983, pp. 48–54.

114 Tom Hurley interview with Gerry Smyth recorded 26 June 2003.

115 Tom Hurley interview with Gerry Smyth recorded 26 June 2003.

116 Tom Hurley interview with Seán Clancy recorded 2 April 2003.

117 Tom Hurley interview with Daniel O'Donovan recorded 1 July 2003.

118 Tom Hurley interview with John Parkinson recorded 22 July 2003.

119 www.history.com.

120 Grayson, Richard S. *Belfast Boys*. Continuum, London, 2009, p. 85.

121 Tom Hurley interview with John Parkinson recorded 14 July 2003.

122 www.firstworldwar.com; https://www.nam.ac.uk/explore/battle-somme.

123 Tom Hurley interview with John Parkinson recorded 14 July 2003.

124 Tom Hurley interview with Norman Douglas recorded 22 July 2003.

125 www.findmypast.ie.

126 Tom Hurley interview with Norman Douglas recorded 22 July 2003.

127 Tierney, Mark. *Ireland Since 1870*. CJ Fallon, Dublin, 1988, p. 201.

128 Tom Hurley interview with Dan Keating recorded 13 January 2003.

129 Military Archives Military Service Pensions Collection, Patrick Holmes.

130 Tom Hurley interview with Patsy Holmes recorded 13 June 2003.

131 Military Archives Military Service Pensions Collection, Patrick Holmes; BMH. WS1376, John O'Sullivan.

132 Tom Hurley interview with Patsy Holmes recorded 13 June 2003.

133 Tierney, Mark. *Ireland Since 1870*. CJ Fallon, Dublin, 1988, p. 203.

134 Tom Hurley interview with Patrick Greene recorded 4 March 2003.

135 The *Longford Leader*, 28 April 1917.

136 Tom Hurley interview with Patrick Greene recorded 4 March 2003.

137 Tom Hurley interview with Patrick Greene recorded 4 March 2003.

138 Tom Hurley interview with Patrick Greene recorded 4 March 2003.

139 Tom Hurley interview with Seán Clancy recorded 2 April 2003.

140 Tom Hurley interview with Seán Clancy recorded 2 April 2003.

141 The *Limerick Leader*, 9 August 1939; the *Nenagh Guardian*, 30 June 1917.

142 www.ancestry.com; 1901 & 1911 Censuses; www.irishgenealogy.ie.

143 Tom Hurley interview with William Geary recorded 15 July 2004.

144 McNamara, Patrick J. *The Widow's Penny*. Santa Lucia, Ballykeelaun, Parteen, Co. Clare, 2000; email from Patrick J. McNamara dated 21/7/2006.

145 www.cwgc.org.

146 Tierney, Mark. *Ireland Since 1870*. CJ Fallon, Dublin, 1988, p. 206.

147 Tom Hurley interview with Seán Clancy recorded 2 April 2003.

148 Dwyer, T. Ryle. *Tans, Terror and Trouble – Kerry's Real Fighting Story*. Mercier Press, Cork, 2001, pp. 120–121.

149 The *Clare Champion*, 4 December 1971.

150 1901 Census.

151 https://web.archive.org/web/20180307101742/http:/markhams-of-derryguiha.com/.

152 Tom Hurley interview with Mai McMahon née Grogan recorded 22 June 2003.

153 Tierney, Mark. *Ireland Since 1870*. CJ Fallon, Dublin, 1988, p. 205.

154 Tierney, Mark. *Ireland Since 1870*. CJ Fallon, Dublin, 1988, p. 204.

155 Tom Hurley interview with Anthony McGinley recorded 27 May 2003.

156 Tierney, Mark. *Ireland Since 1870*. CJ Fallon, Dublin, 1988, p. 100.

157 www.irishgenealogy.ie.

158 Tom Hurley interview with Ellen Troy née Maloney recorded 15 June 2003.

159 The *Nationalist and Leinster Times*, 26 January 1918.

160 The *Nationalist and Leinster Times*, 16 February 1918.

161 The *Nationalist and Leinster Times*, 2 March 1918; https://laoislocalstudies.ie/the-portarlington-sawmills-lockout-of-1918/.

162 The *Freeman's Journal*, 25 February 1918.

163 The *Leinster Express*, 15 June 1918.

164 Tierney, Mark. *Ireland Since 1870*. CJ Fallon, Dublin, 1988, pp. 207–209.

165 Tom Hurley interview with Seán Clancy recorded 2 April 2003.

166 Military Archives, Military Service Pensions Collection, Seán Clancy.

167 Tom Hurley interview with Seán Clancy recorded 2 April 2003.

168 Email from Theresa O'Farrell, St Patrick's College dated 14/2/2008.

169 The *Longford News*, 2000.

170 Conway, Joe. *In Shades Like These: Irish Teacher Life-Histories from the Twentieth Century*. Comhar Linn, Dublin, 2000; www.irishgenealogy.ie.

171 Conway, Joe: *In Shades Like These: Irish Teacher Life-Histories from the Twentieth Century*. Comhar Linn, Dublin, 2000.

172 The *Longford Leader*, 29 December 2000.

173 Tom Hurley interview with Patrick Greene recorded 4 March 2003.

174 http://www.theirishstory.com/2013/05/16/ireland-and-the-great-flu-epidemic-of1918/#.VGcw7cJybIU.

175 http://www.historyireland.com/20th-century-contemporary-history/greatest-killer-of-the-twentieth-century-the-great-flu-of-1918-19/.

176 The *Meath Chronicle*, 25 May 2011; https://web.archive.org/web/20160605064636/http://www.slanetimes.com/index.php?option=com_content&view=article&id=50&Itemid=56.

177 Conway, Joe. *In Shades Like These: Irish Teacher Life-Histories from the Twentieth Century*. Comhar Linn, Dublin, 2000; www.irishgenealogy.ie.

178 Tom Hurley interview with Patrick Greene recorded 4 March 2003.

179 Carpenter, George. *The Life & Times of Cork's George Carpenter*. Innisfree Press, Kinsale, 2002, p. 32.

180 Tom Hurley interview with Michael Casey recorded 7 June 2003.

181 Mitchelstown WWI figures researched by Bill Power, https://www.facebook.com/photo/?fbid=6111972975479343&set=a.312194828790549.

182 Tom Hurley interview with Michael Casey recorded 7 June 2003.
183 Tom Hurley interview with Mai McMahon née Grogan recorded 22 June 2003.
184 www.clarelibrary.ie, Browne, Ger. *'A Tribute to Kilrush in the Great War'.*
185 www.clarelibrary.ie, *'Clare Men & Women in WWI, Where they lived'*; *'The Clare War Dead WWI'.*
186 Tom Hurley interview with George Carpenter recorded 7 January 2003.
187 www.triskelartscentre.ie.
188 The *Cork Constitution,* 27 October 1919.
189 Tom Hurley interview with Patrick Greene recorded 4 March 2003.
190 Tom Hurley interview with Gerry Smyth recorded 26 June 2003.
191 Tom Hurley interview with Mai McMahon née Grogan recorded 22 June 2003.
192 1911 Census; www.irishgenealogy.ie.
193 The *Laois Nationalist,* 4 July 2003.
194 Tom Hurley interview with Ellen Troy née Maloney recorded 15 June 2003.
195 www.ancestry.com.
196 Tom Hurley interview with Ellen Troy née Maloney recorded 15 June 2003.
197 The *Laois Nationalist,* 4 July 2003; the *Nationalist and Leinster Times,* 30 October 1970; 1911 Census.
198 Tom Hurley interview with George Cooper recorded 3 April 2003.
199 Tom Hurley interview with George Carpenter recorded 7 January 2003.
200 Tom Hurley interview with George Carpenter recorded 7 January 2003.
201 Tierney, Mark. *Ireland Since 1870.* CJ Fallon, Dublin, 1988, p. 212.
202 Tom Hurley interview with Michael Casey recorded 7 June 2003.
203 Military Archives, Military Service Pensions Collection, John Kelly.

CHAPTER 3

1 Parkinson, John. *A Belfastman's Tale.* Minprint Ltd, Belfast, 2003, p. 19.
2 Tom Hurley interview with John Parkinson recorded 14 July 2003.
3 Tom Hurley interview with John Parkinson recorded 22 July 2003.
4 *Guy's City and County Cork Almanac and Directory for 1916,* p. 11; *Guy's City and County Cork Almanac and Directory for 1921,* p. 113; 1911 Census.
5 Carpenter, George. *The Life & Times of Cork's George Carpenter.* Innisfree Press, Kinsale, 2002, p. 42.
6 Tom Hurley interview with George Carpenter recorded 7 January 2003.
7 Tom Hurley interview with John Parkinson recorded 14 July 2003.
8 Tom Hurley interview with John Parkinson recorded 22 July 2003.
9 Tom Hurley interview with John Parkinson recorded 22 July 2003.
10 Tom Hurley interview with George Cooper recorded 3 April 2003.
11 Tom Hurley interview with John Parkinson recorded 22 July 2003.
12 Tom Hurley interview with Norman Douglas recorded 22 July 2003.
13 Tierney, Mark. *Ireland Since 1870.* CJ Fallon, Dublin, 1988, p. 213.
14 Breen, Dan. *My Fight for Irish Freedom.* Anvil Books, Dublin, 1981, p. 33.
15 Breen, Dan. *My Fight for Irish Freedom.* Anvil Books, Dublin, 1981, p. 38; Twohig, Patrick J. *Green Tears for Hecuba - Ireland's Fight for Freedom.* Tower Books, Ballincollig, 1994, p. 32; Dwyer, T. Ryle. *Tans, Terror and Trouble - Kerry's Real Fighting Story.* Mercier Press, Cork, 2001, p. 1; *Ballingeary Historical Society Journal 1996.*
16 'Donegal on Sunday', 13 January 2008; Mac Fhionnghaile, Niall. *Dr. McGinley and His Times.* An Crann, Letterkenny, 1985, p. 35.
17 Tom Hurley interview with Dan Keating recorded 13 January 2003.
18 BMH.WS981, Patrick Riordan.

19   Tom Hurley interview with Dan Keating recorded 13 January 2003.

20   Tom Hurley interview with Michael Casey recorded 7 June 2003.

21   The *Clare Champion*, 20 July 2001; Military Archives, Military Service Pensions Collection, Seán Clancy.

22   Tom Hurley interview with Seán Clancy recorded 2 April 2003.

23   Tom Hurley interview with Seán Clancy recorded 2 April 2003.

24   Military Archives, Military Service Pensions Collection, Seán Clancy; the *Clare Champion*, 20 July 2001.

25   Military Archives, IRA Membership Series.

26   Tom Hurley interview with Seán Clancy recorded 2 April 2003.

27   The *Island Journal*, vol. 1, no. 1, Winter 2006/2007.

28   Tom Hurley interview with Patsy Holmes recorded 13 June 2003.

29   The *Irish Times*, 21 June 1919; O'Sullivan, John L. *Cork City Gaol*. Litho Press, Midleton, 1996, p. 75.

30   The *Meath Chronicle*, 5 July 1919.

31   Tom Hurley interview with Gerry Smyth recorded 26 June 2003.

32   The *Drogheda Independent*, 3 October 1903.

33   www.militaryarchives.ie

34   Tierney, Mark. *Ireland Since 1870*. CJ Fallon, Dublin, 1988, pp. 222–223.

35   Military Archives, Military Service Pensions Collection, Patrick Holmes.

36   Military Archives, IRA Membership Series.

37   BMH.WS808, Richard Willis & John Bolster.

38   Military Archives, IRA Membership Series; Ryan, Meda. *The Real Chief – The Story of Liam Lynch*. Mercier Press, Cork, 2005, p. 79.

39   Military Archives, Medal Series, Patrick Holmes.

40   Tom Hurley interview with Patsy Holmes recorded 13 June 2003.

41   Military Archives, Military Service Pensions Collection, Patrick Holmes.

42   Tom Hurley interview with Patsy Holmes recorded 13 June 2003.

43   Tom Hurley interview with Patsy Holmes recorded 13 June 2003.

44   BMH.WS1151, Patrick Luddy.

45   Tom Hurley interview with Michael Casey recorded 7 June 2003.

46   Tom Hurley interview with Jack Duff recorded 25 June 2003.

47   Military Archives, Medal Series, Kathleen Noonan.

48   Tom Hurley interview with Kathleen Noonan née Charles recorded 28 May 2003.

49   Tom Hurley interview with Kathleen Noonan née Charles recorded 28 May 2003.

50   Tom Hurley interview with Kathleen Noonan née Charles recorded 28 May 2003.

51   Military Archives, Medal Series, Kathleen Noonan; Military Archives, Military Service Pensions Collection, Annie Sugrue; www.irishgenealogy.ie.

52   Military Archives, Medal Series, Kathleen Noonan.

53   Tom Hurley interview with Kathleen Noonan née Charles recorded 28 May 2003.

54   Tom Hurley interview with Kathleen Noonan née Charles recorded 28 May 2003.

55   *Rebel Cork's Fighting Story 1916–1921*. The Kerryman Limited, Tralee, 1947, p. 276.

56   Military Archives, Military Service Pensions Collection, Alice Hayes.

57   Tom Hurley interview with Kathleen Noonan née Charles recorded 28 May 2003.

58   Tom Hurley interview with Kathleen Noonan née Charles recorded 28 May 2003.

59   Tom Hurley interview with Kathleen Noonan née Charles recorded 28 May 2003.

60   Tom Hurley interview with Kathleen Noonan née Charles recorded 28 May 2003.

61   Tom Hurley interview with William Geary recorded 15 July 2004.

62   Tom Hurley interview with Mai McMahon née Grogan recorded 22 June 2003.

63   Tom Hurley interview with Mai McMahon née Grogan recorded 22 June 2003.

64   Tom Hurley interview with Mai McMahon née Grogan recorded 22 June 2003.

65 Tom Hurley interview with Mai McMahon née Grogan recorded 22 June 2003.
66 Ryan, Meda. *The Real Chief – The Story of Liam Lynch*. Mercier Press. Cork, 2005, pp. 36–3; the *Irish Independent*, 9 September 1919.
67 Tom Hurley interview with Patsy Holmes recorded 13 June 2003.
68 Tom Hurley interview with Patsy Holmes recorded 13 June 2003.
69 Tom Hurley interview with Patsy Holmes recorded 13 June 2003.
70 Tom Hurley interview with Patsy Holmes recorded 13 June 2003.
71 The *Irish Independent*, 10 September 1919; BMH.WS0978, Leo Callaghan; BMH. WS1030, John Joseph Hogan.
72 The *Cork Examiner*, 22 July & 18 October 1920; http://homepage.eircom.net/~corkcounty/.
73 www.gaa.ie.
74 Tom Hurley interview with Dan Keating recorded 14 April 2003.
75 https://web.archive.org/web/20170118130139/http:/www.esatclear.ie/~hurlingclub/clubhistory.html.
76 Conway, Joe. *In Shades Like These: Irish Teacher Life-Histories from the Twentieth Century*. Comhar Linn, Dublin, 2000.
77 Tom Hurley interview with Patrick Greene recorded 4 March 2003.
78 Tom Hurley interview with George Carpenter recorded 7 January 2003.
79 Tom Hurley interview with George Carpenter recorded 7 January 2003.
80 Parkinson, John. *A Belfastman's Tale*. Minprint Ltd, Belfast, 2003, p. 12.
81 Parkinson, John. *A Belfastman's Tale*. Minprint Ltd, Belfast, 2003, p. 17.
82 The *Belfast Telegraph*, 4 July 2008.
83 Breen, Dan. *My Fight for Irish Freedom*. Anvil Books, Dublin, 1981, pp. 81–92.
84 The *Evening Herald*, 24 February 1920; the *Kilkenny People*, 29 April 1922.
85 Tom Hurley interview with Patsy Holmes recorded 13 June 2003.

CHAPTER 4

1 Military Archives, IRA Membership Series.
2 Tom Hurley interview with Dan Keating recorded 13 January 2003.
3 MacEoin, Uinseann. *The IRA in the Twilight Years 1923-1948*. Argenta Publications, Dublin, 1997, p. 617; Tom Hurley notes taken post interview with Dan Keating recorded 14 April 2003.
4 Tom Hurley interview with Dan Keating recorded 13 January 2003.
5 Tom Hurley interview with Dan Keating recorded 13 January 2003.
6 Tom Hurley interview with Dan Keating recorded 13 January 2003.
7 Tom Hurley interview with Dan Keating recorded 13 January 2003.
8 Tom Hurley interview with William Geary recorded 15 July 2004.
9 Tom Hurley interview with William Geary recorded 15 July 2004.
10 Report of William Geary, Wireless Operator Voyage, 9 February 1920 to 21 January 1921, 23/3/2004.
11 Tom Hurley interview with William Geary recorded 15 July 2004.
12 Report of William Geary, Wireless Operator Voyage, 9 February 1920 to 21 January 1921, 23/3/2004.
13 The *Irish Independent*, 24 February 1920.
14 The *Freeman's Journal*, 25 February 1920.
15 The *Irish Independent*, 21 March 1921.
16 Tom Hurley interview with Seán Clancy recorded 2 April 2003.
17 The *Cork Examiner*, 4 & 13 March 1920; the *Connacht Tribune*, 6 March 1920.
18 https://landedestates.ie/family/854.
19 Campbell, Fergus. *Land and Revolution: Nationalist Politics in the West of Ireland 1891-1921*. Oxford University Press, 2005, pp. 18, 242, 252.

20   1911 Census.

21   The *Connacht Tribune*, 6 March 1920 & 3 July 1920.

22   The Castle Lambert Tape, http://homepage.eircom.net/~oreganathenry/
     oreganathenry/index.html?history/social/castlelamberttape%205.html.

23   Tom Hurley interview with John Kelly recorded 24 May 2003.

24   Campbell, Fergus. *Land and Revolution: Nationalist Politics in the West of Ireland 1891–1921.*
     Oxford University Press, 2005, p. 253.

25   Tom Hurley interview with John Kelly recorded 24 May 2003.

26   The *Connacht Tribune*, 13 March & 3 & 10 April 1920.

27   Campbell, Fergus. *Land and Revolution: Nationalist Politics in the West of Ireland 1891–1921.*
     Oxford University Press, 2005, p. 266.

28   Tom Hurley interview with John Kelly recorded 24 May 2003.

29   The *Connacht Tribune*, 6 March 1920; 1911 Census; the *Cork Examiner*, 3 November
     1913; photo of her headstone in St Mary's, Athenry.

30   Military Archives, Military Service Pensions Collection, John Kelly.

31   Tom Hurley interview with Seán Clancy recorded 2 April 2003.

32   Tom Hurley interview with Seán Clancy recorded 2 April 2003.

33   Tom Hurley interview with John Parkinson recorded 22 July 2003.

34   Tom Hurley interview with George Carpenter recorded 7 January 2003.

35   Jim Herlihy, Royal Irish Constabulary Register Extract – Public Records Office, Kew,
     Richmond, Surrey, England.

36   Tom Hurley interview with Norman Douglas recorded 22 July 2003.

37   Tom Hurley interview with Ellen Troy née Maloney recorded 15 June 2003.

38   Tom Hurley interview with Ellen Troy née Maloney recorded 15 June 2003.

39   Tom Hurley interview with Ellen Troy née Maloney recorded 15 June 2003.

40   Tom Hurley interview with Ellen Troy née Maloney recorded 15 June 2003.

41   Military Archives, Military Service Pensions Collection, Mary Kelly.

42   Tom Hurley interview with Ellen Troy née Maloney recorded 15th June 2003.

43   Military Archives, Military Service Pensions Collection, Margaret Power; Military
     Archives, Cumann na mBan Series.

44   Tom Hurley interview with Margaret Power née Cahill recorded 9 July 2004.

45   Military Archives, Cumann na mBan Series.

46   Military Archives, Military Service Pensions Collection, Margaret Power; Military
     Archives, Military Service Pensions Collection, Siobhán O'Sullivan.

47   Military Archives, Cumann na mBan Series; Military Archives, Military Service
     Pensions Collection, Bridget Kavanagh.

48   Military Archives, Military Service Pensions Collection, Margaret Power.

49   Tom Hurley interview with Margaret Power née Cahill recorded 9 July 2004.

50   Military Archives, IRA Membership Series; Military Archives, Cumann na mBan
     Series; 1901 & 1911 Censuses.

51   Military Archives, IRA Membership Series.

52   Military Archives, Military Service Pensions Collection, Margaret Power.

53   Tom Hurley interview with Margaret Power née Cahill recorded 9 July 2004.

54   Military Archives, Cumann na mBan Series.

55   Military Archives, Military Service Pensions Collection, Margaret Power.

56   Tom Hurley interview with Margaret Power née Cahill recorded 9 July 2004.

57   Tom Hurley interview with Margaret Power née Cahill recorded 9 July 2004.

58   Military Archives, IRA Membership Series; Military Archives, Military Service
     Pensions Collection, Margaret Power; BMH.WS0999, James Fitzgerald.

59   Military Archives, Military Service Pensions Collection, Michael Cahill.

60   Tom Hurley interview with Margaret Power née Cahill recorded 9 July 2004.

61 Tom Hurley interview with Daniel O'Donovan recorded 1 July 2003.

62 Tom Hurley interview with Daniel O'Donovan recorded 1 July 2003.

63 The *Southern Star*, 26 August 2006; Military Archives, IRA Membership Series; Information from Eddie O'Donovan dated 2/3/2023.

64 Tom Hurley interview with Daniel O'Donovan recorded 1 July 2003.

65 Tom Hurley interview with Daniel O'Donovan recorded 1 July 2003.

66 Tom Hurley interview with Michael Casey recorded 7 June 2003.

67 Military Archives, Medal Series, Michael Casey; Military Archives, IRA Membership Series.

68 Tom Hurley interview with Michael Casey recorded 7 June 2003.

69 Tom Hurley interview with Michael Casey recorded 7 June 2003.

70 Tom Hurley interview with Michael Casey recorded 7 June 2003.

71 Tom Hurley interview with Michael Casey recorded 7 June 2003.

72 Tom Hurley interview with Michael Casey recorded 7 June 2003.

73 Military Archives, IRA Membership Series.

74 Military Archives, Medal Series, Michael Casey.

75 Tom Hurley interview with Michael Casey recorded 7 June 2003.

76 The *Cork Examiner*, 17 May 1920.

77 BMH.WS1036, John Moloney; Military Archives, Military Service Pensions Collection, Patrick Holmes.

78 Tom Hurley interview with Patsy Holmes recorded 13 June 2003.

79 The *Freeman's Journal*, 26 May 1920.

80 BMH.WS1018, Martin Fahy.

81 Military Archives, Military Service Pensions Collection, John Kelly; BMH.WS1138, Gilbert Morrissey.

82 Military Archives, Military Service Pensions Collection, John Kelly.

83 The *Cork Examiner*, 14 June 1920.

84 The *Cork Examiner*, 23 June 1920.

85 Tom Hurley interview with Daniel O'Donovan recorded 1 July 2003.

86 BMH.WS1478, Ted O'Sullivan.

87 The *Cork Examiner*, 26 June 1920.

88 The *Cork Examiner*, 26 & 28 August 1920.

89 The *Cork Examiner*, 28 July 1920 & 3, 16 & 23 August 1920.

90 Tom Hurley interview with Daniel O'Donovan recorded 1 July 2003.

91 *Cork County Eagle and Munster Advertiser*, 3 July 1920.

92 Tom Hurley interview with John Parkinson recorded 14 July 2003.

93 Tom Hurley interview with John Parkinson recorded 22 July 2003.

94 Tom Hurley interview with Dan Keating recorded 13 January 2003.

95 Tom Hurley interview with Patsy Holmes recorded 13 June 2003.

96 Dwyer, T. Ryle. *Tans, Terror and Trouble – Kerry's Real Fighting Story*. Mercier Press, Cork, 2001, p. 211.

97 Tom Hurley interview with Dan Keating recorded 13 January 2003.

98 BMH.WS0746, Seán Culhane.

99 https://en.wikipedia.org/wiki/Daniel_O%27Donovan_(Irish_republican).

100 Tom Hurley interview with Patsy Holmes recorded 13 June 2003.

101 Tom Hurley interview with Dan Keating recorded 13 January 2003.

102 The *Cork Examiner*, 21 July 1920.

103 Kenna, G.B. *Facts & Figures of the Belfast Pogrom, 1920-1922*. The O'Connell Publishing Company, Dublin, 1922, p. 159.

104 The *Journal of British Studies*, volume 47, no. 2, April 2008, pp. 375–391.

105 Tom Hurley interview with Norman Douglas recorded 22 July 2003.

106 1901 & 1911 Censuses; www.irishgenealogy.ie; www.nidirect.gov.uk.
107 Tom Hurley interview with Norman Douglas recorded 22 July 2003.
108 The *Belfast Newsletter*, 23 July 1920.
109 Tom Hurley interview with John Parkinson recorded 22 July 2003.
110 www.nidirect.gov.uk.
111 Tom Hurley interview with John Parkinson recorded 22 July 2003.
112 Tom Hurley interview with Norman Douglas recorded 22 July 2003.
113 O'Brien, Paul. *Havoc: The Auxiliaries in Ireland's War of Independence*. The Collins Press, Cork, 2017, pp. 30–35.
114 Tom Hurley interview with Dan Keating recorded 13 January 2003.
115 Military Archives, Military Service Pensions Collection, Patrick Holmes.
116 Tom Hurley interview with Patsy Holmes recorded 13 June 2003.
117 Military Archives, Military Service Pensions Collection, Patrick Holmes.
118 Tom Hurley interview with Patsy Holmes recorded 13 June 2003.
119 http://homepage.eircom.net/~corkcounty/; the *Cork Examiner*, 17 August 1920; www.cwgc.org.
120 Tom Hurley interview with Kathleen Noonan née Charles recorded 28 May 2003.
121 Tom Hurley interview with Kathleen Noonan née Charles recorded 28 May 2003.
122 The *Cork Examiner*, 2 & 19 August 1924.
123 BMH.WS883, John M. MacCarthy; Military Archives, Military Service Pensions Collection, Patrick Clancy.
124 Military Archives, Military Service Pensions Collection, John O'Connell.
125 Tom Hurley interview with Kathleen Noonan née Charles recorded 28 May 2003.
126 Tom Hurley interview with Kathleen Noonan née Charles recorded 28 May 2003.
127 Tom Hurley interview with Kathleen Noonan née Charles recorded 28 May 2003.
128 Tom Hurley interview with Michael Casey recorded 7 June 2003.
129 Military Archives, Military Service Pensions Collection, Patrick O'Brien & Daniel O'Brien.
130 Tom Hurley interview with Michael Casey recorded 7 June 2003.
131 The *Irish Independent*, 17 August 1970; *The Corkman*, 8 August 1970.
132 The *Cork Examiner*, 21 August 1920.
133 Tom Hurley interview with Kathleen Noonan née Charles recorded 28 May 2003.
134 Tom Hurley interview with Kathleen Noonan née Charles recorded 28 May 2003.
135 Tom Hurley interview with Kathleen Noonan née Charles recorded 28 May 2003.
136 Tom Hurley interview with Kathleen Noonan née Charles recorded 28 May 2003.
137 Tom Hurley interview with Kathleen Noonan née Charles recorded 28 May 2003.
138 www.thepeerage.com.
139 Tom Hurley interview with Kathleen Noonan née Charles recorded 28 May 2003.
140 Tom Hurley interview with Kathleen Noonan née Charles recorded 28 May 2003.
141 Tom Hurley interview with Kathleen Noonan née Charles recorded 28 May 2003.
142 Tom Hurley interview with Kathleen Noonan née Charles recorded 28 May 2003.
143 Tom Hurley interview with Kathleen Noonan née Charles recorded 28 May 2003.
144 Tom Hurley interview with Kathleen Noonan née Charles recorded 28 May 2003.
145 www.cwgc.org & www.thepeerage.com.
146 https://web.archive.org/web/20220314215213/http:/landedestates.nuigalway.ie/.
147 The *Cork Examiner*, 2 December 1925.
148 *The Corkman*, 7 October 1994.
149 www.thepeerage.com.
150 Tom Hurley interview with Kathleen Noonan née Charles recorded 28 May 2003.
151 The *Irish Independent*, 24 July 1926.
152 Tom Hurley interview with Kathleen Noonan née Charles recorded 28 May 2003.

153 Tom Hurley interview with Patrick Greene recorded 4 March 2003.

154 Tom Hurley interview with Kathleen Noonan née Charles recorded 28 May 2003.

155 Tom Hurley interview with Mai McMahon née Grogan recorded 22 June 2003.

156 Tom Hurley interview with Ellen Troy née Maloney recorded 15 June 2003.

157 Tom Hurley interview with Mai McMahon née Grogan recorded 22 June 2003.

158 The *Laois Nationalist*, 4 July 2003.

159 Tom Hurley interview with Ellen Troy née Maloney recorded 15 June 2003.

160 The *Belfast Newsletter*, 31 August 1920; the *Irish News*, 15 July 2020.

161 Tom Hurley interview with Norman Douglas recorded 22 July 2003.

162 The *Belfast Newsletter*, 1 & 11 September 1920; the *Freeman's Journal*, 1 September 1920; O'Halpin, Eunan & Ó Corráin, Daithí. *The Dead of the Irish Revolution*. Yale University Press, New Haven, 2020, p. 170.

163 Tom Hurley interview with Norman Douglas recorded 22 July 2003.

164 The *Irish News*, 15 July 2020.

165 Tom Hurley interview with John Parkinson recorded 22 July 2003.

166 The *Evening Echo*, 6 September 1920.

167 Tom Hurley interview with Kathleen Noonan née Charles recorded 28 May 2003.

168 The *Evening Echo*, 18 February 1965.

169 Tierney, Mark. *Ireland Since 1870*. CJ Fallon, Dublin, 1988, p. 381.

170 Tom Hurley interview with Norman Douglas recorded 22 July 2003.

171 Tom Hurley interview with John Parkinson recorded 22 July 2003.

172 Tom Hurley interview with John Parkinson recorded 22 July 2003.

173 Tom Hurley interview with Anthony McGinley recorded 27 May 2003.

174 https://web.archive.org/web/20180307101742/http:/markhams-of-derryguiha.com/.

175 Tom Hurley interview with Mai McMahon née Grogan recorded 22 June 2003.

176 BMH.WS1251, Martin Chambers.

177 BMH.WS1251, Martin Chamber; *The Kerryman*, 18 September 1920; the *Evening Echo*, 16 September 1920.

178 Tom Hurley interview with Mai McMahon née Grogan recorded 22 June 2003.

179 The *Cork Examiner*, 20 August 1920.

180 BMH.WS474, Liam Haugh; the *Cork Examiner*, 15 July 1920.

181 Tom Hurley interview with Mai McMahon née Grogan recorded 22 June 2003.

182 Tom Hurley interview with Mai McMahon née Grogan recorded 22 June 2003.

183 Tom Hurley interview with Mai McMahon née Grogan recorded 22 June 2003.

184 O'Donovan, Donal. *Kevin Barry and His Time*. Glendale Press Ltd, Dublin, 1989.

185 Military Archives, Military Service Pensions Collection, Seán Clancy.

186 Tom Hurley interview with Seán Clancy recorded 2 April 2003.

187 Military Archives, Military Service Pensions Collection, Seán Clancy.

188 Tom Hurley interview with Jack Duff recorded 25 June 2003.

189 Military Archives, Military Service Pensions Collection, Tom Scully; BMH.WS491, Tom Scully.

190 BMH.WS1376, John O'Sullivan; *The Corkman*, 23 & 30 July 1982.

191 Tom Hurley interview with Patsy Holmes recorded 13 June 2003.

192 *The Corkman*, 30 July 1982.

193 Tom Hurley interview with Patsy Holmes recorded 13 June 2003.

194 *The Corkman*, 30 July 1982.

195 Tom Hurley interview with Patsy Holmes recorded 13 June 2003.

196 *The Times*, 18 June 1921; http://homepage.eircom.net/~corkcounty/; *Rebel Cork's Fighting Story 1916–1921*. The Kerryman Limited, Tralee, 1947, p. 199; the *Irish Independent*, 18 June 1921.

197 BMH.WS1163, Patrick MacCarthy.

198 Military Archives, Military Service Pensions Collection, Patrick Holmes.

199 Tom Hurley interview with Patsy Holmes recorded 13 June 2003.

200 Military Archives, IRA Membership Series; Military Archives, Medal Series, Patrick Fitzgerald.

201 Tom Hurley interview with Patrick Fitzgerald recorded 7 June 2003.

202 Military Archives, IRA Membership Series.

203 Tom Hurley interview with Patrick Fitzgerald recorded 7 June 2003.

204 Military Archives, Medal Series, Patrick Fitzgerald.

205 Tom Hurley interview with Patrick Fitzgerald recorded 7 June 2003.

206 http://homepage.eircom.net/~corkcounty/ & BMH.WS1547, Michael Murphy; the *Irish Independent*, 9 October 1920.

207 Tom Hurley interview with George Carpenter recorded 7 January 2003.

208 The *Cork Examiner*, 11 October 1920.

209 Tom Hurley interview with George Carpenter recorded 7 January 2003.

210 Tom Hurley interview with Dan Keating recorded 13 January 2003.

211 Breen, Dan. *My Fight for Irish Freedom*. Anvil Books, Dublin, 1981, p. 149; Conway, Joe. *In Shades Like These: Irish Teacher Life-Histories from the Twentieth Century*. Comhar Linn, Dublin, 2000.

212 Breen, Dan. *My Fight for Irish Freedom*. Anvil Books, Dublin, 1981, pp. 150–158.

213 The *Clare Champion*, 20 July 2001; Colonel Clancy's Hall of Fame; the *Freeman's Journal*, 18 October 1920.

214 Tom Hurley interview with Seán Clancy recorded 2 April 2003.

215 www.irishgenealogy.ie; 1901 & 1911 Censuses.

216 Murphy, Allison. *When Dublin Was the Capital - Northern Life Remembered*. Belcouver Press, Belfast, 2000, p. 112.

217 Tom Hurley interview with Norman Douglas recorded 22 July 2003.

218 The *Belfast Telegraph*, 18 October 2014.

219 The *Belfast Newsletter*, 6 December 1918.

220 The *Cork Examiner*, 25 October 1920; Information from Eddie O'Donovan dated 2/3/2023.

221 Charles Roy, James. *The Fields of Athenry - A Journey through Irish History*. West View Press, USA, 2001, pp. 240-24; the *Cork Examiner*, 26 October 1920; the *Connacht Tribune*, 30 October 1920.

222 The Castle Lambert Tape, http://homepage.eircom.net/~oreganathenry/oreganathenry/index.html?history/social/castlelamberttape%205.html; the *Tuam Herald*, 21 October 2020.

223 Military Archives, Military Service Pensions Collection, Michael Kelly; Military Archives, Military Service Pensions Collection, John Kelly.

224 Tom Hurley interview with John Kelly recorded 24 May 2003.

225 Military Archives, Military Service Pensions Collection, Michael Kelly.

226 Tom Hurley interview with John Kelly recorded 24 May 2003.

227 Tom Hurley interview with Patsy Holmes recorded 13 June 2003.

228 Tom Hurley interview with Margaret Power née Cahill recorded 9 July 2004.

229 The *Cork Examiner*, 18 October 1920.

230 http://homepage.eircom.net/~corkcounty/.

231 The *Cork Examiner*, 26 & 27 October & 1 November 1920.

232 Carpenter, George. *The Life & Times of Cork's George Carpenter*. Innisfree Press, Kinsale, 2002, p. 35.

233 Tom Hurley interview with George Carpenter recorded 7 January 2003.

234 Tom Hurley interview with George Carpenter recorded 7 January 2003.

235 The *Cork Examiner*, 13 November 1920.

236 The *Irish Times*, 2, 3 & 5 November 1920; BMH.WS1716, Seán MacEoin; BMW.WS440, Seamus Conway.

237 Tom Hurley interview with Patrick Greene recorded 4 March 2003.

238 Tom Hurley interview with Gerry Smyth recorded 26 June 2003.

239 Tom Hurley notes taken post interview with Dan Keating recorded 14 April 2003.

240 BMH.WS1181, John O'Connor.

241 O'Halpin, Eunan & Ó Corráin, Daithí. *The Dead of the Irish Revolution*. Yale University Press, New Haven, 2020, p. 208.

242 Tom Hurley interview with Dan Keating recorded 14 April 2003.

243 Tom Hurley interview with John Parkinson recorded 22 July 2003.

244 Tom Hurley interview with Seán Clancy recorded 2 April 2003.

245 Tom Hurley interview with Jack Duff recorded 25 June 2003.

246 The *Irish Times*, 11 November 1920; *Kerry's Fighting Story 1916-21*. The Kerryman Limited, Tralee, 1945, p. 242.

247 The *Cork Examiner*, 5 October 1920.

248 Tom Hurley interview with Patsy Holmes recorded 13 June 2003.

249 Tom Hurley interview with Patsy Holmes recorded 13 June 2003.

250 Tom Hurley interview with Patsy Holmes recorded 13 June 2003.

251 Tom Hurley interview with Patsy Holmes recorded 13 June 2003.

252 Tom Hurley interview with Patsy Holmes recorded 13 June 2003.

253 The *Cork Examiner*, 15 November 1941.

254 The *Irish Independent*, 15 November 1941.

255 *The Liberator*, 18 November 1920.

256 Military Archives, Military Service Pensions Collection, Patrick Holmes.

257 Tom Hurley interview with Michael Casey recorded 7 June 2003.

258 Breen, Dan. *My Fight for Irish Freedom*. Anvil Books, Dublin, 1981, pp. 159-160.

259 Power, Bill. *From the Danes to Dairygold - A History of Mitchelstown*. Mount Cashell Books, Mitchelstown, 1996, p. 96.

260 Breen, Dan. *My Fight for Irish Freedom*. Anvil Books, Dublin, 1981, pp. 39-50.

261 *Rebel Cork's Fighting Story 1916-1921*. The Kerryman Limited, Tralee, 1945, pp. 257-258.

262 BMH.WS1186, Michael O'Sullivan.

263 Tom Hurley interview with Michael Casey recorded 7 June 2003.

264 Coogan, Tim Pat. *Michael Collins - A Biography*. Hutchinson, London, 1990, p. 159; *The Times*, 23 November 1920.

265 Military Archives taped interview with Jack Duff conducted by Commandant Peter Young in 1992.

266 Connell, Joseph E.A. Jnr. *Michael Collins: Dublin 1916-22*. Wordwell Ltd, Dublin, 2015, pp. 132-135.

267 Coogan, Tim Pat. *Michael Collins - A Biography*. Hutchinson, London, 1990, p. 161.

268 Tom Hurley interview with Seán Clancy recorded 2 April 2003.

269 Tom Hurley interview with Seán Clancy recorded 2 April 2003.

270 Tom Hurley interview with Seán Clancy recorded 2 April 2003.

271 The *Irish Independent*, 13 August 1951; the *Clare Champion*, 18 August 1951; email dated 8/2/2023 from Edel McMahon, principal of Cranny National School.

272 Tom Hurley interview with George Cooper recorded 3 April 2003.

273 www.bloodysunday.co.uk.

274 BMH.WS0445, Jim Slattery.

275 The *Irish Independent*, 26 January 1921.

276 O'Sullivan, Niamh. *Every Dark Hour - A History of Kilmainham Jail*. Liberties Press, Dublin, 2007, pp. 130-134.

277 The *Cork Examiner*, 24 November 1920.

278 Military Archives, Medal Series, Patrick Holmes; Military Archives, Military Service Pensions Collection, Patrick Holmes.

279 Tom Hurley interview with Patsy Holmes recorded 13 June 2003.

280 Tom Hurley interview with Patsy Holmes recorded 13 June 2003.

281 Tom Hurley interview with Patsy Holmes recorded 13 June 2003.

282 Tom Hurley interview with Patsy Holmes recorded 13 June 2003.

283 BMH.WS0978, Leo Callaghan.

284 BMH.WS808, Richard Willis & John Bolster.

285 BMH.WS965, Tadg McCarthy.

286 Tom Hurley interview with Patsy Holmes recorded 13 June 2003.

287 *The Kerryman*, 6 November 1920; BMH.WS1066, Manus Moynihan.

288 1901 & 1911 Censuses; the *Irish Press*, 7 May 1945.

289 BMH.WS1547, Michael Murphy; the *Cork Examiner*, 27 October 1920; BMH.WS0551, Canon Thomas Duggan.

290 The *Cork Examiner*, 13 August 2019.

291 Tom Hurley interview with Patsy Holmes recorded 13 June 2003.

292 Tom Hurley interview with Patsy Holmes recorded 13 June 2003.

293 Tom Hurley interview with Patsy Holmes recorded 13 June 2003.

294 Tom Hurley interview with Patsy Holmes recorded 13 June 2003.

295 Murphy, William. *Political Imprisonment and the Irish, 1912–1921*. Oxford University Press, Oxford, 2014, p. 179.

296 The *Roscommon Herald*, 16 October 1920; the *Cork Examiner*, 12 & 20 October 1920; BMH.WS1720, John Manning.

297 The *Donegal News*, 27 November 1920.

298 Military Archives, Brigade Activity Reports.

299 Military Archives, IRA Membership Series; Military Archives, Medal Series, Anthony McGinley.

300 Military Archives, Medal Series, Anthony McGinley; the *Donegal News*, 27 February 2004.

301 Military Archives, IRA Membership Series; Military Archives, Medal Series, Anthony McGinley; Military Archives, Military Service Pensions Collection, Anthony McGinley.

302 Tom Hurley interview with Anthony McGinley recorded 27 May 2003.

303 Lynch, Robert. *The Northern IRA and the Early Years of Partition 1920–22*. Irish Academic Press, Dublin, 2006, p. 57.

304 Tom Hurley interview with Anthony McGinley recorded 27 May 2003.

305 Tom Hurley interview with Anthony McGinley recorded 27 May 2003.

306 Tom Hurley interview with Anthony McGinley recorded 27 May 2003.

307 Tom Hurley interview with Anthony McGinley recorded 27 May 2003.

308 Military Archives, IRA Membership Series; Military Archives, Brigade Activity Reports.

309 Tom Hurley interview with Anthony McGinley recorded 27 May 2003.

310 Military Archives, Medal Series, Anthony McGinley.

311 Tom Hurley interview with Anthony McGinley recorded 27 May 2003.

312 Tom Hurley interview with Anthony McGinley recorded 27 May 2003.

313 *The Story of the Drumboe Martyrs 1923–2003*. 80th Anniversary Edition, pp. 13–14.

314 Tom Hurley interview with Anthony McGinley recorded 27 May 2003.

315 Military Archives, Military Service Pensions Collection, Anthony McGinley.

316 Whyte, Louis. *The Wild Heather Glen – The Kilmichael Story of Grief and Glory*. Tower Books, Ballincollig, 1995.

317 White, Gerry & O'Shea, Brendan. *The Burning of Cork*. Mercier Press, Cork, 2006, pp. 94–95.

318 Tom Hurley interview with George Carpenter recorded 7 January 2003.

319 *The Times*, 4 December 1920.

320 Tom Hurley interview with George Carpenter recorded 7 January 2003.

321 *The Times*, 4 December 1921; the *Irish Times*, 3 December 1920.

322 Tom Hurley interview with George Carpenter recorded 7 January 2003.

323 Cooke, Richard T. *My Home by the Lee*. Irish Millenium Publications, Ballincollig, 1999.

324 www.cwgc.org.

325 The *Skibbereen Eagle*, 11 December 1920.

326 Tom Hurley interview with Daniel O'Donovan recorded 1 July 2003.

327 Information from Eddie O'Donovan dated 2/3/2023.

328 The *Skibbereen Eagle*, 19 February 1921; the *Evening Echo*, 19 February 1921; the *Freeman's Journal*; 9 March 1921; Information from Eddie O'Donovan dated 2/3/2023.

329 Tom Hurley interview with Daniel O'Donovan recorded 1 July 2003.

330 Deasy, Liam. *Towards Ireland Free: The West Cork Brigade in the War of Independence 1917-21*. Royal Carbery Books, Cork, 1973, p. 88.

331 Tom Hurley interview with George Carpenter recorded 7 January 2003.

332 Tom Hurley interview with Patsy Holmes recorded 13 June 2003.

333 Tom Hurley interview with Patsy Holmes recorded 13 June 2003.

334 Walsh, Louis J. *'On My Keeping' and in Theirs: A record of experiences 'on the run', in Derry Gaol, and in Ballykinlar Internment Camp*. The Talbot Press, Dublin, 1921, pp. 47, 103.

335 Newmann, Kate. *The Dictionary of Ulster Biography*. The Institute of Irish Studies, The Queen's University of Belfast, 1993.

336 Military Archives, Military Service Pensions Collection, Peadar Kearney.

337 BMH.WS952, Maurice Horgan.

338 Tom Hurley interview with Patsy Holmes recorded 13 June 2003.

339 Barry, Tom. *Guerilla Days in Ireland*. Anvil Books, Dublin, 1981, p. 90; the *Cork Examiner*, 30 November 1920.

340 Deasy, Liam. *Towards Ireland Free: The West Cork Brigade in the War of Independence 1917-21*. Royal Carbery Books, Cork, 1973, p. 154.

341 Deasy, Liam. *Towards Ireland Free: The West Cork Brigade in the War of Independence 1917-21*. Royal Carbery Books, Cork, 1973. p. 164.

342 Deasy, Liam. *Towards Ireland Free: The West Cork Brigade in the War of Independence 1917-21*. Royal Carbery Books, Cork, 1973. p. 73.

343 Tom Hurley interview with Patsy Holmes recorded 13 June 2003.

344 BMH.WS1093, Thomas Treacy.

345 The *Cork Examiner*, 20 January 1921.

346 Tom Hurley interview with Patsy Holmes recorded 13 June 2003.

347 Walsh, Louis J. *'On My Keeping' and in Theirs: A record of experiences 'on the run', in Derry Gaol, and in Ballykinlar Internment Camp*. The Talbot Press, Dublin, 1921, p. 44.

348 Walsh, Louis J. *'On My Keeping' and in Theirs: A record of experiences 'on the run', in Derry Gaol, and in Ballykinlar Internment Camp*. The Talbot Press, Dublin, 1921, pp. 47- 51.

349 Walsh, Louis J. *'On My Keeping' and in Theirs: A record of experiences 'on the run', in Derry Gaol, and in Ballykinlar Internment Camp*. The Talbot Press, Dublin, 1921, p. 54.

350 Tom Hurley interview with Patsy Holmes recorded 13 June 2003.

351 http://www.bbc.co.uk/northernireland/yourplaceandmine/.

352 Tom Hurley interview with Patsy Holmes recorded 13 June 2003.

353 Ó Duibhir, Liam. *Prisoners of War: Ballykinlar Internment Camp 1920-21*. Mercier Press, Cork, 2013, p. 75.

354 Walsh, Louis J. *'On My Keeping' and in Theirs: A record of experiences 'on the run', in Derry Gaol, and in Ballykinlar Internment Camp*. The Talbot Press, Dublin, 1921, p. 50.

355 Tom Hurley interview with Patsy Holmes recorded 13 June 2003.

356 Tierney, Mark: *Ireland Since 1870*. CJ Fallon, Dublin, 1988, p. 233.

357 Tom Hurley interview with George Carpenter recorded 7 January 2003.

358 Tom Hurley interview with George Carpenter recorded 7 January 2003.

359 Tom Hurley interview with George Cooper recorded 3 April 2003.

360 The *Freeman's Journal*, 5 August 1920.

361 The *Cork Examiner*, 28 April 1921.

362 The *Cork Examiner*, 21 June 1921.

363 Tom Hurley interview with Michael Casey recorded 7 June 2003.

364 Tom Hurley interview with Patrick Greene recorded 4 March 2003.

365 Tom Hurley interview with Gerry Smyth recorded 26 June 2003.

366 White, Gerry & O'Shea, Brendan. *The Burning of Cork*. Mercier Press, Cork, 2006, chapter 8; Whyte, Louis. *The Wild Heather Glen – The Kilmichael Story of Grief and Glory*. Tower Books, Ballincollig, 1995, pp. 149– 150.

367 Carpenter, George. *The Life & Times of Cork's George Carpenter*. Innisfree Press, Kinsale, 2002, p. 36.

368 Tom Hurley interview with George Carpenter recorded 7 January 2003.

369 Power, Bill. *Images of Mitchelstown – Stories and Pictures from my Own Place*. Mount Cashell Books, Mitchelstown, 2002, pp. 83–88; the *Freeman's Journal*, 20 December 1920; the *Nenagh Guardian*, 25 December 1920.

370 BMH.WS430, Thomas Barry; BMH.WS946, Patrick Clifford.

371 Tom Hurley interview with Michael Casey recorded 7 June 2003.

372 Military Archives, Military Census 1922.

373 BMH.WS0940, Leo Skinner.

374 Tom Hurley interview with Michael Casey recorded 7 June 2003.

375 Tierney, Mark. *Ireland Since 1870*. CJ Fallon, Dublin, 1988, p. 234.

376 Tom Hurley interview with Norman Douglas recorded 22 July 2003.

377 The *Cork Examiner*, 23 & 30 December 1920.

378 Deasy, Liam. *Brother Against Brother*. Mercier Press, Cork, 1998, p. 12.

379 The *Cork Examiner*, 3 January 1921.

380 Tom Hurley interview with Daniel O'Donovan recorded 1 July 2003.

381 Military Archives, IRA Membership Series.

382 Tom Hurley interview with Patrick Fitzgerald recorded 7 June 2003.

CHAPTER FIVE

1 The *Cork Examiner*, 21 January 1921

2 Tom Hurley interview with Patsy Holmes recorded 13 June 2003.

3 BMH.WS1093, Thomas Treacy.

4 The *Cork Examiner*, 20 & 21 January 1921.

5 BMH.WS952, Maurice Horgan.

6 Walsh, Louis J. *'On My Keeping' and in Theirs: A record of experiences 'on the run', in Derry Gaol, and in Ballykinlar Internment Camp*. The Talbot Press, Dublin, 1921, pp. 75–76.

7 Tom Hurley interview with Patsy Holmes recorded 13 June 2003.

8 The *Freeman's Journal*, 14 January 1921.

9 Walsh, Louis J. *'On My Keeping' and in Theirs: A record of experiences 'on the run', in Derry Gaol, and in Ballykinlar Internment Camp*. The Talbot Press, Dublin, 1921, p. 76.

10 Ó Duibhir, Liam. *Prisoners of War: Ballykinlar Internment Camp 1920-21*. Mercier Press, Cork, 2013, p. 122.

11 Walsh, Louis J. *'On My Keeping' and in Theirs: A record of experiences 'on the run', in Derry Gaol, and in Ballykinlar Internment Camp*. The Talbot Press, Dublin, 1921, chapter 14.

12 The *Freeman's Journal*, 9 February 1921.

13   The *Freeman's Journal*, 17 February 1921.

14   Ó Duibhir, Liam. *Prisoners of War: Ballykinlar Internment Camp 1920–21*. Mercier Press, Cork, 2013, p. 127.

15   Ó Duibhir, Liam. *Prisoners of War: Ballykinlar Internment Camp 1920–21*. Mercier Press, Cork, 2013, p. 129.

16   Walsh, Louis J. *'On My Keeping' and in Theirs: A record of experiences 'on the run', in Derry Gaol, and in Ballykinlar Internment Camp*. The Talbot Press, Dublin, 1921, chapters 15 & 16.

17   The *Cork Examiner*, 21 January 1921.

18   Murphy, William. *Political Imprisonment and the Irish, 1912–1921*. Oxford University Press, Oxford, 2014, p. 206.

19   Military Archives, IRA Membership Series.

20   Tom Hurley interview with William Geary recorded 15 July 2004.

21   Tom Hurley interview with William Geary recorded 15 July 2004.

22   Tom Hurley interview with William Geary recorded 15 July 2004.

23   Tom Hurley interview with Patsy Holmes recorded 13 June 2003.

24   BMH.WS0978, Leo Callaghan; BMH.WS1036, John Moloney.

25   BMH.WS1036, John Moloney.

26   Lankford, Siobhan. *The Hope and the Sadness: Personal Recollections of Troubled Times in Ireland*. Tower Books, Cork, 1980, pp. 186–185.

27   http://homepage.eircom.net/~corkcounty/; the *Irish Independent*, 2 February 1921.

28   The *Mallow Field Club Journal 1984*, pp. 28–30.

29   As told to me by Mallow historians Derry Twomey and John Caplice, February 2009.

30   Dwyer, T. Ryle. *Tans, Terror and Trouble - Kerry's Real Fighting Story*. Mercier Press, Cork, 2001. pp. 266–267.

31   BMH.WS707, Michael Noyk.

32   1911 Census.

33   Tom Hurley interview with Patsy Holmes recorded 13 June 2003.

34   Walsh, Louis J. *'On My Keeping' and in Theirs: A record of experiences 'on the run', in Derry Gaol, and in Ballykinlar Internment Camp*. The Talbot Press, Dublin, 1921, pp. 45–46.

35   www.offalyhistory.com, *'Diary of Patrick Wrafter 1921-1925'* by Michael Byrne; the *Irish Independent*, 21 March 1921.

36   BMH.WS665, Francis O'Duffy.

37   Tom Hurley interview with Mai McMahon née Grogan recorded 22 June 2003.

38   Tom Hurley interview with Mai McMahon née Grogan recorded 22 June 2003.

39   https://web.archive.org/web/20180307101742/http:/markhams-of-derryguiha.com/

40   Tom Hurley interview with Mai McMahon née Grogan recorded 22 June 2003.

41   Dwyer, T. Ryle. *Tans, Terror and Trouble - Kerry's Real Fighting Story*. Mercier Press, Cork, 2001, p. 306.

42   Tom Hurley interview with Dan Keating recorded 13 January 2003.

43   Ryan, Meda. *Tom Barry - IRA Freedom Fighter*. Mercier Press, Cork, 2003, p. 101.

44   Boylan, Henry. *A Dictionary of Irish Biography*. Gill & Macmillan, Dublin, 1998.

45   Tom Hurley interview with Norman Douglas recorded 22 July 2003.

46   Tom Hurley interview with John Parkinson recorded 22 July 2003.

47   Tom Hurley interview with John Parkinson recorded 22 July 2003.

48   The Castle Lambert Tape, http://homepage.eircom.net/~oreganathenry/oreganathenry/index.html?history/social/castlelamberttape%205.html & www.irishgenealogy.ie.

49   Military Archives, Military Service Pensions Collection, Michael Kelly.

50   Tom Hurley interview with John Kelly recorded 24 May 2003.

51   Tom Hurley interview with John Kelly recorded 24 May 2003.

52   Military Archives, Military Service Pensions Collection, John Kelly.

53 The Castle Lambert Tape, http://homepage.eircom.net/~oreganathenry/
    oreganathenry/index.html?history/social/castlelamberttape%205.html.

54 Tom Hurley interview with John Kelly recorded 24 May 2003.

55 Tom Hurley interview with John Kelly recorded 24 May 2003.

56 Tom Hurley interview with John Kelly recorded 24 May 2003.

57 Notes: The Castle Lambert Tape, http://homepage.eircom.net/~oreganathenry/
    oreganathenry/index.html?history/social/castlelamberttape%205.html.

58 Military Archives, Military Service Pensions Collection, Martin Ruane.

59 Tom Hurley interview with John Kelly recorded 24 May 2003.

60 Tom Hurley interview with John Kelly recorded 24 May 2003.

61 Military Archives, Military Service Pensions Collection, Michael Kelly; Military
    Archives, Military Service Pensions Collection, John Kelly.

62 Tom Hurley interview with John Kelly recorded 24 May 2003.

63 Tom Hurley interview with John Kelly recorded 24 May 2003.

64 Tom Hurley interview with John Kelly recorded 24 May 2003.

65 The Castle Lambert Tape, http://homepage.eircom.net/~oreganathenry/
    oreganathenry/index.html?history/social/castlelamberttape%205.html. Military
    Archives, Military Service Pensions Collection, Martin Ruane.

66 Military Archives, Military Service Pensions Collection, John Kelly; Military
    Archives, Military Service Pensions Collection, Martin Ruane.

67 Military Archives, Military Service Pensions Collection, Martin Ruane.

68 Military Archives, Military Service Pensions Collection, John Kelly.

69 Military Archives, Medal Series, John Kelly.

70 Military Archives, IRA Membership Series.

71 Tom Hurley interview with John Kelly recorded 24 May 2003.

72 Deasy, Liam. *Towards Ireland Free: The West Cork Brigade in the War of Independence
    1917-21*. Royal Carbery Books, Cork, 1973, p. 222; Barry, Tom. *Guerilla Days in Ireland*.
    Anvil Books, Dublin, 1981, p. 94; the *Cork Examiner*, 7 April 1921; the *Freeman's Journal*,
    22 March 1921; www.irishgenealogy.ie.

73 www.irishgenealogy.ie.

74 The *Southern Star*, 26 August 2006.

75 Tom Hurley interview with Kathleen Noonan née Charles recorded 28 May 2003.

76 The *Cork Examiner*, 12 & 13 October 1920.

77 The *Cork Examiner*, 17 August 1920.

78 Ryan, Meda. *The Real Chief - The Story of Liam Lynch*. Mercier Press, Cork, 2005, pp. 72-74.

79 BMH.WS0978, Leo Callaghan.

80 Tom Hurley interview with Patsy Holmes recorded 13 June 2003.

81 Tom Hurley interview with Patrick Fitzgerald recorded 7 June 2003.

82 Murphy, Seán & Síle. *The Comeraghs 'Gunfire and Civil War': The Story of the Deise Brigade
    IRA 1914-24*, Litho Press, Midleton, 2003, pp. 79-94.

83 Begley, Diarmuid. *The Road to Crossbarry - The Decisive Battle of the War of Independence*.
    Deso Publications, Bandon, 1999, p. 96; Barry, Tom. *Guerilla Days in Ireland*. Anvil
    Books, Dublin, 1981, p. 130.

84 O'Halpin, Eunan & Ó Corráin, Daithí. *The Dead of the Irish Revolution*. Yale University
    Press, New Haven, 2020, p. 345.

85 www.cairogang.com; www.irishgenealogy.ie; the *Freeman's Journal*, 22 March 1921.

86 www.cairogang.com.

87 Tom Hurley interview with Daniel O'Donovan recorded 1 July 2003.

88 Tom Hurley interview with Daniel O'Donovan recorded 1 July 2003.

89 Barry, Tom. *Guerilla Days in Ireland*. Anvil Books, Dublin, 1981, back cover; Ryan,
    Meda. *Tom Barry - IRA Freedom Fighter*. Mercier Press, Cork, 2003, pp. 163, 177.

90 Tom Hurley interview with Dan Keating recorded 13 January 2003.

91 Begley, Diarmuid. *The Road to Crossbarry – The Decisive Battle of the War of Independence.* Deso Publications, Bandon, 1999, pp. 80–81.

92 Information from Eddie O'Donovan dated 2/3/2023.

93 Tom Hurley interview with Daniel O'Donovan recorded 1 July 2003.

94 Tom Hurley interview with Daniel O'Donovan recorded 1 July 2003.

95 O'Malley, Ernie. *The Men Will Talk to Me, West Cork Interviews.* Mercier Press, Cork, 2015, p. 129; BMH.WS1478, Ted O'Sullivan.

96 Tom Hurley interview with Daniel O'Donovan recorded 1 July 2003.

97 Tom Hurley interview with Dan Keating recorded 13 January 2003.

98 Tom Hurley interview with Dan Keating recorded 13 January 2003.

99 Tom Hurley interview with Dan Keating recorded 13 January 2003.

100 www.cairogang.com.

101 Dwyer, T. Ryle. *Tans, Terror and Trouble – Kerry's Real Fighting Story.* Mercier Press, Cork, 2001, pp. 289–295; the *Irish Times*, 23 March 1921.

102 *Kerry's Fighting Story 1916–21.* The Kerryman Limited, Tralee, 1945, pp. 245–247; *The Liberator*, 24 March 1921; the *Irish Times*, 24 & 26 March 1921; BMH.WS1189, Thomas O'Connor.

103 Tom Hurley interview with Dan Keating recorded 13 January 2003.

104 BMH.WS0999, James Fitzgerald.

105 BMH.WS1189, Thomas O'Connor.

106 Tom Hurley interview with Dan Keating recorded 13 January 2003.

107 BMH.WS1189, Thomas O'Connor; the *Irish Times*, 26 March 1921; BMH.WS0999, James Fitzgerald; O'Malley, Ernie. *The Men Will Talk to Me, Kerry Interviews.* Mercier Press, Cork, 2012, pp. 114–117.

108 Tom Hurley interview with Dan Keating recorded 13 January 2003.

109 BMH.WS0999, James Fitzgerald; Military Archives, Military Service Pensions Collection, Maurice Fitzgerald.

110 Military Archives, Military Service Pensions Collection, Bridget Kavanagh.

111 1911 Census; Military Archives, Military Service Pensions Collection, Maurice Fitzgerald; Military Archives, Military Service Pensions Collection, Siobhán O'Sullivan.

112 Military Archives, Military Service Pensions Collection, Michael Cahill.

113 *Guy's City and County Cork Almanac and Directory for 1921.*

114 Military Archives, IRA Membership Series.

115 Tom Hurley interview with Michael Casey recorded 7 June 2003.

116 Tom Hurley interview with Michael Casey recorded 7 June 2003.

117 BMH.WS0940, Leo Skinner; the *Cork Examiner*, 2 April 1921; the *Freeman's Journal*, 2 April 1921.

118 The *Freeman's Journal*, 12 April 1921.

119 The *Skibbereen Eagle*, 16 April 1921.

120 The *Freeman's Journal*, 12 April 1921.

121 Tom Hurley interview with Seán Clancy recorded 2 April 2003; Military Archives, Military Service Pensions Collection, Seán Clancy & Peter Freyne & Frank Freyne.

122 The *Freeman's Journal*, 13 & 14 April 1921.

123 BMH.WS1584, Patrick A. Murray.

124 Tom Hurley interview with George Carpenter recorded 7 January 2003.

125 Carpenter, George. *The Life & Times of Cork's George Carpenter.* Innisfree Press, Kinsale, 2002, pp. 33.

126 Tom Hurley interview with Gerry Smyth recorded 26 June 2003.

127 Tom Hurley interview with Gerry Smyth recorded 26 June 2003.

128 Dwyer, T. Ryle. *Tans, Terror and Trouble - Kerry's Real Fighting Story*. Mercier Press, Cork, 2001, p. 305; BMH.WS1011, Patrick Garvey.

129 MacEoin, Uinseann. *The IRA in the Twilight Years 1923-1948*. Argenta Publications, Dublin, 1997, p. 617; Tom Hurley notes taken post interview with Dan Keating recorded 14 April 2003.

130 BMH.WS1189, Thomas O'Connor.

131 The *Irish Independent*, 23 April 1921.

132 Military Archives, Military Service Pensions Collection, Seán Clancy.

133 BMH.WS0882, William James Stapleton.

134 BMH.WS946, Patrick Clifford.

135 Tom Hurley interview with Michael Casey recorded 7 June 2003.

136 Power, Bill. *Another Side of Mitchelstown*. Psyops Books, Mulberry House, Mitchelstown, 2008, p. 192.

137 BMH.WS946, Patrick Clifford.

138 Power, Bill. *Mitchelstown Through the Ages*. Éigse Books, Cork, 1987, p. 96; the *Cork Examiner*, 26 April, 7, 9, 11 & 12 May 1921 & 14 January 1922.

139 Tom Hurley interview with Michael Casey recorded 7 June 2003.

140 The *Freeman's Journal*, 13 January 1922.

141 Power, Bill. *Another Side of Mitchelstown*. Psyops Books, Mulberry House, Mitchelstown, 2008, p. 192.

142 Tom Hurley interview with Michael Casey recorded 7 June 2003.

143 The *Freeman's Journal*, 4 May 1921; the *Irish Independent*, 4 May 1921.

144 Military Archives, Military Service Pensions Collection, Seán Clancy.

145 BMH.WS0882, William James Stapleton.

146 Military Archives, Military Service Pensions Collection, Seán Clancy; the *Freeman's Journal*, 16 May 1921; the *Irish Independent*, 16 May 1921.

147 Tom Hurley interview with Seán Clancy recorded 2 April 2003.

148 Military Archives, Military Service Pensions Collection, Seán Clancy.

149 Tierney, Mark. *Ireland Since 1870*. CJ Fallon, Dublin, 1988, pp. 236-237.

150 Parkinson, John. *A Belfastman's Tale*. Minprint Ltd, Belfast, 2003, p. 16.

151 Tom Hurley interview with John Parkinson recorded 22 July 2003.

152 Notes: http://en.wikipedia.org/wiki/Joseph_Devlin.

153 The *Southern Star*, 28 May 1921 & 26 August 2006.

154 *Cork County Eagle and Munster Advertiser*, 30 April 1921.

155 *Cork County Eagle and Munster Advertiser*, 7 May 1921.

156 Deasy, Liam. *Towards Ireland Free: The West Cork Brigade in the War of Independence 1917-21*. Royal Carbery Books, Cork, 1973, p. 272.

157 Tom Hurley interview with Daniel O'Donovan recorded 1 July 2003.

158 The *Southern Star*, 28 May 1921.

159 O'Malley, Ernie. *The Men Will Talk to Me, West Cork Interviews*. Mercier Press, Cork, 2015, p. 123; BMH.WS1478, Ted O'Sullivan.

160 The *Southern Star*, 26 August 2006; Information from Eddie O'Donovan dated 2/3/2023.

161 The *Island Journal*, vol. 1, no. 1, Winter 2006/2007.

162 BMH.WS1410, Michael O'Kelly.

163 www.theauxiliaries.com.

164 Military Archives, Military Service Pensions Collection, Seán Clancy.

165 O'Shea, Owen. *Ballymacandy: The Story of a Kerry Ambush*. Merrion Press, Newbridge, 2021, p. 86.

166 MacEoin, Uinseann. *The IRA in the Twilight Years 1923-1948*. Argenta Publications, Dublin, 1997, p. 618.

167 Tom Hurley interview with Dan Keating recorded 13 January 2003.

168 *The Kerryman*, 17 December 1955.

169 BMH.WS1181, John O'Connor.

170 Dwyer, T. Ryle. *Tans, Terror and Trouble – Kerry's Real Fighting Story*. Mercier Press, Cork, 2001, p. 317; the *Southern Star*, 4 June 1921; the *Irish Independent*, 8 June 1921.

171 Power, Bill. *Images of Mitchelstown – Stories and Pictures from my Own Place*. Mount Cashell Books, Mitchelstown, 2002, pp. 63, 66, 85; *The Nationalist*, 12 September 1906.

172 Tom Hurley interview with Michael Casey recorded 7 June 2003.

173 The *Cork Examiner*, 8 June 1921; the *Irish Independent*, 4 June 1921.

174 Tom Hurley interview with Anthony McGinley recorded 27 May 2003.

175 Tom Hurley interview with Anthony McGinley recorded 27 May 2003.

176 Tom Hurley interview with Anthony McGinley recorded 27 May 2003.

177 Military Archives, IRA Membership Series.

178 Military Archives, Military Service Pensions Collection, Seán Clancy.

179 The *Irish Independent*, 6 June 1921.

180 The *Irish Independent*, 2 February 1921.

181 Tom Hurley interview with Seán Clancy recorded 2 April 2003.

182 Military Archives, Military Service Pensions Collection, John Kelly; Military Archives, Brigade Activity Reports.

183 Military Archives, Brigade Activity Reports.

184 www.findmypast.ie – Cork County Gaol General Register 1915–1924; the *Southern Star*, 28 May 1921.

185 Tom Hurley interview with Daniel O'Donovan recorded 1 July 2003.

186 The *Southern Star*, 18 June 1921.

187 www.findmypast.ie – Cork County Gaol General Register 1915–1924.

188 The *Southern Star*, 18 June 1921.

189 The *Southern Star*, 18 June 1921.

190 Tom Hurley interview with Daniel O'Donovan recorded 1 July 2003.

191 *Guy's City and County Cork Almanac and Directory for 1921 & 1901*; 1911 Census; Information from Eddie O'Donovan dated 2/3/2023.

192 Tom Hurley interview with Daniel O'Donovan recorded 1 July 2003.

193 www.findmypast.ie – Cork County Gaol General Register 1915–1924.

194 Tom Hurley interview with George Cooper recorded 3 April 2003.

195 The *Freeman's Journal*, 16 June 1921.

196 The *Fall River Globe*, 21 January 1922.

197 Tom Hurley interview with John Parkinson recorded 22 July 2003.

198 Tom Hurley interview with John Parkinson recorded 22 July 2003.

199 Tom Hurley interview with Norman Douglas recorded 22 July 2003.

200 Tom Hurley interview with Patsy Holmes recorded 13 June 2003.

201 Tom Hurley interview with Patsy Holmes recorded 13 June 2003.

202 The *Freeman's Journal*, 14 October 1921.

203 BMH.WS0639, Maurice Donegan.

204 The *Irish Independent*, 17 February 1921; the *Freeman's Journal*, 17 February 1921, the *Freeman's Journal*, 21 February 1921.

205 BMH.WS0838, Seán Moylan.

206 BMH.WS0845, Tomas Malone.

207 The *Freeman's Journal*, 2 June 1921.

208 McCarthy, Kieran & Christensen, Maj-Britt. *Cobh's Contribution to the Fight for Irish Freedom*. Oileánn Mór Publications, Cobh, 1992, p. 102.

209 Tom Hurley interview with Daniel O'Donovan recorded 1 July 2003.

210   Maher, Jim. *The Flying Column 1916-1921 - West Kilkenny*. Geography Publications, Dublin, 1988, p. 166.

211   BMH.WS0838, Seán Moylan.

212   Tom Hurley interview with Daniel O'Donovan recorded 1 July 2003.

213   Tom Hurley interview with Daniel O'Donovan recorded 1 July 2003.

214   www.findmypast.ie - Cork County Gaol General Register 1915-1924.

215   *Cork County Eagle and Munster Advertiser*, 23 April 1921; the *Southern Star Centenary Supplement 1889-1989*, p. 90.

216   The *Southern Star*, 13 August 1921; Military Archives, Military Service Pensions Collection, Seán Hayes.

217   Maher, Jim: *The Flying Column 1916-1921 - West Kilkenny*. Geography Publications, Dublin, 1988, p. 166.

218   BMH.WS1487, Jerry Ryan.

219   Deasy, Liam. *Brother Against Brother*. Mercier Press, Cork, 1998, p. 89; Hopkinson, Michael. *Green Against Green - The Irish Civil War*. Gill & MacMillan Ltd, Dublin, 2004, p. 168; www.oireachtas.ie.

220   BMH.WS0838, Sean Moylan; BMH.WS1547, Michael Murphy.

221   Coogan, Tim Pat. *Michael Collins - A Biography*. Hutchinson, London, 1990, p. 177-178.

222   Tom Hurley interview with Daniel O'Donovan recorded 1 July 2003.

223   The *Meath Chronicle*, 7 May 1921.

224   BMH.WS1506, Henry O'Mahony; the *Cork Examiner*, 17 November 1921; the *Freeman's Journal*, 18 November 1921; McCarthy, Kiran & Christensen, Maj-Britt. *Cobh's Contribution to the Fight for Irish Freedom*, Oileánn Mór Publications, Cobh, 1992, p. 99.

225   Ó'Ruairc, Pádraig Óg. *Truce: Murder, Myth and the Last Days of the Irish War of Independence*. Mercier Press, Cork, 2016, pp. 260, 301, 311-313.

226   Tom Hurley interview with Dan Keating recorded 13 January 2003.

227   Tom Hurley interview with Dan Keating recorded 13 January 2003.

228   BMH.WS1181, John O'Connor.

229   Tom Hurley interview with Dan Keating recorded 13 January 2003.

230   Dwyer, T. Ryle. *Tans, Terror and Trouble - Kerry's Real Fighting Story*. Mercier Press, Cork, 2001, p. 28; BMH.WS1181, John O'Connor; BMH.WS1106, Denis Prendiville.

231   The *Irish Independent*, 12 July 1921; www.cwgc.org.

232   The *Cork Examiner*, 12 July 1921; Power, Bill. *White Knights, Dark Earls - The Rise and Fall of an Anglo-Irish Dynasty*. Collins Press, Cork, 2000, p. 21; BMH.WS0940, Leo Skinner.

233   Tom Hurley interview with Michael Casey recorded 7 June 2003.

234   Power, Bill. *Mitchelstown Through the Ages*. Eigse Books, Cork, 1987, p. 97, the *Cork Examiner*, 12 July 1920.

235   Tom Hurley interview with Michael Casey recorded 7 June 2003.

236   BMH.WS1151, Patrick Luddy; BMH.WS0940, Leo Skinner; BMH.WS1362, William Roche.

237   *Rebel Cork's Fighting Story 1916-1921*. The Kerryman Limited, Tralee, 1947, pp. 271-272.

238   Tom Hurley interview with Michael Casey recorded 7 June 2003.

239   O'Halpin, Eunan & Ó Corráin, Daithí. *The Dead of the Irish Revolution*. Yale University Press, New Haven, 2020, p. 544.

240   Hopkinson, Michael. *The Irish War of Independence*. Gill & MacMillan Ltd, Dublin, 2002, p. 201; Tierney, Mark. *Ireland Since 1870*. CJ Fallon, Dublin, 1988, p. 238.

241   Ó'Ruairc, Pádraig Óg. *Blood on the Banner*. Mercier Press, Cork, 2009, p. 259.

CHAPTER 6

1   http://www.difp.ie/docs/1921/Anglo-Irish-Treaty/138.htm.

2   Tierney, Mark. *Ireland Since 1870*. CJ Fallon, Dublin, 1988, pp. 242–243.

3   Tom Hurley interview with Jack Duff recorded 25 June 2003.

4   http://treaty.nationalarchives.ie/.

5   Tierney, Mark. *Ireland Since 1870*. CJ Fallon, Dublin, 1988, pp. 243–246.

6   Tom Hurley interview with Patsy Holmes recorded 13 June 2003.

7   Tom Hurley interview with Michael Casey recorded 7 June 2003.

8   Tom Hurley interview with Seán Clancy recorded 2 April 2003.

9   Military Archives, Military Service Pensions Collection, Seán Clancy.

10 Military Archives, Military Service Pensions Collection, John Kelly.

11 Military Archives, Military Service Pensions Collection, Margaret Power.

12 Tom Hurley interview with Patrick Fitzgerald recorded 7 June 2003.

13 Tom Hurley interview with Patrick Fitzgerald recorded 7 June 2003.

14 The Castle Lambert Tape, http://homepage.eircom.net/~oreganathenry/ oreganathenry/index.html?history/social/castlelamberttape%205.html.

15 Military Archives, Brigade Activity Reports.

16 The *Connacht Tribune*, 9 July 1921.

17 The *Connacht Tribune*, 24 September 1921.

18 The Castle Lambert Tape, http://homepage.eircom.net/~oreganathenry/ oreganathenry/index.html?history/social/castlelamberttape%205.html.

19 Military Archives, Military Service Pensions Collection, John Kelly.

20 www.familysearch.org; www.myheritage.com; https://athenry.org/record/michael-kelly-of-castle-lambert-his-fight-for-irish-freedom-59/; the *Connacht Tribune*, 31 January 1953 & 13 October 1956; the *Tuam Herald*, 22 June 1968.

21 The *Southern Star*, 19 November 1921.

22 BMH.WS0838, Sean Moylan.

23 Tom Hurley interview with Daniel O'Donovan recorded 1 July 2003.

24 The *Freeman's Journal*, 30 August 1921 & 3 September 1921.

25 The *Freeman's Journal*, 31 August 1921.

26 The *Irish Independent*, 3 September 1921; the *Freeman's Journal*, 2 September 1921; the *Southern Star*, 3 September 1921; the *New York Times*, 30 August 1921.

27 The *Freeman's Journal*, 14 October 1921.

28 Tom Hurley interview with Daniel O'Donovan recorded 1 July 2003.

29 MacEoin, Uinseann. *Survivors*. Argenta Publications, Dublin, 1980, p. 94; www. corkandross.org; the *Freeman's Journal*, 18 October 1921.

30 BMH.WS0845, Tomas Malone.

31 The *Cork Examiner*, 4 June 1921.

32 Tom Hurley interview with Daniel O'Donovan recorded 1 July 2003.

33 The *Irish Independent*, 25 & 29 October 1921.

34 The *Cork Examiner*, 18, 19, 20, 21 October & 7 & 9 November 1921.

35 BMH.WS1487, Jerry Ryan.

36 The *Freeman's Journal*, 12 November 1921.

37 The *Irish Independent*, 21 November 1921.

38 Tom Hurley interview with Daniel O'Donovan recorded 1 July 2003.

39 The *Sunday Independent*, 13 November 1921.

40 Tom Hurley interview with Patsy Holmes recorded 13 June 2003.

41 Walsh, Louis J. *'On My Keeping' and in Theirs: A record of experiences 'on the run', in Derry Gaol, and in Ballykinlar Internment Camp*. The Talbot Press, Dublin, 1921, pp. 65, 68.

42 Tom Hurley interview with Patsy Holmes recorded 13 June 2003.

43   Ó Duibhir, Liam. *Prisoners of War: Ballykinlar Internment Camp 1920–21*. Mercier Press, Cork, 2013; p. 283; the *Belfast Newsletter*, 20 March 1920.

44   www.irishgenealogy.ie; 1901 & 1911 Censuses.

45   The *Belfast Newsletter*, 28 March 1920.

46   www.cwgc.org.

47   The *Belfast Newsletter*, 30 March 1920.

48   The *Belfast Newsletter*, 31 March 1920.

49   The *Irish Independent*, 4 November 1921.

50   BMH.WS1322, Art O'Donnell.

51   BMH.WS1093, Thomas Treacy.

52   Tom Hurley interview with Patsy Holmes recorded 13 June 2003.

53   https://web.archive.org/web/20110222044540/http:/ballykinlar.down.gaa.ie/history.html.

54   The *Freeman's Journal*, 17 November 1921.

55   The *Freeman's Journal*, 17 November 1921.

56   The *Cork Examiner*, 16 November 1921.

57   BMH.WS640, Hugh Gribben.

58   The *Cork Examiner*, 17 November 1921.

59   The *Irish Independent*, 15 November 1922.

60   https://web.archive.org/web/20110222044540/http:/ballykinlar.down.gaa.ie/history.html.

61   BMH.WS1093, Thomas Treacy.

62   Power, Bill. *Another Side of Mitchelstown*. Psyops Books, Mulberry House, Mitchelstown, 2008, p. 26–27.

63   www.irishgenealogy.ie.

64   Murphy, Allison. *When Dublin was the Capital – Northern Life Remembered*. Belcouver Press, Belfast, 2000, p. 147.

65   The *Belfast Newsletter*, 23 November 1921.

66   Tom Hurley interview with John Parkinson recorded 22 July 2003.

67   Tom Hurley interview with Norman Douglas recorded 22 July 2003.

68   Tom Hurley interview with Norman Douglas recorded 22 July 2003.

69   Tom Hurley interview with John Parkinson recorded 22 July 2003.

70   Parkinson, Alan F. *Belfast's Unholy War – The Troubles of the 1920s*. Four Courts Press Ltd, Dublin, 2004, pp. 171–17; the *New York Times*, 23 November 1921; the *Washington Post*, 26 November 1921.

71   The *Belfast Newsletter*, 29 June 1922; Kenna, G.B. *Facts & Figures of the Belfast Pogrom 1920–1922*. The O'Connell Publishing Company, Dublin, 1922, p. 141.

72   The *Cork Examiner*, 6 December 1921; the *Skibbereen Eagle*, 10 December 1921.

73   Coogan, Tim Pat. *Michael Collins – A Biography*. Hutchinson, London, 1990, p. 177.

74   Conway, Joe. *In Shades Like These: Irish Teacher Life-Histories from the Twentieth Century*. Comhar Linn, Dublin, 2000.

75   The *Longford Leader*, 29 December 2000.

76   Tom Hurley interview with Patrick Greene recorded 4 March 2003.

77   The *Longford Leader*, 29 December 2000.

78   1911 Census.

79   Tom Hurley interview with Patrick Greene recorded 4 March 2003.

80   The *Irish Independent*, 11 March 1992; www.irishgenealogy.ie.

81   The *Irish Times*, 27 January 1997; www.irishgenealogy.ie.

82   Tom Hurley interview with Michael Casey recorded 7 June 2003.

83   Tom Hurley interview with Dan Keating recorded 14 April 2003.

84   Tom Hurley interview with George Cooper recorded 3 April 2003.

85   BMH.WS0626, John Donnelly.

86 Dwyer, T. Ryle. *Tans, Terror and Trouble – Kerry's Real Fighting Story*. Mercier Press, Cork, 2001, p. 334.

87 The *Cork Examiner*, 9 December 1921.

88 Tom Hurley interview with Patsy Holmes recorded 13 June 2003.

89 The *Cork Examiner*, 10 December 1921.

90 Tom Hurley interview with Patsy Holmes recorded 13 June 2003.

91 The *Cork Examiner*, 10 December 1921.

92 Tom Hurley interview with Patsy Holmes recorded 13 June 2003.

93 The *Cork Examiner*, 10 December 1921.

94 The *Cork Examiner*, 10 December 1921.

95 Ó Duibhir, Liam. *Prisoners of War: Ballykinlar Internment Camp 1920-21*, Mercier Press, Cork, 201, p. 271.

96 Tom Hurley interview with Patsy Holmes recorded 13 June 2003.

97 Tom Hurley interview with Patsy Holmes recorded 13 June 2003.

98 The *Cork Examiner*, 9, 10, 12, 16, 17 & 19 December 1921; BMH.WS1093, Thomas Treacy.

99 *Tipperary Historical Journal 1998*, p. 103; BMH.WS1100, John Sharkey.

100 The *Irish Times*, 16 December 1921.

101 Military Archives, Military Service Pensions Collection, Patrick Holmes.

102 Tom Hurley interview with Patsy Holmes recorded 13 June 2003.

103 The *Freeman's Journal*, 12 November 1921.

104 Tom Hurley interview with Patsy Holmes recorded 13 June 2003.

105 Tom Hurley interview with Patsy Holmes recorded 13 June 2003.

106 Ó Duibhir, Liam. *Prisoners of War: Ballykinlar Internment Camp 1920-21*. Mercier Press, Cork, 2013, p. 91; Ó Riordán, Tomás. *Where Martyred Heroes Rest*. Published by the Liam Lynch National Commemoration Committee, 1987, p. 63.

107 Coogan, Tim Pat. *Michael Collins – A Biography*. Hutchinson, London, 1990, pp. 303-30; Dwyer, T. Ryle. *Tans, Terror and Trouble – Kerry's Real Fighting Story*. Mercier Press, Cork, 2001, p. 336.

108 The *Clare Champion*, 20 July 2001.

109 Tom Hurley interview with Seán Clancy recorded 2 April 2003.

110 Tom Hurley interview with Seán Clancy recorded 2 April 2003.

111 Tierney, Mark. *Ireland Since 1870*. CJ Fallon, Dublin, 1988, p. 249.

112 Tom Hurley interview with Jack Duff recorded 25 June 2003.

113 Tom Hurley interview with Daniel O'Donovan recorded 1 July 2003.

114 Tom Hurley interview with John Parkinson recorded 22 July 2003.

115 Tierney, Mark. *Ireland Since 1870*. CJ Fallon, Dublin, 1988, pp. 249-250.

116 Dorney, John. *The Civil War in Dublin: The Fight for the Irish Capital 1922-1924*. Merrion Press, Newbridge, 2017, p. 30.

117 Tom Hurley interview with Seán Clancy recorded 2 April 2003.

118 Tom Hurley interview with Jack Duff recorded 25 June 2003.

119 Tom Hurley interview with Anthony McGinley recorded 27 May 2003.

120 Military Archives, Medal Series, Kathleen Noonan.

121 Tom Hurley interview with Patsy Holmes recorded 13 June 2003.

122 Coogan, Tim Pat. *Michael Collins – A Biography*. Hutchinson, London, 1990, p. 333.

123 Coogan, Tim Pat. *Michael Collins – A Biography*. Hutchinson, London, 1990, p. 339.

124 Tom Hurley interview with Patsy Holmes recorded 13 June 2003.

125 The *Irish Examiner*, 22 February 2003; http://news.bbc.co.uk/2/hi/uk_news/northern_ireland/2789253.stm.

126 The *Irish Examiner*, 21 & 22 February 2003; http://news.bbc.co.uk/2/hi/uk_news/northern_ireland/2789253.stm.

127 Tom Hurley interview with Patsy Holmes recorded 13 June 2003.
128 The *Cork Examiner*, 16 & 17 January 1922.
129 The *Mallow Field Club Journal*, 1991, p. 11.
130 Tom Hurley interview with Patsy Holmes recorded 13 June 2003.
131 *The Examiner*, 27 & 30 January 1922 & 9, 13 & 27 February 1922.
132 Tom Hurley interview with Patsy Holmes recorded 13 June 2003.
133 Tom Hurley interview with Seán Clancy recorded 2 April 2003.
134 The *Cork Examiner*, 17 January 1922.
135 White, Gerry & O'Shea, Brendan. *Irish Volunteer Soldier 1913–23*. Osprey Publishing, Oxford, 2003, p. 15.
136 The Garda Museum.
137 Tom Hurley interview with George Carpenter recorded 7 January 2003.
138 The *Cork Examiner*, 4 March 1922.
139 The *Cork Examiner*, 21 January 1922.
140 The *Cork Examiner*, 18 March 1922.
141 Information from Eddie O'Donovan dated 2/3/2023.
142 Tom Hurley interview with Daniel O'Donovan recorded 1 July 2003.
143 Tom Hurley interview with Patrick Greene recorded 4 March 2003.
144 Tom Hurley interview with Anthony McGinley recorded 27 May 2003.
145 Tom Hurley interview with Anthony McGinley recorded 27 May 2003.
146 Hopkinson, Michael. *Green Against Green – The Irish Civil War*. Gill & MacMillan Ltd, Dublin, 2004, pp. 145–147.
147 Tom Hurley interview with William Geary recorded 15 July 2004.
148 Military Archives, IRA Membership Series; Military Archives, Brigade Activity Reports.
149 Military Archives, Military Service Pensions Collection, Anthony McGinley.
150 Military Archives, Abstract of Service, Anthony McGinley.
151 Military Archives, Military Service Pensions Collection, Anthony McGinley.
152 Tom Hurley interview with Anthony McGinley recorded 27 May 2003.
153 Tom Hurley interview with Anthony McGinley recorded 27 May 2003.
154 Tom Hurley interview with Anthony McGinley recorded 27 May 2003.
155 Mac Fhionnghaile, Niall. *Dr McGinley and His Times*. An Crann, Letterkenny, 1985.
156 The *Derry Journal*, 12 May & 14 November 1924.
157 Tom Hurley interview with Anthony McGinley recorded 27 May 2003.
158 Military Archives, IRA Membership Series.
159 Email dated 5/7/23 from Military Archives.
160 Tom Hurley interview with Anthony McGinley recorded 27 May 2003.
161 Tom Hurley interview with George Cooper recorded 3 April 2003.
162 Kelly, Adrian. *Compulsory Irish: Language and Education in Ireland 1870s–1970s*, Irish Academic Press, Dublin, 2002, p. 18.
163 Tom Hurley interview with Patrick Greene recorded 4 March 2003.
164 Tom Hurley interview with George Carpenter recorded 7 January 2003.
165 Gallagher, Julieanne. *Elementary Science in Irish Primary Schools from the Late 1800s to the Present Day*. Dublin City University, 2007, p. 72.
166 Tom Hurley interview with William Geary recorded 15 July 2004.
167 Tom Hurley interview with Dan Keating recorded 13 January 2003.
168 Tierney, Mark. *Ireland Since 1870*. CJ Fallon, Dublin, 1988, pp. 255–256; Ryan, Meda. *The Real Chief – The Story of Liam Lynch*. Mercier Press, Cork, 2005, pp. 113–114.
169 Tom Hurley interview with Michael Casey recorded 7 June 2003.
170 Military Archives, IRA Membership Series.
171 Tom Hurley interview with Daniel O'Donovan recorded 1 July 2003.
172 Tom Hurley interview with Daniel O'Donovan recorded 1 July 2003.

173 The *Southern Star*, 26 August 2006; Military Archives, IRA Membership Series.

174 Tom Hurley interview with Daniel O'Donovan recorded 1 July 2003.

175 Tom Hurley interview with Daniel O'Donovan recorded 1 July 2003.

176 Tom Hurley interview with Jack Duff recorded 25 June 2003.

177 Tom Hurley interview with Patrick Fitzgerald recorded 7 June 2003.

178 Tom Hurley interview with Patrick Fitzgerald recorded 7 June 2003.

179 Tom Hurley interview with Patrick Fitzgerald recorded 7 June 2003.

180 The *Freeman's Journal*, 27 March 1922.

181 The *Freeman's Journal*, 27 March 1922.

182 The *Freeman's Journal*, March 1922.

183 Tierney, Mark. *Ireland Since 1870*. CJ Fallon, Dublin, 1988, p. 387.

184 Tom Hurley interview with Patrick Greene recorded 4 March 2003.

185 The *New York Times*, 11 March 1922; Kenna, G.B. *Facts & Figures of the Belfast Pogrom 1920-1922*. The O'Connell Publishing Company, Dublin 1922, p. 159.

186 Tom Hurley interview with John Parkinson recorded 14 July 2003.

187 Tom Hurley interview with Norman Douglas recorded 22 July 2003.

188 *The Times*, 12 March 1922; the *New York Times*, 11 March 1922; the *Freeman's Journal*, 15 March 1922; the *Evening Herald*, 11 March 1922.

189 Tom Hurley interview with Anthony McGinley recorded 27 May 2003.

190 Tom Hurley interview with Anthony McGinley recorded 27 May 2003.

191 Tom Hurley interview with John Parkinson recorded 22 July 2003.

192 Tom Hurley interview with George Cooper recorded 3 April 2003.

193 Tom Hurley interview with George Cooper recorded 3 April 2003.

194 Ryan, Meda. *The Real Chief - The Story of Liam Lynch*. Mercier Press, Cork, 2005, p. 114.

195 Tom Hurley interview with Dan Keating recorded 13 January 2003.

196 The *Freeman's Journal*, 9 January 1922; www.oireachtas.ie.

197 Maye, Brian. *Arthur Griffith*. Griffith College Publications Ltd, Dublin, 1997, p. 253.

198 Tom Hurley interview with George Cooper recorded 3 April 2003.

199 Boylan, Henry. *A Dictionary of Irish Biography*. Gill & Macmillan, Dublin, 1998.

200 Deasy, Liam. *Brother Against Brother*. Mercier Press, Cork, 1998, pp. 41–47.

201 The *Longford Leader*, 29 December 2000.

202 Tom Hurley interview with Patrick Greene recorded 4 March 2003.

203 *Ballingeary and Inchigeela Local History Society Journal 2000*.

204 Tom Hurley interview with Patrick Greene recorded 4 March 2003.

205 Tom Hurley interview with Patrick Greene recorded 4 March 2003.

206 Tom Hurley interview with Patrick Greene recorded 4 March 2003.

207 Tom Hurley interview with Patrick Greene recorded 4 March 2003.

208 The *Evening Echo*, 1 June 1963; BMH.0103, Seán O'Hegarty, Seán Lynch, Tadhg Twomey, Jeremiah O'Shea.

209 *Ballingeary and Inchigeela Local History Society Journal 2000*.

210 Tom Hurley interview with Patrick Greene recorded 4 March 2003.

211 Dwyer, T. Ryle. *Tans, Terror and Trouble - Kerry's Real Fighting Story*. Mercier Press, Cork, 2001, p. 347.

212 Tom Hurley interview with Dan Keating recorded 13 January 2003.

213 Langton, James. *The Forgotten Fallen, Volume 1*. Kilmainham Tales Teo, Dublin, 2019, pp. 258–261; Dwyer, T. Ryle. *Tans, Terror and Trouble - Kerry's Real Fighting Story*. Mercier Press, Cork, 2001, p. 361.

214 Tom Hurley interview with Dan Keating recorded 13 January 2003.

215 Doyle, Tom. *The Civil War in Kerry*. Mercier Press, Cork, 2008, p. 181.

216 Tom Hurley interview with Dan Keating recorded 13 January 2003.

217	Dwyer, T. Ryle. *Tans, Terror and Trouble – Kerry's Real Fighting Story*. Mercier Press, Cork, 2001, p. 346.

218	Tom Hurley interview with Dan Keating recorded 13 January 2003.

219	Military Archives, IRA Membership Series.

220	The *Skibbereen Eagle*, 6 May 1922.

221	Tom Hurley interview with Patsy Holmes recorded 13 June 2003.

222	Ryan, Meda. *Tom Barry – IRA Freedom Fighter*. Mercier Press, Cork, 2003, pp. 211–212; the *Skibbereen Eagle*, 6 May 1922.

223	The *Evening Echo*, 29 April 1922; the *Skibbereen Eagle*, 6 May 1922.

224	Keane, Barry. *Massacre in West Cork: The Dunmanway and Ballygroman Killings*. Mercier Press, Cork, 2014, pp. 143–146.

225	The Castle Lambert Tape, http://homepage.eircom.net/~oreganathenry/ oreganathenry/index.html?history/social/castlelamberttape%205.html.

226	The *Irish Independent*, 9 April 1922.

227	The *Evening Herald*, 8 July 1924.

228	The *Tuam Herald*, 10 March 1923; Military Archives, Military Service Pensions Collection, Michael Kelly.

229	http://www.westmeathcoco.ie/en/ourservices/planning/conservationheritage/ decadeofcentenariesblog/thepreludetocivilwarinwestmeaththeprotestant experience.html.

230	Tom Hurley interview with William Geary recorded 15 July 2004.

231	Tom Hurley interview with William Geary recorded 15 July 2004.

232	McNiffe, Liam. *A History of the Garda Síochána*. Wolfhound Press Ltd, Dublin, 1997, pp. 18–19; Brady, Conor. *Guardians of the Peace*. Gill & Macmillan, Dublin, 1974, p. 54.

233	Military Archives, Military Census 1922; Military Archives taped interview with Jack Duff conducted by Commandant Peter Young in 1992; Military Archives, Abstract of Service, John Duff.

234	Tom Hurley interview with Jack Duff recorded 25 June 2003.

235	Military Archives, Military Census 1922; Military Archives, Abstract of Service, John Duff.

236	Military Archives.

237	Harrington, Niall C. *Kerry Landing*. Anvil Books Limited, Dublin, 1992, p. 171.

238	Military Archives, Military Service Pensions Collection, Tom Scully; BMH.WS491, Tom Scully.

239	Military Archives taped interview with Jack Duff conducted by Commandant Peter Young in 1992.

240	Military Archives taped interview with Jack Duff conducted by Commandant Peter Young in 1992.

241	McNiffe, Liam. *A History of the Garda Síochána*. Wolfhound Press Ltd, Dublin, 1997, p. 18.

242	Allen, Gregory. *The Garda Síochána – Policing Independent Ireland 1922–82*. Gill & MacMillan Ltd, Dublin, 1999, p. 32.

243	Tom Hurley interview with William Geary recorded 15 July 2004.

244	McNiffe, Liam. *A History of the Garda Síochána*. Wolfhound Press Ltd, Dublin, 1997, p. 20.

245	Brady, Conor. *Guardians of the Peace*. Gill & Macmillan, Dublin, 1974, p. 65.

246	McNiffe, Liam. *A History of the Garda Síochána*. Wolfhound Press Ltd, Dublin, 1997, p. 21.

247	Memoirs, typed and signed by William Geary 28/1/2003.

248	The *Cork Examiner*, 22 June 1922; the *Kildare Observer*, 5 August 1922.

249	The *Kildare Observer*, 5 August 1922.

250	The *Kildare Observer*, 24 June 1922 & 5 August 1922.

251	Allen, Gregory. *The Garda Síochána – Policing Independent Ireland 1922–82*. Gill & MacMillan Ltd, Dublin, 1999, p. 42.

252 The *Kildare Observer*, 24 June 1922.
253 McNiffe, Liam. *A History of the Garda Síochána*. Wolfhound Press Ltd, Dublin, 1997, pp. 22–24.
254 Tom Hurley interview with John Parkinson recorded 22 July 2003.
255 The *Belfast Newsletter*, 18 May 1922; Parkinson, John. *A Belfastman's Tale*. Minprint Ltd, Belfast, 2003, p. 16.
256 The *Freeman's Journal*, 18 May 1922; the *Skibbereen Eagle*, 20 May 1922.
257 Military Archives, Military Census 1922; Military Archives, Abstract of Service, Seán Clancy.
258 Tom Hurley interview with Seán Clancy recorded 2 April 2003.
259 Military Archives, IRA Membership Series.
260 Tom Hurley interview with Patrick Fitzgerald recorded 7 June 2003.
261 Military Archives, IRA Membership Series.
262 Military Archives, IRA Membership Series.
263 Tom Hurley interview with Patrick Fitzgerald recorded 7 June 2003.
264 Parkinson, Alan F. *Belfast's Unholy War - The Troubles of the 1920s*. Four Courts Press Ltd, Dublin, 2004, p. 273.
265 Parkinson, John. *A Belfastman's Tale*. Minprint Ltd, Belfast, 2003, p. 11.
266 Tom Hurley interview with John Parkinson recorded 22 July 2003.
267 Tom Hurley interview with John Parkinson recorded 22 July 2003.
268 Parkinson, John. *A Belfastman's Tale*. Minprint Ltd, Belfast, 2003, p. 11.
269 Tom Hurley interview with John Parkinson recorded 22 July 2003.
270 Parkinson, John. *A Belfastman's Tale*. Minprint Ltd, Belfast, 2003, p. 11.
271 Tom Hurley interview with John Parkinson recorded 22 July 2003.
272 The *Belfast Newsletter*, 14 November 1923.
273 Tom Hurley interview with Norman Douglas recorded 22 July 2003.
274 www.psni.police.uk; email dated 15/9/2006 from Hugh Forrester - curator of the RUC Museum in Belfast.
275 www.irishgenealogy.ie.
276 Tom Hurley interview with George Cooper recorded 3 April 2003.
277 The *Cork Examiner*, 6 June 1922.
278 Deasy, Liam. *Brother Against Brother*. Mercier Press, Cork, 1998, p. 29; Ryan, Meda. *The Real Chief - The Story of Liam Lynch*. Mercier Press, Cork, 2005, p. 96; Deasy, Liam. *Towards Ireland Free: The West Cork Brigade in the War of Independence 1917-21*. Royal Carbery Books, Cork, 1973, p. 16.
279 Tom Hurley interview with Kathleen Noonan née Charles recorded 28 May 2003.
280 Tierney, Mark. *Ireland Since 1870*. CJ Fallon, Dublin, 1988, p. 258.
281 Tom Hurley interview with Seán Clancy recorded 2 April 2003.
282 Tom Hurley interview with Jack Duff recorded 25 June 2003.
283 Tom Hurley notes taken post interview with Dan Keating recorded 14 April 2003.
284 Tom Hurley interview with Dan Keating recorded 14 April 2003.
285 Tom Hurley interview with Dan Keating recorded 14 April 2003.
286 Boylan, Henry. *A Dictionary of Irish Biography*. Gill & Macmillan, Dublin, 1998; the *Longford Leader*, 29 December 2000.
287 The *Longford Leader*, 29 December 2000.
288 Tom Hurley interview with Patrick Greene recorded 4 March 2003.
289 Tierney, Mark. *Ireland Since 1870*. CJ Fallon, Dublin, 1988, pp. 259–260.

CHAPTER 7

1   Military Archives taped interview with Jack Duff conducted by Commandant Peter Young in 1992.

2   Military Archives taped interview with Jack Duff conducted by Commandant Peter Young in 1992.

3   Military Archives taped interview with Jack Duff conducted by Commandant Peter Young in 1992.

4   Tom Hurley interview with Jack Duff recorded 25 June 2003.

5   Tom Hurley interview with Jack Duff recorded 25 June 2003.

6   Power, Bill. *Doomed Inheritance: Mitchelstown Castle Looted & Burned August 1922.* Scriptorium Mulberry, Mitchelstown, 2022, p. 175.

7   Power, Bill. *White Knights, Dark Earls – The Rise and Fall of an Anglo-Irish Dynasty.* Collins Press, Cork, 2000, pp. 220–224.

8   Tom Hurley interview with Michael Casey recorded 7 June 2003.

9   Tom Hurley interview with Michael Casey recorded 7 June 2003.

10 Tom Hurley interview with Michael Casey recorded 7 June 2003.

11 Tom Hurley interview with Michael Casey recorded 7 June 2003.

12 Yeats, Pádraig. *A City in Civil War.* Gill & Macmillan, Dublin, 2015, p. 82.

13 Tom Hurley interview with Jack Duff recorded 25 June 2003.

14 Military Archives taped interview with Jack Duff conducted by Commandant Peter Young in 1992.

15 Tom Hurley interview with Jack Duff recorded 25 June 2003.

16 Military Archives taped interview with Jack Duff conducted by Commandant Peter Young in 1992.

17 Dwyer, T. Ryle. *Tans, Terror and Trouble – Kerry's Real Fighting Story.* Mercier Press, Cork, 2001, p. 353; Hopkinson, Michael. *Green Against Green – The Irish Civil War.* Gill & MacMillan Ltd, Dublin, 2004, pp. 163–165; the *Cork Examiner,* 3 & 4 July 1922.

18 Tom Hurley interview with Dan Keating recorded 14 April 2003.

19 Military Archives, Cumann na mBan Series; Military Archives, Military Service Pensions Collection, Margaret Power.

20 Military Archives, Cumann na mBan Series; Military Archives, Military Service Pensions Collection, Bridget Kavanagh.

21 Military Archives, Cumann na mBan Series; Military Archives, Military Service Pensions Collection, Margaret Power.

22 Tom Hurley interview with Patrick Greene recorded 4 March 2003.

23 *Ballingeary Historical Society Journal 2006.*

24 Tom Hurley interview with Patrick Greene recorded 4 March 2003.

25 Tom Hurley interview with Patrick Greene recorded 4 March 2003.

26 Military Archives, IRA Membership Series.

27 The *Southern Star,* 8 July 1922.

28 Tom Hurley interview with Jack Duff recorded 25 June 2003.

29 Tom Hurley interview with George Cooper recorded 3 April 2003.

30 Ryan, Meda. *The Real Chief – The Story of Liam Lynch.* Mercier Press, Cork, 2005, p. 148.

31 Tom Hurley interview with Dan Keating recorded 14 April 2003.

32 Ryan, Meda. *The Real Chief – The Story of Liam Lynch.* Mercier Press, Cork, 2005, pp. 103–104.

33 https://catalogue.nli.ie/Collection/vtls000749188.

34 O'Malley, Cormac H. & Dolan, Anne. *'No Surrender Here!' – The Civil War Papers of Ernie O'Malley 1922-1924.* The Lilliput Press, Dublin, 2007, p. 197.

35 Tom Hurley interview with Anthony McGinley recorded 27 May 2003.

36 The *Irish Times,* 11 July 1922.

37   The *Irish Times*, 11 & 12 July 1922; the *Derry Journal*, 12 July 1922.
38   BMH.WS1741, Michael V. Donoghue.
39   The *Strabane Chronicle*, 15 July 1922.
40   Tierney, Mark. *Ireland Since 1870*. CJ Fallon, Dublin, 1988, p. 262; Coogan, Tim Pat. *Michael Collins – A Biography*. Hutchinson, London, 1990, p. 392.
41   The *Irish Times*, 17, 18 & 21 July 1922.
42   Tom Hurley interview with Anthony McGinley recorded 27 May 2003.
43   Military Archives, Military Service Pensions Collection, Anthony McGinley.
44   Military Archives, Military Service Pensions Collection, John Kelly.
45   Military Archives, Military Service Pensions Collection, Michael Kelly.
46   The *Connacht Tribune*, 22 July 1922.
47   The *Connacht Tribune*, 22 July 1922.
48   Tom Hurley interview with John Kelly recorded 24 May 2003.
49   Military Archives, IRA Membership Series; Military Archives, Military Service Pensions Collection, James Murray.
50   Military Archives, Military Service Pensions Collection, John Kelly.
51   Military Archives, Military Service Pensions Collection, Michael Kelly.
52   Tom Hurley interview with John Kelly recorded 24 May 2003.
53   Ryan, Meda. *The Real Chief – The Story of Liam Lynch*. Mercier Press, Cork, 2005, p. 149.
54   Tom Hurley interview with Dan Keating recorded 14 April 2003.
55   MacEoin, Uinseann. *The IRA in the Twilight Years 1923–1948*. Argenta Publications, Dublin, 1997, p. 618.
56   Tom Hurley interview with Dan Keating recorded 14 April 2003.
57   MacEoin, Uinseann. *The IRA in the Twilight Years 1923–1948*. Argenta Publications, Dublin, 1997, p. 618.
58   Tom Hurley interview with Dan Keating recorded 14 April 2003.
59   Military Archives, Civil War Internment Collection.
60   O'Malley, Ernie. *The Men Will Talk to Me, Kerry Interviews*. Mercier Press, Cork, 2012, p. 34; Military Archives, Military Service Pensions Collection, Denis Quille.
61   The *Nenagh Guardian*, 22 July 1922; the *Anglo-Celt*, 22 July 1922; the *Freeman's Journal*, 17 July 1922.
62   O'Malley, Ernie. *The Men Will Talk to Me, Kerry Interviews*. Mercier Press, Cork, 2012, p.34.
63   The *Irish Independent*, 19 July 1922; the *Tipperary Star*, 22 July 1922.
64   Tom Hurley interview with Anthony McGinley recorded 27 May 2003.
65   Mac Fhionnghaile, Niall. *Dr. McGinley and His Times*. An Crann, Letterkenny, 1985, p. 96.
66   Military Archives, IRA Membership Series; Military Archives, Military Service Pensions Collection, James Scanlan.
67   Military Archives, Military Service Pensions Collection, James Scanlan; letter from Military Archives dated 5 April 2005.
68   Mac Fhionnghaile, Niall. *Dr. McGinley and His Times*. An Crann, Letterkenny, 1985, p. 96.
69   The *Irish Independent*, 31 July 1922.
70   BMH.WS1741, Michael V. Donoghue.
71   Military Archives, Civil War Internment Collection.
72   O'Malley, Ernie. *The Men Will Talk to Me, Kerry Interviews*. Mercier Press, Cork, 2012, p. 35.
73   Tom Hurley interview with Dan Keating recorded 14 April 2003.
74   BMH.WS1427, Laurence Brady; Military Archives, Military Service Pensions Collection, Thomas Brady.
75   Tom Hurley interview with Dan Keating recorded 14 April 2003.
76   MacEoin, Uinseann. *Survivors*. Argenta Publications, Dublin, 1980, p. 99; Military Archives, Military Service Pensions Collection, Thomas Malone.

77 Tom Hurley interview with Dan Keating recorded 14 April 2003.

78 The *Irish Times*, 29 July 1922.

79 Deasy, Liam. *Towards Ireland Free: The West Cork Brigade in the War of Independence 1917-21*. Royal Carbery Books, Cork, 1973, p. 148.

80 Tom Hurley interview with Anthony McGinley recorded 27 May 2003.

81 Deasy, Liam. *Brother Against Brother*. Mercier Press, Cork, 1998, p. 99.

82 Lynch, Robert. *The Northern IRA and the Early Years of Partition 1920-22*. Irish Academic Press, Dublin, 2006, p. 165.

83 The *Irish Times*, 29 July 1922.

84 Hopkinson, Michael. *Green Against Green - The Irish Civil War*. Gill & MacMillan Ltd, Dublin, 2004, p. 162; Deasy, Liam. *Brother Against Brother*. Mercier Press, Cork, 1998, p. 99; Lynch, Robert. *The Northern IRA and the Early Years of Partition 1920-22*. Irish Academic Press, Dublin, 2006, pp. 171-174.

85 Military Archives taped interview with Jack Duff conducted by Commandant Peter Young in 1992.

86 Tom Hurley interview with Jack Duff recorded 25 June 2003.

87 Military Archives taped interview with Jack Duff conducted by Commandant Peter Young in 1992.

88 Tom Hurley interview with Jack Duff recorded 25 June 2003.

89 Military Archives taped interview with Jack Duff conducted by Commandant Peter Young in 1992; the *Freeman's Journal*, 5 August 1922.

90 Tom Hurley interview with Jack Duff recorded 25 June 2003.

91 Military Archives taped interview with Jack Duff conducted by Commandant Peter Young in 1992.

92 'Meirligh, An Saighdiúir Tréigthe - Liam O Loingsígh', TG4, 2005.

93 The *Freeman's Journal*, 5 August 1922; BMH.WS1763, Dan Breen.

94 https://web.archive.org/web/20180307101742/http://markhams-of-derryguiha.com/.

95 www.irishgenealogy.ie; the *Freeman's Journal*, 8 September 1917; the *Cork Examiner*, 9 May 1925.

96 Tom Hurley interview with Mai McMahon née Grogan recorded 22 June 2003.

97 https://web.archive.org/web/20180307101742/http://markhams-of-derryguiha.com/; the *Irish Independent*, 15 May 1925.

98 The *Clare Champion*, 5 April 2002.

99 Tom Hurley interview with Mai McMahon née Grogan recorded 22 June 2003.

100 Ó'Ruairc, Pádraig Óg. *Blood on the Banner*, Mercier Press, Cork, 2009, p. 332; BMH. WS1195, Patrick Doherty; the *Leitrim Observer*, 11 September 1920; www.findmypast.ie.

101 O'Malley, Ernie. *Rising Out: Seán Connolly of Longford*. University College Dublin Press, 2007, pp. 157-163; www.findmypast.ie.

102 Tom Hurley interview with Mai McMahon née Grogan recorded 22 June 2003.

103 Tom Hurley interview with Mai McMahon née Grogan recorded 22 June 2003.

104 Military Archives, Military Service Pensions Collection, Anthony McGinley.

105 The *Derry Journal*, 4 August 1922.

106 Tom Hurley interview with Dan Keating recorded 13 January 2003.

107 Tom Hurley interview with Dan Keating recorded 13 January 2003.

108 Doyle, Tom. *The Civil War in Kerry*. Mercier Press, Cork, 2008, p. 118.

109 Tom Hurley interview with Dan Keating recorded 14 April 2003.

110 The *Irish Times*, 7 August 1922.

111 Tom Hurley notes written post interview with Seán Clancy 2 April 2003.

112 The *Irish Times*, 7 August 1922; Langton, James. *The Forgotten Fallen, Volume 1*. Kilmainham Tales Teo, Dublin, 2019.

113 *Ballingeary Historical Society Journal 2000*; the *Cork Examiner*, 13 October 1977.

114　The *Cork Examiner*, 28 June 1928.

115　The *Irish Independent*, 9 October 1922.

116　*Ballingeary Historical Society Journal 2006.*

117　*Ballingeary Historical Society Journal 2000.*

118　Tom Hurley interview with Patrick Greene recorded 4 March 2003.

119　Tom Hurley interview with Patrick Greene recorded 4 March 2003.

120　The *Kerry Champion*, 28 July 1951.

121　*Ballingeary Historical Society Journal 2000.*

122　*Poblacht na h-Éireann* (Scot. Edn), 21 October 1922.

123　Borgonovo, John. *The Battle for Cork.* Mercier Press, Cork, 2011, p. 106.

124　Boyne, Sean. *Emmet Dalton: Somme, Soldier, Irish General, Film Pioneer.* Merrion Press, Sallins, 2015, p. 193; Twohig, Patrick J. *The Dark Secret of Béal na Bláth.* Tower Books, Ballincollig, 1991, p. 17.

125　*Ballingeary Historical Society Journal 2000*; *Ballingeary Historical Society Journal 2006*; Twohig, Patrick J. *Green Tears for Hecuba – Ireland's Fight for Freedom.* Tower Books, Ballincollig, 1994, pp. 32–38; the *Cork Examiner*, 15 August 1922; *Poblacht na h-Éireann* (Scot. Edn), 21 October 1922; Borgonovo, John. *The Battle for Cork.* Mercier Press, Cork, 2011, pp. 105–106.

126　Boyne, Sean. *Emmet Dalton: Somme, Soldier, Irish General, Film Pioneer.* Merrion Press, Sallins, 2015, p. 193; the *Southern Star*, 19 August 1922.

127　Military Archives, Military Service Pensions Collection, Christopher O'Toole, James Madden, Patrick Perry, Henry Quinn, James Gavigan & Patrick Maguire; Langton, James. *The Forgotten Fallen, Volume 1.* Kilmainham Tales Teo, Dublin, 2019, pp. 93, 142, 225, 233, 234, 250, 267, 272, 277; Boyne, Sean. *Emmet Dalton: Somme, Soldier, Irish General, Film Pioneer.* Merrion Press, Sallins, 2015, p. 190.

128　Military Archives, Military Service Pensions Collection, Jeremiah Hourigan & Christopher Olden; www.irishgenealogy.ie; Borgonovo, John. *The Battle for Cork.* Mercier Press, Cork, 2011, p. 147.

129　*Ballingeary Historical Society Journal 1997*; the *Cork Examiner*, 11 November 1920.

130　Military Archives taped interview with Jack Duff conducted by Commandant Peter Young in 1992; the *Cork Examiner*, 14 August 1922.

131　Tom Hurley interview with Jack Duff recorded 25 June 2003.

132　Military Archives taped interview with Jack Duff conducted by Commandant Peter Young in 1992.

133　Tom Hurley interview with Jack Duff recorded 25 June 2003.

134　Military Archives taped interview with Jack Duff conducted by Commandant Peter Young in 1992.

135　Coogan, Tim Pat. *Michael Collins – A Biography.* Hutchinson, London, 1990, pp. 398–399; the *Cork Examiner*, 14 August 1922.

136　www.generalmichaelcollins.com.

137　Tom Hurley interview with George Cooper recorded 3 April 2003.

138　Tom Hurley interview with Jack Duff recorded 25 June 2003.

139　Power, Bill. *White Knights, Dark Earls – The Rise and Fall of an Anglo-Irish Dynasty.* Collins Press, Cork, 2000, pp. 224–233.

140　Power, Bill. *Images of Mitchelstown – Stories and Pictures from my Own Place.* Mount Cashell Books, Mitchelstown, 2002, p. 87; the *Cork Examiner*, 19 January 1990.

141　Power, Bill. *Images of Mitchelstown – Stories and Pictures from my Own Place.* Mount Cashell Books, Mitchelstown, 2002, p. 87; the *Cork Examiner*, 19 January 1990.

142　Military Archives, Military Census 1922.

143　Tom Hurley interview with Michael Casey recorded 7 June 2003.

144　www.familysearch.org.

145 Power, Bill. *Doomed Inheritance: Mitchelstown Castle Looted & Burned August 1922.* Scriptorium Mulberry, Mitchelstown, 2022, p. 198.

146 The *Leinster Express*, 1 March 1924.

147 Power, Bill. *Doomed Inheritance: Mitchelstown Castle Looted & Burned August 1922.* Scriptorium Mulberry, Mitchelstown, 2022, p. 181.

148 *The Cork Examiner*, 29 April 1926.

149 The *Cork Examiner*, 5 May 1928.

150 Dooley, Terence. *Burning the Big House.* Yale University Press, New Haven & London, 2022, p. 178.

151 Power, Bill. *Mitchelstown Through the Ages.* Eigse Books, Cork, 1987, pp. 98–100.

152 Power, Bill. *White Knights, Dark Earls – The Rise and Fall of an Anglo-Irish Dynasty.* Collins Press, Cork, 2000, p. 227.

153 *The Tipperary Historical Journal 1993.* Published by the County Tipperary Historical Society, Thurles, 1993, p. 57.

154 Military Archives taped interview with Jack Duff conducted by Commandant Peter Young in 1992.

155 The *Irish Times*, 15 August 1922; the *Cork Examiner*, 16 August 1922.

156 The *Tipperary Historical Journal 1991.* Published by the County Tipperary Historical Society, Thurles, 1991, p. 36; the *Irish Times*, 15 August 1922.

157 Tom Hurley interview with Jack Duff recorded 25 June 2003.

158 The *Tipperary Historical Journal 1992*, p. 36.

159 Tom Hurley interview with William Geary recorded 15 July 2004.

160 Brady, Conor. *Guardians of the Peace.* Gill & Macmillan, Dublin, 1974, p. 68.

161 Tom Hurley interview with William Geary recorded 15 July 2004.

162 The *Irish Times*, 18 August 1922.

163 Tom Hurley interview with William Geary recorded 15 July 2004.

164 Coogan, Tim Pat. *Michael Collins – A Biography.* Hutchinson, London, 1990, p. 399.

165 Tom Hurley interview with Dan Keating recorded 14 April 2003.

166 Coogan, Tim Pat. *Michael Collins – A Biography.* Hutchinson, London, 1990, p. 400; MacEoin, Uinseann. *Survivors.* Argenta Publications, Dublin, 1980, p. 99.

167 The *New York Times*, 19 August 1922; the *Cork Examiner*, 19 August 1922.

168 Tom Hurley interview with Patsy Holmes recorded 13 June 2003.

169 Deasy, Liam. *Brother Against Brother.* Mercier Press, Cork, 1998, p. 79.

170 Twohig, Patrick J. *The Dark Secret of Béal na Bláth.* Tower Books, Ballincollig, 1991, p. 19.

171 Tom Hurley interview with Patrick Greene recorded 4 March 2003.

172 Tom Hurley interview with Patrick Greene recorded 4 March 2003.

173 Tom Hurley interview with Dan Keating recorded 14 April 2003.

174 Tom Hurley interview with Patsy Holmes recorded 13 June 2003.

175 Military Archives, Military Service Pensions Collection, Con Crowley.

176 The *Cork Examiner*, 6 February 1957.

177 The *Cork Examiner*, 17 December 1958.

178 Tom Hurley interview with Patsy Holmes recorded 13 June 2003.

179 Boylan, Henry. *A Dictionary of Irish Biography.* Gill & Macmillan, Dublin, 1998.

180 Deasy, Liam. *Brother Against Brother.* Mercier Press, Cork, 1998, pp. 76–78.

181 Tom Hurley interview with Jack Duff recorded 25 June 2003.

182 Diarmaid Ferriter, email dated 2/9/22.

183 David McCullagh, email dated 2/9/22.

184 Tom Hurley interview with Jack Duff recorded 25 June 2003.

185 Tom Hurley interview with Daniel O'Donovan recorded 1 July 2003.

186 Tom Hurley interview with Daniel O'Donovan recorded 1 July 2003.

187 Tom Hurley interview with Daniel O'Donovan recorded 1 July 2003.

188 Yeats, Pádraig and Wren, Jimmy. *Michael Collins – An Illustrated Life*. Tomar Publishing Ltd, Dublin, 1989, p. 32.

189 Tom Hurley interview with Seán Clancy recorded 2 April 2003.

190 Tom Hurley interview with Seán Clancy recorded 2 April 2003.

191 Tom Hurley interview with Dan Keating recorded 14 April 2003.

192 Tom Hurley interview with Dan Keating recorded 14 April 2003.

193 Tom Hurley interview with Dan Keating recorded 13 January 2003.

194 Tom Hurley interview with Michael Casey recorded 7 June 2003.

195 Tom Hurley interview with Anthony McGinley recorded 27 May 2003.

196 Tom Hurley interview with John Parkinson recorded 22 July 2003.

197 Tom Hurley interview with Jack Duff recorded 25 June 2003.

198 Tom Hurley interview with Seán Clancy recorded 2 April 2003.

199 Tom Hurley interview with William Geary recorded 15 July 2004.

200 Tom Hurley interview with Seán Clancy recorded 2 April 2003.

201 Tom Hurley interview with Patrick Greene recorded 4 March 2003.

202 Military Archives, Military Census 1922; Military Archives, Military Service Pensions Collection, Jeremiah Sullivan; Military Archives, Military Service Pensions Collection, Michael Connolly.

203 BMH.WS1477, Thomas Reidy; the *New York Times*, 19 August 1922.

204 Tom Hurley interview with Daniel O'Donovan recorded 1 July 2003.

205 Tom Hurley interview with Daniel O'Donovan recorded 1 July 2003.

206 Harrington, Niall C. *Kerry Landing*. Anvil Books Limited, Dublin, 1992, p. 171.

207 Military Archives, Abstract of Service, Daniel O'Donovan.

208 The *Cork Examiner*, 1 & 5 September 1922; the *Irish Times*, 31 August 1922 & 1 September 1922.

209 Tom Hurley interview with Daniel O'Donovan recorded 1 July 2003.

210 The *Cork Examiner*, 5 September 1922.

211 Tom Hurley interview with Dan Keating recorded 14 April 2003.

212 MacEoin, Uinseann. *Survivors*. Argenta Publications, Dublin, 1980, pp. 99–100.

213 Tom Hurley interview with Dan Keating recorded 14 April 2003.

214 The *Irish Times* 30 & 31 August & 6 September 1922; the *New York Times*, 31 August 1922; MacEoin, Uinseann. *Survivors*. Argenta Publications, Dublin, 1980, pp. 99–100.

215 Tom Hurley interview with Gerry Smyth recorded 26 June 2003.

216 www.irishgenealogy.ie.

217 Military Archives, Military Service Pensions Collection, Joseph Smyth.

218 The *Irish Times*, 8 September 1922; the *Meath Chronicle*, 9 September 1922; Military Archives, Military Service Pensions Collection, Joseph Smyth.

219 The *Meath Chronicle*, 16 September 1922.

220 Tom Hurley interview with Gerry Smyth recorded 26 June 2003.

221 Doyle, Tom. *The Civil War in Kerry*. Mercier Press, Cork, 2008, pp. 135, 167; MacEoin, Uinseann. *The IRA in the Twilight Years 1923-1948*. Argenta Publications, Dublin, 1997, p. 619.

222 Tom Hurley interview with Dan Keating recorded 13 January 2003.

223 Doyle, Tom. *The Civil War in Kerry*. Mercier Press, Cork, 2008, p. 232; the *Cork Examiner*, 11 December 1922.

224 Tierney, Mark. *Ireland Since 1870*. CJ Fallon, Dublin, 1988, p. 264.

225 Tom Hurley interview with Jack Duff recorded 25 June 2003.

226 Enright, Seán. *The Irish Civil War: Law, Execution and Atrocity*. Merrion Press, Newbridge, 2019, p. 69.

227 Tom Hurley interview with Daniel O'Donovan recorded 1 July 2003.

228 Tom Hurley interview with Patrick Greene recorded 4 March 2003.

229 Coogan, Tim Pat & Morrison, George. *The Irish Civil War*. Weidenfeld and Nicolson, UK, 1998. p. 47.

230 Tom Hurley interview with Patsy Holmes recorded 13 June 2003.

231 The *Freeman's Journal*, 17 August 1922.

232 The *Irish Independent*, 18 September 1922; https://www.theirishstory.com/2022/09/13/the-media-war-robert-erskine-childers-in-west-cork/#_edn14.

233 Tom Hurley interview with Patrick Greene recorded 4 March 2003.

234 Tom Hurley interview with Mai McMahon née Grogan recorded 22 June 2003.

235 Tom Hurley interview with Gerry Smyth recorded 26 June 2003.

236 Military Archives, Military Service Pensions Collection, Anthony McGinley; Military Archives, Abstract of Service, Anthony McGinley.

237 Military Archives, Military Service Pensions Collection, Anthony McGinley.

238 Tom Hurley interview with William Geary recorded 15 July 2004.

239 Tom Hurley interview with William Geary recorded 15 July 2004.

240 The *Anglo Celt*, 4 & 11 November 1922; the *Freeman's Journal*, 11 November 1922.

241 Tom Hurley interview with William Geary recorded 15 July 2004.

242 Tom Hurley interview with William Geary recorded 15 July 2004.

243 Enright, Seán. *The Irish Civil War: Law, Execution and Atrocity*. Merrion Press, Newbridge, 2019, pp. 44–46, 65.

244 Tom Hurley interview with Seán Clancy recorded 2 April 2003.

245 Tom Hurley interview with Jack Duff recorded 25 June 2003.

246 Tom Hurley interview with Patsy Holmes recorded 13 June 2003.

247 Tom Hurley interview with Patsy Holmes recorded 13 June 2003.

248 Tom Hurley interview with Patsy Holmes recorded 13 June 2003.

249 Military Archives, IRA Membership Series.

250 Tom Hurley interview with Patsy Holmes recorded 13 June 2003.

251 *Rebel Cork's Fighting Story 1916-1921*. The Kerryman Limited, Tralee, 1947, p. 276; Military Archives, Military Service Pensions Collection, Lily Neenan.

252 Ryan, Meda. *Michael Collins and the Women Who Spied for Ireland*. Mercier Press, Cork, 2006, p. 46.

253 Tierney, Mark. *Ireland Since 1870*. CJ Fallon, Dublin, 1988, p. 389.

254 Tom Hurley interview with Michael Casey recorded 7 June 2003.

255 Enright, Seán. *The Irish Civil War: Law, Execution and Atrocity*. Merrion Press, Newbridge, 2019, pp. 7, 138.

256 Military Archives, Military Census 1922.

257 Military Archives, Abstract of Service, Seán Clancy.

258 Tom Hurley interview with Seán Clancy recorded 2 April 2003.

259 Ó'Ruairc, Pádraig Óg. *Blood on the Banner*. Mercier Press, Cork, 2009, pp. 326, 329; Knocklong History Weekend Seminar 2023, research by John Flannery.

260 Military Archives, Abstract of Service, Seán Clancy; the *Clare Champion*, 20 July 2001.

261 Tom Hurley interview with Seán Clancy recorded 2 April 2003.

262 Military Archives, IRA Membership Series.

263 The *Irish Independent*, 17 November 1922.

264 Allen, Gregory. *The Garda Síochána - Policing Independent Ireland 1922-82*. Gill & MacMillan Ltd, Dublin, 1999, p. 231; Brady, Conor. *Guardians of the Peace*. Gill & Macmillan, Dublin, 1974, p. 81; McNiffe, Liam. *A History of the Garda Síochána*. Wolfhound Press Ltd, Dublin, 1997, p. 27.

265 The *Cork Examiner*, 28 September 1922; www.policehistory.com; 1911 Census.

266 The *Irish Independent*, 6 October 1922.

267 Tom Hurley interview with William Geary recorded 15 July 2004.

268 Enright, Seán. *The Irish Civil War: Law, Execution and Atrocity*. Merrion Press, Newbridge, 2019, p. 6.

269 Tom Hurley interview with Michael Casey recorded 7 June 2003.

270 Tom Hurley interview with Anthony McGinley recorded 27 May 2003.

271 Enright, Seán. *The Irish Civil War: Law, Execution and Atrocity*. Merrion Press, Newbridge, 2019, pp. 49, 56.

272 BMH.WS1763, Dan Breen; the *Irish Times*, 6 December 1922.

273 Military Archives taped interview with Jack Duff conducted by Commandant Peter Young in 1992.

274 Military Archives taped interview with Jack Duff conducted by Commandant Peter Young in 1992.

275 Military Archives taped interview with Jack Duff conducted by Commandant Peter Young in 1992.

276 Military Archives, Military Service Pensions Collection, Seamus Robinson.

277 www.ancestry.com.

278 *The Nationalist*, 15 December 1926.

279 www.ancestry.com.

280 www.familysearch.org.

281 The *New York Times*, 8 December 1922.

282 Enright, Seán. *The Irish Civil War: Law, Execution and Atrocity*. Merrion Press, Newbridge, 2019, pp. 50–51.

283 Tom Hurley interview with Daniel O'Donovan recorded 1 July 2003.

284 Deasy, Liam. *Brother Against Brother*. Mercier Press, Cork, 1998, p. 94; the *Southern Star Centenary Supplement 1889-1989*, p. 77; Ryan, Meda. *Tom Barry - IRA Freedom Fighter*. Mercier Press, Cork, 2003, p. 110.

285 Tom Hurley interview with Seán Clancy recorded 2 April 2003.

286 Hopkinson, Michael. *Green Against Green - The Irish Civil War*. Gill & MacMillan Ltd, Dublin, 2004, p. 191.

287 The *Irish Examiner*, 10 July 2017.

288 The *Cork Examiner*, 14 December 1922.

289 O'Malley, Ernie. *The Men Will Talk to Me, Galway Interviews*, Mercier Press, Cork, 2013, pp. 241–242; Military Archives, Military Service Pensions Collection, Thomas Malone.

290 Tom Hurley interview with Dan Keating recorded 14 April 2003

291 O'Malley, Ernie. *The Men Will Talk to Me, Galway Interviews*. Mercier Press, Cork, 2013, pp. 246–247; O'Malley, Ernie. *The Men Will Talk to Me, the Northern Divisions*. Merrion Press, Newbridge, 2018, p. 173.

292 The *Southern Star*, 9 December 1922.

293 The *Irish Independent*, 28 June 1923 & 20 May 1971.

294 'Sliabh na mban "the jewel in the crown"' by Bob Webster & Sister Veronica Treacy (http://www.esatclear.ie/~curragh/sliabh_na_mban.htm); the *Cork Examiner*, 12 December 1922.

295 *Ballingeary Historical Society Journal 2000*.

296 Tom Hurley interview with Patrick Greene recorded 4 March 2003.

297 Tom Hurley interview with Patrick Greene recorded 4 March 2003.

298 www.irishgenealogy.ie; 1911 Census.

299 Anderson, Brian. *Gone But Not Forgotten*. Browne Printers, Letterkenny, 2022, p. 109.

300 Military Archives, IRA Membership Series; Military Archives, Brigade Activity Reports; www.irishgenealogy.ie; 1911 Census.

301 Anderson, Brian. *Gone But Not Forgotten*. Browne Printers, Letterkenny, 2022, p. 109.

302 Tom Hurley interview with George Cooper recorded 3 April 2003.

303 The *Freeman's Journal*, 13 January 1923.

304 Military Archives, Military Service Pensions Collection, Michael Cahill.

305 Tom Hurley interview with Margaret Power née Cahill recorded 9 July 2004.

306 Military Archives, Military Service Pensions Collection, Michael Cahill.

307 Military Archives taped interview with Jack Duff conducted by Commandant Peter Young in 1992.

308 The *Cork Examiner*, 22 January 1923.

309 BMH.WS1763, Dan Breen.

310 Military Archives taped interview with Jack Duff conducted by Commandant Peter Young in 1992.

311 Doyle, Tom. *The Civil War in Kerry*. Mercier Press, Cork, 2008, p. 181; Enright, Seán. *The Irish Civil War: Law, Execution and Atrocity*. Merrion Press, Newbridge, 2019, pp. 65, 69, 74.

312 Tom Hurley interview with Dan Keating recorded 13 January 2003.

313 O'Malley, Ernie. *The Men Will Talk to Me, Kerry Interviews*. Mercier Press, Cork, 2012, pp. 106, 107; Enright, Seán. *The Irish Civil War: Law, Execution and Atrocity*. Merrion Press, Newbridge, 2019, p. 75.

314 Enright, Seán. *The Irish Civil War: Law, Execution and Atrocity*. Merrion Press, Newbridge, 2019, pp. 79, 80, 124.

315 Tom Hurley interview with Daniel O'Donovan recorded 1 July 2003.

316 Dwyer, T. Ryle. *Tans, Terror and Trouble - Kerry's Real Fighting Story*. Mercier Press, Cork, 2001, p. 377.

317 Tom Hurley interview with Dan Keating recorded 13 January 2003.

318 Rafter, Michael. *The Quiet County*. Arderin Publishing Company, Portlaoise, 2005, p. 146.

319 McCarthy, Pat. *The Irish Revolution 1912-23, Waterford*. Four Courts Press, Dublin, 2015, p. 115.

320 Tom Hurley interview with Patrick Fitzgerald recorded 7 June 2003.

321 Tom Hurley interview with Patrick Fitzgerald recorded 7 June 2003.

322 Tom Hurley interview with Patrick Fitzgerald recorded 7 June 2003.

323 Military Archives, Military Service Pensions Collection, Liam Deasy.

324 Tom Hurley interview with Seán Clancy recorded 2 April 2003.

325 Deasy, Liam. *Brother Against Brother*. Mercier Press, Cork, 1998. pp. 111–115.

326 Deasy, Liam. *Brother Against Brother*. Mercier Press, Cork, 1998. pp. 109–122.

327 Military Archives taped interview with Jack Duff conducted by Commandant Peter Young in 1992.

328 Deasy, Liam. *Brother Against Brother*. Mercier Press, Cork, 1998, p. 123.

329 Tom Hurley interview with William Geary recorded 15 July 2004.

330 Memoirs, typed and signed by William Geary 28/1/2003.

331 Military Archives, Civil War Internment Collection; O'Malley, Ernie: *The Men Will Talk to Me, Kerry Interviews*. Mercier Press, Cork, 2012, p. 243.

332 Durney, James. *The Civil War in Kildare*. Mercier Press, Cork, 2011, pp. 148–151; O'Malley, Ernie. *The Singing Flame*. Anvil Books Limited, Dublin, 1978, p. 272.

333 MacEoin, Uinseann. *The IRA in the Twilight Years 1923-1948*. Argenta Publications, Dublin, 1997, p. 619; O'Malley, Ernie. *The Men Will Talk to Me, Kerry Interviews*. Mercier Press, Cork, 2012, p. 37; Military Archives, Civil War Internment Collection; Military Archives, Military Service Pensions Collection, Denis Quille.

334 Tom Hurley interview with Dan Keating recorded 14 April 2003.

335 O'Malley, Ernie: *The Men Will Talk to Me, Galway Interviews*. Mercier Press, Cork, 2013, pp. 258–259.

336 O'Malley, Ernie. *The Men Will Talk to Me, Kerry Interviews*. Mercier Press, Cork, 2012, p. 37; the *Leinster Leader*, 27 January 1923.

337 MacEoin, Uinseann. *The IRA in the Twilight Years 1923–1948*. Argenta Publications, Dublin, 1997, p. 619.

338 O'Malley, Ernie. *The Men Will Talk to Me, Mayo Interviews*. Mercier Press, Cork, 2014, p. 300.

339 Durney, James. *The Civil War in Kildare*. Mercier Press, Cork, 2011, p. 149.

340 O'Malley, Ernie. *The Singing Flame*. Anvil Books Limited, Dublin, 1978, p. 272.

341 O'Malley, Ernie. *The Men Will Talk to Me, Kerry Interviews*. Mercier Press, Cork, 2012, p. 37.

342 Military Archives, Military Service Pensions Collection, Michael Kelly.

343 Military Archives, Military Service Pensions Collection, John Kelly.

344 The *Connacht Tribune*, 10 March 1923; the *Evening Herald*, 8 July 1924.

345 The *Connacht Tribune*, 20 October 1923.

346 https://athenry.org/record/michael-kelly-of-castle-lambert-his-fight-for-irish-freedom-59/ & https://athenryparishheritage.com/castlelambert/.

347 Military Archives, Military Census 1922; Military Archives, Abstract of Service, Daniel O'Donovan.

348 Military Archives, Military Service Pensions Collection, Jeremiah Sullivan.

349 Tom Hurley interview with Daniel O'Donovan recorded 1 July 2003.

350 Tom Hurley interview with Daniel O'Donovan recorded 1 July 2003.

351 The *Cork Examiner*, 22 August 1922; the *Evening Echo*, 8 September 1922.

352 The *Cork Examiner*, 25 October 1923.

353 The *Cork Examiner*, 1 & 8 February 1923.

354 Military Archives, Military Service Pensions Collection, Thomas Murray.

355 The *Cork Examiner*, 10 October 1922.

356 Military Archives, Military Service Pensions Collection, Laurence Galvin.

357 Tom Hurley interview with Jack Duff recorded 25 June 2003.

358 Military Archives taped interview with Jack Duff conducted by Commandant Peter Young in 1992; The *Cork Examiner*, 22 January 1923; Military Archives.

359 Langton, James. *The Forgotten Fallen, Volume 1*. Kilmainham Tales Teo, Dublin, 2019, pp. 333–339.

360 Military Archives, Abstract of Service, Seán Clancy.

361 The *Cork Examiner*, 27 February 1923; the *Irish Independent*, 27 February 1923.

362 *Éire The Irish Nation*, 14 April 1923; www.irishgenealogy.ie; Military Archives, Military Service Pensions Collection, Thomas Gibson.

363 Military Archives, Military Census 1922; the *Midland Tribune*, 2 January 2008, article by Philip McConway.

364 The *Freeman's Journal*, 12 & 17 January 1923; the *Cork Examiner*, 27 February 1923.

365 Tom Hurley interview with Dan Keating recorded 14 April 2003.

366 *The Kingdom*, 11 October 2007.

367 O'Dwyer, Martin (Bob). *Seventy-Seven of Mine Said Ireland*. Litho Press, Cork, 2006. p. 4.

368 O'Dwyer, Martin (Bob). *Seventy-Seven of Mine Said Ireland*. Litho Press, Cork, 2006, p. 264.

369 Military Archives, Military Service Pensions Collection, Thomas Gibson; www.irishgenealogy.ie.

370 Rafter, Michael. *The Quiet County*. Arderin Publishing Company, Portlaoise, 2005, p. 145.

371 O'Malley, Ernie. *The Men Will Talk to Me, the Northern Divisions*. Merrion Press, Newbridge, 2018, p. 170.

372 Philip McConway emails dated 18 February 2009 & 10 February 2023.

373 The *Midland Tribune*, 2 January 2008, article by Philip McConway.

374 Philip McConway emails dated 18 February 2009 & 10 February 2023.

375 The *Midland Tribune*, 2 January 2008, article by Philip McConway.

376 Military Archives, Military Service Pensions Collection, Thomas Gibson.

377 The *Cork Examiner* 21, 22, 23 February & 1 March 1923.

378 Tom Hurley interview with Patsy Holmes recorded 13 June 2003.

379 The *Cork Examiner*, 1 March 1923.

380 Dwyer, T. Ryle. *Tans, Terror and Trouble – Kerry's Real Fighting Story*. Mercier Press, Cork, 2001, pp. 367–368.

381 Tom Hurley interview with Dan Keating recorded 13 January 2003.

382 Dwyer, T. Ryle. *Tans, Terror and Trouble – Kerry's Real Fighting Story*. Mercier Press, Cork, 2001, p. 368.

383 Tom Hurley interview with Dan Keating recorded 13 January 2003.

384 Dwyer, T. Ryle. *Tans, Terror and Trouble – Kerry's Real Fighting Story*. Mercier Press, Cork, 2001, p. 369.

385 Tom Hurley interview with Daniel O'Donovan recorded 1 July 2003.

386 Tom Hurley interview with Daniel O'Donovan recorded 1 July 2003.

387 Doyle, Tom. *The Civil War in Kerry*. Mercier Press, Cork, 2008, p. 274.

388 Tom Hurley interview with Dan Keating recorded 13 January 2003.

389 Notes: Doyle, Tom. *The Civil War in Kerry*. Mercier Press, Cork, 2008, p. 275.

390 Dwyer, T. Ryle. *Tans, Terror and Trouble – Kerry's Real Fighting Story*. Mercier Press, Cork, 2001, p. 371.

391 Dwyer, T. Ryle. *Tans, Terror and Trouble – Kerry's Real Fighting Story*. Mercier Press, Cork, 2001, p. 371; *The Kerryman*, 7 January 2009.

392 Tom Hurley interview with Dan Keating recorded 13 January 2003.

393 Tom Hurley interview with Dan Keating recorded 13 January 2003.

394 Macardle, Dorothy. *Tragedies of Kerry*. Elo Press Ltd, Dublin, 1998, p. 73.

395 Tom Hurley interview with Anthony McGinley recorded 27 May 2003.

396 Tom Hurley interview with Dan Keating recorded 14 April 2003.

397 *The Story of the Drumboe Martyrs 1923-2003*. 80th Anniversary Edition, p. 30.

398 BMH.WS1741, Michael V. Donoghue.

399 *The Story of the Drumboe Martyrs 1923-2003*. 80th Anniversary Edition; the *Irish Times*, 15 March 1923.

400 Mac Fhionnghaile, Niall. *Dr. McGinley and His Times*. An Crann, Letterkenny, 1985, p. 82.

401 *The Story of the Drumboe Martyrs 1923-2003*. 80th Anniversary Edition, p. 87; the *Freeman's Journal*, 14 December 1922.

402 O'Malley, Cormac H. & Dolan, Anne. *'No Surrender Here!' – The Civil War Papers of Ernie O'Malley 1922-1924*. The Lilliput Press, Dublin, 2007, p. 199; Hopkinson, Michael. *Green Against Green – The Irish Civil War*. Gill & MacMillan Ltd, Dublin, 2004, p. 162.

403 Lynch, Robert. *The Northern IRA and the Early Years of Partition 1920-22*. Irish Academic Press, Dublin, 2006, p. 174; *The Story of the Drumboe Martyrs 1923-2003*. 80th Anniversary Edition, p. 99.

404 BMH.WS1741, Michael V. Donoghue.

405 Tom Hurley interview with Anthony McGinley recorded 27 May 2003.

406 Tom Hurley notes written post interview with Anthony McGinley recorded 27 May 2003.

407 The *Irish Independent*, 19 March 1923; the *Cork Examiner*, 19 March 1923.

408 *The Nationalist*, 12 August 1922.

409 Military Archives taped interview with Jack Duff conducted by Commandant Peter Young in 1992.

410 Tom Hurley interview with Jack Duff recorded 25 June 2003.

411 The *Irish Independent*, 19 March 1923.

412 The *Freeman's Journal*, 6 April 1923.

413 The *Longford News*, 2000; the *Longford Leader*, 28 February 2007.

414 Tom Hurley interview with Patrick Greene recorded 4 March 2003.

415 https://www.cso.ie/en/releasesandpublications/ep/p-1916/1916irl/society/education/.

416 Tom Hurley interview with Patrick Greene recorded 4 March 2003.

417 Murphy, Allison. *When Dublin was the Capital – Northern Life Remembered*. Belcouver Press, Belfast, 2000, p. 18.

418 Tom Hurley interview with Norman Douglas recorded 22 July 2003.

419 The *Freeman's Journal*, 9 April 1923.

420 *An Cosantóir*, Dec. 2019/Jan. 2020, p. 15.

421 Harvey, Dan. *Soldiers of the Short Grass: A History of the Curragh Camp*. Merrion Press, Newbridge, 2016, pp. 91–92.

422 Military Archives taped interview with Jack Duff conducted by Commandant Peter Young in 1992.

423 Ryan, Meda. *The Real Chief – The Story of Liam Lynch*. Mercier Press, Cork, 2005, p. 189.

424 'Meirligh, An Saighdiúir Tréigthe – Liam O Loingsígh', TG4, 2005.

425 Military Archives taped interview with Jack Duff conducted by Commandant Peter Young in 1992.

426 Military Archives taped interview with Jack Duff conducted by Commandant Peter Young in 1992.

427 'Meirligh, An Saighdiúir Tréigthe – Liam O Loingsígh', TG4, 2005.

428 Ryan, Meda. *The Real Chief – The Story of Liam Lynch*. Mercier Press, Cork, 2005, pp. 189–192; Bourke, Marcus. *The Tipperary Historical Journal 1993*. Published by the County Tipperary Historical Society, Thurles, 1993, p. 58.

429 'Meirligh, An Saighdiúir Tréigthe – Liam O Loingsígh', TG4, 2005.

430 Ryan, Meda. *The Real Chief – The Story of Liam Lynch*. Mercier Press, Cork, 2005, pp. 189–192; Bourke, Marcus. *The Tipperary Historical Journal 1993*. Published by the County Tipperary Historical Society, Thurles, 1993, p. 58.

431 Tom Hurley interview with Dan Keating recorded 13 January 2003.'

432 Doyle, Tom. *The Civil War in Kerry*. Mercier Press, Cork, 2008, pp. 283–284; Ryan, Meda. *The Real Chief – The Story of Liam Lynch*. Mercier Press, Cork, 2005, pp. 181–184.

433 Tom Hurley interview with Dan Keating recorded 13 January 2003.

434 BMH.WS1093, Thomas Treacy.

435 Tom Hurley interview with Patsy Holmes recorded 13 June 2003.

436 Ryan, Meda. *The Real Chief – The Story of Liam Lynch*. Mercier Press, Cork, 2005, pp. 198–199.

437 Tom Hurley interview with Michael Casey recorded 7 June 2003.

438 Tom Hurley interview with Michael Casey recorded 7 June 2003.

439 Tom Hurley interview with Seán Clancy recorded 2 April 2003.

440 Dwyer, T. Ryle. *Tans, Terror and Trouble – Kerry's Real Fighting Story*. Mercier Press, Cork, 2001, p. 377; BMH.WS1763, Dan Breen.

441 Tom Hurley interview with Dan Keating recorded 13 January 2003.

442 Tom Hurley interview with Anthony McGinley recorded 27 May 2003.

443 Tom Hurley interview with Anthony McGinley recorded 27 May 2003.

444 http://web.archive.org/web/20141104140509/http://www.ucd.ie/archives/html/collections/cumann-na-gael.htm.

445 The *Irish Independent*, 15 & 16 May 1923; the *Freeman's Journal*, 15 May 1923.

446 The *Derry Journal*, 25 June 1924.

447 The *Derry Journal*, 7 July 1924.

448 The *Irish Independent*, 16 May 1923.

449 The *Derry Journal*, 20 June 1924; the *Irish Press*, 14 April 1975.

450 Tierney, Mark. *Ireland Since 1870*. CJ Fallon, Dublin, 1988, p. 267.
451 Hopkinson, Michael. *Green Against Green – The Irish Civil War*. Gill & MacMillan Ltd, Dublin, 2004, p. 273; Tierney, Mark. *Ireland Since 1870*. CJ Fallon, Dublin, 1988, p. 271; Langton, James. *The Forgotten Fallen, Volume 1*. Kilmainham Tales Teo, Dublin, 2019, p. 7.
452 Tom Hurley interview with Michael Casey recorded 7 June 2003.
453 Tom Hurley interview with Michael Casey recorded 7 June 2003.
454 Tom Hurley interview with Michael Casey recorded 7 June 2003.

CHAPTER 8

1   Military Archives, IRA Membership Series.
2   Murphy, Seán and Síle. *The Comeraghs – Gunfire and Civil War. The Story of the Deise Brigade IRA 1914-24*. Litho Press, Midleton, 2003. p. 168; National Graves Association. *The Last Post*. Elo Press Ltd, Dublin, 1985, p. 166; Ó Riordán, Tomás. *Where Martyred Heroes Rest*. Published by the Liam Lynch National Commemoration Committee, 1987, p. 57; United Parishes Press. *Backward Glances: A Compilation of Fact and Old Stories from the United Parishes of Glendine, Kilwatermoy and Knockanore*. Litho Press, Midleton, 2001, p. 126.
3   Tom Hurley interview with Patrick Fitzgerald recorded 7 June 2003.
4   Tom Hurley interview with Patrick Fitzgerald recorded 7 June 2003.
5   The *Munster Express*, 13 August 1937.
6   Tierney, Mark. *Ireland Since 1870*. CJ Fallon, Dublin, 1988, p. 267.
7   Tom Hurley interview with Gerry Smyth recorded 26 June 2003.
8   The *Meath Chronicle*, 1 September 1923.
9   The *Donegal News*, 15 September 1923.
10 The *Donegal Democrat*, 14 September 1923.
11 *Sinn Féin*, 17 September 1923.
12 *Sinn Féin*, 15 September 1923.
13 Tom Hurley interview with Anthony McGinley recorded 27 May 2003.
14 Tom Hurley interview with Anthony McGinley recorded 27 May 2003.
15 1901 Census; www.ancestry.com; www.irishgenealogy.ie.
16 Tom Hurley interview with Anthony McGinley recorded 27 May 2003.
17 Tom Hurley interview with Anthony McGinley recorded 27 May 2003.
18 Military Archives, Military Service Pensions Collection, Con Quinn; Military Archives, Military Service Pensions Collection, Anthony McGinley.
19 Military Archives, Military Service Pensions Collection, Anthony McGinley.
20 Tom Hurley interview with Anthony McGinley recorded 27 May 2003.
21 Military Archives, Military Service Pensions Collection, Con Quinn.
22 Military Archives, IRA Membership Series; the *Donegal News*, 9 October 1954; 1901 Census.
23 The *Irish Independent*, 24 September 1924.
24 The *Cork Examiner*, 4 October 1923.
25 The *Cork Examiner*, 14 November 1923.
26 The *Cork Examiner*, 1 & 14 November 1923 & 31 May 1924.
27 The *Cork Examiner*, 21, 23 & 30 January 1924 & 7, 13 & 14 February 1924.
28 The *Cork Examiner*, 31 May 1924
29 Military Archives, Abstract of Service, Daniel O'Donovan; Information from Eddie O'Donovan dated 2/3/2023.
30 Tom Hurley interview with Daniel O'Donovan recorded 1 July 2003.
31 Tom Hurley interview with Daniel O'Donovan recorded 1 July 2003.
32 The *Freeman's Journal*, 19 October 1923.

33   The *Freeman's Journal*, 16 October 1923.

34   The *Freeman's Journal*, 16 October 1923.

35   The *Freeman's Journal*, 24 November 1923.

36   Durney, James. *The Civil War in Kildare*. Mercier Press, Cork, 2011, p. 162, 163.

37   The *Freeman's Journal*, 24 November 1923.

38   The *Freeman's Journal*, 29 October 1923.

39   The *Cork Examiner*, 31 October 1923; Durney, James. *The Civil War in Kildare*. Mercier Press, Cork, 2011, p. 164.

40   The *Irish Examiner*, 21 November 1923.

41   The *Irish Examiner*, 21 November 1923.

42   The *Freeman's Journal*, 27 November 1923.

43   MacEoin, Uinseann. *The IRA in the Twilight Years 1923-1948*. Argenta Publications, Dublin, 1997, p. 619; the *Cork Examiner*, 31 October 1923.

44   The *Kilkenny People*, 20 October 1923.

45   The *Kilkenny People*, 20 October 1923.

46   Military Archives taped interview with Jack Duff conducted by Commandant Peter Young in 1992.

47   MacEoin, Uinseann. *The IRA in the Twilight Years 1923-1948*. Argenta Publications, Dublin, 1997, p. 620; Military Archives, Civil War Internment Collection.

48   Military Archives, Civil War Internment Collection.

49   Tom Hurley interview with Dan Keating recorded 14 April 2003.

50   Durney, James. *The Civil War in Kildare*. Mercier Press, Cork, 2011, pp. 162-170; the *Irish Independent*, 17 December 1923; the *Sunday Independent*, 16 December 1923; Military Archives, Military Service Pensions Collection, Joseph Bergin; O'Malley, Ernie. *The Men Will Talk to Me, Galway Interviews*. Mercier Press, Cork, 2013, pp. 246-247; O'Malley, Ernie. *The Men Will Talk to Me, the Northern Divisions*. Merrion Press, Newbridge, 2018, pp. 173, 226; O'Malley, Ernie. *The Men Will Talk to Me, Mayo Interviews*. Mercier Press, Cork, 2014, p. 301.

51   Tom Hurley interview with Dan Keating recorded 13 January 2003.

52   Tom Hurley interview with Dan Keating recorded 13 January 2003.

53   Tom Hurley interview with Dan Keating recorded 14 April 2003.

54   Military Archives, Abstract of Service, John Duff.

55   Tierney, Mark. *Ireland Since 1870*. CJ Fallon, Dublin, 1988, p. 275.

56   Tierney, Mark. *Ireland Since 1870*. CJ Fallon, Dublin, 1988, p. 277; the *Irish Examiner*, 4 March 2014.

57   Military Archives taped interview with Jack Duff conducted by Commandant Peter Young in 1992.

58   Military Archives, Abstract of Service, John Duff.

59   Military Archives, Abstract of Service, Seán Clancy.

60   www.generalmichaelcollins.com; www.military.ie, Press Release 31 August 2005; Military Archives, Abstract of Service, Seán Clancy.

61   Tom Hurley notes written post interview with Seán Clancy 2 April 2003.

62   www.generalmichaelcollins.com; www.military.ie, Press Release 31 August 2005; Military Archives, Abstract of Service, Seán Clancy.

63   Crowley, John, Ó Drisceoil, Donal & Murphy, Mike. *Atlas of the Irish Revolution*. Cork University Press, Cork, 2017, pp.881–885.

64   Military Archives, Military Service Pensions Collection, Patrick Holmes.

65   Tom Hurley interview with Patsy Holmes recorded 13 June 2003.

66   Military Archives, Medal Series, Patrick Holmes.

67   Tom Hurley interview with William Geary recorded 15 July 2004.

68   Memoirs, typed and signed by William Geary 28/1/2003.

69 Lynch, Robert. *The Northern IRA and the Early Years of Partition 1920-22*. Irish Academic Press, Dublin, 2006, p. 174; *The Story of the Drumboe Martyrs 1923-2003*. 80th Anniversary Edition, p. 99.

70 *The Kerryman*, 8 November 1924.

71 Tom Hurley interview with Dan Keating recorded 14 April 2003.

72 The *Kerry People*, 24 June 1922; the *Kerry Reporter*, 22 June 1929.

73 Tom Hurley notes taken post interview with Dan Keating recorded 14 April 2003.

74 *The Story of the Drumboe Martyrs 1923-2003*. 80th Anniversary Edition, pp. 54-55; the *Donegal News*, 1 November 1924; the *Derry Journal*, 5 November 1924.

75 *The Story of the Drumboe Martyrs 1923-2003*. 80th Anniversary Edition, pp. 93-98.

76 The *Kerry Reporter*, 21 March 1925.

77 Tom Hurley interview with William Geary recorded 15 July 2004.

78 The *Irish Independent*, 22 May 1925.

79 Tom Hurley interview with William Geary recorded 15 July 2004.

80 The *Cork Examiner*, 25 March 1925.

81 The *Cork Examiner*, 27 May 1925; the *Nenagh Guardian*, 14 November 1925.

82 The *Cork Examiner*, 13 & 14 November 1925.

83 Information from Eddie O'Donovan dated 2/3/2023.

84 The *Evening Herald*, 21 February 1925.

85 www.garda.ie.

86 www.policehistory.com.

87 Tom Hurley interview with Daniel O'Donovan recorded 1 July 2003.

88 The Garda Museum. Email from Gerry Kilgallon, The Garda Museum, dated 19 January 2015.

89 Tom Hurley interview with Daniel O'Donovan recorded 1 July 2003.

90 Tom Hurley interview with Daniel O'Donovan recorded 1 July 2003.

91 Tom Hurley interview with Daniel O'Donovan recorded 1 July 2003.

92 Tom Hurley interview with Daniel O'Donovan recorded 1 July 2003.

93 Tom Hurley interview with Daniel O'Donovan recorded 1 July 2003.

94 The *Southern Star*, 26 August 2006.

95 Mac Fhionnghaile, Niall. *Dr. McGinley and His Times*. An Crann, Letterkenny, 1985, p. 267.

96 www.libertyellisfoundation.org.

97 Tom Hurley interview with Anthony McGinley recorded 27 May 2003.

98 Tom Hurley interview with Anthony McGinley recorded 27 May 2003.

99 Ferriter, Diarmaid. *Between Two Hells: The Irish Civil War*. Profile Books Ltd, London, 2021, p. 127.

100 Tom Hurley interview with Anthony McGinley recorded 27 May 2003.

101 www.ancestry.com.

102 The *Donegal News*, 9 October 1954; the *Donegal Democrat*, 15 July 1966; www.familysearch.org.

103 The *Donegal News*, 10 March 1956; Military Archives, Military Service Pensions Collection, Bridget MacNamee.

104 The *Donegal News*, 27 February 2004.

105 www.libertyellisfoundation.org.

106 The *Donegal Democrat*, 1 January 1971.

107 The *Donegal Democrat*, 14 September 1940.

108 The *Irish Times*, 23 June 2012; the *Donegal Democrat*, 25 February 1993.

109 Mac Fhionnghaile, Niall. *Dr. McGinley and His Times*. An Crann, Letterkenny, 1985, pp. 267-269.

110 www.ancestry.com.

111 www.findmypast.ie.

112 www.irishgenealogy.ie; 1911 Census.
113 Tom Hurley interview with Mai McMahon née Grogan recorded 22 June 2003.
114 The *Clare Champion*, 5 April 2002.
115 Tom Hurley interview with Seán Clancy recorded 2 April 2003.
116 Tom Hurley interview with William Geary recorded 15 July 2004.
117 Memoirs, typed and signed by William Geary 20/1/1992.
118 Bury, Robin. *Buried Lives: The Protestants of Southern Ireland*. The History Press Ireland, Dublin, 2017, pp.13–15.
119 Tom Hurley interview with Patrick Greene recorded 4 March 2003.
120 www.buildingsofireland.ie; https://theirishaesthete.com/.
121 Tom Hurley interview with George Cooper recorded 3 April 2003.
122 Tom Hurley interview with Norman Douglas recorded 22 July 2003.
123 Carpenter, George. *The Life & Times of Cork's George Carpenter*. Innisfree Press, Kinsale, 2002, p. 121; the *Cork Examiner*, 22 October 1938.
124 The *Irish News*, 23 September 2022.
125 www.ancestry.com.
126 *The Kerryman*, 5 January 2006; Military Archives, Military Service Pensions Collection, Margaret Power.
127 Tom Hurley interview with Margaret Power née Cahill recorded 9 July 2004.
128 Tom Hurley interview with Margaret Power née Cahill recorded 9 July 2004.
129 Military Archives; Cumann na mBan Series; Military Archives, Military Service Pensions Collection, Bridget Kavanagh; Military Archives, Military Service Pensions Collection, Maurice Fitzgerald.
130 Ferriter, Diarmaid. *Between Two Hells: The Irish Civil War*. Profile Books Ltd, London, 2021, p. 127.
131 www.irishgenealogy.ie.
132 *The Kerryman*, 26 July 1924; Military Archives, Military Service Pensions Collection, Michael Cahill.
133 Military Archives, Military Service Pensions Collection, Michael Cahill.
134 *The Kerryman*, 3 October 1975.
135 www.familysearch.org; the *Clare Champion*, 5 April 2002.
136 The *Irish Examiner*, 10 July 2017.
137 Tom Hurley interview with Dan Keating recorded 13 January 2003.
138 The *Sligo Champion*, 24 January 1925.
139 MacEoin, Uinseann. *Harry*. Argenta Publications, Dublin, 1985, p. 106; the *Irish Examiner*, 10 July 2017.
140 Tom Hurley interview with William Geary recorded 15 July 2004.
141 Tom Hurley interview with William Geary recorded 15 July 2004.
142 www.libertyellisfoundation.org.
143 www.ancestry.com.
144 www.familysearch.org.
145 Memoirs, typed and signed by William Geary 28/1/2003.
146 www.findmypast.ie.
147 *Jottings and Recollections of William Geary, New York - 14 June 1974*.
148 Wallace, Colm. *The Fallen*. The History Press Ireland, Dublin, 2017, pp. 104–108.
149 MacEoin, Uinseann. *The IRA in the Twilight Years 1923–1948*. Argenta Publications, Dublin, 1997, p. 620.
150 Tom Hurley interview with Seán Clancy recorded 2 April 2003.
151 The *Irish Press*, 20 April 1932.
152 Military Archives, Abstract of Service, Seán Clancy.
153 Military Archives, Abstract of Service, John Duff.

154 Tom Hurley interview with Jack Duff recorded 25 June 2003.

155 Military Archives, Abstract of Service, John Duff.

156 Military Archives, Abstract of Service, John Duff.

157 Tom Hurley interview with Jack Duff recorded 25 June 2003.

158 Military Archives taped interview with Jack Duff conducted by Commandant Peter Young in 1992.

159 Military Archives taped interview with Jack Duff conducted by Commandant Peter Young in 1992.

160 McCullagh, David. *De Valera: Rise 1882–1932*. Gill Books, Dublin, 2017, p. 417; McCullagh, David. *De Valera: Rule 1932–1975*. Gill Books, Dublin, 2018, p. 7.

161 Grob-Fitzgibbon, Benjamin. *The Irish Experience During the Second World War: An Oral History*. Irish Academic Press, Dublin, 2004, pp. 100–101.

162 Tom Hurley interview with Jack Duff recorded 25 June 2003.

163 'The Emergency – A Brief Overview' by John Dorney, https://web.archive.org/web/20230625135226/https://www.theirishstory.com/2018/05/21/the-emergency-a-brief-overview/.

164 Tom Hurley interview with Dan Keating recorded 13 January 2003.

165 Tom Hurley interview with Dan Keating recorded 14 April 2003.

166 www.ucfl.ie.

167 The *Belfast Newsletter*, 29 March 1932.

168 Tom Hurley interview with John Parkinson recorded 22 July 2003.

169 The *Belfast Newsletter*, 29 March 1932; 1911 Census; the *Dublin Evening Mail*, 23 December 1933 & 3 March 1934.

170 The *Belfast Newsletter*, 24 March & 7 April 1931.

171 1911 Census.

172 The *Dublin Evening Mail*, 8 November 1932; the *Irish Press*, 13 January 1958; the *Evening Herald*, 24 May 1968 & 19 July 1973.

173 Tom Hurley interview with John Parkinson recorded 22 July 2003.

174 Tom Hurley interview with Dan Keating recorded 13 January 2003.

175 *An Phoblacht*, 29 April & 26 May 1933.

176 Tom Hurley interview with Dan Keating recorded 13 January 2003.

177 The *Evening Herald*, 26 April 1933.

178 *An Phoblacht*, 6 May 1933.

179 The *Irish Press*, 1 May 1933.

180 Tom Hurley interview with Dan Keating recorded 13 January 2003.

181 Tom Hurley interview with Dan Keating recorded 13 January 2003.

182 *An Phoblacht*, 29 April 1933.

183 www.irishgenealogy.ie.

184 Military Archives, Military Service Pensions Collection, Andrew Noonan; *The Corkman*, 7 July 1973.

185 The *Cork Examiner*, 13 November 1934.

186 Tom Hurley interview with Kathleen Noonan née Charles recorded 28 May 2003.

187 Tom Hurley interview with Kathleen Noonan née Charles recorded 28 May 2003.

188 Military Archives, Military Service Pensions Collection, Andrew Noonan.

189 The *Irish Press*, 6 July 1935.

190 The *Cork Examiner*, 6 July 1935.

191 Tom Hurley interview with George Carpenter recorded 7 January 2003.

192 https://www.holocaust.org.uk/hitler-youth-jacket.

193 Tom Hurley interview with George Carpenter recorded 7 January 2003.

194 Carpenter, George. *The Life & Times of Cork's George Carpenter*. Innisfree Press, Kinsale, 2002, p. 115.

195 *The Guardian*, 12 January 2008.

196 Tom Hurley interview with George Carpenter recorded 7 January 2003.

197 Carpenter, George. *The Life & Times of Cork's George Carpenter*. Innisfree Press, Kinsale, 2002, p. 116.

198 Tom Hurley interview with George Carpenter recorded 7 January 2003.

199 Tom Hurley interview with George Carpenter recorded 7 January 2003.

200 Carpenter, George. *The Life & Times of Cork's George Carpenter*. Innisfree Press, Kinsale, 2002, p. 116.

201 The *Irish Press*, 6 July 1935.

202 Tom Hurley interview with Anthony McGinley recorded 27 May 2003.

203 Tom Hurley interview with Anthony McGinley recorded 27 May 2003.

204 Tom Hurley interview with Anthony McGinley recorded 27 May 2003.

205 Tom Hurley interview with Anthony McGinley recorded 27 May 2003.

206 Tierney, Mark. *Ireland Since 1870*. CJ Fallon, Dublin, 1988, pp. 302–305.

207 Tierney, Mark. *Ireland Since 1870*. CJ Fallon, Dublin, 1988, p. 281.

208 Military Archives, Abstract of Service, John Duff.

209 Tom Hurley interview with Michael Casey recorded 7 June 2003.

210 Tom Hurley interview with Michael Casey recorded 7 June 2003.

211 The *Irish Examiner*, 3 June 2003; https://web.archive.org/web/20220314215213/http:/landedestates.nuigalway.ie/.

212 The *Cork Examiner*, 6 May 1921.

213 Bury, Robin. *Buried Lives: The Protestants of Southern Ireland*. The History Press Ireland, Dublin, 2017, p. 11.

214 Tom Hurley interview with Michael Casey recorded 7 June 2003.

215 Tom Hurley interview with Jack Duff recorded 25 June 2003.

216 The *Irish Examiner*, 27 June 2008; Dolan, Anne. *Commemorating the Irish Civil War: History and Memory 1923-2000*. Cambridge University Press, Cambridge, 2006, pp. 15, 25; Augusteijn, Joost. *The Irish Revolution 1913-1923*. Palgrave Macmillan, London, 2002, Chapter 12.

217 Tom Hurley interview with Patrick Greene recorded 4 March 2003.

218 Parkinson, John. *A Belfastman's Tale*. Minprint Ltd, Belfast, 2003, p. 25.

219 Tom Hurley interview with John Parkinson recorded 14 July 2003.

220 Tierney, Mark. *Ireland Since 1870*. CJ Fallon, Dublin, 1988, p. 325.

221 Grob-Fitzgibbon, Benjamin. *The Irish Experience During the Second World War: An Oral History*. Irish Academic Press, Dublin, 2004, p. 103.

222 The *Meath Chronicle*, 25 May 2011.

223 The *Fingal Independent*, 8 February 2006.

224 Military Archives taped interview with Jack Duff conducted by Commandant Peter Young in 1992.

225 Tom Hurley interview with George Carpenter recorded 7 January 2003.

226 Tom Hurley interview with George Carpenter recorded 7 January 2003.

227 Tom Hurley interview with George Carpenter recorded 7 January 2003.

228 Tom Hurley interview with Patrick Greene recorded 4 March 2003.

229 Tom Hurley interview with John Kelly recorded 24 May 2003.

230 The *Leitrim Observer*, 16 September 1939.

231 The *Tuam Herald*, 16 September 1939; the *Connacht Tribune*, 9 September 1939.

232 MacEoin, Uinseann. *The IRA in the Twilight Years 1923-1948*. Argenta Publications, Dublin, 1997, p. 625; Kirby, Dick. *IRA Terror on Britain's Streets 1939-40*. Pen & Sword Books Ltd, Yorkshire, 2021, pp. 5, 92, 109–110.

233 Tom Hurley interview with Dan Keating recorded 14 April 2003.

234 The *Cork Examiner*, 3 August 1940; MacEoin, Uinseann. *The IRA in the Twilight Years 1923-1948*. Argenta Publications, Dublin, 1997, p. 625.

235 *The Nationalist*, 7 August 1940.

236 Tom Hurley interview with Dan Keating recorded 13 January 2003.

237 Grob-Fitzgibbon, Benjamin. *The Irish Experience During the Second World War: An Oral History*. Irish Academic Press, Dublin, 2004, p. 101.

238 www.militaryarchives.ie.

239 Grob-Fitzgibbon, Benjamin. *The Irish Experience During the Second World War: An Oral History*. Irish Academic Press, Dublin, 2004, p. 105.

240 Harvey, Dan. *Soldiers of the Short Grass: A History of the Curragh Camp*. Merrion Press, Newbridge, 2016, p. 107; the *Irish Times*, 8 May 2017.

241 Grob-Fitzgibbon, Benjamin. *The Irish Experience During the Second World War: An Oral History*. Irish Academic Press, Dublin, 2004, p. 103.

242 The *Irish Times*, 8 May 2017.

243 The *Irish News*, 29 December 2020.

244 'The Emergency – A Brief Overview' by John Dorney, https://web.archive.org/web/20230625135226/https://www.theirishstory.com/2018/05/21/the-emergency-a-brief-overview/.

245 Doherty, Richard. *The Thin Green Line: The History of the Royal Ulster Constabulary GC, 1922-2001*. Pen & Sword, Barnsley, 2012, Chapter 2.

246 *An Cosantóir*, October 1996, p. 25.

247 Grob-Fitzgibbon, Benjamin. *The Irish Experience During the Second World War: An Oral History*. Irish Academic Press, Dublin, 2004, p. 104.

248 Grob-Fitzgibbon, Benjamin. *The Irish Experience During the Second World War: An Oral History*. Irish Academic Press, Dublin, 2004, p. 106.

249 Tom Hurley interview with Norman Douglas recorded 22 July 2003.

250 https://www.ed.ac.uk/news/all-news/ireland-120609#:~:text=The%20Roll%20of%20Honour%2C%20compiled,British%2C%20Commonwealth%20and%20Dominion%20Forces.

251 Tom Hurley interview with George Carpenter recorded 7 January 2003.

252 Carpenter, George. *The Life & Times of Cork's George Carpenter*. Innisfree Press, Kinsale, 2002, p. 164.

253 Tom Hurley interview with George Carpenter recorded 7 January 2003.

254 Colvert, Brendon K. *On My Honour*. Mercier Press, Cork, 2011, pp. 70–71.

255 Tom Hurley interview with Norman Douglas recorded 22 July 2003.

256 Tom Hurley interview with Norman Douglas recorded 22 July 2003.

257 Parkinson, John. *A Belfastman's Tale*. Minprint Ltd, Belfast, 2003, pp. 17–18.

258 Tom Hurley interview with John Parkinson recorded 22 July 2003.

259 Tom Hurley interview with George Cooper recorded 3 April 2003.

260 Tom Hurley interview with Jack Duff recorded 25 June 2003.

261 Tom Hurley interview with Seán Clancy recorded 2 April 2003.

262 Tom Hurley interview with Daniel O'Donovan recorded 1 July 2003.

263 Military Archives, Abstract of Service, Seán Clancy.

264 Tom Hurley interview with Seán Clancy recorded 2 April 2003.

265 Military Archives, Abstract of Service, Seán Clancy.

266 Tom Hurley interview with Seán Clancy recorded 2 April 2003.

267 Tom Hurley interview with Michael Casey recorded 7 June 2003.

268 Tom Hurley interview with Michael Casey recorded 7 June 2003.

269 Tom Hurley interview with Anthony McGinley recorded 27 May 2003.

270 Tom Hurley interview with Dan Keating recorded 13 January 2003.

271 Tom Hurley interview with Dan Keating recorded 13 January 2003.

272 Tom Hurley interview with Dan Keating recorded 13 January 2003.
273 Tom Hurley interview with Daniel O'Donovan recorded 1 July 2003.
274 Tom Hurley interview with Patrick Greene recorded 4 March 2003.
275 Tom Hurley interview with Jack Duff recorded 25 June 2003.
276 Tom Hurley interview with Dan Keating recorded 13 January 2003.
277 Tom Hurley interview with Dan Keating recorded 14 April 2003.
278 Tom Hurley interview with Patsy Holmes recorded 13 June 2003.
279 O'Sullivan, Michael. *Seán Lemass – A Biography*. Blackwater Press, Dublin, 1994, p. 15.
280 Tom Hurley interview with Patsy Holmes recorded 13 June 2003.
281 Tom Hurley interview with Patsy Holmes recorded 13 June 2003.

CHAPTER 9

1 The *Cork Examiner*, 16 August 2005; Carpenter, George. *The Life & Times of Cork's George Carpenter*. Innisfree Press, Kinsale, 2002.
2 The *Irish Examiner*, 3 June 2003, *The Corkman*, 19 February 2004 & 2 March 2001.
3 http://readywriterpublications.wordpress.com/2010/05/22/%E2%80%9Ci-have-a-friend%E2%80%9D-the-testimony-of-george-cooper/; www.irishgenealogy.ie.
4 Murphy, Allison. *When Dublin was the Capital – Northern Life Remembered*. Belcouver Press, Belfast, 2000, p. 19; http://www.passedaway.com/notice/norman_douglas/2838/.
5 Military Archives taped interview with Jack Duff conducted by Commandant Peter Young in 1992.
6 www.irishgenealogy.ie.
7 The *Irish Examiner*, 20 October 2003.
8 Tom Hurley interview with William Geary recorded 15 July 2004.
9 Tom Hurley interview with William Geary recorded 15 July 2004.
10 The *Longford News*, 2000.
11 www.irishgenealogy.ie; *The Corkman*, 15 January 1988.
12 *The Corkman*, 8 May 2003, 28 April 2005 & May 2002.
13 The *Connacht Tribune*, 26 April 2002.
14 https://web.archive.org/web/20100524080050/www.vuw.ac.nz/staff/marian_evans/women-filmmaker/films/erin.html; www.mcginleyclan.org; the *Donegal News*, 27 February 2004.
15 The *Clare Champion*, 5 April 2002; https://web.archive.org/web/20180307101742/http://markhams-of-derryguiha.com/.
16 *The Corkman*, 8 January 1998 & 29 November 2002; the *Irish Examiner*, 26 January 2006; www.irishgenealogy.ie.
17 The *Southern Star*, 26 August 2006.
18 Parkinson, John. *A Belfastman's Tale*. Minprint Ltd, Belfast, 2003.
19 *The Kerryman*, 5 January 2006; Home News Tribune Online, 20 December 2005; Military Archives, Military Service Pensions Collection, Margaret Power.
20 The *Meath Chronicle*, 28 February 2004 & 25 May 2011; the *Irish Times*, 21 May 2011.
21 www.irishgenealogy.ie; the *Laois Nationalist*, 4 July 2003.
22 The *Leinster Express*, 29 July 1995.

Bibliography

BOOKS

Allen, Gregory. *The Garda Síochána – Policing Independent Ireland 1922–82.* Gill & MacMillan Ltd, Dublin, 1999.

Ambrose, Joe. *Dan Breen and the IRA.* Mercier Press, Cork, 2006.

Anderson, Brian. *Gone But Not Forgotten.* Browne Printers, Letterkenny, 2022.

Augusteijn, Joost. *The Irish Revolution 1913–1923.* Palgrave Macmillan, London, 2002.

Barberis, Peter, McHugh, John & Tyldesley, Mike. *Encyclopedia of British and Irish Political Organizations: Parties, groups and movements of the 20th century.* International Publishing Group, UK, 2002.

Barry, Tom. *Guerilla Days in Ireland.* Anvil Books, Dublin, 1981.

Begley, Diarmuid. *The Road to Crossbarry – The Decisive Battle of the War of Independence.* Deso Publications, Bandon, 1999.

Borgonovo, John. *The Battle for Cork.* Mercier Press, Cork, 2011.

Boylan, Henry. *A Dictionary of Irish Biography.* Gill & Macmillan, Dublin, 1998.

Boyne, Sean. *Emmet Dalton: Somme, Soldier, Irish General, Film Pioneer.* Merrion Press, Sallins, 2015.

Bury, Robin. *Buried Lives: The Protestants of Southern Ireland.* The History Press Ireland, Dublin, 2017.

Brady, Conor. *Guardians of the Peace.* Gill & Macmillan, Dublin, 1974.

Breen, Dan. *My Fight for Irish Freedom.* Anvil Books, Dublin, 1981.

Campbell, Fergus. *Land and Revolution: Nationalist Politics in the West of Ireland 1891–1921.* Oxford University Press, 2005.

Carpenter, George. *The Life & Times of Cork's George Carpenter.* Innisfree Press, Kinsale, 2002.

Carroll, Michael J. *A History of Bantry & Bantry Bay.* The Square, Bantry, 2008.

Charles Roy, James. *The Fields of Athenry: A Journey through Irish History.* West View Press, USA, 2001.

Colvert, Brendon K. *On My Honour.* Mercier Press, Cork, 2011.

Connell, Joseph E.A. Jnr. *Michael Collins: Dublin 1916–22.* Wordwell Ltd, Dublin, 2017.

Conway, Joe. *In Shades Like These: Irish Teacher Life-Histories from the Twentieth Century.* Comhar Linn, Dublin, 2000.

Coogan, Oliver. *Politics and War in Meath 1913–23.* Folens & Co. Ltd, Dublin, 1983.

Coogan, Tim Pat. *Michael Collins – A Biography.* Hutchinson, London, 1990.

Coogan, Tim Pat & Morrison, George. *The Irish Civil War.* Weidenfeld and Nicolson, UK, 1998.

Cooke, Richard T. *My Home by the Lee.* Irish Millenium Publications, Ballincollig, 1999.

Cooper, G.J. *Titanic Captain: The Life of Edward John Smyth.* The History Press, Gloucestershire, 2012.

Crowley, John, Ó Drisceoil, Donal & Murphy, Mike. *Atlas of the Irish Revolution.* Cork University Press, Cork, 2017.

Deasy, Liam. *Brother Against Brother.* Mercier Press, Cork, 1998.

Deasy, Liam. *Towards Ireland Free: The West Cork Brigade in the War of Independence 1917–21.* Royal Carbery Books, Cork, 1973.

Doherty, Richard. *The Thin Green Line: The History of the Royal Ulster Constabulary GC, 1922-2001*. Pen & Sword, Barnsley, 2012.

Dolan, Anne. *Commemorating the Irish Civil War: History and Memory 1923-2000*. Cambridge University Press, Cambridge, 2006.

Dooley, Terence. *Burning the Big House*. Yale University Press, New Haven & London, 2022.

Dorney, John. *The Civil War in Dublin: The Fight for the Irish Capital 1922-1924*. Merrion Press, Newbridge, 2017.

Doyle, Tom. *The Civil War in Kerry*. Mercier Press, Cork, 2008.

Durney, James. *The Civil War in Kildare*. Mercier Press, Cork, 2011.

Dwyer, T. Ryle. *Tans, Terror and Trouble - Kerry's Real Fighting Story*. Mercier Press, Cork, 2001.

Enright, Seán: *The Irish Civil War: Law, Execution and Atrocity*. Merrion Press, Newbridge, 2019.

Ferriter, Diarmaid. *Between Two Hells: The Irish Civil War*. Profile Books Ltd, London, 2021.

Gallagher, Julieanne. *Elementary Science in Irish Primary Schools from the Late 1800s to the Present Day*. Dublin City University, 2007.

Gaynor, Éamon. *Memoirs of a Tipperary Family: The Gaynors of Tyone 1887-2000*. Geography Publications, Dublin. 2003.

Grayson, Richard S. *Belfast Boys*. Continuum, London, 2009.

Grob-Fitzgibbon, Benjamin. *The Irish Experience During the Second World War: An Oral History*. Irish Academic Press, Dublin, 2004.

Harvey, Dan. *Soldiers of the Short Grass: A History of the Curragh Camp*. Merrion Press, Newbridge, 2016.

Harrington, Niall C. *Kerry Landing*. Anvil Books Limited, Dublin, 1992.

Harris, Henry. *The Irish Regiments in the First World War*. Mercier Press, Cork, 1968.

Hart, Peter. *The IRA and its Enemies - Violence and Community in Cork 1916-1923*. Clarendon Press, Oxford, 1998.

Hopkinson, Michael. *The Irish War of Independence*. Gill & MacMillan Ltd, Dublin, 2002.

Hopkinson, Michael. *Green Against Green - The Irish Civil War*. Gill & MacMillan Ltd, Dublin, 2004.

Keane, Barry. *Massacre in West Cork: The Dunmanway and Ballygroman Killings*. Mercier Press, Cork, 2014.

Kelly, Adrian. *Compulsory Irish: Language and Education in Ireland 1870s-1970s*. Irish Academic Press, Dublin, 2002.

Kenna, G.B. *Facts & Figures of the Belfast Pogrom, 1920-1922*. The O'Connell Publishing, Dublin, 1922.

Kirby, Dick. *IRA Terror on Britain's Streets 1939-40*. Pen & Sword Books Ltd, Yorkshire, 2021.

Lankford, Siobhán. *The Hope and the Sadness: Personal Recollections of Troubled Times in Ireland*. Tower Books, Cork, 1980.

Langton, James. *The Forgotten Fallen, Volume 1*. Kilmainham Tales Teo, Dublin, 2019.

Lynch, Robert. *The Northern IRA and the Early Years of Partition 1920-22*. Irish Academic Press, Dublin, 2006.

Macardle, Dorothy. *The Irish Republic*. Wolfhound Press, Dublin, 1999.

Macardle, Dorothy. *Tragedies of Kerry*. Elo Press Ltd, Dublin, 1998.

MacEoin, Uinseann. *Harry*. Argenta Publications, Dublin, 1985.

MacEoin, Uinseann. *Survivors*. Argenta Publications, Dublin, 1980.

MacEoin, Uinseann. *The IRA in the Twilight Years 1923-1948*. Argenta Publications, Dublin, 1997.

Mac Fhionnghaile, Niall. *Dr. McGinley and His Times*. An Crann, Letterkenny, 1985.

Maher, Jim. *The Flying Column 1916-1921 - West Kilkenny*. Geography Publications, Dublin, 1988.

Maye, Brian. *Arthur Griffith*. Griffith College Publications Ltd, Dublin, 1997.

McCarthy, Kirean & Christensen, Maj-Britt. *Cobh's Contribution to the Fight for Irish Freedom*. Oileánn Mór Publications, Cobh, 1992.

McCarthy, Pat. *The Irish Revolution 1912-23, Waterford*. Four Courts Press, Dublin, 2015.

McCullagh, David. *De Valera: Rise 1882-1932*. Gill Books, Dublin, 2017.

McCullagh, David. *De Valera: Rule 1932-1975*. Gill Books, Dublin, 2018.

McNamara, Patrick J. *The Widow's Penny*. Santa Lucia, Ballykeelaun, Parteen, Co. Clare, 2000.

McNiffe, Liam. *A History of the Garda Síochána*. Wolfhound Press Ltd, Dublin, 1997.

Murphy, Allison. *When Dublin was the Capital – Northern Life Remembered*. Belcouver Press, Belfast, 2000.

Murphy, Seán & Síle. *The Comeraghs – Gunfire and Civil War. The Story of the Deise Brigade IRA 1914-24*. Litho Press, Midleton, 2003.

Murphy, William. *Political Imprisonment and the Irish, 1912-1921*. Oxford University Press, Oxford, 2014.

Nevin, Donal. *James Connolly – A Full Life*. Gill & MacMillan Ltd, Dublin, 2005.

Newmann, Kate. *The Dictionary of Ulster Biography*. The Institute of Irish Studies, The Queen's University of Belfast, 1993.

O'Brien, Paul. *Havoc: The Auxiliaries in Ireland's War of Independence*. The Collins Press, Cork, 2017.

O'Connor, John. *The 1916 Proclamation*. Anvil Books, Dublin, 1986.

O'Donovan, Donal. *Kevin Barry and His Time*. Glendale Press Ltd, Dublin, 1989.

Ó Duibhir, Liam. *Prisoners of War: Ballykinlar Internment Camp 1920-21*. Mercier Press, Cork, 2013.

O'Dwyer, Martin (Bob). *Seventy-Seven of Mine Said Ireland*. Litho Press, Cork, 2006.

O'Halpin, Eunan & Ó Corráin, Daithí. *The Dead of the Irish Revolution*. Yale University Press, New Haven, 2020.

O'Mahony, Sean. *Frongoch – University of Revolution*. FDR Teoranta, Dublin, 1987.

O'Malley, Cormac H. & Dolan, Anne. *'No Surrender Here!' – The Civil War Papers of Ernie O'Malley 1922-1924*. The Lilliput Press, Dublin, 2007.

O'Malley, Ernie. *Rising Out: Seán Connolly of Longford*. University College Dublin Press, 2007.

O'Malley, Ernie. *The Men Will Talk to Me, Galway Interviews*. Mercier Press, Cork, 2013.

O'Malley, Ernie. *The Men Will Talk to Me, Kerry Interviews*. Mercier Press, Cork, 2012.

O'Malley, Ernie. *The Men Will Talk to Me, Mayo Interviews*. Mercier Press, Cork, 2014.

O'Malley, Ernie. *The Men Will Talk to Me, the Northern Divisions*. Merrion Press, Newbridge, 2018.

O'Malley, Ernie. *The Men Will Talk To Me, West Cork Interviews*. Mercier Press, Cork, 2015.

O'Malley, Ernie. *The Singing Flame*. Anvil Books Limited, Dublin, 1978.

Ó Riordán, Tomás. *Where Martyred Heroes Rest*. Published by the Liam Lynch National Commemoration Committee, 1987.

Ó'Ruairc, Pádraig Óg. *Blood on the Banner*. Mercier Press, Cork, 2009.

Ó'Ruairc, Pádraig Óg. *Truce: Murder, Myth and the Last Days of the Irish War of Independence*. Mercier Press, Cork, 2016.

O'Shea, Owen. *Ballymacandy: The Story of a Kerry Ambush*. Merrion Press, Newbridge, 2021.

Ó Súilleabháin, Mícheál. *Where Mountainy Men Have Sown*. Anvil Books, Tralee, 1965.

O'Sullivan, John L. *Cork City Gaol*. Litho Press, Midleton, 1996.

O'Sullivan, Michael. *Seán Lemass – A Biography*. Blackwater Press, Dublin, 1994.

O'Sullivan, Niamh. *Every Dark Hour – A History of Kilmainham Jail*. Liberties Press, Dublin, 2007.

Parkinson, Alan F. *Belfast's Unholy War – The Troubles of the 1920s*. Four Courts Press Ltd, Dublin, 2004.

Parkinson, John. *A Belfastman's Tale*. Minprint Ltd, Belfast, 2003.

Pettit, Dr. S.F. *This City of Cork 1700–1900*. Studio Publications, Cork, 1977.

Power, Bill. *Another Side of Mitchelstown*. Psyops Books, Mulberry House, Mitchelstown, 2008.

Power, Bill. *Doomed Inheritance: Mitchelstown Castle Looted & Burned August 1922*. Scriptorium Mulberry, Mitchelstown, 2022.

Power, Bill. *From the Danes to Dairygold – A History of Mitchelstown*. Mount Cashell Books, Mitchelstown, 1996.

Power, Bill. *Images of Mitchelstown – Stories and Pictures from My Own Place*. Mount Cashell Books, Mitchelstown, 2002.

Power, Bill. *Mitchelstown Through the Ages*. Eigse Books, Cork, 1987.

Power, Bill. *White Knights, Dark Earls – The Rise and Fall of an Anglo-Irish Dynasty*. Collins Press, Cork, 2000.

Rafter, Michael. *The Quiet County*. Arderin Publishing Company, Portlaoise, 2005.

Ryan, Meda. *Michael Collins and the Women Who Spied for Ireland*. Mercier Press, Cork, 2006.

Ryan, Meda. *The Real Chief – The Story of Liam Lynch*. Mercier Press, Cork, 2005.

Ryan, Meda. *Tom Barry – IRA Freedom Fighter*. Mercier Press, Cork, 2003.

Shelly, John R. *A Short History of the 3rd Tipperary Brigade*. Phoenix Publishing, Cashel, 1996.

Sisson, Elaine. *Pearse's Patriots: St Endas's and the Cult of Boyhood*. Cork University Press, Cork, 2004.

Tierney, Mark. *Ireland Since 1870*. CJ Fallon, Dublin, 1988.

Twohig, Patrick J. *The Dark Secret of Béal na Bláth*. Tower Books, Ballincollig, 1991.

Twohig, Patrick J. *Green Tears for Hecuba – Ireland's Fight for Freedom*. Tower Books, Ballincollig, 1994.

Wallace, Colm. *The Fallen*. The History Press Ireland, Dublin, 2017.

Walsh, Louis J. *'On My Keeping' and in Theirs: A record of experiences 'on the run', in Derry Gaol, and in Ballykinlar Internment Camp*. The Talbot Press, Dublin, 1921.

White, Gerry & O'Shea, Brendan. *Irish Volunteer Soldier 1913–23*. Osprey Publishing, Oxford, 2003.

White, Gerry & O'Shea, Brendan. *The Burning of Cork*. Mercier Press, Cork, 2006.

Whyte, Louis. *The Wild Heather Glen – The Kilmichael Story of Grief and Glory*. Tower Books, Ballincollig, 1995.

Yeats, Pádraig. *A City in Civil War*. Gill & Macmillan, Dublin, 2015.

Yeats, Pádraig & Wren, Jimmy. *Michael Collins – An Illustrated Life*. Tomar Publishing Ltd, Dublin, 1989.

NEWSPAPERS

The *Anglo Celt*, the *Ballina Herald*, the *Belfast Newsletter*, the *Belfast Telegraph*, the *Church of Ireland Gazette*, the *Clare Champion*, the *Connacht Tribune*, the *Cork County Eagle and Munster Advertiser*, the *Cork Constitution*, the *Cork Examiner*, *The Corkman*, the *Derry Journal*, the *Donegal Democrat*, the *Donegal News*, *Éire*, the *Drogheda Independent*, the *Dublin Evening Mail*, the *Enniscorthy Guardian*, the *Evening Echo*, the *Evening Herald*, the *Evening Telegraph*, the *Fall River Globe*, the *Fingal Independent*, the *Freeman's Journal*, *The Guardian*, the *Holly Bough*, the *Irish Examiner*, the *Irish Independent*, the *Irish Nation*, the *Irish News*, the *Irish Press*, the *Irish Times*, the *Kerry Champion*, *The Kerryman*, the *Kerry People*, the *Kerry Reporter*, the *Kildare Observer*, the *Kilkenny People*, *The Kingdom*, the *Laois Nationalist*, the *Leinster Express*, the *Leitrim Observer*, *The Liberator*, the *Limerick Leader*, the *Longford Leader*, the *Longford News*, the *Meath Chronicle*, the *Midland Tribune*, *The Nationalist*, the *Nationalist and Leinster Times*, the *Nenagh Guardian*, the *Nenagh News*, the

New York Times, An Phoblacht, Poblacht na h-Éireann, (Scot. Edn), the *Roscommon Herald, Sinn Féin*, the *Skibbereen Eagle*, the *Sligo Champion*, the *Southern Star*, the *Sunday Independent, The Times*, the *Tipperary Star*, the *Tuam Herald*, the *Ulster Herald*, the *Washington Post*, the *Waterford News & Star*, the *Western People*.

ARCHIVE SOURCES & JOURNALS

An Cosantóir.
An t-Óglách.
The *Tipperary Historical Journal 1991, 1992, 1993, 1998*. Published by the County Tipperary Historical Society, Thurles.
Ballingeary Historical Society Journal 1996, 1997, 2000, 2006.
Browne, Ger. *A Tribute to Kilrush in the Great War.*
Cathal Brugha Barracks, Military Archives, Dublin. (Witness Statements: BMH.WS0639, Maurice Donegan & BMH.WS1181, John O'Connor & BMH.WS1487, Jerry Ryan & BMH.WS1093, Thomas Treacy & BMH.WS1151, Patrick Luddy & BMH.WS0940, Leo Skinner & BMH.WS1362, William Roche & BMH.WS0845, Tomas Malone & BMH. WS1036, John Moloney & BMH.WS0838, Seán Moylan & BMH.WS491, Tom Scully & BMH.WS1506, Henry O'Mahony & BMH.WS707, Michael Noyk & BMH.WS665, Francis O'Duffy & BMH.WS1376, John O'Sullivan & BMH.WS946, Patrick Clifford & BMH.WS1547, Michael Murphy & BMH.WS1322, Art O'Donnell & BMH.WS0551, Canon Thomas Duggan & BMH.WS1741, Michael V. Donoghue & BMH.WS1100, John Sharkey & BMH.WS640, Hugh Gribben & BMH.WS0746, Seán Culhane & BMH.WS965, Tadg McCarthy & BMH.WS1011, Patrick Garvey & BMH.WS474, Liam Haugh & BMH.WS1251, Martin Chambers & BMH.WS808, Richard Willis & John Bolster & BMH.WS430, Thomas Barry & BMH.WS1477, Thomas Reidy & BMH. WS1030, John Joseph Hogan & BMH.WS1189, Thomas O'Connor & BMH.WS0999, James Fitzgerald & BMH.WS1195, Patrick Doherty & BMH.WS1106, Denis Prendiville & BMH.WS1584, Patrick A. Murray & BMH.WS0626, John Donnelly & BMH.WS1716, Seán MacEoin & BMH.WS981, Patrick Riordan & BMH.WS, Seán Gaynor & BMW. WS440, Seamus Conway & BMH.WS0445, Jim Slattery & BMH.WS952, Maurice Horgan & BMH.WS1427, Laurence Brady & BMH.WS883, John M. MacCarthy & BMH.WS1410, Michael O'Kelly & BMH.WS1720, John Manning & BMH.WS1066, Manus Moynihan & BMH.0103, Seán O'Hegarty, Seán Lynch, Tadhg Twomey, Jeremiah O'Shea & BMH.WS1478, Ted O'Sullivan & BMH.WS1763, Dan Breen & BMH.WS1163, Patrick MacCarthy & BMH.WS1018, Martin Fahy & BMH.WS1138, Gilbert Morrissey & Military Archives, Civil War Internment Collection.)
Clare Men & Women in WWI, Where they lived.
The Clare War Dead WWI.
Cork County Gaol General Register 1915–1924.
1841–1864 Freedom Roll book, Dublin City Library and Archive.
Guy's City and County Cork Almanac and Directory for 1916.
Guy's City and County Cork Almanac and Directory for 1921.
Guy's Postal Directory for Cork City and County 1914.
Island Journal, Vol. 1, no. 1, Winter 2006/2007.
Jottings and Recollections of William Geary, New York – 14th June 1974.
Kerry's Fighting Story 1916–21. The Kerryman Limited, Tralee, 1945.
Memoirs, typed and signed by William Geary 20/1/1992.
Memoirs, typed and signed by William Geary 28/1/2003.
The *Journal of British Studies*, volume 47, no. 2, April 2008, pp. 375–391.
Rebel Cork's Fighting Story 1916–1921. The Kerryman Limited, Tralee, 1945.

The Saturday Record, 1919.

United Parishes Press: *Backward Glances: A Compilation of Fact and Old Stories from the United Parishes of Glendine, Kilwatermoy and Knockanore*. Litho Press, Midleton, 2001.

Military Archives, Brigade Activity Reports.

Military Archives, Civil War Internment Collection.

Military Archives, Cumann na mBan Series.

Military Archives, IRA Membership Series.

Military Archives, Medal Series.

Military Archives, Military Census 1922.

Military Archives, Military Service Pensions Collection.

Military Archives taped interview with Jack Duff conducted by Commandant Peter Young in 1992.

Rebel Cork's Fighting Story 1916–1921. The Kerryman Limited, Tralee, 1947.

Report of William Geary, Wireless Operator Voyage, 9 February 1920 to 21 January 1921, 23/3/2004.

Jim Herlihy, Royal Irish Constabulary Register Extract – Public Records Office, Kew, Richmond, Surrey, England.

'Sliabh na mban "the jewel in the crown"' by Bob Webster & Sister Veronica Treacy (https://web.archive.org/web/20180708054255/http://www.esatclear.ie/~curragh/sliabh_na_mban.htm).

The *Mallow Field Club Journal* 1984, 1985 & 1991.

National Graves Association. *The Last Post*. Elo Press Ltd, Dublin, 1985.

The Story of the Drumboe Martyrs 1923–2003. 80th Anniversary Edition.

Waterford News & Star Christmas Supplement 2000.

TELEVISON & RADIO

'Meirligh, An Saighdiúir Tréigthe – Liam O Loingsígh', TG4, 2005.

WEBSITES

www.ancestry.com

athenry.org

athenryparishheritage.com

https://web.archive.org/web/20110222044540/http:/ballykinlar.down.gaa.ie/history.html

www.bbc.co.uk/history

http://news.bbc.co.uk/2/hi/uk_news/northern_ireland/2789253.stm

www.bbc.co.uk/northernireland/yourplaceandmine/

www.bloodysunday.co.uk

www.buildingsofireland.ie

www.cairogang.com

https://catalogue.nli.ie/Collection/vtls000749188

www.census.nationalarchives.ie

www.clarelibrary.ie

www.communistpartyofireland.ie

www.corkandross.org

https://www.cso.ie/en/releasesandpublications/ep/p-1916/1916irl/society/education/

www.cwgc.org

https://databases.dublincity.ie/freemen/viewdoc.php?searchid=25139&source=integration

http://homepage.eircom.net/~corkcounty/

http://www.difp.ie/docs/1921/Anglo-Irish-Treaty/138.htm

http://www.dublin1313.com/site/lodge-history/
www.dungarvanmuseum.org
https://www.ed.ac.uk/news/all-news/ireland-120609#:~:text=The%20Roll%20of%20Honour%2C%20compiled,British%2C%20Commonwealth%20and%20Dominion%20Forces.
www.familysearch.org
Mitchelstown WWI figures researched by Bill Power, https://www.facebook.com/photo/?fbid=6111972975479343&set=a.312194828790549
www.findmypast.ie - Cork County Gaol General Register 1915-1924
www.firstworldwar.com
www.garda.ie
www.gaa.ie
www.generalmichaelcollins.com
www.greatwar.ie
www.history.com
http://www.historyireland.com/20th-century-contemporary-history/greatest-killer-of-the-twentieth-century-the-great-flu-of-1918-19/
http://www.historyireland.com/volume-22/dublins-loyal-volunteers/
https://www.holocaust.org.uk/hitler-youth-jacket
www.irishgenealogy.ie
https://livesofthefirstworldwar.iwm.org.uk/lifestory/47070
http://www.kildare.ie/ehistory/index.php/in-the-four-courts/
https://web.archive.org/web/20220314215213/http:/landedestates.nuigalway.ie/
www.landedestates.ie
https://laoislocalstudies.ie/the-portarlington-sawmills-lockout-of-1918/
www.libertyellisfoundation.org
https://web.archive.org/web/20180307101742/http://markhams-of-derryguiha.com/
www.mcginleyclan.org
www.military.ie
www.militaryarchives.ie
www.myheritage.com
https://www.nam.ac.uk/explore/battle-somme
https://www.nam.ac.uk/explore/south-lancashire-regiment-prince-waless-volunteers
www.nidirect.gov.uk
www.offalyhistory.com, Diary of Patrick Wrafter 1921-1925 by Michael Byrne
http://www.passedaway.com/notice/norman_douglas/2838/
www.policehistory.com
www.oireachtas.ie
http://readywriterpublications.wordpress.com/2010/05/22/%E2%80%9Ci-have-a-friend%E2%80%9D-the-testimony-of-george-cooper/
http://web.archive.org/web/20220124172335/http://royalulsterconstabulary.org/
http://web.archive.org/web/20050407153847/www.rte.ie/culture/millennia/people/m_history.html
https://web.archive.org/web/20160605064636/http://www.slanetimes.com/index.php?option=com_content&view=article&id=50&Itemid=56
www.sommeassociation.com
www.templemore.ie
www.theauxiliaries.com
http://www.theirishstory.com/2013/05/16/ireland-and-the-great-flu-epidemic-of1918/#.VGcw7cJybIU
https://web.archive.org/web/20230625135226/https://www.theirishstory.com/2018/05/21/the-emergency-a-brief-overview/

https://www.theirishstory.com/2022/09/13/the-media-war-robert-erskine-childers-in-west-cork/#_edn14

https://theirishaesthete.com/

www.titanic-titanic.com

http://treaty.nationalarchives.ie/

www.triskelartscentre.ie

https://web.archive.org/web/20141104140509/http://www.ucd.ie/archives/html/collections/cumann-na-gael.htm

https://web.archive.org/web/20100524080050/www.vuw.ac.nz/staff/marian_evans/women-filmmaker/films/erin.html

http://www.westmeathcoco.ie/en/ourservices/planning/conservationheritage/decadeofcentenariesblog/thepreludetocivilwarinwestmeaththeprotestantexperience.html

http://en.wikipedia.org/wiki/Frank_Shawe-Taylor

http://homepage.eircom.net/~oreganathenry/oreganathenry/index.html?history/social/castlelamberttape%205.html (The Castle Lambert Tape)

www.1914-1918.net

PHOTOGRAPHS

Thanks to those who provided photographs.